Cases in

STRATEGIC MANAGEMENT

Tenth Edition

Paul W. Beamish

Richard Ivey School of Business
The University of Western Ontario

The McGraw·Hill Companies

McGraw-Hill
Ryerson
Connect. Learn. Succeed.

Cases in Strategic Management
Tenth Edition

The Internet addresses listed in the text were accurate at the time of publication. The inclusion of a website does not indicate an endorsement by the authors or McGraw-Hill Ryerson, and McGraw-Hill Ryerson does not guarantee the accuracy of information presented at these sites.

ISBN-13: 978-0-07-040182-2
ISBN-10: 0-07-040182-9

1 2 3 4 5 6 7 8 9 10 QDB 1 9 8 7 6 5 4 3 2

Printed and bound in the United States of America

Care has been taken to trace ownership of copyright material contained in this text; however, the publisher will welcome any information that enables it to rectify any reference or credit for subsequent editions.

Executive Sponsoring Editor: *Kim Brewster*
Marketing Manager: *Cathie Lefebvre*
Developmental Editor: *Kamilah Reid-Burrell*
Supervising Editor: *Cathy Biribauer*
Senior Editorial Associate: *Christine Lomas*
Proofreader: *Ashley Rayner*
Production Coordinator: *Tammy Mavroudi*
Cover/Inside Design: *Michelle Losier*
Composition: *Laserwords Private Limited*
Cover Photo: © *Robertosch/Dreamstime.com*
Printer: *Quad/Graphics*

Library and Archives Canada Cataloguing in Publication Data

Beamish, Paul W., 1953-
    Cases in strategic management / Paul W. Beamish. — 10th ed.
Includes bibliographical references.
ISBN 978-0-07-040182-2

    1. Strategic planning—Canada—Case studies. 2. Industrial management—
Canada—Case studies. I. Title.

HD30.28.B3322 2011   658.4'0120971   C2011-903125-6

To the memory of two splendid teachers:

John and Catherine Beamish

About the Author

Paul W. Beamish is Professor of International Strategy at the Richard Ivey School of Business, University of Western Ontario. He is the author or co-author of over 50 books, over 100 refereed articles and over 100 case studies. His articles have appeared in *Strategic Management Journal, Journal of International Business Studies, Academy of Management Journal, Academy of Management Review, Organization Science* and elsewhere. His consulting and management training activities have been in both the public and the private sector for such organizations as Boeing, Labatt/Interbrew, The World Bank, the Canadian Foreign Service Institute and the Harvard Institute for International Development. He has received case writing awards from the European Foundation for Management Development, The Management Development Centre of Hong Kong, The Academy of International Business and the Administrative Sciences Association of Canada. Over 2.5 million copies of his cases have been studied worldwide. He worked for the Procter & Gamble Company of Canada and Wilfrid Laurier University before joining Ivey's faculty in 1987. He is the founding Director of Ivey's Asian Management Institute, and is the Director of Ivey Publishing. He is a Fellow of the Royal Society of Canada, The Academy of International Business and the Asia Pacific Foundation of Canada.

Contents

Preface and Acknowledgements   xiii

Part 1 Strategic Management: Creating Competitive Advantages

Case 1 Research in Motion: Managing Explosive Growth   1

In early January 2008, David Yach, chief technology officer for software at Research In Motion (RIM), had just come back from Christmas break. Returning to his desk in Waterloo, Ontario, relaxed and refreshed, he noted that his executive assistant had placed the preliminary holiday sales figures for BlackBerry on top of his in-box with a note that read "Meeting with Mike tomorrow." Knowing 2007 had been an extraordinarily good year, with the number of BlackBerry units sold doubling, Dave was curious: Why did Mike Lazaridis, RIM's visionary founder and co-CEO want a meeting? A sticky note on page 3 flagged the issue. Mike wanted to discuss Dave's research and development (R&D) plans—even though R&D spending was up $124M from the prior year, it had dropped significantly as a percentage of sales. In an industry driven by engineering innovations and evaluated on technological advances, this was an issue.

Case 2 CIBC Mellon: Managing a Cross-border Joint Venture   21

During his 10-year tenure, the president and chief executive officer (CEO) of CIBC Mellon had presided over the dramatic growth of the jointly owned, Toronto-based asset servicing business of CIBC and The Bank of New York Mellon Corporation (BNY Mellon). In mid-September 2008, the onset of the worst financial crisis since the Great Depression threatened to impact all players in the financial services industry worldwide. Although joint ventures (JVs) were uncommon in the financial sector, the CEO believed that the CIBC Mellon JV was uniquely positioned to withstand the fallout associated with the financial crisis. Two pressing issues faced the JV's executive management team. First, they needed to discuss how to best manage any risks confronting the JV as a consequence of the financial crisis. How could the policies and practices developed during the past decade be leveraged to sustain the JV through the broader financial crisis? Second, they needed to continue discussions regarding options for refining CIBC Mellon's strategic focus, so that the JV could emerge from the financial meltdown on even stronger footing.

Part 2 Analyzing the External Environment of the Firm

Case 3 Swimming in the Virtual Community Pool with PlentyofFish   36

PlentyofFish.com is the world's most profitable website on a per capita basis, the 96th most popular website in terms of page views and the most popular online dating site in existence. Remarkably, it is managed by its owner and founder and only one other employee. It is a free dating site that generates $10 million in ad revenues per year and a profit to the owner in excess of $9 million. PlentyofFish.com has achieved stellar growth in the face of stringent competition. Is it sustainable? A number of possible alternatives are offered for analysis.

Case 4 Loblaw Companies Limited   46

The president of Loblaw Companies Limited must decide what to do in response to the rumoured introduction of Wal-Mart's SuperCenters (combining grocery and non-food items) in Canada. The potential launch of SuperCenters in Canada was seen by observers as a threat to Loblaw, the market leader in Canadian grocery. Wal-Mart is a vigorous competitor, and the Every Day Low Prices strategy of Wal-Mart's SuperCenters could wean away traffic from Loblaw's various banners.

Case 5 Alcan (A): Anticipating Industry Change   65

In December 2006, Alcan was the second-largest producer of aluminum in the world, but the industry was consolidating. The case traces the development of the aluminum industry since World War II to the recent emergence of China as an economic power and the accompanying rise in commodity prices. Alcan had to decide between two offers: to be acquired or to go it alone. The first offer was from Alcoa and the other from Rio Tinto. Alcoa was the world leader in the production of aluminum and, like Alcan, was engaged in significant technological research and development. Meanwhile, Rio Tinto was one of the largest mining companies in the world, but had minor aluminum operations and, in general, few downstream processing plants or technologies. Students are asked to identify Alcan's key resources and consider which strategy would make best use of them.

Case 6 The Chinese Fireworks Industry—Revised   80

The Chinese fireworks industry thrived after China adopted the "open door policy" in the late 1970s, and grew to make up 90 per cent of the world's fireworks export sales. However, starting from the mid-1990s, safety concerns led governments both in China and abroad to set up stricter regulations. At the same time, there was rapid growth in the number of small, family-run fireworks workshops, whose relentless price-cutting drove down profit margins. Students are asked to undertake an industry analysis, estimate the industry attractiveness and propose possible ways to improve the industry attractiveness from an individual investor's point of view. Jerry Yu is an American-born Chinese in New York who has been invited, in 2009, to buy a fireworks factory in China.

Part 3 Assessing the Internal Environment of the Firm

Case 7 IKEA (Canada) Ltd.—1986 (Condensed)   92

The new Sears catalogue contained a 20-page section called Elements. This section bore a striking resemblance to the format of an IKEA catalogue, and the furniture being offered was similar to IKEA'S knocked-down self-assembly line. The head of IKEA'S North American operations wondered how serious Sears was about its new initiative and what, if anything, IKEA should do in response.

Case 8 The Prince Edward Island Preserve Company: Turnaround   103

In April 2008, Bruce MacNaughton, president of Prince Edward Island Preserve Co. Ltd. (P.E.I. Preserves), was focused on turnaround. The company he had founded in 1985 had gone into receivership in May 2007. Although this had resulted in losses for various mortgage holders and unsecured creditors, MacNaughton had been able to buy back his New Glasgow shop/café, the adjacent garden property and inventory, and restart the business. He now needed a viable product-market strategy.

Case 9 Rogers' Chocolates (A)   121

A new president has been hired to double or triple the size of Rogers' Chocolates, a high-end chocolate producer and retailer in Victoria, British Columbia. The case allows a comprehensive analysis of marketing, manufacturing, human resource, financial and strategic positioning issues in a small company with manufacturing, retailing, wholesaling and Internet operations.

Part 4 Recognizing a Firm's Intellectual Assets: Moving Beyond a Firm's Tangible Resources

Case 10 Time Warner Inc. and the ORC Patents   141

Optical Recording Corporation (ORC) of Toronto secured the rights to a technology known as digital optical audio recording. During the time it took to negotiate the final transfer of the technology ownership, it was rumoured that some major electronics manufacturers were developing compact disc (CD) players that recorded digital optical audio signals. A patent lawyer advised ORC that the compact disc players and compact discs recently released by these companies might be infringing the claims of ORC's newly acquired patents. Based on this information, the company negotiated licensing agreements with the two largest CD manufacturers. The third-largest manufacturer, WEA Manufacturing, a subsidiary of Time Warner Inc., maintained a position of non-infringement and invalid patents. With the U.S. patent expiry date looming, ORC decided to sue Time Warner for patent infringement. When the defense counsel presented testimony that questioned the integrity of the licensing agreement, ORC's president realized that the entire licensing program was in jeopardy and must decide whether he should accept a settlement or proceed with the lawsuit.

Case 11 Majestica Hotel in Shanghai?   157

Majestica Hotels Inc., a leading European operator of luxury hotels, was trying to reach an agreement with Commercial Properties of Shanghai regarding the management contract for a new hotel in Shanghai. A series of issues require resolution for the deal to proceed, including length of contract term, name, staffing and many other control issues. Majestica was reluctant to make further concessions for fear that doing so might jeopardize its service culture, arguably the key success factor in this industry. At issue was whether Majestica should adopt a contingency approach and relax its operating philosophy, or stick to its principles, even if it meant not entering a lucrative market.

Case 12 Immunovaccine (IMV): Preparing to Cross the "Valley of Death"   171

The case describes the challenges faced by Immunovaccine (IMV), a small biotechnology company founded in Halifax, Nova Scotia. The company has seen early success in the effectiveness of its technology in animal health and is looking for ways to exploit the potential of its technology more broadly, particularly in human health. The company's challenges are presented in the context of the evolving relationship between the pharmaceutical and biotechnology industries. The case describes the various issues the company faces around 2008, shortly after the new president and CEO has taken over. It then provides details on strategy formulation and execution under the new CEO.

Part 5 Business-Level Strategy: Creating and Sustaining Competitive Advantages

Case 13 Maple Leaf Consumer Foods—Fixing Hot Dogs (A)   189

Maple Leaf Foods is Canada's largest and most dominant food processor. The recently appointed senior marketing director discovers on her first day on the job that the hot dog business at the company is completely broken: Market share is down, profits are in free-fall, the products taste bad, there is a proliferation of brands and her team is a mess. To make matters worse, she inherits a job where there is little market data in the files and little to go by to help guide her decisions. She must prepare a short-term plan and a clear strategy for the future.

Case 14 Ganong Bros. Limited   201

Ganong Bros. Limited is a fifth-generation family chocolate company based in New Brunswick that is facing financial difficulties. The firm has been spreading its resources too thinly and needs to develop a plan to not only return to profitability, but also to grow the business while upholding its responsibility to the local community.

Case 15 Holey Soles   213

The president and chief executive officer (CEO) of Holey Soles—a B.C.-based developer, manufacturer and distributor of injected-molded footwear—was optimistic and upbeat. Sales had grown at 300 per cent in each of the past two years, it ranked number four in a leading publication's 2006 Canada's Emerging Growth Companies, and the CEO herself was a finalist for the 2007 Ernst & Young Entrepreneur of the Year Award. Sustaining the momentum that had been building since the company had been bought in 2004 was proving to be a challenge.
Fast growth was stretching the capabilities of Holey Soles in all areas: securing financing, sourcing, developing new markets, maintaining high quality, expanding the product portfolio and management talent. The CEO wondered what the available options, priorities and next steps would be to continue to build a strong foundation for growth, and to reach her aggressive target of $40 million in sales by 2009.

Part 6 Corporate-Level Strategy: Creating Value through Diversification

Case 16 Yunnan Baiyao: Traditional Medicine Meets Product/Market Diversification   231

In 2003, 3M initiated contact with Yunnan Baiyao Group Co. (YB), Ltd. to discuss potential cooperation opportunities in the area of transdermal pharmaceutical products. YB was a household brand in China for its unique traditional herbal medicines. In recent years, the company had been engaged in a series of product/ market diversification strategies to respond to the change in the Chinese pharmaceutical industry and competition at a global level. YB was already a vertically integrated, product-diversified group company with an ambition to become an international player. The proposed cooperation with 3M was attractive to YB, not only as an opportunity for domestic product diversification, but also for international diversification. YB had been attempting to internationalize its products and an overseas department had been established in 2002. On the other hand, YB had also been considering another option; namely, whether to extend its brand to toothpaste and other health care products. YB had to make decisions about which of the two options to pursue and whether it was feasible to pursue both.

Case 17 Vincor and the New World of Wine   247

Vincor International Inc. was Canada's largest wine company and North America's fourth-largest in 2002. The company had decided to internationalize and, as the first step, had entered the United States through two acquisitions. The company's chief executive officer felt that, to be among the top 10 wineries in the world, Vincor needed to look beyond the region. To that end, he was considering the acquisition of an Australian company, Goundrey Wines. He must analyze the strategic rationale for the acquisition of Goundrey, as well as to probe questions of strategic fit and value.

Case 18 CIBC-Barclays: Should their Caribbean Operations be Merged?   263

At the end of 2001, the Canadian Imperial Bank of Commerce (CIBC) and Barclays Bank PLC were in advanced negotiations regarding the potential merger of their respective retail, corporate and offshore banking operations in the Caribbean. Some members of each board wondered whether this was the best direction to take. Would the combined company be able to deliver superior returns? Would it be possible to integrate, within budget, companies that had competed with each other in the region for decades? Would either firm be better off divesting regional operations instead? Should the two firms just continue to go it alone with emphasis on continual improvement? A decision needed to be made with the coming week.

Case 19 SunOpta, Inc.   277

The chairman and chief executive officer of SunOpta, Inc., is wondering whether or not to unlock shareholder value. The company has grown at a rapid pace, with sales growing to more than $400 million in 2005. Its stock price has tripled over five years, but has slumped recently. The case describes SunOpta's history, as well as operations in its three business units: Stake Technology, Opta Mineral and the Food Group.

Part 7 International Strategy: Creating Value in Global Markets

Case 20 Guest-Tek Interactive Entertainment: International Sales   297

The chief executive officer of Calgary-based Guest-Tek Interactive Entertainment Ltd., a leading provider of high-speed Internet access to the hotel industry, must consider whether, and how, his company should grow its business overseas. Ninety-seven per cent of Guest-Tek's fiscal year 2003 revenue was derived from North American hotels—a market he knew would eventually become saturated. Guest-Tek had listed publicly in January 2004. Both internal and external investors now demanded results. Other geographic markets held the promise of new growth and competitors were already pursuing those opportunities.

Case 21 Palliser Furniture Ltd.: The China Question   313

Palliser is Canada's second-largest furniture company. The Manitoba-based company has production facilities in Canada, Mexico and Indonesia, and experimented with cutting and sewing leather in China. The company is looking at further expanding the relationship with China. Ever since Palliser set up a plant in Mexico, the company had faced increasing competitive pressure from Asia, especially from China. The president of Palliser must decide what form this relationship should follow: Should it be an investment, either wholly or partly owned, or should it be through subcontracting?

Case 22 Canadian Solar   324

In late September 2009, the CEO of the NASDAQ-traded solar cell and module manufacturer, Canadian Solar, was at an inflection point in the formation of its international strategy. The company had experienced dynamic growth during the past five years, buoyed largely by aggressive incentive schemes to install solar photovoltaic (PV) technology in Germany and Spain. The credit crunch, coupled with changes in government incentive programs, caused a major decline in the demand for solar PV technology, and analysts were predicting that full year 2009 sales would decline. Furthermore, competition in the industry was fierce, with diverse players ranging from Japanese electronic giants to low-cost Chinese producers. Canadian Solar had decided to focus on 10 major markets in the next 2 to 3 years where strong renewable policies existed. Students are challenged with deciding if any changes to the company's global strategy are necessary.

Case 23 Resuming Internationalization at Starbucks   343

Starbucks enjoyed tremendous growth over the previous two decades. In 2007, it had a global reach of over 17,000 stores in 56 countries. Between 2007 and 2009, however, Starbucks' relentless march was slowed by three forces: increasingly intense competition, rising coffee bean prices and a global economic recession. In order to remain profitable, the company started to scale back its overseas operations. In 2010, Starbucks was faced with a critical strategic decision: Should the company resume its international expansion and once again intensify its commitments in overseas markets? If so, what approach should the company take? Had the pace of Starbucks' internationalization (i.e., the rate of opening new stores abroad), the rhythm of its internationalization (i.e., the regularity by which stores were opened abroad) and geographical scope of its internationalization (i.e., number of new countries entered) had an impact on the company's performance in previous years? Could Starbucks learn from its prior internationalization within the coffee industry in order to guide its future international strategy?

Case 24 Chabros International Group: A World of Wood   361

The Chabros case examines how a Lebanese multinational wood company confronts a drastic drop in its largest subsidiary's sales after 2008's global economic crisis. Antoine Chami, Chabros' owner and president, was reviewing his company's 2009 end-of-year financial statements and, in particular, a 30 per cent drop in sales in Dubai. In 2007, a year before the global economic crisis, Chami had invested more than $11 million to acquire and expand a sawmill in Serbia to meet Chabros' growing lumber sales demand. With a much higher capacity to produce lumber and a much lower probability to sell it, Chami had to decide what to do to overcome this challenge. Should he close parts of his Serbian sawmill? Should he try to boost his company's sales to use all of his sawmill's available capacity? If so, should Chabros try to increase sales within the countries where it already operated (UAE, Saudi Arabia, Qatar, Oman, Egypt) or should it expand into a new country (Algeria, Bahrain, Iran, Iraq, Jordan, Kuwait, Libya, Syria, Tunisia)? Would Morocco, among other countries, be the best country to expand into? Was it the right time to embark on such an expansion?

Part 8 Industry Change and Competitive Dynamics

Case 25 Dell Inc. in 2009   376

The Dell story is well-known in the business world: A young Michael Dell, while attending the University of Texas in Austin, founds a computer sales company that eventually revolutionizes the industry. The case puts students in the position of a senior executive at Dell who is preparing for an investor relations meeting. As the senior executive reviews information on his company, he wonders how best to convey to skeptical investors that Dell's strategy will return the company to growth. In examining the Dell story, students learn about how Dell built up a set of competitive advantages that seemed unassailable until the early 2000s. The second part of the case illustrates the impermanence of competitive advantages—it describes how Dell is attempting to remake itself after falling behind its competitors.

Case 26 Coral Divers Resort (Revised)   395

The owner of a small scuba diving operation in the Bahamas is reassessing his strategic direction in the light of declining revenues. Among the changes being considered are shark diving, family diving, exit and shifting operations to another Caribbean location. These options are not easily combined, nor are they subtle. The case requires understanding of the relationship between strategy, organization and performance, and how changes in strategy may affect the organization. The case also highlights the importance of understanding demographic changes as part of an environmental analysis.

Case 27 Tavazo Co.   413

In June 2010, Naser Tavazo, one of the three owner/manager brothers of both Tavazo Iran Co. and Toronto-based Tavazo Canada Co., was considering the company's future expansion opportunities, including further international market entry. Candidate cities of interest were Los Angeles, Dubai and other cities with a high Iranian diaspora. Another question facing the owners was where to focus on the value chain. Should the family business use its limited resources to expand its retailer business into more international markets, or to expand their current retailer/wholesale activities within Canada and Iran?

The objectives of this case are: (A) to discuss the typical problems that small companies confront when growing internationally and the implication of being a family business in this transition; (B) to provide a vehicle for developing criteria for market selection; (C) to highlight the importance of focus in the value chain regarding horizontal vs. vertical integration.

Part 9 Creating Effective Organizational Designs

Case 28 Victoria Heavy Equipment Limited   426

Victoria Heavy Equipment (Victoria) was a family owned and managed firm that had been led by an ambitious, entrepreneurial chief executive officer who now wanted to take a less active role in the business. His son and daughter were not yet ready to succeed him, so he wondered what kind of person he should hire to become president. Victoria had been through two reorganizations in recent years, which contributed to organizational and strategic issues which would need to be addressed by a new president. Among these was the need to align the organization design (staffing, structure, systems) to fit the desired strategy.

Case 29 Bombardier Transportation and the Adtranz Acquisition   436

Bombardier Transportation, one of the world's largest manufacturers of passenger rail cars, has successfully negotiated the purchase of Adtranz, a large European manufacturer of rail equipment. The newly appointed chief executive officer has been brought in to manage the acquisition. The new CEO faces many challenges including decisions about the pace of integration, location of headquarters, organization structure, personnel retention and personal management style.

Case 30 Challenges of Growth at Protegra   454

Protegra is a small company in Winnipeg, Manitoba, which specializes in computer software development and business performance consulting. Protegra features a unique organizational design, characterized by a lack of hierarchy and a collegial, professional culture centred on employee and customer values. Various information systems support Protegra's design. In the process of expanding into foreign markets and enlarging staff, Protegra has been concerned with preserving its way.

Part 10 Strategic Control and Corporate Governance

Case 31 CCL Industries Inc.: Building and Maintaining an Effective Board   466

CCL Industries Inc. is one of the top packagers of consumer products in the world. Over its 50-year history, the company had grown from a small room to a multinational firm employing 7,500 people with over $1.6 billion in sales. CCL faces an uncertain environment that had already led to a major strategic reorientation when its plan to sell its largest division was cancelled. A global economic slowdown and lower consumer confidence, coupled with extensive international operations, significantly increased the risk to CCL's sales and already slim profits. In the past, the company prospered through product diversification gained through acquisition. The economic slowdown and increased uncertainty meant that this strategy may not be appropriate in the future. The chief executive officer recognizes the time, attention, advice, composition and operations of the board of directors would likely have to be altered to reflect this new reality.

Case 32 Currie Road Construction Limited (A)   475

A successful B.C.-based Canadian road construction and maintenance company is contemplating U.S. market entry via a subsidiary in Texas. The case deals with market entry considerations: speed of entry, the need to invest in learning about a market and decisions regarding who would manage the subsidiary, as well as the proposed governance and control structure.

Part 11 Strategic Leadership: Creating a Learning Organization and an Ethical Organization

Case 33 Online Piracy: Jaywalking or Theft?   487

In September 2009, Brian Lee purchased a computer game developed by a major company and, like other customers, he was experiencing difficulty running it. The source of the problems was a highly restrictive system of digital rights management (DRM), which, while more or less universally disliked, was causing serious technical problems for a minority of users. Lee began to share his experience on the company's message board and was engaging in a debate about online piracy with a company representative. He was curious about piracy in the file-sharing age and wondered why it would be wrong to download a pirated version of the game with the DRM circumvented. The case deals with an ethical issue which resonates with students.

Case 34 Barrick Gold Corporation—Tanzania   496

This case examines the giant Canadian mining corporation, Barrick Gold Corporation (Barrick), called Africa Barrick Gold PLC since 2009, and the way it engages in sustainable community developments that surround its mining activities in Tanzania. Following recent organized tensions and heightened criticism from local communities, media, international social lobbyists and local not-for-profit organizations (NFOs), Barrick has attempted to deal with the local communities in a responsible manner. At issue for senior management was whether there was much more that it could reasonably do to resolve the tensions.

The case considers: how MNEs seek social license and local legitimacy; the relevance of hybrid institutional infrastructures; and the evolving global roles for MNEs and their subsidiaries.

Case 35 FIJI Water and Corporate Social Responsibility—Green Makeover or "Greenwashing"?   511

This case traces the establishment and subsequent operation of FIJI Water LLC. and its bottling subsidiary, Natural Waters of Viti Limited, the first company in Fiji extracting, bottling and marketing artesian water coming from a virgin ecosystem found on Fiji's main island of Viti Levu. The case reviews the growth and market expansion of this highly successful company. The company has grown rapidly over the past decade and a half, and now exports bottled water into many countries in the world, including Canada, from its production plant located in the Fiji Islands. In 2008, FIJI Water was the leading imported bottled water brand in the United States. In the context of great marketing success of the FIJI brand, the case focuses on how the company has responded to a number of corporate social responsibility (CSR) issues, including measuring and reducing its carbon footprint, responsibilities to key stakeholders and concerns of the Fiji government with regard to taxation and transfer pricing issues.

Case 36 Strategic Leadership at Coca-Cola: The Real Thing   535

Muhtar Kent had just been promoted to the CEO position in Coca-Cola. He was reflecting upon the past leadership of the company, in particular the success that Coca-Cola enjoyed during Robert Goizueta's leadership. The CEOs that had followed Goizueta were not able to have as positive an impact on the stock value. When his promotion was announced, Kent mentioned that he did not have immediate plans to change any management roles, but that some fine-tuning might be necessary.

Part 12 Managing Innovation and Fostering Corporate Entrepreneurship

Case 37 GE Energy Management Initiative (A)   550

The business development manager for General Electric (GE) Canada met with executives from GE Supply, a U.S.-based distribution arm of GE. The purpose of the meeting was to discuss new business opportunities in energy management and efficiency. The business development manager had identified some opportunities for business development in Canada, while leveraging GE's strategic capabilities did not fit well with GE's corporate structure. He was keen to work with GE Supply, but wanted to retain a high level of operating autonomy. The challenge was to put together an appropriate organizational structure and find a home for the new development idea.

Case 38 IMAX: Larger Than Life   558

IMAX was involved in several aspects of the large-format film business: production, distribution, theatre operations, system development and leasing. The case illustrates IMAX's use of its unique capabilities to pursue a focused differentiation strategy. IMAX was initially focused on large-format films that were educational yet entertaining, and the theatres were located in institutions such as museums, aquariums and national parks. However, IMAX found that its growth and profitability were constrained by its niche strategy. In response, IMAX sought to grow by expanding into multiplexes. Additionally, IMAX expanded its film portfolio by converting Hollywood movies, such as Harry Potter and Superman, into the large film format. This shift in strategy was supported by the development of two technological capabilities—DMR for conversion of standard 35 mm film into large format, and DMX to convert standard multiplexes to IMAX systems. The shift in strategy was partially successful, but carried the risk of IMAX losing its unique reputation.

Preface and Acknowledgements

This book was made possible with the academic and intellectual support from colleagues at the Ivey Business School at the University of Western Ontario (UWO), and others across the country. The primary stimulus for this book was the ongoing need for new, high-quality Canadian material.

Having decided to produce a book of cases in strategic management, a number of other decisions were made: (1) to bring together primarily Canadian cases written not only at Ivey, but by faculty across North America, Europe and Asia; (2) to include only decision-oriented cases, which arguably provide the best training for future managers; and (3) to include cases dealing with international business, high-technology industries, service industries, not-for-profit industries and business ethics.

Much useful feedback was solicited and received on the ninth edition from colleagues at dozens of institutions across Canada. This included detailed reviews from the following individuals:

Paul Doherty, University of Waterloo
Naheed K. Nenshi, Mount Royal University
Jean-Marie Nkongolo-Bakenda, University of Regina
Barry O'Brien, York University
Clem Ramchatesingh, Humber College
Mark Simpson, George Brown College
Laura A. Thurnheer, Okanagan College
Bernie Williams, University of Lethbridge

This edition contains 17 new cases (CIBC Mellon: Managing a Cross-border Joint Venture; Dell Inc. in 2009; Alcan (A): Anticipating Industry Change; Rogers' Chocolates (A); Immunovaccine (IMV): Preparing to Cross the "Valley of Death"; SunOpta, Inc.; Canadian Solar; Resuming Internationalization at Starbucks; Chabros International Group: A World of Wood; Holey Soles; Tavazo Co.; Challenges of Growth at Protegra; Online Piracy: Jaywalking or Theft?; Barrick Gold Corporation—Tanzania; FIJI Water and Corporate Social Responsibility—Green Makeover or "Greenwashing"?; Strategic Leadership at Coca-Cola: The Real Thing; IMAX: Larger Than Life); and two updated cases (The Chinese Fireworks Industry—Revised; Currie Road Construction Limited (A)). New cases were written or selected not only for their ability to achieve the desired pedagogical objectives, but with an eye to retaining student interest. Some of the new cases deal with such topical issues as online piracy, solar energy, financial crisis, CSR, internationalization and entrepreneurial start-ups.

Professors wishing to delve deeply into certain industries have the option of reorganizing the available material. The book contains multiple cases in each of the following industry groups:

- Recreation
- Furniture
- Consumer Products
- Financial Services
- Internet services
- Mining
- Health
- Retail

The cases themselves have been organized into the 12 subject areas that follow. These subject areas follow closely the current, mainstream approach to the teaching of strategic management.

1. Strategic Management: Creating Competitive Advantages
2. Analyzing the External Environment of the Firm
3. Assessing the Internal Environment of the Firm
4. Recognizing a Firm's Intellectual Assets: Moving Beyond a Firm's Tangible Resources
5. Business-Level Strategy: Creating and Sustaining Competitive Advantages
6. Corporate-Level Strategy: Creating Value through Diversification
7. International Strategy: Creating Value in Global Markets
8. Industry Change and Competitive Dynamics
9. Creating Effective Organizational Designs
10. Strategic Control and Corporate Governance
11. Strategic Leadership: Creating a Learning Organization and an Ethical Organization
12. Managing Innovation and Fostering Corporate Entrepreneurship

A comprehensive Case Teaching Notes package is available to text adopters. This Case Teaching Notes manual contains detailed teaching notes for each of the cases. It also includes an overview of the cases, possible industry groupings,case sequencing and possible course outlines, follow-up cases and Web addresses.

I am indebted to several groups of people for assisting in the preparation of this book. First, I am grateful to the case contributors from Ivey, and, from the faculty side, wish to thank Rod White, Stewart Thornhill, Eric Morse, Bob Nourse, Christopher Williams, Jean-Louis Schaan, the late Larry Tapp, Glenn Rowe and Nick Fry (emeritus). In addition, I acknowledge the contributions of the following current doctoral and research assistants at Ivey: Daina Mazutis, Michael Sartor, Ken Mark, Ramasastry Chandrasekhar, Jordan Mitchell, Bassam Farah, Majid Eghbali-Zarch and my assistant, Mary Roberts.

A number of one-time Ivey PhD students who contributed to the cases in this book are now faculty members in their own right. These include:

Julian M. Birkinshaw, London Business School, UK
Nikhil Celly, The University of Hong Kong
Trevor Hunter, Kings University College, University of Western Ontario
Ruihua Jiang, Oakland University, Michigan
Jane Lu, National University of Singapore

Nathan Lupton, Fordham University, New York
Kent E. Neupert, Boise State University, Idaho
George Peng, University of Regina
Andreas Schotter, Thunderbird School of Global Management, Arizona
Vanessa Strike, Erasmus University, The Netherlands
Jing'an Tang, Sacred Heart University, Connecticut
Huanglin Wang, Utica College, New York

Case contributors from other institutions include:

John Adamson, Cereson Inc.
Alex Beamish, Writer and Editor, London, Ontario
Ella Korets-Smith, Immunovaccine Inc.
James McMaster, University of The South Pacific, Fiji
Laurie Milton, University of Calgary
Karl Moore, McGill University
Allen Morrison, INSEAD
Amrita Nain, McGill University
Anil Nair, Old Dominion University, Virginia
Aloysius Newenham-Kahindi, University of Saskatchewan
Jan Nowak, Central European University, Hungary
Michael Parent, Simon Fraser University
Tom A. Poynter, St. John's, Newfoundland
Suhaib Riaz, University of Massachusetts Boston
Bob Travica, University of Manitoba
Gregory Vit, McGill University
Don Wood, University of West Indies
Charlene Zietsma, University of Victoria

The following doctoral and research assistants from other institutions are also acknowledged: Rob Alkema, David Barrett, Johnny Boghossian, Wilfred Cheung, Chris Ellison, Nigel Goodwin, Scott Hill, Mario Koster, Prarthana Kumar, Jeremy Kyle and Stacey Morrison.

In addition, I wish to thank the various executives who provided the required access to complete the cases in this book, and to recognize those students on whom the cases were tested for classroom use.

I look forward to your feedback.

Paul W. Beamish

Superior Service

Service takes on a whole new meaning with McGraw-Hill Ryerson and Cases in Strategic Management, Tenth Edition. More than just bringing you the textbook, we have consistently raised the bar in terms of innovation and educational research. These investments in learning and the education community have helped us understand the needs of students and educators across the country and allowed us to foster the growth of truly innovative, integrated learning.

Integrated Learning

Your Integrated-Learning Sales Specialist is a McGraw-Hill Ryerson representative who has the experience, product knowledge, training, and support to help you assess and integrate our products, technology, and services into your course for optimum teaching and learning performance. Whether it's how to use our test bank software, helping your students to improve their grades, or how to put your entire course online, your *i*Learning Sales Specialist is there to help. Contact your *i*Learning Sales Specialist today to learn how to maximize all McGraw-Hill Ryerson resources!

*i*Learning Services Program

At McGraw-Hill Ryerson, we take great pride in developing high-quality learning resources while working hard to provide you with the tools necessary to utilize them. We want to help bring your teaching to life, and we do this by integrating technology, events, conferences, training, and other services. We call it *i*Services. For more information, visit **www.mcgrawhill.ca/olc/iservices.**

National Teaching and Learning Conference Series

The educational environment has changed tremendously in recent years and McGraw-Hill Ryerson continues to be committed to helping you acquire the skills you need to succeed in this new milieu. Our innovative National Teaching and Learning Conference Series brings faculty together from across Canada with 3M Teaching Excellence award winners to share teaching and learning best practices in a collaborative and stimulating environment. Preconference workshops on general topics, such as teaching large classes and technology integration, are also offered. We will also work with you at your own institution to customize workshops that best suit the needs of the faculty at your institution.

Coursesmart

CourseSmart brings together thousands of textbooks across hundreds of courses in an eTextbook format, providing unique benefits to students and faculty. By purchasing an eTextbook, students can save up to 50 percent on the cost of a print textbook, reduce their impact on the environment, and gain access to powerful Web tools for learning including full-text search, notes and highlighting, and email tools for sharing notes between classmates. For faculty, CourseSmart provides instant access for reviewing and comparing textbooks and course materials in their discipline area without the time, cost, and environmental impact of mailing print exam copies. For further details contact your *i*Learning Sales Specialist or go to **www.coursesmart.com.**

Research In Motion: Managing Explosive Growth

In early January 2008, David Yach, chief technology officer for software at Research In Motion (RIM), had just come back from Christmas break. Returning to his desk in Waterloo, Ontario, relaxed and refreshed, he noted that his executive assistant had placed the preliminary holiday sales figures for BlackBerry on top of his in-box with a note that read "Meeting with Mike tomorrow." Knowing 2007 had been an extraordinarily good year, with the number of BlackBerry units sold doubling, Dave was curious: Why did Mike Lazaridis, RIM's visionary founder and co-chief executive officer, want a meeting? A sticky note on page three flagged the issue. Mike wanted to discuss Dave's research and development (R&D) plans—even though R&D spending was up $124 million from the prior year, it had dropped significantly as a percentage of sales. In an industry driven by engineering innovations and evaluated on technological advances, this was an issue.

R&D was the core of the BlackBerry's success—but success, Dave knew, could be a double-edged sword. Although RIM's engineers were continually delivering award-winning products, explosive growth and increased competition were creating pressures on his team to develop new solutions to keep up with changes in the global smartphone marketplace. With 2007 revenue up 98 per cent from the previous year, his team of approximately 1,400 software engineers should also have doubled—but both talent and space were getting increasingly scarce. The current model of "organic" growth was not keeping pace and his engineers were feeling the strain. As the day progressed, Dave considered how he should manage this expansion on top of meeting existing commitments, thinking "How do you change the engine, while you're speeding along at 200 kilometres per hour?" As his BlackBerry notified him of dozens of other urgent messages, he wondered how to present his growth and implementation plan to Mike the next morning.

Daina Mazutis wrote this case under the supervision of Professors Rod White and Paul W. Beamish solely to provide material for class discussion. The authors do not intend to illustrate either effective or ineffective handling of a managerial situation. The authors may have disguised certain names and other identifying information to protect confidentiality.

IVEY

Richard Ivey School of Business
The University of Western Ontario

RIM: RESEARCH IN MOTION LTD.

RIM was a world leader in the mobile communications market. Founded in 1984 by 23-year-old University of Waterloo student Mike Lazaridis, RIM designed, manufactured and marketed the very popular line of BlackBerry products that had recently reached 14 million subscribers worldwide and had just over $6 billion in revenue (see Exhibits 1 and 2). In early 2008, RIM was one of Canada's largest companies with a market capitalization of $69.4 billion.[1]

The BlackBerry wireless platform and line of handhelds could integrate e-mail, phone, Instant Messaging (IM), Short Message Service (SMS), Internet, music, camera, video, radio, organizer, Global Positioning System (GPS) and a variety of other applications in one wireless solution that was dubbed "always on, always connected." These features, especially the immediate pushed message delivery, in addition to the BlackBerry's small size, long battery life and ease of use, made the product extremely popular with busy executives who valued the safe and secure delivery of corporate mail and seamless extension of other enterprise and Internet services.

In particular, organizations that relied on sensitive information, such as the U.S. government and large financial institutions, were early and loyal adopters of BlackBerry and RIM's largest customers. RIM's enterprise e-mail servers, which were attached to the customer's e-mail and IM servers behind company firewalls, encrypted and redirected e-mail and other data before forwarding the information to end consumers through wireless service providers (see Exhibit 3). Having been the first to market with a "push" e-mail architecture and a value proposition built on security, RIM had more than 100,000 enterprise customers and an estimated 42 per cent market share of converged devices, and significantly higher market share of data-only devices, in North America.[2]

RIM generated revenue through the "complete BlackBerry wireless solution" which included wireless devices, software and services. Revenues, however, were heavily skewed to handheld sales (73 per cent), followed by service (18 per cent), software (6 per cent) and other revenues (3 per cent). In handhelds, RIM had recently introduced the award-winning BlackBerry Pearl and BlackBerry Curve, which were a significant design departure from previous models and for the first time targeted both consumer and business professionals (see Exhibit 4). RIM had accumulated a wide range of product design and innovation awards, including recognition from Computerworld as one of the Top 10 Products of the Past 40 Years.[3] Analysts and technophiles eagerly awaited the next-generation BlackBerry series expected for release in 2008.

Although originally built for busy professionals, BlackBerry had made considerable headway in the consumer market and had become something of a social phenomenon. Celebrity sightings put the BlackBerry in the hands of Madonna and Paris Hilton among others. The term "crackberry," used to describe the addictive or obsessive use of the BlackBerry, was added to Webster's New Millennium dictionary. Just six months after launching Facebook for BlackBerry, downloads of the popular social networking software application had topped one million, indicating that younger

[1]D. George-Cosh, "Analysts cheer RIM results, hike targets," Financial Post, April 4, 2008, http://www.nationalpost.com/scripts/story.html?id = 420318; accessed April 22, 2008.
[2]Of converged device shipments (smartphones and wireless handhelds). Canalys Smart Mobile Device Analysis service, Press Release, February 5, 2008, http://www.canalys.com/pr/2008/r2008021.htm, accessed April 2, 2008.
[3]http://www.rim.com/newsroom/news/awards/index.shtml

consumers were gravitating towards the popular handhelds.[4] RIM also actively sought partnerships with software developers to bring popular games such as Guitar Hero III to the BlackBerry mobile platform,[5] suggesting a more aggressive move to the consumer, or at least prosumer,[6] smartphone space.

Wireless carriers, such as Rogers in Canada and Verizon in the United States, were RIM's primary direct customers. These carriers bundled BlackBerry handhelds and software with airtime and sold the complete solution to end users. In 2007, RIM had over 270 carrier partnerships in more than 110 countries around the world. Through the BlackBerry Connect licensing program, other leading device manufacturers such as Motorola, Nokia, Samsung and Sony Ericsson could also equip their handsets with BlackBerry functionality, including push technology to automatically deliver e-mail and other data. Expanding the global reach of BlackBerry solutions was therefore a fundamental part of RIM's strategy. In 2007, 57.9 per cent of RIM's revenues were derived from the United States, 7.3 per cent from Canada and the remaining 34.8 per cent from other countries. To date, RIM had offices in North America, Europe and Asia Pacific; however, it had only three wholly owned subsidiaries—two in Delaware and one in England.

THE WIRELESS COMMUNICATIONS MARKET AND SMARTPHONES

Mobile wireless communication involved the transmission of signals using radio frequencies between wireless networks and mobile access devices. Although RIM was one of the first to market with two-way messaging, recent technological developments had encouraged numerous handheld and handset vendors to go beyond traditional "telephony" and release new "converged"[7] devices including smartphones, Personal Digital Assistants (PDA), phone/PDA hybrids, converged voice and data devices and other end-to-end integrated wireless solutions. A shift in the telecommunication industry was moving demand beyond just cellphones to smartphones—complete communications tools that married all the functions of mobile phones with fully integrated e-mail, browser and organizer applications. In 2007, key competitors to RIM's BlackBerry line-up included the Palm Treo 700 and 750, the Sony Ericsson P900 Series, the Nokia E62, the Motorola Q and the Apple iPhone.

The number of wireless subscriber connections worldwide had reached three billion by the end of 2007. China led with over 524 million subscribers, followed by the United States at 254 million and India with 237 million (see Exhibit 5). Year over year growth in the United States, however, was only 9.5 per cent, with an already high market penetration rate (87 per cent). In contrast, China's growth was 18.3 per cent with only 39 per cent penetration. In sheer numbers, India was experiencing the fastest growth rate with a 60 per cent increase and room to grow with 21 per cent market

---

[4]AFX International Focus, "RIM: Facebook for BlackBerry downloads top 1M," April 1, 2008, http://global.factiva.com, accessed April 1, 2008.

[5]Business Wire, "Guitar Hero III Mobile will rock your BlackBerry Smartphone," April 1, 2008, http://global.factiva.com, accessed April 1, 2008.

[6]Prosumer refers to "professional consumers," customers that use their mobile devices for both business and personal communications.

[7]"Converged" refers to the convergence of the digital wireless communication industry (cellular telephony) and information technology industries, signaled by the arrival of 2G networks which merged voice and data transmissions.

penetration. To put that into context, in late 2007 there were almost 300,000 new wireless network subscribers in India every day.[8]

Since the launch of Apple's iPhone in June 2007, competition in the smartphone segment of the mobile telecommunications industry had intensified. The iPhone "set a new standard for usability."[9] In 2007, smartphones represented only 10 per cent of the global mobile phone market in units. However, this segment was projected to reach over 30 per cent market share within 5 years.[10] In the U.S., the number of smartphone users had doubled in 2007 to about 14.6 million[11] while global shipments of smartphones rose by 53 per cent worldwide, hitting 118 million in 2007.[12] Some analysts saw the opportunity for smart phones as "immense," predicting that during 2008 and 2009, 500 million smart devices would be sold globally and cumulative global shipments would pass the one billion mark by 2012.[13]

Worldwide demand for wireless handhelds had been fuelled by several global trends, including the commercial availability of high-speed wireless networks, the emergence of mobile access to corporate intranets and the broad acceptance of e-mail and text messaging as reliable, secure and indispensable means of communication. Coupled with the growth of instant messaging as both a business and personal communications tool, the demand for wireless handhelds and smartphones was robust.

COMPETING PLATFORMS

Symbian, a proprietary Operating System (OS) designed for mobile devices and jointly owned by Nokia, Ericsson, Sony Ericsson, Panasonic, Siemens AG and Samsung, held an estimated 65 per cent worldwide share of the converged devices, shipping 77.3 million smartphones in 2007 (up 50 per cent from 2006).[14] This was significantly ahead of Microsoft's Windows Mobile OS (12 per cent) and RIM's BlackBerry OS (11 per cent). However, in North America, RIM led with 42 per cent of shipments, ahead of Apple (27 per cent), Microsoft (21 per cent) and Palm (less than 9 per cent and shrinking).[15]

However, RIM could not afford to rest on its laurels. In the North American market place, Apple had recently announced that it would be actively pursuing the business segment. Conceding that push-e-mail and calendar integration were key to securing enterprise users, Apple licensed ActiveSync Direct Push, a Microsoft technology. Apple hoped to entice corporate users to adopt the iPhone as their converged device of choice.[16] Similarly, Microsoft, which had struggled to gain widespread acceptance for

---

[8]GSMA 20 year factsheet, http://www.gsmworld.com/documents/20_year_factsheet.pdf, accessed April 5, 2008.

[9]P. Svensson, "Microsoft Upgrades Windows Mobile," Associated Press Newswire, April 1, 2008, http://global.factiva.com, accessed April 1, 2008.

[10]Esmerk Finish News, "Global: Survey: Nokia has best innovation strategy," March 25, 2008, http://global.factiva.com, accessed April 1, 2008.

[11]N. Gohring, "Smartphones on the rise? Thank the iPhone, panel says," Washington Post, March 31, 2008, http://www.washingtonpost.com/wp-dyn/content/article/2008/03/31/AR2008033102392.html, accessed online April 1, 2008.

[12]Canalys Smart Mobile Device Analysis service, Press Release, February 5, 2008, http://www.canalys.com/pr/2008/r2008021.htm, accessed April 2, 2008.

[13]Chris Ambrosio, Strategy Analytics, January 2008; and Pete Cunningham, Canalys, as quoted on www.symbian.com, accessed April 3, 2008.

[14]www.symbian.com, accessed April 3, 2008.

[15]Canalys Smart Mobile Device Analysis service, Press Release, February 5, 2008, http://www.canalys.com/pr/2008/r2008021.htm, accessed April 2, 2008.

[16]A. Hesseldahl, "How the iPhone is suiting up for work," Business Week, March 6, 2008, www.businessweek.com, accessed March 21, 2008.

its Windows Mobile OS, had recently revamped its marketing efforts and announced an end-to-end solution for enterprise customers as well as desktop-grade web browsing for Windows Mobile enabled phones.[17] Even Google had entered the fray with Android, an open and free mobile platform which included an OS, middleware and key applications. Rivalry, it seemed, was intensifying.

In early 2008, an analyst commented about the increasing competition in the converged device (smartphone and wireless handheld) segment:

> Apple's innovation in its mobile phone user interface has prompted a lot of design activity among competitors. We saw the beginnings of that in 2007, but we will see a lot more in 2008 as other smart phone vendors try to catch up and then get back in front. Experience shows that a vendor with only one smart phone design, no matter how good that design is, will soon struggle. A broad, continually refreshed portfolio is needed to retain and grow share in this dynamic market. This race is a marathon, but you pretty much have to sprint every lap.[18]

Another analyst observed:

> The good news for RIM? There still aren't many trusted alternatives for business-class mobile e-mail. This company could be one of the world's biggest handset manufacturers one day. It's hard for me to believe there won't be e-mail on every phone in the world. RIM is going to be a major force in this market.[19]

Given the rapid advances in the mobile communications industry, no technological platform had become the industry standard. In light of the dynamic market situation, RIM needed to ensure that its investment in R&D kept up with the pace of change in the industry.

R&D AT RIM

R&D and engineering were the heart and soul of RIM. In March 2007, RIM employed just over 2,100 people with different R&D areas of expertise: radio frequency engineering, hardware and software design, audio and display improvement, antenna design, circuit board design, power management, industrial design, and manufacturing engineering, among others. R&D efforts focused on improving the functionality, security and performance of the BlackBerry solution, as well as developing new devices for current and emerging network technologies and market segments. The ratio of software to hardware developers was approximately 2:1 and about 40 per cent of the software engineers were involved in core design work while another 40 per cent were engaged in testing and documentation (the remaining 20 per cent were in management, and support functions like documentation and project management).

R&D had increased significantly both in terms of the total number of employees as well as the geographic scope of its operations. Since 2000, the R&D group had grown more than tenfold, from 200 to 2,100 people and expanded to two more locations in Canada (Ottawa and Mississauga), several in the United States (Dallas, Chicago,

---

[17]"Microsoft unveils smartphone advancements to improve ability to work and play with one phone," April 1, 2008, Press Release; and "Microsoft announces enterprise-class mobile solution," April 1, 2008, Press Release, www.microsoft.com/prespass/press/2008/apr08

[18]Canalys Smart Mobile Device Analysis service, Press Release, February 5, 2008, http://www.canalys.com/pr/2008/r2008021.htm, accessed April 2, 2008.

[19]Ken Dulaney of Gartner, as quoted in A. Hesseldahl, "RIM: Growth rules the day," February 22, 2008, www.businessweek.com

Atlanta, Seattle and Palo Alto) and one in England. Waterloo was still the principal location—home to a vibrant and collaborative culture of young and talented engineers.

RIM's cryptographic and software source code played a key role in the success of the company, delivering the safe and secure voice and data transmission on which the Black-Berry reputation was built. Chris Wormald, vice-president of strategic alliances, who was responsible for acquisitions, licensing and partnerships described the challenge as follows:

> At the end of the day, our source code is really among our few enduring technical assets. We have gone through extraordinary measures to protect it. Extraordinary is probably still too shallow of a word. We don't give anyone any access under any circumstances. RIM was founded on a principle of "we can do it better ourselves"—it is a philosophy that is embedded in our DNA. This vertical integration of technology makes geographic expansion and outsourcing of software development very difficult.

Intellectual property rights were thus diligently guarded through a combination of patent, copyright and contractual agreements. It was also strategically managed through a geography strategy that divided core platform development from product and technology development, with most of the core work (on the chip sets, software source code, product design) still occurring in Waterloo. However, the exponential growth in sales, competition and industry changes was placing tremendous pressures on the R&D teams at the Canadian headquarters.

Similar to other players in the telecommunications industry (see Exhibit 6), it was RIM's policy to maintain its R&D spending as a consistent percentage of total sales. Investment analysts often looked to this number to gauge the sustainability of revenue growth. R&D expenses were seen as a proxy for new product or service development and therefore used as a key indicator of future revenue potential. Human capital represented the bulk of R&D dollars and the organizational development team in charge of hiring at RIM was working overtime to try and keep up with the growing demand for the qualified engineers needed to deliver on both customer and investor expectations.

ORGANIZATIONAL DEVELOPMENT FOR R&D AT RIM

The 2,100 R&D employees made up about 35 per cent of RIM's 6,254 employees.[20] Total headcount had also been growing in double digits over the last five years (see Exhibit 7). However, if investment analysts were correct and sales grew by almost 70 per cent again in 2008,[21] the large numbers involved could hinder RIM's ability to rely on its historic growth strategy: sourcing from the local talent pool, through employee referrals and new graduate recruitment, and making selective acquisitions of small technology companies. It needed to find upwards of 1,400 new software developers just to maintain the status quo in R&D. And not only did they have to find large numbers of talented individuals, they also had to figure out where they would be located and how to integrate them into RIM's culture.

The culture at RIM headquarters was seen as one of its differentiators and was a key factor in RIM's low employee turnover rate. In fact, the company had recently

[20]The remaining groups included 836 in sales, marketing and business development; 1,098 in customer care and technical support; 1,158 in manufacturing; and 1,002 in administration, which included information technology, BlackBerry network operations and service development, finance, legal, facilities and corporate administration.
[21]http://finance.yahoo.com/q/ae?s5RIMM

been recognized as one of "Canada's 10 Most Admired Corporate Cultures."[22] In describing the way things worked in the software development group at RIM, Dayna Perry, director of organizational development for R&D, commented:

> What we have here is flexibility, adaptability and the ability to work collaboratively and collegially. We haven't had a lot of process or the kind of bureaucracy that you may see in other larger organizations. . . . It is what has allowed us to be very responsive to market opportunities. It is sort of the "magic" or the "secret sauce" of how things just work and we get things done.

A software developer leading a team working on BlackBerry's many multi-lingual devices agreed, saying:

> RIM, in comparison to some of its competitors, is a nice and dynamic environment . . . RIM is a place engineers like to work. Some of our competitors treat their engineers as something unimportant. They don't participate in decisions. They are interchangeable. There is a very, very strong bureaucracy . . . it's crazy. RIM is very different.

Maintaining its unique culture was a priority for RIM. Remaining centred in Waterloo nurtured this ability. But it was becoming clear that growing mostly in Waterloo was going to become increasingly difficult. Not only did RIM already employ most of the best developers in the area, it already attracted the best and brightest of the nearby University of Waterloo's engineering and computer science graduates. About 300 students came on board every semester through the company's coveted co-op program and many were asked to remain with RIM after graduation. In fact, the talent at the University of Waterloo was so widely recognized that even Bill Gates made frequent visits to the university to court the best students[23] and Google had recently opened facilities there, acknowledging that "Waterloo is an incredible pool of talent"[24] and that it was ready to start hiring the best and the brightest "as quickly as possible."[25]

Attracting outside talent to Waterloo was difficult given the competitive nature of the global software development industry. Most of the big players in the smartphone space were also ramping up. For example, Sony Ericsson had posted 230 design and engineering jobs in Sweden, China and the United States. Nokia was looking for 375 R&D employees in Finland, the United States, India and Germany, among other development sites. In California's Silicon Valley, Apple and Google had scooped up many of the top mobile browser developers in a technology cluster famous for its exaggerated employee benefits and unbeatable climate. Motorola could be the exception to the rule, having announced layoffs of engineers. Although Waterloo, Ontario, had recently been named ICF's "Intelligent Community of the Year," the city of 115,000 people[26] might not be perceived by some candidates to be as attractive as other high tech centres which were more cosmopolitan, for example: Silicon Valley, or previous winners of the ICF, Taipei (2006), Mitaka (2005) or Glasgow (2004).[27]

---

[22]Canada's 10 Most Admired Corporate Cultures for 2006, www.waterstonehc.com, accessed on April 5, 2008.

[23]D. Friend, "Microsoft hunting IT grads," London Free Press, March 22, 2008.

[24]"Google expands Waterloo base," http://atuw.ca/feature-google-expands-waterloo-base/, accessed April 11, 2008.

[25]A. Petroff, "A Recruiter's Waterloo?" http://www.financialpost.com/trading_desk/technology/story.html?id=389305, accessed April 11, 2008.

[26]The greater Kitchener-Waterloo area had approximately 450,000 inhabitants.

[27]Intelligent Community Forum, 2007 Intelligent Community of the Year Awards, Press release May 18, 2007, http://www.intelligentcommunity.org/displaycommon.cfm?an=1&subarticlenbr=221, accessed April 5, 2008.

Compounding the problem was a shortage of physical space at RIM's Waterloo campus that was a running joke around headquarters. Even company founder Mike Lazaridis had to laugh about it—responding to a reporter's question about his most embarrassing moment, Lazaridis replied: "Scraping my Aston Martin in RIM's driveway. I was leaving a space and a car came from nowhere. The scratches have been fixed, but not the too-busy parking lot. It's a hazard of a growing company."[28]

On top of it all, RIM was looking to hire a very particular mix of engineers. Although new graduates were essential, to be ahead of the game a good proportion of the incoming employees was going to have to be senior hires. RIM needed people who could fit with the culture and hit the ground running. Dayna noted: "We just don't have the luxury of time to grow all our own talent. We do that in parallel and do a lot of internal promotion, but that is an investment you make in the future, it is not going to help you solve your problem today." And it wasn't just a question of the number of engineers. In software, breakthrough innovations often came from small teams led by a visionary. Many at RIM believed that "software is as much about art as it is about engineering." And in the dynamic wireless communications market, exceptional software developers were scarce.

MANAGING EXPLOSIVE GROWTH

The approach to growth used by RIM in the past would not deliver the scale and scope of R&D resources required to maintain its technical superiority. RIM had several options.

Do What We Do Now, Only More of It

RIM had been very successful in its local recruiting strategy as well as nation-wide campus recruitment drives. It relied heavily on the personal and professional networks of existing employees as an ear-on-the-ground approach to finding new talent. One option was to expand co-op programs to other universities as well as increase the frequency and intensity of its new graduate recruitment efforts. Microsoft's intern program, for example, included subsidized housing and transportation (car rental or bike purchase plan), paid travel to Redmond, health club memberships and even subsidized housecleaning![29]

Likewise, RIM could follow Microsoft's lead and form a global scouting group dedicated to finding the best talent worldwide and bringing them into RIM. Canada ranked as one of the best countries in the world to live in terms of life expectancy, literacy, education and other standards of living.[30] These and other benefits could attract young developers particularly from emerging markets. As well, the stronger dollar made Canada more attractive.

Similar to other players in the industry (e.g. Apple, Motorola, Sony Ericsson, Nokia), RIM posted many of its job openings online and potential employees searched and applied for the positions best suited for their skills and interests. However, with over 800 worldwide job postings, finding the right job was often a daunting task. RIM also had no formal way to manage qualified candidates that may have simply applied to the wrong team and hence good leads were potentially lost. Some competitors

---

[28]J. Shillingford, "A life run by BlackBerry," Financial Times, March 19, 2008, http://global.factiva.com, accessed on April 1, 2008.

[29]http://www.microsoft.com/college/ip_overview.mspx

[30]United Nations Human Development Index 2007/2008.

allowed candidates to build an open application (similar to Monster or Workopolis) that could then be viewed by anyone in the organization looking for talent. Revamping the careers website and being more creative in the way in which they structured recruiting was being considered.

Some competitors had also formalized hiring and the onboarding processes of computer scientists by hiring in "waves." Rather than posting individual job openings, Symbian, for example, solicited résumés once a year, which were then reviewed, and successful candidates invited to the London, U.K.-based head office to attend one of nine Assessment Days. If the attendees passed a series of tests and interviews, they were then inducted into the company during a formal "bootcamp" training session that lasted five weeks.[31] Symbian had also set up extensive collaborations with 44 universities in 17 countries including China, Russia and India as well as Ethiopia, Kuwait, Lebanon, Thailand and the United States. Dubbed the Symbian Academy, this network allowed partners and licensees to post jobs for Symbian Academy students and for professors to collaborate on the research and development of innovative applications such as pollution monitors on GPS-enabled Symbian smartphones[32]. Although RIM enjoyed an excellent relationship with the University of Waterloo, it did not currently have a recruiting strategy of this scope.

Grow and Expand Existing Geographies

RIM had established R&D operations beyond Waterloo, in Ottawa, Mississauga, Dallas and Chicago over the last five years. It was also expanding the number of product and technology development facilities in locations such as Fort Lauderdale by recruiting through general job fairs. This strategy, however, had to be balanced with a number of trade-offs. First, RIM wanted to ensure that its geographic expansion was not haphazard, but rather strategically executed. Second, the cost of talent in various locations had to be considered. Software engineers in Palo Alto, for example, commanded much higher wages than in Waterloo and the competition there was even more intense, with high turnover costs incurred when employees were wooed away by the many other high tech companies in the area.

There was also some internal resistance to expanding R&D to locations outside of Waterloo. Although there was a growing realization that RIM could no longer continue to grow locally, one senior executive commented:

> There are people here, even leaders and senior people, who have said: "What? Products being built elsewhere? No! We can't do that! Then we won't have any control!" So some of it is a cultural shift and a mind shift for the people that have been here and it is hard for them to let go and to be part of a really big company. And RIM is getting to be a big company now. And for some people, from an organizational culture perspective, it just doesn't resonate well with them.

This sentiment was not uncommon among software-centric organizations. Despite some geographic expansion, Microsoft, for example, had recently recommitted to its Redmond, Washington, campus, spending over $1 billion on new and upgraded facilities there with room to house an additional 12,000 employees.[33] Google was also strongly

---

[31]http://www.symbian.com/about/careers/graduate%20program/index.html, accessed April 3, 2008.
[32]www.symbian.com, accessed April 3, 2008.
[33]B. Romano, "Microsoft campus expands, transforms, inside out," The Seattle Times, November 23, 2007, http://seattletimes.nwsource.com/cgi-bin/PrintStory.pl?document_id=2004007121&zsection_id=2003750725&slug=microsoft11&date=20071111, accessed April 22, 2008.

committed to maintaining its Mountain View, California headquarters, with only a few satellite offices. Its unique company culture, built on attracting and keeping the best talent in a young and fun environment was part of Google's incredible success story, and helped it achieve the status of the number one company to work for according to Fortune Magazine[34]. Other large software companies such as Oracle and Apple also kept their software developers in one location to foster innovation. In some ways, RIM was already more geographically distributed than many larger software organizations.

Although establishing a geographic expansion plan posed difficulties, RIM had nevertheless laid out several criteria for selecting new locations for product and technology development sites. First, the area had to already have a pool of talent that housed a mature skill set; the city or region had be home to an existing base of software or hardware companies, thus ensuring that a critical mass of highly skilled employees was available. RIM's strategic expansion into Ottawa, for example, was influenced by the availability of talented software engineers in the area in the wake of Nortel's massive layoffs.[35] Lastly, the city or region had to have universities with strong technical programs. This allowed RIM to expand on its successful co-op programs and graduate recruitment initiatives. Once a satellite development site was set up, however, there was still the issue of how to transfer RIM's young and dynamic corporate culture to these locations.

Increase Acquisitions

RIM had success in bringing people on board through acquisition. Several years earlier, RIM had acquired Slangsoft, a high-tech start-up in Israel that was developing code which allowed for the ability to display and input Chinese characters—key to tailoring BlackBerry for Asian and other foreign markets. As part of the acquisition, RIM worked with Immigration Canada to relocate 11 of the engineers to Waterloo, 10 of whom were still with RIM more than six years later.

Growth by acquisition was a common practice in the high-tech and telecommunicationssectors. Google had made its initial move to Waterloo in 2006, for example, through the acquisition of a small wireless software company, subsequently discontinuing the company's web browser product, making it a purchase of talent and intellectual property.[36] Other companies had also made strategic acquisitions of technology. In 2002, Apple, for example, purchased EMagic, a small German company whose software was then used in the development of the popular Mac program Garage Band.[37] In larger and more public acquisitions, Nokia and Motorola had both recently acquired software companies in the hopes of gaining faster access to the growing smartphone market. In 2006, Nokia purchased Intellisync Corporation, a wireless messaging and mobile-software developer for $430 million, creating Nokia's "business mobility solutions" group.[38] Also in 2006, Motorola purchased Good Technology for a rumoured $500 million and released Good

---

[34]http://money.cnn.com/magazines/fortune/bestcompanies/2007/snapshots/1.html, accessed April 22, 2008.

[35]Estimated at over 15,000 total jobs in the last eight years; B. Hill, "Nortel to keep Ottawa as main R&D centre," April 4, 2008, The Montreal Gazette, http://www.canada.com/montrealgazette/news/business/story.html?id524aa8d53-154a-4d88-aa9d-593ce9794e10, accessed April 11, 2008.

[36]M. Evans, "Waterloo gets Googled," January 6, 2006, http://www.financialpost.com/story.html?id=c4f6f084-d72f-43ea-8a82-affe38df3830&k=58579, accessed April 11, 2008.

[37]A. Hesseldahl, "What to do with Apple's cash," Business Week, March 1, 2007, http://www.businessweek.com/technology/content/mar2007/tc20070301_402290.htm, accessed April 11, 2008.

[38]TelecomWeb News Digest, "Nokia completes Intellisync purchase," February 10, 2006, http://global.factiva.com, accessed April 11, 2008.

5.0, allowing for secure access to corporate intranets so enterprise users could download, edit and send documents remotely.[39]

Given the depressed economic climate in the United States in early 2008, many smaller firms and technology start-ups were struggling financially as were some larger competitors. There were persistent rumours that Palm, for example, was in severe financial trouble.[40] Further, growth by acquisition could also allow for the tactical expansion in other strategic markets.

The European mobile telecommunications market, in particular, was highly "nationalistic," with end users favoring home grown companies over foreign solutions. Establishing a presence there through acquisition could buy RIM goodwill and serve as a portal to this lucrative market. The economic downturn in the United States and recent competitor plant closures in Europe presented RIM with the potential for opportunistic acquisitions, either of technology or of software engineering talent.

Go Global

In early 2008, most of the R&D was still done in Waterloo, with some core work also being done in Ottawa and product and technology sites throughout the United States and in the United Kingdom. RIM was exploring a broader global expansion. It already had customer service operations in Singapore and sales and marketing representative offices in France, Germany, Italy, Spain, China, Australia, Hong Kong and Japan. Yet it had stopped short of establishing core research and development sites outside of Canada. Nonetheless, despite a strong desire to keep R&D close to home, RIM estimated that of all the new hires in 2008, likely half would have to be outside of Canada. In addition to the United States, it was looking to Europe, the Middle East and Africa (EMEA) and Eastern Europe. The same selection criteria of a mature skill set and strong technological universities applied to choosing R&D sites outside North America.

Some of RIM's key competitors had a long history of global expansion of their R&D activities. Symbian, for example, opened an R&D centre in Beijing in August 2007, already having three others in the United Kingdom and India.[41] Motorola, had been present in China since 1993 when it established its first R&D centre there as part of its Global Software Group (GSG). It had since set up R&D activities in Beijing, Tianjin, Shanghai, Nanjing, Chengdu and Hangzhou, investing an estimated US$800 million and employing more than 3,000 R&D staff in China. In 2007, Motorola added R&D sites in Vietnam and South Korea[42] and announced it would open an additional R&D complex in Wangjing, China, with another 3,000 employees.[43]

China in particular was beginning to gain worldwide recognition as a centre for innovation. The number of patent applications was doubling every two years and the R&D to GDP ratio had also doubled in the last decade. In addition to Motorola, Nokia had set up a number of research bases in China.[44] In 2005, Nokia had five R&D units there, employing more than 600 people; an estimated 40 per cent of its

---

[39]RCR Wireless News, "Motorola set to leverage Good in competitive e-mail market," June 25, 2007, http://global.factiva.com, accessed April 11, 2008.
[40]S. Weinberg, "Palm acquisition not considered threat to RIM," Dow Jones Newswire, http://global.factiva.com, accessed April 11, 2008.
[41]Business Monitor International, Asia Pacific Telecommunications Insight, April 2008, Issue 24.
[42]Business Monitor International, Asia Pacific Telecommunications Insight, January 2008, Issue 21.
[43]Press Release, "Twenty years' commitment ensures a more successful future," November 8, 2007, http://www.motorola.com/mediacenter/news/detail.jsp?globalObjectId=8923_8852_23&page=archive
[44]Business Monitor International, Asia Pacific Telecommunications Insight, November 2007, Issue 19.

global Mobile Phones Business Group handsets were designed and developed in the Beijing Product Creation Center.[45] The company had also recently announced a long-term joint research program with Tsinghua University in Beijing that would see 20 Nokia researchers working alongside 30 professors and associates and up to 50 students.[46] Globally, Nokia Research Centers (NRC) described its R&D strategy as:

> NRC has a two-fold approach to achieving its mandate of leading Nokia into the future. The work for core technology breakthroughs supporting Nokia's existing businesses takes place in the Core Technology Centers, the CTCs. More visionary, exploratory systems research that goes well beyond any current business model is conducted at the many System Research Centers, the SRCs.[47]

Nokia's Core Technology Centers were in Finland, with the SRCs in China, Germany, the United Kingdom, United States, Finland and Japan. The company employed 112,262 people of which 30,415, or 27 per cent, were in R&D.[48]

The Motorola Global Software Group (GSG) was more decentralized. In addition to China, it had R&D centres in Australia, Singapore, Mexico, Argentina, the United Kingdom, Poland, Russia, Italy, Canada and India, among others and employed approximately 27,000 R&D employees worldwide. The Motorola GSG in India had nearly 3,500 engineers and was responsible for designing 40 per cent of the software used in Motorola phones worldwide, including the MOTORAZR and MOTO Q. However, Motorola was not noted for having world-class smartphone software. The GSG structure was speculated to have contributed to Motorola's inability to deliver a successful follow-up product to the RAZR, as well as to have precipitated the company's recent financial downturn.[49]

Nonetheless, partnering with major research institutes to source top talent appeared to be a fairly common strategy. Motorola India collaborated with six of the seven Indian Institutes of Technology (IIT), as well as the Indian Institute of Science (IISC) and the Indian Institute of Information Technology (IIIT).[50] Other technology firms were also partnering with emerging market governmental and educational institutions to secure a foothold in future markets. Cisco Systems, for example, a leading manufacturer of network equipment, had recently announced a US$16 billion expansion plan into China, including investments in manufacturing, venture capital and education. Working with China's Ministry of Education, Cisco had established 200 "Networking Academies" in 70 cities in China and had trained more than 90,000 students.[51]

These types of collaborations and international research consortiums, however, raised not only logistical but also legal issues. Source code loss, software piracy and product imitations were more common in developing countries where IP protection laws (or enforcement) lagged the United States or Canada, leading to both explicit and tacit knowledge "leakage." For example, despite its strong commitment to China, Nokia was recently forced to file suit against two Beijing firms for manufacturing and selling mobile phones that were a direct copy of its proprietary and legally protected

[45]Press Release, May 21, 2004, "Nokia Expands R&D in China," http://press.nokia.com/ PR/200405/946603_5.html

[46]Press Release, May 28, 2007, "Nokia and Tsinghua University announce new research framework," http://www.nokia.com/A4136001?newsid=1129236

[47]http://research.nokia.com/centers/index.html

[48]Nokia annual report 2007.

[49]"What's on Motorola's agenda?" Business Week, January 9, 2008, http://www.businessweek.com/ innovate/content/jan2008/id2008014_304911_page_2.htm, accessed April 16, 2008.

[50]Motorola 2007 10-K and http://www.motorola.com/mot/doc/6/6294_MotDoc.pdf

[51]Business Monitor International, Asia Pacific Telecommunications Insight, January 2008, Issue 21.

industrial designs.[52] Other large high-tech companies such as Cisco and Microsoft had also suffered source code breaches. In late 2006, China Unicom, the state-run telecommunications company, had launched its own wireless e-mail service which it boldly named the Redberry, announcing that their Redberry brand not only continued the already familiar "BlackBerry" image and name, it also fully reflected the symbolic meaning of China Unicom's new red corporate logo.[53] For much of East Asia, reverse engineering and copying foreign products were important sources of learning, helping to transition these markets from imitators of technology to innovators and competitive threats.[54]

Wormald described the difficulties with emerging market dynamics as follows:

> I was just talking to a Fortune 500 CEO the other day who is closing up shop in India. This company had a 45 per cent employee turnover rate. They just walk down the street and go work for his competitor and he was tired of his source code just walking out the door.

For RIM, going global was therefore problematic on a number of fronts, most notably because the BlackBerry source code had to be protected. In addition, expanding to emerging markets was also complicated by restrictions regarding cryptographic software. Most governments, including those of Canada and the United States, along with Russia and China, regulated the import and export of encryption products due to national security issues. Encryption was seen as a "dual-use technology" which could have both commercial and military value and was thus carefully monitored. The U.S. government would not purchase any product that had not passed the "Federal Information Processing Standard" (FIPS) certification tests. This would preclude any product that had encrypted data in China because "if you encrypt data in China, you have to provide the Chinese government with the ability to access the keys."[55] India had also recently notified RIM that it planned to eavesdrop on BlackBerry users, claiming that terrorists may be hiding behind the encrypted messages to avoid detection.[56]

Even if these hurdles could be overcome, going global also brought with it additional challenges of organizational design, communication, and integration between head office and other geographically dispersed locations. Some competitors had chosen to expand globally by product line, while others had outsourced less sensitive functions such as testing and documentation. Eastern European countries such as Poland and Hungary, for example, were emerging as strong contenders for quality assurance testing. The lower cost of labor in developing and transitional economies, however, was showing signs of inflationary pressures in some locales and any planned savings might be somewhat offset by the increased monitoring, coordination and integration costs. Furthermore, RIM was not set up to manage a multi-country research

---

[52]Shanghai Daily, "Nokia files suit over alleged copy of model," June 29, 2006, http://global.factiva.com, accessed April 16, 2008.

[53]Hesseldahl, A. "BlackBerry vs. Redberry in China," September 25, 2006, Business Week http://www.businessweek.com/technology/content/apr2006/tc20060413_266291.htm?chan=search, accessed April 16, 2008.

[54]United Nations World Investment Report 2005, Transnational Corporations and the Internationalization of R&D, New York and Geneva, 2005, p. 165.

[55]E. Messmer, "Encryption restrictions" and "Federal encryption purchasing requirements," Network World, March 15, 2004, http://www.networkworld.com/careers/2004/0315man.html?page=1, accessed April 22, 2008.

[56]N. Lakshman, "India wants to eavesdrop on BlackBerrys," Business Week, April 1, 2008, http://global.factiva.com, accessed April 7, 2008.

consortium and the mindset in Waterloo was still very much such that core engineers needed to be seen to be perceived as valuable. On the other hand, the potential could not be ignored. In China, where the penetration rate was only 38 per cent, the Symbian OS system used in Nokia, Samsung, Sony Ericsson and LG smartphones enjoyed a 68.7 per cent share, and iPhone sales had reached 400,000 "unlocked" units.[57] In India, where the penetration rate stood at 21 per cent, Virgin Mobile had recently struck a brand franchise agreement with Tata Teleservices, announcing plans to gain at least 50 million young subscribers to its mobile services, generating estimated revenues of US$350 billion.[58] The sheer number of potential new users was overwhelming.

CONCLUSION

Looking at the holiday sales numbers and the projected growth for 2008, Yach took a minute to think about the path he was on. He knew that first quarter revenue projections alone were estimated at $2.2 billion to $2.3 billion and that RIM was expecting to add another 2.2 million BlackBerry subscribers by the end of May 2008.[59] At that rate, analysts projected that 2008 would bring at least another 70 per cent growth in sales.[60] Furthermore, Mike Lazaridis had recently said in an interview:

> If you really want to build something sustainable and innovative you have to invest in R&D. If you build the right culture and invest in the right facilities and you encourage and motivate and inspire both young and seasoned people and put them all in the right environment—then it really performs for you. It's what I call sustainable innovation. And it's very different from the idea that you come up with something and then maximize value by reducing its costs. But building a sustainable innovation cycle requires an enormous investment in R&D. You have to understand all the technologies involved.[61]

Yach knew that his software developers were key to RIM's continued success; he was committed to delivering on the expectations for continued and sustainable growth in 2008 and beyond. Although he wanted to keep growing organically, sourcing talent locally and bringing his engineers into the cultural fold of RIM in Waterloo, he suspected this era was ending. In light of the unprecedented and exponential growth of the last year, coupled with the increasing competition and untapped global opportunities, he needed a plan.

Leaving the office after a hectic and frenetic first day back, Yach thought to himself: "How can I plan for this growth when it is just one of 10 burning issues on my agenda? We can't take a time-out to decide how to execute the growth." Grabbing the sales numbers to prepare for tomorrow's meeting, Yach knew he had the evening to consider the way ahead. The vacation was definitely over.

---

[57]Business Monitor International, Asia Pacific Telecommunications Insight, April 2008, Issue 24.
[58]Business Monitor International, Asia Pacific Telecommunications Insight, April 2008, Issue 24.
[59]Press Release, April 2, 2008: http://www.rim.com/news/press/2008/pr-02_04_2008-01.shtml
[60]http://finance.yahoo.com/q/ae?s=RIMM
[61]A. Hesseldahl, "BlackBerry: Innovation Behind the Icon," Business Week, April 4, 2008, http://www.businessweek.com/innovate/content/apr2008/id2008044_416784.htm?chan5search, accessed April 6, 2008.

EXHIBIT 1

BlackBerry Subscriber Account Base (in Millions)

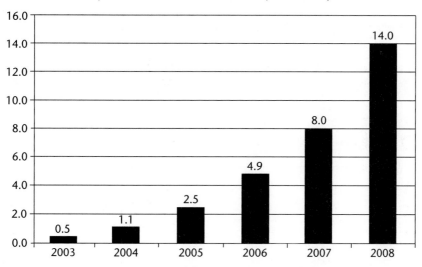

RIM Annual Revenue (in Millions of U.S. Dollars)

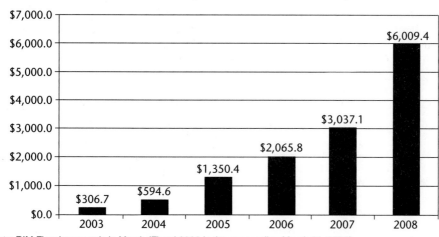

Note: RIM Fiscal year ends in March (Fiscal 2008 is the year ending March 31, 2008).
Source: RIM Fiscal 2007 Annual Report and Fiscal 2008 Press Release (April 2, 2008).

EXHIBIT 2   Consolidated Statement of Operations

	Mar. 1, 2008 (Projected)	Mar. 3, 2007	Mar. 4, 2006	Feb. 26, 2005	Feb. 28, 2004
Revenue	$6,009,395	$3,037,103	$2,065,845	$1,350,447	$594,616
Cost of sales	2,928,814	1,379,301	925,598	636,310	323,365
Gross margin	3,080,581	1,657,802	1,140,247	714,137	271,251
Gross margin %	51.30%	54.60%	55.20%	52.88%	45.62%
Expenses					
Research and development	359,828	236,173	158,887	102,665	62,638
Selling, marketing & admin.	881,482	537,922	314,317	193,838	108,492
Amortization	108,112	76,879	49,951	35,941	27,911
Litigation			201,791	352,628	35,187
	1,349,422	850,974	724,946	685,072	234,228
Income from operations	1,731,159	806,828	415,301	29,065	37,023
Investment income	79,361	52,117	66,218	37,107	10,606
Income before income taxes	1,810,520	858,945	481,519	66,172	47,629
Provision for income taxes					
Current	587,845	123,553	14,515	1,425	
Deferred	−71,192	103,820	92,348	(140,865)	
	516,653	227,373	106,863	(139,440)	−4,200
Net Income	$1,293,867	$ 631,572	$ 374,656	$ 205,612	51,829
Earnings per share					
Basic	$ 2.31	$ 1.14	$ 1.98	$ 1.10	$ 0.33
Diluted	$ 2.26	$ 1.10	$ 1.91	$ 1.04	$ 0.31

Table header: Research In Motion Limited / Incorporated under the Laws of Ontario / (United States dollars, in thousands except per share data) — For the year ended

Source: Company Annual Reports; Fiscal 2008 form; Press Release, April 2, 2008, Research In Motion reports Fourth Quarter and Year-End Results for Fiscal 2008, http://www.rim.com/news/press/2008/pr-02_04_2008-01.shtml

EXHIBIT 3 BlackBerry Enterprise Solution Architecture

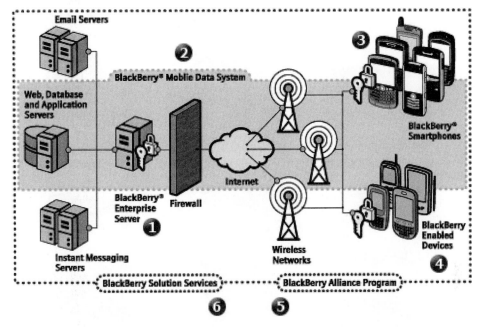

1. **BlackBerry® Enterprise Server:** Robust software that acts as the centralized link between wireless devices, wireless networks and enterprise applications. The server integrates with enterprise messaging and collaboration systems to provide mobile users with access to e-mail, enterprise instant messaging and personal information management tools. All data between applications and BlackBerry® smartphones flows centrally through the server.

2. **BlackBerry® Mobile Data System (BlackBerry MDS):** An optimized framework for creating, deploying and managing applications for the BlackBerry Enterprise Solution. It provides essential components that enable applications beyond e-mail to be deployed to mobile users, including developer tools, administrative services and BlackBerry® Device Software. It also uses the same proven BlackBerry push delivery model and advanced security features used for BlackBerry e-mail.

3. **BlackBerry Smartphones:** Integrated wireless voice and data devices that are optimized to work with the BlackBerry Enterprise Solution. They provide push-based access to e-mail and data from enterprise applications and systems in addition to web, MMS, SMS and organizer applications.

4. **BlackBerry ® Connect™ Devices:** Devices available from leading manufacturers that feature BlackBerry push delivery technology and connect to the BlackBerry Enterprise Server.

5. **BlackBerry ® Alliance Program:** A large community of independent software vendors, system integrators and solution providers that offer applications, services and solutions for the BlackBerry Enterprise Solution. It is designed to help organizations make the most of the BlackBerry Enterprise Solution when mobilizing their enterprises.

6. **BlackBerry Solution Services:** A group of services that include: BlackBerry® Technical Support Services, BlackBerry® Training, RIM® Professional Services and the Corporate Development Program. These tools and programs are designed to help organizations deploy, manage and extend their wireless solution.

Source: http://na.blackberry.com/eng/ataglance/solutions/architecture.jsp

EXHIBIT 4   The Evolution of the BlackBerry Product Line (select models)

RIM Inter@ctive Pager 850   RIM 957   BlackBerry 6200

BlackBerry 8820   BlackBerry Pearl 8110   BlackBerry Curve 8330

Source: http://www.rim.com/newsroom/media/gallery/index.shtml and Fortune, "BlackBerry: Evolution of an icon," Jon Fortt, Sept 21, 2007, accessed April 7, 2008; http://bigtech.blogs.fortune.cnn.com/blackberry-evolution-of-an-icon-photos-610/

EXHIBIT 5   Mobile Telephone Users Worldwide (in Millions)

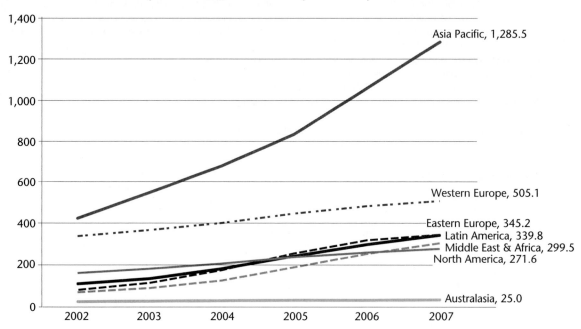

Source: Created from data accessed from the Global Market Information Database, April 4, 2008, http://www.portal.euromonitor.com.proxy1. lib.uwo.ca:2048/portal/server.pt?control=SetCommunity&CommunityID=207&PageID=720&cached=false&space=CommunityPage

EXHIBIT 6 Competitive R&D Spend (Select Competitors)

In Millions (US$)

Nokia		Dec. 31/04	Dec. 31/05	Dec. 31/06	Dec. 31/07
Revenue		$46,606	$54,022	$64,971	$80,672
R&D		$ 5,784	$ 6,020	$ 6,157	$ 8,229
		12.41%	11.14%	9.48%	10.20%
Microsoft	June 30/03	June 30/04	June 30/05	June 30/06	June 30/07
Revenue	$32,187	$36,835	$39,788	$44,282	$51,122
R&D	$ 6,595	$ 7,735	$ 6,097	$ 6,584	$ 7,121
	20.49%	21.00%	15.32%	14.87%	13.93%
Motorola	Dec. 31/03	Dec. 31/04	Dec. 31/05	Dec. 31/06	Dec. 31/07
Revenue	$23,155	$29,663	$35,310	$42,847	$36,622
R&D	$ 2,979	$ 3,316	$ 3,600	$ 4,106	$ 4,429
	12.87%	11.18%	10.20%	9.58%	12.09%
Apple	Sept. 27/03	Sept. 25/04	Sept. 24/05	Sept. 30/06	Sept. 29/07
Revenue	$ 6,207	$ 8,279	$13,931	$19,315	$24,006
R&D	$ 471	$ 491	$ 535	$ 712	$ 782
	7.59%	5.93%	3.84%	3.69%	3.26%
RIM	Feb. 28/04	Feb. 26/05	Mar. 4/06	Mar. 3/07	Proj. Mar./08
Revenue	$ 595	$ 1,350	$ 2,066	$ 3,037	$ 6,009
R&D	$ 63	$ 103	$ 159	$ 236	$ 360
	10.59%	7.63%	7.70%	7.77%	5.99%
Palm	May 31/03	May 31/04	May 31/05	May 31/06	May 31/07
Revenue	$ 838	$ 950	$ 1,270	$ 1,578	$ 1,561
R&D	$ 70	$ 69	$ 90	$ 136	$ 191
	8.35%	7.26%	7.09%	8.62%	12.24%

Note: Nokia 2007 includes Nokia Siemens.
Source: Company Annual Reports.

EXHIBIT 7   Employee Growth at RIM

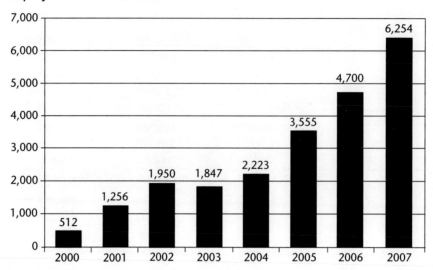

Source: RIM Annual Reports.

CIBC Mellon: Managing A Cross-Border Joint Venture

Thomas MacMillan leaned back in his chair and glanced out of his office window down onto Bay Street, the epicentre of the Canadian financial industry. During his 10-year tenure as president and CEO of CIBC Mellon, MacMillan had presided over the dramatic growth of the jointly owned, Toronto-based asset servicing business of CIBC and the Bank of New York Mellon Corporation (BNY Mellon). However, now it was an overcast day in mid-September 2008 and MacMillan had a front-row seat to witness the onset of the worst financial crisis since the Great Depression.

CIBC Mellon was facing this oncoming global financial storm with a solid balance sheet and was secure in the knowledge that both of its parents were also well capitalized. However, the well-publicized impending collapse of several long-standing financial titans threatened to impact all players in the financial services industry worldwide. Despite the fact that joint ventures (JVs) were uncommon in the financial sector, MacMillan believed that the CIBC Mellon JV was uniquely positioned to withstand the fallout associated with the financial crisis and that it would be able to weather the most significant risks facing the JV—execution risk and the potential exodus of assets and clients who were panicked by the wider financial pandemonium. MacMillan and his team recognized that it would be critical for the JV to continue to deliver a high level of client service and to avoid any major operational missteps.

MacMillan's moment of introspection was interrupted by a knock on the door. He was scheduled to meet with three members of the company's executive management

Professor Paul W. Beamish wrote this case with the assistance of Michael Sartor solely to provide material for class discussion. The authors do not intend to illustrate either effective or ineffective handling of a managerial situation. The authors may have disguised certain names and other identifying information to protect confidentiality.

Ivey
Richard Ivey School of Business
The University of Western Ontario

committee, Paul Marchand, Mark Hemingway and James Slater, to discuss two pressing issues facing the JV. First, they needed to discuss how to best manage any risks confronting the JV as a consequence of the financial crisis. Given the massive size and global reach of the largest financial service giants, and the likelihood that some of these behemoths might now be teetering on the edge of bankruptcy, CIBC Mellon, like other players in the financial services industry, would be forced to move adeptly to protect its operations from any potential exposure to the larger players' fates. While the systems, structure and culture that prevailed at CIBC Mellon served as evidence of MacMillan and his team's diligent efforts over the past 10 years to focus on risk management and to foster a culture of synergistic cooperation, the question remained—how could the policies and practices developed during the past decade be leveraged to sustain the JV through the broader financial crisis? Second, the four men were scheduled to continue discussions regarding options for refining CIBC Mellon's strategic focus, so that the JV could emerge from the financial meltdown on even stronger footing. Notwithstanding the immediate urgency of the financial crisis, the JV's management team recognized the need to continue to manage the business with a view towards future growth.

BACKGROUND

The Asset Servicing/Global Custody Business

When the JV was conceived in 1996, its principal emphasis was on asset servicing—the global custody business—which was generally viewed as "a dull business, with dull services, in a dull little corner of the financial services sector." Asset servicing delivers securities-related administrative services to support the investment processes and goals of clients. Such services include global custody, securities lending, cash management, multicurrency accounting and reporting, global performance measurement and analytics, transition management, commission recapture and foreign exchange. Clients include pension plans, investment managers, mutual funds, insurance companies and global financial institutions. The fees charged to provide such administrative services would typically be much less than one half of one per cent of the value of the asset being supported.

In 1996, CIBC was one of the big five Schedule I (domestic) banks in Canada. At that time, it had an average custodial operation, with approximately 14 competitors, principally trust companies and the security departments of the major banks. CIBC had $100 billion in custody assets and a handful of clients. Its technology platform was poor and needed significant investment. It had three choices to make:

1. Invest—the problem there was that it would have had to invest a lot of money ($300, $400, $500 million)—to come up with a world-class custodial system. It was concerned that the revenue potential from the Canadian marketplace would not have resulted in it receiving adequate returns for its investment.
2. Exit the business—as a lot of companies in Canada subsequently did.
3. Form a joint venture if it could find the right partner. CIBC believed there was the potential of creating a good, viable Canadian-based business, but it needed a partner.

In 1996, Pittsburgh-based Mellon Bank had a Schedule II (Canadian bank which was a subsidiary of a foreign bank) banking operation in Canada, which MacMillan ran. Its Canadian custody market share was about one per cent—specifically one client,

CDN$8 billion in assets under administration, which was being administered out of Boston. However, Mellon had a world-class technology platform, had scale (in a scale business) and was committed to growing its market share but was having difficulty breaking into the Canadian marketplace. It knew it would be a difficult and slow process to get established in Canada by setting up a greenfield operation.

CIBC approached several potential partners, but it was Mellon's technology and people that impressed it the most. CIBC had a Canadian presence and a client base, but no technology and its service was average. Mellon had great technology, products and services, but no presence in Canada and few clients in the country. And it was receptive to CIBC's overtures. It seemed the ideal circumstance for the birth of a joint venture—a great fit. Both parties needed each other and there was very little overlap. The opportunity to create a world-class Canadian asset servicing company—when not many existed in Canada at the time—was too enticing to pass up for both organizations. CIBC Mellon was the first significant JV for either parent.

Given the relative rarity of JVs in the financial services sector, the two sole shareholders in the proposed JV (CIBC and BNY Mellon) devoted a considerable amount of thought and planning during 1996 to the design and structure of the entity. A significant volume of legal agreements was negotiated to establish the parameters that would govern the relationship between the two shareholders. Buried within the reams of legal documents were provisions drafted to prohibit each of the shareholder parents from competing against the JV; to detail the limitations surrounding the JV's use of the parent shareholders' trademarks and other intellectual property; to outline the basis upon which each parent would provide services to the JV, including, in the case of BNY Mellon, the basis upon which it would provide and "Canadianize" its technology for the JV; and to require each of the shareholders to utilize the JV as a supplier of asset servicing and global custody services.

One of the most critical governance clauses pertained to voting rights. Under the JV's shareholder agreement, each of the parties would enjoy a 50 per cent vote on every issue. In effect, this eliminated the need to vote on any issue—only consensus could yield a decision and the JV managers needed to secure the approval of both shareholders before taking any major issues to the board. Accordingly, at the outset MacMillan and his team recognized that in order for the JV to execute on its mission both strategically and operationally, it would be critical for the two shareholders, their employees and the JV's employees to develop an acute understanding and respect for the unique capabilities that each shareholder brought to the JV. MacMillan acknowledged that "the governance processes developed for this JV effectively facilitated our ability to leverage the expertise of each shareholder." While both parties were strong players in the credit markets, BNY Mellon had a strong understanding of credit in the global custody market and enjoyed a strong reputation with federal regulators in the United States. CIBC, on the other hand, had a strong understanding of credit in the Canadian marketplace and was known for its strong global trading platform (CIBC World Markets).

Equally important were provisions pertaining to risk management. The shareholders agreed to the formation and to the membership on the JV's Asset & Liability Committee (ALCO). ALCO was tasked with the responsibility of overseeing the formulation of risk management policies and asset investment policies associated with the JV's treasury and securities lending activities—principal activities under which financial services firms could become exposed to credit risk and market risk. This pivotal committee was populated by senior management from CIBC, BNY Mellon and the JV itself. MacMillan acknowledged that both shareholders had sought to structure the JV to develop a discrete, low-risk business and that risk tolerance would be maintained in the parents' businesses. As such, the JV only engaged in very conservative transactions and did not engage in proprietary trading. Appropriately managing risk necessitated clear and constant communication in order to ensure that the JV was aligned with its shareholders. It also effectively positioned the JV's management team to tap into the knowledge assets and accumulated experience of two major financial institutions.

When formed at the end of 1996, the JV had fewer than 200 employees, $110 billion in assets under administration, a market share of less than 10 per cent and revenues of about $25 million. However, over the next decade, the business grew dramatically. In 1997, it acquired the Canada Trust custody business. In 1999, it acquired the Bank of Montreal custody business, in 2002, the TD Bank third-party custody business, and in 2006, it was awarded the IG/Mackenzie custody business. By 2006, there were 1,400 employees and 1,140 custody clients. At this point, the asset servicing business offered a wide and integrated range of products and services from custody to risk management which could be grouped into two broad categories: core asset servicing functions and capital markets functions (see Exhibit 1). Historically, each of these two categories of business functions contributed approximately 50 per cent of the profits generated by the JV's asset servicing business. While the core asset servicing business functions supplied a stream of recurring-fee revenue to the JV, the income stream generated by the capital markets functions could be more volatile, depending upon the state of the capital markets. The global securities lending component of the capital markets functions involved acting as an agent in facilitating the lending of debt and equities from the JV's clients to other clients, who were typically brokers. While they did not disclose to CIBC Mellon why they were undertaking any particular loan, it could be expected that the brokers that borrowed the assets from CIBC Mellon would utilize the assets both for their own proprietary trading and to loan to the brokers' clients, sometimes including hedge funds that pursued short positions in equities. Short positions were established by traders who sold equities that they did not currently own. In essence, short sales involved selling borrowed equity assets. Consistent with regulatory requirements and its low-risk culture, CIBC Mellon routinely secured the loans that it extended to its broker clients by requiring the borrowers to pledge high-quality assets in excess of the value of the underlying loans as collateral. Exhibit 2 illustrates the interactions that occurred between external parties and CIBC Mellon's securities lending service.

By 2007, assets under administration for the JV's asset servicing business exceeded $800 billion and were growing. The JV had become the second-largest asset servicing business in Canada, with a market share over 30 per cent. It was settling 15,000 transactions each day. Total revenues for CIBC Mellon exceeded $350 million, and healthy quarterly dividends were being paid to each partner.

The Stock Transfer and Corporate Trust Businesses

In 1997, the JV entered the trust services business through CIBC's purchase of a 50 per cent interest in Mellon's R-M Trust Company. The purchase was undertaken because the JV required a trust company as a deposit-taker for its asset servicing business and because R-M also had established stock transfer and corporate trust businesses. Through this business, Canadian companies that issued securities that traded on major stock exchanges relied on CIBC Mellon to manage administrative duties like security holder record keeping, securities transfers, investor communication, dividend payments and employee plan administration. The JV also acted as a corporate trustee for its trust clients' assets. In its corporate trustee role, the JV acted as indenture trustee for a number of series of asset-backed commercial paper (ABCP). ABCPs were typically short-term commercial paper investments that were collateralized by other financial assets which were characterized by very low risk. As of 2006, the JV had 1,200 trust clients. CIBC Mellon did not borrow or lend any securities in connection with this line of business.

In a November 2006 speech to the Financial Services Institute, MacMillan was asked to reflect on both the reasons he felt many joint ventures failed (see Exhibit 3) and the reasons why CIBC Mellon had been so successful.

> Let me start with the one main reason that towers over all of them: our people. They are amazing and we have together somehow created an atmosphere where we can all thrive. Our people are our big differentiator. This can happen in any company. It has happened in our JV. We have succeeded because:

- **The original business plan made sense.** CIBC Mellon is profitable, growing, with good returns because the original business rationale was solid. It wasn't two "lousy" businesses coming together. Outstanding Mellon technology and service was introduced into Canada relatively quickly through a JV that had CIBC in its name and made an immediate positive market impact.

- **The parents receive benefit from the JV itself in the form of dividends but also from outside of the JV.** Both parents make significant FX revenues for their own books from JV clients. We help Mellon win global custody bids, we help CIBC win additional banking business that is often tied to asset servicing, for example cash management. We contribute to the building of strong client relationships for both parents. Mellon gets to appropriately allocate costs to the joint venture connected with their technology spend—and this spend is significantly larger than what they could otherwise afford because of the JV.

- **Both parents cooperate.** I see it at every board meeting—they respect and appreciate the contribution of the others; work collaboratively to make the JV a success. Despite the historical, jurisdictional and managerial differences, we've managed to put these differences to the side to make the JV work. And when there are differences of opinion (and frankly there's not that many) they work it out; and both organizations complement each other: CIBC defers to Mellon's expertise in the global custody business; Mellon defers to CIBC's knowledge/expertise relative to Canadian business and banking. I think it helps that both banks had a good solid friendship for many decades prior to the formation of the JV. They were (and are) comfortable with each other. They don't really compete against each other in any major business lines. Canadians are generally comfortable working with Americans and vice versa. Both parents' head offices are in the same time zone.

- **Commitment of the parents.** They have from the very beginning wanted to see the JV succeed and grow and they spent time making this happen. When more capital was required for acquisitions (the asset servicing business of Canada Trust, BMO, TD)—both parents were there. Early on in our history we had teething pains (our level of client service was not what it is today)—the parents didn't waiver and constructively helped us overcome issues and push on.

- **The JV has effectively leveraged the strength of both parents.** Mellon has 50 per cent ownership, but we benefit 100 per cent from their ongoing technology spend—over US$200 million a year. On a stand-alone basis, we couldn't afford US$200 million each year for technology in support of asset servicing business. This is an enormous plus for us.

From CIBC, we consistently leverage their client banking relationships to win new business for CIBC Mellon. We also leverage governance standards and risk management practices from both partners.

- **And finally—our company is well managed.** We have a strong board composed of mature, competent executives who can speak for their organizations. There has been minimal board turnover and when it has happened the transitions have been smooth. My lead board members from both organizations have been there since day one.

But equally important, I am blessed with an extremely strong executive management team. This team gets direction from the board and we run with it. They are also very skillful at working with both shareholders to ensure that all interests are balanced and satisfied and the strengths of both parents are fully realized. This is a skill requirement unique to joint ventures. For example:

- Leveraging technology development at Mellon and sales development at both parents.
- Working with both parents' risk, audit and compliance.
- It is a skill to unleash the power of our parents without being overwhelmed by them.

And while we are proactive in leveraging the strengths of our shareholders, we never forget we are a stand-alone organization that needs to be managed effectively. We have developed a strong internal culture quite independent of our parents, including our own strategy, brand, vision and core values. And we've shown enormous skills in initiating and successfully concluding major acquisitions at critical times.

- **We have also been a little bit lucky.** The markets have been generally favourable the last 10 years. There has been tremendous growth in the mutual fund industry, a major sector for us. There has been an accelerating trend to globalization of the capital markets, including increased complexity of financial instruments, and heightened requirements for reporting and transparency and real time information. These all play to our strengths. Not all of this was anticipated back in 1996. Over the past 10 years, we've had a good tailwind. You are better to be lucky than good, but we have been good.

2007–2008: FROM TAILWIND TO HEADWIND

The growth that had characterized the global financial sector up until 2006 began to materially change in 2007. A rapid series of problems began to either emerge or become more widely acknowledged. Fundamental differences that existed between the Canadian and U.S. banking sectors posed a unique set of concerns for financial institutions with operations on both sides of the border. Discrepancies in consumer debt and equity levels, divergent banking regulations and differences in the structure of each country's mortgage security industry comprised some of the most significant concerns.

The Canadian Financial Sector[1]

Canada as a whole was entering the crisis with a strong balance sheet and economic position. Consumers had lower debt and more savings than in the United States.

Mortgages were originated and held by Canadian banks, not packaged up and sold as securities. Canadian mortgages were generally five years or less, and mortgage interest was not tax deductible in Canada, so homebuyers were not encouraged to buy beyond their means. There were no 40-year terms, and buyers had to be able to have a down payment. Canadian banks could not lend more than 80 per cent of the value of a house without mortgage insurance from the Canada Mortgage and Housing Corporation.

Canadian banks were large, stable and sophisticated national entities (an oligopoly). With branches across the country and often in other countries, Canadian bank risk was dispersed. Canadian bankers tended to be more risk-averse than their U.S. and international counterparts. Canadian banks were required to maintain a tier one capital ratio of seven per cent and generally exceeded it. They had to cap overall leverage at 20X capital.

Canadian banks were regulated by a single piece of legislation, the Bank Act, which was reviewed every five years, and one national body, the Office of the Superintendant of Financial Institutions (OSFI). OSFI had broad oversight—there was no "shadow banking system" that fell outside the regulations. Canada also had strong monetary policy set by the Bank of Canada and the Department of Finance.

In Canada, most investment banks were owned by commercial banks, providing them with access to capital during a crisis.

The U.S. Financial Sector

Despite the close geographic proximity, the nature of the United States banking and mortgage industry differed significantly from the system that prevailed in Canada.

Decades ago, the U.S. government launched two agencies to promote home ownership in the United States—the Federal National Mortgage Association ("Fannie Mae") and the Federal Home Loan Mortgage Corporation ("Freddie Mac"). These agencies were designed to increase the availability of funds for originating mortgages and to encourage the emergence of a secondary market for mortgages. Subsequently, mortgages could be traded without the involvement of either the original borrower or the original lender.

In the 1990s, to further encourage home ownership in the United States, policymakers lowered the amount of equity that homebuyers were required to invest in the purchase of a home. As a consequence of this policy shift, borrowers who were previously unable to secure a mortgage were able to enter the housing market. Further, the overall degree of leverage in the U.S. housing market increased substantially and a housing bubble emerged as homeowners began to speculate by moving into more expensive homes.

The coincident emergence of three financial innovations in the United States—interest-only mortgages, asset securitizations and credit default swaps—ultimately set the stage for the perfect storm that had converged over the U.S. financial system by 2007.

---

[1]This section is from "You can take it to the bank," *Ivey in Touch Magazine,* Fall 2009, p. 14.

Unlike self-amortizing mortgages in which the mortgage principal was retired through regular payments of principal and interest over the life of a mortgage, interest-only mortgages were mortgages in which the borrower was given the opportunity to pay only the interest portion of a regularly scheduled mortgage payment. Interest-only mortgages were designed to open home ownership to low-income earners who demonstrated enhanced future earning potential, at which point their mortgage would be converted into a self-amortizing mortgage. Interest-only mortgages benefitted these low-income homeowners by facilitating their entry into the housing market through payments which were lower than the payments under a self-amortizing mortgage. However, the emergence of interest-only mortgages also contributed to speculation in the housing market, as some investors purchased homes, made the interest payments while waiting for the value of their homes to increase and then sold the homes, paying back the mortgage principal with the proceeds from the home sale and pocketing the surplus.

Asset securitization involved aggregating a series of future cash flows into a security which was then sold to investors. Mortgage-backed securities (MBSs) were a type of asset securitization in which the underlying asset backing the security was a mortgage which generated cash flows from the interest payments. A securitization was a structured finance product that was originally designed to distribute risk. In fact, when conceived, MBSs were regarded as low-risk investments because they were backed by mortgages and mortgage defaults were relatively rare occurrences.

Credit default swaps (CDSs) resembled insurance policies in the sense that one party paid a series of cash flows to a counter-party in exchange for the promise that the counter-party would reimburse the payer if the underlying asset defaulted. A significant portion of the market for CDSs was built around MBSs. Investors in asset-backed securities such as MBSs regularly insured their investments by purchasing CDSs. The premium revenue stream associated with a CDS on an MBS was considered particularly attractive due to the low level of perceived risk, again due to the relatively rare occurrence of mortgage defaults. Despite their resemblance to insurance policies, CDSs were traded as contracts in the derivatives markets and were free from insurance industry regulations. Consequently, the relative ease with which CDSs could be issued, coupled with the fact that it was not necessary to own the underlying asset in order to purchase a CDS, effectively fuelled speculative behaviour in the CDS market.

Two phenomena associated with these three financial innovations further compromised the precarious foundation upon which the U.S. banking and mortgage industry was perched—subprime mortgages and individual compensation systems prevailing in the financial sector. While mortgages issued to creditworthy borrowers were known as prime mortgages, subprime mortgages were issued to borrowers with poor credit. MBSs based on subprime mortgages became particularly attractive investment vehicles due to their high returns and low levels of perceived risk (due to the assumption that widespread mortgage defaults were highly unlikely). At the same time, mortgage originators and derivative traders were being compensated on the volume of mortgages originated and derivatives sold (MBSs and CDSs). Increased trading volumes in these assets were fuelled by the fact that compensation was rarely adjusted to the riskiness of either the borrower or the underlying asset.

By 2007, the robust growth in U.S. home prices slowed dramatically. As home prices began to decline, the value of mortgages began to exceed the market value of many homes. A flood of mortgage defaults ensued to the point that mortgage-backed securities began to decline in value. The complex nature of these securities further undermined their value. Given that it was not possible to link an MBS to specific properties, investors could not evaluate the risk of default on specific MBSs and, therefore, were unable to ascertain market values for these MBSs. The secondary market for mortgages was near collapse.

The difficulty associated with valuing these securities proved to be particularly problematic for financial institutions that owned the devalued MBSs and for financial institutions facing insurance-like claims on the CDSs they had written on the bet that widespread mortgage defaults would never occur. Consequently, these financial institutions were required to raise more capital to shore up their capital ratios. However, the increasing pervasiveness of uncertainty effectively turned off the taps in both credit and capital markets, making the task of raising capital almost impossible.

As the cost of capital skyrocketed and credit stopped flowing in the United States, financial institutions began to fail. Several "runs on the bank" were triggered in which customers lined up to fully withdraw their deposits. In June 2008, panicked customers of IndyMac Bank in the United States withdrew $1.5 billion in deposits (approximately 7.5 per cent of total bank deposits). Similarly, over the course of 10 days in September 2008, customers withdrew more than $16 billion from Washington Mutual Bank (totaling 9 per cent of total bank deposits). The uncertainty spilled over U.S. borders, triggering bank runs and failures overseas as well. Most notable was the bank run and subsequent failure of the U.K.-based Northern Rock bank, which was subsequently nationalized, in part, to subdue the panic.

CONCLUSION

The Challenge of Refining the Future Direction of the Joint Venture

As early as the summer of 2007, credit spreads for certain financial companies and instruments widened dramatically. In Canada, the marketplace for ABCP began to show signs of stress. The JV's ALCO Committee, on the recommendation of CIBC Mellon's risk management group, and leveraging the respective credit market specialties of both shareholders, directed the JV to refrain from using any of CIBC Mellon's treasury or client funds (the latter in the form of cash collateral for securities lending transactions) to purchase non-bank-owned ABCP. Eventually, in August 2007, the $30 billion market for non-bank-owned ABCP essentially froze. The looming financial crisis did not portend a quick or strong recovery in the credit markets, particularly in the ABCP market.

MacMillan and his team suspected that the future growth potential for the stock transfer and corporate trust business segments was more limited than it was for the asset servicing business. Notwithstanding the onset of the financial crisis, MacMillan debated whether the JV should retain or divest these business lines in order to focus more intensely on the asset servicing business for which the JV was formed.

The Challenge of Avoiding Major Operational Missteps

The brewing financial storm became fodder for the media and it started to rattle financial markets. Despite the fact that there were reasons to believe that the impending financial crisis might not be as bad in Canada as it was likely to be in the United States and elsewhere, numerous challenges remained. Not least of these was the fact that the crisis would likely bring out the worst in many long-term business relationships. As liquidity was tightening, many financial sector lenders, borrowers and partners alike were putting aside years, even decades, of cooperation in order to ensure their own survival. This was in contrast to the approach adopted by CIBC Mellon in the months leading up to and during the crisis. It retained its long-standing practice of emphasizing very extensive communication with its clients and its shareholders, ensuring shared understanding of issues, including having representatives from both parents on ALCO and maintaining transparency.

By mid-September 2008, the most significant risks facing CIBC Mellon were credit risk, operational risk and market risk, as well as the potential exodus of assets and clients who were panicked by the wider financial chaos. MacMillan and his team recognized that it would be critical for the JV to continue to deliver a high level of client service and to avoid any major operational missteps. A key challenge facing the JV pertained to efforts to remain loyal to both long-time and newer business clients, while not exposing the JV to excessive risk in the context of an increasingly volatile market. While CIBC Mellon's global securities lending operations had extended considerable credit to some of the now more precariously perched financial giants, the JV was comfortable that these loans were adequately collateralized. Nevertheless, in order to ensure that the loaned assets were not subsumed into any debtors' possible bankruptcy proceedings, the JV would need to execute against legal agreements with rigour, to preserve its legal rights, including, if necessary, taking possession of collateral assets and then liquidating these assets in an increasingly turbulent market. Critical decisions were faced by MacMillan, Marchand, Hemingway and Slater, ranging from short-run decisions such as how to determine when to call in credit extended to some of the JV's global securities lending clients and how to liquidate any collateral that the JV was forced to take into possession, to longer-run decisions surrounding how to manage the JV's relationships with its solvent clients, so as to stem any risk of client or asset flight.

MacMillan closed the door to his office. Notwithstanding the 110 years of collective experience between MacMillan, Marchand, Hemingway and Slater, the four men recognized that the markets were headed for uncharted waters. MacMillan opened the meeting, reminding the group, "Gentlemen, now more than ever, we need to leverage our JV's administrative heritage, the guidance of our shareholders and the respective strengths of the parents to move through these unprecedented times . . ."

EXHIBIT 1   CIBC Mellon Asset Servicing Business Functions

CORE ASSET SERVICING BUSINESS FUNCTIONS:

The following eight functions constituted the core asset servicing business functions:

CUSTODY The CIBC Mellon custody system is a real-time, multicurrency processor of security and currency movement for the institutional trust/custody business. It maintains automated interfaces to/from depositories and subcustodians, supporting trade affirms/confirmation, trade instructions, settlement confirmations, cash instructions and cash and security position status.

TRADE PROCESSING & SETTLEMENT Trades entering the custody system are auto-matched and confirmed to CDS *(Canadian Depository for Securities)* and its U.S. equivalent, DTC *(Depository Trust Company)*. Discrepancies are flagged, reported to the client and updated with fail codes. If matched, trades automatically settle on the settlement date and the clients' securities and cash positions are updated. Each day, the service team validates the CDS Daily Settled Trades Report against the settled transactions in the system. CIBC Mellon offers contractual settlement of buys, sells and maturities for issues publicly traded on recognized exchanges in 47 countries. All other markets across all asset classes and registration locations, including physical delivery of securities, settle on the actual settlement date.

ACCOUNTING The CIBC Mellon accounting system integrates both Canadian and international securities on a single platform. This trade date, multicurrency system reflects cash movements on the actual settlement date and security transactions on the trade date. Integrated with its custody system, the accounting system manages derivative investments and accommodates both pending trades and income accruals.

SAFEKEEPING CIBC Mellon provides a secure facility for the safekeeping of stocks, bonds, notes and other securities—in both physical and book-based environments. It ensures assets are held securely and recorded accurately in its custody system. These two objectives are accomplished by performing an annual depository risk assessment along with regular reconciliation of physical vault and depository positions.

CORPORATE ACTIONS CIBC Mellon has a Corporate Actions Security Capture and Delivery Engine (Cascade) to keep it informed on all relevant announcements, while providing clients and their investment managers with instant access to information. It provides notification within hours of receipt of notice, with immediate encumbrance of position on receipt of response, and instant settlement on receipt of payment. Its online, real-time mandatory and voluntary corporate action and class action notifications enable clients to respond to events quickly. The most comprehensive sources of corporate action information for Canadian, U.S. and international markets are used, comparing vendor data to ensure accuracy and timely notification is provided to clients.

INCOME COLLECTION The system automatically accrues for all interest and dividend income for each security, providing the amount in local currency prior to the payable date. A contractual income policy for dividends, interest and maturities is offered in which CIBC Mellon guarantees to pay income on the day it is due; amounts are credited to client accounts regardless of receipt of payment. In non-contractual markets, income is credited upon actual receipt of funds. Assets must be held in the depository or registered in CIBC Mellon's name or its agent's nominee name. The funds are credited in local currency on the pay-date, unless otherwise specified.

ONLINE REPORTING Workbench offers a wide array of browser-based information capabilities allowing customers to effectively manage, evaluate and report on their individual or consolidated portfolios. The key features range from access to market news and analysis to a fully secured virtual meeting place to performance analytics and monthly statements. Workbench cash availability and forecast reports are updated in real-time during business hours and also include custody share reports, pending trades, transaction settlements, corporate action notifications and cash balance projections of portfolios. The reporting feature, Workbench Express, facilitates the automatic distribution of reports to a designated printer, a local network drive, an e-mail account or an FTP server, all without manual intervention.

EXHIBIT 1   (continued)

PERFORMANCE & RISK ANALYTICS (P&RA) This unit provides performance measurement, attribution, and investment analysis services to over 1,800 institutional investors in 50 countries and is responsible for US$8.2 trillion in assets under measurement. In Canada, it has 151 clients using performance measurement services and products. Its suite of value-added products and services includes tools for performance measurement, portfolio analytics and universe comparison. Its performance measurement systems are fully integrated with CIBC Mellon's systems.

CAPITAL MARKETS FUNCTIONS:

The following two functions constituted the asset servicing business's capital markets functions:

FOREIGN EXCHANGE CIBC Mellon executes foreign exchange (FX) transactions through the trading desk of one of its corporate parents. From the perspective of the counter-party to the transaction, CIBC or BNY Mellon deals as principal directly with its clients. Only one step is required to execute a trade and instruct for settlement, reducing operational risks and duplication of tasks. CIBC Mellon has neither a principal nor broker role in the transaction but acts simply as a service provider. It facilitates the transactions required to support clients' global trading activity, providing a complex FX trading solution from initiation and execution to settlement and reporting.

GLOBAL SECURITIES LENDING The company delivers client-tailored solutions to the 120 institutional clients participating in its in-house program. Beneficial owners for whom securities are lent include pension funds, government agencies, insurance companies, mutual funds, asset managers and pooled funds. The focus is on the strategic development of new products and services to enhance client revenue performance, with a commitment to product collateral and risk management. Global One is used—the lending system of choice for more than 70 financial institutions in over 20 countries—designed by top market participants.

Source: Company materials.

EXHIBIT 2   The Interactions Between External Parties and CIBC Mellon's
Global Securities Service

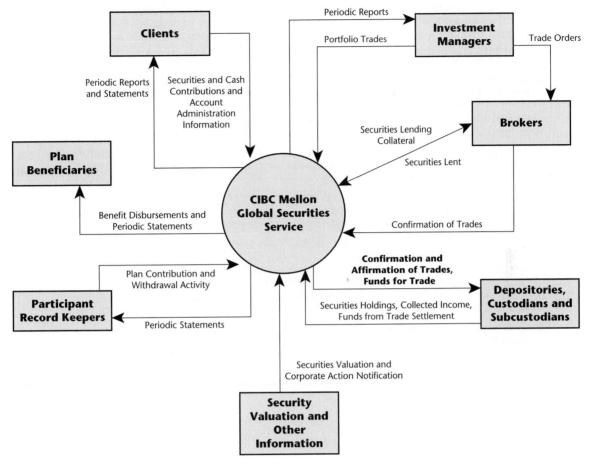

Source: CICA 5970 Report, CIBC Mellon, 2009.

EXHIBIT 3   Top General Reasons for Joint Venture Failures

1. **The rationale for setting up the JV wasn't a good one**—Two lousy businesses put together will not make one good business. Two lousy businesses put together give you one big lousy business. Double the fun! At the core there has to be a good business proposition that creates adequate returns to the shareholding partners. It helps when the founding partners each bring something special to the joint venture that the other doesn't have.

2. **Insufficient planning**—Parties need to agree up front to a comprehensive plan outlining the business transaction, which includes governance, dispute resolution, ownership of intellectual property, how each party will contribute to the JV (whether it's money, expertise, technology, etc.). It's also very important to identify and agree on exit arrangements. Parameters of any business transaction will change. You need to agree to how the exit occurs, up front.

3. **Inadequate capitalization**—Starting out, each partner must commit a set amount of capital that is adequate enough to get the business off the ground. Also, both partners need to agree on how they will fund additional capital calls.

4. **Lack of leadership**—This may be the most important factor of all. If you don't have strong leadership, you are going to fail. In any business, you always need outstanding leadership, but never more so than on the board of a joint venture and within the JV itself.

5. **Lack of commitment**—Poor performance by the JV can result in one or both parties getting disinterested quickly. Results do count. But even if the JV is successful, things can happen to one of the parents quite unrelated to what is happening at the JV that will lead to a lack of commitment. For example, one parent can get into operational difficulties which will cause them to take their eye off the JV ball or even force them to exit the JV. Or one of the parents can have a perfectly legitimate change in strategy that results in the joint venture no longer being core to them.

6. **Cultural differences and differences of opinion emerge between the two partners.** There is definitely a JV mindset—it's different working with another partner than just on your own. You have to sometimes temper your own culture to accommodate a quite different culture or approval of your partner to the benefit of the JV. Some companies are good at it, and some aren't.

Source: Tom MacMillan, November 2006.

EXHIBIT 4   Organization Chart of Senior Officers of CIBC Mellon as of September 2008

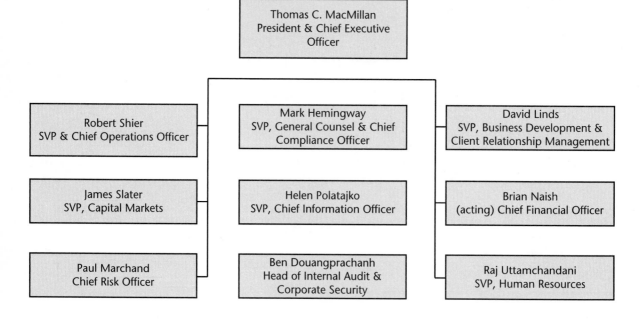

EXHIBIT 5   Brief Bios of Select Senior Officers

Thomas C. MacMillan was president and chief executive officer of CIBC Mellon. He had 35 years of extensive experience in the financial services industry in both Canada and the United States. From 1994–1998, he was chairman, president and chief executive officer of Mellon Bank Canada. Mr. MacMillan was instrumental in the formation of the CIBC Mellon joint venture, and previously held various senior positions with the Bank of Montreal, Chase Manhattan Bank of Canada and Montreal Trust. A native of Toronto, Mr. MacMillan received a bachelor's degree from Princeton University and a master's degree from the London School of Economics and Political Science. He also had significant board experience in both the private and not-for-profit sectors.

Mark R. Hemingway was senior vice president, general counsel and chief compliance officer, and a member of the company's executive management committee. He was responsible for the legal, compliance, corporate secretarial and privacy functions at CIBC Mellon. Mr. Hemingway had 20 years of experience in the legal profession. Prior to joining CIBC Mellon, he held general counsel and corporate secretary positions in a number of large Canadian companies, and was previously a litigation lawyer at Torys. He received his law degree from Queen's University and his master of laws degree from Cambridge University. He articled at the Supreme Court of Canada.

James E. R. Slater was senior vice president, capital markets, and a member of the company's executive management committee. Mr. Slater had overall leadership responsibility for CIBC Mellon's capital markets function, which included global securities lending, treasury and cash management. Mr. Slater's accountabilities also included providing strategic client service engagement in relation to his trading and financial markets responsibilities. He also chaired the company's asset liability committee. Mr. Slater had 20 years of experience in the financial services industry with CIBC World Markets and CIBC Mellon. While at CIBC World Markets, he was part of the team charged with the formation of CIBC Mellon.

C. Paul Marchand was the head of risk management. He joined CIBC Mellon in 2002, after 35 years with a major Canadian bank. At CIBC Mellon, he was responsible for designing and overseeing the company's Risk Management frameworks and programs for both CIBC Mellon Trust Company and CIBC Mellon Global Securities Services Company. His mandate included bringing together comprehensive oversight and reporting of all risk issues affecting CIBC Mellon including credit, market and operational risks up to and including the boards of directors and joint venture partners. He also served as the enterprises' chief compliance officer and chief anti-money laundering officer from 2002 to 2006. Marchand held a bachelor of commerce degree from McGill University.

David S. Linds was senior vice president, business development and client relationship management, and a member of the company's executive management committee. Mr. Linds also oversaw the company's product management and client integration solutions group, which was responsible for ensuring existing and future development of products and services as well as client reporting needs of institutional clients for asset servicing and ancillary services. Mr. Linds had more than 25 years of experience in the financial services industry, including 18 years with CIBC World Markets and CIBC Mellon. While at CIBC World Markets, he was part of the team charged with the formation of CIBC Mellon.

Robert M. Shier was senior vice president and chief operations officer, and a member of the company's executive management committee. Mr. Shier was responsible for CIBC Mellon's operational divisions, including client and investment management services, asset servicing, investment fund accounting for the CIBC Mellon Global Securities Services Company and investor services, stock transfer and employee plan administration for CIBC Mellon Trust Company. He joined CIBC Mellon in 1997, and had more than 25 years of operational experience in financial services including brokerage, banking, asset servicing and transfer agency services.

CASE 3

Swimming in the Virtual Community Pool with PlentyofFish

On a Monday morning in January of 2008, Markus Frind, chief executive officer (CEO) and founder of PlentyofFish.com, was undoubtedly the topic of many conversations as people grabbed their morning coffees from a local vendor. The *New York Times* had just published an article about the Vancouverite's free online dating site, PlentyofFish (PoF). Now that the world was watching and salivating at the $10 million per year that the site was generating, one had to question whether its business model could be sustained. Could Frind maintain his strong foothold in the virtual world of social networking sites? Could PlentyofFish continue to maintain its financial success with advertising as its only source of revenue?

If the concept of offering a free online dating site was so fatally flawed, PoF would not have experienced the success that it had. Frind did not spend the $10 million a month on marketing that some of his competitors like Match.com, eHarmony and Lavalife did. What he was doing was working just fine—for now, and continued to generate a substantial annual profit.

Frind had proudly announced, on many occasions, that his company consisted of just one employee—himself. While he had hired another employee in late 2007, it was only to assist in providing customer service. As the sole operator of the site, Frind had been able to handle massive amounts of traffic. In fact, for the week of April 28, 2007, PlentyofFish was ranked by HitWise as the 96th-busiest website in the United States. To put this into perspective, PoF outranked Apple.com in terms of traffic! How then, was he able to do all of this alone? Did his success lie in his web design philosophy that allowed users to take part in running the site? Was it the automation of the processing? Could he chalk it all up to efficiency? Other concerns included whether this model could be easily replicated, and should PlentyofFish be concerned about others entering the market with better technology and fancier sites?

Richard Ivey School of Business
The University of Western Ontario

Wilfred Cheung, Chris Ellison, Prarthana Kumar, Jeremy Kyle and Stacey Morrison wrote this case under the supervision of Professor Michael Parent solely to provide material for class discussion. The authors do not intend to illustrate either effective or ineffective handling of a managerial situation. The authors may have disguised certain names and other identifying information to protect confidentiality.

As people milled around the corner, some on bikes and others on rollerblades, several couples casually walked along the street, holding hands. With millions having surfed websites looking for that special someone, one had to wonder how many of these people met through PlentyofFish and how much longer others would continue to do so.

THE CONCEPT

Social Networking

The term "social network" was coined by J.A. Barnes who defined it as a group of 100 to 150 people drawn together by family, work or a hobby. In 2008, thanks mainly to the Internet, social networking had expanded to hundreds of millions of people around the world, creating a virtual community for people to interact with one another about anything and everything. Members created their own online "profiles" with biographical data, pictures, likes, dislikes and any other information they chose to post and share. They communicated with each other by voice, instant messaging, video conference and blogs. In many cases, these sites also served as a vehicle for meeting in person. One could find dating sites, friendship sites, and sites with a business networking purpose or hybrids that offered a combination of these applications.

Looking for Mr. or Ms. Right or looking at your neighbour's pictures from vacation while checking your e-mail at the same time seemed to define the growing industry of social networking websites. The genius of these sites lay in their ability to capture the essence of informal exchanges while expanding the matrix of searchable, linked pages. Social networking on the Internet was a growing phenomenon which could be broadly categorized into three segments—virtual communities like Facebook; classified listing sites such as Craigslist; and the growing plethora of dating sites like PlentyofFish.

As participants in a social network started to become more entrenched in the social aspect of their network they often became members of that particular virtual community. A virtual community described "People who use computers to communicate, form friendships that sometimes form the basis of communities, but you have to be careful to not mistake the tool for the task and think that just writing words on a screen is the same thing as real community."[1] Much like a real community, a virtual social networking community was based on the idea that once one joined, they needed to actively participate. There was a reciprocal nature to being part of a virtual community; they depended upon social interaction and exchange among users. A person in a virtual community was motivated to contribute valuable information to the group, starting with a valid profile or an honest response with the expectation that they would receive the same in return.

The lifecycle of a membership in a virtual community went through the same stages as that of any other community. Members of virtual communities began their lifecycle first as visitors, clicking through and around a site to determine whether they could connect with other users and fit into the group. After deciding to break into the community and set up a profile or username, they began participating in the virtual community. Those who contributed for a sustained period of time became regulars. If they took the initiative to recruit others to join the community, they became leaders.

---

[1]Howard Rheingold, *The Virtual Community*, http://www.rheingold.com/vc/book/intro.html, accessed January 27, 2008.

Another category of social networking sites were ones that focused on classified listings and operated as a hub aggregating buyers and sellers. Buyers listed a variety of goods ranging from private planes to services such as housekeeping. Craigslist was one of the most popular sites of this kind.

Dating websites allowed individuals to post their profile, view others' and perhaps develop a romantic or intimate relationship. The market was dominated by several large commercial websites such as Lavalife, eHarmony, and Match.com as well as the newer PlentyofFish. These sites targeted teens to retirees, with a number of new sites targeting niche markets based on religion, race and occupation. They were based on a shift in thinking about web applications, built on interactivity between developer and users, called Web 2.0.

Web 2.0

Web 2.0 was a term first coined in 2004 at a Web conference whose theme was "The Web has become a platform, a foundation upon which thousands of new forms of business would emerge."[2] According to Tim O'Reilly,[3] one of the conference's moderators,

> Web 2.0 is the business revolution in the computer industry caused by the move to the Internet as platform, and an attempt to understand the rules for success on that new platform. Chief among those rules is this: Build applications that harness network effects to get better the more people use them. (This is what I've elsewhere called "harnessing collective intelligence.")
>
> Tim O'Reilly

Web 2.0 systems were theoretically unconstrained as they would harness "the power of user contribution, collective intelligence, and network effects."[4] PlentyofFish was able to take advantage of this new business model by encouraging user contributions and their collective intelligence, while also capitalizing on the network effects it had built with these very users.

PLENTYOFFISH.COM

Business Model

Founded in 2003, PlentyofFish was free to users, a feature that differentiated it from other online dating sites. This was reinforced in the site's slogan: "100% Free. Put away your credit card." However, this came at a cost to users. While other online dating sites provided customer support as part of their service, PlentyofFish did not have that same support structure. It only responded to fraudulent identity notifications and subpoena requests. For example, instead of providing customer service, ". . . users rely on fellow members, whose advice is found in online forums. The Dating & Advice

---

[2]Web 2.0 SUMMIT, *About Web Summit 2.0*, http://conferences.oreillynet.com/pub/w/62/about.html, accessed January 27, 2008.

[3]Tim O'Reilly, "Web 2.0. Compact Definition: Trying Again," *O'Reilly Radar: O'Reilly Media Inc.*, December 10, 2006, http://radar.oreilly.com/archives/2006/12/web_20_compact.html, accessed January 27, 2008.

[4]Ibid.

category listed more than 320,000 posts, making up in sheer quantity what it lacked in a soothing live presence available by phone."[5] However, this also meant that users had to be willing to comb through the wide array of content before finding the information they needed. Therefore, while the growth of Web 2.0 aided Frind in achieving his goal of allowing users to drive the website, this setup raised questions about the quality of content being provided.

Despite it, the site had proven popular, with more than three million members in January 2008—double the membership in the past year, and despite an attrition rate of 30 per cent of members per month who were purged from the site for inactivity. These members generated traffic volume of more than 600,000 unique logins per day and more than 1.5 billion page views per month (an average of roughly 50 million page views per day!). PlentyofFish had managed to grow its membership not only in number, but in terms of active members, despite the growing number of alternative online dating services. This was especially appealing to advertisers.

With the overwhelming supply of online dating sites in the market, one had to marvel at what set PlentyofFish apart: PlentyofFish had built an engaged, passionate community of users who felt emotionally attached to the site. This created high switching costs for users as well as allowing PlentyofFish to benefit from network effects.

PlentyofFish was sustained by revenue from companies advertising on the site. The advertising mix currently returned an estimated $10 million per year through banner ads, Google ads (AdSense) and affiliated dating sites. Ads sent users to other sites, even other dating sites, which in turn generated revenue for PlentyofFish. For example, when a user clicked on a banner ad for a dating and relationship book, PlentyofFish might receive the full revenue from the sale of the book as the advertiser gained another customer who might become profitable. In this way, the other site cheaply outsourced customer acquisition to PlentyofFish.

The Technology Behind PlentyofFish—ASP.NET

While Frind originally created the site to learn the ASP.NET web application framework, it was still being used for PlentyofFish in 2008. Frind claimed that he had stuck with using ASP.NET "because it's trivial and easy and gets the job done."[6] Additionally, Frind believed that he had "gotten really, really good at it" pointing out that, "(what he had) done is about 10 to 20 times more efficient than what anybody else has done with ASP.NET."[7] In fact, PlentyofFish had grown to the scale where "nothing can be brought off the shelf and everything must be built from the ground up."[8] Therefore, while there was no one software package that could accommodate PlentyofFish's needs, Frind believed that he could adapt ASP.NET to meet its needs.

---

[5]Randall Stross, "From 10 hours a week, $10 million a year," *NY Times [US]*, January 13, 2008, http://www.nytimes.com/2008/01/13/business/13digi.html?_r=2&scp=1&sq=plenty+of+fish&st=nyt&oref=slogin&oref=slogin, accessed January 22, 2008.

[6]Plentyoffish.com, "Changing the online dating industry," *Plentyoffish Media Inc.* http://www.PlentyofFish.com/about_team.aspx, accessed January 27, 2008.

[7]Ibid.

[8]Markus Frind, "The paradigm shift—adapt or die," *Plentyoffish Media Inc.* http://PlentyofFish.wordpress.com/2007/08/08/looking-for-3-senior-software-developers, accessed January 27, 2008.

In June 2006, when PlentyofFish was receiving approximately "500 million pageviews a month," Frind believed that he would have "no problem running it by [himself] even if it gets to three times its current size."[9] This stemmed from his belief that he could be successful in automating more and more as the site grew. In early 2008, PlentyofFish was serving 1.2 billion pageviews.

ASP.NET coding enabled the site to maintain itself through automated recognition of spam on its forums and the allowance of user-screening for the thousands of photos uploaded daily. This combination of site automation and user engagement made it possible for only one person to operate the site. For example, the Love and Dating forum had 320,000+ posts in January 2008, all of which had to be monitored for unwanted postings and spam. Frind had been able to effectively rid his site of spam by refining "a formula for analysing customer feedback and arriving at a determination of whether a given forum post is spam and should automatically be deleted."[10] Posted photos were checked by users to ensure they did not contain nudity and were of a person. In fact, some 120 "member volunteers"—unpaid members dedicated to monitoring photographs posted to the site—reportedly checked 100,000 photos each year. The founder explained this behaviour as a means of giving back to the free site: "Lots of people feel they want to give back to the site because it is free."[11] Frind likened this automation to putting his website on autopilot, with users supporting themselves through online forums, while receiving minimal support from the site administrator.

Servers

PoF was able to minimize the amount of servers it employed by being more efficient. Frind stated that he used "one web server, one mail server, two database servers now and a couple of little web servers to run the Userplane instant messenger. So under 10 but I've started to scale up."[12] To bring this into perspective, similar social networking sites such as Friendster and AmericanSingles.com (with less traffic) used 200 servers each. Having fewer servers meant that there was less or, in Frind's case, no need to employ technicians to ensure that the servers were kept up and running. This translated to significantly lower operating costs.

PoF's servers ran on SQL Server 2005. The growth of the website meant that they would need to add new servers. On February 27, 2008, Microsoft released a number of upgrades—Windows Server 2008, Visual Studio 2008 and SQL Server 2008. Frind's need to add additional servers in the near future meant that he would likely have to make a decision on which servers—SQL Server 2005 or 2008—to employ. With Frind's heavy reliance on creating efficiencies for his website, could he afford to wait to employ SQL Server 2008? Conversely, if he did switch to SQL

---

[9]Richard Macmanus, "Plenty of cash for one-man band," ReadWriteWeb.com, June 10, 2006, http://www.readwriteweb.com/archives/plenty_of_cash.php, accessed January 27, 2008.

[10]Randall Stross, "From 10 hours a week, $10 million a year," *NY Times [US]*, January 13, 2008, http://www.nytimes.com/2008/01/13/business/13digi.html?_r=2&scp=1&sq=plenty+of+fish&st=nyt&oref=slogin&oref=slogin, accessed January 22, 2008.

[11]Randall Stross, "From 10 hours a week, $10 million a year," *NY Times [US]*, January 13, 2008, http://www.nytimes.com/2008/01/13/business/13digi.html?_r=2&scp=1&sq=plenty+of+fish&st=nyt&oref=slogin&oref=slogin, accessed January 22, 2008.

[12]Plentyoffish.com, "Changing the online dating industry," Plentyoffish Media Inc. http://www.PlentyofFish.com/about_team.aspx, accessed January 27, 2008.

Server 2008, could he afford to work out the kinks which might ultimately cause problems for the site?

Scalability

At the heart of most database applications was a database management system (DBMS). For most mid-to-large scale databases, this was either Oracle or Microsoft SQL Server. Understanding the nuanced differences between the two products could be difficult for even the most seasoned database professional. One very important difference between the two was that SQL Server ran only on the Windows platform, while Oracle ran on a variety of platforms like UNIX or Linux.

Frind's choice for a DBMS was SQL Server 2005, but other popular sites, such as Craigslist, had chosen Oracle to manage their databases. Craigslist received over nine billion page views per month. This was six times the number of page views that PoF received.

On the issue of scalability, there were two basic concepts—scaling up and scaling out. Scaling up meant adding additional expensive hardware to handle higher loads, while scaling out meant distributing the load using low-cost multiple servers. Frind needed to consider what route he wanted to take if he continued to grow. Would he be able to achieve the scale that Oracle allowed for Craigslist with SQL Server 2005 as PlentyofFish's DBMS?

The PlentyofFish User Experience

From the moment that you entered the website until the moment you left, you were bombarded by pictures of users of the site. Intrigued by the fuzzy and distorted photos, one click and you were viewing a user's profile page. Simplistic in design, the profile page offered information such as height, age, body type and ethnicity. You read the brief description and curiously continued to scroll down the page. More pictures of your "fish" appeared and as you ran your cursor over each one, they expanded to give a much larger, clearer view. Hooked, you might have thought "How can I meet this attractive and witty individual?"

In order to contact any of the 600,000 "fish," a user first had to become a member. This was easily done by moving through the registration screens—two very simple and user-friendly pages. The entire process took only a couple of minutes to complete and the majority of information requested (aside from secure information such as a password) was presented on a profile page. By accurately representing themselves with respect to age, location and preferences, the user was instantly given the opportunity to connect with potential matches in the immediate area that were similar. The prospect of meeting new people immediately was one of the most important driving factors for the website's popularity.

This ability to connect with others so readily had been leveraged by PlentyofFish to create the company's successful online dating community. The longer the user was active, the greater the chance of building a network and finding the "right" match. This idea was reinforced by PlentyofFish's design, which matched users that would be most interested in each other based on their past messaging and searches. Moreover, new users were constantly adding themselves to the website's profile database, creating a new source of people to meet. Thus, how deep a "fish" chose to swim in the virtual community pool was user-determined.

Catching a Fish

Once the user had initiated contact or been contacted, the process of communication was quite simple. Assuming that the parties involved fulfilled the requirements outlined by the other individual such as age range or, more specifically, "must not be looking for an intimate encounter," the user could openly send and receive messages. These messages were placed directly in the inbox and easily accessible as the system was similar in design to many other e-mail platforms. Frind had also recently added a VoIP (voice-over-Internet protocol) which allowed users to send voice messages to other members as well.[13] This ease of use allowed members to immediately "jump into the pool," establishing online conversations with whomever they chose. The type of message sent—voice, e-mail or instant message—was entirely up to the user.

However, not every match that a user made was going to be positive. Even the most optimistic user might have run into individuals that were rude, creepy or downright shocking. Thus, the user had to wade through the pools looking for "fish" that met their needs. If the user did establish contact with a disreputable individual, they could block that other user. However, if someone was bent on creating havoc, a new user profile could always be created. There were no user services available to help deal with these types of issues, which made it difficult to fix any problems that did occur. In this sense, PlentyofFish could be thought of as the Wild West of online dating, whereby users policed themselves.

What was Lurking in the Sea?

There were several forces that posed serious threats to PlentyofFish. A significant force that PlentyofFish had to contend with was the threat of new entry. The capital, or rather lack of capital, required to start a dating site similar to that of PlentyofFish was minimal. All that one needed was the purchase of a domain name and servers to hold information. This meant that there were numerous potential competitors, ranging from major corporations such as Google to minor ones such as freelance web designers. Also, despite the scale that PlentyofFish had been able to achieve, there were no cost disadvantages for any new competitors. A second threat to PlentyofFish was from other, unrelated sites. While sites such as Craigslist and Facebook were not seen as dating sites, they had each branched into that area to attract more users. Craigslist had a personals section, while Facebook added dating applications to its site. Dating sites, such as PlentyofFish, also had to contend with fierce rivalry from their current competitors. Whether they were first movers such as Lavalife or niche players such as HonestyOnline, the market for dating sites was becoming increasingly saturated. With spectacular success stories such as PlentyofFish, one could only expect firm rivalries to become more intense.

OTHER VIRTUAL COMMUNITIES

Friendster

With more than 58 million members worldwide, Friendster was the pioneer in the field of social networking. Driven by simplicity, Friendster prided itself on delivering a

---

[13]Matt Harley, "Money and relationships: It's Love 3.0," *The Globe and Mail*, February 14, 2008, pp. B1 & B6.

clean, user-friendly and interactive environment where users could easily connect with anyone around the world. Friendster targeted the 25-and-under market with no professional or group affiliation. Friendster set itself apart by being the first at introducing innovative features such as a network graph server, as well as launching a choice of languages to navigate the site, thus expanding its ability to tap non-English markets. Friendster continued to innovate and recently expanded its targeted demographic to include older adults.

LinkedIn

LinkedIn was an online network of more than 17 million professionals from around the world, representing over 150 industries. LinkedIn prided itself on claiming that it was not networking—it was what networking should be. The mission of the website was to help the user be more effective in their work and open doors to opportunities using the professional relationships they already had.

The registration process for LinkedIn closely resembled completing a professional résumé. LinkedIn focused on information such as current or most recent job position, job industry, past experience and professional overview. Firms used this site to keep internal and remote employees connected with each other, search out potential employees and as a knowledge management site where they could compare their job postings to their competitors'.

Members could join LinkedIn through invitations or by starting a network of their own. LinkedIn was not purely a free service, but rather offered levels of service ranging from free membership to premium accounts that charged users anywhere from $19.95 to $200 a month. In 2007, LinkedIn was the fourth most popular networking website, behind Yahoo 360, MySpace and Facebook.

Facebook

Facebook was a social utility that connected people through its website, requiring only a valid e-mail address to register. To connect with coworkers or classmates, members used their school or work e-mail addresses to join a network. Since its launch in February 2004, Facebook enrolled over 63 million users worldwide.

Facebook was completely free and, like PoF, supported by ads. In August 2006, Facebook signed a three-year deal with Microsoft to provide and sell ads on their site in return for a revenue split. The deal followed an announcement from Facebook's direct competitor, MySpace who signed a similar deal with Google. The youthful demographic that both services attracted was highly prized amongst advertisers and a number of companies were eager to jump on the bandwagon. In July of 2006, Apple signed an agreement with Facebook to give away 10 million free iTunes samplers to Facebook members. There was even rumour of a Facebook credit card.

MySpace

MySpace was an online community that encouraged its members to create their "own" space online reflecting their personality in music, movies, photos, journal entries and interests that they might share with their growing network of friends. MySpace was for everyone—from friends to family, from singles to colleagues and from classmates to those looking for long-lost friends. Although MySpace called itself a private community, it gained great popularity through the increasing number of bands using this site to get their music heard and to connect with fans. Even Presidential candidates, such as Hillary Clinton, used MySpace as a means to journal their days on the campaign trail. MySpace was constantly expanding rapidly all over the world, with the latest addition being China in 2007.

LISTING SITES

Craigslist

Craigslist was much like other social networking sites in its structure and revenue generation, operating as a hub that aggregated buyers and sellers. One of the top 10 busiest English-language sites in the world, Craigslist was a free website which offered very little customer support. Since it only employed 25 staff, they only fixed problems sporadically, requiring users to serve themselves or request other members' assistance. Craigslist served buyers and sellers in 50 countries and 450 localities. Their sites generated 10 billion total pageviews and 6 million unique visitors a month, more than any other site of its kind. Craigslist, like other listing sites, charged fees for a few of its listings but did not contain commercial listings other than postings.

DATING SITES

Match.com

Launched in 1995, Match.com was an online dating site that charged for its service. It brought people together by creating the opportunity for them to post their profiles and pictures for others to view. With more than 15 million members worldwide, members of the site had the ability to interact with an enormous group of potential matches. Match.com was available on 6 different continents, in 30 different countries and 18 different languages. This large scale approach increased members' chances of finding the person and relationship they were searching for. Match.com estimated 200,000 people entered into relationships because of the site. If, however, a member was finding it hard to find a match, then he or she could browse through Match.com's free online magazine, Happen. This magazine contained helpful articles about romance, sex and relationships. Although communication between members required a fee, Match.com allowed visitors to browse the extensive library of profiles and pictures. This gave prospective users a sneak peak at the types of matches available to them if they joined. The site provided secure and anonymous interactions between members whether they communicated via e-mail, instant messaging or audio and video. In addition to the traditional online communications, the company also offered a wireless dating experience whereby members could match via their cellular phones.

SINK OR SWIM?

There were several challenges that PlentyofFish might have to face, the most obvious of which was competition. The PlentyofFish website was also replete with unfinished patches and quirks that made the site visually unappealing.

Should Frind expand PlentyofFish globally? Should he follow the likes of Friendster and MySpace and develop sites in Korean, Japanese, Chinese and other languages? Should he increase the number of applications available on the site? If he did so, should he imitate Facebook and invite third-party developers to provide applications suited to his target market?

To increase or protect revenues, Frind could change the membership structure of the site to have members pay for basic access and optional services. If he chose to add these functions or features, would ASP.NET be sufficient? If PlentyofFish continued to grow at its current rate, would SQL Server 2005 or 2008 handle the load? To what extent did the business need to invest in new technology?

As commuters scrambled to get to work during the Monday morning rush hour, some of them might have thought of what it was like to be Markus Frind—not having to work 9 to 5. Frind had nicely summed up the situation he had created for himself, stating: "Most of the time I don't have to do anything."[14] Would this continue to be the case, or did he need to invest substantial time, money and effort in protecting his business? After five successful years of operation, had PlentyofFish run its course?

[14]Randall Stross, "From 10 hours a week, $10 million a year," *NY Times [US]*, January 13, 2008, http://www.nytimes.com/2008/01/13/business/13digi.html?_r=2&scp=1&sq=plenty+of+fish&st=nyt &oref=slogin&oref=slogin, accessed January 22, 2008.

CASE 4

Loblaw Companies Limited[1]

It was 8 a.m. on Wednesday October 1, 2003, when John A. Lederer, president of Loblaw Companies Limited, saw the following news item.[2]

> Wal-Mart Canada Corp. is accelerating the pace of its expansion with plans for an undetermined number of Sam's Club wholesale mega-outlets. Some industry insiders have speculated that the company will launch as many as 10 to 15 Sam's Clubs next year to add to the first 4 it will open in Canada this fall. Many observers believe that setting up the grocery distribution network for Sam's Club will be the first step to U.S.-based Wal-Mart Stores Inc. eventually bringing its giant Supercenters, carrying a complete supermarket assortment, to Canada.

Although Wal-Mart had entered Canada in 1994, it had been uncharacteristically cautious. Even a decade later, it had not expanded fully into groceries despite its own global experience that the addition of a grocery line in a store pushed the sales of the more profitable general merchandise upwards by over 30 per cent.[3] Canada was Wal-Mart's only overseas market in which it had not deployed its powerful Supercenter concept. The launch of its wholesale brand, Sam's Club, suggested that the arrival of Supercenters in Canada was imminent.

Richard Ivey School of Business
The University of Western Ontario

Ramasastry Chandrasekhar prepared this case under the supervision of Professor Charlene Zietsma solely to provide material for class discussion. The authors do not intend to illustrate either effective or ineffective handling of a managerial situation. The authors may have disguised certain names and other identifying information to protect confidentiality.

---

[1]This case has been written on the basis of published sources only. Consequently, the interpretation and perspectives presented in this case are not necessarily those of Loblaw Companies Limited or any of its employees.

[2]www.globeandmail.com/reportonbusiness/retail, accessed October 9, 2003.

[3]Kevin Libin, "The Last Retailer in Canada," *Canadian Business*, March 18, 2002, p. 38.

TIME-TESTED STRATEGY

It was time for Loblaw to take a fresh look at its own strategy. The strategy had worked so far: Loblaw was the market leader in Canadian grocery, with a market share in excess of the combined market shares of its four nearest competitors, and it was the 24th largest grocery retailer in the world (see Exhibits 1 and 2).

The Loblaw strategy was both consistent and transparent, listing the following elements in the company's annual reports:[4]

- Use the cash flow generated in the business to invest in the future.
- Own real estate to maximize flexibility for future business opportunities.
- Use a multi-format approach to maximize market share over the longer term.
- Focus on food but serve the customer's everyday needs.
- Create customer loyalty and enhance price competitiveness through a superior control label program.
- Implement and execute plans and programs flawlessly.
- Constantly strive to improve the value proposition.

The strategy was driven by two objectives: driving down costs through size and operational efficiencies, and differentiating both its products (by pioneering its President's Choice brand and other private label brands) and its stores (by following a multi-banner, multi-format approach).

INDUSTRY OVERVIEW

Growing at an average rate of four per cent, food retailing was a $66.8 billion business in 2002 (see Exhibit 3). The rate of growth was impressive in light of two factors: Canadians paid the lowest prices for food in the world, and food inflation was less than two per cent per annum.[5] Grocery retailers also occupied 4 of the top 10 retailer rankings in Canada in 2002.

A broad spectrum of competitors prevailed in the Canadian grocery sector—from stand-alones with limited market presence to integrated firms involved in manufacturing, importing, wholesaling and retailing. They also operated at various levels: local, regional and national. The presence of high levels of discount stores and private labels and the high degree of market concentration had made Canadian grocery rank among "the most advanced grocery markets in the world."[6]

Canadian grocery stores often co-operated on the supply side even as they competed on the demand side. Smaller stores pooled up with large buying groups to negotiate volume discounts from suppliers. Integrated firms sold to independents. Retailers owned wholesalers and vice versa.[7] Such interactions made Canadian grocery a fertile area for mergers and acquisitions. By contrast, Loblaw's approach was characterized by an equal focus on organic growth.

---

[4]Loblaw Companies Limited, 2002 Annual Report, p. 3.

[5]Ibid, p. 7.

[6]Perry Caicco, "Loblaw Companies Ltd.: A company in transition," *CIBC World Markets Equity Research Report,* February 18, 2004.

[7]"The abuse of dominance provisions as applied to Canadian grocery sector," *Competition Bureau November 2002 Bulletin,* www.cb-bc.gc.ca, accessed October 5, 2003.

CONSUMERS

Grocery shoppers were creatures of habit. They went to the same store to buy the same goods and services at almost the same time and day of a shopping period, making the business amenable to relationship building. The advent of supermarkets in the 1930s and the focus on self-service that gathered momentum in later decades had made shopping impersonal. Re-establishing that link with the customers, through the use of technology, was now being seen by mega-grocers as a means of gaining leverage over competitors. Most grocers offered a frequent-shopper loyalty card. The data gathered through it was also used to secure better terms with manufacturers and distributors.

There were three generic ways in which grocers built their revenues: penetration (increasing the number of households shopping in their stores), frequency (increasing the number of shopping trips the shoppers made) and basket size building (getting shoppers to spend more on each shopping trip). Low price, quality service, quality products and breadth of product assortment were important.

The increasing incidence of double income families fuelled the demand for ready-to-heat and ready-to-eat convenience foods. Fast-food chains, take-outs and restaurants were growing in response. This, in turn, reduced the share of unprocessed cooking ingredients in the overall food bill of a household, estimated at $6,438 per annum in 2002, or 11.12 per cent of annual household expenditure. However, 70 per cent of Canadian meals were consumed at home, even though most were not cooked from scratch.[8] Grocers developed new categories like home meals replacement (HMR) and offered on-site cooking demonstrations. Some had franchised restaurants in their premises both to lure traffic into the stores and to provide a value-added facility.

SUPPLIERS

Retailer–supplier relationships were characterized by power plays. The scale would tilt in favour of the one wielding the most clout at a point in time.

A supermarket was like a landlord letting out shelf space for rent. The rent was a combination of different allowances that a manufacturer paid to the retailer to get secure shelf and warehouse position of its products, to encourage advertising and to reward high volume purchases.[9] They included, for example, listing fees, slotting fees, over and above allowances, vendor allowances for merchandise returns, quantity discounts and merchandising allowances. There was no standard basis on which the amount of each allowance was determined. The category manager[10] usually had the last word in deciding how the shelves were stocked.

Smaller suppliers often were at the mercy of their grocery customers since a large percentage of their business was in the hands of just a few buyers. Producers of category-leading products were in a better position: Grocers had to carry their products (often as loss leaders) to attract and retain their customers. The higher a supplier's market share relative to a grocer's, the more power it commanded and vice versa.

---

[8]Canadian Grocer, "2001–2002 Executive Report," p. 15.

[9]Anne Kingston, *The edible man*, Macfarlane, Walter and Ross, 1994, Chapter 2.

[10]A category was a group of products that were inter-related. A manager with profit centre responsibility headed each category. Examples of categories were produce, meat, housewares, dairy and grocery.

Consolidation among either suppliers or grocers would shift the balance of power temporarily, and consolidation was increasing on both sides.

Mega-grocers took a long-term view of the relationships with suppliers as part of ensuring cost-efficiencies and seamlessness in operations. They involved suppliers in merchandising, category management and supply chain management, using enterprise resource planning (ERP) technologies. Suppliers used their industry associations to push for standardization in the ERP programs of the mega-grocers to avoid having overlapping systems, one for each customer.

COMPETITORS

According to the National Market Survey 2002 conducted by *Canadian Grocer,* there were 1,791 supermarkets, 8,342 convenience stores, 3,906 affiliated independents and 10,109 unaffiliated independents in the Canadian grocery business (see Exhibit 4). The independent sector accounted for 39.3 per cent of the grocery market sales in 2002.[11] The unaffiliated independents (usually smaller stores) were facing tough times: 418 of them went out of business during 2002.

Grocery Chains

In 2003, there were 44 grocery chains in Canada (see Exhibit 5). Loblaw faced competition from four leading chains: Sobeys, Metro, A&P and Canada Safeway. Each had a distinctive profile.

Sobeys Inc. In 1907, Sobeys Inc. set up in Nova Scotia, had over 1,500 stores in 10 provinces. It was the second-largest national distributor with an estimated 15 per cent share of the Canadian food market. Employing 33,000 people, Sobeys had sales of $10.41 billion in 2002. Its retail banners included IGA and PriceChopper.

Metro Inc. Metro Inc., another home-grown enterprise of over 50 years standing, was the leading supermarket chain in Quebec. It had sales of $5.15 billion in 2002, and employed 10,733 people in its 833 stores. Metro had several banners, including the discounter Super C, and three private labels: The Irresistible, Econochoix and Super C.

Atlantic and Pacific (A&P) Established in 1927, A&P had 240 stores in prime locations in Ontario generating sales of $3.99 billion in 2002 under three banners: discount grocer Food Basics; Dominion, mainly in Toronto; and A&P in the rest of Ontario. A&P Canada was the best performing division of the U.S.-based The Great Atlantic and Pacific Tea Co. Inc., which was in serious financial trouble. Having recently gone through major capital rejuvenation and a change in marketing strategy emphasizing freshness, A&P Canada was in a growth mode.

Canada Safeway Canada Safeway was started in 1929 as a subsidiary of Safeway Inc., the third-largest supermarket operator in the United States. Canada Safeway had 214 stores located primarily in Western Canada, capturing a 28 per cent share there. Employing 28,000 people, it had sales of $3.48 billion in 2002. Canada Safeway served its own stores and independents through its three distribution centres.

---

[11]Jerry Tutunjian, "What's up and what's down," *Canadian Grocer*, February 2003, p. 26.

Wholesale Clubs

Wholesale clubs charged an annual fee (ranging between $30 and $50), and offered a broad range of products and services at low prices for bulk purchases. They lured away high volume "stock-up shoppers" from the grocery chains. Stores were functional, sans frills. The wholesale club was a profitable format in Canada.

Costco Wholesale Canada was the leading wholesale club in Canada. It had 61 outlets and about four million members, which included small businesses and many individual consumers. The launch of Sam's Clubs in Canada by Wal-Mart posed a direct threat to Costco, which had enjoyed a first mover advantage in Canada since 1985. In the United States, Costco had dealt with competition from Wal-Mart through differentiation. Unlike Sam's Club, which went after bargain-hunting Wal-Mart customers, Costco U.S. had positioned itself towards small-business owners. The focus on a slightly higher-end customer had not only led to a significantly higher average sale per customer but also limited its competition with Sam's Clubs in the United States, which was generally perceived as downscale.

Specialty Chains

Specialty chains operated smaller stores in niche segments, such as ethnic groceries and organic foods. The ethnic foods market, estimated to be of the order of $6 billion,[12] was likely to grow due to immigration patterns. Its customers comprised the five major ethnic communities in Canada—Chinese, South Asian, Middle Eastern, Central and South American and Caribbean. The $1.8 billion organic foods market was growing at 20 per cent per annum.[13] The world's largest natural and organic foods chain, based in the United States, had opened its first overseas store in Toronto in May 2002. Whole Foods Inc. products competed directly with Loblaw's PC Organics natural food products.

Convenience Stores

Convenience stores complemented supermarkets by allowing consumers to fill up between shopping trips. The convenience store segment had grown faster than grocery supermarkets, increasing in number from 6,629 in 1997 to 8,342 in 2002.

Online Shopping

Online grocery shopping accounted for only $100 million in sales in Canada. Grocery Gateway, a Toronto-based e-grocer, dominated the market, growing its customer base from 7,000 in 1999 to 14,200 by mid-2002.[14]

AC Nielsen studies indicated that 57 per cent of Canadians were Internet users in 2000, up from 31 per cent in 1997. A survey in 2000 showed that grocery orders through the Internet numbered between 800 to 1,000 per day, and the average size of

[12]John Schofield, "The ethnic market in Canada," *Food in Canada Magazine*, November/December 2002, p. 28.
[13]Lisa Rostoks, "Romancing the organic crowd," *Canadian Grocer*, August 2002.
[14]Lynne Davidson, "The milkman returneth," *pwcglobal.com/RealEstateTrendsSummer 2002*, accessed October 7, 2003.

an order was $120. New families and young singles were driving contemporary online grocery sales in Canada, but electronic security was a major barrier to shopping online for some consumers.[15]

Competitive Outlook

Small entrants in the independent category entered the market frequently. Two of the most recent large entrants to the Canadian grocery were Whole Foods, which had entered a niche market of organics, and Wal-Mart, which had entered Canadian retail by acquiring 122 Woolco stores. Grocers in the mid-sized category were potential acquisitions for global firms pursuing expansion. European grocers were known to be on the prowl for acquisitions since their home markets had reached saturation levels and the rate of growth was slowing down.[16] However, the limited market size in Canada and lower margins were major disincentives. Each of the four leading grocers in Canada—including Loblaw—had been the subject of regular media speculation as a take-over target of various global firms.

GROCERY OPERATIONS

Supply Chain and Logistics

An average Canadian grocery store carried 25,000 to 40,000 stock keeping units (SKUs). Strong supply chain and logistics functions were thus crucial. Demand forecasts were, in large part, judgment-driven, despite the use of computers. Poor forecasting or logistics led to expired or obsolete products, which drained profitability, or conversely, to out-of-stocks, which reduced sales and customer satisfaction.

Technology

Canadian retail was leading the revolution in technology, ahead of U.S. retail, with its ECCnet. Put into place in mid-2003, ECCnet was a national, online, standardized product registry for synchronized data exchange. It provided the foundation on which subsequent technology platforms, like Radio Frequency Identification, could be deployed without delay. Potential savings for grocers were estimated at one per cent of sales.[17]

Scale

The average size of a Canadian supermarket was 28,000 square feet, generating average weekly sales of about $300,000. Goliath stores averaging 110,000 square feet could generate a million dollars in sales a week.[18] Scale advantages included lower costs of handling incoming materials and lower procurement costs, but backroom support was crucial, and the store had to run at full capacity.

---

[15]Canadian Grocer, "2001–2002 Executive Report," p. 30.

[16] Peter Diekmeyer, "Are Canada's retailers ripe for the picking?" www.cdngrocer.com, accessed October 7, 2003.

[17]Canadian Grocer, "2001–2002 Executive Report," p. 32.

[18]George H. Condon, "Taming a Goliath," *Canadian Grocer*, March 2002.

Profitability

The margins of a supermarket chain were among the lowest of all industries. Post-tax profits averaged between 0.5 per cent and 2 per cent. Independents had higher margins of up to five per cent but on lower sales (see Exhibit 6). Since store profitability was linked to space, costs were calculated per square foot (see Exhibit 7). The data on product profitability or even on category profitability was not always reliable due to the number of variables in cost allocation and cost apportionment.[19]

LOBLAW

Company Background

Loblaw Companies Limited was a part of George Weston Limited, a broadly based Canadian company operating in two distinct business segments: food processing and food distribution. Founded in 1919 by Theodore Pringle Loblaw and J. Milton Crok, Loblaw Grocetarias, as it was then known, was a prosperous chain of 113 stores spread in Ontario, with sales of $50 million in 1947, when Garfield Weston, a young baker in Toronto, acquired a small stake in the company.[20] Now controlled by a third generation member of the Weston family and spearheaded by a professional team led by John Lederer, Loblaw was Canada's largest food distributor with sales of $23.1 billion in 2002 (see financial statements in Exhibits 8–10), and 122,300 employees. The Weston family held majority ownership.

Strategy Execution

The company's overall strategy, as reiterated regularly in its annual reports, was evident at the level of execution in the following ways.[21]

Real Estate As opposed to its competitors who leased stores, Loblaw owned 63 per cent of its corporate stores in Canada, many of which were in very favourable locations.[22] Ownership provided flexibility at the operational level. Loblaw upgraded its stores every five years in contrast to the industry norm of seven years, and redesigned its formats to meet changing customer needs.

Control Label Program Grocery stores were compelled to carry very popular branded products and sell them as loss leaders in order to keep their customers happy. Through its very successful control label program, Loblaw was able to take significant market share away from the big brands, competing with them strongly on prices yet ensuring margins due to lower costs. The popularity of its control label products also produced customer loyalty.

---

[19]www.georgemorris.org/HMR update, accessed October 12, 2003.

[20]Charles Davies, *Bread men*, Key Porter Books, 1987, p. 92.

[21]Ann Leamon, Ray A. Goldberg and David E. Bell, "Loblaw Companies Ltd.: The road ahead," *Harvard Business School Case 9-901-015*, p. 9.

[22]Loblaw Companies Ltd., 2002 Annual Report, p. 34.

A Multi-Format Approach A multi-banner, multi-format approach had enabled Loblaw to cover all price points in the grocery market and cater to all segments ranging from discount to bulk and gourmet. Each store had a local appeal.

Meeting Everyday Needs Groceries were the core of Loblaw business, but a rich fare of non-food items was offered to meet the daily needs of every household. The control label initiative had also been extended to general merchandise by the company. Loblaw also operated over 100 gas stations in Canada.

Increasing Market Share per Store Instead of pursuing national market share, Loblaw focused on increasing the market share of each individual store.

Organizational Structure and Human Resources

The organization structure of Loblaw is shown in Exhibit 11. Line managers reported to both regional heads and banner heads. Regional vice-presidents oversaw profitability in the Ontario, Quebec, Atlantic and Western regions. Senior banner managers held profit centre responsibility across regions. Corporate support departments included real estate, information technology (IT) and supply chain, legal, control label, finance and treasury and labour relations.

The tenure of Loblaw's senior operating team averaged 18 years.[23] Stock options were a major performance driver for senior managers. One of the largest private sector employers in Canada, Loblaw offered top wages and benefits. The United Food and Commercial Workers represented Loblaw's employees.

Marketing

Loblaw stores advertised 35 to 50 sale items in a weekly flyer. Non-sale items earned higher margins. Beyond store marketing, Loblaw's three broad marketing initiatives were Stores-as-a-Brand, Control Label and Customer Loyalty.

Stores-As-A-Brand Loblaw had acquired strong regional stores like *Fortinos* in Hamilton, *Zehrs* in Kitchener and *Provigo* in Quebec without changing their names or diluting their community character.

The Real Canadian Superstore, reigning in Western Canada, was the first major Canadian attempt at establishing mega-stores. Averaging 125,000 square feet, the stores sold a variety of food and non-food merchandise including clothing, housewares, electronics, etc.; 60 per cent of the sales in Superstores came from higher margin non-food merchandise.[24]

The Real Canadian Wholesale Club was positioned against Costco/Price Club, with good prices on bulk purchases of mostly branded products (including President's Choice). *Extra Foods* focused on bulk purchases of inexpensive products, with a higher concentration of no-name products in the store. *SuperValue* and *Shop Easy*

---

[23]Loblaw Companies Ltd., 2000 Annual Report, p. 23.

[24]Susan Thorne, "Loblaws 84 years old; still biggest grocer by far," www.icsc.org/srch/set/current/page24.html, accessed March 19, 2004.

Foods were smaller stores that operated in downtown areas offering smaller package sizes and semi-processed foods. *Lucky Dollar* featured Asian ethnic foods. *No frills* provided low-cost, mostly no-name products in bulk and a limited range of produce and perishables. *Your Independent Grocer* and *ValuMart* were smaller stores, affiliates and independents, often located in small towns where the personal relationship between the store owner and the community was important. In the Maritimes, *Atlantic SaveEasy* was similar in concept to *No frills*. *Atlantic Superstore* was positioned similarly to Western Canada's *Real Canadian Superstore,* though the stores were smaller. *Dominion* (in Newfoundland) had a profile similar to *Loblaw* in Ontario.

Control Label Products In 1984, Loblaw introduced its President's Choice (PC) private label program. High quality products were sourced, labelled as PC, and marketed through the "Insider's Report," a personal communiqué from Dave Nichol, the then-president of Loblaw Supermarkets. At one time, the Insider's Report attracted more readership than the mainstream newspapers in Canada. Other European and North American retailers also sold private label products, but Loblaw was the first to build a brand for its private label that could compete with national brands. In pioneering PC products, Loblaw paved the way for every major grocery chain in Canada to develop a private label program unique to its customer base. Private labels comprised about 25 per cent of grocery sales in Canada and their growth rate (7 per cent) outpaced that of national brands (6 per cent), according to a study by AC Nielsen.[25]

Customer Loyalty Programs Loblaw had developed, in 1997, a loyalty program that worked across its store banners. Launched as an extension of the *President's Choice* brand and offered under the aegis of *President's Choice Financial,* the benefits were two-fold. Customers could earn points redeemable for free groceries based on their purchases at any store in the chain. They could also obtain low-cost financial services such as everyday banking, loans, investments and mortgages through electronic banking and pavilions at select Loblaw family stores. The *PC MasterCard,* launched in 2001, reinforced the program. Planned expansions for PC Financial Services included more stores and more products, such as home and auto insurance.

Distribution Loblaw had four types of stores as part of its distribution network: corporate stores; franchised stores; associated stores; and independent accounts. The corporate stores were managed directly by the chain while the others were business affiliations aimed at enlarging the reach of the chain. The company had a total of 632 corporate stores, 406 franchised stores, 659 associated stores and 7,069 affiliated independents. They were all serviced by 34 warehouses across Canada.[26]

New supermarkets being opened in Canada by existing grocers were getting progressively larger in size. This was accompanied by a gradual decline in sales per square foot. But Loblaw was different. Its annual average sales per square foot of corporate stores grew from $502 in 1994 to $575 in 2002, even as the average store size went up from 37,700 square feet to 48,900 square feet during the period. Future extensions of the large-format *Real Canadian Superstore* into other Canadian markets were planned, and five of them were under various stages of execution in 2003.

---

[25]Lisa Rostoks, "Mastering private label," *Canadian Grocer*, February 2002.
[26]Loblaw Companies Ltd., 2002 Annual Report, p. 18.

THE WAL-MART THREAT

Wal-Mart was the world's largest retailer with $245 billion in revenues in 2002[27] (see financial statements in Exhibits 12 and 13) and 1,383,000 employees. Wal-Mart had 516 million square feet of retail space with an average store size of 116,795 square feet. It was three times the size of the world's second largest retailer, France's Carrefour. Its "Every Day Low Prices" (EDLP) strategy was an extremely popular alternative to the weekly sale items advertised by other retailers. The company was wringing billions of dollars in cost efficiencies out of the retail supply chain and passing them on to shoppers as bargain prices. According to an estimate by New England Consulting, the company saved its U.S. customers $100 billion in 2002 alone, both through lowering its own prices and forcing competitors to do so. The "Wal-Mart effect" has helped suppress inflation and distribute productivity gains through the U.S. economy year after year. The company was known to derive cost advantages amounting to 22 per cent over U.S. competitors, based on the way it managed its "ecosystem" of business partners.[28] Wal-Mart earned US$403 per square foot in its domestic stores, with gross margins of 21.2 per cent.[29] Wal-Mart established close relationships with its suppliers, and although it drove a hard bargain on price, the company shared information and systems with its suppliers that made each company more efficient. A fierce competitor, Wal-Mart was widely touted as the cause of Kmart's bankruptcy, as that chain had tried to compete directly with Wal-Mart. Target, Wal-Mart's other major U.S. competitor, operated slightly up-market from Wal-Mart to avoid head on competition with the retail dynamo.

The company had internationalized with the opening of a Sam's Club in Mexico in 1991 (see Exhibit 14). Its international experience was mixed. While credited with "helping to hold down inflation in Mexico, improving Britain's cost of living and revolutionizing the distribution system in China,"[30] Wal-Mart did less well in Germany and Japan. Only 4 of its 10 overseas ventures were profitable.

When asked about Wal-Mart's plans for the future, chief executive officer H. Lee Scott, Jr., indicated the company wanted "to be where we're not."[31] More than two-thirds of the value implicit in Wal-Mart's stock price was based on growth possibilities rather than on current operations.[32] Scott foresaw decades of growth in the core business, including more stores in smaller geographic centres than had previously been thought possible. Growth plans included significant expansion of their Supercenter format, with over 200 set to open during 2003 and 1,000 expected to open in the U.S. alone in the next five years. Wal-Mart's Supercenter concept was a larger format store that added a full line of groceries and specialty services to its discount store. Food made up approximately 35 per cent of sales, and, though margins were slimmer

[27]Anthony Bianco and Wendy Zellner, "Is Wal-Mart too powerful?" *BusinessWeek*, October 6, 2003.

[28]Marco Iansiti and Roy Levien, "Strategy as ecology," *Harvard Business Review*, March 2004.

[29]Pankaj Ghemawat, Ken A. Mark and Stephen P. Bradley, "Wal-Mart Stores in 2003," *Harvard Business School Case Study, 9-704-430*, p 5.

[30]Robert Slater, *The Wal-Mart decade*, Penguin USA 2003, p. 133.

[31]Bill Saporito, "Can Wal-Mart get any bigger?" *Time*, January 5, 2003.

[32]Luciano Catoni, Nora F. Larssen, James Naylor and Andrea Zocchi, "Travel tips for retailers," *The McKinsey Quarterly*, No. 3. 2002.

(6.6 per cent for Supercenters versus 9 to 10 per cent for discount stores), inventory turned faster than in discount stores, and so return on assets was higher. A population base of 76,000 people was needed to support a Supercenter.[33] Sam's Club stores, which competed directly with Costco, did not perform as well as Supercenters and thus were scheduled for more limited growth.

The company also expected to grow geographically: It had targeted a third of its sales and profit growth to come from its international operations by 2005, doubling from 16 per cent in 2002.[34] Wal-Mart also announced the introduction of financial services for its customers in 2003.

Wal-Mart in Canada

Wal-Mart had entered Canada in 1994 by taking over 122 Woolco stores. It had raced past established retailers like Eaton's, Hudson's Bay Co. and Sears Canada to be ranked, by 2002, as No. 1 retailer in Canada. Wal-Mart Canada had become profitable by the second year of operations, providing a measure of confidence about the company's international operations in general.

Even as its Every Day Low Prices strategy had become popular with Canadian consumers, Wal-Mart had acceptance problems of a different kind. The UFCW Canada had filed charges of unfair labour practices against the company.[35] The first signs of discord had surfaced when Wal-Mart refused to buy any of the nine Woolworth stores where workers were enjoying UFCW Canada union contracts and benefits. The parent company, Wal-Mart Inc., had been a particular target for UFCW, even in the United States where it had successfully prevented unionization at all its stores. The largest private sector employer in the United States was widely blamed for the sorry state of retail wages in America.[36] Raids on U.S. Wal-Mart stores in 2003 found illegal immigrants working as sub-contracted cleaning staff for low wages, with no overtime or benefits pay and no taxes withheld.[37]

Traditionally, supermarkets like Loblaw used size and scale to achieve cost leadership. But Wal-Mart, already the world's largest retailer, was using technology to cut costs further. A centralized information system in Arkansas linked the operations of its 4,750 stores and 30,000 suppliers around the world, in real time. Wal-Mart also developed in-house, retail technology solutions to drive costs continuously down.[38]

According to an industry analyst,[39] Wal-Mart had quickly dominated most markets outside the United States within years of entry because the grocery markets in those countries lacked depth. The Canadian grocery market, in contrast, was characterized by several discount formats and many private labels. Wal-Mart also had limited expertise in perishables (which comprised 67 per cent of total grocery sales in 2001).[40]

---

[33]This paragraph draws on information in Pankaj Ghemawat, Ken A. Mark and Stephen P. Bradley, "Wal-Mart stores in 2003," *Harvard Business School Case Study, 9-704-430.*

[34]Chester Dawson, "Will Wal-Mart conquer Japan?" *BusinessWeek US Edition*, April 1, 2002.

[35]"Threat of Wal-Mart expansion," www.ufcw.ca, press release dated November 25, 2002, accessed October 12, 2003.

[36]www.businessweek.com, accessed October 3, 2003.

[37]"Illegal immigrants arrested in raids sue Wal-Mart," *Associated Press,* November 9, 2003, www.cnn.com, accessed January 23, 2004.

[38]"The IT inside the world's biggest company," *CIO Magazine*, July 2002.

[39]Interview with Perry Caicco of CIBC World Markets.

The launch of Sam's Club wholesale mega-stores suggested that Wal-Mart was feeling confident about its ability to compete in Canada. Would Wal-Mart Supercenters be next?

THE RESPONSE

What should Lederer do, given the expected entry of Wal-Mart into the grocery business? Was it time to shake up the company's stable strategy?

EXHIBIT 1   Canadian Grocers' Market Shares—2002

	Sales (in million $)	Market Share (%)
Statistics Canada Supermarket Sales	58,191	78.0
Grocery Products in Other Channels	16,409	22.0
Total	74,600	100.0
Loblaw	**23,894**	**32.0**
Sobeys	10,960	14.7
Safeway	5,492	7.4
Metro	5,201	7.0
A&P	4,400	5.9
Costco Food	3,550	4.8
Convenience Stores	3,250	4.4
Wal-Mart	**2,758**	**3.7**
Co-Op	2,667	3.6
Drug Stores	2,659	3.6
Overwaitea	2,380	3.2
Commisso Wholesale	757	1.0
Hy Louie	595	0.8
Other Mass Merchandisers	494	0.6
Commisso Food Markets	466	0.7
Thrifty Foods	374	0.5
North West Co.	333	0.4
T&T Foods	170	0.2
Other Independents	4,200	5.6

Source: Canadian Grocer, Executive report 2003–2004.

---

[40]Jerry Tutunjian, "The numbers are in," *Canadian Grocer*, November 2002, p. 31.

EXHIBIT 2   World's Top Grocery Retailers 2001

Ranking	Company	Country	Stores Owned	Sales (in US$ million)
1	Carrefour	France	8,926	61,398
2	Ahold	The Netherlands	8,062	58,842
3	Metro	Germany	2,169	43,758
4	Kroger Co.	USA	2,354	37,900
5	Albertson's	USA	2,533	37,900
6	**Wal-Mart (Food sales)**	**USA**	**4,190**	**36,865**
7	Safeway	USA	1,688	34,300
8	Tesco	UK	907	32,380
9	Rewe Zentrale	Germany	11,788	31,880
10	Aldi	Germany	4,388	26,480
11	Edeka/AVA	France	12,000	26,450
12	ITM Enterprises	France	8,545	26,140
13	J. Sainsbury	UK	626	26,130
14	It-Yokado	Japan	35,600	25,850
15	Group Casino	France	6,650	24,940
16	Daiei	Japan	7,800	23,740
17	Tengelmann	Germany	6,689	23,120
18	Supervalu	USA	1,194	21,300
19	Jusco	Japan	1,780	21,020
20	Auchan	France	243	20,130
21	E. Leclerc	France	555	17,940
22	Fleming Cos	USA	250	15,600
23	Delhaize "Le Lion" Group	Belgium	2,310	15,550
24	**Loblaw**	**Canada**	**606**	**15,100**
25	Winn-Dixie Stores	USA	1,079	13,000

Source: Canadian Grocer, Executive report 2003–2004.

EXHIBIT 3   Volume of Food Retail Trade in Canada

$ in million	2002	2001	2000	1999	1998
A. Supermarkets & Stores	62,049	58,858	56,592	54,500	53,346
B. All Other Food Stores	4,778	4,793	4,498	4,389	4,318
C. Total Food Sales (A + B)	**66,827**	63,652	61,090	58,889	57,664
D. Total Retail Trade Sales	306,578	289,130	277,033	260,779	246,675
E. % of Food in Retail Sales	21.8	22.0	22.1	20.2	23.38

Source: www.statcan.ca.

EXHIBIT 4   Number of Grocery Stores in Canada

Year	Supermarkets	Convenience Stores	Affiliated Independents	Unaffiliated Independents	Total
2001	1,538	7,295	4,782	10,517	**24,132**
2000	1,581	6,812	5,269	11,850	**25,512**
1999	1,611	6,290	5,212	13,217	**26,330**
1998	1,687	6,401	5,078	12,926	**26,092**
1997	1,656	6,629	5,091	12,371	**25,747**

Source: Canadian Grocer, Annual National Market Surveys February 2003.

EXHIBIT 5 Grocery Chains in Canada with More Than 20 Stores

Name of the Chain	Banners	Year Est.	No. of Stores	Ownership	Private Labels
A&P Canada	A&P	1927	81	Corporate	Body Basics Master
	Dominion	1919	56	Corporate	Choice Basics for Less
	Food Basics	1995	88	Corporate	Equality
Bulk Barn Foods	Bulk Barn	1982	63	Franchise	
Canada Safeway	Safeway	1929	213	Corporate	
Co-op Atlantic	Co-op Atlantic	1927	181	Cooperative	
The Grocers People	Bigway	1960	102	Family	West Best
Loblaw Companies	Atlantic Save Easy	–	56	Corp/Franch	Club Pack
	Atlantic Superstore	1986	50	Corporate	Exact
	Cash & Carry	1980	10	Corporate	Green
	Dominion in NFL	–	15	Corporate	President's Choice
	Extra Foods	1980	90	Corp/Franch	Today's Choice
	Fortino's	1961	18	Franchise	Too Good To Be True
	Loblaw	1920	98	Corporate	no name
	Lucky Dollar	–	102	JV/Franch	
	Maxi	1984	85	Corporate	
	Provigo	1969	138	Corp/Franch	
	Real Canadian SS	1980	57	Corporate	
	RealCanadianWSC	1991	32	Corporate	
	Shop Easy	1912	56	Franchise	
	SuperValue	1903	29	Corp/Franch	
	Valu-Mart	1925	71	Franch/JV	
	Your Independent …	1987	54	Franch/AD	
	Zehrs Markets	1950	58	Corporate	
	No Frills	1978	110	Franchise	
Metro Inc.	Metro	1947	251	Family/Fran	The Irresistible
	Ami	1962	95	Family	Econochoix
	Gem	1960	268	Family	Super C
	Loeb	1912	43	Family/Fran	
	Marche	1952	142	Family	
	Super C	–	49	Corporate	
Overwaitea	Overwaitea Foods	1915	34	Corporate	Value-Priced
	Save-on-Foods	1982	50	Corporate	Western Classics
					Western Family
Rabba's Fine Foods	Rabba's	–	26	Corporate	
Sobeys Inc.	Boni Choix	1982	104	Franchise	Our Compliments
	Food Town	–	104	Corp/Franch	Smart Choice
	Food Land	–	94	Franchise	
	GardenMarket IGA	–	94	Corp/Franch	
	IGA	1951	433	Corp/Franch	
	IGA Extra	–	31	Corp/Franch	
	Knechtel	1930	46	Corp/Franch	
	Omni	1982	117	AD	
	Price Chopper	1992	88	Corp/Franch	
	Sobeys	1907	119	Corporate	
H Y Louie	IGA	1914	43	Corp/Franch	

Source: 2003 Directory of retail chains in Canada.

EXHIBIT 6 Operating Expenses of Canadian Grocetarias as % of Sales

Item of Expenditure	Conventional Stores	Supermarkets
Store Labour	10.0	9.9
Benefits	1.7	2.7
Occupancy	2.4	2.6
Utilities	1.2	1.0
Advertising	1.3	1.6
Maintenance	0.7	0.8
Stores Supplies	1.1	1.0
Interest	0.4	0.6
Others	3.1	4.0
Total	**21.9**	**24.2**

Source: Canadian Grocer, Executive report 2000–2001.

EXHIBIT 7 Productivity of Canadian Supermarkets

Productivity Measure	Conventional Stores	Supermarkets
Total Store Area (Sq Ft)	17,400	42,000
% of Selling Area to Total Area	73.90	74
Weekly Sales per Sq Ft of Selling Area ($)	9.10	11.06
Weekly PBT per Sq Ft of Selling Area ($)	0.20	0.26
Average Weekly Sales per Store ($)	102,574	310,567
Sales per Labour Hour ($)	82.33	107.17
Payroll Cost per Labour Hour ($)	7.76	10.44
Occupancy Cost per Sq Ft ($)	10.47	15.84
% of Occupancy Cost to Total Expenditure	15.40	13.40
Overall Store Inventory Turns (No. of Times)	15.70	17.40
Average Number of Checkouts	6	10
Average Transaction Size ($)	14.60	21.34
Weekly Transactions/Checkouts (Nos.)	1,356	1,269
Total Gross Margin as % of Sales	24.3	27.1
Total Store Labour Expenses as % of Sales	11.7	12.6
Profit Before Tax as % of Sales	2.2	3.0

Source: Canadian Grocer, Executive report 2000–2001.

EXHIBIT 8

$ in million	**LOBLAW COMPANIES LIMITED** **Consolidated Balance Sheet**						
$ in million	**2002**	**2001**	**2000**	**1999**	**1998**	**1997**	**1996**
Assets							
Cash & S/Term Investments	1,127	1,001	1,050	726	672	562	720
Accounts Receivables	605	472	381	417	352	364	157
Inventories	1,702	1,512	1,310	1,222	1,141	707	659
Others	92	101	175	50	84	48	16
Total Current Assets	3,526	3,086	2,916	2,415	2,249	1,681	1,552
Fixed Assets	5,587	4,931	4,174	3,549	3,194	2,093	1,738
Investments & Advances	–	–	189	160	134	113	112
Intangible Assets	1,599	1,599	1,641	1,685	1,363	38	40
Other Assets	398	409	105	170	165	88	88
Total Assets	**11,110**	**10,025**	**9,025**	**7,979**	**7,105**	**4,013**	**3,530**
Liabilities							
Short-term Borrowings	639	367	889	746	1,150	374	421
Accounts Payables	2,336	2,291	2,240	2,066	1,806	1,084	931
Other Current Liabilities	179	138	78	0	0	21	47
Total Current Liabilities	3,154	2,796	3,207	2,812	2,956	1,479	1,399
Provisions	68	49	78	113	122	77	57
Long-term Debt	3,420	3,333	2,377	1,979	1,364	915	733
Other Liabilities	344	278	239	171	68	47	30
Total Liabilities	6,986	6,456	5,901	5,075	4,510	2,518	2,220
Retained Earnings	2,929	2,375	1,930	1,721	1,429	1,221	1,046
Common Share Capital	1,195	1,194	1,194	1,183	1,166	274	265
Total Shareholders' Equity	4,124	3,569	3,124	2,904	2,595	1,495	1,310
Total Liabilities & **Shareholders' Equity**	**11,110**	**10,025**	**9,025**	**7,979**	**7,105**	**4,013**	**3,530**

Source: Company files.

EXHIBIT 9

$ in million	2002	2001	2000	1999	1998	1997	1996
LOBLAW COMPANIES **Statement of Earnings**							
Sales	23,082	21,486	20,121	18,783	12,497	11,008	9,848
Cost of Sales	21,425	20,035	18,862	17,706	11,785	10,435	9,367
Depreciation	354	315	283	266	185	147	122
Oper. Income	1,303	1,136	976	811	527	426	359
Interest	161	158	143	112	68	44	46
Income Taxes	414	372	317	280	198	169	139
Goodwill	–	43	43	43	–	–	–
Net Earnings	728	563	473	376	261	213	174

Source: Company files.

EXHIBIT 10

$ in million	2002	2001	2000	1999	1998	1997	1996
LOBLAW COMPANIES **Retained Earnings**							
Year Beginning	2,375	1,930	1,721	1,429	1,221	1,046	902
Less: Misc. Charges	25	–	152	–	2	–	–
Add Net Earnings	728	563	473	376	261	213	174
Less Dividend Paid	149	118	112	84	51	38	30
Year End	2,929	2,375	1,930	1,721	1,429	1,221	1,046

Source: Company files.

EXHIBIT 11 Loblaw Companies Ltd. Organization Chart **(Figures in brackets indicate age and tenure of service)**

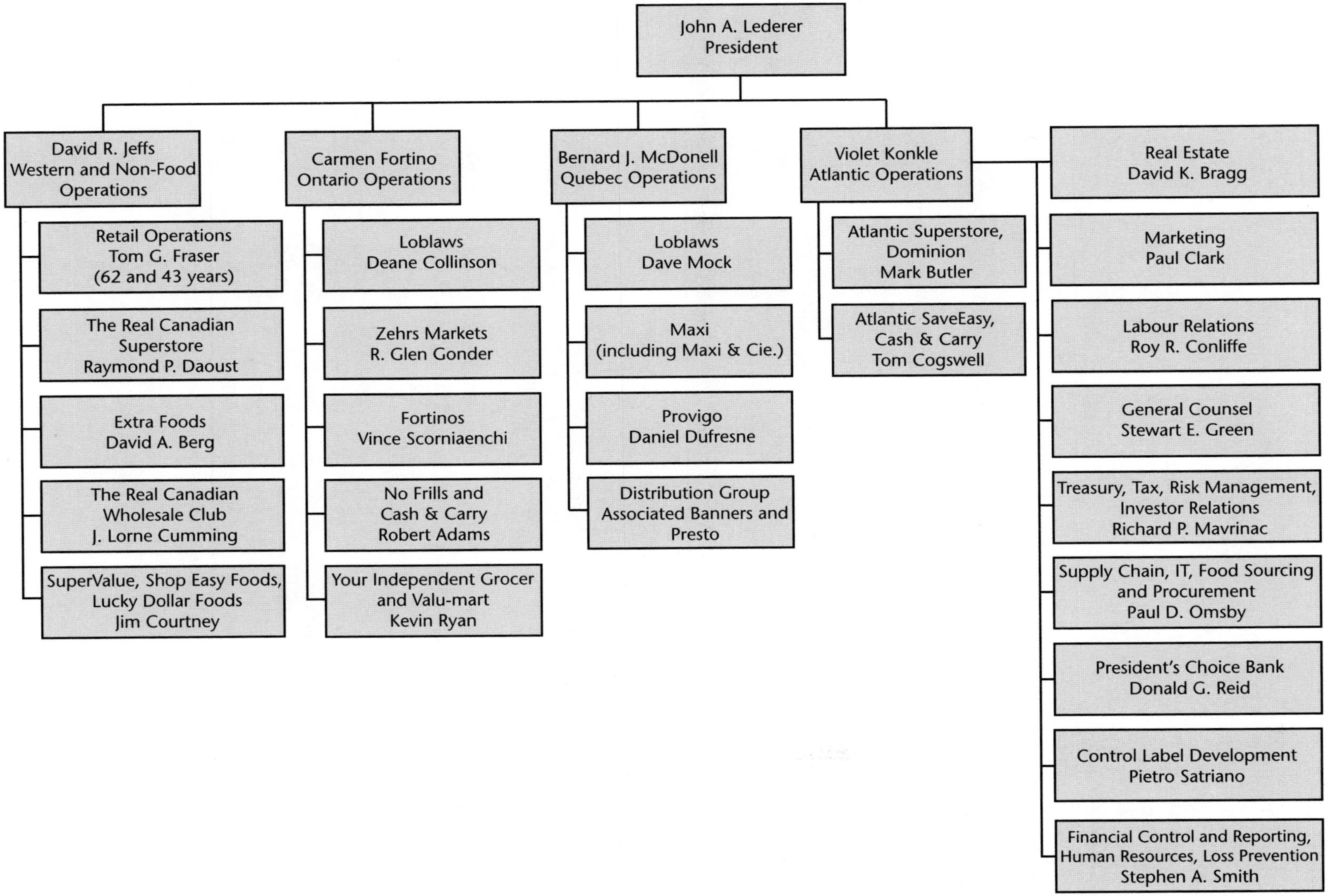

John A. Lederer
President

Staff functions (right column):
- Real Estate — David K. Bragg
- Marketing — Paul Clark
- Labour Relations — Roy R. Conliffe
- General Counsel — Stewart E. Green
- Treasury, Tax, Risk Management, Investor Relations — Richard P. Mavrinac
- Supply Chain, IT, Food Sourcing and Procurement — Paul D. Omsby
- President's Choice Bank — Donald G. Reid
- Control Label Development — Pietro Satriano
- Financial Control and Reporting, Human Resources, Loss Prevention — Stephen A. Smith

Violet Konkle — Atlantic Operations
- Atlantic Superstore, Dominion — Mark Butler
- Atlantic SaveEasy, Cash & Carry — Tom Cogswell

Bernard J. McDonell — Quebec Operations
- Loblaws — Dave Mock
- Maxi (including Maxi & Cie.)
- Provigo — Daniel Dufresne
- Distribution Group Associated Banners and Presto

Carmen Fortino — Ontario Operations
- Loblaws — Deane Collinson
- Zehrs Markets — R. Glen Gonder
- Fortinos — Vince Scorniaenchi
- No Frills and Cash & Carry — Robert Adams
- Your Independent Grocer and Valu-mart — Kevin Ryan

David R. Jeffs — Western and Non-Food Operations
- Retail Operations — Tom G. Fraser (62 and 43 years)
- The Real Canadian Superstore — Raymond P. Daoust
- Extra Foods — David A. Berg
- The Real Canadian Wholesale Club — J. Lorne Cumming
- SuperValue, Shop Easy Foods, Lucky Dollar Foods — Jim Courtney

EXHIBIT 12

WAL-MART INC. Consolidated Balance Sheet					
$ in Millions	2002	2001	2000	1999	1998
Current Assets	28,170	26,555	24,356	21,132	19,352
Total Assets	83,375	78,130	70,349	49,996	45,384
Current Liabilities	27,173	28,949	25,803	16,762	14,460
Shareholders' Equity	35,102	31,343	25,834	21,112	18,503

EXHIBIT 13

WAL-MART INC. Statement Of Earnings					
$ in Millions	2002	2001	2000	1999	1998
Net Sales	217,800	191,329	165,013	137,634	117,958
Other Income	2,013	1,966	1,796	1,574	1,341
Cost of Sales	171,562	150,255	129,664	108,725	93,438
Operating & Admin Costs	36,173	31,550	27,040	22,363	19,358
Operating Income	11,937	11,311	10,105	8,061	6,503
Interest	1,186	1,195	841	614	733
Taxes	3,897	3,692	3,338	2,740	2,115
Net Income	6,671	6,295	5,576	4,430	3,526

EXHIBIT 14 Wal-Mart Outside USA

Year of Entry	Country	Mode of Entry	Initial No. of Stores	No. of Stores in 2002	No. of Employees in 2002	Sales in 2002 ($ mn)	Op.Income in 2002 ($ mn)
1991	Mexico	JV	1	595	92,708	10,980	656
1992	Puerto Rico	Expansion	1	55	7,500	2,000	104
1994	Canada	Acquisition	122	213	52,000	5,643	485
1995	Brazil	Expansion	5	22	6,000	421	−3
1995	Argentina	Expansion	3	11	4,000	100	−3
1996	China	JV	2	26	15,000	517	−8
1996	Indonesia	JV	—	—	—	—	—
1997	Germany	Acquisition	95	94	15,500	2,408	108
1998	South Korea	Acquisition	4	15	3,000	741	−18
1999	Britain	Acquisition	229	259	125,000	17,430	941
2002	Japan	Stakeholder	400	400	30,000	NA	NA

Source: Pankaj Ghemawat, Ken A. Mark and Stephen P. Bradley, "Wal-Mart stores in 2003", *Harvard Business Review case 9-704-430*.

Alcan (A): Anticipating Industry Change

As Richard Evans looked out over the frosty Montreal skyline, his thoughts were focused on Alcan's future. It was December 2006, and he had only been appointed president and chief executive officer (CEO) of Alcan in March of that year. Despite his short time as head of the world's second-largest aluminum producer, he knew full well that the industry was changing and that Alcan might soon change with it.

He thought of the record year that was coming to an end and the options available for the one ahead. Despite surging commodity prices, many unknowns lay ahead regarding the industry and what Alcan's future role would be. The industry was consolidating and he had been approached with two offers to be acquired.

A boom in aluminum production was under way around the world. Rising costs and the increasing scarcity of good sites for new development made acquisition an attractive option for many firms. He had been approached by two firms interested in Alcan and he had to decide between them, or to go it alone.

One of the earliest phone calls congratulating Evans on his new job had come from Alain Belda, CEO of Alcoa. There was more to the phone call than just congratulations, however. When the two met in May 2006, Belda asked Evans about his thoughts on a merger between the two companies.

Belda was not the only one to express his interest. In October 2006, Leigh Clifford, CEO of mining giant Rio Tinto, contacted Evans about acquiring Alcan. The two interested companies were very different and Evans knew that a deal with either would have very different consequences.

Gregory Vit, Johnny Boghossian, Amrita Nain and Karl Moore wrote this case solely to provide material for class discussion. The authors do not intend to illustrate either effective or ineffective handling of a managerial situation. The authors may have disguised certain names and other identifying information to protect confidentiality.

Ivey Management Services prohibits any form of reproduction, storage or transmittal without its written permission. Reproduction of this material is not covered under authorization by any reproduction rights organization. To order copies or request permission to reproduce materials, contact Ivey Publishing, Ivey Management Services, c/o Richard Ivey School of Business, The University of Western Ontario, London, Ontario, Canada, N6A 3K7; phone (519) 661-3208; fax (519) 661-3882; e-mail cases@ivey.uwo.ca.

Copyright © 2009, Ivey Management Services   Version: (A) 2009-12-04

Richard Ivey School of Business
The University of Western Ontario

ALCAN OVERVIEW

On December 31, 2006, Alcan had approximately 64,700 employees in 61 countries and approximately 3,300 employees in joint ventures. In terms of output, Alcan was the second-largest producer in the world after Alcoa, as shown in Exhibit 1. Employees were distributed between four operating segments consisting of Bauxite and Alumina, Primary Metal, Engineered Products and Packaging.

Aluminum production requires several steps and large amounts of energy. For a detailed description of the technologies involved, refer to Exhibit 2. The raw material used in aluminum is bauxite, which is mined and transformed into alumina through the refining process. Alumina is then transformed into aluminum through the electricity-intensive smelting process.

The Bauxite and Alumina segment, based in Montreal, included Alcan's mines and alumina refineries. Production ranged from standard grades to specialty alumina used in non-aluminum applications. The company planned to be self-sufficient in bauxite and alumina by 2008.

The Primary Materials segment, also based in Montreal, managed the company's electrical installations, smelting facilities, research and development (R&D) and sales of smelting technologies. Company-owned power plants generated a substantial part of the company's required electricity.

Technology sales were focused on the AP18-22 and AP3X families of smelting systems, which already provided industry-leading productivity levels. These capabilities were to be further enhanced by the breakthrough AP50 technology, which was now ready to move into the industrial development phase. Alcan expected a 20 per cent reduction in the energy consumed during smelting.[1] A breakdown of the costs of production is given in Exhibit 3.

The Engineered Products segment manufactured a broad range of aluminum and other composite products for applications ranging from automotive, mass transport, aerospace, marine, construction and beverage containers. This segment provided clients with high levels of expertise in the design of complex components. It also had the facilities to manufacture specialty parts according to client specifications.

The Packaging segment was built upon the packaging businesses of recently acquired Alusuisse and Pechiney. It had a strong global presence in the packaging of a wide range of food products. The segment benefited from dedicated research and development centres in North America and Europe. It was active in the packaging of pharmaceuticals, cosmetics and tobacco products, with over 130 plants in 30 countries.

Alcan revenues for 2006 totalled $23.6 billion.[2] Broken down by business segment and including inter-segment transactions, Exhibit 4 provides sales and profit figures. Comparative industry data is provided in Exhibit 5.

Recent Acquisitions

In the late 1990s, Alcan had spearheaded a three-way merger between itself, Alusuisse and Pechiney. The merger fell through after European Union regulators disapproved. However, Alcan did subsequently manage to acquire the smaller of the two, Alusuisse

---

[1]Alcan Inc., "Alcan launches breakthrough aluminum technology initiative in France," December 14, 2006, www.alcan.com/web/publishing.nsf/Content Alcan+Launches+Breakthrough+Aluminum+Technology+Initiative+in+France

[2]All funds in US$ unless otherwise noted.

Group Ltd., in 2000. The acquisition, valued at $3.5 billion, generated $200 million in synergies and greatly expanded Alcan's packaging business.[3]

In 2003, Evans' predecessor, Travis Engen, was determined to finish the job and embarked on an outright acquisition of the then-fourth largest aluminum producer, Pechiney. The acquisition started out hostile, but then became friendly once Alcan raised the value of its offer. Evans was instrumental throughout this process.

Pechiney was comparable in size to Alcan at the time and the acquisition, valued at $5.5 billion, promised synergies of $360 million annually.[4] The acquisition also provided Alcan access to Pechiney's AP smelting technology, which Alcan continued to develop at its main research and development sites in Quebec and those acquired from Pechiney in France.

Social Obligations

This time it was Alcan that was the target for acquisition, but Evans had to consider factors most CEOs in his position would not be confronted with. Only one month earlier, in November 2006, Alcan's representatives returned from a retreat with government officials and unveiled the "Continuity Agreement."

The company had recently signed a major deal with the province to receive large, interest-free loans and access to more public electricity. In return, it would make $1.88 billion in investments over the next 10 years. The Quebec government wanted to ensure that any possible acquirer would respect Alcan's side of the bargain.[5] If not, the province maintained the right to revoke the new entitlements it had granted the company.

The novelty of the Continuity Agreement was in who would participate in the acquisition talks. Rather than requiring three-way negotiations between Alcan, the acquirer, and the government, the Alcan board would be charged with ensuring the province's interests. The board was now legally obligated to negotiate on behalf of the social and economic well-being of Quebec communities.

STRATEGIC OPTIONS

Evans knew that the two offers represented very different futures for Alcan and he had to make the best choice for the company based on the changing structure of the industry.

(Option #1) Merge with Alcoa

The traditional model for the aluminum producer had been that of complete vertical integration. After years of consolidation, Alcan and Alcoa were the two remaining firms based on this model. They had large in-house engineering and packaging divisions. They worked closely with clients, providing them with design and manufacturing expertise as well as aluminum-based solutions difficult to find elsewhere.

Over the previous few years, many large, integrated aluminum producers had merged to unlock synergies and fend off competition. By consolidating operations and

---

[3]Alcan Inc., Form 10-K405, 2001.

[4]Alcan Inc., 2004 Annual Report, 2004.

[5]"Building a social bulwark in an age of takeovers," *The Globe and Mail*, February 19, 2008.

research efforts and combining their technologies, they had increased their levels of productivity as well as the size of their markets. This was the rationale behind Alcan's acquisition of Pechiney in 2003 and Alusuisse in 2000.

American-based Alcoa was the number one producer of aluminum in the world (see Exhibit 1) and had a structure very similar to Alcan's. Its operations were divided into four business units comprised of Bauxite and Aluminum, Primary Metal, Engineered Products and Packaging.

According to Belda, the proposed merger was driven by the desire to create a more competitive North American firm that could better compete against the feared glut of Russian and Chinese aluminum.[6] The Russian RusAl and Chinese Chalco, backed by their national governments, were threatening Alcoa's dominance.

Belda's synergy projections for the merger reflected the similarity of the two firms. He saw savings in the range of $1 billion annually from consolidation, sharing of best practices and more effective procurement. Alcoa had an excellent base of refineries, but many of its smelters were approaching their fourth decade of operation. Meanwhile, Alcan smelters, using the latest proprietary technologies, operated at industry-leading productivity levels (see Exhibit 6).

Regulatory approval, however, might be a hurdle in such a deal. The combined firm would produce 30 per cent of world alumina and 23 per cent of aluminum,[7] causing fears that it would have undue market power. The combination could also upset major aluminum-dependent clients such as Airbus, which sourced aluminum from both firms. Important divestitures would be necessary to satisfy regulators.

(Option #2) Be Acquired by Rio Tinto

Headquartered in England but with the majority of its aluminum operations in Australia, Rio Tinto was run with a very different business model. It was a mining giant, holding a portfolio of minerals and few downstream operations.

The company followed opportunities wherever they appeared in the mining and processing of minerals. Its mantra was "long life, low cost assets." Rio Tinto's operations were structured around product groups which consisted of copper, iron ore, aluminum, energy, industrial minerals and diamonds.

A strategy review initiated by Leigh Clifford, CEO of Rio Tinto, identified approximately $600 million in synergies between Rio Tinto and Alcan. Rio Tinto generated revenues of $22.46 billion. Aluminum, however, only represented 15.5 per cent of sales and 9.6 per cent of earnings, as shown in Exhibit 7.

Production of aluminum at Rio Tinto was too small for the firm to enjoy economies of scale. Managers had to make the decision soon whether to get out of aluminum or expand that segment. With good, undeveloped sites difficult to come by, acquisition was seen as the way to proceed.

If the acquisition went through, however, Alcan's Packaging and Engineered Products segments would be the first of their kind at Rio Tinto. Already for Alcan, Packaging required unique skills to run. It was marketing-driven rather than technology- and efficiency-driven, like its other business segments. It therefore risked being even more difficult to manage for Rio Tinto.

---

[6]Alcoa Inc., Form S-4, 2007.

[7]John C. Tuzamos and Andrew Tseng, "Lots of possible outcomes to the take-over battle," Prudential Equity Group, LLC., May 23, 2007.

(Option #3) Go It Alone

Alcan was based in the province of Quebec and there were benefits of remaining the local giant. Soon after Evans became CEO, he entered into negotiations with the Quebec government for support to build an AP50 pilot plant in the province.

"We're continuing in the 21st century the great history of aluminum, so intimately linked to this region and all of Quebec," announced Jean Charest, the premier of Quebec, when the new deal was unveiled on live television. It involved Alcan receiving interest-free loans, extensions to certain water rights to produce power and securing access to more public power. Exhibit 8 accompanied the announcement and presents the basic agreement.

Over a long history of close ties with the provincial government, Alcan was the best positioned in the industry when it came to electricity supply. Water rights allowed it to generate power at its own hydroelectric facilities. Some of these rights were based on long-term leases, while others extended into perpetuity. Alcan also had long-term power contracts with Hydro-Quebec to purchase low-cost electricity. In sum, Alcan was self-sufficient for 50 per cent of its power needs, while another 25 per cent was secured under contract.

The company was not confined to the provincial borders either. In fact, of all the aluminum companies in the world, it was the most international. After its large European acquisitions, it was spread all across the globe. This provided it with an advantage because some of the most attractive and fastest growing regions were not keen to allow foreign firms to enter.

Entering developing markets required a keen knowledge of the region and an ability to develop joint ventures with local governments. What is more, developing countries often demanded only the latest technologies. This meant that even Alcan's competitors would come to Alcan to purchase its efficient and cleaner technologies.

In early October 2006, Alcan released to shareholders the company's near-term strategy describing its pipeline of projects. The smelter projects Alcan had under development are shown in Exhibit 9. The Sohar smelter was closest to completion and was 20 per cent owned by Alcan. Kitimat and Isal would be 100 per cent owned by the company. Coega was still in the planning stages and ownership was expected to be in the range of 25 to 40 per cent for Alcan. All the new projects were to be in the lowest quartile of the industry cost curves.[8]

THE ALUMINUM INDUSTRY

The importance of aluminum in manufacturing was recognized over a century ago. Governments had long seen the major investments required to produce the material as crucial to national security and prosperity.

Early Years

Charles Martin Hall was the inventor of the modern process to manufacture aluminum. In 1890, he established the company which would later become Alcoa. The company built its first smelter in the province of Quebec in 1901, lured by the region's cheap

---

[8]Cynthia Carroll, *Alcan investor workshop*, October 3, 2006.

sources of hydroelectricity.[9] Alcan was born when all the international holdings of Alcoa were spun off starting in the 1920s.

Golden Age

The World Wars generated a large demand for aluminum in military applications, but after they ended, manufacturers turned to the civilian market. Because the civilian market was still small, companies focused on expanding the range of applications for aluminum and increasing the public's awareness.

They launched packaging and engineering divisions in order to expand the applications of aluminum. Although after the advent of plastics, packaging no longer utilized much aluminum, in these years it soaked up much of the excess aluminum capacity left over from the wars.

The stage was set for major industry changes after the market liberalization of the 1980s and the introduction of aluminum to the London Metals Exchange (LME). Independent smelters in countries around the globe were now able to compete with the large, integrated Western firms.

Recent Times

In 2006, aluminum was experiencing yet another run-up in prices. Exhibit 10 shows the swings in global aluminum prices over the last 30 years. The demand was fuelled by China's economic expansion and supported by steady Russian and Middle Eastern growth.

The demand for commodities was impacting aluminum especially. In an era of rising fuel costs, its lightweight properties were making it the metal of choice for the transport sector. Total world demand in 2006 outstripped production, driving inventory levels down and prices up. This resulted in aluminum prices hitting $3,310 per ton, an all-time high.

The China Factor

China already had the largest smelting capacity in the world and this was growing fast. Over the coming decades, China's growth was expected to result in a major shift in world production centres, as shown in Exhibits 11 and 12.

Despite the Chinese government's emphasis on meeting the country's resource needs, the environment was increasingly becoming an issue. Chinese smelters were often smaller, independent operations. These made less efficient use of electricity and were often more polluting.

The government had announced that it would like to see consolidation in the industry. The national producer Chalco was already the largest Chinese aluminum producer and the only one with both mining and refining operations. It therefore had considerable supplier power over many smelters that could not afford to backward integrate.[10]

Electricity costs continued to rise as the economy expanded. The development of the electrical grid throughout the country was connecting increasingly remote regions to the national network. Previously isolated power producers were now able to sell

---

[9]Alcan Inc., "Our history," 2009, www.alcan.com/web/publishing.nsf/Content/Media+Our+History, accessed February 1, 2009.

[10]Datamonitor, *Aluminum in China industry profile,* 2007.

their electricity nationally rather than rely on local smelters.[11] This meant local aluminum producers could no longer benefit from privileged access to electricity.

Despite high costs of production in China, the country still remained the lowest-cost location to establish new refineries and smelters. Exhibit 13 shows the average capital expenditures required to found new (greenfield) plants and modernize existing ones (brownfield).

THE ROAD AHEAD

Evans had to decide soon, as Alcoa and Rio Tinto would not wait forever. It was up to Alcan's board to read the changes in the industry and set a path for Alcan and its thousands of employees. How was the industry changing? What were the implications of the Continuity Agreement? How would Russian and Chinese competition impact Alcan's future? What kind of structure should Alcan assume?

Gregory Vit, Johnny Boghossian, Amrita Nain and Karl Moore are from the Desautels Faculty of Management, McGill University.

EXHIBIT 1   2006 Aluminum Output of Largest Producers (in thousand metric tons)

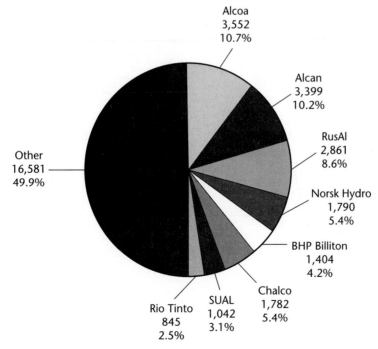

Source: Citigroup, Company in depth: Alcoa, April 11, 2007.

___

[11]*UBS*, Rio Tinto PLC, 2007.

EXHIBIT 2   The Aluminum Manufacturing Process

The production of aluminum still relies today on the Hall-Héroult process discovered in 1886. The three major steps are listed below:[12]

Bauxite Mining

Aluminum is produced through a three-step process. Production begins with the mining of bauxite ore. Bauxite is the third-most plentiful mineral on the planet's surface. It is extracted through strip mining and the largest producers are Australia, which accounts for 35 per cent of global production, followed by Brazil and China, each with 12 per cent, Jamaica and Guinea, each with 8 per cent, and India with 7 per cent.[13]

Alumina Refining

Bauxite is transported to a refining facility in order to produce the intermediary material called alumina. In this process, four tons of bauxite results in two tons of alumina. Because of the costs of transport, often refineries are located near the bauxite mines.

Aluminum Smelting

The intermediary material, alumina, is then transported to a smelter for processing into aluminum. This stage is based on the Hall-Héroult process and occurs in large carbon- or graphite-lined steel containers. The alumina is subjected to a high-power direct current (DC). The immense amounts of electricity required to process the alumina into aluminum make this stage highly energy-intensive and thus smelters will tend to locate near cheaper sources of energy such as hydroelectricity. Two tons of alumina and between 13.5 and 18.5 MWh of electricity are required to produce one ton of aluminum.[14]

EXHIBIT 3   Breakdown of Aluminum Production Costs Based on 2006 World Averages

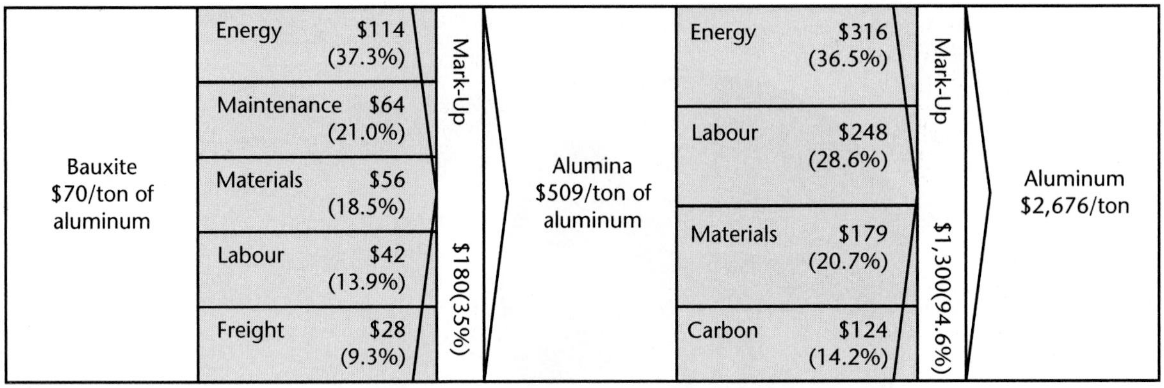

Bauxite $70/ton of aluminum	Energy $114 (37.3%)	Mark-Up $180(35%)	Alumina $509/ton of aluminum	Energy $316 (36.5%)	Mark-Up $1,300(94.6%)	Aluminum $2,676/ton
	Maintenance $64 (21.0%)			Labour $248 (28.6%)		
	Materials $56 (18.5%)			Materials $179 (20.7%)		
	Labour $42 (13.9%)			Carbon $124 (14.2%)		
	Freight $28 (9.3%)					

Source: Citigroup, *Company in depth: Alcoa,* April 11, 2007.

[12]G.E. Totten and D.S. Mackenzie, *Handbook of aluminum*, Marcel Dekker Inc., New York, 2003.

[13]U.S. Geological Survey, Mineral commodity summaries, January 2008.

[14]Alcan Inc., Form 10-K, 2006.

EXHIBIT 4 2006 Alcan Business Segment Performance (in millions $)

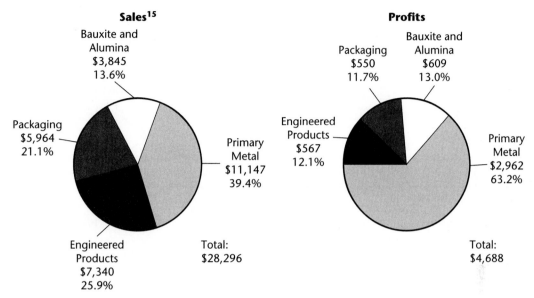

Source: Alcan Inc., Form 10-K, 2006.

EXHIBIT 5 Financial Ratios of Selected Aluminum Producers (%)

	Alcan	Aluminum Industry
Return on Assets	2.0	8.3
Return on Investment	2.6	27.1
Return on Equity	5.8	14.6
Operating Profit Margin	4.7	16.9
Net Profit Margin	2.7	10.2

	Alcan		Alcoa		Rio Tinto		Chalco		BHP Billiton		Norsk Hydro	
	2006	2005	2006	2005	2006	2005	2006	2005	2006	2005	2006	2005
Return on Assets[16]	6.2	0.5	6.0	3.7	22.8	18.4	15.9	12.3	21.7	15.8	7.4	6.9
Return on Equity[17]	16.1	1.3	15.4	9.2	40.6	34.9	25.9	21.2	43.1	37.0	18.0	16.5
Profit Margin[18]	7.6	0.6	7.4	4.8	35.0	28.9	20.0	19.2	32.8	24.8	8.9	9.2

Source: Company reports; Datamonitor, *Alcan Inc. company profile,* May 2007.

[15] Includes both intersegment and third-party sales.
[16] ROA=Net Income/Total Assets.
[17] ROE=Net Income/Shareholder's Equity.
[18] Profit Margin=Net Income/Revenues.

EXHIBIT 6   Production Cost Curves

Alumina Refining Cash Cost Curve for 2006

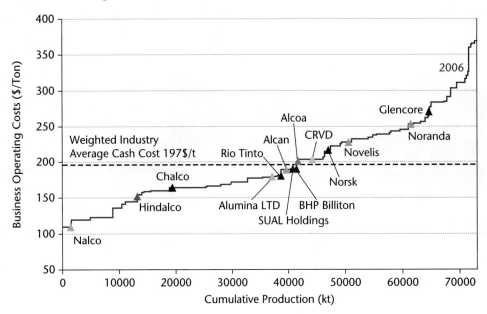

Aluminum Smelting Cash Cost Curve for 2006

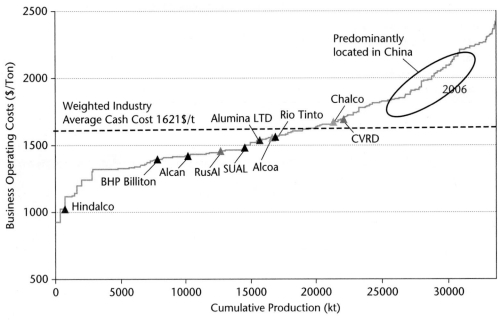

Source: CRU, 2006.

EXHIBIT 7 2006 Rio Tinto Performance by Product Group (in millions $)

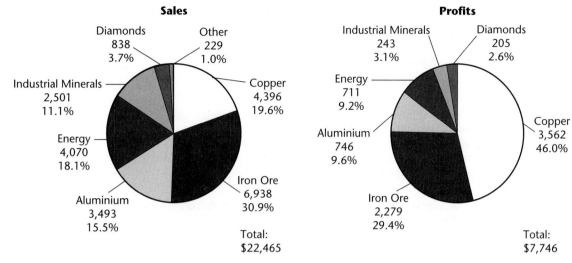

Sales

Diamonds 838 3.7%
Other 229 1.0%
Industrial Minerals 2,501 11.1%
Copper 4,396 19.6%
Energy 4,070 18.1%
Iron Ore 6,938 30.9%
Aluminium 3,493 15.5%

Total: $22,465

Profits

Industrial Minerals 243 3.1%
Diamonds 205 2.6%
Energy 711 9.2%
Aluminium 746 9.6%
Copper 3,562 46.0%
Iron Ore 2,279 29.4%

Total: $7,746

Source: Datamonitor, *Rio Tinto company profile*, November 2007.

EXHIBIT 8 Summary of Deal Between Alcan and The Province of Quebec

Backgrounder

ALCAN TO PILOT ADVANCED AP50 TECHNOLOGY THROUGH US$550 MILLION FACILITY IN QUEBEC

QUEBEC TO BECOME CRADLE FOR AP50 GLOBAL DEVELOPMENT

December 14, 2006—With today's agreement, Alcan reaffirms the outstanding partnership it has historically enjoyed with Quebec, its government and communities through the following mutually beneficial commitments:

ALCAN:

- Build a world-leading US$500 [CAN$600] million AP50 technology platform in the Saguenay–Lac-Saint-Jean region;
- Invest more than US$1.8 [CAN$2.0] billion over the next decade in the Saguenay–Lac-Saint-Jean region;
- Create up to 450,000 tonnes of new generation AP smelting capacity;
- Create 740 highly skilled jobs, in addition to an expected 1,200–1,500 related to construction;
- Facilitate the development of a local network of globally competitive suppliers to AP50—proactively facilitated through a Regional Industrial Development Office;
- Create a US$9 [CAN$10] million fund to support equipment manufacturers and support the industrial development of the Beauharnois and Shawinigan regions;
- Maintain Arvida Research and Development Center (ARDC) and Regional Indusrial Development offices at similar or increased levels of activity.

EXHIBIT 8   (continued)

QUEBEC:

- Finance:
    - A 30-year US$355 [CAN$400] million interest-free loan;
    - US$100 [CAN$112] million of various tax benefits;
    - Federal and Provincial R&D tax incentives, subject to further discussions.

- Energy:
    - Extension of current energy (342 MW) and power contracts with Hydro-Quebec from 2023 to 2045;
    - Extension of Alcan's existing water rights to the Peribonca River until 2058. This lease support 900 MW of self-generated power;
    - An additional 225 MW power block at the L-rate beninning in 2010.

- Environment:
    - Implementation of a rapid approval process to protect the confidentiality of AP50's first industrialization phase;
    - Consolidation of Alcan's SO^2 commitment across Quebec.

- In connection with the agreement, the Government of Quebec has retained various rights which allow it to cancel some or all of the new entitlements and benefits relating to water and power, including financial support, should there be either an acquisition of control of Alcan or a change in the location of its headquarters which has a negative impact on the company's positive commitment to or presence in Quebec.

Canadian Auto Workers (CAW):

- Labour stability with long-term labour contracts;
- Skilled and dedicated workforce.

This backgrounder document must be read in context with the appended press release of the same date.

Source: Alcan.

EXHIBIT 9 Alcan 2006 Pipeline of Projects

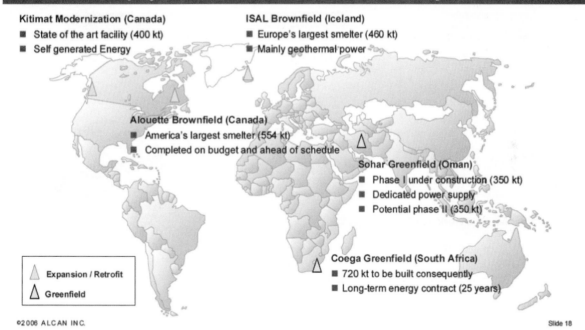

Source: C. Carroll, *Alcan investor workshop*, October 3, 2006.

EXHIBIT 10 Historical Aluminum Prices

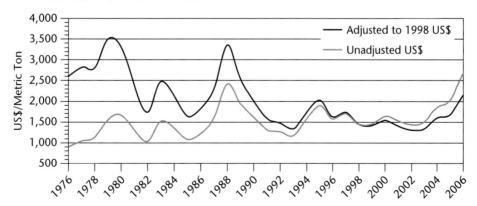

Source: U.S. Geological Survey, "Aluminum statistics," 2008, http://minerals.usgs.gov/ds/2005/140/aluminum.pdf

EXHIBIT 11   Projected Shift in Global Aluminum Production

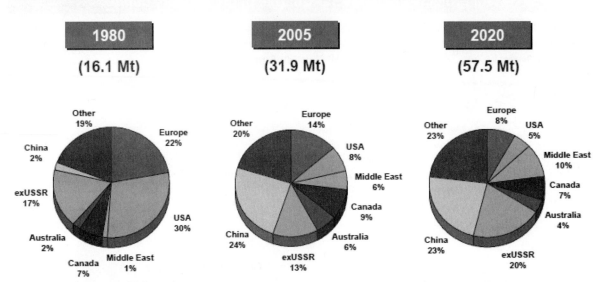

Source: C. Carroll, *Alcan investor workshop,* October 3, 2006.

EXHIBIT 12   Year on Year Aluminum Ingot Production Growth in China and Rest of World

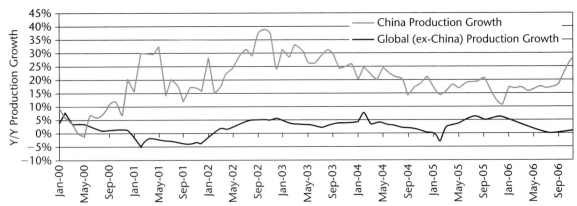

Source: Citigroup, *Company in depth: Alcan Inc.,* April 24, 2007.

EXHIBIT 13 Industry and Chinese Average Capex to Build New Plants

Alumina Refineries			Aluminum Smelters		
CapEx/Ton	Global	China	CapEx/Ton	Global	China
-Greenfield	$600–900	$450–600	-Greenfield	$4,000–6,000	$2,000–3,000
-Brownfield	$300–900	$250–600	-Brownfield	$2,000–4,000	$1,000–2,000

Source: Citigroup, *Company in depth: Alcan Inc.,* April 24, 2007.

CASE 6

The Chinese Fireworks Industry—Revised

In February 2009, Jerry Yu was spending the Chinese New Year holidays in Liuyang (lee-ou-yang), a city known as "the home of firecrackers and fireworks," located in Hunan Province in China. Jerry was an ABC (America-Born-Chinese). With an MBA, he was running a small, family-owned chain of gift stores in Brooklyn, New York. Liuyang was his mother's hometown. During his visit, his relatives invited him to invest in a fireworks factory that was owned by a village. Mr. Yu had been impressed by the extravagant fireworks shows he had seen during the festival; however, he wanted to assess how attractive the Chinese fireworks industry was before he even looked at the financial details of the factory.

HISTORY OF FIREWORKS AND FIRECRACKERS

Fireworks referred to any devices designed to produce visual or audible effects through combustion or explosion. The art of making fireworks was formally known as pyro-technics. Firecrackers were a specific kind of fireworks, usually in the form of a noise-making cylinder. Firecrackers were often strung together and fused consecutively, a staple of Chinese New Year celebrations, weddings, grand openings, births, deaths and other ceremonial occasions.

The main ingredients of fireworks had remained almost the same over the past thousand years: 75 parts-by-weight potassium nitrate, 15 parts charcoal and 10 parts sulfur. It burned briskly when lighted, but did not erupt or make any noise. When it was found that a projectile could be thrust out of a barrel by keeping the powder at one end and igniting it, black powder became known as gunpowder. Today, smokeless pow-der has replaced black powder as the propellant in modern weaponry, but black powder remains a main ingredient in fireworks, both as a propellant and as a bursting charge.

Richard Ivey School of Business
The University of Western Ontario

Ruihua Jiang wrote this case under the supervision of Professor Paul W. Beamish solely to provide mate-rial for class discussion. The authors do not intend to illustrate either effective or ineffective handling of a managerial situation. The authors may have disguised certain names and other identifying information to protect confidentiality.

It was generally believed that the Chinese were the first makers of fireworks. The Chinese made war rockets and explosives as early as the sixth century. One legend said that a Chinese cook, while toiling in a field kitchen, happened to mix together sulfur, charcoal and saltpetre, and noticed that the pile burned with a combustible force when ignited. He further discovered that when these ingredients were enclosed in a length of bamboo sealed at both ends, it would explode rather than burn, producing a loud crack. This was the origin of firecrackers. In fact, the Chinese word for firecrackers—*bao-zhu*—literally means "exploded bamboo."

The loud reports and burning fires of firecrackers and fireworks were found to be perfect for frightening off evil spirits and celebrating good news at various occasions. For more than a thousand years, the Chinese had been seeing off past years and welcoming in new ones by firing firecrackers.

Fireworks made their way first to Arabia in the 7th century, then to Europe sometime in the middle of the 13th century. By the 15th century, fireworks were widely used for religious festivals and public entertainment. Most of the early pyrotechnicians in Europe were Italians. Even today, the best-known names in the European and American fireworks industry were Italian in origin. From the 16th to the 18th century, Italy and Germany were the two best-known areas in the European continent for fireworks displays.

In 1777, the United States used fireworks in its first Independence Day celebration, and fireworks have become closely associated with July Fourth celebrations ever since.

Up until the 1830s, the colours of the early fireworks were limited, but by 2009, there were six basic colours used in fireworks.

LIUYANG—THE HOMETOWN OF FIRECRACKERS AND FIREWORKS

According to historical records in China, firecrackers and fireworks "emerged during the Tang dynasty (618–907 AD), flourished during the Song Dynasty (960–1279 AD), and originated in Liuyang." For more than 1,000 years, Liuyang had been known as the "hometown of firecrackers and fireworks of China," a title that was officially conferred to Liuyang by the State Council of China in 1995. As early as 1723, Liuyang fireworks were chosen as official tributes to the imperial family and were sold all over the country. Exports started early: By 1875, firecrackers and fireworks were being shipped to Japan, Korea, India, Iran, Russia, Australia, England, the U.S., and other countries. In China, the name Liuyang had become almost synonymous with firecrackers and fireworks. Liuyang-made firecrackers and fireworks won numerous awards over its long history of fireworks making.

The long history and tradition had made fireworks more than just a livelihood for the Liuyang people. Almost every native person in the area knew something about fireworks making, or had actually made firecrackers or fireworks in their lifetime. As a result, Liuyang claimed an impressive pool of skilled labour. Firecrackers and fireworks had become the pillar industry of Liuyang, accounting for nearly 50 per cent of all jobs or about one-third of the total population in the Liuyang District (including Liuyang City and the surrounding counties). In 2008, Liuyang claimed 2,702 fireworks manufacturers with an additional 2,144 in the surrounding area. In total, there were 6,458 fireworks producers in China. While there has been some trend towards consolidation in the industry, most factories were still owned either by villages or families.

Among them, about a dozen or so were medium to large factories with employment between 100 to 500 workers. The rest were small workshops employing anywhere from 10 to 50 people, depending on market demand.

Liuyang was the top fireworks exporter in the world, making up 60 per cent of global production. The trademarked brand "Red Lantern" had become well known to fireworks-lovers around the world. China now accounted for 89 per cent of world-wide fireworks exports with the vast majority of that coming from Liuyang. In addition, over the past 10 years, China had become the largest market for fireworks. The ratio of domestic use to exports was 6:4, and Chinese imports of fireworks were negligible.

The increase in demand in the Chinese market had only intensified the competition. All new demand was more than met by the Chinese fireworks industry. Thus, instead of seeing increased margins, the profit margins for many small manufacturers had shrunk over the past decade. In order to make up the difference, manufacturers were cutting corners. However, some of these cost-cutting efforts came at the expense of safety. A 2007 factory explosion that left 11 workers dead was blamed primarily on decreased safety standards, which were blamed on a lack of money due to cutthroat competition. In response, the government and company officials from Luiyang and surrounding areas agreed to regulate the price of fireworks with the hope of increasing profit margins. With higher profit margins, company officials vowed to increase workers' safety.

The Product

Fireworks could be classified into two categories: display fireworks and consumer fireworks. The display fireworks, such as aerial shells, maroons and large Roman candles, were meant for professional (usually licensed) pyrotechnicians to fire during large public display shows. They were devices that were designed to produce certain visual or audio effect at a greater height above the ground than the consumer fireworks, which the general public could purchase in convenience stores and enjoy in their own backyards. Display fireworks were known as Explosives 1.3 (Class B prior to 1991) in the U.S. The consumer fireworks belonged to Explosives 1.4 (Class C prior to 1991). The difference lay mainly in the amount of explosive components contained in the product. Canada had a similar classification system. In the U.K., it was more carefully divided into four categories: indoor fireworks; garden fireworks; display fireworks; and display fireworks for professionals only.

There were many varieties of fireworks. Liuyang made 13 different types with more than 3,000 varieties. The major types included fountains, rockets, hand-held novelties, nail and hanging wheels, ground-spinning novelties, jumping novelties, floral shells, parachutes and firecrackers.

Historically, firecrackers made up 90 per cent of the total production and sales. Over the past 50 years or so, however, there had been a shift away from firecrackers to fireworks. In 2009, firecrackers made up less than 20 per cent of the total sales. The skill levels of fireworks-making had been greatly improved. For instance, the old-day fireworks could reach no more than 20 metres into the sky, while the new ones could go as high as 400 metres.

Not much had changed in fireworks-making. Over the last few decades, numerous novelties were added to the fireworks family. However, innovation had never reached beyond product variations. The ingredients had remained more or less the same. The process technology had not changed much either, although some manual processes, such as cutting the paper, rolling the cylinders, mixing powder and stringing the cylinders could now be done by machines.

Safety Issues

The fact that fireworks were made with gunpowder and listed under explosives brought about the issue of safety. Numerous accidents related with fireworks had resulted in tragic human injuries and considerable property damages. As a result, fireworks had become heavily regulated in most countries.

According to the manufacturers, fireworks were the most dangerous during the production process. Powder mixing and powder filling, in turn, were the two most dangerous procedures. The workers had to abide by strict safety measures. Even a tiny spark caused by the dropping of a tool on the floor or the dragging of a chair could start a major explosion. The quality of the ingredients was also of significant importance. Impure ingredients could greatly increase the possibility of accidents. In Liuyang, almost every year, there would be one or more accidents that resulted in deaths and damages. With an ever increasing number of firms entering the industry, safety was an ongoing concern.

Once the fireworks were made, they were relatively safe to transport and store. Even in firing, good quality fireworks rarely caused any problems if everything was done properly. Most of the fireworks-related accidents occurred during private parties or street displays, and quite often involved children playing with fireworks that needed to be handled by adults, or adults firing shells that required professional expertise. Most accidents were linked to consumer backyard events rather than to public displays.

According to the United States Consumer Products Safety Commission's (CPSC) data, injuries related to fireworks had declined substantially, even though their use had increased (see Exhibit 2). For 2009, there were an estimated 5,244 fireworks-related injuries, 30 per cent of which were caused by firecrackers and bottle rockets. Of all the injuries related to firecrackers and fireworks, most were treated in the emergency department. Eight per cent of patients had to be admitted to hospital, and seven people died due to sustained injuries.

Children from ages 5 to 14 were the most frequently involved in fireworks-related injuries. However, fireworks were not the only consumer product that might cause injuries to this age group. According to a 2008 CPSC Injury Surveillance Report, fireworks were actually safer than swing sets and baseballs. However, fireworks-related injuries were usually the most dramatic and the most widely publicized accidents, which partly explained the fact that fireworks was the only category among the products listed in Exhibit 3, for which prohibition, instead of education and adult supervision, was often urged.

In the United States, multiple government agencies were involved in regulating fireworks. The Bureau of Alcohol, Tobacco and Firearms (BATF) controlled the manufacture, storage, sales and distribution of explosives, i.e., Class B fireworks. The CPSC regulated Class C consumer fireworks, and the Department of Transportation dealt with the transportation of fireworks. Although at the federal level fireworks and firecrackers were allowed as long as the safety features were up to the standard, local governments would have their own different regulations regarding fireworks consumption. Out of the 50 states, 1 would allow only novelty fireworks, 5 had banned all consumer fireworks but allowed professional pyrotechnics, and 4 allowed customers only wire or wood stick sparklers and other novelty items. However, the remaining 40 would allow essentially all consumer fireworks. For display fireworks, permits would have to be obtained from federal and local authorities and fire departments.

All legal consumer fireworks offered for sale in the United States had been tested for stability by the Bureau of Explosives and approved for transportation by the

U.S. Department of Transportation. Because of the limited amount of pyrotechnic composition permitted in each individual unit, consumer fireworks would not ignite spontaneously during storage, nor would they mass-explode during a fire. Therefore, no special storage was required.

In most of Europe, similar regulations were in place for safety considerations, only the requirements were regarded as less stringent. In Canada, however, regulations were extremely restrictive. However, over the past decade Chinese fireworks companies had made great strides in the Canadian market. In 1999, there were no Chinese companies allowed to sell fireworks in Canada. By 2009, over 75% of all fireworks imports to Canada were from China.

THE FIRECRACKERS AND FIREWORKS INDUSTRY IN CHINA

The firecrackers and fireworks industry in China was dominated by small, family-owned-and-operated workshops. It was essentially a low-tech, highly labour-intensive industry. After 1949, government-run factories replaced the family-owned workshops. The increased scale and government funds made possible the automation of some processes. However, the key processes like installing powder, mixing colour ingredients, and putting in fuses, were still manually done by skilled workers.

The factories themselves were made up of small workshops that stood away from each other, so that in case of an accident the whole factory would not explode. For the same safety consideration, the workshops were usually located near a water source and in sparsely populated rural areas, to reduce the noise and explosion hazard.

After the reform towards a market economy started in 1979, most of the factories were broken up and became family-run units of production again. It was hoped that this privatization might help to motivate people to increase their productivity and raise output. However, this move also served to restrict further technological innovations. There were hardly any research and development (R&D) facilities, nor human and capital resources allocated to R&D in most fireworks companies. The few resources that were available were all spent on product varieties. Even in Liuyang, out of the 400,000 or so people working in the industry, very few were engineers with advanced professional training.

In response, the Hunan and other local governments began initiatives aimed at upgrading the traditional fireworks industry. Substantial amounts of money were spent on R&D. The Liuyang Firecrackers and Fireworks Authority reported that they had spent RMB 2,000 million in projects with the Beijing University of Technology and the Nanjing University of Science. Among these initiatives were environmentally-friendly fireworks, which used cold flame fireworks technology.

The majority of the manufacturing workers were regular farmers who had learned how to make fireworks just by watching and following their elders. They would come to work in fireworks workshops when there were jobs to be done, and return to till their fields if there were none. In Liuyang, for instance, few factories operated year-round. Most workshops would operate as orders came in. Since the fireworks-making communities were very concentrated geographically and had lasted for generations, only a few places (like Liuyang) could claim a large pool of skilled fireworks-makers.

Although Liuyang was by far the most well-known place for making fireworks in China, it faced increasing competition within the country. Also located in Hunan Province, Liling was another major manufacturing community of fireworks. Liling fireworks did not enjoy the same reputation and variety as Liuyang products, but they were fierce in price competition. In the neighbouring Jiangxi Province, Pingxiang and Wanzai fireworks had become strong competitors both in price and quality, especially on the low- and medium-priced market. In the high-end product market, especially in large-type display fireworks and export market, Dongguan in Guangdong Province had taken advantage of its closeness to Hong Kong and more sophisticated management and marketing practices, and snatched market share from Liuyang. By 2009, however, more than one-third of all firms and 60 per cent of Chinese production remained in Luiyang.

The initial capital requirement for starting a fireworks-manufacturing facility was relatively low. To set up a factory with the necessary equipment for making large display shells would require around RMB1,250,000.[1] However, setting up a small family workshop making consumer firecrackers and fireworks would require less than RMB125,000. Consequently, the number of small manufacturers mushroomed after the government started to encourage private business ventures.

While labour costs in the area were still low, they were steadily increasing. As a result of Chinese economic growth, wages had almost doubled over the past 5 years. This was in part because many workers were moving into less dangerous occupations. Skilled workers engaged in major processes would earn an average of RMB1,200 to RMB1,800 per month. A non-skilled worker would be paid only RMB500 to RMB700 every month. In larger factories, labour costs were between 20 and 30 per cent of total costs.

The main raw materials for fireworks were gunpowder, colour ingredients, paper, fuse and clay soil. None would be difficult to procure. However, because of the growth in the Chinese domestic fireworks market, costs of raw materials were steadily rising. Another possible problem in supply was quality. Major manufacturers would usually establish long-term relationships with their suppliers to guarantee the quality of the materials. The small workshops would often go with the lowest prices, sometimes at the cost of quality, which could lead to fatal results.

The number of small companies intensified competition. The private workshops were flexible and quick in responding to market demand. They did not entail much administrative cost. Compared to government-owned or some collectively owned factories, they did incur the costs of providing health care, retirement benefits and housing. They usually did not do any product research or design. Oblivious to intellectual property protection, they would copy any popular product design and sell it for much less. The resulting price drop had become a serious problem for the whole industry. As the profit margin kept shrinking, some workshops would hire cheap unskilled workers, and use cheap equipment and raw materials to cut down on cost. The results could be disastrous.

THE DOMESTIC MARKET

Firecrackers and fireworks had long been an integral part of any ceremonies held in China. Until recently, demand had been stable, but had risen in the past three decades because of increased economic development and living standards. Economically, market reform and unprecedented growth had given rise to the daily appearance of multitudes of new companies and new stores. As people's income level and living standards kept rising, fancier and pricier fireworks and firecrackers were desired over the cheap simple firecrackers, thereby creating more profit opportunities for fireworks manufacturers. Almost every household would spend at least a couple of hundred RMB on firecrackers and fireworks during the Spring Festival.

---

[1]In 2009, the exchange rate was around 6.60 yuan per US$1.00.

However, during the 1990s, increased concerns over environmental pollution and safety of human life and property led more and more cities to regulate the consumption of fireworks and firecrackers. Every year, high profile fireworks-related accidents were reported and emphasized on mass media before and after the traditional Spring Festival. Some articles even condemned firecrackers and fireworks as an old, uncivilized convention that created only noise, pollution and accidents. In a wave of regulations, city after city passed administrative laws regarding the use of fireworks. By 1998, one-third of the cities in China had completely banned the use of firecrackers and fireworks. Another one-third only allowed fireworks in designated places. This led to a decline in domestic market demand.

However, all this began to change in the mid-2000s. Demand began to soar when Beijing lifted a 12-year ban on fireworks in 2005. Other cities followed suit. In 2005, 106 cities eased restrictions on fireworks; in 2006, another 54 cities eased restrictions. This was followed by 40 cities in 2007 and another 79 cities in 2009. All this lead to an explosion in the Chinese domestic fireworks market.

In the meantime, domestic competition grew intensely. The reform towards a market economy made it possible for numerous family-run workshops to appear. They competed mainly on price. Almost every province had some fireworks-making workshops or factories, many set up and run with the help of skilled workers who had migrated from Liuyang. These small establishments usually were located in rural, underdeveloped areas where labour cost was low. The manufacturing was done manually, sometimes without safety measures, using cheap raw materials and simplified techniques. The products were sold locally at low prices, making it difficult for Liuyang fireworks to sell in those areas. To make things worse, these products would often copy any new or popular product designs coming out of Liuyang or other traditional fireworks communities, even using their very brand names.

In the past, fireworks were sold through the government-run general merchandise companies. Eventually, private dealers took over a large part of the business. Overall, the distribution system was rather fragmented. The old government-run channels were not very effective, especially for general merchandise. In the new distribution channels, wholesale dealers would get shipments directly from the manufacturers, and then resell to street peddlers and convenience stores.

In the countryside, wholesale markets would appear in focal townships, with wholesale dealers and agents of the manufacturers setting up booths promoting their products. Small peddlers in the surrounding areas would get supplies from the market and then sell them in small towns or villages. The wholesale markets in China were important outlets for distributing general merchandise like fireworks.

In the display fireworks market, the buyers were often central and local governments, who would purchase the product for public shows on national holidays or special celebrations. Obviously, a local company would have advantages in supplying to local government in its area. Large fireworks shows usually would use invited bidding to decide on suppliers. The amount of fireworks used could range from RMB100,000 to several million yuan, depending on the scale of a fireworks show.

Account receivables and bad debt control was a problem not just for fireworks manufacturers, but for all businesses in China. Bad debts and lack of respect for business contracts had created a credit crisis in China. The bad debt problem greatly increased transaction costs, slowed down the cash turnover and had become a headache for fireworks manufacturers. Some had chosen to withdraw from selling in the domestic market, although the profit margin was higher than in the export market.

Legal restrictions, local protectionism, cutthroat price competition, hard-to-penetrate distribution channels and bad debt were impacting negatively on the domestic sales of

Liuyang fireworks. In 1997, seeing the decline of its fireworks sales, Liuyang Firecrackers and Fireworks Industry Department, the government agency in charge of the overall development of the pillar industry, decided to start an offensive strategy. First, it opened local offices in most of the 29 provinces, major cities and regions to promote Liuyang fireworks. Second, it regulated the prices that Liuyang fireworks companies could quote and sell in export sales. Third, it resorted to a government-to-government relationship in order to secure contracts for large public fireworks displays in each province. One year after introducing the offensive strategy, Liuyang fireworks sales had increased. By 2009, they controlled an estimated 60 per cent of the global market.

Over the next 10 years, many legal restrictions were lifted. One of the most notable legal restrictions to be eased was foreign direct investment. With huge growth in both the Chinese domestic market and with China nearing a virtual lock on export market, the Chinese fireworks industry had become a magnet for foreign investors. Liuyang remained the centre of the Chinese fireworks industry and an attractive region for foreigners and foreign firms looking at controlling the entire fireworks value chain.

THE EXPORT MARKET

Since the opening of the Chinese economy in 1979, exporting had become a major market for the Chinese fireworks industry. As one of the most celebrated products out of China, export sales of fireworks had risen dramatically between 1978 and 2009. According to independent research, the recorded exports of firecrackers and fireworks reached US$675 million in 2009. This was up from an estimated US$143 million in 1994.

The products from China were rich in variety and low in price, but also had a lower reputation in quality control, packaging and timing control, compared to the products made in Japan and Korea. China-made fireworks also would wholesale for much lower prices, usually 80 per cent lower than similar products made in Japan or Korea.

There had been little overall co-ordination of export sales. As more and more companies were allowed to export directly, competition kept intensifying and the profit margins on export sales kept slipping. As a result, underpricing each other became a common practice. Therefore, despite its dominant share of the world market, the Chinese fireworks export industry enjoyed limited profitability. The export price of Chinese fireworks was between one-fifth and one-third the wholesale price in the United States.

The importers enjoyed a high markup even after paying the 2.4 per cent U.S. import duty. Of course, the importers had to absorb the cost of getting permits, shipping, storing and carrying the inventory for three to four months before making the sales. This gap pushed both domestic and foreign companies to find ways to control more of the value chain from production to retail.

Besides suffering from low profit margin, the Chinese fireworks makers were also risking losing their brand identities. Given the low cost and reasonably good quality of the Chinese fireworks, many large fireworks manufacturers and dealers in the West started to outsource the making of their brand-name fireworks. Failing to see the importance of brand equity, the Chinese fireworks manufacturers were sometimes reduced to mere manufacturing outfits for foreign companies, gradually losing their own brands. There were also fireworks merchants in Korea, Japan or Spain, who would buy the products from China, and then repackage them, or replace the fuses with better quality ones, then resell them for much higher prices.

The export market was usually divided into five blocks: Southeast Asia, North America, Europe, South America and the rest of the world. The most popular market had been Europe, where the regulations on fireworks were less stringent, and orders were of larger quantities and better prices. The United States was considered a tough market because of complex regulations and high competition; nevertheless a necessary one if a company wanted to remain a viable world-player. While in the past the Canadian market was virtually closed to the Chinese fireworks due to its regulations, by 2009 Chinese imports dominated the entire Canadian market.

The foreign importers were powerful buyers for several reasons. First, they were very well informed, both through past dealings with China and the internet. Second, they were able to hire agents who were very familiar with the industry in China. Third, they could deal directly with the factories that were willing to offer lower prices. Fourth, there were basically no switching costs, so they could play the suppliers against each other.

The diversity of the cultures in the destination countries greatly reduced the seasonality of the fireworks production and sales. As a result, orders evened out throughout the year. However, the peak season was still towards the end of the year. For the U.S., it was before July 4. Usually, the importers would receive the shipment two or three months beforehand. While the U.S. was still China's major export market for fireworks, other countries were also importing large quantities of Chinese-made fireworks (see Exhibit 4).

The internet had become a marketing outlet for Chinese fireworks. Twenty per cent to twenty five per cent of the worldwide sales were through the internet. However, export sales were still made mainly through foreign trade companies or agents.

In recent years, foreign investments were also funneled into the fireworks industry. In Liuyang, four of the large fireworks factories had foreign investments, made mainly by the fireworks trading companies in Hong Kong. In 2009, the Liuyang Fireworks Company was listed on the Toronto Stock Exchange (TSE), a first for a Chinese fireworks manufacturer.

The Future of the Fireworks Industry in China

The managers of the Chinese fireworks companies that Jerry talked to expressed mixed feelings towards the future outlook of their industry. One pessimistic view was that fierce competition and more stringent safety regulations were killing the industry. As the Chinese economy advanced, the government was forcing more manufacturing regulations onto firms that were driving up costs. Moreover, as people became more environmentally conscious and more distracted by the endless diversities of modern entertainment, traditional celebrations using firecrackers and fireworks would die a gradual death. As to the function of attracting public attention for promotional purposes, fireworks also faced challenges from new technologies, such as laser beams combined with sound effects.

In fact, "make-believe firecrackers" already appeared as substitutes in China. These were made of red plastic tubes strung together like firecrackers with electric bulbs installed inside the tubes. When the power was turned on, the lights would emit sparks, accompanied by crackling reports that sounded like firecrackers. These were being used at weddings and grand openings in cities where firecrackers and fireworks were banned. More interesting substitutes were spotted at some weddings in Beijing, where people paved the road with little red balloons, and made the limousine carrying the bride and groom run over the balloons to make explosive cracking sounds as well as leave behind red bits and pieces of debris. Also, more and more young couples were getting married in Western styles, in a church or a scenic green meadow outdoors, where serene and quiet happiness prevailed over the traditional noisy way of celebrating. Therefore, some managers believed that firecrackers and fireworks were doomed to fade off into history.

The more optimistic view, however, was that the industry would not die at all. If the right moves were made by the industry, it could even grow. Some said that tradition would not die so easily. It was in their national character for the Chinese to celebrate with an atmosphere of noisy happiness. Moreover, even in the West, the popularity of fireworks was not suffering from all the regulations. No real substitutes could replace fireworks, which combined the sensual pleasures of visual, audio and emotional stimuli. For instance, the U.S. Congressional resolution in 1963 to use bells to replace fireworks in celebrating Independence Day never really caught on.

Fireworks were also being combined with modern technologies like laser beams, computerized firing and musical accompaniment to make the appeal of fireworks more irresistible. The safety problem was not really as serious as people were made to believe, and would only improve with new technological innovations like smokeless fireworks. With the success of the fireworks displays at the Beijing Olympics, China's brand as a world-class fireworks producer was on the rise. With better management practices, perhaps margins could be increased.

However, both sides agreed that the Chinese fireworks industry would have to change its strategy, especially in international competition, to stay a viable and profitable player.

THE DECISION

While the Liuyang fireworks industry dominated the worldwide industry, Jerry had to decide whether he should invest in the industry. If he did invest, what was the best way to capitalize on the potential that remained unexploited in this industry? He wondered whether he could apply the industry analysis framework he had studied in his MBA program.

EXHIBIT 1 China & Liuyang Firecrackers and Fireworks: Total Revenue (US$000s)

	2007	2009
Total Revenue Domestic (estimated)		
All China	742,395	1,009,757
Liuyang	450,000	757,500
Total Revenue Exports		
All China	494,930	673,171
Liuyang	300,000	505,000
Total Revenue (estimated)		
All China	1,237,325	1,682,928
Liuyang	750,000	1,262,500

Sources: International Fireworks Association; ICON Group Ltd. "The world market for fireworks: A 2009 global trade perspective."

Notes:

1. Domestic Revenue estimate based on a 6:4 domestic to export ratio as reported by http://www. articlesbase.com.

2. Alternative sources put the Chinese domestic market much higher.

3. 2009 data and 2007 data are from different sources. Caution should be used when making comparisons. Growth rates of 15 to 18 per cent per year have been reported by other news sources (especially: http:// www.newsreelnetwork.com).

EXHIBIT 2   Total Fireworks Consumption and Estimated Fireworks-
Related Injuries in U.S.: 2000 to 2008

Year	Fireworks Consumption, Millions of Pounds	Estimated Fireworks-Related Injuries	Injuries per 100,000 Pounds
2000	152.6	11,000	7.2
2001	161.6	9,500	5.8
2002	190.1	8,800	4.6
2003	220.8	9,700	4.4
2004	236.2	9,600	4.1
2005	281.5	10,800	3.8
2006	278.2	9,200	3.3
2007	265.5	9,800	3.7
2008	213.2	7,000	3.3

Source: American Pyrotechnics Association.

EXHIBIT 3   Estimated Emergency Room Treatment per 100,000 Youths
(Ages 5 to 14) from Outdoor Activities (June 22 to July 22,
2008)

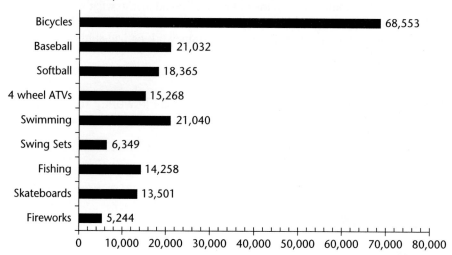

Source: American Pyrotechnics Association. As cited from the CPSC National Injury Information
Clearinghouse.

EXHIBIT 4 Fireworks Exports from China, 2009

Country of Destination	Rank	Value (000 US$)	% Share	Cumulative %
United States	1	301,500	44.8	44.8
Germany	2	83,553	12.4	57.2
United Kingdom	3	33,645	5.0	62.2
The Netherlands	4	32,586	4.8	67.0
Japan	5	26,764	4.0	71.0
Russia	6	16,157	2.4	73.4
Italy	7	15,967	2.4	75.8
France	8	13,574	2.0	77.8
Spain	9	13,009	1.9	79.7
Denmark	10	9,935	1.5	81.2
Canada	11	9,817	1.5	82.7
Poland	12	9,580	1.4	84.1
Taiwan	13	8,130	1.2	85.3
Finland	14	6,002	0.9	86.2
South Africa	15	5,623	0.8	87.0
Austria	16	5,488	0.8	87.8
Ukraine	17	5,445	0.8	88.7
Sweden	18	4,868	0.7	89.4
Albania	19	4,835	0.7	90.1
Argentina	20	4,793	0.7	90.8
Turkey	21	4,592	0.7	91.5
Belgium	22	4,583	0.7	92.2
Norway	23	4,336	0.6	92.8
Czech Republic	24	4,312	0.6	93.5
Venezuela	25	4,257	0.6	94.1
New Zealand	26	4,024	0.6	94.7
Switzerland	27	3,316	0.5	95.2
South Korea	28	3,104	0.5	95.6
Thailand	29	2,720	0.4	96.0
Indonesia	30	1,925	0.3	96.3
Other	31	24,731	3.7	100.0
Total		**673,171**	**100.00**	**100.00**

Source: Professor Philip M. Parker, INSEAD, copyright © 2009, www.icongrouponline.com

Ikea (Canada) Ltd. 1986 (Condensed)

Founded as a mail order business in rural Sweden in 1943, IKEA had grown to more than US$1 billion in sales and 70 retail outlets by 1985, and was considered by many to be one of the best-run furniture operations in the world. Although only 14 per cent of IKEA's sales were outside Europe, the company's fastest growth was occurring in North America.

Success, however, brought imitators. In mid-1986, Bjorn Bayley and Anders Berglund, the senior managers of IKEA's North American operations, were examining a just-published Sears Canada catalogue, which contained a new 20-page section called "Elements." This section bore a striking resemblance to the format of an IKEA Canada catalogue (see Exhibits 1 and 2 for sample pages), and the furniture being offered was similar to IKEA's knock-down, self-assembled line in which different "elements" could be ordered by the customer to create particular designs. Bayley and Berglund wondered how serious Sears was about its new initiative, and what, if anything, IKEA should do in response.

THE CANADIAN FURNITURE MARKET

Canadian consumption of furniture totalled more than $2 billion in 1985, an average of well over $600 per household. Imports accounted for approximately 18 per cent of this total, half of which originated in the United States. The duties on furniture imported into Canada were approximately 15 per cent.

Furniture was sold to Canadian consumers through three types of stores: independents, specialty chains and department stores. Although the independents held a 70 per cent market share, this figure was declining due to their inability to compete with the chains in terms of advertising, purchasing power, management sophistication and

Richard Ivey School of Business
The University of Western Ontario

Professor Paul W. Beamish prepared this case solely to provide material for class discussion. The author does not intend to illustrate either effective or ineffective handling of a managerial situation. The author may have disguised certain names and other identifying information to protect confidentiality.

Ivey Management Services prohibits any form of reproduction, storage or transmittal without its written permission. This material is not covered under authorization from any reproduction rights organization. To order copies or request permission to reproduce materials, contact Ivey Publishing, Ivey Management Services, c/o Richard Ivey School of Business, The University of Western Ontario, London, Ontario, Canada, N6A 3K7; phone (519) 661-3208; fax (519) 661-3882; e-mail cases@ivey.uwo.ca.

Copyright © 1988, Ivey Management Services   Version: (A) 2003-03-17

sales support. The average sales per square metre in 1985 for furniture stores of all three types was $1,666 (the figure was $2,606 for stores which also sold appliances) and the average cost of goods sold was 64.5 per cent.

While the major department stores such as Eaton's and Sears tended to carry traditional furniture lines close to the middle of the price/quality range, chains and independents operated from one end of the spectrum to the other. At the upper end of the market, specialty stores attempted to differentiate themselves by offering unique product lines, superior service and a specialized shopping atmosphere. The lower end of the market, on the other hand, was dominated by furniture warehouses which spent heavily on advertising, and offered lower price, less service and less emphasis on a fancy image. The warehouses usually kept a larger inventory of furniture on hand than the department stores, but expected customers to pick up their purchases. Over half the warehouse sales involved promotional financing arrangements, including delayed payments, extended terms and so on.

The major firms in this group—both of whom sold furniture and appliances—were The Brick and Leon's. The Brick had annual sales of $240 million from 15 Canadian stores and was rapidly expanding from its western Canada base. With 30 additional stores in California under the Furnishings 2000 name, The Brick intended to become the largest furniture retailing company in the world. Leon's had annual sales of $160 million from 14 stores, and was growing rapidly from its Ontario base. These 14 stores were operated under a variety of names. Leon's also franchised its name in smaller cities in Canada. For part of their merchandise requirements, The Brick and Leon's often negotiated with manufacturers for exclusive products, styles and fabrics and imported from the U.S., Europe and the Far East. Although both firms had had problems earlier with entry to the U.S. market, each intended to expand there.

Most furniture retailers in Canada purchased their products from Canadian manufacturers after examining new designs and models at trade shows. There were approximately 1,400 Canadian furniture manufacturers, most of whom were located in Ontario and Quebec. Typically, these firms were small (78 per cent of Canadian furniture plants employed fewer than 50 people), undercapitalized and minimally automated. One industry executive quipped that one of the most significant technological developments for the industry had been the advent of the staple gun.

Canadian-produced furniture typically followed American and European styling, and was generally of adequate to excellent quality but was often more costly to produce. The reason for high Canadian costs was attributed to a combination of short manufacturing runs and high raw material, labour and distribution costs. In an attempt to reduce costs, a few of the larger manufacturers such as Kroehler had vertically integrated—purchasing sawmills, fabric warehouses, fibreboard and wood frame plants—but such practices were very much the exception in the industry.

THE IKEA FORMULA

IKEA's approach to business was fundamentally different from that of the traditional Canadian retailers. The company focused exclusively on what it called "quick assembly" furniture, which consumers carried from the store in flat packages and assembled at home. This furniture was primarily pine, had a clean European-designed look to it, and was priced at 15 per cent below the lowest prices for traditional furniture. Its major appeal appeared to be to young families, singles and frequent movers, who were looking for well-designed items that were economically priced and created instant impact.

According to company executives, IKEA was successful because of its revolutionary approach to the most important aspects of the business: product design, procurement, store operations, marketing and management philosophy, which stressed flexibility and market orientation rather than long-range strategy. Each of these items is discussed in turn.

Product Design

IKEA's European designers, not the company's suppliers, were responsible for the design of most of the furniture and accessories in IKEA's product line, which totalled 15,000 items. The heart of the company's design capability was a 50-person Swedish workshop which produced prototypes of new items of furniture and smaller components such as "an ingenious little snap lock for table legs which makes a table stronger and cheaper at the same time" and a "clever little screw attachment which allows for the assembly of a pin back chair in five minutes." IKEA's designers were very cost-conscious, and were constantly working to lower costs in ways that were not critical to the consumer. "The quality of a work top," for example, would be superior to that of the back of a bookshelf which would never be seen. "Low price with a meaning" was the theme.

Although it was not impossible to copyright a particular design or process, IKEA's philosophy was "if somebody steals a model from us, we do not bring a lawsuit, because a lawsuit is always negative. We solve the problem by making a new model that is even better."

Procurement

IKEA's early success in Sweden had so threatened traditional European furniture retailers that they had promised to boycott any major supplier that shipped products to the upstart firm. As a result, IKEA had no choice but to go to the smaller suppliers. Since these suppliers had limited resources, IKEA began assuming responsibility for the purchase of raw materials, packaging materials, storage, specialized equipment and machinery and engineering. What began as a necessity soon became a cornerstone of IKEA's competitive strategy, and by 1986, the firm had nearly 100 production engineers working as purchasers. Together with IKEA's designers, these engineers assisted suppliers in every way they could to help them lower costs, dealing with everything from the introduction of new technology to the alteration of the dimensions of a shipping carton.

Although IKEA sometimes leased equipment and made loans to its suppliers, the firm was adamant that it would not enter the furniture manufacturing business itself. In fact, to avoid control over—and responsibility for—its suppliers, the company had a policy of limiting its purchases to 50 per cent of a supplier's capacity. Many products were obtained from multiple suppliers, and frequently suppliers produced only a single standardized component or input to the final product. Unfinished pine shelves, for example, were obtained directly from saw mills, cabinet doors were purchased from door factories and cushions came from textile mills.

In total, IKEA purchased goods from 1,500 suppliers located in 40 countries. About 52 per cent of the company's purchases were from Scandinavia, 21 per cent from other countries of Western Europe, 20 per cent from Eastern Europe and 7 per cent elsewhere.

Store Operations

IKEA stores were usually large, one or two-storey buildings situated in relatively inexpensive stand-alone locations, neither in prime downtown sites nor as part of a shopping mall. Most stores were surrounded by a large parking lot, adorned with billboards explaining IKEA's delivery policy, product guarantee and the existence of a coffee shop and/or restaurant.

On entering a store, the customer was immediately aware of the children's play area (a room filled with hollow multi-coloured balls), a video room for older children, and a receptionist with copies of IKEA catalogues, a metric conversion guide, index cards for detailing purchases and a store guide. The latter, supplemented by prominent signs, indicated that the store contained lockers and benches for shoppers, a first-aid area, restrooms, strollers and a baby-care area, an "As-Is" department (no returns permitted), numerous check-outs, suggestion boxes and, in many cases, a restaurant. All major credit cards were accepted.

Traffic flow in most IKEA stores was guided in order to pass by almost all of the merchandise in the store, which was displayed as it would look in the home, complete with all accessories. Throughout the store, employees could be identified by their bright red IKEA shirts. Part-time employees wore yellow shirts which read "Temporary Help—Please Don't Ask Me Any Hard Questions." The use of sales floor staff was minimal. The IKEA view was that "salesmen are expensive, and can also be irritating. IKEA leaves you to shop in peace."

While IKEA stores were all characterized by their self-serve, self-wrapping, self-transport and self-assembly operations, the company's philosophy was that each new store would incorporate the latest ideas in use in any of its existing stores. The most recent trend in some countries was an IKEA Contract Sales section, which provided a delivery, invoicing and assembly service for commercial customers.

Marketing

IKEA's promotional activities were intended to educate the consumer public on the benefits of the IKEA concept and to build traffic by attracting new buyers and encouraging repeat visits from existing customers. The primary promotional vehicle was the annual IKEA catalogue which was selectively mailed out to prime target customers who, in the Toronto area for instance, had the following characteristics:

Income $35,000 +	Primary Age Group 35–44
Owner Condominium or Townhouse	Secondary Age Group 25–34
University Degree	Husband/Wife both work
White Collar	Two Children
	Movers

With minor variations, this "upscale" profile was typical of IKEA's target customers in Europe and North America. In Canada, IKEA management acknowledged the target market, but felt that, in fact, the IKEA concept appealed to a much wider group of consumers.

IKEA also spent heavily on magazine advertisements, which were noted for their humorous, slightly off-beat approach. In Canada, IKEA spent $2.5 million to print 3.6 million catalogues, $2 million on magazine advertising and $1.5 million on other forms of promotion in 1984.

Management Philosophy

The philosophy of Ingvar Kamprad, the founder of IKEA, was "to create a better everyday life for the majority of people." In practice, this creed meant that IKEA was dedicated to offering, and continuing to offer, the lowest prices possible on good quality furniture, so that IKEA products were available to as many people as possible. Fred Andersson, the head of IKEA's product range for the world, stated: "Unlike other companies, we are not fascinated with what we produce—we make what our customers want." Generally, IKEA management felt that no other company could match IKEA's combination of quality and price across the full width of the product line.

IKEA also made a concerted effort to stay "close to its customers," and it was not unusual for the general manager of IKEA Canada, for instance, to personally telephone customers who had made complaints or suggestions. Each week, an employee newsletter detailed all customer comments and indicated how management felt they should be dealt with.

Another guiding philosophy of the firm was that growth would be in "small bites." The growth objective in Canada, for instance, had been to increase sales and profits by 20 per cent per year, but care was given to sequence store openings so that managerial and financial resources would not be strained.

Internally, the company's philosophy was stated as "freedom, with responsibility," which meant that IKEA's managers typically operated with a good deal of autonomy. The Canadian operation, for instance, received little in the way of explicit suggestions from head office, even in the one year when the budget was not met. The Canadian management team travelled to head office as a group only once every several years. As Bjorn Bayley explained:

> We are a very informal management team, and try to have everyone who works for us believe that they have the freedom to do their job in the best way possible. It's almost impossible to push the philosophy down to the cashier level, but we try.

IKEA IN CANADA

IKEA's formula had worked well in Canada. Under the direction of a four-man management team, which included two Swedes, the company had grown from a single store in 1976 to nine stores totalling 800,000 square feet and, as shown in Exhibit 3, predicted 1986 sales of more than $140 million. The sales of IKEA Canada had exceeded budget in all but one of the past five years, and usually by a wide margin. Net profits were approximately five per cent of sales. Profit and loss statements for 1983 and 1984, the only financial statements available, are presented in Exhibit 4.

IKEA Canada carried just less than half of the company's total product line. Individual items were chosen on the basis of what management thought would sell in Canada, and if IKEA could not beat a competitor's price by 10 to 15 per cent on a particular item, it was dropped. Most of the goods sold in the Canadian stores were supplied from central warehouses in Sweden. To coordinate this process, a five-person stock supply department in Vancouver provided Sweden with a three-year forecast of Canada's needs and placed major orders twice a year. Actual volumes were expected to be within 10 per cent of the forecast level. As Bayley noted, "you needed a gambler in the stock supply job."

Individual stores were expected to maintain 13.5 weeks of inventory on hand (10.5 weeks in the store and 3 weeks in transit), and could order from the central warehouse in Montreal or, if a product was not in stock in Montreal, direct from Sweden. Shipments from Sweden took six to eight weeks to arrive, shipments from Montreal two to three weeks. In practice, about 50 per cent of the product arriving at a store came via each route.

IKEA's success in Canada meant that the firm was often hard pressed to keep the best selling items in stock. (Twenty per cent of the firm's present line constituted 80 per cent of sales volume.) At any given time in Canada, IKEA stores might have 300 items out of stock, either because actual sales deviated significantly from forecasts or because suppliers could not meet their delivery promises. While management estimated that 75 per cent of customers were willing to wait for IKEA products in a stock-out situation, the company, nevertheless, began a deliberate policy of developing Canadian suppliers for high-demand items, even if this meant paying a slight premium. In 1984, the stock control group purchased $57 million worth of goods on IKEA's behalf, $12 million of which was from 30 Canadian suppliers, up from $7 million the previous year.

As indicated in Exhibit 3, IKEA Canada sold products, rather reluctantly, by mail order to customers who preferred not to visit the stores. A senior manager explained:

> To date we have engaged in defensive mail order—only when the customer really wants it and the order is large enough. The separate handling, breaking down of orders and repackaging required for mail orders would be too expensive and go against the economies-through-volume approach of IKEA. Profit margins of mail order business tend to be half that of a store operation. There are more sales returns, particularly because of damages—maybe four per cent—incurred in shipping. It is difficult to know where to draw the market boundaries for a mail order business. We don't want to be substituting mail order customers for store visitors.

In 1986, the management team which had brought success to IKEA's Canadian operations was breaking up. Bjorn Bayley, who had come to Canada in 1978, was slotted to move to Philadelphia to spearhead IKEA's entry into the U.S. market, which had begun in June 1985 with a single store. With early sales running at a level twice as high as the company had predicted, Bayley expected to be busy, and was taking Mike McDonald, the controller, and Mike McMullen, the personnel director, with him. Anders Berglund who, like Bayley, was a long-time IKEA employee and had been in Canada since 1979, was scheduled to take over the Canadian operation. Berglund would report through Bayley to IKEA's North American Sales Director, who was located in Europe.

NEW COMPETITION

IKEA's success in Canada had not gone unnoticed. IDOMO was a well-established Toronto-based competitor and Sears Canada was a new entrant.

IDOMO

Like IKEA, IDOMO sold knocked-down furniture which customers were required to assemble at home. IDOMO offered a somewhat narrower selection than IKEA but emphasized teak furniture to a much greater extent. With stores in Hamilton, Mississauga (across from IKEA), Toronto and Montreal, IDOMO appeared to have capitalized on the excess demand that IKEA had developed but was not able to service.

The products and prices offered in both the 96-page IDOMO and 144-page IKEA catalogues were similar, with IKEA's prices slightly lower. Prices in the IKEA catalogues were in effect for a year. IDOMO reserved the right to make adjustments to prices and specifications. A mail order telephone number in Toronto was provided in the IDOMO catalogue. Of late, IDOMO had begun to employ an increased amount of television advertising. IDOMO purchased goods from around the world and operated a number of their own Canadian factories. Their primary source of goods was Denmark.

Sears

The newest entrant in the Canadian knocked-down furniture segment was Sears Canada, a wholly owned subsidiary of Sears Roebuck of Chicago and, with $3.8 billion in annual revenues, one of Canada's largest merchandising operations. Sears operated 75 department stores in Canada, selling a wide range (700 merchandise lines comprising 100,000 stock keeping units) of medium price and quality goods. Sears Canada also ran a major catalogue operation which distributed 12 annual catalogues to approximately 4 million Canadian families. Customers could place catalogue orders by mail, by telephone, or in person through one of the company's 1,500 catalogue sales units, which were spread throughout the country.

A quick check by Bayley and Berglund revealed that Sears' Elements line was being sold only in Canada and only through the major Sears catalogues. Elements products were not for sale, nor could they be viewed, in Sears' stores. In the fall/winter catalogue that they examined, which was over 700 pages in length, the Elements line was given 20 pages. Although Sears appeared to offer the same "type" of products as IKEA, there was a narrower selection within each category. Prices for Elements products seemed almost identical to IKEA prices. One distinct difference between the catalogues was the much greater emphasis that IKEA placed on presenting a large number of coordinated settings and room designs.

Further checking indicated that at least some of the suppliers of the Elements line were Swedish, although it did not appear that IKEA and Sears had any suppliers in common.

The IKEA executives knew that Sears was generally able to exert a great deal of influence over its suppliers, usually obtaining prices at least equal to and often below those of its competitors, because of the huge volumes purchased. Sears also worked closely with its suppliers in marketing, research, design and development, production standards and production planning. Many lines of merchandise were manufactured with features exclusive to Sears and were sold under its private brand names. There was a 75 per cent buying overlap for the catalogue and store, and about a 90 per cent overlap between regions on store purchases.

Like any Sears' product, Elements furniture could be charged to a Sears charge card. Delivery of catalogue items generally took about two weeks and, for a small extra charge, catalogue orders would be delivered right to the consumer's home in a Sears truck. If a catalogue item was out of stock, Sears' policy was either to tell the customer if and when the product would be available, or to substitute an item of equal or greater value. If goods proved defective (10 per cent of Sears Roebuck mail-order furniture purchasers had received damaged or broken furniture), Sears provided home pick-up and replacement and was willing, for a fee, to install goods, provide parts and do repairs as products aged. Sears emphasized that it serviced what it sold, and guaranteed everything that it sold—"satisfaction guaranteed or money refunded." In its advertising, which included all forms of media, Sears stressed its "hassle-free returns" and asked customers to "take a look at the services we offered . . . they'll bring you peace of mind, long after the bill is paid."

In their assessment of Sears Canada, Bayley and Berglund recognized that the company seemed to be going through something of a revival. Using the rallying cry that a "new" Sears was being created, Sears executives (the Canadian firm had 10 vice presidents) had experimented with new store layouts, pruned the product line and improved customer service for catalogue orders. Richard Sharpe, the chairman of Sears Canada, personally addressed as many as 12,000 employees per year, and the company received 3,000 suggestions from employees annually. Perhaps as a result of these initiatives, and a cut in workforce from 65,000 to 50,000 over several years, Sears Canada posted its best-ever results in 1985.

CONCLUSION

With the limited data they had on Sears, IKEA management recognized that their comparison of the two companies would be incomplete. Nonetheless, a decision regarding the Sears competitive threat was required. Any solution would have to reflect Kamprad's philosophy:

> Expensive solutions to problems are often signs of mediocrity. We have no interest in a solution until we know what it costs.

EXHIBIT 1   Sample Page from IKEA Catalogue

GUTE. EIGHTEEN DIFFERENT CHESTS OF DRAWERS TO FIT IN ALMOST ANYWHERE.

GUTE chests of drawers ●möbelfakta White lacquered or pine veneered particleboard, natural or nutbrown stained. W80 cm, D40 cm. QA.
49/2. 2 drawers. H49 cm. White **$94.** Natural or nutbrown **$98.**
49/6. 6 drawers. H49 cm. White **$115.** Natural or nutbrown **$125.**
87/4. 4 drawers. H87 cm. White **$130.** Natural or nutbrown **$145.**

87/8. 8 drawers. H87 cm. White **$170.** Natural or nutbrown **$185.**
126/6. 6 drawers. H126 cm. White **$175.** Natural or nutbrown **$195.**
126/10. 10 drawers. H126 cm. White **$215.** Natural or nutbrown **$225.**

EXHIBIT 2   Sample Page from Elements Section of Sears Catalogue

Dressers and chests whose quality and practicality are inherent—
in the colors and sizes you want. Assemble them yourself with ease.

Your choice of clear knot-free pine veneer over non-warp platewood core
or White baked-on European-quality low gloss enamel on a platewood core.

3 Drawer Units. 38 cm deep, 54 cm high (15 x 21¼").
Wide. 75 cm wide (29½").
012 065 012 DLT – *Pine* Each.139.98
012 065 002 DLT – *White* Each.139.98
Narrow. 50 cm wide (19½").
012 065 015 DLT – *Pine* Each.119.98
012 065 005 DLT – *White* Each.119.98

4 Drawer Units. 38 cm deep, 69 cm high (15 x 27¼").
Wide. 75 cm wide (29½").
012 065 011 DLT – *Pine* Each.159.98
012 065 001 DLT – *White* Each.159.98
Narrow. 50 cm wide (19½").
012 065 014 DLT – *Pine* Each.139.98
012 065 004 DLT – *White* Each.139.98

6 Drawer Units. 38 cm deep, 99 cm high (15 x 39")
Wide. 75 cm wide (29½").
012 065 010 DLTJ – *Pine* Each.219.98
012 065 000 DLTJ – *White* Each.219.98
Narrow. 50 cm wide (19½").
012 065 013 DLT – *Pine* Each.189.98
012 065 003 DLT – *White* Each.189.98

EXHIBIT 3   IKEA Canada Sales by Store (including mail order; CDN $000s)

	1981	1982	1983 (Actual)	1984	1985	1986 (Forecasted)	Mail* Order (%)
Vancouver	$12,122	$11,824	$12,885	$19,636	$19,240	$25,500	6.8
Calgary	7,379	8,550	7,420	7,848	9,220	11,500	8.6
Ottawa	5,730	6,914	8,352	9,015	10,119	12,500	1.8
Montreal			8,617	12,623	15,109	22,000†	2.2
Halifax	3,634	4,257	4,474	6,504	7,351	9,000	22.9
Toronto	11,231	13,191	16,249	18,318	22,673	30,500	1.8
Edmonton	6,506	7,474	8,075	8,743	9,986	16,000	15.4
Quebec City		5,057	8,284	9,027	10,037	12,000	6.1
Victoria					2,808	3,500	
Total	**$46,602**	**$57,267**	**$74,356**	**$91,714**	**$106,543**	**$142,500**	**6.7**

* 1984 most recent data available
† Projected growth due to store size expansion

EXHIBIT 4   Statement of Earnings and Retained Earnings Year Ended August 31, 1984 (with comparative figures for 1983)

	1984	1983
Sales	$92,185,188	$74,185,691
Cost of merchandise sold	49,836,889	38,085,173
Gross profit	42,348,299	36,100,518
General, administrative and selling expenses	28,016,473	23,626,727
Operating profit before the undernoted	14,331,826	12,473,791
Depreciation and amortization	1,113,879	1,066,285
Franchise amortization	257,490	257,490
Franchise fee	2,765,558	2,225,571
	4,136,927	3,549,347
Earnings from operations	10,194,899	8,924,444
Rental income	769,719	815,683
Less: rental expense	245,803	258,296
	523,916	557,387
Interest expense	2,453,116	3,042,471
Less: other income	438,683	65,757
	2,014,433	2,976,714
Earnings before income taxes	8,704,382	6,505,117
Income Taxes:		
Current	3,789,773	2,716,645
Deferred	(70,400)	175,500
	3,719,373	2,892,145
Net earnings for the year	4,985,009	3,612,972
Retained earnings beginning of year	5,501,612	1,888,640
Retained earnings, end of year	$10,486,621	$ 5,501 ,612

Source: Consumer and Corporate Affairs, Canada.

The Prince Edward Island Preserve Company: Turnaround

In April 2008, Bruce MacNaughton, president of Prince Edward Island Preserve Co. Ltd. (P.E.I. Preserves), was focused on turnaround. The company he had founded in 1985 had gone into receivership in May 2007. Although this had resulted in losses for various mortgage holders and unsecured creditors, MacNaughton had been able to buy back his New Glasgow shop/café, the adjacent garden property and inventory, and restart the business. He now needed a viable product-market strategy.

BACKGROUND

Prince Edward Island Preserve Co. was a manufacturing and retail company located in New Glasgow, P.E.I., which produced and marketed specialty food products. The company founder and majority shareholder, Bruce MacNaughton, had realized that an opportunity existed to present P.E.I. strawberries as a world-class food product and to introduce the finished product to an "up-scale" specialty market. MacNaughton had made good on the opportunity he had perceived years earlier. It had not been easy, however.

MacNaughton arrived in Prince Edward Island from Moncton, New Brunswick, in 1978. Without a job, he slept on the beach for much of that first summer. Over the next few years he worked in commission sales, waited tables in restaurants, and then moved to Toronto. There he studied to become a chef at George Brown College. After working in the restaurant trade for several years, he found a job with "Preserves by Amelia" in Toronto. After six months, he returned to Prince Edward Island where he opened a restaurant. The restaurant was not successful and MacNaughton lost the $30,000 stake

Nathaniel C. Lupton wrote this case under the supervision of Professor Paul W. Beamish solely to provide material for class discussion. The authors do not intend to illustrate either effective or ineffective handling of a managerial situation. The authors may have disguised certain names and other identifying information to protect confidentiality.

Copyright © 2008, Ivey Management Services   Version: (A) 2008-09-05

IVEY

Richard Ivey School of Business
The University of Western Ontario

he had accumulated. With nothing left but 100 kilograms of strawberries, MacNaughton decided to make these into preserves in order to have gifts for Christmas 1984. Early the following year, P.E.I. Preserves was founded.

The products produced by the company were priced and packaged for the gift/gourmet and specialty food markets. The primary purchasers of these products were conscious of quality and were seeking a product which they considered tasteful and natural. P.E.I. Preserves felt its product met the highest standard of quality at a price that made it attractive to all segments of the marketplace.

Over the next few years as the business grew, improvements were made to the building in New Glasgow. The sense of style which was characteristic of the company was evident from the beginning in its attractive layout and design.

In 1989, the company diversified and opened "The Perfect Cup," a small restaurant in Prince Edward Island's capital city of Charlottetown. This restaurant continued the theme of quality, specializing in wholesome, home-made food featuring the products manufactured by the company. The success of this operation led to the opening in 1990 of a small tea room at the New Glasgow location. Both of these locations showcased the products manufactured by P.E.I. Preserves.

In 1989, the company also opened a small (22-square-metre) retail branch in the CP Prince Edward Hotel. MacNaughton hoped this locale would expand visibility in the local and national marketplace, and serve as an off-season sales office. P.E.I. Preserves had been given very favourable lease arrangements and the location would require minimal financial investment. Two years later, the CP hotel location was closed and the company opened the Piece of Cake restaurant and a retail location a short distance away in the Confederation Court Mall. As Table 1 suggests, various forms of diversification had occurred over the years.

TABLE 1

Operation (Year Opened–Closed)
Charlottetown—Manufacturing and Retail (1985–1987)
New Glasgow—Manufacturing and Retail (1988–Present)
Charlottetown—Restaurant (Perfect Cup) (1989–1990)
Charlottetown—Retail (CP Hotel) (1989–1991)
New Glasgow—Restaurant (Tea Room) (1990–Present)
Charlottetown—Restaurant (Piece of Cake) (1991–1992)
Charlottetown—Retail (1991–1993)
Moncton, N.B.—Retail Franchise (1992–1994)
New Glasgow—Garden (bought 1994, opened 2003)
New Glasgow—Theatre (2003–Present)
Charlottetown—Sweater Shop (2006–2006)

MARKETPLACE

Prince Edward Island was Canada's smallest province, both in size and population. Located in the Gulf of St. Lawrence, it was separated from Nova Scotia and New Brunswick by the Northumberland Strait. The major employer in Prince Edward Island was the various levels of government. Many people in Prince Edward Island worked seasonally in farming (especially potato), fishing, or tourism. During the peak tourist months of July and August, the island population would swell dramatically from its base of 138,000. Prince Edward Island's one million annual visitors came "home" to enjoy the long sandy beaches, picturesque scenery, lobster dinners, arguably the best-tasting strawberries in the world and slower pace of life. Prince Edward Island was best known in Canada and elsewhere for the books, movies and television series about Lucy Maud Montgomery's turn-of-the-century literary creation Anne of Green Gables. 2008 was a special year for many tourists as it marked the 100th anniversary of the publication of Anne of Green Gables.

P.E.I. Preserves felt it was competing in a global market. Its visitors were from all over the world, and in 2008, it expected the numbers to exceed 150,000 in the New Glasgow location alone. New Glasgow (population 100) was located in a rural setting equidistant (15 kilometres) from Charlottetown and Prince Edward Island's best-known north shore beaches. In its mailings, it planned to continue to promote Prince Edward Island as "Canada's Garden Province" and the "little jewel that was in everyone's heart!" It had benefited, and would continue to benefit, from that image.

MARKETING

Products

The company had developed numerous products since its inception. These included many original varieties of preserves as well as honey, vinegar, mustard and repackaged tea (Exhibit 1 contains a 2008 price list, order form and a page from the mail order catalogue). The company had also added to the appeal of these products by offering gift packs composed of different products and packaging. With over 80 items, MacNaughton felt that a diverse product line had been achieved, and efforts in developing new product lines were expected to decrease in the future. Approximately three-quarters of total retail sales (including wholesale and mail order) came from the products the company made itself. Of these, three-quarters were jam preserves.

With the success of P.E.I. Preserves, imitation was inevitable. Several other small firms in Prince Edward Island also retailed specialty preserves. Another company which produced preserves in Ontario emphasized the Green Gables tie-in on its labels.

Price

P.E.I. Preserves was not competing with "low-end" products, and felt its price reinforced its customers' perception of quality. The 13 types of jam preserves retailed for $6.95 for a 250-millilitre jar, significantly more than any grocery store product. However, grocery stores did not offer jam products made with such a high fruit content and with champagne, liqueur or whisky. The food products were not subject to the 5 per cent national goods and services tax or Prince Edward Island's 10 per cent provincial sales tax, an advantage over other gift products which the company would be stressing.

Promotion

Product promotion had been focused in two areas: personal contact with the consumer and catalogue distribution. Visitors to the New Glasgow location (approximately 125,000 in 2007) were enthusiastic upon meeting MacNaughton "resplendent in the family kilt," reciting history and generally providing live entertainment. MacNaughton and the other staff members realized the value of this "island touch" and strove to ensure that all visitors to New Glasgow left with both a positive feeling and purchased products.

Visitors were also encouraged to visit the New Glasgow location through a cooperative scheme whereby other specialty retailers provided a coupon for a free cup of coffee or tea at P.E.I. Preserves. In 2007, roughly 2,000 of these coupons were redeemed.

Approximately 25,000 people received their mail order catalogue annually. They had experienced an order rate of 7.5 per cent with the average order being $66. They hoped to devote more time and effort to their mail order business in an effort to extend their marketing and production period.

In addition to mail order, the company operated with an ad hoc group of wholesale distributors. These wholesalers were divided between Nova Scotia, Ontario and other locations. For orders as small as $150, buyers could purchase from the wholesalers' price list. Wholesale prices were on average 60 per cent of the retail/mail order price. Total wholesale trade for the coming year was projected at $211,000, under the assumption of a three per cent increase over the previous year.

Over the past few years, the company had received numerous enquiries for quotations on large-scale shipments. Mitsubishi had asked for a price on a container load of preserves. Airlines and hotels were interested in obtaining preserves in 28- or 30-gram single-service bottles. One hotel chain, for example, had expressed interest in purchasing three million bottles if the cost could be kept under $0.40 per unit. (MacNaughton had not proceeded due to the need to purchase $65,000 worth of bottling equipment, and uncertainty about his production costs.) This same hotel chain had more recently been assessing the ecological implications of the packaging waste which would be created with the use of so many small bottles. It was now weighing the hygiene implications of serving jam out of larger, multi-customer use containers in their restaurants.

FINANCIAL

Growth, although indicative of the success of the company's products, had also created its share of problems. Typical of many small businesses, the company had not secured financing suitable to its needs. This, coupled with the seasonal nature of the manufacturing operation, had caused numerous periods of severe cash shortages.

Recent years, however, had been especially difficult for the company. The company had lost over $313,000 to start 2007, and this deficit grew to over $365,000 by the end of March. After going through four different bookkeepers, an unsuccessful attempted acquisition of an unrelated store in Charlottetown which proved costly, and general "distractions" with his garden and other projects, MacNaughton realized his company was not going to be able to manage payments to creditors any longer. The company officially went into receivership on May 10, 2007, after the bank reduced its line of credit to zero. Exhibit 2 presents the balance sheet of the P.E.I. Preserve Co. Ltd. The new company, Prince Edward Island Preserve Co., with a fiscal year end of April 30, opened shortly thereafter.

Sales of the new company up to the end of March 2008 were a little over $1,570,000. These sales were made up of $1,065,000 from retail and wholesale (including mail order) of what they manufactured and/or distributed, $494,000 from the café and dairy bar and $13,000 in sales and donations from visitors to the garden. Exhibit 3 provides a departmental income statement from these operations, while Exhibit 4 contains a consolidated balance sheet.

At this time, MacNaughton was attempting to provide a sound financial base for the continued operation of the company. Projected sales for the period from May 1, 2008, to April 30, 2009, are summarized in Table 2 (see Exhibit 5 for details).

TABLE 2

New Glasgow Restaurant	$565,000
Retail (New Glasgow)	$708,000
Wholesale (New Glasgow)	$211,000
Mail Order (New Glasgow)	$163,000
Kiosk (Charlottetown Mall)	$140,000
Garden Donations	$24,600
Gallery and Tea Room	$15,000
Shipping	$50,230
Total	$1,876,830

OPERATIONS

Preserve production took place on site, in an area visible through glass windows from the retail floor. Many visitors, in fact, would videotape operations during their visit to the New Glasgow store, or would watch the process while tasting the broad selection of sample products freely available.

Production took place on a batch basis. Ample production capacity existed for the $30,000 main kettle used to cook the preserves. Preserves were made five months a year, on a single shift, five-day-per-week basis. Even then, the main kettle was in use only 50 per cent of the time.

Only top quality fruit was purchased. As much as possible, P.E.I. raw materials were used. For a short period, the fruit could be frozen until it was time for processing.

The production process was labour intensive. MacNaughton was considering the feasibility of moving to an incentive-based salary system to increase productivity and control costs. While there were some minor differences due to ingredients, the variable costs for the 250-ml size are shown in Table 3 for both the traditional line of products and a new certified organic line developed for export to Japan (discussed later). The Japanese retailer required a unique style of jar and shrink-wrapping for the lid which increased the overall cost in addition to the premium price for organically grown fruit.

TABLE 3

	Traditional Line	Certified Organic
Ingredients	$1.24	$2.37
Labour	$0.47	$0.47
Packaging	$0.40	$0.90
Total	$2.11	$3.74

Café, Gallery and Tea Room

Restaurant operations were the source of many of MacNaughton's headaches. The New Glasgow Restaurant had evolved over time from offering dessert and coffee/tea to its present status where it was also open for meals all day from late May until mid-October. McNaughton spent about 40 per cent of his time on restaurant-related activities.

Retail and Mail Order

Retail accounted for the greatest portion of both sales and income for the company (see Exhibit 3). Most retail took place in the New Glasgow store as visitors stopped in individually or on bus tours. Although road travel vacations were on a steady decline due to record high gas prices, cruise ship travel received a major boost after the opening of a new pier in 2008, as shown in Table 4. With major expansions to the port still under way in Charlottetown, the number of visiting cruise ships was expected to rise to about 80 within two years. In the past, cruise ships would stay in Prince Edward Island for about half a day before heading off to other ports. However, due to the popularity of the location, they began staying for a full day in 2007. MacNaughton estimated that about 30 per cent of the ship's passengers would stop in New Glasgow in the morning, and another 30 per cent in the afternoon. Based on this, he forecast that the number of visitors would increase from about 125,000 to 150,000.

TABLE 4

Year	Cruise Ships	Passengers
2004	28	23,118
2005	23	23,894
2006	25	28,830
2007	16	21,360
2008	40	69,380

Source: http://historiccharlottetownseaport.com/cruiseships/

About 85 per cent of the passengers of these ships were American with the majority of the remaining 15 per cent divided evenly between Canadians and Germans. MacNaughton noted that the European consumers were not interested in purchasing products to take back with them but preferred items they could consume on the premises. American consumers were also beginning to shy away from purchases of preserves and other products as new air travel regulations disallowed liquids and gels in containers with volumes greater than 100-ml in carry-on luggage. When MacNaughton suggested these customers place the bottles in their checked luggage, customers expressed fears about the bottles breaking. For these customers, MacNaughton agreed to ship the products to their homes for the same fee used for mail orders (see Exhibit 1). The goal of P.E.I. Preserves was to operate shipping on a breakeven basis, but in actuality, it was proving to be an expense (see Exhibit 3).

Some of the customers who purchased products while visiting the New Glasgow location would become repeat customers who would order using the P.E.I. Preserve mail order catalogue or through the company's website (www.preservecompany.com). Shipping to the United States had become difficult over the last few years. The Food and Drug Administration's (FDA) Bioterrorism Act required that any shipment of food products be announced well in advance of the shipment date. In addition, the FDA notified P.E.I. Preserves early in 2008 that their labels were not compliant with new regulations in terms of the print location and presentation of the size of the container and the ingredients. As a result, the 40,000 labels the company had printed were now useless and mail order was halted for a period of two months while new labels were designed and printed.

In addition to the retail location in New Glasgow and mail order, P.E.I. Preserves Co. opened a small kiosk in the Charlottetown Mall to gain access to the estimated $150,000 local market. MacNaughton felt the kiosk was an efficient way of educating customers about his products. The kiosk operated during the summer months only in 2007, but MacNaughton decided to keep it in operation from July 1 to December 25 in 2008 in order to increase sales during the holiday season.

Wholesale

The company's wholesale operation largely resulted from market pull forces. Prior visitors to the New Glasgow location who did not want the inconvenience and added cost of purchasing products through mail order requested that their local high-end food distributors import P.E.I. Preserves products. The company established several relationships with these distributors in locations from Eastern Ontario to the Maritimes, and a few in Alberta and British Columbia. In general, however, MacNaughton was always worried about how his products were marketed in these stores and how that might affect his brand. He strongly believed customers needed to sample the products, as they regularly did in the New Glasgow shop, in order to be convinced that the premium price was justified. He felt he should visit locations that wished to sell his products, but he did not have the time to do so, given the demands of managing his business.

The Country Garden

P.E.I. Preserves purchased 12 acres of land adjacent to the New Glasgow location in 1994 and committed substantial time, energy and money in landscaping and adding new structures beginning in 2003. One structure was an old church which was donated to the company and was to serve as a gallery for local artists in 2008. Another was a pavilion where local classical musicians were paid to perform on occasion during the summer. The third building was a butterfly observatory which was popular with visitors to the location.

After the first year of operation for the garden, MacNaughton discovered that while visitors truly enjoyed the scenery, most were not willing to pay for the experience. From that point on, the garden was operated on a breakeven basis funded through donations and staffed by local volunteers. In 2007, the garden managed a very slight profit and the company planned to hire back a caretaker on a part-time basis in 2008.

The long-term plan for the gardens was to build a respite for chronically ill patients and their caretakers. As the land was now designated by the provincial government as a hospice and wildlife park, property taxes were negligible.

Japanese Exports

In 2005, Kosaku Morita visited Prince Edward Island from Japan to meet with Mac-Naughton and Raymond Loo, a local organic farmer and president of P.E.I. Certified

Organic Producers Co-op. Morita was specifically interested in the organic black currants grown by Loo, which Japanese consumers appreciated for their health benefits, most notably their high levels of antioxidants. Morita was so impressed with the quality of P.E.I. Preserves' products he invited both Loo and MacNaughton to Foodex in Japan in March of the following year.

Foodex was an annual event held in Japan in which 2,000 food and beverage producers showcased their wares to roughly 100,000 restauranteurs, caterers, distributors and wholesalers. MacNaughton was impressed with the interest in his preserves, so he decided to extend his line of organics and return the following year in 2007.

P.E.I. Preserves made an initial shipment of 90,000 125-ml and 250-ml bottles of their new organic line of products to a Japanese distributor in 2007. The bottles retailed for ¥1,000 (about $10) and ¥1,800 (about $18), respectively, of which the distributor and retailer took the majority of the margin. P.E.I. Preserves' wholesale price for these organic products was $3.00 for the 125-ml and $4.92 for the 250-ml bottle, both priced to obtain a margin of about $1.00 per bottle. The freight cost of about $0.30 per bottle was paid by the importer. In 2008, the company's Japanese partners were running a two-week trial of the organic products during which time they expected to place two orders of 90,000 bottles each.

Together, P.E.I. Preserves, local organic farmers and their Japanese business associates marketed products under the name "Anne's P.E.I. Farm" and created a new Japanese language website (www.annespeifarm.com) which contained information about the products and their health benefits. The website also provided information about the province of Prince Edward Island, including sustainable energy projects, organic farming, photographs capturing the natural beauty of the land and, of course, Anne of Green Gables. In addition, the site recounted the "stories" of the individuals involved in the production and delivery of the end product including the farmers, MacNaughton and P.E.I. Preserves and the Japanese business associates.

Management

During the peak summer period, P.E.I. Preserves employed 65 people among the restaurants, manufacturing area and retail locations. Of these, five were managerial positions. The company was considered a good place to work, with high morale and limited turnover. Nonetheless, most employees (including some management) were with the company on a seasonal basis. This was a concern to MacNaughton who felt that if he could provide year-round employment, he would be able to attract and keep the best quality staff.

MacNaughton felt that the company had survived on the basis of word-of-mouth. Few follow-up calls on mail order had ever been done, although MacNaughton read every e-mail sent to the customer service address. MacNaughton did not enjoy participating in trade shows—even though he received regular solicitations for them from across North America. He participated in one retail show in 2007 and four in 2008, all of them in or close to Prince Edward Island. He hoped to be able to eventually hire a sales/marketing manager.

The key manager continued to be MacNaughton. He described himself as "a frugal but fair person to deal with when it comes to purchasing. However, I like to spend enough money to ensure that what we do—we do right." Financial and managerial constraints meant that MacNaughton felt stretched ("I haven't had a vacation in years") and unable to pursue all of the ideas he had for developing the business. Other key members of the administrative staff included Lynn Whitlock in charge of production and purchasing, Sian Morris in charge of bookkeeping and administration, retail and human resources manager Judy Clark, and Don Croiter, chef and product development manager.

THE JAPANESE CONSUMER

Japan was one of Canada's most important sources of foreign tourists. In 2006, there were 364,000 Japanese visitors to Canada. The number of visits by Japanese tourists to each province is shown in Table 5. Most Japanese visitors entered through the Vancouver or Toronto airports. Within Canada, the most popular destination was the Rocky Mountains (in Banff, Alberta, numerous stores catered specifically to Japanese consumers). Excluding airfare, these visitors to Canada spent an estimated $500 million in 2006, making it the third-largest international market for tourism. These figures were expected to decline slightly for 2007, and rebound in 2008.

The Japanese fascination with Prince Edward Island could be traced to the popularity of Anne of Green Gables. The Japanese translation of this and other books in the same series had been available for many years. However, the adoption of the book as required reading in the Japanese school system since the 1950s had resulted in widespread awareness and affection for "Anne with red hair" and Prince Edward Island.

TABLE 5

Province	Japanese Visitors, 2006
Newfoundland	200
Prince Edward Island	4,100
Nova Scotia	5,400
New Brunswick	2,000
Quebec	36,900
Ontario	168,800
Manitoba	7,300
Saskatchewan	1,100
Alberta	87,900
British Columbia	183,000
Yukon	3,000
Northwest Territories	2,300

Source: 2006 facts & figures: Canada Tourism Commission
www.canada.travel/research

The Japanese Jam Market

Japanese annual consumption of jam was approximately 80,000 tons. Imports made up six to nine per cent of consumption, with higher-grade products (¥470 or more per kilo wholesale CIF) making up a third of this total. Several dozen firms imported jam, and utilized a mix of distribution channels. Prices varied, in part, according to the type of channel structure used. Exhibit 6 provides a common structure.

Future Directions

P.E.I. Preserves needed a viable product-market strategy. Many options existed to expand manufacturing and serve a larger market size in order to grow. The factory in

New Glasgow was adequate for existing business but too small to meet the demands of a larger market.

One option MacNaughton considered was setting up a manufacturing operation independent of P.E.I. Preserves, in which he would be a minority shareholder and would manage initially. Once the operation was up and running, P.E.I. Preserves could continue to license its brand name to the products, provided strict quality standards were maintained. This would allow MacNaughton the freedom to devote his time to the existing New Glasgow operations.

Before expanding production, however, MacNaughton had to decide what product market should be targeted, and to establish what the demand from that market would be. He could attempt to expand one or more of his retail, wholesale, mail order or Japanese export operations. There were also decisions to be made around pursuing his established product lines and the new organic line. He wondered if there were other potential opportunities he had not considered as well.

MacNaughton was the first to acknowledge that, while the business had been "built on gut and emotion, rather than analysis," this was insufficient for the future. The challenge was to determine the direction and timing of the desired change.

EXHIBIT 1 Prince Edward Island Preserve Co. Mail Order Catalogue

Order Date_____

PRESERVES						
Description	250ml	Price	Qty.	250ml	Price	Qty.
Blackcurrant	997	$6.95		9944	$4.95	
Blueberry Raspberry	993	$6.95		9942	$4.95	
Blueberry Lemon	996	$6.95		9949	$4.95	
Cabernet/Sauvignon/Jelly	9918	$6.95		9954	$4.95	
Lemon Ginger/Marmalade	9911	$6.95		9946	$4.95	
Lime Marmalade	9912	$6.95		N/A	$4.95	
Orange Marmalade	9910	$6.95		9945	$4.95	
Raspberry Champagne	992	$6.95		9941	$4.95	
Raspberry Jelly	9919	$6.95		9952	$4.95	
Raspberry Peach	995	$6.95		9943	$4.95	
Sour Cherry Marmalade	999	$6.95		9951	$4.95	
Strawberry Rhubarb	994	$6.95		9947	$4.95	
Strawberry Grand Mariner	991	$6.95		9940	$4.95	
Very Berry	9914	$6.95		9948	$4.95	

Preserves 375ml	375ml	Price	Qty.
Strawberry Grand Mariner	9930	$9.95	
Raspberry Champagne	9931	$9.95	
Blue Raspberry Champagne	9932	$9.95	
Very Berry	9933	$9.95	
Strawberry Rhubarb	9934	$9.95	
Blueberry Lemon	9935	$9.95	

Gift Boxes	125ml	Price	Qty
2 x 125ml	99171	$10.95	
3 x 125ml	99172	$15.95	
6 x 125ml	99173	$29.95	
2 x 250ml	99174	$15.95	
3 x 250ml	99175	$22.95	
6 x 250ml	99170	$43.95	
9 x 250ml	99176	$66.95	
2 x 375ml	99177	$23.50	
3 x 375ml	99178	$34.95	

BBQ Sauce 375ml	375ml	Price	Qty
Tomato & Herb	99140	$6.95	
Smoked Hickory & Maple	99141	$6.95	
Habanero & Mango	99142	$6.95	

Salsa	250ml	Price	Qty
Peach Salsa 250ml	9923	$6.95	
Cherry Salsa 250ml	9924	$6.95	
Cherry Salsa 375ml	9937	$8.95	
Peach Salsa 375ml	9936	$8.95	

Miscellaneous Items

_____

_____

_____

_____

SOLD TO INFO   Telephone: _____

Name: _____

Address: _____

_____

_____

City: _____

State/Province: _____ ZIP/Postal Code: _____

☐ same as ship to

SHIP TO INFO   Telephone: _____

Name: _____

Address: _____

_____

_____

City: _____

State/Province: _____ ZIP/Postal Code: _____

Gift Message: _____

_____

_____

METHOD OF PAYMENT

☐ Visa   ☐ Mastercard   ☐ American Express
☐ JCB   ☐ Cheque/Money Order   ☐ Diners Club

Exp. Date MM/YY   3 Digit Security Code

Name on Card _____

Shipping Cost

STANDARD RATES FOR CANADA AND USA*

For delivery please allow up to 15 business days.

Value or Order	Shipping Cost
$25 - $40.99	$12.00
$41 - $55.99	$13.00
$56 - $65.99	$14.00
$66 - $75.99	$15.00
$76 - $100.99	$16.00
$101 & over	20% of order

*Surcharge of 20% for Northern Canada, Newfoundland Labrador, Alaska and Hawaii.

FREE * SHIPPING with a minimum order per address of 24 jars valued @ $3.50 or more.

Subtotal	$
Shipping IF ASSISTANCE NEEDED CALL 1-800-565-5267	$
GST/HST NO TAX CHARGED TO U.S. DESTINATIONS *Amount paid is set by the province to which the order is being shipped. NF, NB and NS is HST (14%) The rest of Canada is GST (6%)	$
TOTAL ORDER	$

EXHIBIT 1   (continued)

PRESERVES•JELLY•MARMALADE

Using only the finest and freshest fruits possible, we produce a wonderful low sugar, high fruit content preserve. Our ingredients are only the highest quality and for flavour enhancement we use freshly squeezed orange and lemon juices. No added preservatives! See complete listings at www.preservecompany.com

Strawberry & Grand Marnier
991 250ml   9940 125ml   9930 375ml
Using only Prince Edward Island Strawberries we have created a high in Strawberry flavour product complemented by the addition of Grand Marnier Liqueur. You can taste summer! *Texture: Smooth*

Wild Blueberry and Lemon
996 250ml   9949 125ml   9935 375ml
This recipe has the least amount of sugar and the freshest taste. The fresh lemon and the fresh mint work to enhance the flavour of Wild Blueberries. *Texture: Loose/Smooth*

Raspberries and Champagne
992 250ml   9941 125ml   9931 375ml
This one bursts of fresh raspberry flavour only to be enhanced further by the addition of Champagne. *Texture: Loose/Smooth*

Very Berry
9914 250ml   9948 125ml   9933 375ml
The staff's favourite. Combined – Strawberries, Raspberries, Cherries and Wild Blueberries, we have created a flavour that is delicious and unique. Great topping as well as preserve. *Texture: Loose/Smooth*

Wild Blueberry and Raspberry w/Champagne
993 250ml   9942 125ml   9932 375ml
My personal favourite. Adding two of the world's most favourite flavours together and adding Champagne to complement is ambrosia in a jar. *Texture: Smooth*

Strawberry and Rhubarb
994 250ml   9947 125ml   9934 375ml
A flavour trip back in time. This combination of flavours is a memory of time past for many people. Delicious! *Texture: Smooth/Loose*

Raspberry and Peach
995 250ml   9943 125ml
This preserve is looser than most and suitable for desserts or ice cream. *Texture: Loose*

Black Currant
997 250ml   9944 125ml
Good morning sunshine! This very flavorful berry and the use of little sugar are sure to wake your mouth up any time of day. Quite tart! *Texture: Smooth*

Lime Marmalade
9912 250ml
Wow! If you like lime and you like marmalade, you will have thought you reached the nirvana of flavour when you taste this marmalade. *Texture: Chunky*

Sour Cherry Marmalade
999 250ml   9951 125ml
Unique, colourful, flavourful are a few words that describe this marmalade. *Texture: Smooth/Chunky*

Lemon and Ginger Marmalade with Amaretto
9911 250ml   9946 125ml
A very unique combination. One of our best selling marmalades. We use fresh lemons, fresh ginger and real Italian Amaretto. *Texture: Smooth/Chunky*

Orange Marmalade with Chivas Regal
9910 250ml   9945 125ml
One way to their hearts. Sweet oranges, a little sugar, time and Chivas Regal is a combination of flavours certain to be enjoyed by anyone who enjoys marmalade. *Texture: Smooth/Chunky/Loose*

Cabernet Sauvignon Wine Jelly
9918 250ml   9954 125ml
This is a full bodied wine jelly loaded with flavour. *Texture: Smooth*

Strawberry & Grand Marnier
– our most popular flavour!

$4.95 125ml/4.4oz.
$6.95 250ml/8.8oz.
$9.95 375ml/13.5oz.

3

EXHIBIT 2   P.E.I. Preserve Co. Ltd. Balance Sheet as at March 31, 2007

Assets	$
Current assets	
Accounts receivable	14,927
Accounts receivable—related parties	127,224
Prepaid expenses	6,312
Inventory	358,204
	506,667
Investment tax credits receivable	19,048
Property and equipment	1,642,265
Due from related parties	602,387
Intangible assets	29,787
Funds held on deposit	200,000
	3,000,154
Liabilities	
Current liabilities	
Bank advances	4,704
Accounts payable and accrued liabilities	248,595
Accounts payable—related parties	86,472
Current portion of capital lease	1,229
Current portion of long-term debt	1,652,814
	1,993,814
Advances from shareholders	155,468
Long-term debt, less current portion	126,748
Deferred government assistance	76,681
Preferred shares	200,000
	2,552,711
Shareholders' Equity	800,000
Capital stock	13,300
Contributed surplus	(365,857)
Deficit	447,443
	3,000,154

EXHIBIT 3 Prince Edward Island Preserve Co. (New Company) Departmental Income Statement May 11, 2007, to March 31, 2008

	Café/Dairy Bar	Retail	Wholesale	Mail Order	Garden	Preserves Production	Admin.
Revenue							
Sales	505,369	735,087	180,784	132,409	1,225	0	0
Freight revenue	0	6,325	3,362	27,178	0	0	0
Discounts	(11,209)	(17,266)	(1,976)	(269)	0	0	0
Donations	0	0	0	0	11,830	0	0
Interest/Tax/Other	0	0	0	0	0	0	548
Total Revenue	494,160	724,146	182,169	159,318	13,055	0	548
Direct Costs							
Materials	132,894	0	0	0	0	243,567	0
Supplies	25,952	143,268	0	30,708	0	17,423	0
Wages	186,363	44,125	0	0	0	88,870	0
Repair & maint.	6,991	0	0	0	12,739	2,281	0
Cash over/short	(333)	62	0	(28)	0	0	0
Freight expense	0	6,826	13,017	33,538	0	17,523	0
Opening inventory	0	0	0	0	0	166,172	0
Ending inventory	0	0	0	0	0	(197,610)	0
R&D expense	0	0	0	0	0	4,308	0
Total Direct Costs	351,868	194,280	13,017	64,218	12,739	342,533	0
Admin. Expenses							
Adv. & promotion	0	0	0	0	0	0	29,005
Land & equipment	0	0	0	0	0	0	77,261
Interest expense	0	0	0	709	0	0	58,624
Admin. wages	0	0	0	0	0	0	142,253
Wage & empl. exp.	0	0	0	0	0	0	80,591
Office	0	0	0	0	0	0	57,928
Repairs & maint.	0	0	0	0	0	0	24,074
Other	0	0	0	0	0	0	9,511
Foreign exchange	0	0	0	0	0	0	(447)
TOTAL EXPENSE	351,868	194,280	13,017	64,927	12,739	342,533	478,799
NET INCOME	142,292	529,866	169,152	94,391	317	(342,533)	(478,250)

EXHIBIT 4   Prince Edward Island Preserve Co. (New Company) Balance Sheet as at March 31, 2008

ASSETS	
Current Assets	
Cash	7,108
Accounts receivable	5,318
Prepaid expenses	49,525
Inventory	197,610
Total Current Assets	259,560
Long-Term Assets	
Land	143,840
Building	367,743
Equipment	34,588
Automotive Equipment	2,555
Computer Hardware	2,244
Total Long-term Assets	550,970
TOTAL ASSETS	810,530
LIABILITIES	
Current Liabilities	
Accounts payable	12,500
Receiver General payable	−290
PST payable	5
Total Current Liabilities	12,215
Other Liabilities	
Advances from shareholder	−1,918
Loan and Mortgage	685,000
Total Other Liabilities	683,082
TOTAL LIABILITIES	695,297
EQUITY	
Capital Stock	0
Retained Earnings	115,234
TOTAL EQUITY	115,234
LIABILITIES AND EQUITY	810,530

EXHIBIT 5   Prince Edward Island Preserve Co. (New Company) Cash Flow Budget for the Year May 1, 2008–April 30, 2009

Sales	$
Café	565,000
Retail	708,000
Wholesale	211,000
Mail order	163,000
Garden donations	24,600
Gallery & Tea room sales	15,000
Charlottetown Mall location	140,000
Freight (retail—1% sales)	7,080
Freight (wholesale—5% sales)	10,550
Freight (mail order—20% sales)	32,600
TOTAL SALES	**1,876,830**
Wages & Benefits	
Wages—Management gross	143,000
Wages—Café	184,928
Wages—Retail	69,548
Wages—Mail Order	22,920
Wages—Production	77,358
Wages—Garden Maintenance Gross	6,760
Wages—Maintenance Gross	10,920
CPP, EI, Workers Compensation	40,438
Total Wages & Benefits	**555,872**
Cost of Sales	
Café (28% sales)	158,200
Retail (22% sales + 15% mall)	176,760
Mail order	6,460
Production—preserves	260,800
Freight—production (5% of above)	13,040
Freight—retail (1% sales)	7,080
Freight—wholesale (8% sales)	16,880
Freight—mail order (25% sales)	40,750
Total Cost of Sales	**679,970**
Total Professional Fees	**18,000**
Repairs & Maintenance	**32,000**
Utilities	**61,320**
Insurance	**21,909**
Office	**53,475**
Leases	**16,726**
Advertising & Promotion	**41,200**
Vehicle & Travel	**18,000**
Supplies & Miscellaneous	**75,243**

EXHIBIT 5 (continued)

Interest & Bank Charges	
Interest on operating loan—150k	2,367
Interest on long-term debt + principle	73,707
Bank interest and back charges	16,400
Credit card fees	2,650
Total Banking Charges	**95,124**
Rent	**21,000**
Commission Paid	**5,000**
TOTAL EXPENSES	**1,694,839**
CASH IN (OUT)	**181,991**
Corporate income taxes, 2008	−15,300
Corporate income tax installments, 2009	−15,300
Cash out to pay creditors	−60,000
Cash from operating line	−55,000
Cash balance—beginning	**0**
Cash balance—ending	**36,391**

EXHIBIT 6   The Japanese Jam Market

To expand sales of imported jam or enter the Japanese market for the first time, it is necessary to develop products after a precise study of the market's needs. Importers who are making efforts to tailor their products to the Japanese market have been successfully expanding their sales by 10 per cent each year. Based on the analysis of successful cases of imported jam, the following factors may be considered very important.

Diversification of consumer preferences: Strawberry jam occupies about 50 per cent of the total demand for jam and its share is continuing to rise. Simultaneously, more and more varieties of jam are being introduced.

Low sugar content: European exporters have successfully exported low sugar jam that meets the needs of the Japanese market. Jam with a sugar content of less than 65 per cent occupies a share of 65 to 70 per cent of the market on a volume basis.

Smaller containers: Foreign manufacturers who stick to packaging products in large-sized containers (650 grams, 440 grams, 250 grams), even though their products are designed for household use, have been failing to expand their sales. On the other hand, foreign manufacturers who have developed products in smaller containers (14 grams, 30 grams, 42 grams) specifically for the Japanese market have achieved successful results.

Fashionable items: Contents and quantity are not the only important aspects of jam. The shape and material quality of the containers and their caps, label design and product name can also influence sales. It is also important that the label not be damaged in any way.

Development of gift items: Sets of various types of imported jams are popular as gift items. For example, there are sets of 10 kinds of jam in 40-gram mini-jars (retail price ¥2,000) sold as gift sets.

Selection of distribution channel: Since general trading companies, specialty importers and jam manufacturers each have their own established distribution channels, the selection of the most appropriate channel is of the utmost importance.

Pricing Structure: An importer of products typically pays about 50 per cent of the final retail price for the goods and adds about 10–15 per cent when selling to primary and secondary wholesalers. Wholesalers in turn add about 10 per cent of the final cost of the good when selling to retailers, who add the final mark-up of about 30–35 per cent of the retail price to consumers.

Source: Access to Japan's Import Market, *Tradescope,* June 1989.

Rogers' Chocolates (A)

Steve Parkhill was thinking about his options for growing Rogers' Chocolates (Rogers'). It was March 2007, and he had just started his new job as president of the company, after training with the former president for two months. The board of directors had asked him to double or triple the size of the company within 10 years. Each board member of the privately held company, and each member of the management team (most of whom also held shares), had a different idea about what Rogers' needed to do to achieve that growth. Parkhill needed to devise a strategy that would fit the company's culture, and then gain the support of the board, the management team and the employees.

THE PREMIUM CHOCOLATE MARKET

The Canadian market size for chocolates was US$167 million in 2006 and it was projected to grow at two per cent annually.[1] The growth rate in the chocolate industry as a whole had been falling, however, so traditional manufacturers such as Hershey's and Cadbury were moving into the premium chocolate market through acquisitions or upmarket launches. The premium chocolate market was growing at 20 per cent annually,[2] as aging baby boomers purchased more chocolate and emphasized quality and brand in their purchases.

About one-quarter of chocolate sales typically occur in the eight weeks prior to Christmas. Twenty per cent of "heavy users" accounted for 54 per cent of these

Charlene Zietsma wrote this case solely to provide material for class discussion. The author does not intend to illustrate either effective or ineffective handling of a managerial situation. The author may have disguised certain names and other identifying information to protect confidentiality.

Ivey Management Services prohibits any form of reproduction, storage or transmittal without its written permission. Reproduction of this material is not covered under authorization by any reproduction rights organization. To order copies or request permission to reproduce materials, contact Ivey Publishing, Ivey Management Services, c/o Richard Ivey School of Business, The University of Western Ontario, London, Ontario, Canada, N6A 3K7; phone (519) 661-3208; fax (519) 661-3882; e-mail cases@ivey.uwo.ca.

Copyright © 2007, Ivey Management Services   Version: (A) 2009-01-06

Richard Ivey School of Business
The University of Western Ontario

[1] P. M. Parker, "The world outlook for chocolate and chocolate type confectionery," INSEAD, http://www.marketresearch.com/, February 20, 2007.

[2] S. David. Sprinkle, "The U.S. chocolate market, packaged facts." New Orleans: MarketResearch.com, 2005.

pre-Christmas sales in 2006. These heavy users tended to be established families, middle-aged, childless couples and empty-nesters with high incomes, and they tended to purchase more high quality boxed chocolate than bars or lower quality chocolate.[3] The margins in premium chocolate were much better than those in lower quality segments.

Purchasers were also demanding more from chocolate than taste. In line with a broad social trend for healthier diets, the demand for organic products, including organic chocolates, was growing. Consumers looked for products with no trans fats.[4] Demand for dark chocolate, traditionally less popular than milk chocolate in North America, was growing in part because of its heart-healthy, anti-oxidant properties. At the same time, however, larger chocolate manufacturers were seeking a redefinition of the term "chocolate" under USFDA guidelines, so that they could produce cheaper versions of the product and still call it chocolate.

Consumers and employees were also demanding that chocolate companies (like other companies) follow good corporate social responsibility practices. Environmental concerns, which were very strong in Victoria, influenced packaging, procurement and operational decisions. Human rights concerns were also high on the list for consumer expectations of chocolate companies, as forced labour and child labour were still used in some of the production of cocoa beans in West Africa. One customer e-mail received by Rogers' read as follows:

> I am drawing the conclusion that Rogers' buys their raw product from West Africa. Rogers' is uninterested in making a real effort to eradicate this crisis. Furthermore, Rogers' is making contributions to the unethical side of the conflict and in so doing is endorsing the vile acts that continue to occur in West Africa. If any of my conclusions are incorrect, please let me know. I would appreciate it if you kept my e-mail address on file and notified me if Rogers' begins to value the lives of people even though they are not potential consumers.

COMPETITORS

Chocolate competitors in the premium chocolate segment in Canada featured strong regional brands, plus a few larger players. Godiva, backed by Nestle, had taken the business by storm with glitzy packaging, high price points and widespread distribution among retailers of gift items. Godiva's quality was not as high as Rogers', but it was able to obtain about 15 per cent higher price points for standard products on the strength of its packaging, advertising and distribution. For truffle-only collections and seasonal collections, the price points were often two to three times the price of Rogers' chocolates, though these featured exceptionally sleek and modern packaging, significant variations in chocolate moulding and chocolates of various colours.

Bernard Callebaut[5] was a premium chocolate producer out of Calgary that had begun to grow in similar locations to Rogers' (tourist and downtown retail), though it also had mall locations. There were 32 stores, mostly across the West, but with 4 in the United States and 2 in Ontario. The company's quality was good and it excelled in new flavour introductions, with an often seasonal influence. Callebaut's packaging was also superior with copper and gold boxes that could be customized for the consumer at the

---

[3]Company insider citing a presentation by Neilson at the Confectionary Manufacturers' Association of Canada Conference, 2007.

[4]Rogers' was one of the first chocolate companies to announce a trans-fat free product line.

[5]Note that Bernard Callebaut was not the same as the international chocolatier, Callebaut.

store, and great seasonal displays. Bernard Callebaut attracted similar price points to Godiva, but emphasized a retail strategy instead of a wholesale strategy, though bars for immediate consumption could be found in grocery outlets and other retailers.

Lindt was a large and well-established Swiss chocolate producer that offered a large variety of chocolates and distributed them broadly in mass merchandisers, drug and grocery retailers. The product quality and packaging was mid-range and their pricing was about 90 per cent of Rogers' pricing. They emphasized bars and small bags of truffles for immediate consumption though they also produced gift boxes. They also produced the Ghirardelli brand, which was of higher quality but focused on pure chocolate squares.

Purdy's was a Vancouver-based company that was 120 years old, and had been very successful with a variety of products, particularly its hedgehogs. Purdy's had over 50 locations, nearly all of which were based in malls. While they had stores nationally, their biggest and most successful presence was in British Columbia. Purdy's had tried to launch its products in Seattle, but had not done well there. Purdy's price point was significantly lower than Rogers' (about 35 per cent lower), and product quality level was also lower than Rogers', though still high. Their packaging and store displays were very good. Purdy's did a strong business in corporate gifts and group purchases, offering 20 per cent to 25 per cent discounts for high volume orders.

Other premium chocolate companies ranged from the extremely high-end custom chocolatiers that carried a very small line of chocolates in exclusive packaging and often produced custom orders, to Belgian producers that sold in Canada through established retailers or online, to niche players in single varietal bean chocolates or organic chocolates carried only at high-end grocery or retail stores.

There were also companies that commanded price premiums over their quality level because of their distribution and/or store concept. For example, Laura Secord, which emphasized mall stores, and Rocky Mountain Chocolate Company, which sold more candy than chocolate and used a franchise model, had higher price points than Purdy's but lesser quality. Laura Secord had had several ownership changes over the last decade.

ROGERS' COMPANY HISTORY

Founded by Charles "Candy" Rogers in 1885, Rogers' Chocolates, based in Victoria, British Columbia (BC), was Canada's oldest chocolate company and British Columbia's second-oldest company. After Charles's death, his wife ran the company until the late 1920s, when she sold the firm to a customer. Since then the company had changed hands three times. For the last two decades (during which time the company had grown sales by more than 900 per cent), the company had been owned by a private group comprised principally of two financial executives and partners with Connor, Clark & Lunn, a Vancouver-based investment firm; an art dealer and private investor; and a former owner of Pacific Coach Lines, a Victoria-based bus company. These four plus a past president of Rogers' comprised the board of directors.

CURRENT OPERATIONS

Rogers' head office was located above its flagship store in the Inner Harbour area of Victoria, near the world-famous Empress Hotel. The head office consisted of a board room and offices for the management team. Those involved in production worked out of the factory about eight kilometres away, and the national wholesale sales manager worked in Kitchener, Ontario.

Rogers' main products were high-quality, hand-wrapped chocolates including its premiere line, the Victoria Creams, along with truffles, nuts and chews, almond bark, nutcorn and various assortments. In addition to pure milk chocolate, dark chocolate and white chocolate bars and baking/fondue chocolate blocks, Rogers' also produced specialty items, such as chocolate-covered ginger, truffles, caramels, brittles and orange peel. Rogers' also produced no-sugar-added chocolates. Select Rogers' products are shown in Exhibit 1. The company also produced and sold a line of premium ice cream novelty items through its retail stores. Rogers' chocolates were of the highest quality, and the company had many loyal customers around the world. In 2006, the company won a prestigious 2006 Superior Taste Award from the International Taste & Quality Institute (ITQI), an independent organization of leading sommeliers, beverage experts and gourmet chefs, based in Brussels, Belgium. A company press release stated:

> "Classy, refined and elegant," were just a few of the words used to describe the 120-year-old company's chocolate line. The discerning panel of European chefs also identified the Rogers' assortment as a "top-of-the-range-product," filled with "abundant and rich chocolate aromas."[6]

PRODUCTION

Rogers' chocolates were produced in a 24,000-square-foot manufacturing facility on the outskirts of Victoria. There were about 110 non-unionized retail and production employees, with about 35 in production and the remainder in retail. Twenty employees worked seasonally in the two departments for the Christmas season. An additional 20 employees worked in management, administration and sales, as shown in the organization chart in Exhibit 2. Production, which took place on a one-shift operation (day shift), was labour-intensive, since most chocolates were handmade then hand-packed. Since there were so many different product offerings, most production consisted of batch processing, utilizing technology that had been used in the chocolate business for decades. Set-up times and equipment cleaning times were a significant component of costs, especially since they were required at the beginning and end of each eight-hour shift. To date, there had been no meaningful measures of productivity or efficiency in the plant, and thus no way of telling on a day-to-day basis if the plant was doing a good job.

Demand forecasting was difficult due to the seasonality of sales, but a long product shelf life (approximately six months) and a monthly sales forecast allowed Rogers' to deal with the ups and downs of sales patterns through healthy inventories kept on site. Nevertheless, the complicated nature of seasonal production created problems with out-of-stocks: Souvenir items and ice cream were required in the spring and summer, then core Rogers' products and seasonal items were required for the fall and Christmas. The Christmas season was particularly chaotic, with 24 per cent of annual sales occurring in the eight-week run up to Christmas. Valentines and spring items were required for early January, which overlapped with the end of Christmas production. The wholesale business required early production for seasonal needs, whereas the

---

[6]"Canadian chocolate legend receives taste award from top European chefs," *Press Release* , May 9, 2006, available at www.rogerschocolates.com/archives, accessed December 21, 2006.

online and retail business required late production. Art tins used for chocolate assortments came from China, and some were season-specific. The Chinese supplier was sometimes unable to produce tins in a timely way due to lack of electricity. As soon as there were out-of-stocks for one product, the back order production of that product would throw the schedule off for the next product.

Production planning was made even more complicated by the impact of out-of-stocks on the historical information that was used to plan the following year's sales. For example, when an item was out of stock for a month, and the back orders were filled in a short period of time, the sales graph would be distorted with unnatural spikes; yet these spikes would be used for production planning for the following year. When there were over-stock problems on an item, the retail stores would push the items, sometimes discounting them, again creating distortions in the sales data, which would be replicated over time since that data would be used for production planning. Because the same process recurred for hundreds of items, these issues created significant havoc for production planning and inventory management. Ice cream presented a problem in that it was a new item (two years old), and it was difficult to predict sales volume accurately.

The out-of-stock issue was a major one for the company. Each week, numerous products were shorted. Because out-of-stocks in the wholesale channel created problems with customers, and because the previous president had favoured the wholesale channel, short supplies were diverted from the company's own stores and delivered to wholesalers. Furthermore, when a special order arrived in wholesale, it was not uncommon for the president to tell the plant to put production plans on hold to focus on the special order.

The plant was non-union, which was a direct reflection of the company's long history and strong family values. Some production workers were third-generation Rogers' employees. Employees were quite proud of the Rogers' heritage and commitment to quality and were quite passionate about the company. This passion sometimes created resistance to change: Anything new caused concern that the company was compromising its values and its heritage. Employees learned multiple job functions and enjoyed a variety of work and tasks. Employees took great care in hand-wrapping chocolates, folding the traditional gingham packaging "just so", and hand-ribboning boxes, tins and bags. Several disabled people were employed in the plant, and Rogers' supported a local social service agency by allowing a group of brain-damaged individuals in every Friday to help with production. Turnover was low, and wages were competitive. Permanent employees were on a first-name basis with all of the senior leaders, including the president.

MARKETS

Rogers' currently earned revenues in four major areas: retailing chocolate products through company-owned stores, wholesaling chocolate products, online/mail order sales of chocolate products and sales from Sam's Deli, a well-known eatery in Victoria, which Rogers' had purchased in 2004.

Retail

Approximately 50 per cent of the company's sales came from Rogers' 11 retail stores. The stores featured Rogers' many products displayed attractively in glass cases, merchandised to suit the season, with an overall Victorian theme. Rogers' flagship store on Government Street had been designated a Heritage Site by Parks Canada. Uniformed sales staff offered chocolate samples to customers, and the aromas and images in the store contributed to an excellent retail experience. In 2000, Rogers' had won the Retail Council of Canada's Innovative Retailer of the Year award in the small business category, for demonstrating "outstanding market leadership and innovative approaches to customer and employee relations. Through creative ideas and strong delivery, the winning retailer has taken their brand to the top of their class."[7] Each of Rogers' retail stores, other than the factory store itself, was located in a tourist area, such as Whistler, Granville Island and Gastown, or at BC Ferry locations.[8]

Each store was wholly owned by Rogers'. Most were leased, with a minimum of a 10-year lease. The factory store and the downtown Victoria store were owned. The stores were typically about 500 square feet in size, with the exception of the ferry terminal locations, which were booths or catering wagons open on a seasonal basis and selling primarily ice cream. The ferry terminal locations were leased on an annual agreement basis, and rents were fixed as a percentage of sales. Although other retailers sold Rogers' Chocolates, they purchased the products wholesale through direct sales from Rogers'. Exhibit 3 shows the store locations and their approximate annual sales.

The Victoria stores could sell almost anything because of Rogers' positive brand image on the Island. They were often used to clear inventory problems. The two newest stores, Gastown and Granville Island in Vancouver, were showing steady sales growth in their first two years of operations, but significantly shy of expectations. The Granville Island store was located next to the popular Arts Club Theatre, but it was, unfortunately, also behind several large metal refuse bins. Rogers' had waited a number of years for a location to open up on Granville Island, so although the present location wasn't perfect, it was the best that could be obtained. The Gastown store was in a good location, likely to attract considerable cruise ship business.

Wholesale

Approximately 30 per cent of sales came from wholesale accounts in five categories: 1) independent gift/souvenir shops, 2) large retail chains, 3) tourist retailers, such as duty-free stores, airport or train station stores and hotel gift shops, 4) corporate accounts that purchased Rogers' products for gifts for customers or employees and 5) a new segment, specialty high-end food retailers, such as Thrifty Foods on Vancouver Island, Sobeys in Western Canada, Sunterra in Alberta and Whole Foods in Toronto, Oakville and Vancouver. Some large accounts, such as the Bay, Crabtree & Evelyn and Second Cup, had been significant Rogers' customers, but had recently changed their purchasing to focus either on their own products or on less expensive lines. As a result, Rogers' wholesale sales had dropped over the last two years. Sales were strongest in BC, followed by Ontario. Sales in Alberta, Manitoba and Saskatchewan had increased very recently due to the Sobeys roll-out, but sales were weak in Quebec and the Maritimes.

The wholesale business was supported by a sales structure that included a salaried national sales manager based in Ontario, who had been with the company for

---

[7]From www.retailcouncil.org/awards/rcc/innovative, accessed December 7, 2006.

[8]The Whistler store was at the world-class Whistler ski area. Gastown and Granville Island were tourist attractions in Vancouver.

eight years, and nine sales reps across Canada, of which eight were sales agents. The one salaried rep, who had been with the company for 10 years, was located on Vancouver Island. Currently, sales agents were in place in the following territories: Vancouver/Lower Mainland; Interior BC and Alberta; Saskatchewan and Manitoba; Northern Ontario; Niagara Falls and Metro Toronto; east of Toronto to Ottawa area; Quebec and the Maritimes.

Sales agents maintained independent businesses, but made agreements with Rogers' to have exclusive rights to sell Rogers' products within a certain geographical territory. These agreements were not contracted and thus they were open to review at any time. Generally, terminations were given 90 days' notice by either party. Many had been with the company as long as the previous president, who had established the wholesale division nearly two decades earlier. Rogers' sales agents typically carried several non-competing lines, such as maple syrup, gourmet condiments, plush toys, smoked salmon and kitchenware. A couple of sales agents were also customers as they also operated independent retail outlets that carried Rogers' Chocolates. Marketing vice-president Kate Phoenix had the following to say about sales agents and the sales rep on Vancouver Island:

> Some perform very well. They cite many challenges with our brand—niche market, high prices, inadequate shelf life, old-fashioned ("not glitzy or fashionable enough") packaging and an unknown brand in many areas of Canada. We intend to introduce a "Tastes of Canada" product this year that we hope will play well to our wholesale and souvenir buyers.
>
> Some reps have other much stronger lines and just carry Rogers' as an add-on to their existing accounts, which can be effective as their existing relationships with buyers gives us an "in" that a new salesperson would not have. The salaried rep on Vancouver Island receives a constant series of requests for our products, as it is our "home turf" and we do extensive advertising in our local market for our own stores. The brand is very well-established and seen as a desirable product. In the Victoria area, some accounts will say they are honoured to carry Rogers'. In other parts of Canada, they have not heard of us and are dismissive of the products and their price points as they do not understand the brand and the value of the product. If the remote reps are not well trained, they just cannot present the brand adequately and sell it.

Similar to most gift products, retailers typically marked items up by about 100 per cent. Rogers' earned about half the gross margins on wholesale sales as it did on retail and online sales and the company paid its sales agents approximately 10 per cent commission. The salaried sales rep on the island earned a one per cent commission on sales above her salary, but benefited significantly from Rogers' high profile in Victoria and the extensive advertising the company did there.

There were 585 active wholesale customers in 2006. Of those, 346 purchased less than $2,000 per year. Of the 346, 221 purchased less than $1,000 per year. Rogers' provided these smaller customers with the same level of service as other retailers, sometimes crediting them for stale stock, and paying the shipping expenses on orders of more than $350. There had been problems in the past with smaller accounts selling stock past its expiration date.

Some of the wholesale accounts ordered custom products, such as logo bars for special events. Rogers' would custom-produce molds, then chocolate bars for the customers featuring their logos. In the past, some regular customers had created problems by ordering with too little lead time, so the plant typically kept some logo bars in inventory for customers in anticipation of their orders.

Online, Phone and Mail Orders

A further 10 per cent of sales came from the company's online (approximately 4 per cent) and mail order (approximately 6 per cent) business. Sixty per cent of all orders were from regular customers. The average sale per phone or mail order was $138, while the average sale per website order was $91. Parkhill felt that online orders could be increased, since 30 per cent of men, and 18 per cent of women in Canada were shopping online in 2006—these tended to be people in the 18–34 age group (44 per cent), while only 20 per cent of online purchasers were in the 35–54 age group.

Orders received by phone, mail or online were generally processed within three to four days, wrapped in attractive packaging, then shipped via FedEx in a sturdy outer box. In addition to the order, a separate thank you and confirmation letter from Rogers' was sent with a catalogue. In the summer, orders were shipped in insulated containers and packed with frozen ice packs. Shipping charges ranged from $10 for 3- to 5-day delivery within Canada and $15 to the United States for 5-day shipping, to $42 for international air shipping, on products up to a $27 value. As the value of the product increased, shipping charges also increased: With product approaching $500, the costs were $18.50 within Canada for 3- to 5-day shipping, $37.50 to the United States and $122 internationally. For orders over $500, Rogers' paid the shipping charges.

Approximately 60 per cent of phone, mail and online sales were shipped to Canadian destinations, while 35 per cent went to the United States and 5 per cent shipped to 50 countries internationally. Many of the mail order sales came from rural locations in Canada, where the mail order tradition was strong. Rogers' chocolates were delivered to the far North, sometimes via dogsled, and were shipped to lighthouses on both coasts. Many of the rural mail order customers placed very large orders.

Products ordered through the online and mail order business were given priority for inventory allocation, and thus could usually be shipped within one or two working days. If there was a shortage of a particular product, its stock would be transferred back to the factory from the retail stores to meet mail order commitments. The next priority for shipping was wholesale accounts, since wholesale back orders had to be shipped at Rogers' expense, and many accounts would not accept back orders. Yet, given that Rogers' margins on wholesale sales were much lower than in the retail business, this policy meant that sometimes a high-margin retail sale would be foregone for the much lower margins at wholesale.

Sam's Deli

The remaining sales were generated from Sam's Deli, a cafeteria-style restaurant on the Inner Harbour in Victoria, between the Rogers' head office store and the Empress Hotel. Sam's Deli featured made-to-order sandwiches, soups and salads, desserts (many featuring Rogers' chocolate) baked on the premises or at the Rogers' chocolate factory and wine and beer. Sam's had strong sales of ice cream as well. At lunchtime in the summer, the lineup regularly extended out the door.

Sam's Deli had been a Victoria institution for many years. Since Rogers' purchased it, most of the long-term staff had turned over, and recruiting new employees was difficult in Victoria's tight labour market. Sam's had had to curtail its evening hours of operations due to staff recruiting problems. Although Sam's had a liquor license, the volume of alcohol sold was very small. Parkhill felt that Sam's wasn't living up to its potential.

MARKETING

Target Market

Since Rogers' chocolates were fairly expensive relative to others in the market (due to their quality ingredients and their hand-packaging processes), the company targeted affluent customers looking for a luxury experience with a superior taste, or an elegant, prestigious and uncommon gift item. Many were cruise ship visitors and general tourists, though many locals were frequent visitors to the store and loyal to the brand. Some were huge spenders. Many local businesses also saw Rogers' as their corporate gift of choice. According to Phoenix:

> Our best and most loyal client base comes from customers (in all three sales channels) that have an emotional connection to Rogers'. For example, they were in the Victoria store on a holiday or a honeymoon, etc., or it was a traditional gift in their family. By tending this market carefully, it has grown. Many of those people then give Rogers' as a corporate gift or a personal gift to a substantial list and some of those recipients then become loyal customers. It's classic viral marketing.

> Other customers are affluent people who want to give something unique. They've found us on the Internet or in their travels and see us as an obscure but classic gift. What do rich people give each other as a present in this society of indulgence and privilege? Unique wines, flowers, a handmade cake or cookies from a remote little shop, or Rogers'!

> But how do you reach these people to promote to them? Advertising to this target is so expensive and they are scattered across Canada and USA predominantly and of course they are courted by every advertiser around so are ceasing to respond to advertising. The best way in our experience to sell to them is not to make mistakes or disappoint them in any way. If you do, apologize and replace the product immediately—good old-fashioned service. This segment continues to grow for us.

Tourists often became mail order or online customers—especially American tourists, since there were no American resellers. Happy customers from resellers often became mail order or online customers as well since information about Web and mail order sales was available in all packaging. Rogers' also had an easy-to-navigate website and a superior search engine ranking that attracted Web shoppers.

Brand

The Rogers' brand had both significant strengths and some weaknesses. The brand was established around Rogers' long history, with traditional packaging, including pink or brown gingham-wrapped Victoria Creams, Chocolate Almond Brittle and Empress Squares. Chocolates were packed in Rogers' traditional burgundy box, a new gold box, or tins. Some tins featured old-fashioned scenes such as English roses, cornucopias or floral arrangements, while others featured Canadian art, particularly from the west coast. Chocolate and candy bars were also available, with a mixed variety of packaging. In the retail stores, individual chocolates could be purchased for immediate consumption or custom-packed into gift boxes to suit the buyers' tastes. Rogers' was a classic premium brand, Canadian and of high perceived value. Ingredients were mostly natural.

The brand had a very loyal following, particularly in the Victoria area. Parkhill described the brand perception:

> When I first began investigating Rogers', I asked everyone I knew what they thought of the brand. I received one of two reactions. People either said, "I've never heard of it", or they said "Oooooh, Rogers'. That is the best chocolate I've ever tasted". People would tell me stories about what Rogers' meant to them.

> It's become clear to me that the retail experience is key in creating the memories that lead to repeat sales. Through our store décor, sampling, aromas, taste and service, I think we are delivering "chocolate orgasms" to our customers.

If the company wanted to grow, it needed to become known more broadly. The challenge would be to increase awareness without diluting the brand with weak messaging or presentation to wholesale accounts, or without cheapening the product. The premium price scared some consumers and wholesale accounts away. Although those who knew the brand were willing to pay for the product, those who didn't know the brand were often unwilling to try it. Discounting the product, or developing cheaper products to piggyback on the brand, would risk destroying brand integrity.

An additional problem was associated with the traditional image of the brand. As Rogers' loyal customers aged, who would take their place? Younger buyers were less likely to be attracted by the traditional image of Rogers' brand. Developing an organic or fair trade product might be a possibility, but Rogers' chocolate supplier did not yet have organic or fair trade capabilities, and Rogers' was not large enough to pressure its supplier to change. Rogers' would also have to source organic versions of all the other ingredients. Phoenix identified with brands such as Chanel and Lancome, which had developed classic images and refused to compromise the brand, and brands such as Jaguar, Cadillac, BMW and Volvo, which had developed a younger, sexier image while maintaining core design elements to keep the integrity of the brand.

Advertising

Rogers' used several types of advertising. To reach tourists, the company advertised in guide magazines, such as *WHERE;* in flyers available on the ferry boat brochure rack; in hotel magazines and in the *Enroute* magazine available on Air Canada flights. Seasonal print advertising, radio spots and a small amount of TV advertising (in Victoria only) were also used. Rogers' also donated product extensively to charitable events in its markets, and participated in promotional events; for example, Rogers' was the headline sponsor for the Arts Club Theatre, next door to the Granville Island store. Rogers' had also purchased a delivery truck for Victoria last year and covered it with advertising. Rogers' preferred to use advertising that served each of the three major channels; for example, the *Enroute* magazine advertisements promoted Rogers' stores, its wholesale accounts and its website to Air Canada flyers, a demographic with a large number of online shoppers. Direct mail and solid search engine rankings promoted the online business.

Website

Rogers' website was the key point of contact for the online business. It featured beauty shots of the different chocolate assortments, an easy ordering facility, a reminder service that e-mailed customers when a special occasion they had entered was upcoming, frequently updated online links and optimized search engine placement. The website also had links to resellers, which provided added value to those retailers and helped customers find the nearest location that carried Rogers' chocolates. However, the sales agents had not been prompt about responding to requests to provide links for their top accounts, as they did not seem to understand the value provided by such links.

FINANCIALS[9]

Rogers' was in a strong financial position. As a privately held firm, Rogers' was under less pressure than a public firm to manage shareholders' expectations. Therefore, many of its financial strategies were designed to minimize taxable earnings. Assets were depreciated as quickly as possible under the Canada Revenue Agency's guidelines.

Although Rogers' had gone through a period of significant growth just after the current shareholders acquired the company, growth had slowed considerably in the past few years. In part, this decline had resulted from the slowdown in tourism from the United States since September 11, 2001, and the subsequent decline in the U.S. dollar. In fact, chocolate sales had declined since 2004, though the company's revenues had grown slightly, due to the contributions of Sam's Deli. Margins remained strong, however, at about 50 per cent of sales on average. Financial statements are shown in Exhibits 4 to 7.

LEADERSHIP

Jim Ralph had been president and general manager of Rogers' from 1989 until 2007. It was his impending retirement that had launched the search for a new president. Ralph had been a well-networked sales manager in the gift business prior to his appointment as president, and as a result, he had grown Rogers' wholesale business during his tenure. Ralph arrived every morning at 5 a.m. and oversaw Rogers' operations closely.

When Ralph announced his intention to retire in 2005, the controlling shareholders (and board of directors) considered selling Rogers'. It was a healthy company with significant assets, great cash flow and good margins. Yet the board felt that Rogers' had significant potential to grow even more. They decided to hold onto the company and seek a leader who could take the company to the next level. They retained an executive recruitment firm, and the job ad shown in Exhibit 8 was posted on www.workopolis.com. In the two years during the search, managers were aware that Ralph was retiring, and significant decisions were put off until a new leader could be found.

A friend of Steve Parkhill saw the ad and thought it fitted Parkhill perfectly. Parkhill agreed. At the time, he was vice-president of operations for Maple Leaf Foods, in charge of 6 plants and approximately 2,300 employees. Previously, Parkhill

---

[9]Since Rogers' is a privately held company, all financial figures in the case are disguised.

had been president of a seafood company and general manager of a meat processing subsidiary. His career had involved stints in marketing and sales in addition to operations, and he had an MBA from the Richard Ivey School of Business. Parkhill was known as an exceptional leader with an empowering style and significant personal integrity. He missed the strategy involved in his general management days and was looking for a smaller company to settle into: The west coast was very appealing. After several rounds of interviews, Parkhill was offered the position, and he accepted with excitement. Both Parkhill and the board of directors agreed that the position was intended to be a long-term one—10 years or more. To that end, the offer had a provision requiring Parkhill to purchase a significant number of shares in the company each year for the first three years, with an option to increase his holdings further after that.

The senior management team included three others. Kate Phoenix, vice-president of sales and marketing, a Rogers' employee since 1994, managed the retail outlets, developed marketing plans and oversaw the online and wholesale businesses, as well as Sam's Deli. She was also responsible for the ice cream business. She supervised the wholesale sales manager, the retail operations manager, a communications manager and the order desk staff. The product development person and purchasing and sales planning person also reported indirectly to Phoenix, though they worked more directly with Ray Wong. Phoenix worked long hours at the office, had regularly helped out at Sam's Deli during short staff situations and often drove product around to stores on the weekends when they ran out or were short-shipped by the factory. Before coming to Rogers', Phoenix had been an independent systems consultant, and had served as director, information systems and distribution, and assistant divisional manager, retail operations for Gidden Industries. Phoenix was a shareholder in the company.

Ray Wong, vice-president of production, oversaw production and worked at the factory. Wong completed a Bachelor of Food Science from the University of Alberta in 1978, and later took courses in material requirements planning, candy-making, ice-cream making and management. He had worked in progressively responsible operations positions in a variety of food and beverage companies prior to joining Rogers' in 1990. Wong did not own shares in the company. Wong was especially interested in computer programming, and he had developed all of Rogers' internal production planning systems himself.

Bjorn Bjornson, vice-president of finance and chief financial officer, had retired as chief financial officer of Pacific Coach Lines in 1991, but joined Rogers' in 1997 at the urging of his former partner, who was on Rogers' board. Previously, Bjornson had worked in financial management in manufacturing and retail after articling as a chartered accountant with Price Waterhouse. Bjornson's expertise was in reorganizations, acquisitions and dispositions. He maintained Rogers' books by hand, as he had never learned accounting or spreadsheet software programs. Bjornson owned shares in the company.

Phoenix and Bjornson were a cohesive team. In the past, there had been conflict between marketing and production, as marketing sought to reduce out of stocks and launch new products, while production sought to retain control of its own scheduling and production processes. Conflict between Phoenix and Wong had escalated to the board level during the past two years of uncertainty. Furthermore, because the wholesale division was favoured by the past president, the wholesale manager in Kitchener had regularly gone over Phoenix's head to have the president overturn her decisions. Phoenix had indicated significant frustration with her job.

GROWTH OPPORTUNITIES

During the recruitment process, and in his first few months on the job, Parkhill had been probing the managers and board members to get their perspectives on growth options. There was a dizzying array of options. One board member, who was very well connected in the tourism business in Victoria, had said Rogers' approach to cruise ship traffic needed to be reconsidered. Although for years Rogers' had counted on cruise ship passengers for business, representatives from Victoria's Butchart Gardens now boarded the cruise ships in San Francisco and promoted bus tours from the ship north to Butchart Gardens in Victoria. Many of the passengers were thus no longer going downtown.

The idea of franchising Rogers' outlets had been discussed but not truly investigated, because the board was concerned about giving up control of the brand and pricing. Parkhill had visited a store in Banff that had a Rogers' chocolate store attached to a larger gift store. Yet the store was not owned or franchised by Rogers': The gift store had merely displayed the Rogers' chocolates in a separate area for their own purposes. Others who purchased Rogers' chocolates wholesale merely displayed Rogers' merchandise along with their regular merchandise. For example, the Kingsmill's department store in London, Ontario, carried Rogers' chocolates in its food section. Of course, it might also be possible to franchise Sam's Deli.

The online business also appeared exciting. With low costs of sales and no intermediaries, the profits on the online business were exceptional. With such a high reorder rate, the chance to build a loyal following of online customers seemed like a sure winner.

The corporate gift market also seemed promising. Offering discounts of 25 per cent to corporate purchasers enabled Rogers' to still earn stronger margins than wholesale, without the costs of retail. Furthermore, corporate gifting expanded trial of the product.

There were many other possibilities for growth. The Olympics were coming to Vancouver and Whistler in 2010, promising a huge boon for BC tourism. Although Rogers' wasn't big enough to gain official Olympic status, it needed a strategy to take advantage of the crowds. With two stores in Vancouver and one in Whistler, Rogers' should be able to generate increased sales. Should Rogers' obtain more stores in Vancouver? Or should Rogers' extend its product line to take advantage of its strong franchise in British Columbia? Although ice cream had not been the runaway success the company had hoped, its sales were still building. Rogers' had a sugar-free chocolate line that served a small but growing market.

Another option might be for Rogers' to concentrate its efforts outside of BC. If American tourists had stopped coming to Victoria, due to the decline in the American dollar, should Rogers' go to them? Should Rogers' attempt to increase its penetration in Ontario or other parts of Canada? Should Rogers' attempt to extend its wholesale distribution outside of British Columbia? Would the current sales agency structure be appropriate for increased penetration? Should Rogers' consider an acquisition of another niche chocolate company or a joint venture with another firm to increase its geographical reach? Were there opportunities to pair Rogers' chocolates with other high-end products or brands for mutual benefit?

There was also the issue of the brand image. While Rogers' traditional image was treasured by loyal customers and employees alike, it didn't seem to play as well outside of Victoria. The packaging had been described as homey or dowdy by some, yet others were adamant that it should not be changed. Parkhill had spoken to a brand image consultant that had won numerous awards in the wine industry for the spunky brands he had designed. The consultant had suggested that the only dangerous thing in today's market was to play it safe—consumers loved edgy brands. Should Rogers' throw off tradition and try to reinvent itself?

Of course, if sales were to be increased, Rogers' would need more internal capacity to produce products and fill orders. Should more capacity be added in Victoria, with its expensive real estate and significant shipping costs to get product off the island, or should it be placed somewhere with lower costs and easier access to markets?

As Parkhill pondered all these options, he also knew that he had to take into consideration the culture of the organization and the desires of the board of directors and owners. Would the current managers and employees be willing and able to grow the organization? Would the board endorse a growth strategy that would increase the risk profile of the company? And with all these options, what should Rogers' do first?

EXHIBIT 1   Rogers' Products

Empress Squares

Dark Chocolate Almond Brittle

Marquis Assortment

Collectible Gift Tins

Fruit & Nut Collection

Ice Cream and Ice Cream Bars

EXHIBIT 2   Organization Chart

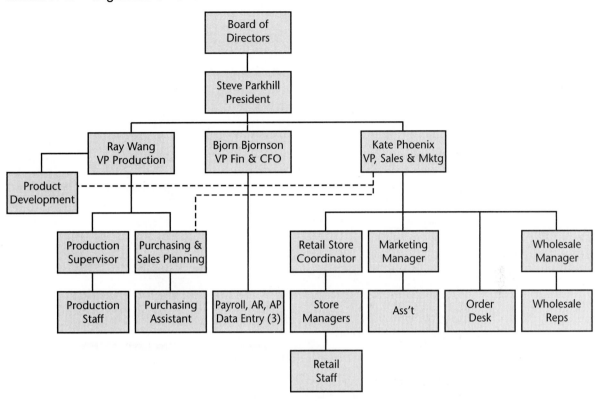

EXHIBIT 3   Retail Stores Sales in Fiscal 2007 (Rounded to Nearest Thousand)

Store	Date Acquired	Approximate Annual Sales	Contribution Margin
Downtown Victoria	1885	$2,775,000	45.3%
Sam's Deli	2004	$1,598,000	8.9%*
Factory	1985	$726,000	36.7%
Granville Island	Dec. 2005	$686,000	(11.5%)
Whistler	1995	$639,000	8.2%
Tudor Sweet Shoppe	1983	$517,000	22.86%
Sidney	2003	$401,000	29.1%
Gastown	April 2006	$138,000	(22.3%)
Swartz Bay–BC Ferries	2000	$60,000 (Mostly ice cream)	15.5%
Departure Bay–BC Ferries	2006	$42,000 (All ice cream; summer only)	18.2%
Duke Point–BC Ferries	2005	$35,000 (All ice cream; summer only)	21.1%

* Reflects full cost of expenses to refurbish the store.

EXHIBIT 4   Rogers' Chocolates Ltd. Consolidated Statement of
Earnings and Retained Earnings

Year Ended March 31	2006	2005
Sales	$11,850,480	$11,991,558
Cost of sales		
Amortization of property and equipment	135,385	108,759
Direct labour	1,545,794	1,677,247
Direct materials	1,770,603	2,745,995
Overhead	1,933,306	846,186
	5,385,088	5,378,187
Gross profit	6,465,392	6,613,371
Interest income	664	1,610
	6,466,056	6,614,981
Expenses		
Interest on long-term debt	91,465	86,943
Selling and administrative	5,221,520	5,007,145
	5,312,985	5,094,088
Earnings before income taxes	1,153,071	1,520,893
Income taxes	261,989	451,567
Net earnings	$ 891,082	$ 1,069,326
Retained earnings, beginning of year	$ 4,748,611	4,381,155
Net earnings	891,081	1,069,326
Dividends	–	(701,870)
Retained earnings, end of year	$ 5,639,692	$ 4,748,611

EXHIBIT 5   Rogers' Chocolates Ltd.—Schedule of Selling and Administrative Expenses

Year ended March 31			2006	2005
Selling		Advertising & Promotion	$ 489,345	$ 536,886
		Bad debts	23,000	12,796
		Credit card charges	125,198	125,544
		Mail order	118,606	133,081
		Office & Telephone	29,975	27,274
		Postage and freight	483,003	476,724
	Stores:	Factory Store	112,885	122,897
		Sam's Deli	572,495	323,995
		Sidney	75,854	84,047
		Swartz Bay	42,709	38,592
		The Bay Vancouver (closed in 2006)	3,938	4,058
		The Bay Victoria (closed in 2006)	4,236	2,759
		Tsawwassen	–	24,179
		Tudor Sweet Shoppe	87,103	119,058
		Whistler	168,157	182,939
		Royalties	29,862	31,099
		Salaries & benefits	812,269	715,325
		Travel	68,364	46,830
		Total	3,246,999	3,013,658
		Less: postage and freight recoveries	343,116	369,823
			2,903,883	2,638,260
Admin		Amortization	196,970	135,267
		Automotive	28,658	24,404
		Bank charges and interest	22,533	20,882
		Consulting	102,241	107,379
		Foreign exchange	–6,272	
		Insurance	80,704	78,777
		Management fees	191,226	183,627
		Office supplies and postage	134,159	118,582
		Professional fees	42,872	67,952
		Rent, property taxes and utilities	61,211	56,815
		Repairs and maintenance	18,378	21,105
	Stores:	Sam's Deli	326,901	179,834
		Sidney	26,559	28,159
		Swartz Bay	22,038	26,927
		The Bay Vancouver	10,082	18,251
		The Bay Victoria	32,123	37,939
		Tsawwassen		14,647
		Tudor Sweet Shoppe	49,849	45,002
		Whistler	112,450	105,720
		Salaries and benefits	810,049	1,030,336
		Telecommunications	27,824	32,588
		Travel and promotion	27,082	34,692
Total Admin Expenses			$ 2,317,637	$ 2,368,885
TOTAL S, G & A Expenses			$ 5,221,520	$ 5,007,145

EXHIBIT 6   Rogers' Chocolates Ltd.—Consolidated Balance Sheet

March 31	2006	2005
Assets		
Current		
Cash	$ 112,185	$ 750,948
Receivables	358,969	461,874
Inventories		
Packaging materials	620,452	576,287
Raw materials	169,235	179,119
Work in progress	89,146	66,467
Manufactured finished goods	643,105	692,517
Finished goods for resale	21,878	36,241
	1,543,816	1,550,631
Investments	103,136	76,822
Income taxes receivable	127,515	–
Prepaids	84,620	56,566
	2,330,241	2,896,842
Property and equipment (see Note 1)	4,364,527	3,922,183
Intangible assets		
Goodwill	916,999	916,999
Trademarks	783,596	783,596
Total Intangible Assets	1,700,595	1,700,595
TOTAL ASSETS	$ 8,395,363	$ 8,519,620
Liabilities		
Current		
Bank indebtedness	$ 186,929	$ 599,146
Payables and accruals	1,098,232	1,226,570
Income taxes payable	–	127,845
Current portion of long-term debt	419,971	373,405
	1,705,132	2,326,966
Long-term debt	1,017,679	1,411,184
TOTAL LIABILITIES	2,722,811	3,738,150
Shareholders' Equity		
Capital stock	32,860	32,860
Retained earnings	5,639,691	4,748,611
TOTAL EQUITY	5,672,551	4,781,471
TOTAL LIABILITIES & EQUITY	$ 8,395,362	$ 8,519,621

EXHIBIT 6   (continued)

Note 1

Property and equipment			2006	2005
		Accumulated	Net	Net
	Cost	Amortization	Book Value	Book Value
Land	1,219,819.20	–	1,219,819.20	1,219,819.20
Buildings	2,799,181.35	1,099,926.90	1,699,254.45	1,770,056.19
Manufacturing equipment	1,693,140.69	1,375,596.00	317,544.69	231,858.99
Furniture and fixtures	749,496.78	385,684.35	363,812.43	249,376.83
Office equipment	108,352.86	90,299.22	18,053.64	24,020.76
Computer equipment	250,683.90	225,157.26	25,526.64	53,214.81
Leasehold improvements	914,332.83	193,817.19	720,515.64	373,836.12
	7,735,007.61	3,370,480.92	4,364,526.69	3,922,182.90

EXHIBIT 7   Rogers' Chocolates Ltd.—Consolidated Statements of Cash Flows

Year Ended March 31	2006	2005
Increase (decrease) in cash and cash equivalents		
Operating		
Net earnings	$ 891,081	$ 1,069,326
Amortization	332,355	244,026
	1,223,436	1,313,352
Change in non-cash oper. working capital	(328,344)	350,045
	895,092	1,663,397
Financing		
(Repayments of) advances from LT debt	(349,168)	661,806
Dividends paid	–	(701,870)
	(349,168)	(40,064)
Investing		
Purchase of assets of Sam's Deli	–	(1,198,500)
Purchase of property and equipment	(772,470)	(419,307)
	(772,470)	(1,617,807)
Net (decrease) increase in cash and cash equivalents	(226,546)	5,526
Cash and cash equivalents, beginning of year	151,802	146,276
Cash and cash equivalents, end of year	$ 74,744	$ 151,802
Comprised of:		
Cash	$ 112,185	$ 750,948
Bank indebtedness	(186,929)	(599,146)
	$ 74,744	$ 151,802

EXHIBIT 8   Workopolis Job Ad

A unique company........ a unique location........... a unique opportunity.

Our client, one of Canada's oldest and respected confectionery companies, is seeking a **PRESIDENT** to oversee the entire business on a day-to-day basis, and provide the vision and guidance for long-term success and profitable growth.

Reporting to the Board of Directors, the President will:

- Deliver superior results and guide the organization to improve.
- Develop formal planning systems and ongoing personnel development.
- Oversee the development of business and marketing strategies to maintain market leadership.
- Provide the necessary leadership to motivate and transform the organization to meet growth expectations.
- Leads, protects and reinforces the positive corporate culture, and is the overseer of the ethics and values in the organization.

An executive level compensation plan commensurate with the importance of this role is offered.

An opportunity that blends an executive level position with the lifestyle only Victoria can offer.

CANDIDATE PROFILE:

Given the high levels of autonomy and accountability, the President must display considerable maturity and business experience.

From a personal perspective, the ideal candidate will be:

- A strong non-authoritative team builder.
- A highly motivated and results-oriented self-starter.
- Extremely customer-, quality- and safety-oriented.
- People oriented with the innate ability to establish a high degree of credibility.
- Capable of providing objective insight in a non-confrontational manner.

The successful candidate will likely be or have been in one of the following positions in a manufacturing environment:

- President or General Manager
- At a VP level in operations/finance/marketing looking to rise to the next level

While food manufacturing experience would be a clear asset, it is not a pre-requisite.

Time Warner Inc. and the ORC Patents

In early July 1992, John Adamson, president of Optical Recording Corporation (ORC), sat depressed and second-guessed his company's decision to sue Time Warner Inc. for patent infringement. An in-house patent counsel from the U.S. Philips Corporation, whose parent firm developed and licensed the compact disc (CD) technology in partnership with Sony Corporation, had just finished his testimony in the Wilmington, Delaware, courtroom.

The Philips attorney had just advised the court that Philips International N.V. had indeed signed a license agreement with ORC but only to "get rid of ORC with a modest nuisance payment." He had gone on to say that in spite of their decision to accept a license from ORC, the Philips engineers and attorneys had never believed that the Russell patents owned by ORC were valid nor that any compact disc products infringed these patents. Adamson watched in shock as the Philips man made his way out of the courtroom.

Given that Time Warner had mounted a very credible defense and that ORC's entire licensing program might be at risk, Adamson needed to decide whether he should make a modest settlement with Time Warner, just to save the licensing program.

BACKGROUND

Optical Recording Corporation (ORC) was incorporated in 1984 to exploit a technology invented by James T. Russell, an American inventor, then working in laboratories in Salt Lake City, Utah. Due to the desperate financial straits of SLC[1], his employer,

---

IVEY

Richard Ivey School of Business
The University of Western Ontario

---

[1]Due to a series of commercial lawsuits lasting 10 years with Russell's former employer, the author prefers to omit any real name reference to this company that had been a party to the technology transfer agreements with ORC. It is referred to here as "SLC." In all other references herein to persons, places or businesses, the actual names are used.

Russell had made little progress in the previous two years and both he and SLC were anxious to secure a buyer for the technology.

Through Wayne White, a fellow MBA 1972 graduate from the University of Western Ontario, then working with Dominion Securities in Toronto, John Adamson was put in contact with Dr. R. Moses and Dr. A. Stein. These two Toronto businessmen had been working for close to a year to buy Russell's technology. By happenstance, Adamson had contacted White looking for business opportunities to start his next business, preferably in electronics or software, just days after Moses and Stein had advised White that they were going to throw in the towel on their Russell project. In spite of the considerable time that they had spent, it appeared unlikely that they would be successful in securing the necessary finances to proceed.

Adamson negotiated an option with these gentlemen to assume their "interests" in the Russell project, on the condition that he secure the necessary funding for a technology transfer by April 1, 1985, a propitious date as it would turn out. In return, Adamson agreed to reimburse their expenses to date and to give to each a five per cent equity interest in the incorporation formed to exploit the Russell project in Toronto.

After completing a "due diligence" investigation of the Russell technology, with the assistance of Warner Sharkey, an alumnus and friend from the Royal Military College of Canada and a senior technology consultant, who operated from offices in New York and Toronto, Adamson began planning in earnest. He wanted to transfer the Russell technology to Toronto, where he expected a well-qualified team of scientists and engineers could be assembled to pursue a cost-effective development of a pocket-portable digital storage device.

For the next nine excruciating months, he worked to find investors for an issue of special debentures from his Toronto start-up. These debentures also offered a very attractive cash-back feature under a research tax credit program of the Canadian government. Funding was secured and the technology transfer agreements were signed on March 28, 1985, only three days before the option agreement with Moses and Stein would have expired. Adamson had resisted the temptation to request an extension of time on his option agreement with Moses and Stein. He feared that, better informed, they might rekindle their interest in the Russell technology and work to obstruct what little chance he still had to find funding prior to the option expiry on the first of April.

With the debenture funding and the transfer agreements signed, the new Toronto company, soon to be called Optical Recording Corporation (ORC), was now ready to hire Russell and transfer SLC's technology to Toronto.

JIM RUSSELL

By 1984, Jim Russell had worked for close to 20 years toward an improvement in recorded music beyond what was possible with the analog magnetic tape technology. This quest was motivated in part by his love of opera and a desire to listen to more accurate playbacks of recorded performances. When Adamson first visited Russell's lab in Salt Lake City, he was treated to the playback of a recording of Richard Wagner's "Ride of the Valkyries" (or "Die Walkure" in the original German). It was a most rousing introduction to a technology!

Russell had accomplished this playback by shining an argon ion laser beam onto a pre-recorded glass plate the size of an index card. This was the latest of his laboratory prototypes designed to demonstrate his patented techniques. These techniques were claimed in his extensive portfolio of 26 U.S. patents with corresponding foreign issues in 7 other countries.

In Russell's way of recording music, the acoustic signal of the music was first pre-processed into a single *digital* bit stream from a series of time-coincident frequency samples. A laser, an *optical* device, was then used as the energy source to mark the music, as digital bits, onto a glass plate in the recording step and then used to read the music, as digital bits, in the playback step. This technology was known as *digital optical* audio recording.

Adamson was not the first to visit Russell's lab, far from it. Over the course of the previous 10 years, both at SLC in Salt Lake City, and at Battelle Northwest Laboratories in Richland, Washington, electronics manufacturers around the world beat a path to Russell's laboratory door and at his invitation. SLC had been trying to sell technology licenses to the Russell technology but with virtually no success. Prominent among the visitors to SLC's labs were representatives from Philips International N.V., the multinational electric/electronics giant headquartered in Eindhoven, the Netherlands. They had made 3 separate visits over that 10-year period.

Prior to the commercial availability of the diode laser in the early 1980s, Russell's recording and playback devices were operated with the use of a gas ion laser and as such could be made no smaller than the dimensions of an office desk. Gas ion lasers were too bulky, complicated and expensive to be used in consumer products. This may explain SLC's lack of success in licensing and their resultant financial distress. With the advent of the diode laser, essentially a powerful light source on a silicon chip, a light, compact and economical consumer product such as the compact disc was possible. Although never well funded, SLC's money troubles really began in 1981, just as the mass commercialization of a digital optical audio recording device became feasible.

From Adamson's viewpoint, Russell's greatest achievement was not any one of his inventions, but his success in demonstrating the technical feasibility of recording a digital audio signal optically. Before Russell had successfully demonstrated this technical feat in 1975, no one else had even attempted it. By early 1984, however, the electronics trade papers were reporting that Sony and Philips were developing a so-called compact disc player. SLC and Russell must have felt that they were being left on the sidelines in Salt Lake City, a bitter fate for the inventor and his investors who had all contributed so much.

In bringing Russell and his technology to Toronto, Adamson had decided that there was little point in continuing audio research toward a digital optical tape recorder. The opportunity to develop a massive random access data storage device using credit card-sized media was seen a less ambitious technical challenge and possibly of greater commercial value than a music device like the CD. With the insight of Russell, Adamson envisioned books, medical records, equipment schematics, maintenance instructions and records on this type of device—and all pocket-portable.

In order to determine what protection the existing Russell patents would provide to the new research focus, Adamson employed the services of John Orange, a patent agent, then with the Toronto law firm of McCarthy & McCarthy. (Orange was recommended by Daniel Cooper, a corporate attorney with the same law firm, who earlier had prepared all of the financing and technology transfer agreements for ORC.)

After working with Russell for several months, Orange advised Adamson in early 1986 that the Russell patents may not provide much protection to the new company's research focus, as the most relevant patents appeared to be limited in their claims to audio applications. Adamson had already understood that it was the precise language of the claims within a patent that determined the patent's intellectual property rights.

DISCOVERING A TREASURE

In completing his study of ORC's patents with the assistance of Russell, Orange also concluded that the newly released compact disc players and discs might infringe one or more of the claims in the Russell patents. What a finding!

Russell had mentioned this possibility to Adamson during their first meeting in the Salt Lake City lab; however, Adamson had put little faith in Russell's remark at the time, as no consumer electronics firm had bothered to license the technology, in spite of SLC's efforts. Furthermore there were no CD products on the market then and its commercial success could not be anticipated.

Encouraged by the report from Orange and the early market success of the compact disc by the spring of 1986, Adamson retained the services of Adrian Horne, an established patent licensing professional of Dolby acoustic research fame. With Horne's assistance, ORC set out to advise every electronics firm likely to market a compact disc player anywhere in the world that "they may infringe the Russell patents" by doing so. Horne was most clear on the point that ORC must not appear to threaten legal action in their notice, as it may give grounds to the recipients to file a preemptive request for Declaratory Judgment and thereby force ORC into premature legal proceedings that ORC could ill afford.

In conjunction with the initial contact of alleged infringers, Adamson prepared cost estimates for the licensing effort and started to gain some early information on what it would cost to sue for patent infringement. He knew that once launched, any investment in the licensing program was certain to be incurred, whereas the return by way of royalty revenues would be anything but certain. He also made early estimates of the royalty potential for the licensing program, but these royalty estimates carried an enormous emotional impact.

Simple arithmetic established that if 100 million CD players were sold in ORC's patent-protected territories at an average manufacturer's selling price of US$100 and if ORC licensed their patent rights for this product at 2 per cent of revenues, ORC's projected royalties would total US$200 million. And this figure ignored the royalties to be earned on the manufacture and sale of the compact disc media itself! It was clear that a successful licensing program could be mounted given these simple estimates. Adamson chose not to dwell on these figures, however, as his typical reaction oscillated between a measured excitement and a raw fear of the business of licensing beyond what little he knew.

ORC's first meeting with a suspected infringer took place in the early summer of 1986 in Tarrytown, New York, in the offices of N.A. Philips Corporation. Legal representatives for both N.A. Philips and their Philips parent in Eindhoven, the Netherlands, and for the DuPont Corporation of Wilmington, Delaware, were in attendance. For ORC there were Cooper, Orange, and Adamson and a lawyer from Battelle Laboratories of Columbus, Ohio, Jim Russell's first employer, and the original owner and assignor of the Russell patents, first to SLC and then to ORC.

This first meeting with the Philips and DuPont people ended three and one-half hours later, after a full exchange of views and some acrimony, but no progress toward a licensing agreement. The attorneys representing both Philips and DuPont were of the view that no patents were infringed and further that there was some question about the validity of the Russell patents in the first place. There seemed little point in a further meeting and it seemed very likely that ORC might get no further without filing a patent infringement suit.

In August 1986, Adamson made a first trip to Tokyo on behalf of ORC, with Horne and Russell. A week-long series of company presentations had been arranged by Horne, with the assistance of Far East Associates, a technology licensing agency based in Tokyo, with whom Mr. Horne had collaborated in his Dolby days. Only one prominent manufacturer was invited to each meeting.

On Horne's advice, ORC had booked conference room space at the prestigious Okura Hotel, located directly across from the American Embassy in Minato-ku, a district of central Tokyo. Adamson choked on the daily expense of US$2,000 per day for a meeting room that comfortably held only six people. Horne, however, had stressed the importance of the location to ensure that the status-sensitive Japanese gained the best initial impression of ORC and its business offering.

The ORC team was overwhelmed by the turnout to their presentations. Each firm sent at least four executives and engineers; and in two instances, a group of over 10 people arrived, forcing the ORC team to scramble for a larger meeting room. Many guests recognized Horne from his previous Dolby research licensing days and more than a few appeared quite knowledgeable of Russell's research and patents. In fact, three firms clearly had comprehensive files on Russell's work and appeared very familiar with the technology.

The ORC presentations were made in English. Horne had advised that the executives in the international departments of all Japanese companies were invariably fluent in English. The younger members, however, tended to be more at ease in English, while some of the more experienced guests appeared to be there simply to witness the process and tone of the meeting and to gage the visitors as adversaries. Adamson concluded that some of the groups had arrived en masse, ready to take notes, in order to do a team translation, once they returned to their corporate offices. This would explain the large numbers of guests from some companies.

Nonetheless, this initial series of meetings convinced the ORC team that their patent infringement claims were being taken seriously by the Japanese firms. Apart from Philips, only the Japanese had announced CD player products by the fall of 1986.

During this initial trip by the ORC team to Tokyo, Yoshihide (Josh) Nakamura, then senior general manager, Intellectual Property, Sony Corporation invited the ORC team to Sony's headquarters for another meeting on their next visit to Japan.

Adamson returned to Tokyo with Orange and Horne in November 1986, for another series of presentations and meetings, but this time at each company's offices as prearranged again by Far East Associates. The most important of these meetings was with Sony Corporation, as the ORC team felt certain that Sony's decision on whether to license the Russell patents, would predetermine ORC's success with all other firms in Japan. (It was a Philips-Sony partnership that had launched the compact disc and taught an industry how to make them.)

On a schedule of two and even three meetings each day, including shuttles between companies located around Tokyo and Osaka, the ORC team made 12 more presentations. All discussions were held in English, again with only a perfunctory objection from the Japanese hosts. Everyone appreciated that the United States represented the largest domestic market for the compact disc industry and as Jim Russell had first filed his patents in the United States, it was also likely to be the site of ORC's most comprehensive patent protection.

In fact, ORC's patents were most comprehensive in the United States, Britain and Canada, but appeared to provide a weaker protection in Germany, France and the Netherlands. The prosecution of ORC's patents before the Japanese Patent Office had been stalled for many years, partly due to SLC's lack of funds. As such, while virtually all of the CD players were being manufactured in Japan, apart from those made by Philips, the greatest exposure of these Japanese manufacturers to ORC's claims of infringement lay in their export shipments to North America and Europe. Their shipments within Japan and to the rest of the world would only be exposed if ORC succeeded in getting the Japanese Patent Office to issue a key patent. (ORC never succeeded at having their Japanese patent issued.)

Some firms, including Sony, had gone to the expense of having a U.S. patent attorney present at all meetings with ORC, but Sony appeared the most ready to enter into substantive discussions. In this second round of discussions, Sony's team of six or seven engineers and executives presented ORC with a package of over 25 U.S. patents, all cited as Prior Art against the Russell patents.

PUBLISHING THE "BLUE BOOK"

Adamson had been warned by both Horne and Orange to expect such a patent defense from Sony. He understood that if the techniques that Russell had claimed in his patents as inventions could be found in any reference that had been published or made public prior to the filing of his patents (i.e., Prior Art), Russell's patents would be found "invalid" and unenforceable. In spite of the warnings, Adamson was highly alarmed and wondered whether ORC was in for a challenge.

On returning to Toronto and on the suggestion of Orange, Adamson tasked him to collaborate with Russell in a review of documents that Sony had provided. Orange prepared a technical response for each reference and compiled these results in a bound booklet for distribution to each prospective licensee. Thus, the so-called "Blue Book" was born. It was thought that by making a general distribution of the "Blue Book," any duplication of effort from one set of technical discussions to another could be minimized, while hopefully speeding all talks toward the signing of licenses.

Adamson had no sense whether one or other of the Prior Art references might hold a "golden arrow" that would pierce the assumed validity for the Russell patents. He knew that a patent was generally assumed to be valid as issued, and therefore enforceable before the courts, but any unanswered Prior Art reference could quickly dispose of ORC's credibility and their licensing prospects.

DISTRACTIONS ALONG THE WAY

Adamson had another, more urgent reason to wish the licensing talks to progress quickly. As a research firm, ORC was funding its operations from its initial financing, gained through a tax credit program of the Canadian government. With an initial net investment of just CDN$6.5 million and a monthly "burn-rate" approaching CDN$250,000 for the research program, Adamson knew that ORC would likely run out of cash by the end of 1987, at the latest. (Luckily for ORC, the mid-1980s were a period of rampant inflation and ORC was earning 10 per cent and 12 per cent per annum on its cash hoard.)

To add to the general instability of the situation, the Canadian government, SLC (the firm that had transferred the Russell technology to ORC) and the inventor himself, Russell, were now all objecting to the terms of the agreements that had brought the technology to Toronto. The Canadian government wished to rescind their tax credits and were demanding an immediate cash reimbursement, while SLC and Jim Russell were both interpreting their respective agreements in their favour, to secure some respective right to ORC's potential licensing windfall from the compact disc industry.

Adamson remained of the view that all claimants were incorrect in their positions and vowed privately to resist their claims even into bankruptcy. Despite all of these distractions, he also knew that ORC had to maintain the appearance of complete stability, control and competence, in order to avoid "losing face" before their Japanese prospective licensees. Many hours of sleep were lost during this desperate period.

THE SONY PROTOCOL

By their second meeting with ORC, the Sony team were stating that they wished to deal directly with ORC and not through Far East Associates, as Sony reportedly had for their patent licence with the Dolby firm. They also indicated that if Sony agreed to a licence, they would want the right to act as ORC's exclusive agent to license all other manufacturers based in Japan for their CD player production. As only Japanese manufacturers were then making CD players, apart from Philips in the Netherlands, this was difficult to agree to, given that ORC had resisted a similar proposal from Far East Associates.

Both the services of Horne and Far East Associates had been contracted on a fee-for-service basis, with ORC retaining all licensing rights to the Russell patents. Both could be terminated without cause in the normal course of business. As consultants, their services were required only as long as the client thought they were adding value. Far East Associates had indicated a desire to assume a full agency role on behalf of ORC with the full authority to license ORC's patents on behalf of ORC, but Adamson had resisted this overture, convinced that ORC would be better served by dealing with each manufacturer directly.

Now Sony was asking ORC to terminate Far East Associates and to make presentations directly to Japanese manufacturers, in anticipation of Sony agreeing to a patent licence. This licence, however, would only apply to CD players, with Sony assuming the role of exclusive agent, possibly for all of Asia. Adamson accepted this protocol with Sony, but he had to trust that Sony was in earnest in their desire to be the exclusive agent and not just leading ORC toward a dead end.

Further, as with Far East Associates, he had no idea how ORC was to monitor the work and licensing progress of an exclusive agent based in the Far East, directly licensing Asian manufacturers. How was one to know when a licence signed and royalties collected, if not by the exclusive agent? In any case, as co-licencer with Philips of the CD technology, Sony's support was clearly paramount to ORC.

So a pattern developed. Every four to eight weeks, Adamson and Orange travelled to Tokyo, Osaka and other cities in Japan to hold patent infringement and licensing discussions with the major Japanese consumer electronics firms such as Matsushita (Panasonic), Toshiba, Hitachi, Sanyo, Pioneer, Sharp and particularly Sony.

With each visit, new Prior Art references were put forward by one or other of the manufacturers, and ORC, in the person of Orange, would respond "on the fly" if an obvious separation from the art could be discerned. If not, ORC would fax a response to all participants upon returning to Toronto.

As the months passed, it was becoming increasingly clear to all that the Russell patents as presented by the ORC team, could withstand the invalidity challenges from the Prior Art. Equally important, the compact disc technical standard that ensured manufactured compatibility across all compliant CD products included techniques claimed in the Russell patents. To comply with this CD standard was to infringe the Russell patents! In short, it appeared that the Russell patents were valid and infringed by all CD products!

To balance this rosy picture, however, it was equally clear that, month by month, ORC's cash was disappearing into its research program. The company had lost any of the financial strength with which to mount a credible court challenge against even one of the established manufacturers: Sony, Philips or any of the 20 other firms of similar bulk.

THE END GAME?

Finally, in the fall of 1987, Adamson realized that neither Sony nor any other firm was likely to accept a license without more pressure being applied and more pressure than ORC could bring to the negotiating table. With nothing left to lose, Adamson flew to Tokyo in mid-January 1988, for a final meeting with Sony Corporation. No other firm was as advanced in discussions with ORC as Sony and Adamson reasoned that Sony had become fairly certain of the profit potential as ORC's master licensee for Japan. Sony would also have something to lose if the talks with ORC failed.

To add to this pressure, he could advise Sony that ORC was close to bankruptcy and, if ORC went into bankruptcy, the Russell patents would revert to their former owner, SLC, a firm that, in his direct experience, proved to be very litigious. The Sony team requested a lunch break.

Over lunch, Josh Nakamura asked Adamson whether he would continue to be involved with the Russell patent licensing if ORC went bankrupt. Adamson replied that while his ownership of the patents would be lost, he could no doubt strike a deal with SLC such that the licensing program would not "skip a beat." However the program would then be well financed by a very litigious American backer and, under the circumstances, Adamson would have little interest in favouring Sony in any way. Given his rocky relations with SLC, Adamson painted a most optimistic view of his future.

Returning to the Sony offices after lunch, the Sony team requested a further break and Adamson and Cooper sat quietly for an hour and a half in the meeting room at the Sony corporate head offices in Kita-Shinagawa, Adamson pondering his fate.

ORC'S FIRST LICENSE

Back in the meeting, Nakamura advised that Sony would be ready to sign a license with ORC. The license, however, would only cover CD players, not compact disc media. Further, ORC had to significantly reduce their royalty demands, accept Sony as the exclusive agent with full authority to license all CD player manufacturers based in Asia and pay Sony an administrative fee for their exclusive agency representation out of the royalties to be received. The proposal also required that ORC transfer the right to sue Asian CD player manufacturers for patent infringement to Sony as their exclusive agent. Adamson felt he had no choice but to accept this proposal if he wished to maintain his control of the Russell patents.

It was then agreed that the outline of the license and agency agreements be developed that very afternoon with a final negotiation of royalty rates to occur by telephone in the following week. Cooper took on the task of drafting the required changes to ORC's standard patent license agreement. Negotiations were then completed by telephone the following week and the Sony CD player agreement was signed in early February 1988.

From this shaky last-minute effort, Adamson had managed to retain his full ownership of the Russell patents through ORC. By licensing Sony, ORC now had a royalty cash flow with which to maintain the research program underway in Toronto, as well as the resources to fend off the lawsuits from the Government of Canada and SLC. For the first time in its existence, ORC was cash flow positive and in that sense, time was now on ORC's side; however, when measured against industry norms, the license with Sony cost ORC plenty. Nakamura and the Sony team had done their job well.

Apart from Sony's hard bargain, they were always gracious but now as business partners, Nakamura and Sony's negotiating team seemed to relish this role even more.

Adamson came to look forward to an invitation to dine at one restaurant in particular. High above Akasaka in central Tokyo, directly overlooking the Diet, Japan's national parliament, there was a restaurant laid out in a series of private dining rooms, each in a unique Western décor of a particular colour and at least one Monet or similar Old Master painting dominating the room. Their chefs were trained at the Paul Bocuse culinary school in France and the wine list read like a vintners' award booklet.

Adamson also came to realize that the superb ambiance and staff service of the Hotel Okura was very habit-forming and in spite of the expense, he opted to stay there whenever he was in Tokyo. Horne had been right. Being invited to lunch or dinner at the Hotel Okura was also a great treat for ORC's licensing prospects and other business associates in Tokyo.

ONWARD

Among the more difficult challenges that ORC faced in mounting the licensing program was the determination of the size of the infringing production unit volumes and sales revenues. A prospective licensee is not about to divulge this data, as it would impair their negotiating position and possibly increase their chances of being sued before one of their competitors. Nevertheless in the case of CD media, it was pretty obvious that the five sisters of sound—Philips (Deutsche Grammophon), Sony (Columbia), Time Warner (Warner), EMI (London and Angel) and Bertelsmann (RCA)—were the largest manufacturers of CD media. After Philips and Sony, Time Warner was likely to be the largest compact disc maker in the United States.

Government agencies and industry trade associations publish trade statistics, but this data is usually on an industry-wide basis (not by company) and for broad product categories, not for individual products such as a CD player. Beyond these sources, there are industry consultants of varying usefulness and reliability. Nevertheless, the licenser must develop estimates of the production and sales volumes for the infringing product by manufacturer and for each year from the start of the infringement to the expiry of the patent or the end of the infringement, whichever comes first.

Without such numbers it is not possible to decide which companies are the more lucrative licensing prospects and, more importantly, whether a licensing program is even feasible. Without this data, the licenser cannot know which infringer to sue or in which jurisdiction to bring the suit, to ensure the most favourable cost-benefit ratio for such an action.

In the ensuing 12 months, Sony sub-licensed over 50 per cent of the remaining Japanese production for CD players and ORC began to develop a substantial "war-chest." Still unresolved were ORC's equivalent infringement claims against the manufacturers of the discs, the compact disc media. Sony had refused to include this item in the initial license as they advised that they needed more time to study the matter. They also stated the view that the Russell patents were less likely to be infringed by the discs.

In the summer of 1988, however, ORC succeeded in licensing the Philips Corporation for both CD players and media and with this success, somewhat confirming Sony's earlier license commitment, Sony agreed to sign a license for CD media in November 1988. By the end of 1988, ORC had a cash position well in excess of US$10 million and the licensing program was on a roll.

The next largest manufacturer of CD media in the United States, by production volume, after American subsidiaries of Sony and Philips-Dupont, was known to be WEA Manufacturing, a subsidiary of Time Warner Inc. Commencing in 1987, Adamson held several discussions, by mail, telephone and face-to-face meetings, with Time Warner's in-house counsel. These discussions lead nowhere, however, as Time Warner's often-repeated view was the standard "non-infringement and invalid patents" position of an alleged infringer.

ENFORCING ORC'S PATENT RIGHTS

In early 1990, ORC had retained Davis Hoxie Faithfull & Hapgood, a patent law firm, just next door to Time Warner's corporate head office in the Rockefeller Center in New York City. Charles Bradley, a senior patent litigating attorney with Davis Hoxie had been recommended to Adamson on a chance encounter, while in Tokyo, with an American attorney who had the misfortune of opposing Bradley in a previous patent case. Bradley and Lawrence Goodwin, his partner, were engaged to pursue ORC's interests with the respect to the alleged infringement by WEA Manufacturing, a subsidiary of Time Warner Inc. Goodwin became the "lead" attorney on the ORC file with Bradley providing oversight, senior counsel and strategic advice to Goodwin.

On ORC's behalf, the Davis Hoxie firm filed a patent infringement complaint against WEA Manufacturing in the Federal District Court in Wilmington, Delaware, in June 1990. Like many other major American corporations, Time Warner and its subsidiary, WEA Manufacturing, were incorporated in the State of Delaware.

Not the least of Adamson's concerns in deciding to sue Time Warner in early 1991 was a looming patent expiry date in July 1992, for a U.S. patent, the key to ORC's infringement claims against CD media manufacturers.

The greatest threat that a patent-holder has against a recalcitrant infringer is a court injunction to stop the infringer's production lines. By 1991, this threat was all but lost to ORC as the July 1992 expiry date of ORC's key U.S. patent was likely to pass before any court could rule on the matter.

Without the threat of a court order to stop an infringing production, the patent-holder's leverage is reduced to the probability of a favourable court award being considerably more arduous for the infringer than the royalty payable if a license had been accepted. Even this leverage is diminished by the reality that, at any time prior to an appeal court ruling on a lower court award, the infringer is free to negotiate a settlement with the licenser, even well past a court decision which declares them to be infringing. The infringer can also hope that the patent-holder will capitulate before the end of a full trial, for lack of sufficient funds.

These considerations were very much on Adamson's mind in March 1992, as he drafted a letter (see Exhibit 1) to be sent directly to Time Warner's in-house counsel with a copy to Goodwin. Goodwin had advised against sending the letter, given that ORC had filed their patent infringement suit against Time Warner almost two years earlier; however, Adamson felt certain that Time Warner should be willing to settle for the modest sum of US$3 million, just to avoid the patent infringement trial now scheduled for June 1992, with all of its costs and disruption. Of no surprise to Goodwin, Time

Warner politely declined ORC's settlement proposal, perhaps thinking that the letter was a clear indication that ORC was about to capitulate, if they had not already, with their modest US$3 million settlement offer.

WILL THEY LIKE US IN WILMINGTON?

Now faced with the certainty of a trial in the United States, Adamson had to deal with a personal overriding concern. Could an American jury be prejudiced against a Canadian company such as ORC? Goodwin had told him not to worry about it, but Adamson was concerned that Goodwin simply did not know.

Too embarrassed to advise Goodwin of his continuing concern with a potential American prejudice toward a Canadian company, Adamson hired the New York office of Goldfarb Consultants, a Canadian market survey firm. Their assignment was to conduct an opinion survey on attitudes toward Canadian companies, of people drawn from the "jury-pool" population around Wilmington, Delaware. The Goldfarb team suggested that they conduct this survey with focus group interviews based on a set of questions pre-cleared by ORC.

In April 1992, Adamson travelled to Wilmington to witness the interviews first-hand by watching the proceedings on a video monitor in an adjacent room. There were three sessions comprising a total of 35 participants, who gave up a part of their evening for the survey in return for dinner and a modest stipend.

The interviews were conducted in two parts. The first part was designed to solicit an unprompted reference to Canada, in its role as a trading partner of the United States. The second part was designed to solicit directly any opinions that they may hold toward Canadian companies and then specifically a Canadian company's right to protect their American rights by suing an American company in Delaware.

The survey was of great benefit to Adamson as it quickly became clear that he should not be concerned about an American prejudice toward Canadian companies. If a prejudice did exist, it could only be positive because the survey, in every focus group, turned into a love-fest for Canada and Canadians.

Each focus group became frustrated with the first part of the survey. In trying to find the trading partner that they might be concerned about, Canada was never mentioned, even in their desperate attempts to finally yell out the "correct answer." This desperation was then followed by groans when Canada was finally noted by the session moderator at the beginning of the second part of the survey. Very few of those surveyed knew that Canada was indeed the largest trading partner of the United States.

With Canada now on the table and not hiding as in a trick question, many positive views were openly expressed. In fact, more than a few had vacationed in Canada, some had close Canadian relatives and one woman was so effusive as to simply say, "I love Canadians," quickly adding that she and her husband vacationed regularly in the Montreal area.

A little sheepishly, Adamson returned to Toronto and phoned Goodwin to advise him that "the ball was now in his court" and that ORC would see the Time Warner case through to appeal, if necessary. He did not mention the survey.

THE RUBBER MEETS THE ROAD

Lead by Goodwin, the Davis Hoxie team was comprised of one other full-time attorney, Robert Cote, and a support staff of three, all of whom stayed in Wilmington for the duration of the trial (with some weekends at home in New York). This Delaware team worked from the offices of a Wilmington law firm. This law firm in turn provided its own legal and support staff to ORC's team on an as-required basis. At Davis Hoxie in New York, at least one additional full-time attorney, Peter Bucci, and various other support staff were employed in research and document preparation for the duration of the trial. This entire trial effort was monitored and when appropriate, coached by Charles Bradley.

The trial began in the last days of May 1992, and it was to run for five and one-half weeks. Throughout the trial period, the Davis Hoxie team worked a daily double shift, one in courtroom and then a second in their law offices and hotel rooms, debriefing the day's events and preparing for the next day's court sessions. This preparation included a review of salient facts, prior affidavits, deposition testimony and then general court procedures with each individual witness, in preparation for the court appearance.

It also included a daily review of defendant witness testimony for discrepancies. The review of the court plan for the following day might include witness questioning, preparing motions that pulled together now-important facts and revising presentation materials imperiled by the day's events.

Adamson had decided to remain in Wilmington and attend every court session, given the importance of its outcome for ORC. Having watched the jury selection a few days before, he was highly stressed on the morning of the first day of the trial. He took some comfort in the size and evident competence of the Davis Hoxie team until the Time Warner team appeared.

Either by chance or design, 20 minutes prior to the official court start-time, opposing attorneys began to file into the courtroom. First they filled to overflowing the small defendant's bench in front of the commons rail, and then gradually they occupied the entire commons observer section on the defendant side of the courtroom, spacing themselves comfortably. Adamson sat as a lone observer for ORC directly behind the Davis Hoxie team of five on the plaintiff's side until three more groups of attorneys whom he had never met, filed in to sit behind him, also on the plaintiff's side.

Possibly the entire recording industry, including a few Japanese firms with still unlicensed CD plants in the United States, had sent attorneys, some 30 in all, to observe the start of the trial. The contrast between the sizes of the defendant and plaintiff legal teams was so evident that, prior to the jury entrance, lead counsel for Time Warner told the attorneys behind him to scatter into the plaintiff's observer benches.

Apparently unfazed by the obvious imbalance, a few minutes later, Goodwin stood up to address judge, jury and courtroom on behalf of ORC in a calm, humble but masterful tone. He was to continue as he had started through five and one-half weeks of trial, through surprise, setback, equipment failure, client panic and one or two staff confusions.

ORC's case was further strengthened by the skill of a superb expert witness, Leonard Laub. Laub was responsible for explaining ORC's highly technical infringement case to a jury with no technical training except for one retired man with an engineering degree dating back to the 1930s. This was accomplished with Laub's testimony, guided by questioning from Goodwin, and with the use of circuit diagram blow-ups and point summaries on white three feet by five feet storyboards. Adamson was satisfied that if there were a chance that the jury could come to understand ORC's case, it would be solely through the ample teaching skills of Goodwin and Laub.

ORC asked the court and jury for an award in lieu of royalty of six cents per disc against Time Warner and their American subsidiaries and a tripling of that award in punitive damages for willful infringement. The decision to ask for six cents per disc was partly based on ORC's initial licensing request of three cents per disc. Legally, licensers are able to change their royalty demands at any point in a negotiation, before or after the filing of a suit, just as infringers are free to agree to previously unacceptable terms.

(In normal licensing practice, it is simply wise to give active infringers some substantial incentive to sign a license prior to the filing of a suit. This is usually accomplished by increasing the royalty rate by some multiple of the original, say two, three, five or even ten times. The practical upper limit of a royalty rate is, of course, at that point where the manufacturer can make little profit after paying the royalty, as it is unlikely that any judge or jury would endorse a more onerous royalty request.)

Hearing Goodwin make this request for six cents per disc in open court was a thrilling moment early in the trial. Weeks later, the Time Warner attorney was obliged to produce for the court, the unit volumes of their subsidiary's infringing production of compact discs. Their infringement for the period covering the start of production in 1986 through July 1992, the month of the expiry of ORC's patent, totalled over 450 million discs and, at six cents per disc, represented a potential court award for ORC of over US$27 million. The addition of pre-judgment interest and a possible tripling of those damages were more than Adamson could fathom or entertain.

In spite of the good efforts of the Davis Hoxie team with Laub and several other strong witnesses, including Russell, the inventor, and the prospect of an enormous court award, all was not well. After the court appearance by the Philips attorney, Adamson believed that ORC's decision to sue Time Warner might have been taken too lightly.

Goodwin had warned that corporate litigation in the United States was a very expensive enterprise. It was also very demanding of management time, given the need to find, assemble and organize relevant business records, to educate the attorneys in the minutiae of events that usually had happened long ago and to attend court hearings as observers and witnesses. He had also noted that, in the normal course of a robust cross-examination, the combatants and their witnesses could expect personal insults and general verbal abuse. Adamson observed somewhat ruefully that Goodwin had been correct on all counts.

Preliminary motions, production and review of plaintiff and defendant business records and correspondence files, witness depositions, private investigators and trial preparations for the attorneys, company personnel and expert witnesses had already consumed close to US$750,000 of ORC's hard-won royalties all before the actual trial had begun. Adamson had budgeted an additional US$1.5 million for fees and expenses to be incurred from the trial itself; however, after the first three weeks of the trial, Adamson saw no end in sight to the trial or its expense.

As was its right as the plaintiff, ORC had chosen to have its case against Time Warner heard before a jury. Even this decision seemed to backfire as it was clear that the jury was putting a good deal of attention and apparent credence into what the defendant's attorneys had to say. The Time Warner litigating team had mounted a very credible defense. They seemed to cloud the technical issues of patent validity and product infringement as these related to the Russell patent claims and the compact disc technology, so that even Adamson found himself confused with ORC's claims from time to time. He had little hope left that the jury would be able to sort through the haze.

With this technical complexity and possible jury confusion, Adamson worried that the direct and damning statements of the Philips attorney toward the Russell patents and ORC's infringement claims could be disastrous for ORC, as these arguments gave the jury a reasonable and easy "out" from all the confusing technical jargon. Perhaps he was simply someone who knew better about these matters than they could ever hope to know.

Adamson also reflected on the fact that he had been forced to curtail the on-going licensing program for the other CD manufacturers. He had been concerned that some event within ORC's licensing program, such as an agreement with a royalty rate for CD discs below the six cents per disc demanded in the court case, might affect the outcome of the case; however, this concern was made mute by the simple fact that the other CD manufacturers had displayed little interest in signing a license with ORC as long as a major record company such as Time Warner was challenging ORC's infringement claims in court.

Should the court case result in anything less than a complete endorsement of ORC's infringement claims, ORC's entire licensing program could collapse, including the all-important quarterly payments from Sony. The CD player license with Sony may have been a "done deal." As a matter of practicality, Adamson wondered whether ORC would be prudent to take Sony to court should Sony simply stop paying royalties to ORC after a jury verdict had cleared Time Warner of ORC's patent infringement claims.

Over the course of the six years from 1986 to 1992, Adamson had been drawn away from ORC's research effort and future prospects and ever deeper into patent licensing and then this litigation struggle. As he had testified in the Time Warner trial, "there seems little point in investing in the creation and development of new intellectual property rights if major industrial firms are prepared to ignore and infringe existing patent rights that you already own." Playing somewhat to the jury, he knew that he had purposefully overstated his predicament but the basic truth of his simple observation resonated in the momentary silence of the court that day.

Adamson had made the very difficult decision early in 1991 to temporarily shelve ORC's research program and to reduce the company's technology development team to a skeleton staff of five team leaders. This move had been made for reasons other than the need to focus the company's resources on the Time Warner litigation. Nonetheless, as he sat in that Delaware courtroom watching the door close after the hasty exit of the Philips attorney, Adamson felt that he had bet ORC's entire future on the outcome of the court case against Time Warner.

The Richard Ivey School of Business gratefully acknowledges the generous support of John Adamson (MBA '72) in the development of this case as part of THE JOHN ADAMSON JAPAN CASE SERIES.

EXHIBIT 1   Draft Letter to Time Warner's In-House Counsel

CONFIRMATION ONLY

FACSIMILE MESSAGE OF TWO PAGES TO: 1 (212) 522-1252

March 4, 1992

WITHOUT PREJUDICE

Dear

RE: ORC vs Time Warner Inc.

Over the past week, we have prepared estimates on the costs and probable outcome of this case. We share this information with you now, in the hope of developing a common understanding from which a mutually satisfactory settlement might result. Our New York counsel is aware of this communication but, the views expressed here may not necessarily coincide with theirs.

Assuming that your costs to date equal ours, Time Warner has spent US$1,000,000. in out-of-pocket expenses alone,. Assuming that we will each spend another US$1,000,000. to the end of trial and then another US$200,000. on an appeal, we will each have spent another US$1,200,000. for a total of US$2,200,000 on this case. Give or take a few $100,000., these costs have a 100% probability of being incurred, if we proceed.

As to the outcome, it is our view that ORC has a significantly stronger case, as Justice Farnan's recent rulings might suggest. Further, we have substantial confidence in our representation. Nevertheless, we accept that the trial process is highly unpredictable. Therefore, we would attach a conservative estimate of perhaps 50% to the probability of ORC winning at both, trial and appeal.

Our licensing program had been based on the royalty rate of US$0.015 per disk and against the estimated and actual production totals for WEA and Allied of 400 million disks, a royalty amount of US$6,000,000. can be estimated. The size of award by the court could vary up or down from this royalty estimate but, it is our view that US$6,000,000 is a good average to assume of all possible court awards. If we assume a 50% probability that ORC will win, then it follows that there is a 50% probability that Time Warner will be required to pay the average award of US$6,000,000.

.../...

OPTICAL RECORDING CORPORATION

141 JOHN STREET, TORONTO, CANADA M5V 2E4 • TELEPHONE (416) 596-6862 • FAX (416) 596-0452

EXHIBIT 1   (continued)

OPTICAL RECORDING CORPORATION

- 2 -

To summarize, at this point in time, Time Warner has a 50% probability of paying out $6,000,000 in award and a 100% probability of paying $1,200,000 in continuing litigation costs, if we proceed.

We believe that a final attempt at settlement is in the interest of both companies at this time. Therefore, we now propose a patent license to Time Warner for their manufacture of Compact Disc in the United States, for $3,000,000.; that is, for 50% of the $6,000,000. which we contend that Time Warner has at least a 50% probability of incurring as a court award.

This offer will remain open until 5:00pm, Friday, March 6, 1992, after which, this and all previous offers will be withdrawn.

We would appreciate your comments on the logic presented here, particularly if you have a significantly divergent view on any point. Please feel free to call me directly if you wish to discuss any point in this letter.

Yours very truly,

G. John Adamson
President

GJA/gj

Majestica Hotel in Shanghai?

On March 20, 2005, Richard Roy, executive vice-president of Majestica Hotels Inc., was in China, for negotiations with Commercial Properties of Shanghai Limited (CPS). They were discussing a possible management contract under which Majestica would be the operator of a new luxury hotel there owned by Shanghai Industrial Holdings.

Majestica Hotels Inc. was one of the world's leading operators of luxury hotels. The expansion into mainland China had been on management's agenda since 1999. The opportunity emerged in late 2003 when a close friend of Majestica's chief executive officer (CEO) revealed that CPS was looking for an operator for its new luxury hotel under construction in Shanghai. Majestica immediately sent representatives to Shanghai to explore the possibility of becoming the operator. Majestica's proposal was welcomed by CPS, and a letter of intent was signed on August 20, 2004.

However, in discussions regarding the management contract, the two parties had reached a deadlock. The key issues to be resolved were the contract term and the responsibilities and rights of Majestica, as the operator, and CPS, as the owner, of the hotel.

This Shanghai deal was important for Majestica's global expansion. It would not only provide Majestica with the opportunity to enter the China market but could also set a precedent for Majestica's future expansion in other emerging markets.

MAJESTICA HOTELS INC.

Majestica was founded in 1970 in Western Europe. It focused exclusively on its niche of developing and operating luxury hotels with 200 to 450 rooms. In 1977, Majestica expanded to the United Kingdom. In 1984, Majestica entered the U.S. market via acquisition. Majestica's expansion in the U.S. market continued with properties in

Richard Ivey School of Business
The University of Western Ontario

seven other major cities. By the end of the 1990s, Majestica had secured a strong position in the luxury hotel industry in North America, competing with such established chains as Four Seasons, Ritz-Carlton, Hilton, Hyatt, Marriott and Westin.

While Majestica expanded quickly in North America, it adopted a gradual expansion strategy in Asia. This gradual expansion strategy shifted when the opportunity arose to acquire a major competitor in Asia in 1998. This acquisition made Majestica one of the world's largest operators of luxury hotels and resort properties. More importantly, it provided Majestica with a much expanded position in Pacific Asia and an immediate presence in the greater China area. Majestica continued its international expansion by amassing a select portfolio of medium-sized luxury hotels in the world's commercial and financial centres. By the end of 2004, Majestica managed 40 properties in 15 countries, with approximately 20,000 employees. The contribution of Majestica's properties in North America, Asia and Europe to its consolidated revenue was 54 per cent, 14 per cent and 32 per cent, respectively. Exhibit 1 provides a five-year review of the occupancy rate, average daily room rate (ADR) and average room revenue per available room (REVPAR) of Majestica hotels in these three regions and worldwide.

In 2004, Majestica had a market capitalization of $1.7 billion[1] and generated revenue of more than $2.3 billion (see Exhibit 2). Majestica earned revenue both from hotel management and hotel ownership operations. In the past five years, Majestica shifted away from owning hotels and focused on managing hotels. In 2004, 80 percent of Majestica's earnings before other operating items were generated by its hotel management business.

Majestica followed a business strategy that offered business and leisure travellers excellent hotel and resort accommodation in each destination it served. Following this strategy, Majestica developed into a luxury hotel chain with service standards among the best in the industry. Majestica hotels and resorts were widely recognized for the exceptional quality of their guest facilities, service and atmosphere. The Majestica brand was generally considered one of the top luxury hotel chain brands in the world, and its hotels and resorts were named frequently among the world's best hotels and travel experiences by Institutional Investor, Condé Nast Traveler, AAA Five Diamond and others. Majestica's success was also reflected in consistently achieving above-market operating results for the properties under its management. During 2003, REVPAR for Majestica core hotels worldwide and in North America was 60 per cent higher than that of its competitors in the luxury segments worldwide and in North America. The room rate for a Majestica hotel in Chicago, for example, averaged $50 higher than those of Hyatt Regency, Hilton, Sheraton and Marriott (see Exhibit 3).

Majestica's superior hotel management results attracted the owners and developers of luxury hotels worldwide. By the end of 2004, in addition to the 40 hotels under its management, Majestica had 16 new hotels and resorts under construction or development, and it was evaluating dozens of additional management opportunities around the world. In summarizing the key success factors, the Majestica management pointed to a service culture that they had fostered for decades.

It emphasized anticipating travellers' needs and meeting those needs with superior hotel structures and a deeply instilled ethic of personal service. This service culture was built into every property, going beyond elegant hotel designs and finishes to

---

[1]All amounts in US$ unless otherwise specified.

the small, thoughtful touches that would add value for the guests. Every detail was deliberate, from mechanical systems that were as quiet as they were efficient, to providing a disposable bathing suit in case hotel guests forgot to bring one. In addition, the design of the hotel rooms highlighted a use of space that enhanced the sense of luxury. On average, standard guest rooms in Majestica hotels were 25 per cent larger than those in Hyatt Regency, Hilton, Sheraton and Marriott.

More importantly, the service culture emphasized the depth of personal service. Majestica deemed ultimate luxury as derived not from furnishings but from personal service. The services at Majestica hotels were comprehensive and highly personalized. Guided by the service culture, Majestica's employees treated every interaction with guests as an opportunity to anticipate and satisfy a need. They provided services ranging from room service that felt like a fine dining experience to replacing worn shoelaces. The strong service culture ensured highly reliable services. For example, room service always arrived on time and conference arrangements were in place as promised.

The service culture encouraged surpassing each guest's highest levels of expectation. Majestica employees would do everything possible to accomplish the guests' purpose of the trip. The stories of Majestica employees' responses to unusual requests were legendary.

It took Majestica decades to foster this unique service culture and to achieve the widely recognized outstanding service standards. The challenge Majestica faced in its global expansion was how to replicate the exceptional Majestica guest experience from hotel to hotel, no matter where it operated in the world. Maintaining consistency in the quality of guest experience across its portfolio was regarded as essential to Majestica's continuing success. Decades of experience in the luxury hotel market had taught Majestica that constancy built trust and loyalty. The challenge in Majestica's global expansion was how to export its service culture to new locations. Majestica successfully handled this challenge with the following two policies.

First, Majestica was careful about the pace of adding new hotels and resorts in the portfolio. Whether there was a compatible service culture in the new location was an important criterion in deciding the direction and pace of Majestica's international expansion. In fact, the perceived lack of service culture in Asia was one of the major reasons that Majestica adopted a gradual expansion strategy in Asia in the mid-1990s. This second-mover strategy allowed Majestica to profit from the development of a service culture in Asia brought about by the earlier entrants, the major American hotels.

Second, it was Majestica's operating philosophy to have full control of the hotels under its management in order to cultivate its service culture and to maintain service consistency in new markets. Majestica's operating philosophy requested the owners of the Majestica hotels to adopt a hands-off approach, from the planning and designing of the hotels, to the daily operating of the hotel such as purchasing hotel equipment, marketing and staffing. The non-interference from the hotel owners was important to the smooth fostering of Majestica's service culture in new markets. For example, the full authority in staffing enabled Majestica to carefully select the right people and imbue them with Majestica's service culture through various training programs and through leadership by example. Following this operating philosophy, Majestica's service culture was passed from one Majestica hotel to another so as to succeed in maintaining consistant service throughout its global expansion.

MAJESTICA IN THE ASIA-PACIFIC REGION

Asia was one of the fastest-growing tourism destinations in the world. However, Asia's importance as a travel destination was not recognized by the major hotel companies in the world until the rising of Asia's tigers in the 1980s. Attracted by the unprecedented economic and construction boom in the region, a growing middle class, increases in passenger miles and an expanding economy, major hotel companies rapidly opened new properties in the Asia-Pacific region in an attempt to ensure a strong presence.

Among the major international luxury hotel chains, Hilton was the earliest entrant to the region. After its initial entry in 1948 with the 450-room Nagoya Hilton, Hilton International had 45 properties spreading across the region by 2000.

Through its 1995 acquisition of Westin Hotels & Resorts and ITT Sheraton Corp., Starwood Hotels & Resorts Worldwide gained a strong presence in the Asia-Pacific region. Prior to being acquired, both Westin and ITT Sheraton had been active in the Asia-Pacific region, and were managing numerous properties.

Marriott and Hyatt were two of the later entrants to the Asia-Pacific region. Hyatt International managed 56 hotels and 18 resorts in 34 countries. In the Asia-Pacific region, it had 18 hotels in operation and 19 properties under development. Marriott entered the Asia-Pacific region in 1990 with its opening of the JW Marriott Hotel Hong Kong. Four more entries over the next seven years brought Marriott's total to five hotels, with a total of 1,941 rooms. Marriott had also secured management contracts for four additional hotels. The company was looking to add more hotels in the four- and five-star categories.

Another competitor, Four Seasons, had 15 Asian-Pacific properties, with a total of 4,950 rooms. This total represented one-third of its rooms worldwide. In addition to these hotels, two more were scheduled to open in 2005. The company's Asian-Pacific portfolio was heavily concentrated in India, Indonesia, Singapore and Thailand.

The Ritz-Carlton Hotel Company was another upscale hotel firm that had targeted the region. In 1997, the company opened hotels in Osaka and Kuala Lumpur to complement its existing properties in Singapore, Hong Kong, Seoul and Sydney. The company also opened a resort in Bali, Indonesia, situated near one of Four Seasons' premier properties.

In addition to these competitors, Asian hotel companies such as Mandarin Oriental, Dusit Thani, CDL, Regal Hotels, Marco Polo, New World Hotels International and the Peninsula Group had been exploring opportunities for expansion in and around their bases in Asia. Hong Kong-based Shangri-La Hotels and Resorts was the most active Asian hotel company. It operated 32 hotels and resorts in China and Southeast Asia, with plans for more.

Compared with the rapid expansion of these companies, Majestica had kept a low profile in the region. It had not entered Asia in the late 1980s because Majestica was not convinced that the political situation was stable and that a service culture existed there.

However, the 1990s brought a change in Majestica's strategy. In 1994, after two years of negotiation, Majestica acquired two Tokyo hotels as its first properties in the region. In August 1996, with a solid capital base that had been built on the company's outstanding financial performance, Majestica acquired 100 per cent ownership of Le Roi Resorts, including its management contracts, trade names and trademarks. This transaction provided Majestica with a much expanded position in the Asia-Pacific region.

As 2005 approached, China was becoming the centre of Asia's fiercest competition in the hotel industry. With an annual Gross Domestic Product (GDP) growth rate of

9 per cent for the past 20 years, China was the 7th-largest economy and the 10th-largest trading nation in the world. China's booming economy, coupled with its huge potential market comprising more than 1.2 billion people, had attracted many foreign investors. By the end of 2001, China ranked second to the United States as the largest foreign direct investment recipient in the world.

China's economic development and open door policy also attracted many foreign visitors. With over seven million foreign visitors (including people from Hong Kong, Macao and Taiwan) in 2000, China was the sixth-most popular destination for business and leisure travel in the world. The World Tourism Organization predicted that China would become the No. 1 travel destination by 2020.

The hotel industry in China prospered with the boom in tourism. At the end of 2002, China had approximately 5,201 hotels, a growth rate of nearly 20 per cent since 1996. This represented a total of 701,700 available rooms in China. In 2000, the hotels sector recorded growth of over 10 per cent. Over half the hotels in China were categorized as tourist hotels.[2] Of the 1,669 hotels rated by the government, the majority were at the two- and three-star level, while just three per cent had been awarded five-star ratings. Most five-star hotels were operated by international luxury hotel chains such as Shangri-La Hotels and Resorts, ITT Sheraton Asia-Pacific Group, Hilton International and Ritz-Carlton Hotels & Resorts.

COMMERCIAL PROPERTIES OF SHANGHAI LIMITED

Commercial Properties of Shanghai Limited (CPS) was a subsidiary of Commercial Properties Shanghai Investment (Holdings) Co., Ltd. (CPSIH), one of several overseas investment arms of the Shanghai municipal government. Incorporated in Hong Kong in October 1985, CPSIH expanded its businesses quickly, and became a diversified conglomerate active in a wide range of businesses, including international investment, manufacturing, real estate development and investment, banking and finance, trading and cultural activities. By the end of 2001, it was the largest overseas conglomerate wholly owned by the Shanghai municipal government, with interests in more than 200 companies in Shanghai, Hong Kong, other parts of China, and in cities spanning the Americas, Europe, Australia, Africa and Asia.

Hotel development and management was one of the businesses in which CPSIH was engaged. It owned and managed three hotels: the Oceania Hotel, situated on Hong Kong Island; Mandarin United Hotel, situated in Pudong, Shanghai; and Peace Garden Hotel, located near the Yuyuan Gardens in Shanghai. In addition, it also organized mainland China and Hong Kong tours from its properties. Although hotel development and management was a comparatively small business in the company's 2001 business portfolio, it was one of the focuses of the company's future business development. Development of the hotel industry fit well in the company's mission to promote Shanghai and served the need of the Shanghai municipal government for foreign currency. To strengthen its position in the hotel industry and enter the luxury hotel segment, CPSIH had invested $220 million in building the Oceania Hotel in Hong Kong.

---

[2]In China, there are two basic categories of hotels. Tourist hotels are licensed to receive foreigners. The rest are open only to domestic visitors. Tourist hotels are usually better built and better equipped than domestic hotels.

CPS was listed on the stock exchange of Hong Kong in May 2000, and subsequently selected as a Hang Seng Index constituent stock in January 2002. At the time of the listing, the market capitalization of CPS was approximately $700 million. A majority of its shares were held by its parent, CPSIH.

Within the first year after the listing, CPS conducted several successful acquisitions. As well, the parent company also injected assets into CPS. These acquisitions and asset injections together were worth approximately $1.3 billion, making CPS one of the largest "red-chip" stocks listed on the Hong Kong stock market.

For the year ended 31 December, 2001, the company's turnover reached approximately HK$4,978 million (about $795 million), an increase of approximately 60 percent over that in 2001. Profit for the year amounted to approximately HK$1,421 million (about $227 million) and earnings per share HK$1.79 (about $0.29), representing substantial increases over the results of 2000.

THE HOTEL INDUSTRY IN SHANGHAI

Situated in the middle of China's east coastline, Shanghai was China's economic and trade centre. In 2000, Shanghai had a population of 16.74 million and the highest per capita income in China. Shanghai and the surrounding provinces of Jiangsu and Zhejiang (Shanghai's manufacturing hinterland) formed the Yangtze River delta region. This region had a comprehensive industrial base and accounted for nearly one-third of China's industrial output. Moreover, it was home to one-quarter of all foreign investment in China. For these reasons, Shanghai was regarded not only as one of the main engines of China's economic growth but also as one of the leading markets in China. Given its strategic importance in China's economic development, its huge market potential and its popularity among tourists, Shanghai had long been recognized as a key site for companies that operated in the luxury hotel business.

According to the Shanghai Tourism Administrative Commission, Shanghai had 423 hotels at the end of 2004, with 68,000 rooms. By the end of 2005, the number of hotels was expected to rise to around 470, with the number of guest rooms rising to 75,000. The commission expected more than 4 million overseas tourists to stay at least 1 night in the city in 2005, an increase of 11 per cent from 2004. The commission also expected the number of domestic tourists visiting Shanghai to rise by 5 per cent, hitting 90 million. However, only a handful had a top rating of five-stars (see Exhibit 4). Portman Ritz-Carlton had been originally managed by Shangri-La Hotels and Resorts. However, at the end of 1997, the management contract expired and Ritz-Carlton took over the management of Portman. It was then renamed Portman Ritz-Carlton, and was Ritz-Carlton's first hotel in China.

In 1992, the Chinese government announced its initiative to develop Shanghai's Pudong District into Asia's finance centre. Local government offices, the Shanghai Stock Exchange, the Shanghai Cereal & Oil Exchange and the Shanghai Real Estate Trading Market were all to move their offices across the Huangpu River to the Pudong District. Hotel developers quickly seized the opportunity created by this initiative and invested in the Pudong area. International luxury hotel chains soon followed and, by mid-1998, Shangri-La opened the first five-star hotel in Pudong. Several months later, in the fall of 1998, Hyatt International opened its first Chinese Grand Hyatt in Pudong. This luxury hotel occupied the top 36 floors of Pudong's 88-story Jin Mao Tower, making it the tallest hotel in the world. Quickly, other luxury hotels followed these entries, and there was some thought among industry observers that the Shanghai luxury hotel market was saturated, even before Majestica's proposed entry.

MAJESTICA—CPS NEGOTIATION

Shanghai was an ideal location for Majestica's expansion into mainland China. First, the Shanghai location met Majestica's preference for locating in major commercial and financial centres. In fact, Shanghai ranked second to Paris on the company's list of attractive international location choices. Shanghai was also attractive for its investment infrastructure, especially in terms of the service mentality of the Shanghai people. The quality of people was important for the development of a service culture.

In addition to being an ideal location, Majestica was interested in the partner. The partner was seen as having both the appetite and resources, and could provide the potential to enter into multiple cities in China in the future. Such an owner not only reduced Majestica's concern about the political risk in China, but also ensured a long-term commitment to the city and the support of the Shanghai municipal government to the project. The fact that CPS was publicly listed in Hong Kong gave Majestica more confidence about business transparency and independence from government influence. Further, the fact that the hotel was under construction made the opportunity more attractive to Majestica.

Majestica's proposal to operate the luxury hotel satisfied CPS's ambition to build a pre-eminent hotel in Shanghai. Majestica's outstanding financial performance and reputation in the luxury hotel industry convinced CPS that Majestica had the capability to provide the expected rate of return to its investment in the hotel. CPS's confidence in Majestica was reflected in changing the original hotel design from 600 to 700 rooms (the Sheraton standard) to 375 to 450 rooms to meet the high standard of Majestica.

Majestica and CPS signed a letter of intent on August 20, 2004. After the signing of the letter of intent, the two parties started negotiation on the management contract. With respect to the fee structure, CPS was impressed by Majestica's above-market results for existing properties, and was confident that the same could be achieved for the hotel. CPS agreed that Majestica would receive a base fee of three per cent of gross revenues of the hotel, as per its standard arrangement. In addition, Majestica would receive incentive fees based on the hotel's operating performance. Such incentives were in place for 90 per cent of the properties that Majestica managed.

The key issues in the negotiation that required resolution in March 2005 were the length of contract term and the control that Majestica could have over the management of the hotel.

Length of Contract Term

Most of the negotiation time was spent on the issue of the length of contract term. The length of the term of management contract was very important to Majestica. Majestica did not sign short-term management contracts. Based on its typical management contract term of 50 to 60 years elsewhere in the world, Majestica asked for a contract term of 55 years in its negotiation with CPS. CPS was shocked by this request; it had been prepared to offer only 12 years. In China, there were two levels of licensing in hotel development and management. The first level of licensing was from the government to the owner for the use of the land on which the hotel was built. The maximum length of land lease was 50 years. The second level of licensing was from the owner of the hotel to the operator who would manage the hotel on behalf of the owner. The normal hotel management term in China was only 10 years, since one of the objectives of the licensors was to learn hotel management and eventually manage the hotel themselves.

The big gap between the two parties on the contract length was a very difficult issue in the negotiation. After consultation with its parent company and presumably the Shanghai municipal government, CPS countered with an offer of 30 years. Majestica insisted that the hotel management contract term should be at least 50 years, the same as the land use right certificate term that CPS had received from the government. CPS argued that the hotel industry belonged to a sector which limited foreign investment, and government regulations would not allow the duration of hotel operation by foreign investors to be over 30 years. It further suggested that Majestica could enjoy a 30-year operation period and the operation period could be extended when it expired, if both parties agreed to extend.

Pre-opening Assistance

Majestica assumed a substantial pre-opening role by sending senior people, such as its senior vice-president of design and construction, to help CPS in the design and constructing of the hotel. CPS welcomed Majestica's help, but couldn't accept Majestica's request for retaining the approval right over all design aspects relating to the hotel, including the furniture, fixtures and equipment. Majestica argued that it requested this right to keep chain consistency, to make sure that the hotel would be developed and constructed as a world-class luxury hotel and to allow effective functioning of the hotel in operation.

Name of the Hotel

CPS suggested that the hotel be named "Shanghai Oceania–Majestica Hotel." Majestica insisted that the hotel should be under the name "Majestica Hotel, Shanghai." This was essential to, and consistent with, Majestica's international strategic expansion program. Majestica believed that the Majestica brand was critical to the successful operation of the hotel as an international luxury hotel. Majestica would not agree to operate the hotel under any other name.

General Manager

Another major issue under debate was staffing the different levels of the hotel management (Exhibit 5). The hotel's general manager was responsible for the overall operation. In general, the two parties agreed that the general manager, upon the opening of the hotel, would be an expatriate. CPS, however, expressed the wish that in the near future, a Chinese general manager would be used. Majestica told CPS that in the selection of a general manager for the hotel, the competence of the general manager was a more important issue than their ethnic background and that while they could make every effort to locate a suitable person with Chinese background, they could not guarantee such an appointment. There was simply no history of Chinese nationals managing world class hotels at or near this level.

Expatriates

In discussions about the number of expatriates to be employed, the localization issue was raised again and was expressed more strongly. CPS could accept the use of any number of expatriates that Majestica considered necessary to get the hotel up and running. But they insisted that the number of the expatriate managers should be gradually reduced and local managers trained to replace them. The reasons were two-fold. First, such a move would cut down the overall operating costs, as it was very expensive to use expatriates. Second, learning how to operate a world-class luxury hotel was one of CPS's objectives, and CPS expected Majestica to train the local employees and eventually use them to replace the expatriates.

Specifically, CPS requested that Majestica use a deputy general manager and a deputy financial controller sent by CPS. Majestica told CPS that Majestica would like to fill the positions of senior hotel personnel with local people, both from a cost and a cultural perspective. However, at this time, Majestica did not believe that local people would have the prerequisite experience (i.e., having held an equivalent position successfully in a world-class luxury hotel) to perform their duties at the hotel on a basis consistent with its operation as an international world-class luxury hotel. In addition, hotel management was a service business, and it took a long time to build a service culture. On average, it took 12 to 15 years for the culture to be absorbed by hotel professionals. Therefore, it was difficult to reduce the number of expatriates in the foreseeable future. In fact, staffing key positions in the new hotels with experienced hotel operations personnel was one of the secrets to Majestica's success. Richard Roy noted, "Exporting the Majestica work ethic does not depend on manuals, but on seeding new markets with those skilled at finding similar people in new places."

General Staffing

Closely related to the issues of the general manager and expatriates was the responsibility and authority of general staffing. Majestica insisted that it must have the exclusive responsibility and authority on the hiring, paying, supervising, relocating and discharging of all personnel of the hotel, and that CPS should unconditionally employ all the personnel selected and pay all the employment expenses. Majestica emphasized that selecting the appropriate employees and developing their attitudes and job performance in the context of Majestica's operating philosophy was critical to maintaining consistently high-quality performance. Therefore Majestica should have exclusive authority in staffing to achieve a consistency of staff attitude and service standards. CPS argued that it was entitled to share the responsibility and authority in staffing as the ultimate employer of the hotel staff.

Purchasing

Majestica insisted that, commencing on the opening date, the hotel should participate in Majestica's centralized purchasing system for furniture, fixtures, operating equipment and supplies, and CPS should pay Majestica a modest fee relating to such centralized purchasing. Majestica argued that central purchasing could ensure standardized products, economies of scale and control over quality and design. CPS was concerned about the purchase prices and insisted that domestic purchasing should be a first priority.

With regard to personal property, other than the operating equipment and supplies, Majestica agreed that CPS could be responsible for the purchasing, subject to Majestica's approval right over the design of the personal property, as well as the firm used to purchase and install the personal property.

Owner's Access to Hotel Rooms

As the owner of the hotel, CPS requested access to hotel rooms or the use of some hotel rooms as offices. Majestica, however, insisted that the owner should not have any privileges over the use of hotel rooms, as such an arrangement would cause confusion for the hotel management.

Arbitration

Another major issue discussed in the negotiation was related to arbitration. While both parties agreed to an arbitration process in the event of future disputes, they disagreed on the location for dispute resolution. Majestica insisted on a third country, following the norm commonly practised by the company. CPS, however, insisted that any arbitration should take place in China.

On top of the various issues in the negotiation of the management contract, CPS asked Majestica to take a minority equity position in the hotel. Generally, Majestica made only minority investments in properties where it was necessary and justified. It sought to limit its total capital exposure to no more than 20 per cent of the total equity required for the new property. The Foreign Investment Law in China, however, had stipulated until recently that the equity holdings by foreign investor(s) in an equity joint venture should be no less than 25 per cent. Thus, the request by CPS exceeded Majestica's upper limit on minority investment policy.

After many rounds of negotiation in the past three months, several issues remained unresolved. While CPS showed its flexibility and made concessions with a counter offer of a 30-year contract term, it was clear that Majestica was expected to reciprocate CPS's flexibility and make some concessions in the next round of negotiations. However, Majestica found it difficult to make any concessions. Any requests made in the management contract were based on its operating philosophy for building a service culture, the key success factor in the luxury hotel industry.

THE DECISION

Thinking of the prolonged negotiation, Richard Roy felt disappointed because a lot of management time had been invested in this Shanghai project, but no decision had been reached. Reading through the minutes of the negotiation again, it was clear to Roy that many of the issues under dispute reflected the conflict between Majestica's operating philosophy and CPS's hands-on approach as the owner of the hotel. The Shanghai deal was a great opportunity, particularly if the management contract could be settled quickly. Roy was unsure what position Majestica should take. Given the importance of the China market, should Majestica adopt a contingency approach and relax its operating philosophy at this time, or should it stick with its original philosophy, even if this meant not entering the Shanghai market?

EXHIBIT 1 Hotel Occupancy, ADR and REVPAR (in US$ millions)

	2004	2003	2002	2001	2000
Worldwide					
Occupancy	75.44%	74.50%	70.30%	69.50%	68.00%
ADR[1]	$380.18	$354.22	$312.24	$286.53	$239.85
REVPAR[2]	$280.38	$265.16	$223.93	$203.20	$162.15
Gross operating margin[3]	32.50%	33.10%	29.10%	26.70%	22.00%
North America					
Occupancy	76.40%	77.50%	78.00%	71.20%	68.90%
ADR	$413.69	$368.73	$328.87	$303.62	$251.84
REVPAR	$311.02	$277.72	$233.04	$211.71	$172.48
Gross operating margin	32.10%	33.10%	31.20%	25.40%	23.80%
Asia-Pacific					
Occupancy	69.90%	74.50%	73.80%	74.10%	67.80%
ADR	$288.44	$299.56	$267.36	$240.39	$195.80
REVPAR	$204.20	$220.02	$193.93	$175.69	$129.27
Gross operating margin	32.30%	34.50%	31.20%	29.60%	25.80%
Europe					
Occupancy	80.10%	82.30%	77.90%	70.10%	64.50%
ADR	$669.40	$637.95	$576.92	$428.95	$515.70
REVPAR	$530.01	$519.36	$455.44	$296.84	$331.49
Gross operating margin	42.10%	41.30%	39.80%	31.70%	34.10%

[1]ADR is defined as average daily room rate per room occupied.

[2]REVPAR is average room revenue per available room. It is a commonly used indicator of market performance for hotels and represents the combination of the average occupancy rate achieved during the period.

[3]Gross operating margin represents gross operating profit as a percentage of gross revenues.

Source: Company records.

EXHIBIT 2   Five-Year Financial Review (in US$ millions, except per share amounts)

	2004	2003	2002	2001	2000
Statements of Operations Data	268.80	135.18	151.87	143.92	113.23
Consolidated revenues					
Hotel Management Operations					
Fee revenues	118.72	106.06	99.12	89.49	67.54
Hotel management earnings before other operating items	71.34	62.38	58.02	51.41	31.25
Hotel Ownership Operations					
Revenues	151.54	19.71	47.60	48.27	42.56
Distribution from hotel investments	6.72	10.30	6.72	7.62	4.37
Hotel ownership earnings before other operating items	16.91	9.74	16.69	15.90	8.06
Earnings before other operating items	88.14	72.02	74.70	67.20	39.31
Net earnings (loss)	45.70	33.49	(83.55)	7.62	(135.30)
Earnings (loss) per share					
Basic and fully diluted	1.86	1.56	(3.92)	0.36	(6.49)
Weighted average number of shares (millions)	24.60	21.50	21.30	20.90	20.90
Balance Sheet Data					
Total assets	507.58	431.54	427.39	550.48	580.27
Total debt	157.02	268.80	299.71	345.63	400.40
Shareholders' equity	285.04	98.67	64.06	153.66	139.66
Other Data					
Total revenues of all managed hotels	2,373.73	2,129.68	2,058.45	1,901.98	1,514.13
Fee revenues as a % of consolidated revenues	44.20%	78.50%	65.30%	62.20%	59.60%
Percentage of fee revenues derived outside North America	31.20%	38.30%	40.90%	38.80%	35.90%
Hotel management operating margin	60.10%	58.80%	58.50%	57.40%	46.30%
Hotel management earnings before other operating items as a % of earnings before other operating items	80.90%	86.60%	77.70%	76.50%	79.50%
EBITDA	88.14	72.02	74.70	67.20	39.31
Debt, net of cash	128.69	251.55	258.61	335.10	387.07
Market price per share at year-end	50.40	31.08	21.28	18.20	14.56
Shares outstanding (millions)	25.28	21.53	21.38	21.30	20.85
Market capitalization at year-end	1,699.49	892.86	606.26	517.33	404.43
Employees	24,640	23,520	24,080	24,080	22,456

Source: Company records.

EXHIBIT 3   Major Luxury Hotels in Chicago (2005) (in US$)

Name of hotel	Affiliation	Number of guest rooms	Room rate*
Four Seasons Hotel Chicago	Four Seasons Hotels & Resorts	343	435–535
The Ritz-Carlton Hotel Chicago	Four Seasons Hotels & Resorts	435	395–535
Park Hyatt Chicago	Hyatt International	203	375–425
Renaissance Chicago Hotel	Marriott International	513	204
The Drake	Hilton International	535	255–295
The Peninsula Chicago	Peninsula Hotel Group	339	445–455
Le Meridien	Le Meridien Group	311	249
Majestica Miracle Mile	Majestica Hotels	435	455

*Ratings and pricing were obtained from Frommer's Hotel Guide online as of March 2005.
Source: Company files.

EXHIBIT 4   Major Luxury Hotels in Shanghai (2005) (in US$)

Name of hotel	Affiliation	Number of guest rooms	Room rate*
St. Regis Shanghai	St. Regis Hotels International	318	320–340
Portman Ritz-Carlton Shanghai	Ritz-Carlton Hotels & Resorts	564	250
Westin Shanghai	Westin Hotels	301	320
Sheraton (fka Westin) Tai Ping Yang, Shanghai	Sheraton Hotels & Resorts	578	230–280
Grand Hyatt Shanghai	Hyatt International	555	320–335
Pudong Shangri-La	Shangri-La Hotels & Resorts	606	330–350
Hilton Shanghai	Hilton Hotels International	720	264
Four Seasons Shanghai	Four Seasons Hotels	439	312–362

*Ratings and pricing were obtained from Frommer's Hotel Guide online as of March 2005.
Source: Company files.

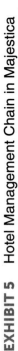

EXHIBIT 5   Hotel Management Chain in Majestica

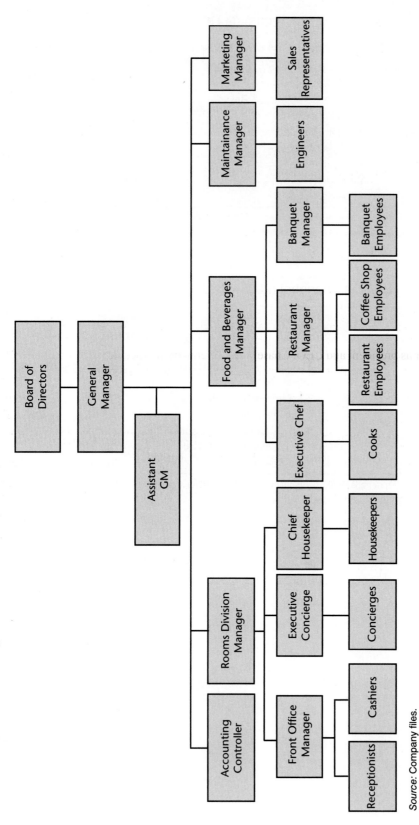

Source: Company files.

Immunovaccine (IMV): Preparing to Cross the "Valley of Death"

In 2008, Immunovaccine (IMV) was a small biotechnology company in Halifax, Nova Scotia, Canada, developing a technology that could have the potential to improve future vaccines. There were attractive external opportunities due to the changing nature of the relationship between the pharmaceutical and biotechnology industries. Nonetheless, IMV had to deal with several internal issues, such as getting the right management and scientific staff, setting the strategic direction and developing the means to raise more finances. The company had undergone a recent change of management, with Dr. Randal Chase taking over as president and CEO. Chase was a veteran of the vaccine industry and hoped to take IMV's technology from a research project to a successful commercial product.

THE PHARMACEUTICAL INDUSTRY: THE BIG PHARMA

The pharmaceutical industry consisted of a handful of large multinational companies (MNCs), such as Pfizer Inc., GlaxoSmithKline, Sanofi-Aventis, Novartis, Merck Inc. and AstraZeneca, along with a few medium-size competitors, such as Wyeth (see Exhibit 1). These large MNCs had operations around the world. At any time, they had hundreds of technologies and products in development and undergoing clinical trials. In 2006, the total revenue for the pharmaceutical industry was more than $555 billion, a 4.9 per cent growth since 2005. The four largest pharmaceutical companies represented 25.6 per cent of the total market share, with Pfizer leading the group at 8.7 per cent market share.[1]

Ella Korets-Smith and Suhaib Riaz wrote this case solely to provide material for class discussion. The authors do not intend to illustrate either effective or ineffective handling of a managerial situation. The authors may have disguised certain names and other identifying information to protect confidentiality.

IVEY

Richard Ivey School of Business
The University of Western Ontario

---

[1]Datamonitor Industry Profile: Global Pharmaceuticals, reference code 0199-0372, December 2006.

The small number of competitors in the industry was due to very high barriers to entry. Companies had to be able to finance long-term product development programs that involved high risks. The average cost of bringing a medication from research to market was estimated to be anywhere from $200 million to $2 billion, with an average cost of about $800 million[2] (see Exhibit 2). The timeline of product development from research to introduction in the market was about 10 years per product. The success rate for developing medications, starting from a research project to a marketed product, was about six per cent. This meant that the companies had to be able to absorb development costs associated with a 94 per cent failure rate. Few other industries had to sustain such losses. In 2006, the pharmaceutical industry spent more than $70 billion on drug development, but only 24 new drugs were approved. The rising costs and timelines of development led to increasing consolidation among pharmaceutical companies, with the few large ones buying out the products and human assets of the smaller companies.

The costs, timelines and success rate of bringing medications to the market had been seriously affected by the increasingly stringent and risk-averse regulatory environment. In order to be approved for use in humans, a new medication had to go through a long and expensive process of clinical trials. For example, a novel breast cancer treatment had to first show positive results in animal models and undergo extensive safety testing in animals before it was allowed for clinical trials in humans. The medication then went through at least three different phases of clinical trials, starting with very small trials to show safety in humans, then slightly larger trials to show effectiveness and lock in the dosing and finally, large sample trials to show statistically significant effectiveness before approval. Any of these steps might have to be repeated several times. Detailed documents had to be submitted and approved at every step. The trial might be stopped at any point if safety concerns arose or no efficacy was seen. Companies incurred most of the expenses in the later stages of the trials. If a medication was not approved after the final stages of clinical trials, companies could often lose around $1 billion in development costs.

However, successful products could reap major rewards. A truly novel medicine could even capture one hundred per cent of the market share for a specific treatment. A medication that was truly effective and the only option for treatment could be sold in large quantities and at a huge profit. Market forces in other industries that typically led to a decrease in price with the passage of time and an increase in volume often did not apply in the pharmaceutical industry. Niche monopolies were created and sustained for long periods of time. For example, Herceptin, an anti-cancer drug, was the first effective drug of its kind to receive United States Food and Drug Administration (FDA) approval and come on the market in 1998.[3] Though other types of cancer drugs became available by 2008, Herceptin remained the most effective and therefore the most used therapy for breast cancer. The costs of manufacturing an approved product were relatively minor compared to the price of that product. The majority of the costs were incurred in the earlier development phase that had started about 10 years prior.

In the investment community, pharmaceutical and biotechnology companies had to compete with more traditional businesses for investment dollars. The differential pattern of returns across industries created a tension when companies in different

---

[2]C. Adams and V. Brantner, "Estimating the cost of new drug development: Is it really 802 million dollars?" *Health Aff (Millwood),* 25:2, pp. 420-428.

[3]"Medsafe grants Herceptin approval," *TVNZ,* March 23, 2006; "Genentech wins approval for new Herceptin indications," *FierceBiotech,* November 16, 2006.

industries competed for the same investors to raise capital. Investors in the pharmaceutical and biotechnology industries often had to forgo short-term returns for the potential of significantly higher long-term returns.

Traditionally, the major players in the pharmaceutical industry had been very profitable and confident about their future profitability. The large pharmaceutical companies invested relatively little money into truly novel research projects since their business model of strong intellectual property protection and incremental improvements was deemed sufficient to sustain profitability.

BIOTECHNOLOGY INDUSTRY AND THE CONNECTION TO BIG PHARMA

Unlike the pharmaceutical industry, the biotechnology industry consisted of a few larger players, e.g., Amgen, Biogen Idec and Genentech, and also hundreds of significant, but small, technology-driven, innovative companies. Since most biotechnology companies were small, they could not compete head-on with the pharmaceutical industry to develop products. Very few biotechnology companies had enough funding to take a novel drug from inception to the market. For this reason, licensing, mergers and acquisitions were very common. Typically, a biotechnology company would be built around one central platform technology that it would apply to a variety of opportunities. The typical strategy for small biotech companies was to innovate, develop and patent a technology or product and then license or sell to large pharma or large biotech companies. For example, Coley Therapeutics, a biotechnology company that developed vaccines and cancer therapeutics, worked on its products up to Phase 2 of development, partnered with Pfizer for Phase 3 development and was then eventually bought by Pfizer.[4]

The key to success in the biotechnology industry was innovation, driven by science and protected by intellectual property. The patent regulatory system had been created in order to encourage innovation. Patents were filed to protect novel ideas. The basic principle was that, in exchange for disclosing the invention in significant detail, the inventor was given a period of exclusivity for 20 years during which no one else was allowed to use the invention. In the pharmaceutical and biotechnology industries, patents on inventions allowed companies to commercialize their inventions and protect their discoveries from use by other companies. However, patents in these industries were often similar in content, and the companies were forced to try novel things to gain competitive advantage.

Large pharmaceutical companies held patents for many of the commonly used medications. The traditional model for Big Pharma was to look inward for new products to continue to fill their pipelines. However, over the years, Big Pharma had become slow and innovation was increasingly difficult in large companies with well-established ways of doing things. Big Pharma were often over-focused in their areas of expertise and did not do enough to invest in, and support, exploratory research internally. In contrast, small and nimble biotechnology companies were known for their creativity. They allowed employees to explore peripheral opportunities and invested research and development dollars in new, unexplored ideas.

In 2008, the pharmaceutical and biotechnology industries were more interrelated then ever. Big Pharma had recognized the benefits of looking outward for innovation

---

[4]"Pfizer buys Coley for $164M," *FierceBiotech,* November 16, 2007.

in order to stay competitive. Biotechnology firms were seen as potential sources of competitive advantage in an environment where many pharma companies were suffering from dwindling patent coverage and fewer product pipelines. Many patents for the most common and most profitable medications were expiring and companies stood to lose billions of dollars in revenues. For example, Pfizer's major product, Lipitor, would come off patent in 2010, followed by Viagra and Geodon by 2014.[5] With the loss of these three products, Pfizer was projected to lose close to $19 billion in revenues through loss of sales to generic medications that were expected to enter the market. Generic medications were copies of the brand name medications and therefore had the same effect and the same safety profile. These medications were often much cheaper because the companies manufacturing generics did not have to take these medications through the costly development process. Though availability of generics was potentially good for consumers in the immediate term, sales of generics resulted in large losses for the pharmaceutical industry.

The year 2008 was both a good and a bad time to be in the biotechnology industry. The growing dependence of Big Pharma on products from the biotechnology industry was providing exciting merger and acquisition (M&A) and partnership opportunities for small technology-driven companies. However, in order to sell a technology, it had to be first developed to a point where Big Pharma could see value in it. For this reason, a significant upfront investment was required. The global financial crisis that started in 2007, and the overall negative outlook for the U.S. economy, made it difficult for biotechnology companies to raise capital. As investors tried to reduce their risk exposure, high-risk industries, such as biotechnology, could be hit hard. Many companies could fall into "the valley of death." This industry phrase referred to the investment period when the technology had to be developed for use on a larger scale and undergo clinical trials. If companies were unable to find financing for this essential development stage, they often did not survive. Such companies had to either give up their technology or make unfavourable deals that did not yield reasonable returns and often cost founders and researchers their jobs and savings. In the harsh world of small biotech companies, a fight for resources in this critical period could truly mean life or death for a new technology.

IMMUNOVACCINE (IMV)

In the 1980s, the fishing industry on the east coast of Canada faced a crisis of declining fish stocks attributed to an infestation of fish with seal worms. An increase in the seal population was held responsible for the increased seal worm infestation. An alternative view on the declining fish stocks was that large populations of seals were consuming too many fish. The focus on the seal population resulted in calls to increase seal hunting, while there was also public pressure to cease the practices of harvesting seals for human consumption. The chair of the biology department at Dalhousie University and a team of three other senior scientists put together a proposal to develop a single-dose birth-control vaccine for seals. A birth-control vaccine was considered a humane way to reduce the seal population. The vaccine could reduce the fertility of seals by more than 90 per cent and sustain the desired immune response for

---

[5]Maureen Martino, "Pfizer's future rests with biotech," *FierceBiotech,* September 13, 2007.

at least 10 years.[6] The single-dose vaccine was thus ideally suited to the situation, as finding and monitoring the seals for multiple doses was practically impossible.

The team filed and obtained patents for the composition and use of the new technology. The scientists wanted to develop the technology further because they saw great potential in the success of the single-dose vaccine in seals. They began evaluating the usefulness of the technology in other areas of animal health. They sought the help of a local businessperson, who used his influence and contacts in the region to secure financing from local angel investors to the order of a million dollars. This allowed Immunovaccine (IMV) to be incorporated and to purchase the patents for its technology from Dalhousie University in the year 2000.

IMV's technology, later called the VacciMax platform, was able to enhance vaccine performance. IMV thus started looking for new problems to solve with its technology. The founders were not sure where the fit was most lucrative, so the technology was initially developed on a "try and see" principle and everything was a bit of an experiment. Since the company started with animal vaccines, this was where the technology was first applied. It soon became apparent that the technology could also be applicable in the human vaccine field. In 2003, IMV hired a cancer biologist to begin experimentation with the VacciMax platform in the area of cancer prevention and treatment in humans.

MANAGEMENT

Out of the four original founders, three remained involved with the company in the roles of president and chief executive officer (CEO), chief science officer and vice-president of business development. They played key roles in the development of the technology and the creation of the company outside the walls of Dalhousie University. During his years as the dean of science, the founder-CEO had seen the problems of a business remaining within a university and believed that IMV was doing the right thing for the technology by taking it out of the academic environment. However, due to the involvement of prominent Dalhousie researchers, the company maintained a relationship with the university and was able to use some university facilities and expertise when required. The founders had a very strong belief in the technology and held an attitude that "they will all come to us soon because we have the answer." This optimistic view made them believe that a major deal with a pharmaceutical company was not very far off and would be easily forthcoming.

IMV had started out small, with almost everyone having a scientific educational background and working in the laboratory facilities. The founder-CEO handled all issues, large and small, strategic and operational. As the company became more involved in a variety of collaborative projects, another person was hired to take care of business development. This individual had prior experience in the biotechnology industry, but little understanding of the IMV technology. Since the company's strategy at this

---

[6]R.G. Brown, W.C. Kimmins, M. Mezei, J.L. Parsons, B. Pohajdak and W.D. Bowen, "Birth control for grey seals," *Nature*, 379, 1996, pp. 30-31; R.G. Brown, W.D. Bowen, W.C. Kimmins, M. Mezei, J.L. Parsons and B. Pohajdak, "Evidence for a long-lasting, single-administration contraceptive vaccine in wild grey seals," *Journal of Reproductive Immunology*, 35 (1997), pp. 43-51; R.G. Brown, W.D. Bowen, W.D. Eddington, W.C. Kimmins, M. Mezei, J.L. Parsons and B. Pohajdak, "Temporal trends in antibody production in captive grey, harp, and hooded seals to a single-administration immunocontraceptive vaccine," *Journal of Reproductive Immunology*, 35 (1997), pp. 53-64.

time was to experiment with all possible uses of its technology, his role and contribution was difficult to assess. Though IMV formed a few new collaborations, it did not succeed in attracting Big Pharma and joining the big league.

IMV's organizational structure at this time was simple (see Exhibit 3). The three founders and the local businessperson held the top executive positions in the company. The remaining staff comprised scientific researchers working under the direction of two head scientists.

FINANCING

The local businessperson's involvement made it possible for IMV to acquire more than one round of seed financing by angel investors and government agencies. IMV's technology and the involvement of a respected businessperson generated a lot of local support in the community and sustained the company in the early stages.

As the company's requirement for capital increased, funding from venture-capital (VC) firms had to be sought as the follow-up to initial angel investment. In comparison to angel investors, VC firms often invested with an eye on returns in a relatively short period of time. They often imposed stringent terms, which could include veto rights, low company valuations and seats on the board of directors. However, VCs were a source of credibility and professional advice for the companies in which they invested. At a certain stage in a company's development, if angel investors had been the only type of financing that the company had received, the investment community began to question the value of the company. Financing was a continuous struggle not just for IMV, but for every small biotech company. Much of management's time was taken up by issues of identifying sources of money, raising the money, allocating money and then repeating this cycle almost every year.

STRATEGIC DIRECTION

Since IMV's beginnings were in the field of animal vaccines, the company had started developing a proof of concept for an animal health business. IMV started a few collaborations in animal health, including one with CSL in Australia. Reflecting the continual consolidation in the industry, CSL was later bought by Pfizer Animal Health. This was a favourable turn of events for IMV, since it now had a collaboration with one of the largest animal health companies in the world. Over time, IMV also started seeing the potential of its technology for human health and decided to invest time and money towards developing proof of concept for this field.

Companies that tried to participate in both the animal and human health fields often faced difficulties due to the differences between the two businesses. In the past few years, the majority of pharmaceutical companies had developed or acquired animal health capabilities. For example, Pfizer acquired CSL to add to its Pfizer Animal Health division. Merck Inc. and Sanofi Pasteur started a very successful joint venture called Merial. Bayer Inc. bought Schering Plough, which had just recently acquired InterVet. Though both animal and human health businesses seemingly existed under one umbrella, they were generally distinct and autonomous. Very little communication went on between the two groups. Even though synergies existed, they were often overlooked.

Timelines for product development in the animal business were shorter, since regulatory barriers were much lower. Though products still had to go through trials approved by United States Department of Agriculture (USDA), these trials were conducted on smaller samples of animals, were shorter in duration and had higher risk tolerance (e.g., some product reactions in a cow could be considered within tolerable limits, whereas almost any product reactions in humans were considered unacceptable). Once the product was on the market, the profits from such products were also lower. The price of most livestock products was very low and was determined largely by what the market was willing to pay. Better, but more expensive, products were rarely introduced unless an unmet need was identified. However, this was not strictly true in the companion animal market. Pet owners would often purchase premium-priced products for their pets.

On average, profitability from developing an animal health product was lower, and therefore deals made with Big Pharma in the animal health field were not as highly valued as deals for human health products. For this reason, relatively few biotechnology companies were working towards developing technologies for animal health and the competition for getting a partnership with Big Pharma in this area was low.

In contrast to animal health, the human health business was based on high risk and high reward. The timelines for product development were longer, mainly because there were more regulatory barriers due to lower risk tolerance by the regulatory agencies. Though the industry had a few large players, there were thousands of small biotechnology firms vying for a piece of the Big Pharma budget to be spent on their technology. This competition allowed Big Pharma players to be choosy with the technologies they would support. It allowed the large players to use a "wait and see" approach, which involved watching a small player develop a technology, show its effectiveness and safety and only then decide to purchase or partner to get access to that technology. This reduced the risk for the large companies, but significantly increased the risk for the small biotech companies that had to bear the costs of the initial risky development. However, the value of the deals made in the human health field was also considerably higher than in the animal health field. Upfront payments to biotech companies in human health could be in hundreds of millions of dollars for a single technology program. Royalty rates paid to biotech companies for their technology were also relatively higher in human health.

The broad potential of IMV's technology in the animal and human health fields, as identified by the management, led to an unfocused partnering strategy. The approach essentially boiled down to work with "whoever comes first to use IMV's technology" and efforts were made to appeal to multiple groups simultaneously. The business development function was based in Toronto, while the research and development function was based in Halifax. This resulted in weak communication between these functional areas and added to the confusion. One example of this was that the information presented to potential partners was not updated regularly.

The company as a whole had very little experience in taking projects past the laboratory stage. There was little expertise in chemistry and manufacturing, which was required to make the products for human trials. No regulatory or medical expertise was available in-house that could anticipate these types of challenges. A longer-term strategic plan was not a priority since the management team believed that the technology was good enough to be picked up by large pharma or large biotech companies at a very early stage (even without trials in humans).

By 2006, it became increasingly clear that IMV was not going to get the attention of Big Pharma with the technology that had not yet left the laboratory area. Big Pharma had a lot of choice when it came to vaccine enhancement. Competing groups were working on technologies that were not like the VacciMax platform but could accomplish the same goal in different ways. This was exactly the type of innovation encouraged by the system of intellectual property protection. For example, instead of liposomes, which were used by IMV, some competing groups used what were called "virus-like particles" to achieve the delivery of antigens to the immune system in an effective way.

A major possible application of the IMV technology platform was delivering cancer vaccines. However, Big Pharma was more risk averse when it came to the area of cancer vaccines. Though a major need for new cancer treatments existed, no cancer vaccine had yet been approved for use in humans. The approval of Gardacil, a preventative cancer vaccine, by Merck Inc. in 2007 had opened the doors to the possibility of an effective therapeutic cancer vaccine. IMV's pre-clinical data for cancer vaccines in animals was extremely strong. The company was able to achieve 100 per cent tumour elimination with a single dose of vaccine in three different tests at the pre-clinical stage. Though most found this interesting and impressive, this was not enough to sign a licensing deal.

It seemed that IMV had to develop its technologies and products further before major partnerships or financial exits could materialize. One approach would be for the company to focus on the technology side of the business and license the technology to multiple partners. However, this meant reduced control over the destiny of its products and its own future. Also, returns from such licensing would always be limited to single-digit royalties.

CHANGE IN MANAGEMENT

In 2006, the company learned that the founder-CEO was not well, and some sort of leader succession planning was required. IMV thus began the search for a new president and CEO, a difficult undertaking considering that very few individuals with the right experience were available and even fewer would be looking to relocate to Nova Scotia.

Dr. Randal Chase was an ideal candidate for the position. Chase was a vaccine industry veteran. He had spent his entire career of more than 30 years in the biotechnology and pharmaceutical industries. He held a Ph.D. from the University of British Columbia and had attended the executive program of the London Business School. His past positions included president of Shire Biologics, senior vice-president — vaccines operations of Biochem Pharma, president and CEO of North American Vaccine, president and CEO of Pasteur Merieux Connaught, president and CEO of Quadra Logic Technologies Inc. and senior vice-president of Glaxo Canada Inc. Dr. Chase was an active board member of four biotechnology companies and was known in the industry for having turned around several organizations. At one point, Jacques Lapointe, president of Glaxo Canada, had introduced Chase to Francesco Belini, another veteran in the industry, by saying "he fixes companies."

Chase was impressed by the data on IMV's technology. He took on the job as interim president and CEO in 2007 and later dropped the "interim" because it looked non-committal on his part. He continued living in the Toronto area and began commuting to Halifax regularly. Shortly after Chase joined IMV, the founder-CEO passed away.

Under Chase, IMV started on the path to take its technology out of the laboratory and into the clinic, the first step towards making a vaccine product. Chase set out to develop a viable strategy for the company. He said:

> The most important thing was to build a strategic backbone for the company and develop a plan with everyone to execute to achieve that purpose. The first goal is to identify the NORTH STAR, the place where you want to end up as a company.

One can't start at the bottom and then wonder where to go. You have to fix the star and identify how to get there, derive a strategy to get there and then derive an execution plan to implement the strategy. In a small technology-driven company, it is important to put into place the strategy and you also HAVE to be a little bit flexible as well as allowing opportunities to arise. You should be ready for things, as if standing by the door waiting to run in. If the door is opened, you run, seize the opportunity and act.

Unlike the founder-CEO, Chase had no desire to deal with all issues, big and small. He had observed how much ended up on the desk of the president and CEO at IMV, and had made it clear that continuing this practice was not his intention. After Chase joined the company, the management team began to hold a series of brainstorming sessions to identify all the issues related to IMV's technology that needed to be addressed. During these meetings, Chase remained an observer, pointing out those issues that he felt were more pressing than others. His contributions were limited to arranging the issues in order of priority for the group. He allowed the team to propose what the issues were, who the best person was to deal with them and what a reasonable time in which the issue would be resolved was. He stressed that the team would be held to the deadlines they set for themselves.

Chase commented:

In small companies, everyone's jobs seem to overlap. It is the leader's major role to give people specific, identifiable responsibilities. One of my most important roles is to assess people. Right from the start, I need to decide who is competent and who are the stars of the organization. These people will play a key role in the organization's success.

Under Chase, IMV was starting on its way towards what is considered the most difficult time in a company's development. IMV had to start thinking about how to take its technology out of the laboratory and into the clinic. This would be the first step towards making a vaccine product. It could mean making IMV a different organization compared to what it had been under the founder-CEO. It could also require large funds to enable the company to commercialize its technology.

NEW STRATEGIC DIRECTION

Chase quickly identified that being a technology platform company and licensing the technology to multiple partners was not a viable strategy. IMV would not be in control of its destiny, would be limited to single-digit royalties and would always be dependant on Big Pharma for revenues. Chase decided that IMV needed to focus exclusively on the human health field and also work towards development of its own vaccine products. IMV would therefore try to divest all of its animal health business. To this end, IMV signed two licensing deals and an agreement with Pfizer Animal Health in January 2008 for use of IMV's technology in future livestock vaccines. IMV also began working to divest the rest of its animal health technology to qualified partners.

Chase started to implement the new strategic direction. He commented:

It was most important for IMV to become credible to its potential partners and investors. This credibility is built through the science and the strong pre-clinical data, which IMV has, but also through taking all the right steps towards commercialization.

In particular, IMV needed to show that we could manufacture the VacciMax platform at a large scale and that it would produce consistent results. Many liposome technology companies have failed to do so in the past, so the manufacturing issue is a real show-stopper for potential partners. We needed to show that we are in control of our product to become credible.

IMV faced a choice between developing its own manufacturing capabilities and outsourcing the manufacturing function to a contract manufacturer. Building a manufacturing capability in-house was difficult since material made for human use needed to be manufactured under Good Manufacturing Practices (GMP) guidelines.[7] All GMP manufacturing facilities needed to go through multiple steps of qualification and inspection, which were both time consuming and extremely costly.

Chase focused on ensuring that IMV's core team was in place. IMV's co-founder and chief science officer had recently retired, and a young and energetic scientist, who had been with the company since its inception in 2000, was promoted to that position. IMV had a strong biological science team but had a marked lack of expertise in most other areas required to take a product from the laboratory to clinical trials. Chase hired a scientist to head the biology group and consolidate its strengths. He also pushed for the creation of an analytical chemistry team to further test the VacciMax platform. Two research associates with chemistry backgrounds were hired as part of the chemistry team and a scientist from GlaxoSmithKline was hired as head of the team (see Exhibit 4).

The newly formed analytical chemistry team spent several months developing a method for manufacturing VacciMax vaccines. When this was accomplished, IMV transferred the method to a manufacturing facility, Dalton Pharma, in Toronto. Using IMV-dedicated equipment and under the direction of IMV's scientists, Dalton manufactured commercial-size batches of the VacciMax platform (50 litres or 200,000 doses). One year after initiation of the project, this was considered a major success for IMV. IMV continued to optimize and implement changes to the methods as necessary.

PRODUCT PIPELINE

To ensure long-term success, IMV needed to have a pipeline of vaccine products that it could move closer to the market over time. IMV's own technology, the VacciMax platform, was just one part of a vaccine product. Under the guidance of Chase, the business development team set off to identify complementary technologies and companies that would be compatible with the VacciMax platform and would provide the pieces of the puzzle for IMV to take its products into the clinic.

In 2008, IMV identified and started the process of acquiring Immunotope Inc., a clinical-stage biotechnology company based in Pennsylvania. Immunotope's technology and intellectual property comprised a large selection of active components for vaccines—the pieces that were missing from the IMV portfolio. The acquisition of Immunotope would allow IMV to start developing its own proprietary vaccine products. Immunotope would bring with it a team of scientists who would continue the discovery of other vaccines, which would then be fed into IMV's vaccine pipeline.

IMV's first product into the clinic was likely to be a small cancer vaccine product. This type of product would be directed towards a niche market and would considerably speed up IMV's progress through clinical trials. After the first clinical trials in

---

[7]*Drug and health products: Guidance documents*, Health Canada, www.hc-sc.gc.ca

cancer patients, IMV planned to initiate further trials for other products with broader market appeal, such as an influenza vaccine.

REGULATORY EXPERTISE

In order to advance the newly formulated vaccine products into the clinic, IMV would need to meet and file documentation with regulatory agencies in the United States and Canada. This required very specific regulatory expertise. Individuals with relevant regulatory experience were difficult to find and expensive to have on staff. Since IMV was a small company, Chase used his extensive network to hire an expert as a part-time consultant. Under the consultant's guidance, IMV began working with regulatory agencies to understand and plan the most efficient way forward for IMV's products.

INTELLECTUAL PROPERTY

Since intellectual property was the key to success for biotechnology companies, Chase pushed for an R&D strategy that would lead to more intellectual property creation and better protection. Several provisional applications were filed for new applications of IMV's technology. It was hoped that this type of focused research would serve to increase the value of the company in the eyes of Big Pharma. Considering the potential of the technologies, a decision was made (contrary to the previous management's decision) to protect the company's intellectual property not just in North America, but also in Europe, Asia and Australia.

COMPANY IMAGE

Besides becoming more credible, IMV needed to become more visible in the industry. Chase felt that, regardless of how good a company's science and product were, if few people knew about the company, it would not succeed in the industry. IMV thus hired a public relations (PR) firm, a small and dedicated group located close to IMV's head office in Halifax. In line with the company's new strategy, the PR firm was given a number of tasks: redesign the IMV logo, move IMV's image away from animal health into human health and get IMV on the radar of potential partners and investors. IMV thus changed to a new logo and a new slogan that positioned it as a vaccine developer, not a technology provider (see Exhibit 5).

EMPLOYEE MORALE

Chase understood that employee empowerment was crucial for a small and innovative company like IMV. In order to motivate the scientific team, Chase initiated an employee personal development program. All employees were interviewed to discuss their future goals and aspirations. Employees were encouraged to identify what they wanted to learn or courses they would like to take. The company made sure they were able to attend such courses for personal development.

Prior to Chase's involvement, the laboratory and the management office of IMV were two separate entities. Employees were rarely told of major company policies, strategic direction or successes. The founders, though very enthusiastic about IMV, often were not able to share this enthusiasm with other employees.

Chase initiated company gatherings and events, which included the monthly Lunch and Learn program. For this program, the company invited various speakers to talk to the entire group on a topic of interest. Regular updates to employees were also initiated, which became a forum for the CEO to share the latest developments, future goals and challenges. Chase emphasized that all accomplishments, even incremental ones, must be celebrated. This was the best way to motivate the scientific staff—the people on whose creativity and hard work the future of the company rested.

BUSINESS DEVELOPMENT

Chase revamped the business development function. It was co-headed by an internal person with a scientific background and experience in the company's R&D function and an experienced external consultant who would bring a wealth of negotiation experience and an extensive list of personal contacts inside Big Pharma.

Several types of partnerships could be important for IMV. Partnerships with small, science-based organizations or academics could provide access to novel technologies and research skills not currently present in the company. This was valuable for validating the technology and creating the product pipeline. Big Pharma partners could provide funding to advance products that the company might not otherwise be able to fund. They could also provide expertise in areas that IMV might not be strong in, such as conducting large clinical trials, marketing and sales. In such partnerships, a small company like IMV would usually get upfront payments for licenses, milestone payments based on progress and royalties when the product was licensed and sold by the large partner.

IMV's strategy involved finding partners for various research programs, which would all be at different stages of product development. IMV would partner for a few programs early on, in order to fund the company's development of more products. For certain programs, IMV would handle the development alone in the initial stages, typically until Phase 2, to show the value of the product through more data. This would lower the risk for partners and also increase the premiums that they would be willing to pay to IMV. Chase understood that the further IMV was able to develop its products, the more a partner would value the product. However, value maximization involved a balancing act between the money IMV was able to invest in development and the value that a potential partnership deal would place on the product.

MORE FINANCING

IMV was entering the difficult valley of death period. Large amounts of capital were required for clinical trials, but not enough data was available to show the value proposition. This was the time when it was most difficult for companies to raise the required funds. IMV needed a significantly larger round of investment than the local angel investors could provide.

Chase felt that several sources of funding would have to be considered. IMV could try to partner with Big Pharma in order to get upfront payments and fund the development of products. This had proven to be difficult so far. Other types of funding available to IMV included VC firms or the public markets accessed through an initial public offering (IPO).

The VC firm route was considered desirable since VCs could bring both money and expertise to the organization. They would also lend credibility to the company through their investment. IMV had been searching for a VC firm that would take the lead on doing due diligence and set the valuation for the financing round. This would create the conditions for others to invest in the company. Going down the VC route could potentially mean a move to the United States, since many VCs were located in the United States. Other Canadian companies were known to have resorted to this approach. IMV's acquisition of Immunotope gave the company a U.S. presence, but it remained to be seen whether this would be enough to attract U.S.-based investors. Chase was hopeful that relocation would not be required since many in IMV preferred that it remain in Canada.

Chase did not prefer the IPO route because he believed it carried many downsides. A company in IMV's position was quite far away from having products on the market. The public markets typically did not value companies in such early stages of development very highly, so even if IMV was able to get a significant amount of funding through the IPO, follow-on financing would be difficult. Investors might become reluctant to invest in a devalued, illiquid company that IMV had the potential of becoming. Several examples of post-IPO negative outcomes were available in the biotech sector, and a number of IPOs had been withdrawn in the last year.

IMV's attempts to raise finances became more challenging in the recessionary environment engendered by the global financial crisis of 2008. Investors typically opted for safe havens in such environments. Given their limited cash flows, many biotechnology companies were expected to struggle for survival through the recession. In this environment, IMV could not get VC funding and, in June 2009, the company announced that it would go public through a reverse-takeover. A reverse-takeover involved acquiring an existing public company that would act as a "shell" to enable IMV to be publicly listed on the TSX Venture (TSX-V) Exchange. The TSX-V Exchange allowed companies that had not yet reached the stringent reporting standards required for the TSX to become publicly listed. The company's financial situation until the end of 2009 is presented in Exhibits 6 through 9.

Chase commented, "All of the strategic changes and directions are currently a work in progress. The next six months will determine in what shape IMV goes forward."

EXHIBIT 1   Pharmaceutical Industry Concentration

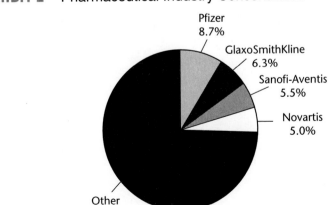

Source: Datamonitor, 2006.

EXHIBIT 2   Drug Development Costs

Stage	Description	Approximate cost
Pre-clinical	In test tubes and on animals; use wide-ranging doses to assess efficacy, toxicity, etc.	Variable
Phase 1	Small sample (20–100) of healthy humans; assess safety and dosage	$0.25–1.5 million
Phase 2	Medium sample (100–500) of healthy and patient humans; assess effectiveness, safety and dose-response	$2–20 million
Phase 3	Randomized, large sample (1,000–5,000) trials on humans; definitive assessment of effectiveness compared to existing treatments, confirm safety	$20–100 million
Phase 4 (optional)	Post-marketing safety surveillance	Variable

Note: Figures shown are approximate; actual values might differ. Costs shown are per trial—standard practice involves multiple trials per phase.

Source: MaRS Discovery District presentation (2007) on "Clinical Trials Strategy."

EXHIBIT 3   Organization Chart

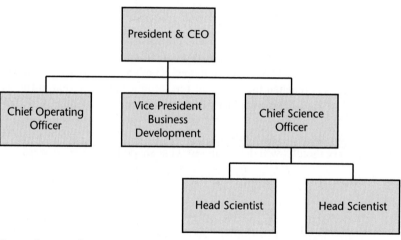

Source: Company files.

EXHIBIT 4   New Organization Chart under Randal Chase

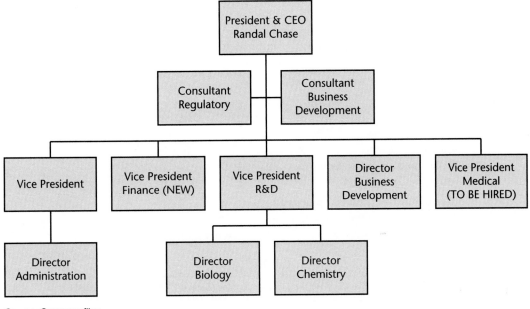

Source: Company files.

EXHIBIT 5   IMV's Logo and Image Re-Design Outcome

This combination of logo, slogan and image appears on all IMV documentation (the logo shows the company's acronym at that time, IVT).

Source: Company files.

EXHIBIT 6   Overview of Immunovaccine Financing up to December 31, 2009

Funds raised

Equity invested 2000–2009	$11.0 M
Government grants & loans	$ 9.0 M
Equity private placement September 2009	$ 8.8 M (24% institutional)
License fees collected – Animal health	$ 1.8 M
Total	**$30.6 M**

Funds remaining

Cash & equivalents	$ 7.8 M
Access to government loans	$ 2.4 M
Total working capital	**$10.2 M**

Use of private placement proceeds

- Completion of Phase 1 clinical trial
- Move an infectious disease vaccine towards the clinical stage
- Working capital to Quarter 1 – Quarter 2, 2011

Notes: All figures are in Canadian dollars. Conversion rates (Bank of Canada) for all financial Exhibits 6 to 9: CDN$1 = US$0.96 (Dec. 31, 2009), US$0.79 (Mar. 31, 2009) and US$0.97 (Mar. 31, 2008).
M stands for million.
Source: Company files.

EXHIBIT 7   Consolidated Balance Sheets

	At December 31, 2009 $	At March 31, 2009 $
Assets		
Current assets		
Cash & cash equivalents	7,777,303	713,872
Amounts receivable	595,436	24,423
Share subscription receivable	28,877	–
Prepaid expenses	183,441	47,073
Investment tax credits receivable	553,448	895,113
	9,138,505	1,680,481
Intangible assets	430,460	–
Property and equipment	322,356	345,749
	9,891,321	2,026,230
Liabilities		
Current liabilities		
Accounts payable and accrued liabilities	720,861	550,625
Current portion of long-term debt	67,821	40,829
Deferred revenues	24,000	–
	812,682	591,454

Long-term debt	5,782,959	4,716,521
	6,595,641	5,307,975
Shareholders' equity (deficiency)		
Capital stock	18,730,299	10,770,437
Contributed surplus and other	633,970	489,400
Warrants	136,672	–
Deficit	(16,205,261)	(14,541,582)
	3,295,680	(3,281,745)
	9,891,321	2,026,230

Note: All figures in Canadian dollars (see conversion rates in Exhibit 6 notes).
Source: Company financial statements.

EXHIBIT 8   Consolidated Statements of Loss, Comprehensive Loss and Deficit

	9 months to December 31, 2009 $	12 months to March 31, 2009 $
Revenue	1,420,412	105,830
Expenses		
General and administrative	942,341	1,134,890
Research and development	1,801,982	2,422,189
Business development	365,134	320,795
Stock-based compensation	154,634	259,200
	3,264,091	4,137,074
Loss from operations	(1,843,679)	(4,031,244)
Investment tax credits	180,000	299,000
Net loss and comprehensive loss for the period	(1,663,679)	(3,732,244)
Deficit–Beginning of period	(14,541,582)	(10,809,338)
Deficit–End of period	(16,205,261)	(14,541,582)
Basic and diluted loss per share	(0.05)	(0.12)
Weighted-average shares outstanding	35,473,757	30,288,44

Note: All figures in Canadian dollars (see conversion rates in Exhibit 6 notes).
Revenue figures for 12 months to March 31, 2008 are $244,815.
Source: Company financial statements.

EXHIBIT 9   Consolidated Statements of Cash Flows

	9 months to December 31, 2009 $	12 months to March 31, 2009 $
Cash provided by (used in)		
operating activities		
Net loss for the period	(1,663,679)	(3,732,244)
Charges to operations not involving cash		
Amortization of intangible assets	16,305	–
Amortization of property and equipment	55,050	95,692
Stock-based compensation	154,634	259,200
Shares issued for professional services	–	34,281
	(1,437,690)	(3,343,071)
Net change in non-cash working capital balances related to operations		
Decrease (increase) in amounts receivable	(281,533)	29,127
Increase in share subscriptions receivable	(28,877)	–
Decrease (increase) in prepaid expenses	(136,368)	125,205
Decrease (increase) in investment tax credits receivable	341,665	(94,988)
Increase in accounts payable and accrued liabilities	170,236	216,992
Increase in deferred revenues	24,000	–
	(1,348,567)	(3,066,735)
Financing activities		
Shares issued for net assets on the reverse take-over	127,511	–
Repayment of employee loan	37,500	–
Proceeds from issuance of capital stock, net of issuance costs	7,747,184	1,482,309
Proceeds from long-term debt	835,101	1,454,475
Repayment of long-term debt	(31,151)	–
Repayment of obligation under capital lease	–	(4,082)
Proceeds from exercise of stock options	174,275	–
	8,890,420	2,932,702
Investing activities		
Acquisition of intangible assets	(446,765)	–
Acquisition of property and equipment	(31,657)	(29,694)
	(478,422)	(29,694)
Net change in cash & cash equivalents during the period	7,063,431	(163,727)
Cash & cash equivalents – Beginning of period	713,872	877,599
Cash & cash equivalents – End of period	7,777,303	713,872
Cash and cash equivalents are comprised of the following:		
Cash on hand and balances (overdrafts) with banks	1,269,506	(86,128)
Short-term investments	6,507,797	800,000
	7,777,303	713,872
Supplementary cash flow information		
Income taxes paid	–	–
Interest paid	3,836	2,737

Note: All figures in Canadian dollars (see conversion rates in Exhibit 6 notes).

Source: Company financial statements.

Maple Leaf Consumer Foods—Fixing Hot Dogs (A)

Kelly Gervin hardly had the chance to get things straightened around in her new office. It was June 5, 2001, and Gervin had been the senior marketing director of the packaged meats group in the Consumer Foods division of Maple Leaf Foods (MLF) for all of four hours. She was still unpacking boxes in her office when the division's vice-president of marketing, Pat Jacobs, came flying in. He tossed a pile of papers on her desk (see Exhibits 2 to 7).

> Kelly . . . these reports I received this morning are scary. We have a serious problem in our hot dog business. Of our nine hot dog brands, five are losing significant market share and another one is down marginally. We've lost as much as 45 per cent relative to last year in one category . . . and that's just the start of it! Kelly, I need you to figure out what is going on and solve this problem, and I need you to do it quickly.

MAPLE LEAF FOODS

The MLF brand had been around in Canada for over 100 years. The organization had grown and evolved out of a number of mergers and amalgamations, but its origins could be traced as far back as 1836 when Grantham Mills opened a flour production and distribution facility in St. Catharines, Ontario. In 1991, U.K.-based Hillsdown Holdings PLC amalgamated with MLF through the purchase and merger of Canada Packers and Maple Leaf Mills. In 1995, McCain Capital Corporation and the Ontario Teachers' Pension Plan Board came together to acquire controlling interest of MLF.

Scott Hill prepared this case under the supervision of Professor Allen Morrison solely to provide material for class discussion. The authors do not intend to illustrate either effective or ineffective handling of a managerial situation. The authors may have disguised certain names and other identifying information to protect confidentiality.

Ivey Management Services prohibits any form of reproduction, storage or transmittal without its written permission. Reproduction of this material is not covered under authorization by any reproduction rights organization. To order copies or request permission to reproduce materials, contact Ivey Publishing, Ivey Management Services, c/o Richard Ivey School of Business, The University of Western Ontario, London, Ontario, Canada, N6A 3K7; phone (519) 661-3208; fax (519) 661-3882; e-mail cases@ivey.uwo.ca

Copyright © 2002, Ivey Management Services   Version: (A) 2009-10-22

Richard Ivey School of Business
The University of Western Ontario

189

Between 1995 and 2001, new systems were introduced, operations streamlined and several new acquisitions were completed.

By 2001, MLF was Canada's largest and most dominant food processor, generating nearly $4.8 billion in annual sales. The MLF organization and its products were also gaining significant momentum on the international scene. The company's operations focused on three core areas of business: bakery products, meat products and agribusiness. Each core business was composed of several independent operating companies (IOCs) and each IOC was run by a president who controlled the overall profitability and competitive strategy of the business. Under the direction of MLF chief executive officer (CEO) Michael McCain, IOCs were encouraged to follow a common set of values and strategic principles that emphasized the importance of brand equity, operating efficiencies, market leadership and continuous improvement (see Exhibit 1).

The meat products group was by far the largest of the company's core groups, with 2000 sales of nearly $2.5 billion and EBITDA (Earnings Before Interest, Taxes, Depreciation and Amortization) of $26.5 million. The group consisted of all the company's meat and meat-related businesses and included four distinct IOCs: Maple Leaf Pork, Maple Leaf Poultry, Maple Leaf International and Maple Leaf Consumer Foods. While each IOC operated independently, efforts were under way in 2001 to optimize the vertical co-ordination of IOCs within the broader MLF organization.

The packaged meats division, in which Kelly Gervin worked, was part of the Consumer Foods IOC. Consumer Foods had full responsibility for the production and distribution of all branded and value-added prepared meat products. This included bacon, ham, hot dogs, cottage rolls, a wide variety of delicatessen products, prepared turkey products, sliced meats, cooked sausage products, frozen entrees, lard and canned meats. In 2000, Consumer Foods generated in excess of half a billion dollars in sales, representing over 10 per cent of MLF's overall revenues.

Excluding commodities, the MLF hot dog portfolio of products was by far the largest meat category at MLF Consumer Foods, with over twice the dollar sales of any other MLF branded, value-added or prepared meat category within the IOC. The MLF organization had been acquiring expertise in the production and distribution of hot dogs for nearly 75 years. The organization first entered the hot dog business when Canada Packers began producing hot dogs in 1927. At that time, hot dog and sausage production was seen as a financially viable method to dispose of beef, pork and chicken trimmings. It was this profitable opportunity to use up raw material—in combination with the increasing momentum the hot dog was gaining as a cultural icon in the marketplace—that traditionally drove the business.

In 2000, total MLF hot dog sales were approximately $50 million. Industry professionals used both dollar sales and volume-by-weight to measure sales performance, and these sales correlated with a total of approximately 10.5 million kilograms of hot dogs sold. In the preceding year, total MLF hot dog sales were also approximately $50 million, but volume-by-weight had actually been approximately 11.2 million kilograms. In Gervin's words, "Our average price per kilo was going up, but there was no question we were selling less. We were losing market share and this became our primary concern."

THE HOT DOG INDUSTRY

A good deal of disagreement exists over the origin of the hot dog. People in Frankfurt, Germany, claim they invented the hot dog in 1487. Others argue that it was Johan Georghehner, a butcher from Coburg who travelled to Frankfurt to promote this product—which he called the "dachshund" because of its shape—in the late 1600s. Others in Vienna point to the name "wiener" as evidence of the product's Austrian roots.

In the United States, the origins of the hot dog industry can be traced to the arrival of a German immigrant by the name of Charles Feltman, who opened up the first Coney Island hot dog stand in 1871. In 1893, Chris Ahe, the owner of the St. Louis Browns baseball team, started selling hot dogs in his ball park. This laid the groundwork for what would become an inseparable connection between hot dogs and the game of baseball.

The actual phrase "hot dog" was coined in 1901. It all started on a cold April day in New York City, when concessionaire Harry Stevens became frustrated with losing money selling ice cream and soda. He ordered his assistant to go out and buy all the long, skinny sausages he could find and to sell them from portable hot-water tanks while yelling "get your red hot dachshund while they last!" Sports cartoonist Ted Dorgan became quite amused with the scene, and did a cartoon strip on it. When he had trouble spelling "dachshund," he substituted the term "dog," and the rest, as they say, is history.

The Industry Today

At the aggregate level, per capita demand for hot dogs was slightly higher in the United States than in Canada. In 2000, consumers in the United States spent nearly $1.7 billion on hot dogs in retail outlets. The average U.S. household purchased 7.65 pounds of hot dogs annually, which translated to about 65 hot dogs per person per year. In 2000, total Canadian hot dog market sales were just over $220 million, which represented approximately 52.5 million kilograms of hot dogs. This translated into an annual consumption rate of about 52 hot dogs per person in Canada. Sixty-four per cent of hot dogs sold in Canada were pork and meat combinations, 24 per cent were all-beef hot dogs and 12 per cent were made from poultry.

Demand for hot dogs was consistently strongest during the summer months. Since the turn of the 20th century, hot dogs in buns at baseball games, summer picnics, backyard barbecues and roadside diners had become a tradition in North American culture. Hot dog sales from May to August represented more than 44 per cent of the annual total, with July—National Hot Dog Month in the United States—leading the pack. In both Canada and the United States, hot dogs were popular at barbecues and entertainment events. Four hot dogs were consumed for every 10 baseball tickets sold, so it was projected that there would be more than 26 million hot dogs consumed in major league ballparks in 2001.

Hot dog consumption preferences were subject to significant regional differences in Canada. Western Canadian consumers had the strongest demand in Canada for beef hot dogs. The Quebec market was partial to hot dogs in a specific (lower) price segment, due to the influence of "steamies" or "toasties"—hot dogs that were prepared using unique cooking methods. (In this market, lower-priced hot dogs were considered adequate since any hot dog could be prepared in the preferred manner.) Atlantic Canada had the largest per capita consumer of low-fat hot dogs, due in part to the higher average age of the population versus other parts of Canada.

Hot dog consumption was consistently uniform throughout all income levels. Wealthy and low-income Canadians appeared to consume approximately the same volume of hot dogs on an annual basis. Larger families with five or more members tended to eat larger numbers of hot dogs, as did younger families where heads of households were under the age of 35. Children were heavy influencers in hot dog purchase decisions.

Despite their broad consumption, hot dogs had always been subject to considerable consumer scrutiny concerning their content and manufacture. For some time, consumers had been concerned about the presence of "mystery" meat in hot dogs. Both the Canadian and U.S. Departments of Agriculture required by law that meats used in hot dogs include only muscle meat. In addition to meeting this requirement, there was a movement in the industry to introduce all-meat, by-product-free hot dogs.

Competitive Landscape

In 2001, the competitive landscape of the hot dog industry in Canada was dominated by two organizations: MLF and Schneider Foods (JMS). Each had over 20 per cent share of the national market (see Exhibit 2). Other competitors were relatively small (less than one-quarter the size of MLF and JMS) and were regionally focused.

Based in Kitchener, Ontario, JMS had over 110 years of experience in producing and distributing meat products throughout the Canadian marketplace. JMS also had a reputation as a tough competitor; it fought for every inch of shelf space and was tactically reactive and retaliatory. It also knew the hot dog business well and had loyal employees.

In June of 2001, JMS led the industry, possessing over 28 per cent of the dollar share of the hot dog market in Canada. The company was not only the largest hot dog producer in Canada, it was the fastest growing. Between mid-2000 and mid-2001, JMS's dollar sales increased by nearly three per cent; in contrast, MLF's overall sales declined by just over two per cent. JMS had strong national brands that it supported with consistently effective promotional campaigns. It was also very aggressive on pricing. While MLF raised hot dog prices in both 2000 and 2001, JMS held firm to its prices and picked up market share.

In assessing JMS's performance in the Canadian hot dog market, one MLF insider commented:

> Schneider has done a great job of managing its product line from a quality perspective and overall consistency. It has done very little to its hot dog product line over the years. It has not proliferated sub-brands as we did. It did not change packaging on a regular basis as we did. It has also had great consistency in its sales and marketing staff—as we did not. Also, Schneider has done a great job managing its trade relations.
> Consumers consistently tell us that JMS means quality, heritage and great-tasting products. This is something that Consumer Foods has to overcome!

Hot Dog Segmentation

For marketing purposes, MLF segmented the hot dog market in two ways: 1) by target consumer (adult or family) and 2) by price (premium, mainstream and value/economy). While there were plenty of small niche players, both JMS and MLF competed in all major hot dog markets in Canada.

Target Segment The adult segment consisted of franks and sausages. Franks had a larger diameter, slightly more coarse emulsion (meat blend), larger particle definition and more spices than wieners. Also, franks were at least 6 inches long and, by weight, were usually about 6 per pound (2.5 ounces each). Sausages were curved and, by weight, were 3 to 5 per pound (3 to 5 ounces each). Unlike franks, which were always sold pre-cooked, sausages could be sold either uncooked or pre-cooked. In 2001, the adult segment was growing at a rate of about 11 per cent industry-wide, but this segment still represented only approximately 16 per cent of the total hot dog industry. In the adult segment, MLF's brands included ML 100's, Overlander and Shopsy's Original Recipe. JMS's primary adult segment hot dog was Juicy Jumbos.

Products targeted towards the family segment were called wieners and represented 84 per cent of overall industry sales. Wieners were also 6 inches long but had a finer emulsion than franks and, by weight, were generally about 12 per pound (1.3 ounces each). Across the industry, the family segment was growing at a rate of about two per cent per year. Industry observers believed that, increasingly, consumers were trading up towards adult categories. In the family segment, JMS offered Red Hots (in Ontario) and an identical product simply called "Wieners" for the rest of Canada. MLF's brands in the family segment included Top Dogs (Regular and BBQ), Lean 'n Lite (Regular and All-Beef), Beef Dogs and Shopsy's Beef.

Price Segment Premium hot dogs sold at a price point greater than $3.50 per pound and contained franks and sausages. In addition, Maple Leaf competed in this segment with Top Dogs Singles, which were premium priced to reflect the quality of their ingredients and high packaging and high labour costs. Mainstream hot dogs were the largest price segment and included all hot dogs priced between $2.50 and $3.50. MLF's Top Dogs, Lean 'n Lite, Beef Dogs and Shopsy's Beef fit into this segment. Hot dogs in the value segment sold for between $1.89 and $2.50 per pound. MLF's products in this segment included Maple Leaf Original (Regular and Beef), Burns (Regular, Beef and 6 + 6), Hygrade (Regular and Beef) and Shopsy's (Regular and BBQ). Wieners in the economy segment were priced under $1.89 per pound; MLF produced several private label brands in this segment, including no name and Smart Choice. JMS's Red Hots and Wieners were both considered mainstream hot dogs. However, during 2001, both products were heavily discounted (to $1.99) which gave them about a 10 to 20 per cent price advantage over MLF's value-price products.

MLF'S CURRENT BRAND STRATEGY

In mid-2001, MLF had nine different brands competing in the Canadian marketplace. Exhibit 3 summarizes the positioning of each of the Maple Leaf hot dog brands. While MLF had strong regional brands, none of the company's brands had a strong national presence. Instead, Shopsy's brands were sold only in Ontario, Burns and Overlander brands competed only in Western Canada and Hygrade was distributed only in Quebec.

For some time, MLF had emphasized different brands for different geographic regions within Canada. This development had resulted in strong brand equity in each of Canada's major regions. The Burns brand was strong in Western Canada. In the late 1990s, Burns lost substantial market share due to a cost-plus pricing structure which drove prices substantially higher than key competitors. MLF had recently fixed the pricing formula and had moved to reduce production costs, thereby stabilizing the brand. The Hygrade brand was a leader in the Quebec hot dog marketplace, possessing a 25 per cent share in that province (8 per cent nationally). The Shopsy's brand boasted an 8 per cent market share in Ontario (2 per cent nationally). All MLF hot dog products were produced at the company's manufacturing facility in Stoney Creek, Ontario. Despite brand distinctions and minor taste differences, there were essentially no major differences in the hot dog products within each price segment. At MLF, the senior marketing director did not have direct authority over, or responsibility for, manufacturing.

When interviewing for her current position, Gervin had asked about the origins of regional hot dog branding at MLF. To her surprise, no one in MLF could fully explain why the company had so many regional brands. Some believed it was the result of the company's numerous mergers and acquisitions and the desire to preserve the strength in each new brand that was acquired. Others felt the brand differences could be traced to the different consumer preferences in each region. Notwithstanding these explanations, one of the first things that Gervin noticed about the MLF hot dog portfolio was that often as many as six different MLF brands competed for shelf space in any given retail outlet at the same time.

In 1994, MLF launched Lean'n Lite brand hot dogs. The product was introduced in an effort to meet increasing consumer demands for low-fat food products. The initial launch was very successful and produced strong profit margins for the company. However, sales for Lean'n Lite peaked in 1997, and between 1998 and 2001, sales dropped every year. Many at MLF believed that the decline was the result of growing consumer unwillingness to compromise taste for low fat. However, this belief had not been substantiated with market research. Furthermore, the company was familiar with national consumer research that showed that 70 per cent of consumers were interested in low-fat products with acceptable taste.

In 1999, MLF introduced Top Dogs as a national hot dog. The launch was in response to consumer trends that seemed to emphasize healthy and natural food products and ingredients. The all-meat product was designed to appeal to both children and parents and was initially launched with vitamins and protein added. Top Dogs were the first—and only—hot dogs sold in North America that were nutritionally enhanced. The product was launched with a value price of $1.99 per package and initial consumer demand was strong. However, in the summer of 2000, the price was increased to $2.49 and sales declined noticeably. The perception was that the new price alienated many price-sensitive shoppers. Also, during this period, the formulation for Top Dogs was altered several times in an attempt to lower per unit costs. The result was a product that was priced too high and that, in the minds of many consumers, lacked good taste. By June 2001, Top Dogs had captured just 2.8 per cent of the national market (4.6 per cent in Western Canada, 2.6 per cent in Ontario, 2.3 per cent in the Maritimes and 1.7 per cent in Quebec).

Based on the initial success of Top Dogs, MLF launched Beef Dogs in 2000. The launch was designed to replace the company's existing beef hot dog product called Maple Leaf All-Beef Hot Dogs. Beef Dogs were fortified with calcium and iron. Initial taste tests were positive. However, the product's formulation came under the scrutiny of the Canadian Food Inspection Agency (CFIA), which raised concerns over the sourcing of calcium for Beef Dogs. Beef Dogs were then reformulated to incorporate a new source of calcium. Several internal taste panels concluded that the newly reformulated Beef Dogs tasted chalky and somewhat artificial. By June 2001, Beef Dog sales were down seven per cent from 2000 levels.

Kelly Gervin

Kelly Gervin had a solid professional marketing management background. Prior to joining the MLF organization, Gervin had been North American director of marketing for Moulinex, a French appliance manufacturer. She had joined Moulinex after graduating from the University of Toronto with a bachelor of science degree in microbiology.

She decided to leave Moulinex after it became apparent that her opportunities for professional growth were stagnating.

Gervin first applied for a job with MLF in 1996, in response to a newspaper advertisement. Always one to embrace a challenge, she jumped at the opportunity to join an organization she could grow with. She initially accepted the position of category manager within Consumer Foods and then spent five years in sales and 18 months in purchasing, where she was presented with the opportunity to take over her current position as senior marketing director. Reporting directly to the vice-president of marketing, Gervin had responsibility for overseeing all marketing decisions (product, price,[1] promotions, packaging and marketing communications strategies) for Maple Leaf's lines of hot dogs, sliced meats and meat snack products. While success in all categories was critical, hot dogs represented by far the largest portion of the portfolio of products for which Gervin was responsible.

Recent Developments

From 1995 through 1999, MLF went through a period of reorganization of the meats business, refocusing on vertically coordinating both its pork and poultry protein value chains. By 2000, Consumer Foods had a new president and vice-president of marketing. The president, Rick Young, had built a very successful career in sales and general management while working within the Maple Leaf companies. The vice-president, Pat Jacobs, had just arrived at Maple Leaf Consumer Foods, having built a marketing career in the packaged goods industry. During 2000, Young focused on strengthening the management team, while Jacobs concentrated on organizing a strong marketing team. As 2001 approached, it was becoming clear to Young that the team was not coming together, and he began to pay increasing attention to the marketing operations. In 2001, Young came to the conclusion that marketing needed additional changes in leadership. It was through this decision that Gervin arrived in her new role.

In Gervin's mind, the market share reports that had come to Jacobs' attention unquestionably reflected the lack of stability in the packaged meats group. Although she knew MLF's hot dog business was struggling, she was hoping that additional market analysis and customer survey data would provide her with the information needed to make appropriate decisions. On her first morning as the new marketing director, she was troubled to find much of the data she needed was simply not available. During the late 1990s, considerable research had been carried out on brands, culminating with the introduction of Top Dogs. But the individual who conducted this research had since been promoted and transferred out of the IOC. The data was now a couple of years old and had not been updated. In addition, there was essentially no consumer research relating to what drove consumers to buy MLF's hot dog products.

In addition to segment sales numbers and market share data referred to by Jacobs, Gervin found two notes of interest. One was written by the previous marketing director, suggesting that his group had been working diligently to become the low-cost producer in the value segment. On this matter, Gervin did a couple of quick calculations and realized that they weren't even close to achieving this goal. The second document of interest was a hand-written note from an unidentified source that indicated growing concerns over recent losses in market share in the adult segment. That was it.

---

[1]Pricing responsibility also fell under category management, which set price in consultation with Gervin.

To complicate matters, the group did not seem to have a business plan. Being new to the team, Gervin was unsure of the backgrounds, skills and commitments of her direct reports. Also, she could sense that morale was low—not surprising, given the recent declines in market share and changes in staff. Beyond the organizational concerns, MLF hot dogs were having real problems in the marketplace. Earlier in the morning, Gervin had placed a call to a major grocery retailer to get a sense of what that customer thought of MLF's hot dog products. The retailer was surprisingly cool to Gervin and offered the following observation: "MLF has an uncompetitive product portfolio. Quite frankly, some of your hot dogs taste lousy." Gervin had no idea whether these sentiments were shared across all of MLF's retail customers, whether this retailer was dissatisfied for other reasons, or whether the retailer was, in fact, satisfied but was playing games with her to win later concessions on price or service.

In organizing a business plan, Gervin knew that she would have to work within the constraints of the broader Consumer Foods organization. As senior marketing director, she had full profit and loss accountability for hot dogs. But others in the organization were also responsible for various determinants of profit. For example, the sales team in the field—account managers, directors and the vice-president of sales for the IOC—were in part measured by hot dog profits. Manufacturing also had a stake in the game. So while she was responsible for profits, people outside her direct control impacted how far she could go and whether her overall approach would succeed.

Decisions

As soon as Jacobs left her office, Gervin closed the door and put her phone on voice mail. She needed time to think. There was clearly good news and bad news in what she had learned on her first day on the job. The bad news was MLF's hot dog business was a mess in almost every sense of the word, and if not handled deftly, the business could go from bad to worse. The good news was that Gervin felt the business could be turned around and that it had huge up-side potential for growth and profitability. She knew this, and she believed that Jacobs and Young also believed in the huge up-side potential in hot dogs. Reversing the negative trends and moving MLF to a leadership position in the marketplace would have positive spill-over effects on the entire Consumer Foods product line and would almost certainly capture the attention of the broader MLF organization.

As the challenges of turning the hot dog business around were becoming more and more apparent, Gervin recognized the need for short-term "fixes" and a clear strategy for the future. She pulled out a pen and scratched down two questions: 1) Which hot dog segments do we most want to be in? and 2) How are we going to grow the business in these segments?

While these were simple questions, the answers would be much more difficult. As Gervin contemplated her next steps, additional questions came to mind. Should MLF even "make" hot dogs? Gervin was aware that an increasing number of companies like Nike, IBM and Matsushita were contracting all or part of their manufacturing over to others. Should hot dogs be any different? She also wondered whether the fact that MLF was Canada's largest supplier of pork and poultry products should influence a decision on the composition of hot dogs and their overall positioning in the marketplace. Gervin was also uncertain how the positioning of hot dogs might influence other products manufactured and sold by Consumer Foods. For example, how might an emphasis on the value segment affect the sales of branded lunch meats? Finally, she wondered what role brands should play in growing hot dog sales in a chosen segment. Should she emphasize a national brand or brands, and if so, what impact might national branding have on existing regional brands?

The more Gervin thought about the challenges she faced, the more questions came to her mind. She had no idea how to answer them, but she knew that a number of senior executives were waiting to hear what she had to say.

EXHIBIT 1   Maple Leaf Foods Core 7 Principles

Maple Leaf Foods' broad strategic direction is shaped by the Core 7 Strategic Principles. Continuously evolving, these 7 principles are strongly grounded in the Maple Leaf culture and provide the guiding framework for the planning and execution of the company's corporate and competitive strategies.

1. Build high-potential leadership
2. Focus on markets and categories where we can lead
3. Develop brand equity
4. Create customer value with Six Sigma processes and products
5. Be the lowest-cost producer
6. Execute with precision and continuous improvement
7. Think global

Source: Company files.

EXHIBIT 2   Canadian Market Share Analysis (as of June 5, 2001)

Company	Share in weight	Share point change in weight	$ Share	Share point change in $
MLF	19.3	−1.6	22.9	−2.1
Hub Larsen	5.0	−0.1	4.0	0.0
JM Schneider	22.6	2.7	28.2	2.9
Fleetwood	1.4	0.2	2.2	0.3
Freybe	0.8	0.2	1.5	0.3
Grimms	0.6	0.0	1.2	−0.1
Harvest	1.0	0.2	1.4	0.2
Fletchers	1.7	0.0	2.1	0.0
Lafleur	3.6	0.0	3.4	0.1
Lesters	0.4	−0.2	0.4	−0.1
Lilydale	0.2	−0.2	0.4	−0.1
Maple Lodge	4.2	−1.5	2.7	−0.7
Mitchells	3.9	0.8	5.0	1.1
Olymel	1.3	−0.2	1.3	−0.2
Control Label	32.3	−0.3	22.9	−0.2

(Latest 52 weeks)

Source: Company files.

EXHIBIT 3   Maple Leaf Foods Hot Dog Product Line (Segmentation)

	Family (wieners)	Adult (franks & sausages)
Premium (>$3.50)	• Top Dogs Singles (450g)	
Mainstream ($2.50 to $3.50)	• Top Dogs (Reg. & BBQ) • Lean 'n Lite (Reg. & Beef) • Beef Dogs • Shopsy's Beef	• Maple Leaf 100's • Overlander • Shopsy's Original Recipe
Value ($1.89 to $2.50)	• Maple Leaf Original (& BBQ) • Burns (Reg., Beef & 6 + 6) • Hygrade (Reg. & Beef) • Shopsy's (Reg. & BBQ)	
Economy (<$1.89)	• Control/private label	

Source: Company files.

EXHIBIT 4   Canadian Hot Dog Market Review (as of June 5, 2001)

	Total	Family	Adult
Last 52 weeks	Category: +2.5% ML: −5.0% JMS: +18.2%	Category: +0.7% ML: +0.7% JMS: +14.5%	Category: +11.2% ML: −44.8% JMS: +35%
Last 12 weeks	Category: +3.2% ML: −8.8% JMS: +9.6%	Category: +2.6% ML: −4.9% JMS: +10.0%	Category: +1.0% ML: −38.4% JMS: +15.5%
Last 4 weeks	Category: +4.0% ML: −9.3% JMS: +10.6%	Category: +3.1% ML: −6.5% JMS: +10.4%	Category: −1.0% ML: −30.5% JMS: +16.4%

Source: Company files.

EXHIBIT 5 Current Brand Share (as of June 5, 2001)

	1998 Volume	Share	1999 Volume	Volume variance to PY	National share	Share variance to PY	2000 Volume	Volume variance to PY	National share	Share variance to PY	2001 LE volume	Volume variance to PY	National share	Regional share	National share variance to PY
Burns	1,071,903	1.7	1,033,266	−4%	1.5	−0.2	810,295	−22%	1.1	(0.4)	711,491	(0.1)	0.9	3.8	−28%
Hygrade	2,065,039	4.6	2,171,784	5%	4.6	0	2,449,504	13%	5.1	0.5	2,630,840	0.1	5.0	22.5	16%
Lean 'n Lite	588,071	1.1	597,365	2%	1.2	0.1	448,795	−25%	0.9	(0.3)	328,384	(0.3)	0.6		−24%
ML Reg./ BBQ	2,917,099	4.9	2,512,953	−14%	3.8	−1.1	2,087,457	−17%	3.7	(0.1)	2,291,438	0.1	3.9		−1%
ML Beef	932,830	1.7	868,634	−7%	1.3	−0.4	798,928	−8%	1.5	0.2	687,283	(0.1)	1.2		−7%
Top Dogs		0	1,467,889		2.6	2.6	1,199,268	−18%	2.6	—	1,243,616	0.0	2.2		−6%
ML 100's	1,019,974	2.4	1,139,581	12%	2.4	0	710,382	−38%	1.5	(0.9)	600,205	(0.2)	1.0		−45%
Top Dogs Singles		0			0		123,572		0.2	0.2	215,655	0.8	0.3		N/A
Overlander	394,373	0.9	470,076	19%	1	0.1	416,278	−11%	0.8	(0.2)	365,957	(0.1)	0.6	2.9	−28%
Shopsy's	2,058,655	3.7	2,230,319	8%	3.5	−0.2	2,154,001	−3%	3.7	0.2	2,255,999	0.1	3.5	9.2	6%
TOTAL	11,047,944	21.4	12,491,867	13%	22.1	0.7	11,198,480	−10%	20.9	(0.8)	11,330,868	0.0	19.3		−5%

Source: Latest 52 weeks, June 2001.

EXHIBIT 6   Maple Leaf Consumer Foods: Hot Dog Margins

	Projected 2001	Actual 2000
Hot dog margins by category		
Regular	$0.44	$0.56
Adult	$0.16	$0.37
Beef	$0.24	$0.27
Better for you	$0.60	$0.75
Total	$0.38	$0.59
	Projected 2001	**Actual 2000**
Hot dog margins by brand		
Maple Leaf Regular	$ 0.71	$0.92
Maple Leaf 100's	$ 0.31	$0.47
Maple Leaf Beef Dogs	$ 0.10	$0.27
Lean 'n Lite	$ 0.35	$0.33
Top Dogs	$ 0.60	$0.78
Overlander	$(0.14)	$0.20
Hygrade	$ 0.23	$0.20
Burns	$(0.14)	$0.23
Shopsy's	$ 0.43	$0.50
Total	$ 0.39	$0.49

GP = Gross Profit

Source: Company files.

EXHIBIT 7   TL Wieners—National Tonnage Trends

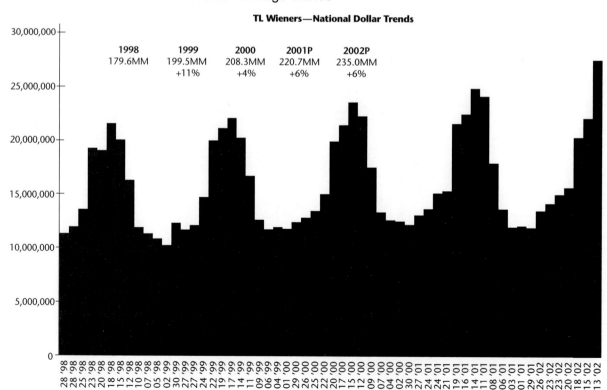

Source: Company files.

Ganong Bros. Limited

On March 30, 1995, David Ganong, president of Ganong Bros. Limited (GBL), walked out of the annual board meeting gravely concerned. Ganong Bros. Limited was a small, private family confectionery firm in St. Stephen, New Brunswick, with a wide variety of sugar confectionery and chocolate product lines. The board of directors had just reviewed the year-end financial statements, which essentially showed two consecutive years of financial losses. The board had pressed Ganong hard for a solution and had given him six weeks to return with a recommendation that would restore the company to profitability. The board had also challenged Ganong to develop a growth plan that would increase company revenues by 50 per cent. Furthermore, this growth was required to take place above and beyond changes that were made to the main business lines and was to be driven by business models, products or services that were not currently considered to be part of the core business.

THE CONFECTIONERY INDUSTRY IN CANADA[1]

The confectionery industry was divided into sugar confectionery, chocolates and other cocoa-based products and chewing gum. The major products in Canada consisted of chocolate bars (34 per cent), boxed and bulk chocolates (28 per cent), hard and soft candies (18 per cent), gum (15 per cent) and other products (5 per cent). Most Canadian confectionery goods were produced in Ontario, accounting for 67 per cent of industry employment and 65 per cent of shipments; Quebec followed closely behind.

Vanessa M. Strike prepared this case under the supervision of Professor Eric Morse solely to provide material for class discussion. The authors do not intend to illustrate either effective or ineffective handling of a managerial situation. The authors may have disguised certain names and other identifying information to protect confidentiality.

IVEY

Richard Ivey School of Business
The University of Western Ontario

---

[1]Industry, Science and Technology Canada; Agriculture and Agri-Food Canada.

Profits tended to be higher in the sugar confectionery industry than in the chocolate industry. Furthermore, return on sales in the chocolate bar industry was less in Canada than in the United States. Canada was the only country in which the four major multinational chocolate bar companies, all essentially equal in size, co-existed in the same market. The intensely competitive market conditions caused by this unique situation kept profits low. In addition, the demand for many domestic confectionery products had decreased recently, due to a lower proportion of children in Canada and a growing number of health-conscious Canadians; conversely, exports showed a slight increase.

Production facilities ranged in size from small one- and two-person operations to several plants with more than 1,000 employees at each plant. Operations with fewer than 20 employees accounted for 70 per cent of total establishments, but only 5 per cent of the industry's employment and 3 per cent of shipments. About 52 per cent of total industry employment was shared among 15 per cent of the firms that contributed 85 per cent of total shipments. Approximately 44 per cent of all products sold at retail made their way from the manufacturers to the final outlets through wholesale distributors. Most of the rest was sold directly to retail stores.

It was estimated that the industry operated at about 75 per cent of production capacity, in large part because specialized equipment was used only for seasonal product lines. Managing production, full-time employees, inventory, marketing and cash flow could thus be particularly challenging for smaller firms.

THE CHANGING CANADIAN ENVIRONMENT

The industry in Canada originally consisted mainly of independents, but in the late 1980s, consolidation led to greater concentration of market shares, resulting in the increased plant efficiencies necessary to compete internationally. There were still several large independent firms but their numbers were dwindling. Many brand-name acquisitions were also being made by American parent firms. These acquisitions were not meant to build international distribution or gain market share, but they provided a way for multinationals to prevent the erosion of their domestic market share.

There were two additional main issues facing confectionery firms in the late 1980s. The first one was free trade. Prior to free trade, the industry was protected behind a tariff wall. Canadian firms had protection from confectioneries coming into the country. Some of the product lines had tariffs as high as 15 per cent and Canadian firms going into the United States faced tariffs as low as 5 to 7.5 per cent; with free trade, the Canadian industry lost this tariff differential.

The second issue was the belief that Canadian firms would find it difficult to penetrate the U.S. market. Canadian plants typically faced scale disadvantages compared with U.S. and European firms; they were smaller, had less capacity and served smaller markets. As a result, their unit costs of production were higher. Even if Canadian firms were able to penetrate the U.S. market, they often did not have the capacity to cope with orders of the magnitude that the market dictated.

In the late 1980s, the growth of retail gourmet candy shops, such as Laura Secord, pointed to a consumer trend toward purchasing high-quality specialty products at premium prices. While many shops sold imported merchandise, they would also sell high-quality domestic products. The industry began to adapt to the more open global trading environment through a series of rationalizations that resulted in more efficient and specialized operations.

By 1994, there were 87 confectionery plants in Canada that employed almost 9,500 people and manufactured products worth more than $1.5 billion. Approximately $400 million of these were exported outside of Canada, and $540 million worth of confectionery products were imported into Canada, mainly from the United States and Europe. Foreign ownership of the industry was high, as multinationals had a major position in the industry. Approximately 60 per cent of industry shipments were accounted for by foreign-controlled enterprises located in Canada, and the number was growing.

THE CHOCOLATE GANONGS

Ganong Bros. Limited was founded in 1873 by two brothers in St. Stephen, New Brunswick (Exhibit 1). The town, situated on the U.S. border, had a population of approximately 5,000 people and was officially named "Canada's Chocolate Town."

GBL was Canada's oldest confectionery company. It had invented the widely-imitated chicken bone—a cinnamon-flavoured, pink, hard candy jacket over a chocolate centre—and was the first company in Canada to make lollipops using butchers' wooden skewers. It had invented the first five-cent chocolate nut bar in North America (originally made to take along on fishing trips), and it was the first in Canada to sell Valentine heart boxes. All GBL products were made with great professional care using only the finest ingredients.

GBL was a small company compared to the international giants, but it had done a good job of becoming "Canadian competitive." It had built a name for itself in boxed chocolates, competing with similar Canadian firms such as Moirs, Laura Secord, Smiles and Chuckles, Neilson and Lowney. GBL maintained its traditional regional markets through local allegiances and seasonal products; for example, the firm enjoyed a 30 per cent market share for its Valentine's Day chocolates in heart-shaped boxes. Yet, although GBL was a strong player in boxed chocolates in Atlantic Canada, it was a fringe player in other product lines.

PRIVATE OWNERSHIP

GBL had survived four generations remaining a private family firm. Private ownership was important to GBL as it ensured that they could remain committed to their community and employees, it provided them with the ability to make long-term decisions and it avoided the time investment of a public company. The firm's success was due in large part to its unique business ethic, where the commitment to both the community and to its workers ranked above all else, including, on occasion, profitability.

As with many family firms in Atlantic Canada, GBL's strong commitment to the community played a significant role in the firm's business decisions over the years. For example, there were several opportunities to sell the firm, but the commitment to the community and to the employees who worked in the company came first. Historically, in other small towns in Atlantic Canada, when the ownership left the community, the firm eventually left as well, and those from the town employed with the company lost their jobs. The economic benefit to Atlantic Canada provided through the location of head offices in that region could not be overstated.

While GBL was "Canadian competitive," it was not North American competitive. Several years earlier, Nicholas Highfield had expressed concerns for the future of GBL. Highfield was the president of the leading manufacturer and marketer of boxed chocolates and chocolate bars in Canada; he was also the president of the Confectioners Association and knew the industry well. Highfield had said that GBL was an "anachronism," having lived beyond its time. It was dated, the world had changed and GBL was too small. He asserted that due to its lack of critical mass, research and development capabilities, financial capacity and managerial capabilities, GBL was not big enough to compete in the world of global giants.

THE GBL BOARD OF DIRECTORS

For a family firm, GBL had a robust governance process. The board of directors was a strong, diverse board consisting of six external members and two family members. Ganong was the only person from the management team on the board, and he reported directly to the board's non-executive chairman. The board approved all business plans, financial statements and compensation. The philosophy for having such a disciplined governance structure came from Arthur Ganong two generations earlier, who said "when ownership and management are the same, you need a board of directors to protect you against yourself; it is important to not get carried away with your own ideas, and the board fills the essential role of providing a sobering second thought." Several of the board members had been selected because they owned and led firms of their own; as a result they were able to provide valuable insights based on their own successes.

DISTRIBUTION

GBL used both its own sales force and independent brokers to sell its chocolate across Canada (see Exhibit 2). In Western Canada, Ontario and the Atlantic Provinces, GBL had its own sales operation with a sales force of 29 personnel. The company employed 10 sales people and 2 managers in the West, 9 sales people and a manager in Ontario and 10 sales personnel and 2 managers in Atlantic Canada. Having its own sales force resulted in fixed costs that would be incurred whether sales were doing well or not; these fixed costs averaged about 10 per cent of sales.

In Quebec, GBL used a broker, which resulted in variable costs of approximately five per cent of sales. Typically, brokers, who carried hundreds of lines of products, were most successful with grocery goods. Brokers were less successful, however, with drug-related goods, a category in which chocolates were usually sold. As a result, despite the lower cost of using brokers, there was sometimes hesitancy to use them for confectionery products.

GANONG'S RESPONSE TO CHANGES IN THE ENVIRONMENT

St. Stephen Factory

The series of rationalizations within the industry in the late 1980s resulted in more efficient operations for most large and mid-sized firms. The modernization of competing plants and the establishment of free trade were the key determinants to build a new factory in St. Stephen. GBL felt it needed to make a quantum change and had initially looked at dramatic expansion to the old facility, but it didn't have the long-term growth prospects. In the modern world, the original factory could not compete effectively. The firm required more automation, more buying leverage for supplies and more volume to cover fixed costs. In 1988, GBL began building the new St. Stephen plant, and it moved into the facility in 1990. GBL now had a facility with the potential for expansion and growth and the ability to reduce unit costs so it could compete with the onslaught of U.S. confectioners that would come with free trade.

The near-term results of the expansion were modest. GBL had had a very solid boxed chocolate performance in the 1980s, and felt that it could capture more of the Canadian market based on extrapolating the success of boxed chocolates. While variable costs fell, fixed costs from the new facility were higher, and the company did not build sales as quickly as projected. GBL had also thought there would be an opportunity to capture some of the U.S. market as a result of changes that were taking place in the U.S. confectionery industry. The U.S. market offered potential for specialty products, particularly in large border markets. Unfortunately, GBL was not successful in extracting the customer support it anticipated and it experienced a direct profit loss from the U.S. drive.

Overseas Market

The domestic market exhibited very little real growth in the late 1980s. As a result, GBL realized it needed to become more aggressive in the export market. The company decided to go into partnership with a firm in Thailand that would provide an opening into the growing Asian market. On Halloween in 1989, GBL opened the new Bangkok factory, which coincided with the building of the St. Stephen plant.

The Thailand factory produced several products that were brought back to Canada. It also produced chocolates that were exported to the Middle East and Japan, where chocolate imports were increasing and there was a strong demand for Western consumer products. The Thailand operation did well; while it did not create purchasing synergies, it made money. It provided a small amount of royalties and dividends, and accounted for approximately seven per cent of total sales, with a four per cent total cost of goods sold.

In conducting business in Asia, the relationship with the partner was critical, and it took time to maintain. Ganong was the primary contact, and he spent significant time travelling to and from Bangkok to nurture the relationship.

Ganong in the 1990s

As GBL entered the mid-1990s, the competitive environment intensified across all lines of business from both U.S. and Canadian producers. GBL employed 207 in the factory and 15 staff. The factory was operating at 50 per cent of capacity, and not one of the individual product lines was pushing its capacity limits. As a result, GBL had to apply twice the amount of fixed cost to its products. Overhead costs were making GBL uncompetitive in various markets. For example, jelly beans were only made for part of the year, but the fixed costs associated with maintaining the floor space (depreciation, interest and taxes) still had to be paid for the entire year, resulting in slim margins and fixed costs that were high relative to the competitors. David Ganong wondered if the firm should cut selling prices to try to increase volume, or increase prices to try to cover fixed costs.

In total, GBL had 400 lines of product in 7 product categories (see Exhibit 3). The firm wanted to use its labour force, equipment and capacity to build volume;

consequently, it ended up with very broad and diverse product lines. Not all of the lines were profitable, and some were more profitable than others (Exhibit 4). With so many independent lines, it was difficult to achieve economies of scale. In addition to its own brands, GBL also made products for private labels. GBL was fairly reactive in this market, providing its services occasionally and only when asked.

ALTERNATIVES

As David Ganong walked out of the meeting, he tried to figure out what his options were, given the board mandate; he recalled some of the strategies board members had previously shared with him, ones that they had used for their own firms. He wasn't sure which ones, if any, made sense for GBL.

Alternative Financing

As a private firm, GBL had limited financial flexibility; the past two years of losses had tapped the financial resources that it required to take the business where it needed to go, and obtaining additional funds was a challenge. In addition, GBL had a covenant with the bank where all of its assets were secured, thus it was difficult to pursue other lines of financing. The firm had hit a crisis point (see Exhibits 5, 6 and 7).

Recently, GBL had been approached by an international chocolate firm who was interested in becoming a partner with a minority position. To accept such an offer was a defensive strategy, a "rear guard action," but Ganong felt they had their back in the corner. He thought this option may be feasible as the company could keep the business in St. Stephen and build the firm, while establishing an umbilical cord for the resources it lacked. Ganong's one concern was whether the partner would continue to be satisfied with a minority position. He had seen the too-often the detrimental results on the community when a family firm was purchased by an outsider, and he was wary of such offers.

Contract Packs

One of the board members had explained how he had built his business by focusing on contractual business lines. These contract packs were with firms who required a reliable source of supply that would meet certain specifications for a particular product. In return for adhering to such specific terms, these firms would sign a long-term contract that allowed the supplying firm to obtain the financing required to purchase the necessary specialized manufacturing equipment and raw materials. Such arrangements were very common in the auto industry. For example, Ford would sign a long-term contract with a car-part supplier to have that firm manufacture parts that met Ford's specific requirements.

Private Labels

The management team had also explored the possibility of becoming more proactive in the private label sector, as they felt the private label trend would grow in Canada. Private label products, also known as in-house or store brands, were products that carried a store's name as its brand or another name owned by the store, where the selling prices were relatively lower. For example, Loblaw's private label, President's Choice, produced by George Weston Ltd., accounted for 80 per cent ($23 billion) of Weston's sales.

Private labels offered wide product lines, including budget, value and premium products. The market for private-label foods was driven both by a desire on the part of retailers to increase their profit margins and by consumer demand for good quality foods at prices lower than those of brand-name products. Retailers retained a greater portion of the margin for private-label products than for brand-name products. This increased gross margin allowed them to pass on savings to their customers, who typically saved from 10 to 25 per cent.

For the manufacturer, private labels provided an opportunity for increased volume and limited competition. This ability to deliver high-quality products at a reduced price was due to lower marketing, lower overhead and lower logistical costs. To keep up with private labels, brand names had to make greater marketing efforts and keep introducing new, value-added products.

Moving the Factory

Another option Ganong considered was to move the GBL operations. As the majority of the Canadian population and a large portion of the company's market were located in Ontario, it could move the enterprise and build a new factory in a more central location. Ganong wondered if such a move would help to increase the firm's presence and thereby increase sales.

Consolidation of Manufacturing and Shared Ownership

The previous year, GBL, along with two other confectionery firms, had hired an outside consultant to complete an extensive study on the prospect of consolidating the operations of the three firms. The purpose of the study was to determine which of the firms were the lowest-cost producers for their shared product lines, and then to explore the possibility of having the lowest-cost producer complete the production runs for all three firms for that particular product. Once produced, the product would be marketed under each separate company name.

A variation of this idea was to go a step further and share the ownership of the confectionery assets that each firm had in common. The three firms would consolidate their candy production and form a new, independent company that each would have stake in. While each firm shared product lines with the other firms, they also had their own unique lines. One company, for example, produced biscuits, which the other two did not, and GBL produced chocolate, while the other two did not. The companies would continue with their own independent product lines under their original firm. GBL, for example, would continue to produce chocolate on its own premises and under the Ganong name.

MARCH 30, 1995

Ganong realized he had to convince the board of a solid plan going forward to solve these issues. At the end of the first year of losses, the management team had convinced the board they did not need to change the business model, that they would do a better job of executing the current strategy. The board was losing patience with its ability to pull out of the red. Ganong realized they had to make fundamental changes to the business model to bring the firm back to profitability, and to develop a new $10 million block of business. It was already several months into the new fiscal year, and Ganong was unsure of where to go next. The gravity of the results was apparent, and he had committed to get back to the board within six weeks. The leadership of Ganong Bros. Limited in chocolate making went back four generations, and David Ganong wanted to preserve and perpetuate the firm's rich heritage.

As he left the board meeting, Ganong thought back to his conversation with Nicholas Highfield. Highfield's comment about GBL being an "anachronism" had stuck with Ganong over the years. This comment had challenged his fundamental belief system and pushed him to succeed. Until this time, he had proven Highfield wrong, but now the words came back to haunt him as he wondered how their small, independent firm, based in the middle of nowhere, could possibly compete among the international giants.

EXHIBIT 1   St. Stephen, New Brunswick, Head Office Location

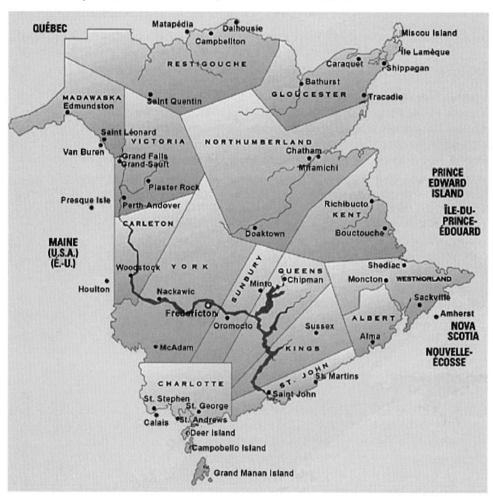

Source: National Geographic Maps, www.nationalgeographic.com/xpeditions/atlas/index.html

EXHIBIT 2 Sales Analysis for 1994 (in $000s)

	1994
Ganong brand sales	
Atlantic	7,082
Quebec	1,798
Ontario	4,485
Prairies	2,013
British Columbia	980
National accounts	3,855
Private label	1,450
Domestic Ganong sales	21,663
Export	950
United States	577
Total Ganong sales	**23,190**
Distributor line sales	
Atlantic	40
Quebec	3
Ontario	50
Prairies	93
British Columbia	42
Special	39
Private label	15
Domestic distributor line sales	282
Export	–
United States	–
Total distributor line sales	**282**
Total sales	**23,472**

Source: Company files.

EXHIBIT 3 Description of Product Categories

Packaged chocolates	Boxed or packaged chocolates; sold as gifts for birthdays, Christmas, Valentine's Day, etc.
Portable confections	Non-chocolate sugar confection bars sold for less than $1; e.g., mint rolls
Chocolate bars	Chocolate pre-packed snack that sold for less than $1
Cellos	Sugar confectionery such as jelly beans, jujubes, mints packaged in flexible packaging
Staples	Bulk product
Fruit snacks	Portable nutritional snack with real fruit content, generally marketed in the cereal section of grocery stores
Distributor lines	Products purchased and resold by Ganong Bros. Limited under another firm's name; these helped to reduce sales cost and allowed the company to employ more sales people
National accounts	Accounts with centralized warehousing where the product was shipped to a customer who redistributed it (e.g., Wal-Mart)

EXHIBIT 4   Parital Income Statement for 1994 (in $000s)

	1994
Sales–Packaged chocolates	11,817
COGS	7,326
Gross margin $	4,491
Gross margin %	38.0%
Sales–Portable confections	447
COGS	286
Gross margin $	161
Gross margin %	36.0%
Sales–Chocolate bars	1,056
COGS	542
Gross margin $	514
Gross margin %	48.7%
Sales–Cellos	4,804
COGS	3,167
Gross margin $	1,637
Gross margin %	34.1%
Sales–Staples	2,485
COGS	1,731
Gross margin $	754
Gross margin %	30.3%
Sales–Fruit snacks	2,580
COGS	1,624
Gross margin $	956
Gross margin %	37.1%
Sales–Distributor lines	283
COGS	249
Gross margin $	34
Gross margin %	12.0%
Total sales	23,472
Total COGS	14,925
Pre-discount gross margin $	8,547
Pre-discount gross margin %	36.4%
Discounts	796
Net gross margin $	7,751
Net gross margin %	33.0%

Source: Company files.

EXHIBIT 5   Partial Balance Sheet (in $000s)

	1994	1993	1992
Current assets			
Cash	48	21	15
Accounts receivables	4,263	5,049	4,155
Inventories:			
Raw materials	2,590	2,254	2,399
Work in process	245	215	260
Finished goods	1,581	1,727	1,708
Prepaid expenses	446	370	477
Total current assets	**9,173**	**9,636**	**9,014**
Long-term assets			
Land & building–Net	8,583	8,953	9,464
Machinery & equipment–Net	3,517	3,818	4,065
Notes & misc. receivables	71	70	68
Investments in/due from affiliates	16	16	16
Other investments	199	189	189
Deferred charges (pension, startup)	496	513	470
Total assets	**22,055**	**23,195**	**23,286**
Current liabilities			
Notes payable–Bank	1,479	1,478	1,238
Accounts payable	3,821	3,620	3,920
Income taxes	203	225	146
Current portion–LTD	399	422	311
Current liabilities	**5,902**	**5,745**	**5,615**
Long-term liabilities			
Long-term debt	6,236	6,593	7,029
Deferred government grants	5,027	5,372	5,663
Deferred taxes	1,135	1,317	1,097
Total liabilities	**18,300**	**19,027**	**19,404**
Capital stock	83	83	83
Retained earnings	1,463	1,864	1,569
Subordinated debt	2,209	2,221	2,230
Net worth	**3,755**	**4,168**	**3,882**
Total liabilities & net worth	**22,055**	**23,195**	**23,286**

Source: Company files.

EXHIBIT 6   Key Operating Ratios

Key operating ratios	1994	1993	1992	Industry medians*
Liquidity				
Current ratio	1.6	1.7	1.6	2.5
Quick ratio	0.7	0.9	0.7	1.1
Days' receivables	61 days	71 days	59 days	21 days
Inventory turnover	3.2	3.3	3.0	4.2
Coverage				
EBIT/interest	(0.0)	1.2	1.5	9.5
Leverage				
Fixed assets/net worth	3.2	3.1	3.5	0.5
Total debt/net worth	4.9	4.6	5.0	0.6
Operating				
Profit before taxes/net worth	−14.9%	13.3%	9.7%	13.3%
Profit before taxes/ total assets	−2.5%	2.4%	1.6%	7.7%
Net sales/fixed assets	1.8	1.9	1.7	5.4
Net sales/total assets	1.0	1.0	1.0	1.6

* For firms $10 million to $50 million in assets.
Source: Robert Morris Associates Annual Statements.

EXHIBIT 7   Statement of Operations 1992 to 1994 (in $000s)

	1994	1993	1992
Net sales	22,346	23,803	23,554
Cost of sales	14,075	13,706	13,182
Gross profit $	8,271	10,097	10,372
Gross profit %	37.0%	42.4%	44.0%
Admininstration and selling expenses	8,279	9,368	9,239
Operating profit $	(8)	729	1,133
Operating profit %	0.0%	3.1%	4.8%
Interest expense	651	625	770
Other (Income) expenses–Net*	(98)	(452)	(15)
Net profit (loss) before taxes	(561)	556	378
Income taxes	(159)	261	167
Net profit after taxes $	(402)	295	211
Net profit after taxes %	−1.8%	1.2%	0.9%

* Includes sale of old factory in 1993.
Source: Company files.

HOLEY SOLES

As of July 2007, the mood at Vancouver-based Holey Soles Holdings Ltd. (Holey Soles) was decidedly optimistic and upbeat. Sales had grown at 300 per cent in each of the last two years; the company had been ranked number four in the 2006 *Profit* magazine ranking of Canada's Emerging Growth Companies (the HOT 50); and Joyce Groote, president and chief executive officer (CEO) of Holey Soles, was a finalist for the 2007 Ernst & Young Entrepreneur of the Year award.

Holey Soles was a developer, manufacturer and distributor of injection-molded footwear. These were exciting times for the company, and Groote wanted to sustain the momentum that had been built since she had bought the company in 2004. Fast growth was stretching the capabilities of Holey Soles on all fronts, including financing, sourcing, developing new markets, maintaining high quality, expanding the product portfolio and management talent. Groote wondered what her priorities and next steps should be to continue to build a strong foundation for growth. Her goal for the company was to reach $40 million in sales by 2009.

INJECTION-MOLDED FOOTWEAR INDUSTRY

The most successful injection-molded footwear were these comfortable, colourful, funky, extremely light, holed and moulded foam clogs that had taken the world by storm.

This type of shoe was first launched in 2001, when a Quebec manufacturer, Finproject (later Foam Creations Inc.) started supplying its injection-molded clogs to several companies in North America, including Holey Soles and the company that later became Crocs Inc.

Huanglin Wang wrote this case under the supervision of Professor Jean-Louis Schaan solely to provide material for class discussion. The authors do not intend to illustrate either effective or ineffective handling of a managerial situation. The authors may have disguised certain names and other identifying information to protect confidentiality.

Ivey

Richard Ivey School of Business
The University of Western Ontario

Although the shoe industry was well established and stable, the multiple-use clogs represented an expanding niche that was enjoying rapidly growing markets as customers were beginning to recognize the benefits of these shoes.

Groote commented:

The actual market size was almost impossible to determine due to its breadth of market segments available. The market was far from saturation in North America and was virtually untouched in many other countries.

The industry operated in 18-month cycles. Most buyers placed orders at trade shows for the following year, whereas large buyers did pre-season ordering. Because most of the trade shows were in July and August, the design drawings for a new product had to be completed by January, and the products needed to be in the warehouses by early November for delivery in the spring of the following year.

The retailing industry was undergoing a major shift as large chains pushed smaller retailers out of the marketplace. Large chains were expanding their market penetration by offering a more diverse array of products. They were also expanding their customer base by entering new geographic regions. As a result, smaller independent retailers were being forced out of the marketplace. Smaller independent retailers responded by focusing on narrow product lines, narrowly defined price points, geographic markets, customer segments or a service offer. The medium-sized retailers followed a strategy of either becoming more specialized or expanding to become "department store–like."

CONSUMERS

The shoes had such a broad appeal that they crossed many traditional demographic markets: from people living an active outdoor lifestyle to those working in institutions, such as hospitals. The shoes were the new favourite footwear of people from various occupations, including gardeners, chefs, nurses, doctors, potters, beach-goers, travellers and those heading back to school. The fans said that wearing them was like walking on "pillows" or "marshmallows" and claimed the shoes could "change your life."

However, some concerns had emerged with the use of these shoes for health-care workers and for children. For example, the shoes could pose a danger if a nurse dropped a needle that landed on the shoe or if body fluids spilled into the shoe's holes. Health-care workers' reaction time was also compromised because it was more difficult to run in clogs than in traditional hospital footwear. The shoes also enabled static electricity to be generated, which could harm medical equipment that was affected by very small changes in electrical fields, such as some monitors in maternity wards. As a result, injected-molded footwear was banned at some hospitals. However, most nurses said these concerns were minor and the shoes offered more benefits than risks. Some children had sustained injuries when their shoes were caught in escalator mechanisms.

Once consumers had tried injection-molded footwear, many became addicted to the shoes and would buy several pairs. The following is a typical customer testimonial:

My wife and I have six pairs of Holey Soles between us. We use them for everything (well, almost). I use my red ones as gardening shoes and my black ones for household slippers. I use my yellow Holey Soles for walking in the water at the beach; they protect my feet from sharp objects on the ocean bottom, and if one falls off, it floats to the surface and its bright yellow colour makes it easily visible and retrievable. They're light, soft, comfortable, warm, breathable, durable, cute and fun. What a marvelous invention![1]

COMPETITION

As the clog style gained popularity, more competitors entered the industry, some of them by making the product in China and distributing it in North America. Manufacturing high-quality clogs required very expensive and specialized equipment, a high level of technical expertise and well-trained production personnel. Although many of the competitors' shoes looked similar, they were vastly different in terms of the injection-molded material, shape and fit. Consumers appeared to quickly grasp the relative merits of higher-quality clogs although some customers based their purchase decision on price alone. Many competitors lacked distribution channels and production capacity. With the exception of Crocs, the competitors that did have a reasonable quality and production capability offered shoes only in limited styles and usually in limited colours and sizes. Although Groote believed that the product was not yet a commodity, with increased players and the evolution of the product in the life cycle she anticipated that prices would decline. Exhibit 1 compares several competitors' products in key areas, including product quality, pricing, distribution channels, and range of colour and style.

Crocs was Holey Soles' main competitor. Payless Shoes, Walden's and Australia Unlimited (Nothinz shoes) had attempted to differentiate themselves by using diamond-shaped (or other-shaped) holes instead of round holes for aeration. These competitors used inferior materials and offered significantly different ranges of styles, colours and sizes. Virtually all the remaining companies made "me-too" shoes, close copies of the Crocs Beach model.

The best-known brand of these shoes, Crocs, originally called Western Brands, was based in Boulder, Colorado. It was founded by three partners who had found the unusual clog made in Canada, and dreamed of the perfect boat shoe while sailing in the Caribbean. When they added a heel strap, which became the answer to their dream shoe, Crocs was born. They launched their first model, Bulbous Beach, in November 2002, months after Holey Soles had launched its gardener's shoe.

Crocs implemented savvy marketing strategies and surged far ahead of Holey Soles. Revenues leaped from US$1.2 million in 2002 to US$109 million in 2006. By 2007, Crocs had developed more than 30 shoe models in 30 different colours, sold in 40 countries. Besides heavy marketing, Crocs moved aggressively on acquisitions. The company bought Foam Creations in 2004 and kept all the supplies for itself. In 2006, it sued Holey Soles and 10 other companies through the U.S. International Trade Commission with a claim to protect its purported intellectual property. As of July 2007, the lawsuits had not yet been resolved. Groote's interpretation was that Crocs was trying to leverage the free media exposure and undermine its competitors' public image.

In 2006, Crocs purchased, for US$20 million, Jibbitz, a manufacturer of accessories that snap into the holes in Crocs. In July 2007, it purchased Washington-based Bite, which had invented the golf sandal. Crocs planned to incorporate the Crocslite material into the soles of golf shoes, running shoes, sandals and other footwear and compete in the running shoe market, with Nike and Adidas as its main targets. Early in 2007, Crocs went public on the NASDAQ exchange, raised US$100 million and

---

[1]Jerry Steinberg, "What a marvelous invention," Holey Soles website, http://holeysoles.com/flashsite/testimonials.htm, accessed July 2007.

attained a market capitalization topping US$1 billion. It was the largest footwear initial public offering (IPO) in history. In mid-2007, Crocs' sales were 33 times that the sales of Holey Soles.

Crocs products retailed from US$25 to US$50, depending on style and whether it was a child or adult size. Crocs manufactured its footwear in China, Mexico, Brazil and Eastern Europe to increase production at a lower cost. The company attempted to supply the Canadian market from its Quebec facility. Groote believed that this activity was part of Croc's strategy to "appear" to be a Canadian company. However, Crocs was only partially successful because only a small fraction of its Beach model was actually made in Canada. Many of the Crocs products were made in China. Holey Soles' public relations department had made efforts to dispel the myth of Crocs being a Canadian company.

Crocs had considerable human and financial resources to market its products and gain market access. As of July 2007, Crocs employed approximately 5,000 employees, 500 of which worked at headquarters in Boulder. Groote described Crocs' approach:

> They use a very aggressive approach in their marketing efforts which focus primarily on serving large accounts. They pressure distributors and retailers to order large volumes or risk being placed at the bottom of the priority list. They require retailers to sign contracts stating that they will not sell any competitor products. Feedback from many of these distributors and retailers has shown that these pressure tactics were disliked. This has allowed us to win over many Crocs accounts. The combination of being a Canadian company with inventory and lower prices, strong customer service, as well as their desire to work with clients of all sizes, has attracted a number of these Crocs clients to Holey Soles.

In addition to working directly with retailers, as opposed to using distributors, Crocs told the media that it planned to open 100 stores by the end of 2007 because its products moved much faster when the full line was available. Although Crocs' initial strategy had focused on small retailers, by 2007, 75 per cent of sales came from large accounts. Crocs had its own retail outlets in eight European cities, including Amsterdam, Maastricht in The Netherlands and Sheffield in the United Kingdom. The United Kingdom was Crocs' largest European Union (EU) market.

HOLEY SOLES' STRATEGY

Early Years

Holey Soles was founded in September 2002 by Vancouver psychologist Ann Rosenberg. She operated the company in her garage and backyard. The company sold the injection-molded foam clogs made by Finproject through retailers in British Columbia. By 2004, when Crocs bought the Quebec-based manufacturer, Holey Soles' revenues were CDN$52,568. At this point, Rosenberg recruited Joyce Groote. Soon Holey Soles had designed improved clogs that were narrower and fit better than competitive offerings. Holey Soles was also the first injection-molded footwear company to outsource manufacturing to China, and it entered the U.S. market to compete with Crocs in its home market. In February 2006, revenues had grown to CDN$3.5 million, with 30 employees and 18,000 square feet of space. By February 2007, revenues had grown to CDN$11.5 million (see Exhibits 2, 3 and 4), and Holey Soles shoes were sold in

35 countries around the world, including throughout North America, Japan, Australia, New Zealand, South Africa and Europe (see Exhibit 4).

Product and Market Portfolio

Until 2005, Holey Soles focused on designing and commercializing injection-molded foam shoes. In the spring of that year, in response to customer input, three new improved styles were introduced to the market: the Social (holed-upper, no strap), the Explorer (holed-upper with strap) and the Provider (solid upper with strap). Design changes included the elimination of the flag pattern across the bridge, an altered tread pattern, an altered pattern of bumps on the heel of the footbed, a stronger black plastic rivet with the company's website address and a nylon washer. The newly designed shoes provided greater ventilation and reduced exposure of the toes. The Holey Soles logo was placed prominently on the side of the shoe and on the heel strap.

In December 2005, the overall vision of Holey Soles shifted from being a footwear company to being "a world leader using injection-foam molding as the basis for a new generation of lifestyle products that were comfortable, functional, stylish and affordable." Lifestyle was defined as "fun, pleasure things you want to do on your own time" (see Exhibit 5).

Key elements of the business strategy included providing innovative lifestyle products for all seasons, identifying new markets in areas where competitors were absent, providing superior customer service and competitive pricing, altering distribution channels as products reached market maturity and pursuing aggressive marketing for new styles. In addition to increasing its market share, Holey Soles' other goals were rapid growth, annual profitability and maintaining a loyal customer base, a satisfied workforce and industry-leading employee retention rates.

The Holey Soles brand was positioned in the upper-moderate level of the ethyl vinyl acetate (EVA) accessories market. The Holey Soles lifestyle products were high-quality, moderate to high fashion and priced at the upper-moderate level, at 10 to 15 per cent lower than Crocs. Holey Soles focused on innovation to gain a competitive edge. Innovation underpinned everything that the company did moving forward. Over time, Holey Soles continued improving the technology and design, while keeping customer service as its top priority.

The Holey Soles target consumer was sophisticated, earned a moderate to upper income and appreciated innovative style and colour coordination. Eighty per cent of purchases were made by adult females. The user breakdown was as follows: 50 per cent adults and 50 per cent children; of the adults, 80 per cent were female, 20 per cent male; and of the children, 60 per cent were female and 40 per cent were male.

By December 2006, the first lifestyle product of the Getaway Collection was launched (the Getaway shoe). This shoe transformed the technology from a single injection-foam product to a product with a cemented thermo-rubber (TR) tread, which enhanced the shoe's longevity, increased its non-slip attributes and allowed multiple colour combinations to be introduced in the same shoe. The remaining products of this collection, which were made available in the spring of 2007, included a sun hat, a beach bag and two new styles of flip-flops (Freedom and Drifter), all with the innovative TR tread system.

The launch of these new products was followed by the launch of the first product in the new Synergy Collection (Dreamerz open-toed shoe) in the spring of 2007, and then the first product in the Critter Collection, the Critter clog for children. Other elements of the Synergy Collection included a locker bag in the summer of 2007. The

Explorer style was improved with the TR tread, and several other design changes were added to make it obviously different from the first-generation product.

Holey Soles also offered private labelling for retailers. This option was available only to companies planning to use Holey Soles shoes as promotional items with their name attached using a cemented PVC logo or pad print.

In 2007, the company became an exclusive international distributor for Foyo charms. Foyo, a U.S. company, provided more than 300 styles of charms and adornments for shoes and other products. Foyo had incorporated Disney characters into their line in 2007.

International Expansion

Holey Soles launched its expansion in 2005, when the company products became available through distributors in the United States (see Exhibit 6). The first distributor was Mountain Sole, which had seen Holey Soles' advertisement and had contacted the company about distribution. By the end of 2005, Holey Soles shoes could also be found in Australia and New Zealand. A distributor based in Australia had approached Holey Soles, whose reaction was "Good, somebody loves us!" No due diligence was conducted. Within a year, the distributor stopped paying (terms were full payment 30 days upon receipt of the shipment, no down payment). After a year of the distributor giving excuses for the non-payment, Groote sent a collector and received only a fraction of what Holey Soles was owed. One year later, the former distributor had set up its own company and was selling poor versions of the shoes.

Following this experience, formal criteria were set up for the selection of distributors (e.g., enthusiasm, an active sales network, verticals served, minimum amounts ordered and a fit with Holey Soles' culture and values) and payment terms were established (30 per cent down with order, 30 per cent upon shipment from China and 40 per cent net 30 days). Holey Soles tried to avoid working with exclusive distributors. It established renewable contracts with minimum volumes, defined geographic territories and verticals. A due diligence process now included both on-site visits and Dunn and Bradstreet verification. When screening potential distributors, Holey Soles classified accounts into A, B, C and D types, according to their importance and priority. The A types were the top customers that sold branded products; B types were those customers that never offered promotional discounts; C types had promotional discounts occasionally; D types were the customers that Holey Soles did not want to establish a relationship with, for example, Wal-Mart and Costco, which under-priced their goods, a practice that would hurt the Holey Soles brand.

Groote decided to first focus on English-speaking countries, and to then roll out the product to other markets. The initial response to the product encouraged the company to participate in the world's major trade shows, where Holey Soles picked up sales in Western Europe. Holey Soles started with the United Kingdom, then Denmark, Norway, Sweden, Benelux[1], Germany and France. Next came Japan.

The international expansion extended the product life cycle. One product could be at different stage of the life cycle in different markets. For example, in July 2007, the Explorer was at the mature stage in North America, but was at the growth stage in Europe and at the launch stage in Japan.

In July 2006, Holey Soles formed a wholly owned subsidiary in Barbados called Lifestyle Products Incorporated (LPI) for the purpose of minimizing its tax burden and maximizing the efficiency of international sales efforts. This subsidiary was also

---

[1]Benelux is comprised of Belgium, The Netherlands and Luxembourg.

responsible for marketing and sales for all customers outside of Canada and Barbados. Because LPI was not able to fully service the accounts in the United States, Holey Soles continued to deal directly with that market. LPI was also responsible for new product development. Groote believed that financial considerations played a key role in shaping her approach to international business. The currency used for sales outside of Canada and for purchases from China was the U.S. dollar; however, because the U.S. dollar was depreciating, Groote was considering changing to another currency for sales in both Europe and Japan. For financial reporting, all currencies were converted to Canadian dollars.

SOURCING

History of China Suppliers and Plans

Prior to sourcing the shoes in China in 2004, Holey Soles determined through its patent attorneys that the existing shoe designs were not protected by either patent or industrial design. The first product from China arrived in Vancouver in April 2004. The moulds were designed to produce clogs that had several distinct differences from the Finproject shoe (e.g., a higher lift from the sole to the bridge of the shoe, a roomier toe box, larger massaging bumps on the footbed and a more robust material).

Initially, Holey Soles depended on a single Chinese manufacturer (YX) to provide all shoe products. The supplier was capable of producing up to 800 pairs per day using a single injection machine. In September 2005, Holey Soles contracted a second manufacturer (DK). Although clear benefits could be reaped by diversifying the supply base, quality control issues increased.

By April 2007, due to recurring quality-control problems, all production was removed from YX and transferred to DK. DK added extra injection equipment, trained its personnel and was able to produce approximately 13,000 pairs per day. Another manufacturing facility (SL) was subcontracted to provide extra production capacity of up to 5,000 pairs per day. DK was in the process of acquiring a second cementing line and installing three new injection machines in its nearby sister facility, which together would add the production of 15,000 pairs per day.

In June 2007, a third factory (XS) was identified and inspected. This facility was able to produce 30,000 pairs per day. XS was in the process of providing material and shoe samples for laboratory testing. If these tests were successful, production could begin in early 2008.

Over the past three years, production capacity had been fully utilized during the months of March through July, often restricting the number of new orders that could be accepted during this period. Through the remainder of the year, however, production capacity was reached on occasion, but generally the factories were running well below capacity. The months of November through January tended to be slow, with production at less than 30 per cent of capacity. During this period, Holey Soles focused on production of non-shoe products and on contract manufacturing. As well, the sales team was training customers to plan ahead by ordering before the busy season. Holey Soles was also seeking new customers in the southern hemisphere to even out the seasonal production demands. Online sales also offered opportunities to offset the seasonal fluctuations, as did the expanded product lines (to some degree). For example, boots and closed shoes were under development, and the Synergy Collection targeted spas and gyms, which were active throughout the year.

The transit time from China to the warehouses in North America was lengthy. Holey Soles was looking for manufacturers in other parts of the world, such as Mexico, to provide prompter delivery. Hats, bags and display racks were manufactured in factories in three Chinese cities. The Foyo charms were also manufactured in China.

Holey Soles had a strong and family-like relationship with the manufacturers in China, characterized by their close connections. Four full-time Holey Soles personnel worked in China, and Rick Walter, vice president of operations, flew to China every six weeks to coach people and to check on the product quality.

Quality Control

For each shoe style, Holey Soles and LPI created a detailed quality control checklist, which it reviewed with senior management and line personnel in the Chinese production facilities and with LPI quality-control inspectors. The packers in North American warehouses were also trained to monitor shoe quality using the same checklist prior to packaging each pair for shipment to customers. The quality was also carefully monitored both in China and in the North American warehouses through random sampling. When shoes did not meet the standards, they were pulled from inventory, and a credit was provided by the relevant Chinese manufacturer.

As new quality issues surfaced as a result of customer feedback and feedback from employees, the quality control checklists were updated, and the staff in China and North America were retrained. Management believed that Holey Soles would be able to maintain the highest quality standards in the industry.

Rejection rates from the manufacturing process ranged from 15 to 18 per cent. Rejection rates could exceed this level, especially during the first few production runs of a new style. Rejection rates in the North American warehouses ranged from 0.5 to 3 per cent, with normal ranges of less than 1 per cent for most products. The higher ranges tended to be encountered during the first few shipments of new styles, prior to the quality control checklist being established for that style. Product return rates from customers due to quality were less than 0.5 per cent; 3 to 5 per cent was the industry acceptable standards at the retail level.

Quality control for non-shoe lines was carried out by the Chinese manufacturer. Incoming shipments required a random check to verify both carton content and product quality. Quality was also verified by the packers prior to shipping product to customers. These products had no reported quality control issues.

SHIPPING

For shipping from China to the warehouses in North America, Holey Soles used Geodis Wilson, which had offices both in Vancouver and China. A&A Customs Brokers was contracted to facilitate the products across U.S. and Canadian borders. LPI customers were required to use their own freight forwarders and take ownership of the containers when they left the factory. LPI customers paid for their own shipping and duties, including the local transportation from the factory to the Chinese port.

Transit time from China to Vancouver was approximately 25 days; from China to Virginia was approximately 35 days; and from China to a European port was approximately 45 days, although this time varied, depending on customs clearance. Transit times from North American warehouses to any destination within continental North America tended to be within five days.

Shipping charges from the North American warehouses to customers were generally handled by UPS, paid by Holey Soles and charged back to the customer with a 20 per cent surcharge for administration. Other firms used for special cases included

Canada Post, the U.S. Postal Service, Federal Express and DHL. In some cases, customers arranged their own transportation from Holey Soles' warehouses.

SALES & MARKETING

Sales Force

The sales force included both internal employees and independent sales representatives. The sales manager for North America had 2 U.S. territory managers, who both supervised the independent sales force of approximately 80 and sought out new corporate accounts. A total of six independent sales representatives were hired throughout Canada. British Columbia and Ontario were both covered by two full-time employees, who supervised the independent sales force in their regions and reported directly to the sales manager. LPI sales efforts were managed by an international sales manager contracted by LPI Barbados and based in Europe. Independent sales representatives, who were able to deliver high-quality service and deal with specified geographic regions and market segments, had a significant existing customer base and reported to territory sales managers in the United States and to provincial sales representatives in Canada (see Exhibit 7).

Distribution

Holey Soles' sales channels included retail stores in North America and international distributors (businesses that bought container volumes and sold either through their own network of stores or directly to consumers in a particular country). Consumers in North America could also buy products online. The North American distribution channels, which had supported the company's high growth, had been primarily independent retailers and medium-sized chain accounts.

The relationship with accounts was important. Holey Soles expended efforts to develop relationships with clients from all levels of the organization, including the vice-president of marketing and sales, the corporate account manager and the warehouse manager. In the changing retail industry structure, Holey Soles focused on the medium-size and large corporate retail base to increase both market penetration and branding opportunities. Private labels accounted for less than five per cent of total sales.

The formalized approach to distributor selection helped Holey Soles to secure strong distributors. For example, in Denmark, Holey Soles was number one in market share. In North America, Holey Soles products were available through mid- to upper-end chain stores, including JoAnn's, Calloway's, WestLake, Home Hardware, Source for Sports, Canadian Tire, Lee Valley, Fosters Distributing and Sheplers. By 2007, the company had established a solid base of key distributors in more than 35 countries worldwide. It had also opened a new office in Brussels to increase business development and on-the-ground management of existing accounts.

Holey Soles planned to continuously develop new retail outlets in North America by approaching at least one outlet in each top priority market as a first entry into that market. Once initial sales were generated, secondary outlets in the same key market segment were approached.

Branding

Holey Soles sought legal protection for its logo and products through trademarks and patents. The company name, Holey Soles, and a stylized "HS" logo were trademarked in Canada, Australia, Europe, Japan and the United States, and an application was pending in China. The logo had been used in point-of-sale (POS) and display racks, as well as in trade show booths and sales kits. Further, LPI had applied for U.S. utility and design patents on the Eclipse hat and the Getaway, Drifter and Freedom shoes. The Critters characters were protected under copyright in the United States.

It was important to create a consistent image through identical messages carried by all communications whether they were at the point of sale or formed part of public relations or promotions. The key messages focused on Holey Soles as an innovative lifestyle company regardless of the products that were developed. A series of messages had been developed to support branding. The corporate message was Holey Soles' phenomenal growth from a garage to worldwide distribution. The brand message embodied the company's focus on innovative lifestyle products. Lastly, the product message featured products that differentiated them from other companies' products. As an example, the new Critter shoe was the first foam shoe to have embossed Critters. The central message to all of Holey Soles' promotional efforts was the focus on innovative lifestyle products and unique SoleTek and SmartCel foam technologies. Secondary messages included customer service and competitive pricing for high-quality products.

Holey Soles put effort into creating common characteristics among the products, in both look and feel. Key characteristics were the comfy foam feel for shoes and the footbed. The SmartCel foam material remained consistent, although minor modifications were made to ensure the suitability of the material for different types of products. A range of colours and sizes would also continue to be offered in new styles.

Brand recognition took time to develop. To maximize the opportunities to gain brand recognition, Holey Soles seized publicity opportunities wherever possible. The company had been very successful in gaining positive media in 2006, including a television feature on the company, which was carried on Careers TV (early 2006) and Good Morning Canada (on CTV) in spring 2007. Holey Soles had also encouraged newspaper coverage on an ongoing basis, and it issued media releases for various charity efforts, such as its donations of 13,000 shoes to the aid effort following Hurricane Katrina and 100,000 pairs of shoes to the Soles4Souls charity. The latter donation was the largest donation in the history of the charity.

An image developed for advertising, and marketing activities used fresh colours and action showing the different uses for the shoes. However, the branding was still not sufficiently strong; more effort was required to develop the Holey Soles "look" and standards that would be used in all marketing activities.

Inventory Management

By July 2007, Holey Soles had leased an 85,000 square foot office and warehouse space in Vancouver. A 55,000 square foot U.S. warehousing operation had been contracted for pick-pack-ship operations in the United States.

To ensure the full range of stock keeping units (SKUs), approximately 1,300 individual items, were constantly available in both North American warehouses, sales analyses were conducted monthly to determine the fast-moving SKUs and to observe any buying trends in styles, colours or sizes. New production orders to China were developed to reflect these trends so that stock in all SKUs would be available. During the spring and summer, these analyses were done more frequently, often weekly. The more-frequent analyses helped to identify slow-moving SKUs that could be eliminated from inventory. Analyses were done separately for the Canadian and the U.S. warehouse operations because of these countries' different preferences for size and colour.

To manage the existing collection, the U.S. warehouse required an estimated inventory level of 400,000 pairs, whereas the Canadian warehouse required an estimated 250,000 pairs. As new styles were introduced, the inventory level would need to increase by 30,000 to 50,000 pairs per style in each warehouse. Keeping enough inventory was made challenging because of several factors: an increase in the number of large customers with large orders, the preference of chain stores to select a narrow range of colours and sizes and the high cost to maintain large inventories. As a partial solution, Holey Soles struck an agreement with DK in June 2007, to enable the production and storage of inventory in China to prepare for periods of extreme demand. Holey Soles and LPI would pay 20 per cent of the purchase price for DK to maintain an inventory of up to 300,000 pairs of shoes in China. This payment would be deducted from the final payment for the inventory when it was used. This process was expected to reduce the time required to fulfill purchase orders and would ensure that Holey Soles would always have adequate quantities of high-moving SKUs ready to be shipped from China. The first implementation would begin in late 2007.

TECHNOLOGY

Research and Development: Design

Product development had been conducted at a senior level, which required part-time resources from the president, vice-president sales and marketing, vice-president operations and a full-time person to deal with day-to-day requirements and communication with China. LPI was responsible for new product development, but contracted that activity to Holey Soles in Canada. Senior-level resources were engaged at the beginning to ensure that the translation of use of SmartCel foam and SoleTek was developed in line with the company vision. The contract between LPI and Holey Soles specified the amount to be invested for product development. A Product Development Committee under LPI had been formed to select the most promising new products. A design consultant had been contracted to work with Holey Soles to develop new shoe styles. He had broad experience working in shoe design, marketing and sales for more than 40 years, mostly with Bata in a senior management position. A different designer had been contracted by Holey Soles to design bags that integrated the foam material with the bag to maximize aesthetics and functionality. Holey Soles planned to launch four to six new products every year. Each year, LPI would develop, through organic growth, two to three new collections that were compatible with key product characteristics, distribution channels and target markets.

Ideas for new products came from feedback from the sales force, distributors, retailers, customers and every employee at Holey Soles. For example, for the development of the beach bag, all the female employees gathered together to brainstorm what kind of bag they liked to have on the beach. Some said that most bags had no place for a swimsuit; others said the stuff inside the bag got wet on the beach. Therefore, Holey Soles developed a beach bag configured with the foam in front with a net for a wet swimsuit and foam on the bottom to isolate moisture.

SmartCel and SoleTek

Two key technologies were involved in the shoes: SmartCel and SoleTek. The shoes and components of the other lifestyle products were made through injection molding of polyolefin/polypropylene and ethyl vinyl acetate (EVA) compounds. The name of the combination of the various elements that comprised the foam was filed for trademark as SmartCel. The foam formed itself to a wearer's feet and offered purported medical benefits, based on comments by a number of podiatrists. The foam shoes were waterproof, slip-resistant, odour-free, lightweight and comfortable. The shoes were easy to clean and sterilize. With the exception of the Social, Provider and Explorer models of the Classic Collection, all Holey Soles footwear had SoleTek (trademark filed) thermal rubber that was fused to the sole of the shoe using the most current technology. Holey Soles was the first company to accomplish this fusing technology. The shoes with SoleTek had increased slip resistance and increased durability. All styles did not scuff or mark surfaces, were UV- and chemical-resistant and resisted fading and cracking. They were extremely lightweight and were comfortable when worn on a variety of surfaces, from concrete to sand. One of the key features of the shoes was that the material offered exceptional cushioning and uniform pressure distribution of weight during and after heel impact.

ORGANIZATION STRUCTURE

Management Team

Holey Soles was divided into four key areas: sales, marketing, operations (included finance) and customer service (see Exhibit 8 for key managers). The vice-president of sales and marketing, Marc Burchell, led the in-house sales team, which, in turn, managed the distributor and sales representative network. Burchell also led the marketing team responsible for all aspects of marketing activity. Vice-president of operations Rick Walter was responsible for finance, legal, production, inventory, shipping and receiving. The comptroller managed accounts receivable and payable, cash flow forecasting and financial reporting; payroll was contracted out to ADP Canada. CEO Joyce Groote was responsible for vision, strategic planning and direction for the entire operation, and was directly responsible for human resources and the innovative design of product development. Groote was also the chair of both the LPI board of directors and the Product Development Committee.

Growth was challenging the employees, some of whom had been with Holey Soles since the beginning. When the company began, employees needed to be generalists able to wear multiple hats. Now the company needed more and more specialists with great depth in their area. Some were able to transition to their new jobs more easily than others, and in 2007, Holey Soles was recruiting high-quality people with large company experience who commanded high salaries.

Organizational Culture

A set of corporate values were developed from the ground up, as led by the Corporate Culture Committee. The committee comprised one non-management employee from each section, and the chair was rotated for every meeting. This committee acted as a watchdog to identify issues in the company and to recommend solutions to conflicts.

This role provided a strong value system that guided many of the decisions made at all levels of the company to build a healthy, happy and productive environment, which, in turn, created a positive experience for staff and customers alike. The values were as follows:

> **Vision**—We strive for clarity and flexibility so that we can embrace the future. We encourage the sharing of new ideas by providing positive feedback and by acknowledging and rewarding superior performance.

> **Customer Service**—We provide a positive customer service experience. Our priority is to thoroughly understand the specific needs of every client, then to develop and deliver top-quality products that meet those needs.

> **Teamwork**—We work in a happy, positive environment because we like each other and enjoy working together.

> **Respect**—Our respect for individual diversity, opinions and cultures empowers us with a solution-oriented environment.

> **Honesty and Integrity**—Trust is built on a foundation of honesty and integrity, and is the cornerstone of our business.

> **Happiness and Health**—Our fun and healthy environment is important to the culture of our company and is critical to our own well being.

> **Competency and Meaningful Employment with a Future**—Individuals are mentored, coached and trained to help us hire from within whenever we can.

> **Quality**—We are committed to, and responsible for, excellence and quality control in all aspects of our work.

> **Community Involvement**—We support charitable endeavours, both as a company and as individuals, to give back to the community.[2]

Organization Development (Talent Growth and Performance Appraisal)

Everyone in the company, other than Groote and Walter, was reviewed for performance annually. Both the employee's supervisor and the human resource manager completed performance appraisals in conjunction with the employee, and then the two managers discussed the employee's performance. Key issues from evaluation and discussion were written down. The items for performance appraisal included personality–job fit, knowledge, communication skills and a series of specific criteria related to each position.

To help employees grow with the company and transform them from generalists to specialists, Groote allocated a budget for training and spent a considerable portion of her time mentoring employees.

OPTIONS

Groote recognized that the target of $40 million by 2009 was aggressive (see Exhibit 1 for previous years' revenue) but she thought it was feasible given the company's track record. She wondered whether the current strategy would deliver the expected

---

[2]Company strategic plan 2007.

results. A concern was that Holey Soles was a one-product company: Should Holey Soles diversify? What should be the role of international expansion? Where would the financing come from? What pressure would result from rapid growth on the supply chain? How should these be arranged? Could the organization and the people grow as fast as the company demanded?

EXHIBIT 1   Holey Soles' Major Competitors

	Quality	Retail price	Wholesale	Distribution	No. of colours	No. of styles
Holey Soles–shoes, accessories	High	US$25–35	US$12.50–15 (incl. shipping)	Stores, Internet	~25	6
Crocs–shoes, sports products	High	US$30–60	avg at $16.75/pr	Stores, Internet	Numerous	Numerous
Waldies–shoes	High	US$29	US$15	Recently established, not very aggressive	~20	4
Dawgs–shoes	Med	US $29	Unknown	Recently established aggressive sales strategy	Unknown	Unknown
Nothinz (Old Friends Slippers)–shoes	Med	US$27.95	US$12.50	Stores		
Airwalks (Payless Shoes)–shoes	Med	US$14.99	N/A	Corporate stores		
All Heart–shoes	Med	US$10.99	N/A	Internet	9	4
Wal-mart–shoes	Low	US$9.99	Not available	Corporate stores	2	1
Veggies–shoes	Low	not available	US$7.50	Only via container	Numerous	Numerous (copies of all others)

Source: Company strategic plan 2007.

EXHIBIT 2   Holey Soles' Financial Performance, 2004–2007 (in CDN $000s)

	FY'04	FY'05	FY'06	FY'07
Revenue	52	686	3,511	11,545

Source: Company strategic plan 2007.

EXHIBIT 3 Holey Soles' Consolidated Balance Sheet (Fiscal 2007) (in CDN$)

	02/29/08
Assets	
Cash and cash equivalent	304,717
Accounts receivable	2,707,015
Inventories	2,943,049
Prepaid expenses and deposits	213,748
Total current assets	6,168,529
Costs of property and equipment	2,469,305
Less accumulated depreciation	−809,424
Net fixed assets	1,659,881
Trademarks	29,293
Less accumulated amortization	−12,416
	16,877
Other assets	8,982
Total assets	7,854,269
Liabilities and equity	
Bank indebtedness–LOC	1,418,000
Bank indebtedness–Term loan	500,000
Accounts payable and accrued liabilities	3,065,884
Income taxes payable	−445,455*
Current portion of capital lease obligation	1,918
Current portion of term loan	50,040
Total current liabilities	4,590,387
Capital lease obligations	5,679
Term loan–BDC	104,250
Due to related parties	0
Due to shareholders	306,315
Future income taxes	26,428
Total long-term liabilities	442,672
Total liabilities	5,033,059
Common stock	120,778
Retained earnings	1,119,727
Year-to-date income	1,580,705
Total equity	2,821,210
Total liabilities and equity	7,854,269

*refund for overpayment in FY'07
Source: Company data.

EXHIBIT 4   Key Milestones in Holey Soles' Growth

Time	
2002/09	The first pair of shoes was distributed from the garage
2003/03	Holey Soles was incorporated
2004/02	Joyce Groote joined Holey Soles; sales reached $60,000
2004/04	Holey Soles switched to a Chinese manufacturer
2004/12	Groote and Walter purchased Holey Soles
2005/03	Three new styles: The Social (holed upper, no strap), the Explorer (holed upper with strap) and the Provider (solid upper with strap) were developed
2005/06	Holey Soles found 2nd Chinese manufacturer
2005/12	Holey Soles changed its vision to a lifestyle company
2006/07	Lifestyle Products Incorporated (LPI) was incorporated to manage the international expansion
2006/09	Holey Soles was named as the fastest-growing company in Canada by *Profit* magazine
2006/12	SoleTek™ was developed
2007/	Holey Soles launched the new collections
2007/08	Increased manufacture capacity

Source: Company strategic plan 2007.

EXHIBIT 5   Holey Soles' Four Collections of Lifestyle Products

Collection	Related lifestyle	Products
Classic Collection	No particular related lifestyle	• Shoes–Social, Explorer, XP2
Getaway Collection	Weekend lifestyle	• Shoes–Getaway, Freedom, Drifter • Sun hat–Eclipse hat • Beach bag
Synergy Collection	Spa and gym lifestyle	• Shoes–Dreamerz • Locker/travel cosmetic bag
Critters Collection	Kids	• Shoes–Explorer, XP2 and Getaway in kids' sizes; Critter clog • Sun hat • Colouring book

Source: Company strategic plan 2007.

EXHIBIT 6   Holey Soles' International Timetable (Selected Countries)

Time	Market entered
2003	Australia, New Zealand, USA
2004	UK, Denmark, Switzerland
2005	South Africa, Germany
2006	Japan, Benelux, Finland, Norway
2007	Italy, France, Korea, Poland, Iceland, Greenland, Caribbean, Chile
2008	Guam, United Arab Emirates, Israel

Source: Company strategic plan 2007.

EXHIBIT 7 Holey Soles' Organizational Chart (including In-house Sales Team)

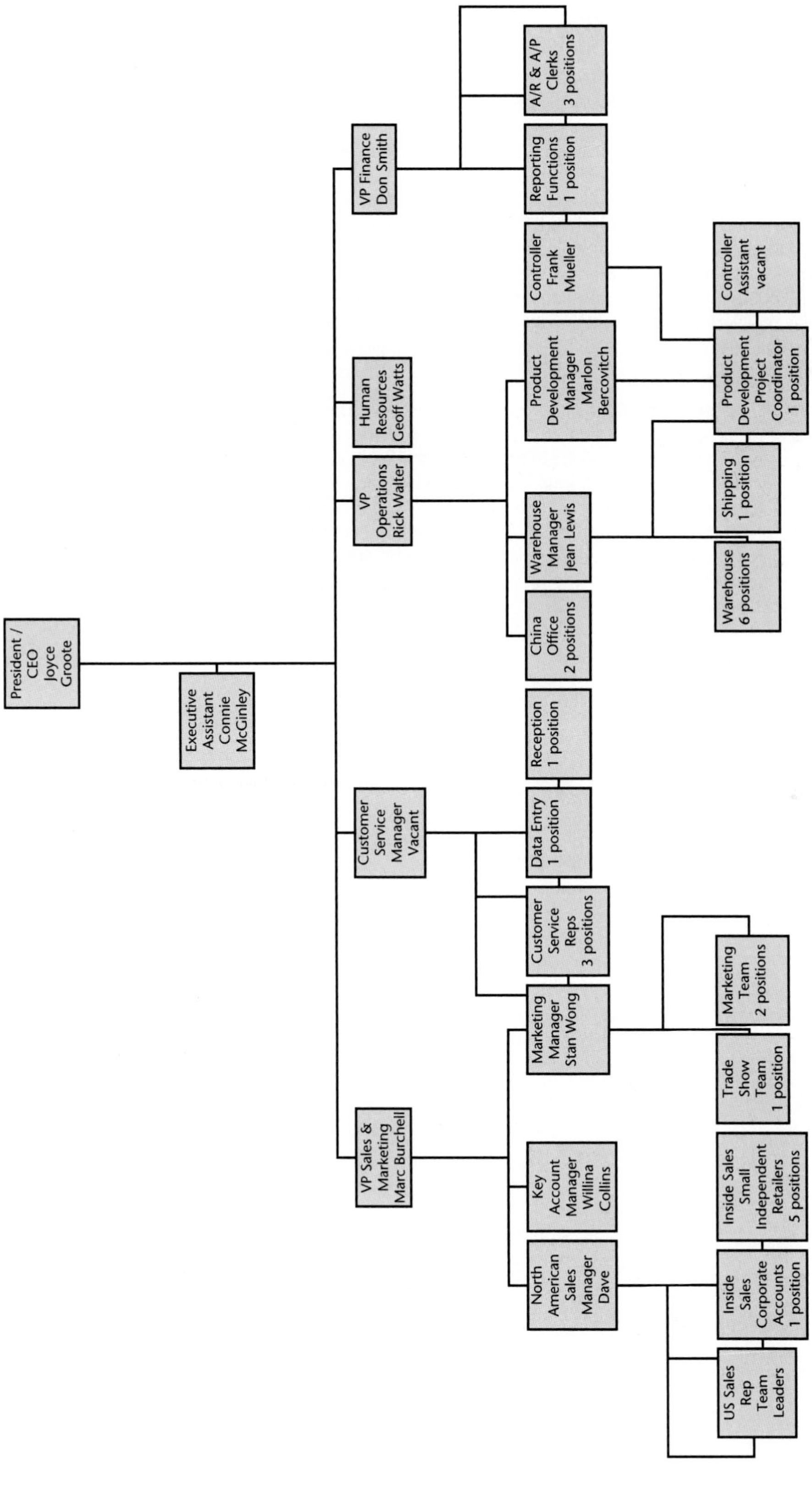

```
                                    President /
                                    CEO
                                    Joyce
                                    Groote
                                       |
                            Executive
                            Assistant
                            Connie
                            McGinley
```

- President / CEO — Joyce Groote
  - Executive Assistant — Connie McGinley
  - VP Sales & Marketing — Marc Burchell
    - Customer Service Manager — Vacant
      - Reception — 1 position
      - Data Entry — 1 position
      - Customer Service Reps — 3 positions
    - Marketing Manager — Stan Wong
      - Marketing Team — 2 positions
      - Trade Show Team — 1 position
    - Key Account Manager — Willina Collins
    - North American Sales Manager — Dave
      - Inside Sales Small Independent Retailers — 5 positions
      - Inside Sales Corporate Accounts — 1 position
      - US Sales Rep Team Leaders
  - VP Operations — Rick Walter
    - China Office — 2 positions
    - Warehouse Manager — Jean Lewis
      - Shipping — 1 position
      - Warehouse — 6 positions
    - Product Development Manager — Marlon Bercovitch
      - Product Development Project Coordinator — 1 position
  - Human Resources — Geoff Watts
  - VP Finance — Don Smith
    - Controller — Frank Mueller
      - Controller Assistant — vacant
    - Reporting Functions — 1 position
    - A/R & A/P Clerks — 3 positions

Source: Company strategic plan 2007.

EXHIBIT 8   Holey Soles' Key Managers

Joyce Groote, BSc, MSc, MBA—CEO Joyce was an experienced entrepreneur with a strong business management background who had successfully established and led seven organizations in the private and not-for-profit sector. She had considerable experience with successful interim management situations and moving organizations through periods of transition. The development of business strategies, business plans and forging partnerships and alliances had all been key elements to this success. She possessed strength in building teams and was a skilled marketing and public/media relations practitioner. She established and chaired the Life Science Angel Investor Network for British Columbia, which had raised a cumulative total of approximately $200 million for the companies that had successfully secured financing. She also started her own venture-capital fund, Building Biotech (VCC) Ltd., and raised $325,000 from 13 investors. The fund was invested in 10 companies. This corporation had managed to generate a return of about 300 per cent to date. There was one very successful exit, Victoria-based Aspreva Pharmaceuticals Corp., that generated 20-fold return. She had also been involved in a number of boards within the British Columbia community, either as a director or as a chair. She was supported by an executive assistant and the management team.

Rick Walter, BSc—VP operations Rick was an expert in start-up transition management. He had led the development or re-development of five organizations in Ontario and British Columbia. His most recent challenge was acting as transition CEO for a specialty food distribution firm with facilities in Canada and the United States. Rick had provided consulting advice to some of Canada's leading firms and organizations for business strategy, strategic partnerships and complex projects. He graduated from McGill University and had held numerous senior positions in both the public and private sector. He had also led a major national health care organization (antibiotic resistance) and had sat on numerous boards and committees. Rick was an active investor in early-stage companies and managed a small venture-capital firm.

Source: Company strategic plan 2007.

Yunnan Baiyao: Traditional Medicine Meets Product/ Market Diversification

In 2003, following an introduction through the State Food and Drug Administration of China, 3M Company, a major U.S. multinational corporation, initiated contact with Yunnan Baiyao Group Co., Ltd. (YB) to discuss potential cooperative opportunities in the area of transdermal pharmaceutical products. YB, the namesake of one of its main products, Yunnan Baiyao, was a household brand in China for its unique traditional herbal medicines that were effective in the treatment of open wounds, fractures, contusions and strains. (Hereafter, we refer to the group company as YB and the product as Baiyao.) In recent years, the company had been engaged in a series of corporate reforms and product/market diversification strategies to respond to the sea change in the Chinese pharmaceutical industry and competition at a global level. By 2003, YB was already a vertically integrated, product-diversified group company with an ambition to become an international player.

The proposed cooperation with 3M was an attractive option to YB: It was not only an opportunity for domestic product diversification, but also an opportunity for international diversification. YB had been attempting to internationalize its products for some time: An overseas department had been established in 2002 specifically for this purpose. On the other hand, YB had also been considering another option for some time, namely, whether to extend its brand to toothpaste and other healthcare products. YB had to decide which of the two options to pursue and whether it would be feasible to pursue both.

George Z. Peng wrote this case under the supervision of Professor Paul Beamish solely to provide material for class discussion. The authors do not intend to illustrate either effective or ineffective handling of a managerial situation. The authors may have disguised certain names and other identifying information to protect confidentiality.

IVEY

Richard Ivey School of Business
The University of Western Ontario

THE HISTORY OF YUNNAN BAIYAO: 1902–1998[1]

Stage 1: 1902–1955 (Qu Huanzhang Panacea Period)

In 1902, Baiyao, originally know as Qu Huanzhang Panacea, was formulated from various natural herbs by Qu Huanzhang, a highly respected practitioner of Chinese medicine. However, he did not develop the medicine solely on his own. Some stories say that he benefited from the Yi, Hani and Yao ethnic minority medicine in Yunnan Province, while others say that he may have developed his herbal formula based on the traditional medicines used by the trading caravans that travelled on the Tea and Horse Caravan Road (known in Chinese as *Chamadao*), an ancient trade route that connected Southwest China and India and functioned as the so-called Silk Road of Southwest China.

Baiyao was destined, to a certain degree, to be formulated in Yunnan Province, a mountainous area characterized by high and dangerous terrain. In bygone eras, it had been routine for local people to suffer injuries, fractures, contusions and strains from work or travel. Local people looked for ways to cure injuries, and herbal medicine was the usual solution. In addition, Yunnan Province was famous for its herbal diversity: 6,500 out of the 11,000 medicinal herbs in China were grown there, and many were unique to Yunnan Province. The combination of the need for medicine and the herbal diversity resulted in a higher likelihood of the formulation of herbal medicines in Yunnan Province.

When Baiyao was first formulated, it was known as Qu Huanzhang Panacea. The name *Baiyao* translates as "white powder," referring to the original form of the product. Because of its effectiveness in the treatment of open wounds, muscular strains, bruising and arthritis and its ability to invigorate blood circulation, this formulation gained rapid fame. It became a household name, initially in Yunnan Province and then throughout the rest of China. In 1916, the Chinese Nationalist government allowed the public sale of the product. By the 1930s, it could be found, in its powder form, on the shelves of many Chinese homes.

In 1937, Qu, the creator of the formulation, donated 30,000 bottles of Baiyao to the Chinese army, which was fighting the Japanese in the Second Sino-Japanese War. The medical power of Baiyao was further spread through word of mouth of the soldiers. The product proved so effective that from that time on, it became part of the first-aid kit of the Chinese armed forces.

The formula and manufacturing process of Baiyao had been kept secret since its formulation in 1902. Because of his refusal to reveal the formula of Baiyao, Qu was imprisoned and tortured by the then-ruling party, the Chinese Nationalist government. Before his death in captivity in 1938, at the age of 58, he secretly passed the details of the formula and manufacturing process over to his wife, Miao Lanying. In order to guard the formula, she closed down their shops and ceased the production of Baiyao.

On the fall of the Chinese Nationalist government in 1949, the new government led by the Chinese Communist Party assisted Miao Lanying in re-establishing the business. She was so grateful for this assistance that, on her death in 1955, she left the formula and manufacturing process to the government.

Stage 2: 1956–1992 (Baiyao Period)

After Miao Lanying transferred the formula and manufacturing process to the government in 1955, the production of Baiyao was started by Kunming Pharmaceutical

---

[1]Please refer to Exhibit 1, Yunnan Baiyao Timeline.

Factory under the original name of Qu Huanzhang Panacea. One year later, the name was changed to Baiyao, and the formula and the manufacturing process were listed as a top national secret and placed under national protection. At that time, Baiyao was of military importance due to the adverse international environment China was facing. Baiyao was so highly guarded and regarded by the central government that, in 1970, premier Zhou En-lai himself gave instructions that efforts should be made "to construct a specialized pharmaceutical factory to expand the production; to establish research institutes to deepen the research into Baiyao; and to establish a herb-planting base for Baiyao."

Subsequently, in 1971, Yunnan Baiyao Pharmaceutical Factory, the predecessor of the current YB, was established on the foundation of the fifth workshop of Kunming Pharmaceutical Factory. Since then, Baiyao had seen rapid development in its mass production, research and application.

Yunnan Baiyao Pharmaceutical Factory carried out a series of product development and product diversification moves. Various forms of Baiyao and related products were developed and mass produced:

- 1975: Baiyao Capsule (for internal use)
- 1984: Baiyao Plaster and Baiyao Tincture
- 1985: Gong Xue Ning Capsule (for vaginal bleeding)
- 1992: Baiyao Aerosol

In the meantime, the active ingredients of Baiyao and its source herbs had been identified, and their pharmacologic activity had been determined. This stage also saw the use of Baiyao in the treatment of a wider spectrum of diseases. Baiyao moved from being an herbal medicine with narrow usage in caring for wounds and injuries to a wide-spectrum medical product line. Baiyao products were widely used in caring for more than 300 applications in areas such as internal medicine, gynecology, pediatrics and dermatology.

Stage 3: 1993–1998

In 1993, Yunnan Baiyao Pharmaceutical Factory was reformed toward a modern enterprise system through the establishment of Yunnan Baiyao Limited Co., which was listed on the Shenzhen Securities Exchange through a successful A-share initial public offering (IPO). This public listing not only brought in much needed funds for technological upgrading, but it also standardized operations and management practices, which were prerequisites for a public company.

Despite efforts to modernize Yunnan Baiyao Pharmaceutical Factory, problems hindered its development. One of the most serious problems was the lack of unified branding. Because of historical reasons, Baiyao was also produced by three other companies in Wenshan, Dali and Lijiang under different trademarks. As a result, there was a vicious price competition that weakened the brand reputation of Baiyao as a whole. Companies sacrificed product quality to lower costs and gain market share, resulting in over-production and predatory use of wild herbal resources.

To strengthen the brand reputation of Baiyao, Yunnan Baiyao Limited Co. and the other three producers were integrated into Yunnan Baiyao Group Co. (YB) through joint shareholding in 1996. Through what was referred to as the five U's—unified production planning, unified permit number, unified trademark, unified quality standards and unified sales management—YB became the sole producer of Baiyao and the sole proprietor of intellectual property related to Baiyao. Production was reduced from 50 million vials/packages to 20 million vials/packages, alleviating the pressure on the wild herbal resources. The acquisition of the other three companies also served a product diversification purpose, because all of the other three companies also marketed a series of other products.

The unified sales management approach also enhanced product standardization and market concentration, transforming the original price competition into a competition based on quality, brand and service. As a result, the brand image and market price of Baiyao recovered quickly. YB subsequently raised the prices of Baiyao products several times to position them as quality products. The five U's also effectively curbed the counterfeiting of Baiyao, and the interest of customers was better protected.

During this period, YB took the first step in its corporate strategy by adopting both a modern enterprise system and a unified management of production and branding. The integration of the companies also diversified YB's products. This stage laid the foundation for the subsequent corporate strategies in product and market dimensions. It should be noted that even though YB was trying to reform toward a modern enterprise system and move toward a market-oriented economy, the strategic moves made during this period were basically directed by the government. It was the government that pushed for the integration of the Baiyao-producing companies and the production of Baiyao by a single company. Without government support, YB could not have repeatedly raised the prices of Baiyao products amid generally declining drug prices as a result of intensified competition and China's rapid transition toward a market economy.

THE REFORM, RESTRUCTURING AND DIVERSIFICATION OF YUNNAN BAIYAO: 1999–2003

Year 1999 (Share Diversification, Vertical Integration and Product Diversification)

In 1999, the Chinese pharmaceutical industry entered an era of drastic transition. The requirements of Good Manufacturing Practices (GMP) and Good Supply Practices (GSP) certification resulted in further industry concentration. Several diversified and vertically integrated pharmaceutical companies had appeared, reshaping the industry landscape. Firms faced the fact that they needed to either grow bigger through integration and diversification or they would be eliminated through competition.

Regardless of Baiyao's reputation and various efforts made in the past to move YB toward a market-oriented economy, by 1999, YB was still basically a state-owned company. Its resources were mainly allocated to production, and its sales department consisted of only a dozen staff members waiting for customers to come. YB could not respond to the rapidly changing market situation. As a consequence, revenue in 1998 dropped RMB8 million compared with the previous year. In 1999, the chief executive officer (CEO) of YB was replaced by Wang Minghui.

Under Wang's leadership, YB underwent a series of reforms, restructurings and strategic moves toward product and market diversification. In 1999, Hongta Group became YB's second-largest shareholder, and as a result, YB diversified its share structure. YB also acquired Yunnan Pharmaceutical Trading Co. and Tian Zi Hong

Pharmaceutical Co. Through the distribution channels of the former, YB achieved forward vertical integration into distribution, while through the latter, YB diversified its offerings into the production of decocted (concentrated) pieces. These simultaneous activities moved YB in the direction of becoming a diversified and vertically integrated player in the Chinese pharmaceutical industry.

In the same year, YB established its e-Commerce Co. Ltd. to build its nation-wide sales network. Previously, YB had a negligible sales force and its resources were mainly allocated to production, like many other state-owned companies. Because Wang had a background in sales, he saw the importance of a sales network during a time when China was moving toward a market economy. YB used the e-Commerce Co. Ltd. as a platform on which to build its sales offices across the country. The e-Commerce Co. Ltd. also served as a platform for internal entrepreneurship: YB regarded the 800-plus salespersons as internal entrepreneurs who used YB's e-commerce platform to set up sales offices. These salespersons were hired based on competition and were motivated to compete with each other through a benchmarked incentive plan on a yearly basis. With the establishment of a sales network, YB allocated more resources to marketing, which played a decisive role in YB's competition with other pharmaceutical companies.

Year 2000 (Research & Development Reforms)

In 2000, YB also made efforts to build its research and development (R&D) system, based on the belief that a competitive enterprise must have strong R&D capabilities. In September, YB established a Medicinal Herb Research Institute (MHRI) by integrating its three originally independent R&D entities: the National Postdoctoral Research Station, the Technology Center and the Research Institute. The integration of the originally dispersed units pooled their resources and laid the foundation for future R&D to exploit synergy and scale.

With the establishment of MHRI, YB also adopted new systems of R&D operation, including the Chief Scientist System and the R&D Cooperative System. The Chief Scientist System motivated scientists by linking their income to their scientific output. A series of awards was set up for the purpose of motivating scientists and spurring their creativity, including the stage output award, the subproject award, the risk reduction award for timely termination of unfruitful projects, the cost reduction award, the project early/on-time delivery award, and so on. Chief scientists and their team members who made significant R&D contribution would be given a substantial reward. Through the R&D Cooperative System, YB in fact established a society-wide and open R&D system, maximally using society-wide resources and successfully implementing a "brain-borrowing" strategy. YB cooperated with a number of universities and research institutes in a series of cooperative agreements. A number of national experts were hired by YB to serve as chief scientists. Through new methods of R&D operation, YB solved more than 20 technical problems and developed a series of new products.

Year 2001 (Organizational Restructuring and Management Reform)

On the foundation of achievements made in 1999 and 2000 in marketing and R&D reform, YB forged ahead to carry out fundamental organizational restructuring in 2001. First, YB streamlined its structure by reducing the number of departments. Functional departments with overlapping functions were either eliminated or merged, and administrative departments were reduced. In all, the number of departments was reduced from 17 to 12, resulting in higher functional and administrative efficiency.

Secondly, YB underwent drastic management reform by adopting a compensation point system, an Enterprise Resource Planning (ERP) system and a production order system. Through cooperation with Tsinghua University, YB clarified 158 jobs by assigning compensation points for each job position, based on detailed job descriptions. YB broke away from the traditional egalitarian compensation system and made a transition towards skills-based and contribution-based compensation systems. YB also established eight cost centres and implemented an ERP system to carry out cost and benefit accounting for these cost centres. The ERP system was also linked to the compensation point system to serve the purpose of employee compensation accounting. The adoption of ERP and the compensation point system greatly motivated employees on a fair basis.

Traditionally, YB had been focused on production and lacked cost and market competition awareness. As a result, the production was not oriented toward market demand, which greatly affected YB's core competence and competitiveness, resulting in high costs, low product quality and low levels of flexibility and agility in production. To change this passive situation, YB decided to adopt a production order system. Through this system, the production became demand-oriented, resulting in better use of resources, cost reduction and production flexibility. The production order system was subsequently introduced in YB in 2003.

In 2001, YB also established Shanghai Yunnan Baiyao Transdermal Technology Ltd. to develop the market for Baiyao Bandage and Baiyao Plaster. In June 2001, Baiyao Bandage appeared on the market and was an immediate success. In this year, YB also made another product diversification move by bringing to market a hemorrhoid ointment. YB succeeded again in extending its brand by leveraging its brand reputation.

Year 2002 (100-Year Anniversary and a New Strategy)

The year 2002 was significant for YB. Not only was it YB's 100-year anniversary, it was also the first year since China had been accepted as a member of the World Trade Organization (WTO). The end of 100 years was a convenient moment to take stock. Looking back, the leadership felt that the progress YB had made was remarkable, and the progress made in the last three years since the current leadership took office had occurred in leaps and bounds. The combination of a rapidly changing market situation and the mission falling upon YB leadership to carry the firm into a new century called for new strategies.

However, YB was facing some problems. The first was how to respond to the significant changes in the Chinese pharmaceutical industry. The reform of the Chinese pharmaceutical industry and China's accession to the WTO brought about drastic changes in the competitive landscape. YB had been essentially a producer of a medicine for the treatment of minor injuries. It would become a minor niche player if it did not follow a diversification and integration strategy. With the opening up of the Chinese market to world competition, YB either had to become a global brand or it would fade out from competition. Even though YB had pursued bold corporate strategies in the past decade, more needed to be done to keep up with global competition.

Secondly, many of YB's products had reached or were reaching maturity. To grow this traditional medicine firm, YB had to look for new growth areas; diversification of its products and markets and vertical integration could help YB extend its life cycle and stabilize its profits.

To respond to these challenges, YB established a series of strategies titled "one core and four growth areas." The "one core" referred the headquarters of YB, its group companies (the other three production-oriented companies acquired in 1996) and its sales network, which was basically what YB had in 2002. The four growth areas—the industrialization of herbal resources, the industrialization of research and development, vertical integration and internationalization—are described below.

Growth Area 1: The Industrialization of Herbal Resources The market for herbs and decocting pieces had been growing at an annual rate of 20 per cent, both for the domestic market and the export market. Yunnan Province was one of the main sources of herbs with its more than 6,500 species. However, the potential of rich herbal resources was not exploited in a managed way. There was no quality assurance system in place. Herbal resource products originating from Yunnan Province lacked not only bioactivity fingerprint standards, which ensured consistency in the identification, chemical separation and quality monitoring of the characteristic chemical substances of the herbs, but also branding and product quantity control. This lack of standards and quality control greatly affected the profitability of these herbal resources.

YB believed that it could benefit from Yunnan's rich herbal resources by industrializing the herbal resources. To achieve this goal, YB decided to set up an herb-planting base and establish a quality assurance system and bioactivity fingerprint standards. The herb-planting base could be used as a platform upon which herbal resources could be industrialized based on established quality systems and fingerprint standards. Herbs would be purchased from farmers through a system of purchase orders. YB could help farmers plant herbs in quantity according to the established quality standards. YB would then use its brand and sales network to market the herbal resources, ensuring consistent quality, controlled quantity and compliance with the fingerprint standards.

Growth Area 2: The Industrialization of Research and Development The development of new medicines had become the rule of the game in the international pharmaceutical industry. In addition, the transfer of intellectual property rights and new medicine certificates was more profitable than producing and selling pharmaceutical products themselves. For example, the annual net profit of the National Institute of Health (NIH), a U.S. medical research institute, was approximately US$12 billion. YB aspired to become a big player in pharmaceutical research by adopting similar approaches to those of NIH. These approaches included research contracts, grants and findings. YB's research institute could serve as a platform for industrializing R&D.

YB had already become a target of those who had herbal know-how for potential cooperation and knowledge transfer. By leveraging its reputation into research, YB believed that further growth could be expected.

Growth Area 3: Vertical Integration into Distribution through the Operation of Chain Stores With competition intensifying as a result of the drastic changes in the Chinese pharmaceutical industry, many companies diversified into distribution. Even though YB had made similar moves by acquiring Yunnan Pharmaceutical Trading Co. in the past, the distribution channels so obtained were not fine-grained and extensive. YB felt the need to strengthen its foothold in Yunnan Province by establishing Baiyao Da Yao Fang (a drugstore chain) to cover the whole province.

Growth Area 4: Internationalization Even though Baiyao was well-known in China and in Singapore, Malaysia, Thailand and Vietnam, where there were visible overseas Chinese communities, Baiyao was not known to customers in other countries, especially those in the two biggest markets, the European Union (EU) and North America. To ultimately become a world player, YB had to internationalize its products. Therefore, YB saw internationalization as another growth area.

Once its strategies had been determined, YB was aggressive in pursuing them. In 2002, the Wuding Traditional Chinese Herb-Planting Base was set up for the planting and domestication of wild herbs. The planting base later obtained a Good Agricultural Practices (GAP) certificate. On the foundation of the Wuding base, the industrialization process of wild herbal resources was sped up. Under the auspices of state funding, two companies, Traditional Chinese Herbal Seed Breeding Company and Yunnan Baiyao State Key Laboratory, were established that attracted a group of top scientists, and were key in the construction of a planting base that met the Good Laboratory Practice (GLP) standards. YB hoped that through quality assurance it could offer the domestic and international markets safe, reliable and consistent herbal products, thus laying the foundation for the modernization and internationalization of traditional Chinese herbal medicine.

Even though the Wuding planting base was set up to industrialize herbal resources, there was another reason for YB to backward integrate into herbal planting. Throughout the past couple of decades, the herbs from which Baiyao was produced had been exploited without regulation. Some herbal medicine species were very rare, and due to increasing demand in alternative treatment, they were getting closer to extinction. Because of over-exploitation, it became questionable whether the supply of herbal sources could keep pace with YB's growth. To a certain degree, YB's move in this direction was a necessity.

The backward integration was also motivated by the associative branding effect for YB because the herbal resources produced through the planting base would be exported using the YB brand name. YB hoped that through the export of good quality herbs it could build its reputation overseas for its pharmaceutical products.

Also in 2002, Baiyao Da Yao Fang Ltd. (a drugstore chain) was established, and it had since been making smooth progress. YB also integrated the operations of the drugstore chain and Yunnan Pharmaceutical Trading Co. because the two subsidiaries shared the same goal of forward vertical integration and had many synergies.

The moves YB made in 2002 were all strategic in nature. Both the Wuding Planting Base and the Baiyao Da Yao Fang drug chain were long-term investments because they would not contribute to YB's profit within the first five years after their establishment.

In summary, during the 1999 to 2002 period, YB had been pursuing systematic reform, restructuring, vertical integration and diversification strategies to modernize the state-owned enterprise. This period coincided with the assumption of office by Wang Minghui. With these strategic moves, YB had been seeing dramatic improvement in its performance (see Exhibits 2, 3 and 4).

THE OPTION OF MARKET AND PRODUCT DIVERSIFICATION: THE 3M PROPOSAL

Consistent with the "one core and four growth areas" strategy, YB had been exploring the possibilities of overseas markets. In 2002, the Yunnan Baiyao Overseas Department was set up to develop international markets. The goal of the department was to solidify Yunnan Baiyao's markets in Southeast Asia and to develop markets in the United States, the European Union and Japan.

YB wasted no time in its internationalization strategy. In 2003, YB registered and received approval from Vietnam and Thailand authorities to market its products. YB adopted the path of least resistance by first exploring geographic regions of low cultural distance and low entry barriers. The company was deliberating about how to enter the United States, the European Union and Japan, and at this juncture, 3M proposed to cooperate with YB in the area of transdermal products. YB had to decide whether to pursue this opportunity.

3M Company

3M Company (NYSE: MMM; formerly Minnesota Mining and Manufacturing Company until 2002) was founded at Two Harbors, Minnesota, in 1902. The company had since become a gigantic multinational enterprise with a worldwide presence. By 2003, 3M was one of the 30 companies included in the Dow Jones Industrial Average, and was ranked number 110 on the 2003 Fortune 500 listing. The company had 132 plants and more than 67,000 employees around the world, with sales offices in more than 200 countries.

Out of 3M's more than a dozen core competencies, adhesives was one of its major successes. Over the years, 3M had leveraged its competencies in adhesives technologies to many industries, including health care, automotive, construction and telecommunications. In health care, 3M's adhesive technology was mainly used in transdermal drug delivery systems. 3M's Drug Delivery Systems Division was a global leader in transdermal drug delivery with a 30-year proven track record, and more than 80 per cent of the transdermal drug delivery products in the United States contained a 3M transdermal component. The Drug Delivery Systems Division utilized nearly 50 per cent of the 3M corporate core technologies to meet customer needs. Transdermal products developed and manufactured by 3M were registered in more than 60 countries.

3M's technology in transdermal delivery systems offered many advantages over other products: They were breathable adhesives, offered pain-free removability and were waterproof. 3M solutions to transdermal delivery were also hypo-allergenic, thus reducing skin irritation.

3M's transdermal technologies could be utilized by pharmaceutical and biotech companies by forming partnerships with 3M. 3M Drug Delivery Systems' technology, product development, global regulatory expertise and commercial manufacturing provided pharmaceutical and biotech companies with differentiated products, speed to market and increased probability of technical and commercial success. For example, 3M had been involved in the development and manufacturing of the following products:

- Minitran™ ([nitroglycerin] transdermal delivery system)[2]
- Climara® (estradiol transdermal system)[3]
- Climara Pro® (estradiol transdermal system)[4]
- Menostar® (estradiol-levonorgestrel transdermal system)[5]

---

[2]Minitran™ is a trademark of 3M Company.
[3]Climara® is a registered trademark of Schering AG.
[4]Climara Pro® is a registered trademark of Schering AG.
[5]Menostar® is a registered trademark of Berlex Laboratories.

YB's Experiments with Transdermal Products

The History of Chinese Traditional Transdermal Products Transdermal drug delivery through a plaster (or plaster bandage) was an important branch of traditional Chinese medicine. The Chinese term for plaster, *Bo Tie,* appeared in the year 682 for the first time, in Sun Si-Miao's *Thousand Golden Prescriptions,* an important medical book containing the main medical achievements before the Tang dynasty [618–907 AD]). In later dynasties, the application of plasters was further developed and perfected with the development of acupuncture and moxibustion (a therapy using moxa, or mugwort herb). According to Chinese medical theory, plasters were applied on acupoints for better curative effect. There were many plaster recipes collected in the famous Ming Dynasty book *Compendium of Materia Medica* (or *Great Pharmacopoeia*), compiled by Li Shi-Zhen in 1578.

The application of plasters culminated in the Qing Dynasty with the publication of *Li Yue Pian Wen* in 1864. Written by Wu Shi-Ji, this book focused on the cutaneous and external applications of various plasters. Wu Shi-Ji, regarded as the master of plasters, used plaster as the main method of drug delivery for most diseases and achieved significant curative effects on patients. Many Chinese doctors learned from his masterpiece on plasters and spread the use of plasters across China.

As a result, plasters were a well accepted form of medicine in China. In an online survey, 99 per cent of respondents answered that they had used plasters before. However, due to the disadvantages of traditional rubber adhesive plasters, and the inroads of Western medicine, Chinese plaster medicine had been under pressure and many thought plasters were a so-called sunset form of treatment. Plasters occupied a very small share in the Chinese pharmaceutical market, and market competition of plaster products was not intense. Within the small market share of plasters in the whole pharmaceutical industry, the share occupied by Baiyao plasters was almost negligible.

However, plasters, as a medium of transdermal drug delivery, were still an attractive alternative drug delivery method. Compared to oral medication and hypodermal injection, transdermal drug delivery had the advantage of direct application to the afflicted areas, thus avoiding both the degradation of medicine in the digestive tract and toxic effects on the liver. The apprehensions people held about plasters were largely caused by non-medicinal components, such as skin allergies to the adhesives, the adhesive's lack of breathability, the pain associated with removing the adhesive from the skin and the failure of the adhesives when they became wet. If these disadvantages could be overcome with technological advances, more and more people would embrace plasters. An online survey showed that 95 per cent of respondents thought that plasters had huge market potential.

YB's History in Transdermal Products YB's interest in diversifying into transdermal products dated back to 1997, when a product called Baiyao Bandage (a product similar to Band-Aid) was developed in the laboratory. Seeing the great market potential of transdermal products, Shanghai Yunnan Baiyao Transdermal Technology Ltd. was consequently established in 2001, charged with the market development for Baiyao Bandage and Baiyao Plaster. In the beginning, the company adopted the concept of a virtual firm, with only an investment of RMB5 million and three persons from Yunnan Baiyao: one responsible for general management, one responsible for sales and the third responsible for technology.

Prior to Baiyao Bandage, the Chinese bandage market had been monopolized by Johnson & Johnson. To compete with such a strong competitor, speed and strategy were needed. If Yunnan Baiyao had adopted its traditional way of doing business by sequentially acquiring land, constructing production workshops and purchasing production facilities, it would have taken at least two years for Baiyao Bandage to go to market. By outsourcing the production of Baiyao Bandage to a French firm, YB was able to not only bring Baiyao Bandage to market within only three months but also to concentrate on brand and market development.

In June 2001, Baiyao Bandage appeared in the market and was an immediate success. In June alone, YB achieved sales of RMB4 million and a profit of RMB1.88 million. From June to December, YB realized sales revenue of RMB30 million. In only a short time, Baiyao Bandage became the most formidable competitor of Band-Aid. This accomplishment was attained not only because YB had adopted a strategy of using second-grade cities to encircle first-grade cities to avoid direct market competition but more importantly because YB had a deep grassroots brand image. In addition, Baiyao Bandage came in two forms, one without medicinal contents, sold in supermarkets to compete with Johnson & Johnson, and the other with medicinal contents, sold in pharmacies. Compared to Band-Aid, Baiyao Bandage with medicinal contents could not only cover the wounds but also had antiphlogistic (inflammation-reducing) and haemostatic (blood-stopping) effects.

The Potential of the 3M Proposal

The Potential for Product Diversification The cooperative opportunity with 3M could potentially be an effective way of diversifying YB's product line into the transdermal market. 3M had numerous transdermal solutions that could overcome customer concerns in terms of the adhesive's breathability, removability, skin irritation and waterproofness. By solving these problems, YB could better serve customers and increase its market share.

The potential cooperation with 3M also had several advantages. First, if YB decided to use 3M transdermal drug delivery systems to deliver its Baiyao medicinal contents, the cooperation would improve the likelihood of success because the proposed products were proven from both sides.

Secondly, YB would enjoy speed to market with low R&D costs. Because the 3M contents were proven products, only minimal R&D would be necessary to tailor 3M's product to YB's medicinal contents. R&D would cost much less and consume less time, resulting in higher speed to market. In addition, most of the R&D was to be carried out by 3M because it had the core competence. 3M would carry out the pre-feasibility assessment, the feasibility study, the product development and the commercialization with input from YB.

The Potential for Internationalization The cooperation with 3M offered not only an opportunity for product diversification but also an opportunity for YB to diversify its markets. 3M's transdermal products were widely registered, and 3M had global regulatory expertise. 3M's global presence and expertise would serve as a platform for YB to internationalize its products, beginning with its transdermal products. 3M had shown interest in helping YB to gain access to the U.S. market using its reputation. This opportunity was just what YB had been looking for.

It was very difficult for a traditional herbal medicine to enter a market like the United States because of the regulatory barriers. Through 3M's regulatory expertise and its status as a reputed American company, YB might gain easier access to the U.S. market. In addition, the regulatory barrier for transdermal products was lower than that for products that were delivered either orally or directly into the bloodstream.

By first introducing transdermal products into the U.S. market, YB could build its brand internationally while incurring minimal risk. If the launch of a transdermal product were successful, there would be potential for brand synergy for YB's other pharmaceutical products in the future.

However, there were also a series of challenges YB had to face. The first challenge was cultural distance, which YB had to overcome in many respects. American customers had different consumer behaviours, and they were not very comfortable with traditional herbal medicine that lacked modern scientific substantiation. Even though the YB transdermal products adopted a form North Americans were familiar with, there was still high potential for customer rejection due to skepticism regarding its herbal contents.

YB also lacked international marketing experience. Even though YB had been building up its marketing capabilities, these efforts were confined within China. Despite an overseas department that was established in 2002, the scope of business of the department was still very limited. This lack of international experience could prove to be a big hurdle to surmount by a long-time domestic firm. Even if YB hired local sales personnel, the management of this personnel could still be a big challenge. On the other hand, entering into a foreign market could provide YB an opportunity to gain precious overseas operations experience.

Yet another challenge was the gap between the levels of economic development in China and the United States. Thus, the marketing expense would be very high in the U.S. market, imposing a burden on a developing country firm that was defending and expanding along both the product and market dimensions.

THE PRODUCT DIVERSIFICATION OPTION: ESTABLISHING A HEALTH CARE DEPARTMENT

Concurrent with the 3M option, YB was also faced with another option. According to the "one core and four growth areas" strategy, YB should not ignore further strengthening its core business. Even though internationalization was one of its growth strategies, YB had to be cautious because it lacked the necessary international experience. In the foreseeable future, the majority of its revenue would still be generated from the Chinese market. Therefore, YB had to maintain a focus on its domestic market. Because many of YB's products had reached or were reaching maturity, YB needed to further diversify its product line and extend its brand to seek new growth opportunities.

In 2003, YB was considering the feasibility of establishing a health care department to diversify into health care products. One such product was Baiyao toothpaste. YB came up with this idea based on two facts: 1) many customers already used Baiyao powder to deal with dental bleeding and 2) many multinational pharmaceutical companies offered health care products, including toothpaste.

First, even though Baiyao had been formulated for the purpose of curing wounds and injuries, customers had been extending its use in innovative ways. Since its formulation, Baiyao had been used by people for every kind of disease related to blood or bleeding. People had been using Baiyao in its powder form for curing periodontitis and gingivitis for many years, even though the powder form was very inconvenient to use in these cases. By formulating a toothpaste as the carrier to deliver the medicinal content, the customer needs could be better served.

Secondly, many international pharmaceutical companies had health care products. Johnson & Johnson (J&J), which had very strong presence in China, was one such example. The sales of J&J in health care products made up approximately 18 per cent of its total sales, and the net revenue had been increasing steadily. Health care products did not cannibalize J&J's main products; on the contrary, they strengthened J&J's brand equity by brand synergy. J&J's health care brands, such as Johnson's

Baby, Band-Aid, Neutrogena and Tylenol, made J&J even more visible to customers. YB thought that it could learn from these multinationals by leveraging its own brand. A successful health care product (such as a Baiyao toothpaste) affiliated with YB could potentially add to YB's brand equity. If foreign multinationals all adopted this approach, YB reasoned it might work in the case of YB too.

Diversifying into health care products could also increase YB's economy of scope and/or economy of scale because a Baiyao toothpaste would share some value chain activities with its original products. Brand extension might bring about greater production and marketing efficiency and lower promotion costs.

Another potential benefit of product diversification was that it offered an opportunity for YB to build its capabilities. Because YB aspired to be a Chinese multinational in the global pharmaceutical industry, it had to build capabilities. In the past decade, YB had been building up its capabilities in both the product and market dimensions and along the value chain. To compete in the new area of affiliated health care, YB needed to build capabilities in this area, otherwise YB would not be on par with the multinationals, even in the Chinese market.

However, this option did have several weaknesses. Although Baiyao toothpaste would have medicinal content, the value chain activities that could be shared were few. Few health care products were related to YB's current businesses. New production facilities would have to be built sooner or later for each health care product.

Health care products did not even share sales channels with the existing products. YB was a traditional herbal medicine firm, and it was not familiar with the sales practices in the Chinese daily chemical industry. YB would have to establish new distribution channels different from that for its medicine-related products.

In addition, the potential intense competition could not be ignored. The toothpaste industry was dominated by multinational firms, such as Colgate and Procter & Gamble (P&G). The competition was already intense and profit margins were very low. YB was in no position to compete with these giants on their turf as a new entrant. On the other hand, if YB tried to avoid direct competition by pricing the toothpaste to target the higher end, it would then only occupy a niche market.

Yet another potential problem was product cannibalism. Toothpaste had been used by Chinese customers for various topical uses in the past. Some even used toothpaste to clean utensils. There was no guarantee that consumers of Baiyao toothpaste would not use it for other external uses and consequently cannibalize the markets of existing products.

Lastly, there was the problem of brand contagion. Because toothpaste was not in YB's core competence, potential failure of toothpaste might cause damage to YB's reputation overall. As such, YB had to make sure that the new product would succeed. The success of Baiyao toothpaste would not only affect the fate of the health care department, but would also affect YB's brand equity.

THE DECISION

The year 2003 was an important one for YB: It marked one year since YB had established its "one core and four growth areas" strategy, and 2003 had been scheduled for implementing those strategies. The company's leadership was also very ambitious to achieve even higher goals.

The possibilities of the cooperative arrangement with 3M and the diversification into health care products were both opportunities and threats to YB. After careful deliberation, YB came to a point where a decision had to be made. Should YB pursue the 3M option or the toothpaste option? Was it feasible to pursue both? YB had to come up with a decision soon.

EXHIBIT 1 Yunnan Baiyao Timeline

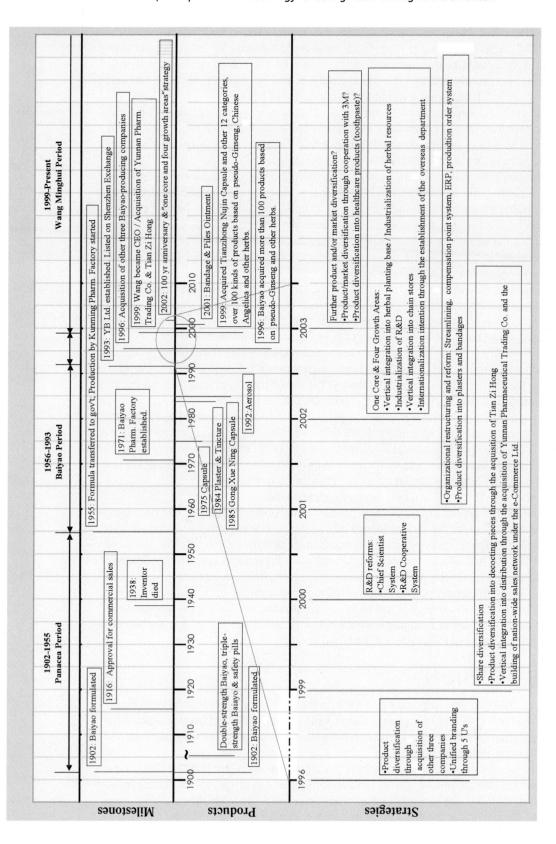

EXHIBIT 2   Total Annual Revenue of Yunnan Baiyao, 1990–2003

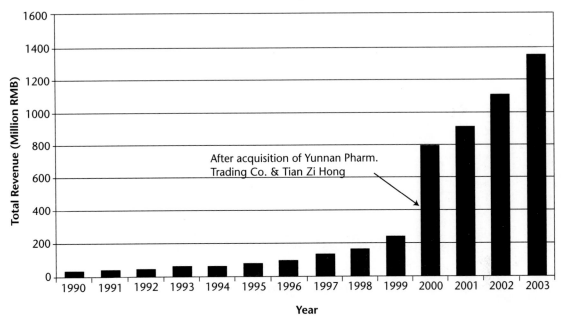

Source: Authors' calculation based on: Yunnan Baiyao Group Co. (various years), *Annual report of Yunnan Baiyao Group Co.;* and Jing Luo, "Yunnan Baiyao company analysis," Shenyin & Wanguo Securities Co., Ltd., February 13, 2006.

EXHIBIT 3   Annual Net Profit of Yunnan Baiyao, 1993–2003

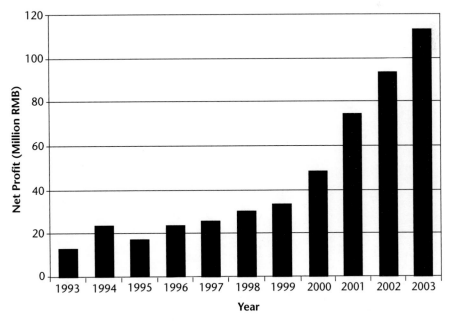

Source: Authors' calculation based on: Yunnan Baiyao Group Co. (various years), *Annual report of Yunnan Baiyao Group Co.;* and Jing Luo, "Yunnan Baiyao company analysis," Shenyin & Wanguo Securities Co., Ltd., February 13, 2006.

EXHIBIT 4   Return on Equity of Yunnan Baiyao 1993–2003

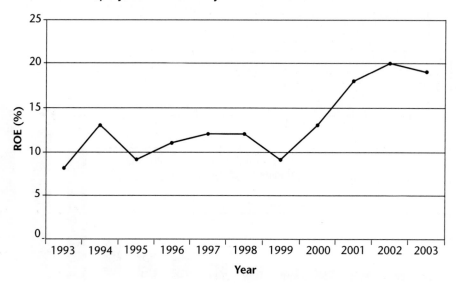

Source: Authors' elaboration, based on: Jing Luo "Yunnan Baiyao company analysis," Shenyin & Wanguo Securities Co., Ltd., February 13, 2006.

Vincor and the New World of Wine

On September 16, 2002, Donald Triggs, chief executive officer (CEO) of Vincor International Inc. (Vincor), was preparing for the board meeting to discuss the possible acquisition of Goundrey Wines, Australia. Vincor had embarked upon a strategic internationalization plan in 2000, acquiring R.H Phillips and Hogue in the United States. Although Vincor was the largest wine company in Canada and the fourth-largest in North America, Triggs felt that to be a major player, Vincor had to look beyond the region. The acquisition of Goundrey Wines in Australia would be the first step. Convincing the board would be difficult, as the United States was a close and attractive market where Vincor had already spent more than US$100 million on acquisitions. In contrast, Australia was very far away.

THE GLOBAL WINE INDUSTRY

Wine-producing countries were classified as either New World producers or Old World producers. Some of the largest New World producers were the United States, Australia, Chile and Argentina. The largest of the Old World producers were France, Italy and Spain (see Exhibit 1). The world's top 10 wine exporters accounted for more than 90 per cent of the value of international wine trade. Of those top 10, half were in Western Europe, and the other half were New World suppliers, led by Australia (see Exhibit 2).

France

France had been a longtime world leader in the production of wine, due to historical and cultural factors. France was the top producer of wine in the world (see Exhibit 1). The French had developed the vins d'appellation d'origine contrôlée (AOC) system

Nikhil Celly prepared this case under the supervision of Professor Paul W. Beamish solely to provide material for class discussion. The authors do not intend to illustrate either effective or ineffective handling of a managerial situation. The authors may have disguised certain names and other identifying information to protect confidentiality.

Version: (A) 2009-10-08

IVEY

Richard Ivey School of Business
The University of Western Ontario

centuries ago to ensure that the quality of wine stayed high. There were many regions in which quality grapes could be grown in France. Some of their better known appellations were Bordeaux, Burgundy and Champagne. France was the second-largest exporter of wine (see Exhibit 2).

Italy

Italy, like France, also had a very old and established wine industry that relied on the appellation method to control the quality. Italy was the second-largest producer of wine in the world (see Exhibit 1) and the largest exporter (see Exhibit 2).

Australia

Grape vines were first introduced to Australia in 1788. The wine "industry" was born in the 1860s when European immigrants added the skilled workforce necessary to develop the commercial infrastructure. The Australian wine industry grew after 1960 with the development of innovative techniques to make higher quality wine while keeping costs down. Australia was the sixth-largest producer of wine in the world (see Exhibit 1). Australia had 5.5 per cent of the total export market and was ranked 4th in the world for its export volume (see Exhibit 2).

Chile

The first vines were introduced to Chile in the 16th century. Due to political and economic instability, the wine industry was not able to develop and take on a global perspective until 1979, when Chile began to focus on the exporting of natural resources to strengthen its economy. Despite being only the 10th-largest producer, Chile had 4.5 per cent of the total export market and was ranked 5th in the world (see Exhibit 2).

Argentina

Argentina had a long history of making wine. However, the quality of the wine from Argentina was never as high, due to the small area of land that was capable of producing high-quality grapes. Argentina was the fifth-largest producer of wine in the world (see Exhibit 1), but did not feature in the top 10 exporters of wine.

All of the countries, with the exception of Argentina, were capable of shipping brands that could compete at a wide range of price points. The French wines typically were capable of competing in the higher price classes, and could retail for more than US$100 per bottle.

MAJOR WORLD MARKETS

After a 2.2 per cent gain in 2001, the global wine market was estimated to have increased another 1.2 per cent in 2002 to 2.55 billion cases, according to *The Global Drinks Market: Impact Databank Review and Forecast 2001 Report.* Wine consumption was projected to expand by 120 million cases by 2010. Most of the growth was expected to come from major wine-consuming nations, such as the United States, the United Kingdom, Australia and South Africa, as well from less-developed wine markets, such as China and Russia.

Wine imports were highly concentrated. The 10 top importing countries accounted for all but 14 per cent of the value of global imports in the late 1980s. In 2001, half the value of all imports were purchased by the three biggest importers: the United Kingdom (19 per cent), the United States (16 per cent) and Germany (14 per cent).

France and Italy were the number one and two countries in the world for per capita consumption (see Exhibit 3). However, the consumption rate in France was relatively stagnant, while Italy was showing a decrease. Italy, unlike France, had a very small market for imported wines. The import market sizes for France and Italy were 13.4 per cent and 2.8 per cent respectively in 2001, based on volume.

The United Kingdom's wine market was considered to be the "crucible" for the global wine market.[1] The United Kingdom had very small domestic wine production and good relationships with many of the wine-producing countries in the world. This, coupled with the long history of wine consumption, resulted in an open and competitive market. The United Kingdom was ranked number seven for consumption in 2001, with a trend of increasing consumption. The United Kingdom wine market was dominated by Old World country imports; however New World imports had grown as Australian wines replaced French wines as the number one import (see Figure 1).

FIGURE 1   United Kingdom Wine Market Share

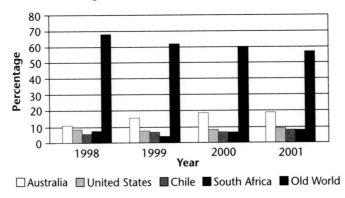

☐ Australia ☐ United States ■ Chile ■ South Africa ■ Old World

Source: Company files.

Other Countries

In 2001, Canada was ranked number 30 in the world for per capita consumption, with an increasing trend. Japan had seen a steady increase in the size of its imported wine market. Asia presented a great opportunity for wine producers around the world because it had populous markets that had yet to be tapped.

THE U.S. WINE INDUSTRY

The international image of the U.S. wine industry until the mid-1970s was that of a low-quality jug wine producer. This changed in 1976 during a blind wine-tasting contest in France, where California wines from Napa Valley beat out several well-established European wines for the top honours. From that time forward, there had been a focus on developing high-quality wines that could compete in the international market from the northern California appellations, such as Napa Valley and Sonoma County. The United States was the fourth-largest producer of wine (1.98 billion litres) in 2001 (see Exhibit 1), with California wines accounting for 90 per cent of production volume. There were more than 3,000 wineries in all 50 states. The nation's top wine-producing states were California, New York, Washington and Oregon.

The United States saw huge gains in the total volume and value of its wine exports, increasing from US$85 million in 1988 to US$548 million in 2002. The major markets for U.S wines included the United Kingdom, Canada and Japan. Together, they represented 66 per cent of the total export market value for the United States (see Exhibit 4).

The United States was the third-largest wine market in the world, consuming 2.13 billion litres a year in 2001. It was also one of the biggest untapped wine markets in the world; 7 per cent of the U.S. population accounted for 86 per cent of the country's wine consumption. The total wine market in the United States in 2001 was $21.1 billion, with an average growth rate of 6 per cent since 1994. Of this, approximately $10 billion were sales of New World wines.

While California wines dominated the domestic market (67 per cent market share) due to the ideal growing conditions and favourable marketing and branding actions taken by some of California's larger wineries, imports were on the rise. The United States had one of the most open markets in the world for wine, with low barriers to entry for imports. Imports represented 530 million litres for a 25 per cent share of the market. By 2002, wine imports grew by 18 per cent (see Figures 2 and 3).

Wine was the most popular alcoholic beverage in the United States after beer, which accounted for 67 per cent of all alcohol consumed. The table wine category

FIGURE 2   United States Wine Markets 1998 to 2001

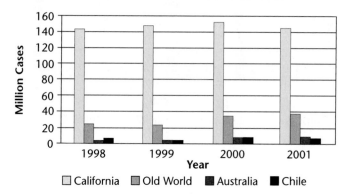

Source: Company files.

FIGURE 3   United States Wine Market Growth Rates

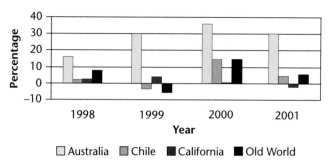

Source: Company files.

represented 90 per cent of all wine by volume, dessert wine was 6 per cent and sparkling wine accounted for 4 per cent. U.S.-produced table wine held an 83 per cent share of the volume and 78 per cent of the value. Premium wine ($7 and more per 750 ml bottle) sales increased 8 per cent over 2001, accounting for 30 per cent of the volume, but a sizeable 62 per cent of winery revenues. Everyday value-priced wines selling for less than $7 per bottle grew about 1.5 per cent by volume. This segment represented 70 per cent of all California table wine shipments and 38 per cent of the value.

The United States wine industry was fragmented, with the largest producer, E. & J. Gallo, supplying 30 per cent and no other producer supplying more than 15 per cent by volume in 2002.

In the United States, a law mandated the implementation of a three-tier distribution system. The wine producers were required to sell to a wholesaler, who then sold to an established customer base of grocery stores, liquor stores, hotels and restaurants. Wineries were capable of using a two-tier distribution system, which allowed wineries to sell directly to the customers through gift shops located at the winery. The role of the distribution channel was growing and taking on greater strategic importance as the trend towards international and domestic consolidation grew.

THE CANADIAN WINE INDUSTRY

Canadians had been making wine for more than two centuries, but Canada's modern-day success in the production of high-quality, vinifera-based wines went back only a quarter-century. The signing of the North American Free Trade Agreement in 1988, together with a ruling under the General Agreement on Tariffs and Trade (GATT), required Canada to abandon the protection it offered its wine industry. While many producers felt threatened, many more responded by reaffirming their belief in their capacity to produce premium wines and redoubled their efforts to prove it. New vineyards were planted with only the finest varieties of grapes: Chardonnay, Riesling, Sauvignon Blanc, Pinot Gris, Gewürztraminer, Pinot Noir, Cabernet Sauvignon, Merlot and others.

During 1988, the Vintners Quality Alliance (VQA) was launched in Ontario, culminating six years of voluntary initiatives by the leaders of Ontario's wine industry. This group set the standards, to which they agreed to comply, to elevate the quality of Canadian wines and provide quality assurances to the consumer. British Columbia adopted similar high standards in 1990, under the VQA mark.

The 1990s was a decade of rapid growth. The number of commercial wineries grew from about 30 in 1990 to more than 100 by the end of the decade, and consumers began to recognize the value represented by wines bearing the VQA medallion. Canadian vintners continued to demonstrate that fine grape varieties in cooler growing conditions could possess complex flavours, delicate yet persistent aromas, tightly focused structure and longer aging potential than their counterparts in warmer growing regions of the world.

In Canada, despite increasing import competition, sales of Canadian quality wines were increasing as consumers moved up the quality and price scale (see Figure 4).

Canadian quality wines began to capture both domestic and international recognition not only in sales, but also by garnering an impressive list of significant wine awards, beginning in 1991 when Inniskillin won the Grand Prix d'Honneur for its 1989 icewine at the prestigious VinExpo, in Bordeaux, France. New access for Canadian

FIGURE 4   The Canadian Wine Market

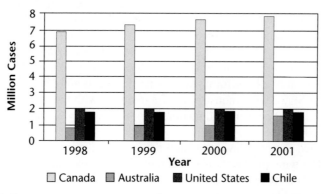

Source: Company files.

wines, especially icewine, in the European market and expanding market opportunities in the United States and Asia were giving Canadian wines greater market exposure.

THE AUSTRALIAN WINE INDUSTRY

The Australian wine industry was structured to be able to deliver large quantities of high-quality branded wine to the world's major markets, at costs less than many of their Old World and New World competitors. Since Australia had a very limited domestic market (population of only 17 million), the wineries realized that if the industry was to continue to grow, it would have to do so internationally.

As a result, Australian wineries had gained, and were expected to continue to gain, market share. Growth had been in exports as well as domestic sales (see Exhibits 5 and 6). Australia had recently overtaken France as the largest exporter to the United Kingdom, where 7 of the top 10 wine brands were Australian. Exports to North America had grown at 27 per cent by volume in 2001. Consumption of Australian wine in Canada was up 24 per cent and in the United States, consumption was up 35 per cent. The growth trends were expected to continue. Export growth had been driven by sales of premium red wine, which accounted for 53 per cent of Australia's wine exports.

Domestic wine consumption had grown from 296 million litres in 1991 to 398 million litres in 2001, an annual growth rate of 4 per cent. The Australian domestic market was relatively unregulated compared to North America, although alcohol taxes were high (42 per cent). Wineries were allowed to have their own retail outlets and sell directly to retailers or on-premise customers. The 7,500 licensed liquor retail outlets accounted for 56 per cent of wine sales, while the 28,000 licensed on-premise outlets accounted for 44 per cent of wine sales.

Although there were 1,300 wineries in Australia, the industry was the most concentrated of any major wine region, with 80 per cent of production being accounted for by 4 players: Southcorp Wines, Beringer Blass, BRL Hardy and Orlando Wyndham. The large wineries had their own sales forces, as well as warehouses in the major markets.

Southcorp Wines was Australia's largest winery and vineyard owner, with sales of AUD$1.5 billion. Beringer Blass was owned by the Foster's Group and had wine revenues of approximately AUD$800 million (7 million cases). The purchase of Beringer (for AUD$2.6 billion) provided the company with significant growth and U.S. market access.

BRL Hardy had revenues of more than AUD$700 million. The company had several top brands and a very strong U.K. market position. A recent joint venture in the United States with Constellation brands had improved their United States market access. Orlando Wyndham was owned by Pernod Ricard, a French publicly traded spirits company.

TRENDS IN THE GLOBAL WINE INDUSTRY

Wine was unique among alcoholic beverages in that its top 25 brands represented only 7 per cent of the global market. In 2002, Martini vermouth was the world's most widely distributed wine, while Gallo's E. & J. Wine Cellars was the largest-selling brand at 25 million cases annually, with most of those sales in the United States.

Globally, vermouth and other fortified wines were projected to continue their long-term decline, but this would be more than offset by expected growth in table wines, which accounted for more than 90 per cent of total wine consumption. The hottest sales category was Australian wines, with brands such as Rosemount Estate, Jacob's Creek and Lindeman's showing double-digit growth rates.

The North American market was expected to exhibit annual growth rates of three per cent. There were positive demographics with the 20-to-39 age group having a per capita consumption of 7.9 litres and the 40+ age group having a per capita of 14.0 litres. The ongoing trends were a shift in consumer preference to red wines and premium wines (see Exhibits 7 and 8).

The global wine market was consolidating in terms of its retail, wholesale and production operations. One key to success seemed to be distribution and marketing. Globalization was also altering the structure of firms both within the wine industry and among those distributing and retailing wine. Rapid growth in supermarkets and in concentration among distributors was driving wine companies into mergers and acquisitions to better meet the needs of those buyers and their customers. Since information about the various niches and the distribution networks in foreign markets was expensive to acquire, new alliances between wine companies were being explored with a view to capitalizing on their complementarities in such knowledge.

Recent examples of such alliances included the purchase of Napa Valley-based Beringer by the owner of Mildara Blass (Foster's Group), the alliance between Southcorp/Rosemount and California's Mondavi, BRL Hardy's joint venture with the second-largest U.S. wine company, Constellation Brands, (to operate as Pacific West Partners) and the purchase by New Zealand's biggest wine firm (Montana) of the country's second-largest winery (Corbans). See Exhibit 9 for the 10 largest wine companies worldwide.

VINCOR INTERNATIONAL INC.

Vincor International Inc. (Vincor) was formed as a combination of a number of Canadian wineries, including Barnes Wines, Brights Wines, Cartier Wines, Inniskillin Wines and Dumont, over the period from 1989 to 1996. Vincor began operations in 1989 with a management buyout of Ridout Wines (Ridout) from John Labatt Ltd. The Ridout management team, led by Allan Jackson, Peter Graigner and John Hall, sought out Donald Triggs to lead the purchase and become CEO. They raised more than CDN$2 million in equity, largely from personal finances, and borrowed $25 million to buy out Ridout. The new company was renamed Cartier Wines and Beverages.

Vincor had grown in three stages to become Canada's largest wine company in 2002. The first stage of growth had been a leveraged buyout (LBO) in turbulent times (1989 to 1995), followed by a period of consolidation and rationalization: Building Canada's Wine Company (1990 to 2000). The third stage of growth was Building an International Wine Company (2000 onwards).

The first stage had seen the formation of Vincor and wine company acquisitions. From 1995 to 2000, Vincor acquired eight wineries, integrated its sales, marketing, production and accounting and merged two wine-kit companies. This lead to economies of scale and a 21 per cent market share in 2000.

During this period, Vincor developed Canada's first premium wine brands: Jackson-Triggs, Inniskillin and Sawmill Creek. The Canadian wine market had seen a shift from popular (less than $7 retail price) to premium ($7 to $10 retail price), leading Vincor to start focusing on the premium and super-premium ($10 to $15 retail price) segments. They developed vineyards and re-capitalized wineries to support premium growth. Product coverage was also achieved in the growing ultra-premium ($15 to $20 retail price) and specialty (more than $20 retail price) segments. The year 2000 saw Vincor at a strategic crossroad. Triggs recalled:

> We were faced with three options. We could choose to be a cash cow by further developing our dominant Canadian position. A second option was to develop a diversified Canadian beverage conglomerate. A third option was to expand to the United States and perhaps beyond.
>
> We went for option 3. The move was driven by opportunities as well as threats. In terms of opportunities, the global trend was one of strong growth and premiumization. There was an industry consolidation favouring global brands. The market was fragmented, with the largest player only having one per cent market share. The markets for New World wine were growing. The dynamics in the U.S. market were highly profitable with very high profit margins. We were already #5 in North America and #22 globally.
>
> On the risk side, wine was an agricultural industry and, as such, susceptible to changing weather conditions. A diversified portfolio in terms of production and markets would only be an asset.

Triggs and Vincor decided to go international. The company's mission statement was drafted to reflect the new strategic plan:

> To become one of the world's top-10 wine companies, producing Vincor-owned New World, premium branded wines, which are marketed and sold through Vincor-controlled sales and distribution systems in all major premium wine consuming regions.

Where Were the Big Markets?

According to Triggs:

> The United States was the largest market with New World wine sales of $10 billion, followed by the United Kingdom and Australia at $3.7 billion each. Canada and the rest of Europe were next at $700 million. Japan was the 6th-largest with sales of about $500 million. To be a New World market player, Vincor needed to be in 5 to 6 markets.

In 2002, the company's strategy was formulated for each region. In Canada, the aim was to build share in premium segments, to develop export capability and to generate cash and improve return on capital employed. In the United States, Vincor decided to focus on portfolio migration to high-end super-premium, enhancement of sales capability, product innovation and a shift to consumer marketing. Vincor's international strategy was to develop new geographic markets for core brands, specifically for icewine, a signature product for Canada that had attained world recognition. It was a luxury product in terms of pricing and margins and one of the top-five wine brands in select Asian duty-free stores. The U.S. launch was in Fiscal 2001 in 1,850 high-end restaurants. By 2002, Inniskillin was being sold in 3,300 premium restaurants across the United States. The European launch of Inniskillin was slated for Fiscal 2002.

U.S. ACQUISITIONS

R.H. Phillips

On October 5, 2000, Vincor acquired R.H. Phillips, a leading California estate winery, which produced a range of super-premium wines. The aggregate purchase price, including acquisition costs, was US$56.7 million. In addition, R.H. Phillips' debt of US$33.8 million was assumed and refinanced by the company. The Phillips acquisition and the refinancing of the assumed debt were funded entirely through borrowing from the company's senior lender.

R.H. Phillips was established in 1981 by John and Karl Giguiere. It was located in the Dunnigan Hills Viticultural Region, near the wine regions of Napa and Sonoma. R.H. Phillips specialized in the production of super-premium wines, marketing its products under the brands R.H. Phillips, Toasted Head, EXP and Kempton Clark. Its wines were sold throughout the United States and in several other countries, including Canada. In 2001, its brands generated sales revenues of approximately US$25 million for Vincor. Its wines were distributed across the United States by a network of 13 sales executives, distributors and brokers.

The Phillips acquisition established a presence for Vincor in the U.S. wine market, in addition to adding strong brands which were well-positioned in the super-premium category, one of the fastest-growing segments of the wine market. With its national network of distributors and sales professionals, R.H. Phillips provided a platform for future acquisitions in the United States (such as the Hogue acquisition), while also facilitating the marketing of Vincor's products in the United States.

Hogue Cellars

On September 1, 2001, Vincor acquired Hogue Cellars for US$36.3 million. Hogue was the second-largest wine producer in Washington state, well known for its super-premium wine. Hogue was a family-controlled and family-operated winery founded in 1982 by Mike and Gary Hogue.

The Washington state wine industry had emerged as the second-largest producer of premium wines in the United States, after California. Hogue produced red varietals, including Cabernet Sauvignon, Merlot and Syrah, as well as white varietals, including Chardonnay, Sauvignon Blanc, Riesling and Pinot Gris. In 2001, sales of Hogue-produced premium wine were 415,400 cases. In addition to its owned brands, Hogue was the U.S. agent for Kim Crawford wines of New Zealand and Heritage Road wines from Brian McGuigan wines of Australia.

The Hogue acquisition added 11 sales people nationally, and immediately increased Vincor's annual U.S. sales volume to more than 1 million cases and its annual U.S. revenues to more than US$60 million.

INTEGRATION WITH R.H. PHILLIPS

Vincor's management believed that Hogue was an excellent complement to the R.H. Phillips portfolio, as Hogue was primarily a super-premium brand, with approximately 88 per cent of its volume in the super-premium category. The strength of the Hogue product range lay in different varietals from the R.H. Phillips range. Different appellations greatly reduced portfolio overlap, as the character and taste of the wines were clearly distinct. Given the price and quality positioning of both businesses, customers were similar and opportunity existed to improve the efficiency and effectiveness of the sales force, while simultaneously developing incremental sales for all brands in the combined portfolio. Vincor incurred expenses of US$4 million from the integration of Hogue and R.H. Phillips and from transaction costs related to the Hogue acquisition. It was management's objective that the integration of Hogue and R.H. Phillips would result in the realization of annual synergies of US$2.8 million.

VINCOR IN 2002

In 2002, Vincor was Canada's largest producer and marketer of wines, with leading brands in all segments of the market in Canada. Vincor had a 22 per cent market share and sales of CDN$376.6 million (see Exhibit 11 for financials). Andrés Wines Ltd., the second-largest winery in Canada, had approximately an 11 per cent market share. Vincor was North America's 4th-largest wine producer in terms of volume and the world's 22nd-largest wine producer in terms of revenue.

The company had wineries in British Columbia, Ontario, Quebec, New Brunswick, California and Washington state, marketing wines produced from grapes grown in the Niagara Peninsula of Ontario, the Okanagan Valley of British Columbia, the Dunnigan Hills of California, the Columbia Valley of Washington state and other countries. The company's California and Washington wines were available throughout the United States and in parts of Canada (see Exhibit 10 for corporate structure).

Canada's government liquor distribution systems and the company's 165-store Wine Rack chain of retail stores sold Vincor's well-known and industry-leading brands: Inniskillin, Jackson-Triggs, Sumac Ridge, Hawthorne Mountain, R.H. Phillips, Toasted Head, Hogue, Sawmill Creek, Notre Vin Maison, Entre-Lacs, L'Ambiance, Caballero de Chile, Bellini, Spumante Bambino, President Canadian Champagne, Okanagan Vineyards, Salmon Harbor and other table, sparkling and fortified wines, Vex and the Canada Cooler brands of coolers and the Growers and Vibe brands of cider.

In the United States, R.H. Phillips, Toasted Head, EXP, Kempton Clark and Hogue wine brands were distributed through a national network of more than 127 distributors, supported by 8 brokers and 40 sales managers. The company's icewines were sold in the United States through a dedicated team of sales managers and internationally, primarily through the duty-free distribution channel. The company had seven employees outside of Canada engaged full-time in the sale of icewine.

Vincor's portfolio had evolved as per Table 1.

The company's objectives in 2002 were to obtain a top-quartile return on capital employed (ROCE) of 16 to 20 per cent and to achieve sales of CDN$1 billion and an Earnings Per Share (EPS) increase of more than 15 per cent. At the time, these objectives were to be met as per Table 2.

TABLE 1   Evolution of Vincor's Portfolio—Table Wine

	F'95		F'02	
	% by vol	% by $	% by vol	% by $
Popular	83	80	47	28
Premium	17	20	53	72

Source: Company files.

TABLE 2 Company Sales Objectives (CDN$ millions)

	Current	5 years
Canada	300	400
United States	100	200
Icewine	15	50
Acquisitions	0	350
Total	415	1,000

Source: Company files.

GOUNDREY WINES PTY. LTD.

Goundrey Wines was one of the pioneer winery operations in Western Australia. The Goundrey family had established the vineyard in 1972, and the first vintage was produced in 1976. By 1995, the business had grown to approximately 17,000 cases in annual sales and was sold to Perth businessman Jack Bendat. Bendat expanded both the vineyards and the winery to reach 2002 sales levels of 250,000 cases annually and revenues of AUD$25 million. Goundrey was one of the largest wineries in Western Australia, selling under two labels: Goundrey and Fox River (see Exhibit 12 for financials).

Bendat was 77 years old, and health and family concerns had resulted in his recent decision to sell the business. Vincor believed it would be able to purchase the assets of Goundrey for AUD$46 million, plus working capital at close (estimated at AUD$16.5 million), plus transaction costs of AUD$2 million for an enterprise value of AUD$64.5 million.

The majority of the Goundrey brand volume (85 per cent) was sold in the AUD$15 to AUD$30 super premium segment of the Australian market. The ultra-premium segment ($30 to $50) accounted for 7 per cent of sales and the premium ($10 to $15) for the remaining 8 per cent. The company's sales were almost entirely in the domestic market with 3 per cent export sales. When asked what Goundrey's export strategy was, Bendat said, "I answer the phone."

Goundrey employed its own sales force in Queensland and New South Wales, with a total of 13 sales reps and 4 sales managers in 2 states. In other states, Goundrey had appointed distributors. In all regions, Goundrey was the most important winery for the distributor. Goundrey had tighter control of its distribution capability in Australia than most of its competitors. Goundrey consumption was running at more than 26 per cent year-over-year growth versus 2001.

Located 350 km south of Perth, the winery could process 3,500 tons of grapes. The winery also had its own bottling capability, enabling it to support an export business where each export market had different labelling requirements.

Triggs felt the Goundrey acquisition would be an important strategic move for Vincor. He saw several major advantages. First, the acquisition would be a significant step in achieving Vincor's strategy of converting from a North American to a global player. The Australian wine industry had captured market share in the world's new wine markets and was poised to continue to do so. Second, the Western Australia region had an established reputation for super- and ultra-premium wines. Although the grape harvest was a mere 4 per cent of the Australian total, more than 25 per cent of Australia's super-premium wines were sourced from that state. Third, the company had developed its own sales force in Queensland and New South Wales. Triggs wanted the proposal to go through.

EXHIBIT 1   Top 10 Producers of Wine in the World 2001

Country	Wine production* (million litres)	Share of world production (%)
France	5,330	19.9
Italy	5,090	19.0
Spain	3,050	11.4
United States	1,980	7.4
Argentina	1,580	5.9
Australia	1,020	3.8
Germany	900	3.4
Portugal	770	2.9
South Africa	650	2.4
Chile	570	2.1
World	27,491	

* Does not include juice and musts (the expressed juice of fruit and especially grapes before and during fermentation; also the pulp and skins of the crushed grapes).

Note: 1 litre=0.26 gallons; each case contains 12, 750 ml bottles=9 litres.

Source: G. Dutruc-Rosset, *Extract of the report on world vitiviniculture*, June 24, 2002.

EXHIBIT 2   Top 10 Exporters of Wine in the World 2001

Country	Wine production* (million litres)	Share of world exports (%)
Italy	1,830	26.5
France	1,580	22.9
Spain	990	14.4
Australia	380	5.5
Chile	310	4.5
United States	300	4.3
Germany	240	3.5
Portugal	200	2.9
South Africa	180	2.6
Moldavia	160	2.3
World	6,897	

Source: G. Dutruc-Rosset, *Extract of the report on world vitiviniculture*, June 24, 2002.

EXHIBIT 3 Top 10 Wine-Consuming Nations 2001

Country	Wine consumption (million litres)	Share of world consumption (%)
France	3,370	15.4
Italy	3,050	13.9
United States	2,133	9.7
Germany	1,966	9.0
Spain	1,400	6.4
Argentina	1,204	5.5
United Kingdom	1,010	4.6
China	580	2.6
Russia	550	2.5
Romania	470	2.1
World	21,892	

Source: G. Dutruc-Rosset, *Extract of the report on world vitiviniculture*, June 24, 2002.

EXHIBIT 4 U.S. Wine Exports Top Countries (by dollar value in 2002)

Country ranking by 2002 dollar value	Value ($000s)	Volume (litres 000)
United Kingdom	188,895	95,446
Canada	92,571	50,348
Japan	81,199	32,342
Netherlands	53,201	26,388
Belgium	18,791	10,884
France	13,326	5,943
Germany	11,818	8,634
Ireland	10,153	5,380
Switzerland	7,199	3,914
Denmark	5,710	3,933
Mexico	5,001	3,705
Taiwan	4,868	2,736
South Korea	3,865	2,439
China	3,370	2,537
Singapore	3,002	1,822
Sweden	2,782	1,145
Hong Kong	2,393	1,140

Source: Wine Institute and Ivie International, using data from U.S. Dept. of Commerce, USA Trade Online. History revised. Numbers may not total exactly due to rounding.

EXHIBIT 5 Australia Wineries

	1998 to 1999	2000 to 2001
Wineries (number)	1,150	1,318
Hectares under vine	122,915	148,275
Wine grape production	793	1,035
Wine consumption	373	398
Wine exports		
million litres	216	339
AUD$ millions	$ 991	$ 1,614
Wine imports		
million litres	24	13
AUD$ millions	$ 114	$ 92

Source: Company files.

EXHIBIT 6 Australia—Top Export Markets 2001

	Million litres	AUD$ millions
United Kingdom	183	762
United States	78	457
Canada	17	106
New Zealand	23	83
Germany	13	55
Other	61	301
All markets	375	1,764

Source: Company files.

EXHIBIT 7 The Wine Market—Canada, Fiscal 2002

	Retail price	% by volume	Trend	% by sales
Popular	< $7	33%	−5%	20%
Premium	$ 7–$10	35%	5%	30%
Super-premium	$10–$15	24%	19%	33%
Ultra-premium	$15–$20	6%	31%	15%
Specialty	>$20	2%	45%	6%

Source: Company files.

EXHIBIT 8 The U.S. Market for California Wine, Fiscal 2002

	Retail price	% by volume	F'02 trend*	% by sales
Jug	<$3	36%	−4%	12%
Premium	$ 3–$7	36%	−2%	27%
Super-premium	$7–$15	18%	8%	28%
Ultra-premium	>$15	10%	3%	33%

* Total U.S. table wine market: +1%; imports: +9%; states other than California: +4%

Source: Company files.

EXHIBIT 9 Top 10 Wine Companies and Sales in 2002 (US$)

Company	Country	Wine sales ($ millions)
E. & J. Gallo Winery	United States	1,500
Foster's Group	Australia	818
Seagram	Canada	800
Constellation Brands	United States	712
Southcorp	Australia	662
Castel Freres	France	625
Diageo	Britain	590
Henkell & Sonlein	Germany	528
Robert Mondavi	United States	506

Note: Excludes France's LVMH, which earned more than 75 per cent of its $1.6 billion in wine sales from champagne.

Source: Direction des Etudes/Centre Français du Commerce Exterieur.

EXHIBIT 10 Vincor's Significant Legal Subsidiaries 2001 (all wholly owned)

Subsidiary	Jurisdiction of incorporation
Hawthorne Mountain Vineyards (2000) Ltd.	Canada
Hogue Cellars, Ltd.	Washington
Inniskillin Wines Inc.	Ontario
Inniskillin Okanagan Vineyards Inc.	British Columbia
R.H. Phillips, Inc.	California
Spagnol's Wine & Beer Making Supplies Ltd.	Canada
Sumac Ridge Estate Winery (2000) Ltd.	Canada
Vincor (Quebec) Inc.	Quebec

Source: Company files.

EXHIBIT 11 Vincor Consolidated Financials (1998 to 2002) (CDN$ millions)

	F'98	F'99	F'00	F'01	F'02	Average annual growth	
						F'01–02	F'98–02
Revenue	206.4	253.2	268.2	294.9	376.6	27.7%	17.7%
EBITDA	28.1	35.0	37.9	49.5	70.5	42.4%	26.1%
% revenue	13.6%	13.8%	14.1%	16.8%	18.7%		
Net income	10.8	11.7	13.3	14.3	26.9	40.1%	25.6%
Avg.capital empl'd	145.5	191.6	222.1	310.4	468.2		
ROCE (EBIT)	14.5%	13.8%	12.7%	13.1%	12.5%		
Funds employed							
Receivables	30.4	33.3	35.7	37.4	55.1		
Inventory	65.1	83.1	70.7	125.9	175.6		
Working capital	57.8	73.3	67.9	111.9	184.9		
Net fixed assets	45.2	60.0	73.3	165.9	178.8		
Other assets	59.8	87.1	82.7	133.4	161.5		
Funds employed	162.8	220.4	223.9	411.2	525.2		
Turnover	1.2x	1.1x	1.2x	.7x	.7x		
Financing							
Debt (net)	50.9	92.5	80.5	254.5	110.1		
Deferred tax	9.6	12.1	14.1	11.4	18.3		
Equity*	102.3	115.8	129.3	145.3	396.8		
Financing	162.8	220.4	223.9	411.2	525.2		

Note: EBITDA—Earnings Before Interest, Taxes, Depreciation and Amortization
* Increased in 2002 due to the fact two equity issues were completed that year.
Source: Company files.

EXHIBIT 12 Goundrey Financials (for years ending June 30) (AUD$ 000s)

	1999	2000	2001
Sales (000)	16,280	21,509	20,942
EBITDA	3,102	6,014	3,548
EBITDA%Sales	19.1%	28.0%	16.9%

Source: Company files.

CIBC—Barclays: Should their Caribbean Operations be Merged?

At the end of 2001, the Canadian Imperial Bank of Commerce (CIBC) and Barclays Bank PLC were in advanced negotiations regarding the potential merger of their respective retail, corporate and offshore banking operations in the Caribbean. Motivated in part by a mutual desire to achieve greater economies of scale, the negotiations had gained momentum ever since the possibility had been raised a year earlier.

Notwithstanding the progress to date, some members of each board could not help but wonder whether this was the best direction to take. Would the combined company be able to deliver superior returns? Would it be possible to integrate, within budget, companies that had competed with each other in the region for decades? Would either firm be better off divesting regional operations instead? Should the two firms just continue to go it alone with an emphasis on continual improvement? These and other issues and options continued to be discussed by the executives at CIBC and their counterparts at Barclays.

Decision time was fast approaching. Both executive teams knew that to prolong discussion further would increase employee, investor and customer anxieties and perhaps do serious harm to both firms. A decision needed to be made within the coming week; there was little time for additional research.

Don Wood and Professor Paul W. Beamish prepared this case solely to provide material for class discussion. The authors do not intend to illustrate either effective or ineffective handling of a managerial situation. The authors may have disguised certain names and other identifying information to protect confidentiality.

IVEY

Richard Ivey School of Business
The University of Western Ontario

AN OVERVIEW OF BANKING IN THE CARIBBEAN

Banking in the Caribbean can best be described as complex and dynamic. Most of the Caribbean countries are islands, with the consequent natural isolation from each other and the main continental world (see Exhibit 1).

Most Caribbean countries were colonies until the latter half of the 20th century. Caribbean banks were originally largely a convenience for the colonial governments and their representatives, and focused on savings, some lending and financing trade. In colonial times, branches of international banks such as Barclays were set up in the region to finance the production and export of commodities such as bananas, sugar, rum, bauxite and petroleum. These banks viewed the Caribbean as a small part of their global operations, and they typically focused on maximizing profits and shareholder returns. They were an oligopoly, involving a small number of players with limited government control. Consequently, the banks co-operated in setting interest rates and terms of credit, and were able to make significant profits.

In the post-colonial period, there was an effort by governments in the region to exert greater control over the economies, and some governments nationalized a number of industries, including the banking sector. By the 1980s, the limitations of state ownership had become evident, and many state-owned banks were privatized. The most significant result was increased competition and an improvement in customer service and product innovation.

The Caribbean banking industry is currently undergoing structural change characterized by mergers and strategic alliances. These mergers and alliances have been driven by the need for economies of scale and scope and the need to be more competitive in the light—globalization in the overall industry. Mergers are complicated, however, because of the many central banks and different currencies—many countries have individual central banks and their own currency, the exception being the Organization of Eastern Caribbean Countries (OECS), comprising eight countries,[1] which share a central bank and currency.

CURRENT OPERATIONS IN THE CARIBBEAN

Barclays PLC (total assets of US$500 billion) and CIBC (total assets of US$200 billion) have extensive operations throughout the Caribbean. Although neither has branches in all countries, between the two, they cover most of the English-speaking Caribbean, as illustrated in Exhibit 2.

CIBC CARIBBEAN OPERATIONS

CIBC Canada is one of North America's leading financial institutions, measured by assets, with more than eight million personal banking and business customers worldwide. It has provided banking services in the West Indies[2] since 1920 and employs approximately 1,600 staff serving 350,000 retail and commercial clients at 42 branches and 4 commercial banking centres.

---

[1]The Organization of Eastern Caribbean Countries comprises Anguilla, Antigua and Barbuda, the Commonwealth of Dominica, Grenada, Montserrat, St. Kitts and Nevis, St. Lucia and St. Vincent and the Grenadines.

[2]For the purpose of this case, the terms "West Indies" and "the Caribbean" are used interchangeably.

The West Indies comprises 29 countries with 4 major language groups. The countries in which CIBC operates represent 9 per cent of the total population of the Caribbean and 57 per cent of the English-speaking population. Although the West Indies is a small market, it is growing faster than North America on a population basis. Economic measures, such as GDP per capita, unemployment and inflation, vary widely across the region.

CIBC is the only major bank serving the Caribbean as a separate, integrated unit, CIBC West Indies Holdings Limited (WIHL). Exhibit 3 displays WIHL and its subsidiaries.

CIBC's Caribbean operations showed net income of US$67.8 million, and total assets were US$4.6 billion for the year ended October 31, 2001. The company is listed on three regional stock exchanges: the Jamaica Stock Exchange, the Barbados Stock Exchange and the Trinidad and Tobago Stock Exchange. In addition, two subsidiaries, CIBC Bahamas Limited and CIBC Jamaica Limited, are also listed on their local stock exchanges. Caribbean headquarters for CIBC is in Barbados.

During 1999 through 2001, CIBC had invested US$48 million in a new banking system, FISERV's International Banking System (ICBS), and related technology and operational improvements. While the conversion to the new system had created operational and customer service problems in the 1999 through 2001 period, the system and its operational platform were now stable and working effectively. The capacity of the ICBS system, however, was built for a bank roughly twice the size of CIBC WI, and full efficiencies would not be realized at the current size of the bank.

CIBC views its strengths and weaknesses in Exhibit 4.

BARCLAYS BANK PLC—CARIBBEAN OPERATIONS

Barclays Caribbean Banking Operations had a net income of US$72.6 million and total assets of US$5.2 billion for the year ended December 31, 2001. Barclays' Caribbean branch network employed 1,584 staff: 157 were management staff, 738 were in front office functions and 846 were in back office functions. Staff were unionized in six countries: Antigua and Barbuda, Barbados, Dominica, Grenada, St. Lucia and St. Vincent and the Grenadines. Apart from salaries and a fully funded pension scheme, local staff received benefits in the form of a medical scheme, loans at preferential rates, 20 to 30 days annual leave, uniforms and profit sharing. Management grades also participated in a bonus scheme, received the use of bank cars and many had club memberships provided.

Corporate and business services are offered in all 14 countries (see Exhibit 5), and offshore banking services are offered in the Bahamas, Barbados, the Cayman Islands, the British Virgin Islands (BVI), and Turks and Caicos. Corporate banking accounts for 45 per cent of corporate income; personal banking, 27 per cent; and offshore banking, 28 per cent.

Barclays' current Caribbean strategy has been rationalization, alongside focused development of the onshore business, together with controlled development of offshore business. Increasing focus has been placed on managing the level of operational risk. Specifically this has meant:

- Organic growth of the corporate and retail presences in existing countries;
- Focus on increased share of existing customers through improvement of consumer lending propositions; and

- Limited investment to rationalize the operating model through centralization initiatives and closure of marginal branches.

Barclays' view of current competitive conditions and their strengths and vulnerabilities can be summarized as follows:

Competition is increasing. For example:

- Traditional Canadian bank competitors are marketing aggressively;
- Regional indigenous banks are expanding their footprints;
- Competitors with new business models (e.g., niche players like CitiGroup) are increasingly entering Barclays' markets;
- In the onshore and retail and corporate businesses, competition comes from large Canadian banks (principally CIBC, Royal Bank of Canada and Scotiabank) and from regional indigenous banks (e.g., Republic Bank of Trinidad);
- Barclays' strong customer relationships have been key to maintaining the bank's market position and have helped to maintain margins;
- Price and convenience are becoming increasingly important as buying factors; as markets become more crowded, price erosion can be expected to reduce currently relatively high margins; and
- Barclays sees its delivery channel "gaps" of real-time electronic banking for corporate accounts and full telephone and Internet offerings for retail customers as becoming increasingly significant.

With no player having an obvious opportunity to develop a sustainable competitive advantage, Barclays believes that the player that achieves the best productivity (and can match the best customer service) is likely to succeed in the medium term. This has led Barclays to increase its focus on how to maximize the cost effectiveness of its operating model.

Barclays' information technology (IT) approach focuses on its Caribbean Regional Data Processing Centre (RPC), located in Nassau, Bahamas. One reason for locating the centre in the Bahamas is the strong Bahamian secrecy laws, which protect confidential client data from being disclosed to third parties. The RPC operates the core banking applications for 13 of the 14 countries in the region.[3] It performs the following:

- BRAINS (Barclays Retail Accounting and Information System), the retail banking software package, which is also used by Barclays Africa;
- Interlink connection for the ATM network (55 units);
- Gateways to the MasterCard and VISA networks;
- BusinessMaster, online access to information and customer service for corporate and offshore customers; and
- BarclayCall, online access to information and customer service for retail customers (available only in the Bahamas and Barbados).

All the applications above are run on stand-alone Caribbean systems, with no dependency on the United Kingdom, except for contingency arrangements.

The BRAINS system had been installed about 10 years previously and lacked the ability to consolidate projects by customer so as to facilitate Internet and telephone

---

[3]The remaining country is British Virgin Islands, which, for historic reasons, uses a stand-alone accounting system.

banking. Barclays operations in both Africa and the Caribbean were faced with a costly decision on whether to replace BRAINS with a more modern banking system. Moreover, Barclays operations tended to be more manually intensive and costly than those of its competitors, Royal, BNS and CIBC, who had installed more modern technology.

THE COMPETITION

The four major international players identified in Exhibit 6 have each developed a different market niche in which to compete successfully in the retail and commercial markets in the West Indies. The Royal Bank is considered the best performer across the region. CIBC summarized its competitive niches as shown in Exhibit 6.

Banking oligopolies existed across the West Indies, with the five largest banks in each country controlling more than 80 per cent market share. CIBC estimated market shares in the various national markets it serves as shown in Exhibit 7.

In addition to the retail and commercial services, major banks in the Caribbean also serve the US$1.1 billion capital markets in the region. The capital markets business in the West Indies is composed mainly of debt financing arrangements. It is considered a new and emerging sector, comprising eight players in this marketplace (see Exhibit 8).

The capital market segment began to develop in the 1980s and is expected to grow at about 10 per cent annually for the next few years. The majority of debt financing is government borrowing, government divestitures of banks, hotels and utilities and large multinational corporations' projects. More recently, the resource sector has brought more sophisticated arrangements to the West Indies capital markets sector. The market is driven mainly by the large economies of Jamaica and Trinidad and Tobago. Revenue in this sector is generated by a typical 1 per cent fee and a 3.5 per cent lending spread. In 2000, the total size of all CIBC WI capital markets deals was estimated at US$118 million, generating about US$3 million of revenue and US$1.5 million in profits.

A few large competitors like CS First Boston, Citibank and ABN AMRO have entered the market and basically manage the region through local relationships with business and government leaders, augmented by head office expertise to complete the transactions. These key relationships are important to gaining business, and many other large competitors like DLJ, Merrill Lynch and Smith Barney have not been able to enter the market successfully. Exhibit 8 summarizes the main players in the West Indies capital markets.

Both CIBC and Barclays now need to assess their options, evaluate the factors and select the best strategy for their respective firms. They must consider whether to merge or not and determine the implications for merging in this complex environment. Exhibits 9 and 10 provide financial information on the two firms' Caribbean operations.

EXHIBIT 1   Map of the West Indies

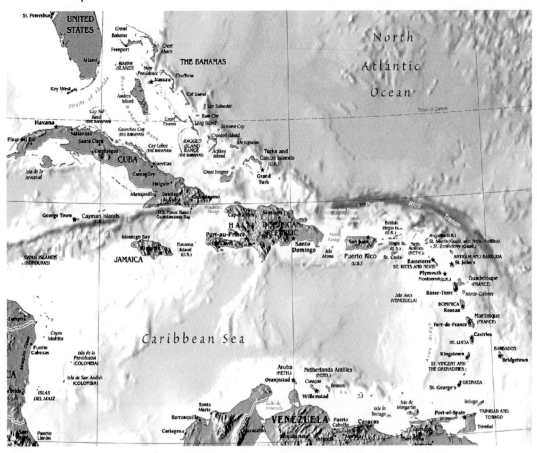

Source: CIA World Factbook, 2004.

EXHIBIT 2   Caribbean Presence

Country	Population	GDP/capita (US$)	CIBC	Barclays
Anguilla	10,000	4,000		•
Antigua and Barbuda	70,000	8,419	•	•
Bahamas	280,000	13,847	•	•
Barbados	270,000	7,750	•	•
Belize	230,000	2,688		•
British Virgin Islands	20,000	12,000		•
Cayman Islands	30,000	24,000	•	
Dominica	70,000	3,233		•
Grenada	100,000	877		•
Jamaica	2,570,000	1,756	•	
St. Kitts and Nevis	40,000	5,761		•
St. Lucia	160,000	3,581	•	•
Netherlands Antilles	200,000	N/A		•
St. Vincent and the Grenadines	110,000	N/A	•	•
Turks and Caicos Islands	20,000	6,000	•	•

Source: CIBC Economics; World Fact Book; Americas Review 1999—Economic indicators.

EXHIBIT 3   Current Situation—CIBC West Indies Holdings Limited (WIHL) and Subsidiaries

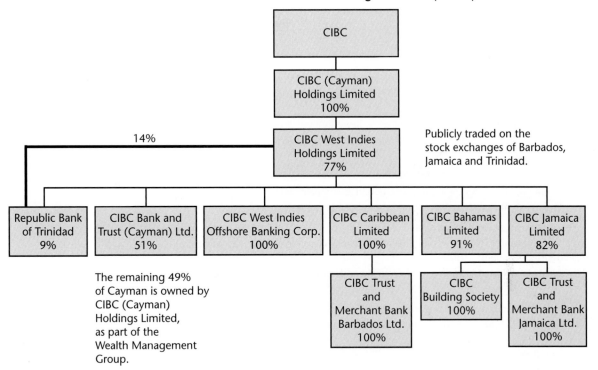

Operating Units:

1. Bahamas—CIBC Bahamas Limited.

2. Jamaica—consists of CIBC Jamaica Limited, CIBC Building Society and CIBC Trust and Merchant Bank Jamaica Limited.

3. Barbados—consists of CIBC Caribbean Limited and CIBC Trust and Merchant Bank Barbados Limited, which includes our operations in Barbados, Antigua, St. Lucia, St. Vincent and Turks and Caicos.

4. Cayman—Fifty-one per cent of operations of CIBC Bank and Trust (Cayman) Ltd., which relate to the Retail and Commercial Operations in Cayman.

Source: Company files.

EXHIBIT 4   CIBC Internal Analysis

STRENGTHS

CIBC ownership
- Strong brand and public image
- Expertise in retail banking
- Effective mix of delivery channels
- High loyalty ratings
- Excellent relationships with governments, important business players and the public
- Enormous value in WIHL franchise on local equity markets–currently selling at 26x earnings

Management
- New leadership with strong management support from CIBC in Canada
- Extensive knowledge of the region (economic and political)
- Important relationships with business and political leaders

Products and delivery channels
- An established strength in product lines currently experiencing tremendous growth in the region (mortgages, cards, ABMs)
- Ability to leverage expertise in all products and services from the Canadian organization

Operations
- Co-ordinated regional operations strengthened by strong linkages to CIBC
- Established branch network with 40 branches in 8 countries
- Ability to leverage CIBC Canadian operations expertise from Intria Items Inc., O&T and National Operations Support

Technology
- An integrated banking system (ICBS) that will enable consistent and efficient operations in the WI and will allow new channels such as Internet banking
- An extended wide area network (EWAN) will provide a dependable robust real-time environment
- Ability to leverage CIBC Canadian technology expertise from Intria Corporation and O&T

WEAKNESSES—Issues (all of which were being resolved)

Credit risk management
- During the conversion period, retail loan losses have increased substantially
- Recent audits have revealed weaknesses in lending practices
- There was not a consistent view on credit risk appetite between local management and the credit risk group, which is largely seconded from CIBC Canada

Items processing
- Three item processing centres have been found to be inefficient and lacking in reliable processes

Systems and technology
- Two years ago, systems were antiquated and not Y2K compliant; however, the new platform is stable and operating effectively
- The investment in technology exceeds the scale of the current operations

Organization
- Until recently, the West Indies operations were organized geographically
- Inefficiencies and overlaps

Jamaica
- Very inefficient operations with high NIX ratios and low returns
- Poor credit risk management

EXHIBIT 5 Barclays Caribbean Business Base

Country	Operating income—1999 (US$ millions)	No. of accounts ('000s)			No. of outlets*
		Personal	Business	Total	
Anguilla	2	4.3	0.1	4.4	1
Antigua and Barbuda	8	28.5	0.7	29.2	1
Bahamas	49	50.1	2.4	52.5	9
Barbados	42	101.0	2.9	103.9	6
Belize	8	16.9	3.1	19.9	4
British Virgin Islands	16	17.6	1.6	19.2	3
Cayman Islands	34	11.9	3.4	15.3	2
Dominica	4	20.0	0.7	20.7	2
Grenada	6	23.6	1.3	24.9	4
St. Kitts and Nevis	5	14.1	0.4	14.5	2
St. Lucia	12	43.1	1.1	44.2	4
Netherlands Antilles	3	5.7	0.6	6.3	3
St. Vincent and the Grenadines	4	20.8	0.4	21.1	1
Turks and Caicos Islands	12	11.0	2.3	13.2	3
Totals	**205**	**368.6**	**21.0**	**389.3**	**45**

*In addition, there is a Card & Mortgage Centre and a Regional Processing Centre in the Bahamas, as well as a Card and Operations Centre in Barbados.

EXHIBIT 6   External Analysis—Retail and Commercial

Each of the four major international players has developed a different market niche in which to compete successfully in the retail and commercial market in the West Indies. Royal Bank is considered the best performer across the region.

Player	Operations	How They Compete in the West Indies
CIBC	• 40 branches in 8 countries serving 350,000 retail and commercial customers • Core business is retail banking with trust, offshore and capital market activities as other lines of business	• Strong in retail and small business and merchant services across the West Indies Region, particularly in Bahamas which has a sizeable market share • Market leader in credit card sales in Barbados but lags behind in Bahamas and Jamaica • Good reputation for corporate and capital markets activities • Newest technology in the region • Only major competitor to manage the West Indies as a separate, integrated unit
Scotia Bank	• 158 branches in 24 countries with a balance sheet of CDN$6.9 billion, built primarily on consumer products, hospitality financing and loans to government • Very efficient at managing expenses • In 1998, Bank of Nova Scotia Jamaica earned $73 million, 5 per cent of total BNS profit • In 1999, International retail operations were larger than domestic operations—the West Indies accounts for the majority of international operations	• Leader in consumer loans, particularly vehicle loans • Competitive advantage by having hard currency lending operations maintained out of Puerto Rico, giving them access to inexpensive government funding, which they have leveraged throughout the West Indies Region • Focus on product offering and strong marketing efforts • Very successful operations in Jamaica • Good development of local staff using secondments to Canada, consistent
Royal Bank	• 33 branches in 9 countries, with the most comprehensive convenience delivery channels in those countries and are leaders in the offshore industry	• Active high-value strategy and a leader amongst high-value clients • Considered best performer of retail banks • Significant offshore and international presence in Barbados and Bahamas • Dominating in certain products in each country
Barclays PLC	• 45 branches in 17 countries and have recently invested US$30 million in new technology for the region	• Strong remittance and offshore business • Strong corporate banking connections • Good Cards business run by Barclaycard US • Offers telephone banking • Strong client relationship building system, (Premiere Service), targeted to its working professional client base

EXHIBIT 7 Selected Market Share Measures

	Measure	CIBC	Barclays	Scotiabank	Royal Bank	NCB*	Others
Antigua	% total assets						
	% deposits	12		14	10	24	40
	% loans	11	9	22	7	20	31
	No. branches	1	3	4	3		15
	No. ATMs	1	3	4	2		10
Barbados	% total assets						
	% deposits	18	22	13	21	17	9
	% loans	19	21	21	10	18	11
	No. branches	10	6	8	7		15
	No. ATMs	11	8	8	13		14
Jamaica	% total assets						
	% deposits	7		41		36	16
	% loans	9		50		27	14
	No. branches	13		45			100
	No. ATMs	8		31			55
St. Lucia	% total assets						
	% deposits	10	23	16	10	24	19
	% loans	12	24	17	10	21	17
	No. branches	2	4	4	4		10
	No. ATMs	3	4	7	3		12
St. Vincent	% total assets	14	14	13			59
	% deposits						
	% loans						
	No. branches	1	1	1			10
	No. ATMs	1	1	1			5
Bahamas	% total assets	19		15	21		45
	% deposits						
	% loans						
	No. branches	8	10	17	21		27
	No. ATMs	9	11	21	21		18
Cayman Islands	% total assets	25	25	15			35
	% deposits						
	% loans						
	No. branches	2	2	4	2		10
	No. ATMs	4	3	3	2		16
Turks and Caicos	% total assets		70	16			14
	% deposits						
	% loans						
	No. branches	1	2	2			
	No. ATMs	1	2	1			

*National Commercial Banks.

EXHIBIT 8   External Analysis—Capital Markets

The West Indies Capital Markets business is dominated by a small number of players. Citibank is the dominant competitor in the region and is estimated to have earned profits of US$20 million in the capital markets sector in each of the last five years.

Financial services company	Industry focus[1]	Product focus[2]	Level of relationship with foreign parent/ partner[3]	Level of physical Caribbean presence	Market share (approx.)	Level of offshore booking (approx.)
CIBC	E&P, H&R,A, Cong, PS	Bnd U/W, PF, LS	Medium	High	10%	100%
Citi bank	E&P, PS, A	Bnd U/W, D, CBF, LS, S	High	Low	50%	80%
Royal Merchant Bank (Trinidad)	E&P, H&R,A, Cong, PS	Bnd U/W, E U/W, S, PF	Medium	High	15%	50%
Republic Bank (Fincor)	E&P, H&R, A, Cong, PS	PF, Bnd U/W, E U/W, LS	Low	Medium	10%	60%
Scotia Bank	E&P, H&R, A, Cong, PS	Bnd U/W, LS	High	High	5%	70%
Credit Swiss First Boston	E&P, PS	Bnd U/W, LS	High	None	5%	100%
ABN Ambro	E&P	LS	High	None	4%	100%
Chase	E&P, PS	Bnd U/W, LS	High	None	1%	100%

1. Energy and Petrochemicals (E&P); Hotel and Resorts (H&R); Agriculture (A); Conglomerates (Cong); Public Sector (PS).

2. Bond Underwriting (Bnd U/W); Project Financing (PF); Equity Underwriting (E U/W); Derivatives (D); Commodity-based Financing (CBF); Loan Syndication (LS); Securatization (S); Advisory Services (AS).

3. This variable measures the relationship with the foreign partner in terms of advisory assistance on financial products structuring.

EXHIBIT 9 Five-year Statistical Review—CIBC West Indies Holdings Condensed Consolidated Balance Sheets (as of October 31, 2001) (BDS $000s)

	2001	2000	1999	1998	1997
Assets					
Cash resources	2,743,877	1,849,630	1,961,285	813,025	772,552
Securities	2,417,865	2,249,992	1,578,942	458,508	450,235
Loans	3,760,574	3,411,184	3,162,052	2,424,544	2,030,889
Customer's liability under acceptances	11,587	42,880	1,651	1,600	4,532
Net investment in leases	3,055	4,221	5,396	6,817	6,061
Fixed assets	138,114	123,427	120,401	75,175	62,281
Other assets	113,982	127,393	127,179	118,460	67,039
	9,189,054	7,808,727	6,956,906	3,898,129	3,393,589
Liabilities and shareholders' equity					
Deposits	8,191,737	6,716,869	6,016,367	3,285,774	2,895,778
Acceptances	11,587	42,880	1,651	1,600	4,532
Other liabilities	101,172	303,874	279,636	173,236	97,697
Minority interests	232,282	195,375	170,298	39,829	37,321
Shareholders' equity common shares	316,380	316,380	316,380	274,980	274,980
Retained earnings	335,896	233,349	172,574	122,710	83,281
	9,189,054	7,808,727	6,956,906	3,898,129	3,393,589

Consolidated Statements of Income (as of October 31, 2001) (BDS $000s)

	2001	2000	1999	1998	1997
Interest income	601,309	594,914	497,534	348,231	317,178
Interest expense	(316,737)	(313,945)	(252,750)	(149,632)	(147,423)
Net interest income	284,572	280,969	244,784	198,599	169,755
Non-interest income	128,378	126,846	120,286	71,640	63,020
Total income	412,950	407,815	365,070	270,239	232,775
Non-interest expenses	218,519	224,891	210,402	159,211	136,167
Provision for credit losses	10,287	28,602	23,908	15,342	10,277
Total expenses	228,806	253,493	234,310	174,553	146,444
Net income before income taxes	184,144	154,322	130,760	95,686	86,331
Income taxes	8,616	7,038	4,027	12,980	15,228
Net income before exception/extraordinary items and minority interests	175,528	147,284	126,731	82,706	71,103
Exceptional/Extraordinary items	–	–	(2,171)	–	583
Minority interests	(39,919)	(29,702)	(29,536)	(7,690)	(4,563)
Net income	135,609	117,582	95,024	75,016	67,123

EXHIBIT 10 Financial Information—Barclays Profit and Loss/Balance Sheets (for years ending December 31) (US$ millions)

	1995	1996	1997	1998	1999
Net interest income	103	107	116	134	153
Commission income	41	42	46	51	54
Total operating income	**144**	**149**	**162**	**185**	**207**
Staff costs	(53)	(57)	(58)	(61)	(66)
Property, equipment and other expenses	(36)	(34)	(42)	(48)	(50)
Depreciation/amortization	–	(6)	(8)	(8)	(10)
Operating costs	**(89)**	**(97)**	**(108)**	**(117)**	**(126)**
Net operating income	**55**	**52**	**54**	**68**	**80**
Provisions	**(8)**	**(11)**	**(2)**	**(1)**	**(9)**
Profit before tax	**47**	**41**	**52**	**67**	**71**
	1,995	**1,996**	**1,997**	**1,998**	**1,999**
Assets					
Loans to banks	54	50	168	55	87
Loans to customers	1,141	1,240	1,360	1,618	1,884
Other assets	255	572	593	752	860
Accruals and prepayments	–	3	14	21	23
Due from BBPLC	2,270	2,017	2,188	2,897	2,855
Property & equipment	54	62	61	60	79
Total assets	**3,774**	**3,944**	**4,384**	**5,403**	**5,788**
Liabilities and capital					
Customer deposits	3,469	3,513	3,836	4,654	4,972
Other liabilites	108	206	279	161	180
Due to BBPLC	166	194	235	549	580
Revenue reserve	31	31	34	39	56
Total liabilities	**3,774**	**3,944**	**4,384**	**5,403**	**5,788**

2000 Full-year Forecast (US$ millions)

	H1 2000 actual	H2 2000 forecast	2000 forecast
Net interest income	91	91	182
Fees and commission	30	29	59
Total operating income	**121**	**120**	**241**
Staff costs	(32)	(30)	(62)
Property and equipment	(11)	(11)	(22)
Other expenses	(14)	(11)	(25)
Depreciation/amortization	(4)	(5)	(9)
Operating costs	**(61)**	**(57)**	**(118)**
Net operating income	**60**	**63**	**123**
Provisions	**(4)**	**(4)**	**(8)**
Profit before tax	**56**	**59**	**115**

*Income analyzed between net interest, fees and commisons and other.

SUNOPTA, INC.

Jeremy Kendall, chairman and chief executive officer (CEO) of SunOpta, Inc., glanced out his window at the rural Ontario landscape. The offices of his $400 million[1] publicly-traded corporation (STKL–Nasdaq/SOY–TSX), set in a converted farmhouse and out-buildings in Norval, Ontario, conveyed a sense of calm and serenity. But Kendall, as he spoke, was clearly frustrated:

> We're supposed to be building value for our shareholders, but that hasn't happened recently. I'm not sure what else we can do. This company is growing dramatically—at $306 million, our sales last year were up more than 50 per cent over 2003. We're on track to top $400 million in 2005. SunOpta is profitable and has a strong balance sheet. There's an ongoing stream of positive news from the company. Yet, over the past 15 months, our market capitalization has dropped from over $500 million to less than half that amount.
>
> Anyone who bought into this company five years ago is still today holding an investment that has tripled, or even quadrupled, in value. But many of our current investors acquired their shares in the last couple of years, and most of them have lost money. That's not what they expected to happen, and they are definitely looking to me for a better outcome.

It was May 17, 2005, and the annual shareholders meeting for SunOpta was just one week away. Kendall knew he'd be pressed to provide some answers. Shareholder value seemed locked, and it was his job to do something about it.

Ken Mark prepared this case under the supervision of Professor Robert Nourse solely to provide material for class discussion. The authors do not intend to illustrate either effective or ineffective handling of a managerial situation. The authors may have disguised certain names and other identifying information to protect confidentiality.

Ivey

Richard Ivey School of Business
The University of Western Ontario

---

[1]All currency in U.S. dollars unless otherwise specified.

COMPANY BACKGROUND

SunOpta, Inc. was a well-established company, having been founded in 1973 as Stake Technology Ltd. Its goal at that time was to develop commercial applications for a patented technology using high-temperature steam and pressure to break down the ligno-cellulose fibres in sugar bagasse, corn stalks and other crop residues that would ordinarily be regarded as waste. The result was a digestible product that could serve as roughage in animal feed and, potentially, as a basis for production of ethanol fuel. Developing a solid customer base proved difficult, however. While the company was continually able to attract capital and generate enough revenue to survive, it had been unable, over a 20-year period, to attain reasonable growth. From a peak of $2.4 million in 1992, sales fell to $124,000 in 1994, with a loss of $740,000. While Stake's balance sheet still showed a positive cash position and no long-term debt, its outlook at that time was not good.

Jeremy Kendall had been at the helm of Stake Technology since 1983 and thus had personally lived through many of its struggling years. His background and experience in entrepreneurial ventures, however, had contributed substantially to keeping the company afloat against difficult odds. At the relatively young age of 24, Kendall had graduated as an Ivey Scholar from Canada's renowned MBA program at the University of Western Ontario. Almost immediately, while holding a full-time job as a product manager for a specialty steel company, he had formed an investment company with a friend, parlaying $2,000 of capital into $100,000 in less than a year and a half. That gain provided him with the equity to buy an obsolete manufacturing plant and sell off its equipment at considerable profit, with the National Museum of Canada among the buyers. Kendall later bought an interest in a company making television commercials in Toronto, and, in a subsequent part-time venture, bought, moved and resold houses being displaced by the construction of the Welland Canal in southern Ontario.

In 1969, Kendall and a partner were able to put up $200,000 to co-found a venture capital company. Over the next 12 years, Venturetek International grew to become Canada's largest venture conglomerate, controlling almost $200 million in new venture assets and numbering major pension funds, international banks and an arm of the Canadian government among its shareholders. Then one of Venturetek's principal investments, a soft drink company with 50 bottling plants throughout North America, ran into serious difficulties. Its financial problems reverberated throughout the portfolio and, in 1982, the venture company was liquidated. Kendall moved on, initially working as a part-time consultant to Stake Technology and, shortly thereafter, being named as its CEO.

When Kendall arrived at Stake in 1983, the company was in serious financial straits. It had gone public in 1981, raised $10 million and spent it all. Explained Kendall:

> We raised another $10 million, spent it and borrowed $10 million more. After some innovative restructuring, we eventually converted all of the debt to preferred shares. Three years later, we redeemed those preferred shares and paid everyone back and never borrowed a penny until the late 1990s because we generated enough internal cash to keep the company going.

For almost a dozen years, Stake Technology survived, but often at a pace slowed by time-consuming feed tests required by Canadian, U.S. and European health authorities. Then, abruptly, a series of events began that would dramatically transform the small, steam-explosion technology company into a very different entity.

OPTA MINERALS

Early in 1995, Kendall was introduced to the owner of a Waterdown, Ontario, company, Barnes Environmental Ltd. Barnes manufactured silica-free abrasives and minerals used in various environment-sensitive industrial processes. The business interested Kendall, who had a lifelong concern for environmental preservation. With $10 million in sales, Barnes was in trouble, unable to service the interest expense and bank monitor fees of $12 million in debentures issued while the company was diversifying into a number of unsuccessful non-core businesses. Essentially, Barnes was bankrupt, with its owner and the debenture holders having little prospect of recovery. Kendall, however, proposed a restructuring deal:

> First, we convinced the debenture holders to foreclose on their security and take possession of the assets. Then, in return for a $4 million, non-interest-bearing note payable as a balloon after three years, the assets relating to the core business were sold to a newly formed company, Barnes Environment, Inc. (later re-named Opta Minerals). Stake Technology was able to buy 51 per cent of the new company for one dollar, while the previous owner, who had to approve the deal, got 49 per cent for a dollar. The new company, with no debt and now focused only on its primary abrasives business, was "profitable from the first second we owned it." Meanwhile, we were able to help the debenture holders recover almost $1.5 million by selling off the remaining non-core assets.

On the strength of Barnes' newfound profitability, Stake was able, by the end of 1995, to buy the original owner's 49 per cent of Barnes Environmental, Inc. for $2.5 million, half as cash and half as stock in Stake Technology. Within a few years, however, Barnes would generate annual cash flows of $2.5 million or more.

With internal growth and four small acquisitions over the next eight years, Opta Minerals, as the group of companies came to be known, grew to become a significant player in North American markets for industrial minerals and environmental recycling. Its abrasives, for example, were used in ship-building and repair and as blasting media on steel bridges and overpasses, and its sands and clays were used to create moulds in the foundry industry and for various products in the brick industry. By 2004, Opta Minerals generated revenue of $32.2 million, a 30 per cent increase over 2003, while operating earnings of $3.6 million were up 40 per cent over the prior year.

Opta competed in an industry characterized by small, regionally based niche companies with limited product offerings. Looking ahead, Kendall saw continued opportunities to grow the business by continuing to acquire other companies in its industry, by developing new products and services and by continuing to expand geographically. His vision was, in effect, a classic rollup. With a broader scale of operations, Opta could compete effectively by offering an unbeatable combination of product quality, customer service and competitive pricing.

In February 2005, the net assets and business of Opta Minerals were transferred to a new, wholly owned subsidiary, Opta Minerals, Inc. Next, a portion of the new subsidiary's shares were sold in an initial public offering (OPM–TSX). The offering raised a net CDN$17.5 million in proceeds and resulted in reducing the parent company's ownership in Opta to 70.8 per cent. Approximately CDN$4 million was used to repay intercompany loans owed to the parent company, with the balance earmarked for investment in new products, technologies and business related to the future growth of Opta Minerals, Inc.

MOVING INTO ORGANICS

Meanwhile, Kendall's early success in turning around Barnes Environment had not gone unnoticed. Attending a Stake Technology meeting in 1999, James Riffenbergh, a board member and wealthy private investor, complained in a casual conversation that his retirement from a large U.S. printing company had been interrupted. Riffenbergh was also an outside director of Sunrich, Inc., a Minnesota-based producer of non-genetically modified (non-GMO) and identity-preserved (IP) organic grains and food ingredients. Following a serious injury to Sunrich's president in a farm accident, he was now acting as interim CEO and looking for a permanent replacement. The time and energy commitment was not what he and his wife had in mind for their retirement.

Kendall, whose family had eaten organically for many years, saw an opportunity. Why couldn't Stake Technology buy Sunrich, which was owned by 350 farmers and generating $17 million in annual revenues? Kendall would run and grow the merged entity, while Riffenbergh could return to a more relaxed life.

The purchase of Sunrich, Inc., for approximately $6.8 million, was completed in August 1999. Of the total purchase price, $392,000 was paid in cash and the balance by approximately 5.5 million shares of Stake Technology. The transaction took Stake, for the first time, into the emerging field of natural and organic foods.

Natural foods were generally described as being minimally processed and free of preservatives and chemical additives, such as artificial colouring or flavouring. To qualify as *organic,* however, food had to be produced, processed and handled according to strict standards verified through inspection by an organic certifying agency. For example, no pesticides, herbicides or fertilizers made with synthetic ingredients or sewage sludge could be used, and no ionizing radiation or bioengineering was permitted. Land on which organic food was grown must have been free of prohibited substances for a minimum of three years.

Reflecting increased consumer interest in healthy lifestyles, the U.S. market for organic foods was growing at 10 to 20 per cent annually and, in the early 2000s, was thought to total more than $10 billion. Nonetheless, this represented less than two per cent of total food sales.

Soybean products, in particular, had experienced exceptional growth, primarily as a result of their association with improved cardiovascular health. Shortly after purchasing Sunrich, therefore, Kendall elected to shift its product mix toward the soy concentrate used by manufacturers of soy milk. The move proved successful and, in August 2000, the Sunrich acquisition was followed by that of Northern Food and Dairy, Inc., an Alexandria, Minnesota, manufacturer of soy milk and related food ingredients. The total purchase price was $11.2 million, including $608,000 in cash and 7 million shares of Stake Technology.

With two acquisitions in a little over a year, food and food ingredients had become Stake's single largest revenue group. Over two-thirds of the company's 2000 consolidated revenue of $68.4 million was food related.

During the next four years, Stake entered a period of unparalled expansion into natural and organic food products, driven both by internal growth and by an aggressive series of 18 additional acquisitions. To soy products, Stake added businesses in oat fibre production, sunflower products and organic fruit snacks. To its manufacturing businesses, Stake added, starting in October 2002, a series of acquisitions aimed at positioning the company as the only national distributor in Canada of natural and organic foods.

Initially, because it didn't have cash, Stake had relied on shares to make acquisitions. But as it started to grow, internally generated funds and new capital made it possible to acquire companies using cash. During 2001, the company completed four private equity placements with a number of investors, including Claridge, Inc., a privately held investment arm of the Bronfman family. Prices ranged from $1.75 to $2.10 per share. Approximately 11.1 million shares and 4.1 million warrants were issued, yielding net proceeds of $20 million.

In August 2003, a public offering of 7.5 million shares at $7 per share yielded net proceeds to the company of $51 million. The proceeds enabled the company to continue its acquisition program, but now largely on the basis of all-cash transactions. Shortly after the public offering, in October 2003, the company's name was changed to SunOpta, Inc., reflecting the names of its two principal businesses, the Sunrich Food Group (later renamed SunOpta Food Group) and Opta Food Ingredients.

The Food Group had grown, in just six years, from a single operating company with $17 million revenue to a vertically integrated business model selling non-GMO, organic, natural and specialty food products and ingredients. The Food Group's 2004 revenue of $273 million represented 89 per cent of total consolidated SunOpta revenue of $306 million, up from $174 million in 2003. Operating earnings were $14.9 million, a 37 per cent increase from $10.9 million in 2003.

SUNOPTA IN 2005

By 2005, SunOpta consisted of three business units, all with a focus on environmental responsibility. Each business unit was substantially different from the other two in size and activity: the Food Group (2004 revenue: $272 million), Opta Minerals, Inc. (2004 revenue: $32 million, 70 per cent owned) and the StakeTech Steam Explosion Group (2004 revenue: $1.3 million, nominal operating profit on low-cost operation). The company's mission statement, however, made SunOpta's future direction clear:

> Our Mission: To rapidly grow sales, profits and shareholder value through an effective balance of internal growth and acquisition, with a focus on integrated business models in the natural, organic and specialty foods markets.

For the past 7 years, SunOpta's revenues had grown at a 62 per cent compound annual growth rate (CAGR). For 7 consecutive years, it had been included in Profit magazine's "Profit 100" list of the fastest-growing companies in Canada. Overall, SunOpta's 23 facilities throughout the United States and Canada employed more than 1,500 people.

Shown in Exhibits 1 and 2 are historical income statements and balance sheets for the period 1998 to 2004, as well as first-quarter results for 2005. Exhibit 3 presents selected key financial statistics for the same period. Exhibit 4 is a summary of key acquisitions.

THE FOOD GROUP

Growth in natural and organic foods was guided at SunOpta by a business model called "Seed to Table." Shown figuratively in Exhibit 5, it had emerged over time from the Food Group's beginnings in soy. Explained Kendall:

> We began by selling seeds to farmers, buying their grains and soybeans, processing it and then shipping to others who made soy milk. We were clear to avoid owning farms—we just provided the seed to farmers and bought what they harvested. Soon after we started this model and had purchased Northern, a gentleman

building a packaging plant for soy milk ran out of money, so we took over his debt and completed it. Now we were making and packaging soy milk, which was the beginning of our vertically integrated strategy. Later, we could extend the same strategy to other grains, such as corn and sunflower, and in Canada, to organic food distribution. We stop at wholesale distribution—we don't want to own retail.

By 2005, the Seed to Table business model was reflected in the organizational structure of the Food Group, which now consisted of four business segments, each also described as a Group:

- *The Grains and Soy Products Group* sourced grain and other agricultural products, sold them in bulk to other customers, but also transferred them to . . .
- *The Ingredients Group,* which processed internally and externally sourced raw materials into food ingredients such as soy milk concentrate. These ingredients were sold to external customers, but also transferred internally to . . .
- *The Packaged Products Group,* which produced finished consumer products, such as soy milk. These products were sold to U.S. and Canadian grocery chains, to organic food distributors in the United States and, in Canada, to . . .
- *The Distributed Products Group,* which distributed organic, kosher, natural and specialty food products in Canada.

While acquisitions had played a major role in the growth of overall Food Group revenues, the Food Group had also shown a capacity to generate internal growth. Since the Sunrich acquisition in 1999, Food Group revenues had grown from $17.3 million to $272.3 million in 2004. On average, over the past 5 years, 60 to 65 per cent of the Food Group's revenue growth had come from acquisitions.

Grains and Soy Products

The Grains and Soy Products Group sourced and marketed non-GMO and organic crops, focusing on soybeans, sunflower, corn, rice and oat products. It sold seeds to, and purchased crops from, 2,100 IP growers in the Midwestern United States, as well as the spot market. Raw materials were tested, processed and sold in bulk domestically and internationally. Revenues in 2004 were $84.3 million.

The Grains and Soy Products Group competed with large companies in the United States and international grain procurement market and, for specialty grains, in smaller, niche U.S. organic grains markets. Availability of supply, access to transportation and relationships with organic food producers were keys to success. Profitability in any given year could be substantially influenced by supply fluctuations caused by drought or insect damage.

Ingredients

Products of the Ingredients Group included oat fibre, soy milk concentrate,[2] food texturizers and organic ingredients. Its hundreds of worldwide customers included some of the largest U.S. packaged food companies and restaurant chains. The Group was also thought to be one of the largest producers of soy milk concentrate in the United States, holding contracts with several major branded soy milk manufacturers. It was also the largest supplier of oat fibre in North America and was continuing to increase

---

[2]Soy milk concentrate is produced in the Ingredients Group, but its revenues and margins are accounted for in the Grains and Soy Products Group.

its oat fibre capacity as a growing number of food manufacturers sought to improve the nutritional content of their foods by addition of fibre.

Ingredients Group sales of $69.8 million in 2004 represented a $20 million increase over the prior year. Almost half the increase, or $8.4 million, came from higher sales of oat fibre driven by consumer interest in low carbohydrate diets. By 2005, however, demand for low-carb products had levelled off and, in some instances, declined.

The Ingredients Group operated mostly in highly competitive niche ingredient markets, often developing and processing products for specific customers or industry segments. Many other small product developers and specialty processors did the same thing. Beyond the specialty segments, large firms with resources and capabilities far greater than SunOpta's dominated. They included major chemical companies with food ingredient divisions and consumer food product manufacturers that also developed and sold food ingredients.

Packaged Products

With 2004 sales of $42.7 million, the Packaged Products Group marketed private label products such as soy milk, healthy convenience foods, organic dairy products, vegetables and meat analogues. These products were sold directly to grocery chains and specialty stores. Under its own brand names of Kettle Valley and Dakota Gourmet, the Group also sold organic fruit bars and snack products. Kendall indicated, however, that he was starting to move away from owning brands, stating that brands were not essential to SunOpta's business model.

Competition came from other suppliers of natural and organic meat and dairy product in North America, while the company's aseptic packaged products competed with numerous regional manufacturers of similar size and capabilities. Branded products competed against a number of larger producers of snack products.

Distributed Products

The Distributed Products Group was the result of a series of acquisitions, starting in late 2002, of small- to medium-sized natural, organic and kosher food distributors in Canada. The Group's 2004 revenue of $75.9 million stood in striking comparison to $25.1 million in 2003. Gross margin of $15.8 million in 2004 was almost triple the $5.4 million in 2003, reflecting increasing synergies between the recent acquisitions and the previously acquired businesses.

By May 2005, continued internal growth and acquisitions had built the Distributed Products Group to annualized revenues of $100 million. The Group was thought to be the largest natural and organic foods distributor in Canada, with operations in the principal cities of Vancouver, Toronto and Montreal. Management hoped to double the Group's size to approximately $200 million by 2007.

Competition was represented by a number of regional natural and organic food distributors of varying size. The Group also competed against much larger conventional food distributors and food companies that included specialty products in their assortments.

LOOKING AHEAD

Management believed that continuing to grow in natural and organic foods would open the door to further integration within and among the food groups and would, as a result, bring about increased efficiencies and cost savings. Steven Bromley, SunOpta's president and chief operating officer (COO), outlined key points in the expansion strategy for 2005:

- Continue to focus on the Seed to Table vertical integration model, with particular emphasis on opportunities in the soy and sunflower segments;
- Expand the company's ability to source organic products worldwide. Invest in healthy convenience food business, which the company believed would continue as a strong growth area;
- Diversify the range of organic and non-GMO grains marketed by SunOpta, particularly businesses that were integrated through to ingredients and packaged products;
- Emphasize private label, as opposed to brands, particularly within the soy and rice beverage categories;
- Achieve 20 per cent internal growth in the Canadian distribution business by introducing new SunOpta SKUs and U.S. private label products. Continue to acquire companies to enhance overall capabilities as the dominant distributor of natural and organic foods;
- Expand the company's presence in markets outside North America;
- Expand range of insoluble and soluble fibre offerings; and
- Expand company's vertically integrated fruit and ingredients processing capabilities.

Meanwhile, Kendall noted that SunOpta had learned a lot about the kinds of companies it should acquire. A recent investor presentation outlined SunOpta's acquisition criteria:

- Target companies must operate in the natural, organic or specialty food sectors, but not in retail or in farming, and must share our values.
- Focus on companies with revenues between $10 million and $50 million to mitigate risk.
- Acquisition must be profitable, growing and immediately accretive with key management committed to remain.
- Purchase price:

    −two to four times EBITDA
    −three to five times EBT
    −Synergies are identified, but are not included in EBITDA
    −Earn out provisions.

MANAGEMENT AND ORGANIZATION

SunOpta was a highly decentralized company, with its corporate offices in Norval employing fewer than 15 people. In addition to Kendall, key corporate management included Steven Bromley, president and COO; John Dietrich, vice-president (VP) and chief financial officer (CFO); Sergio Varela, VP, operations and business development; Benjamin Chhiba, VP and general counsel; and Debra Boyle, corporate VP, public relations.

In acquiring companies, it was SunOpta's policy to retain the former owners in an active role, typically with a two- or three-year contract to ensure continuity in management. At an early stage in negotiations, therefore, a candidate was asked whether they were willing to stay and run the business. If the candidate was not prepared to do so, then "we're out of here," as Kendall put it. Since 1999, SunOpta had been able to retain most senior management of the companies it had acquired.

Steven Bromley, SunOpta's COO, had played a particularly important role in building the company. A certified general accountant (CGA), Bromley joined the company in June 2001, and was appointed as its CFO in September 2001. Previously, he had spent 13 years in the Canadian food industry in a wide range of financial and operational roles, principally with Ault Foods Limited and Natrel, Inc., where he had most recently been VP, business development. Recalled Bromley:

> I joined the company right at the time we were doing the private placement deals with the Bronfmans. Pretty quickly, it became clear that we weren't in any way prepared to take on a sophisticated investor. We needed to build a financial group, with treasury and financial reporting systems, and to do it quickly.

Bromley recruited several key individuals, some of whom had worked with him before, including John Dietrich, who would later succeed him as CFO when Bromley was appointed as SunOpta's COO in 2003; Sergio Varela, who later would become VP, operations and business development, was recruited from outside. By 2005, the financial team Bromley started to build consisted of more than 50 people, the majority of whom were employed in the field.

A brief organization chart for SunOpta is shown in Exhibit 6.

Integration within the company occurred in a number of ways. Common budgeting systems, recording systems and management reports provided reasonably standardized flows of information. SunOpta controllers held regularly scheduled conference calls with their counterparts in the field, while reports from each of the group presidents were consolidated into monthly reports to the board. Nonetheless, in what Bromley described as a "massive undertaking," SunOpta had recently begun installing an Oracle Enterprise Resource Planning package. The system, which SunOpta hoped would improve its ability to absorb and integrate information, included enterprise-wide financial accounting systems, as well as control and reporting systems for both manufacturing and distribution.

To the extent feasible in a regionally diverse organization, SunOpta maintained comparable human resources policies in all of its business units. The company also placed a strong emphasis on instilling a set of ethical values at all levels of the organization. SunOpta's Value System, shown in Exhibit 7, was formally endorsed by the board and management and was distributed to all employees.

STOCK REPURCHASE

The dramatic growth of SunOpta had, for a number of years, created a great deal of market enthusiasm for the company's performance and prospects. From a year-end price of $0.59 per share in 1998, SunOpta stock had grown fivefold to $3.15 by the end of 2002 and, on April 6, 2004, briefly touched a high of $11.45 per share. That point, however, marked the beginning of a steady decline in value, to $7.18 at the end of 2004 and, by May 17, 2005, to $4.38.

Kendall knew that a short-term drop in stock price could be caused by a number of factors unrelated to the company's performance. But there was a longer term trend here that couldn't be easily dismissed. Anxious shareholders began to call more frequently, while some analysts covering SunOpta lowered their ratings from "Strong Buy" or "Buy" to "Market Performer."

On April 5, 2005, SunOpta issued a press release announcing completion of its purchase of an organic ingredients supplier in California. In the same release, Kendall added a statement that he hoped might help to re-establish confidence among the company's shareholders:

> We are very concerned with the recent decline in the Company's share price and are not aware of any recent developments or changes causing this decline. We are currently considering a number of options including a possible buy back of up to 5% of the outstanding common shares of the Company, subject to receipt of necessary regulatory approvals. In the meantime, we are totally committed to building a strong, vibrant and sustainable business that will drive long-term shareholder value. We remain confident that we will continue our pattern established in recent years of growing our sales and profits on an annual basis.

In a subsequent release on April 12, the company announced that the Toronto Stock Exchange had given regulatory approval to SunOpta's plan to buy back up to five per cent of its stock. The authorization, to be in effect for one year, did not actually oblige the company to buy back stock, and no specific number of shares to be acquired was established. The release went on to say, however, that SunOpta believed that its common shares were undervalued at current prices, based on its current earnings and future prospects, and that the buyback was a worthwhile investment in the best interests of SunOpta and its shareholders.

Unfortunately, the announced buyback had only a nominal, short-lived impact. The share price increased by $0.30 on the day of the release, from $5 to $5.30; it then resumed its declining trend. By the end of April, SunOpta's shares closed at $4.61 and, by mid-May, the company had not yet repurchased any material quantity of shares.

Exhibit 8 shows a history of SunOpta share prices at selected points since the end of 1998. Exhibit 9 shows latest 12-month operating statistics for selected comparable companies.

UNLOCKING SHAREHOLDER VALUE

Kendall recalled that, over the past few months, he had received plenty of advice on what needed to be done to build value for the shareholders.

One observation was that SunOpta had not done a good enough job of integrating the many different business units in the company and had therefore failed to realize sufficient cost savings and efficiencies. While Kendall acknowledged there was always room to do better, it was also true that it took time to reap the benefits of integration. A good example was in the Distributed Products Group, where two organic distributors, one French-Canadian and one English-Canadian, were merged into a new facility in Montreal. Before efficiencies from the merged operation could be realized, there were relocation issues, procedural changes and cultural barriers to overcome. The end result would be a tremendous improvement, but it couldn't happen overnight.

Kendall accepted the suggestion that management had focused more on the top line than the bottom. Top-line growth had been necessary to achieve scale and, with it, recognition as a force that could bring about consolidation in the organic foods industry. To a considerable extent, that goal had been accomplished, and management was now much more concerned about profitability and return.

Many analysts and observers seemed to find SunOpta confusing. It was hard enough to grasp a business that was in natural and organic foods, minerals and steam-explosion technology. But within the Food Group, SunOpta's Seed to Table business model took it to a number of different levels of its industry. Without diligent study of the company, an investor could easily become mired in confusion.

Among those who could understand the company, some felt that SunOpta was too widely spread to be effective. For example, in grains, SunOpta was involved in soybeans, corn, sunflower, oat fibre and was now pushing heavily into fruit, including cranberries, strawberries and fruit juices. More focus would, in the eyes of some investors, yield better results. But focus was a double-edged sword: A great way in hindsight to explain success, but a potential disaster if you happened to focus on the wrong thing.

SunOpta, which had delivered 30 consecutive quarters of record revenue, was currently followed by 6 sell-side analysts. Unfortunately, the analysts' enthusiasm for the company had been somewhat diminished by the inherent optimism of management. "We've done a poor job of managing analysts' expectations," said Kendall. "We're always coming in one cent below their projections."

In Jeremy Kendall's mind, however, SunOpta had performed incredibly well and had great prospects for the future. He wondered, therefore, about steps that he should be taking to ensure its shareholders realized full value for their investment.

EXHIBIT 1   SunOpta: Income Statement[3] (US$ millions, except EPS)

Years*	1998	1999	2000	2001	2002	2003	2004	Q1 2005
Revenues	13.86	29.70	68.45	92.36	120.90	199.10	306.25	86.22
Cost of goods sold	10.87	25.20	58.59	79.64	101.43	163.42	247.81	70.59
Gross profit	2.99	4.49	9.86	12.72	19.47	35.68	58.44	15.64
SG&A	2.42	3.44	7.65	11.34	14.35	25.43	43.24	12.39
Earnings before the following	0.57	1.05	2.21	1.39	5.12	10.25	15.20	3.25
Interest	(0.08)	(0.23)	(0.96)	(1.75)	(1.41)	(1.94)	(1.44)	(0.30)
Interest and other income, net	(0.02)	(0.10)	(0.20)	(0.03)	0.22	0.59	2.15	4.04
Write-off of intangible asset	–	–	–	–	–	–	(2.25)	–
Foreign exchange	0.04	(0.05)	0.05	0.36	0.18	1.08	0.57	0.04
Earnings before income taxes	0.52	0.67	1.10	(0.03)	4.10	9.97	14.23	7.01
(Provision for) recovery of income taxes	–	0.28	0.77	(0.20)	(0.40)	(1.00)	(3.14)	(0.24)
Net earnings before minority interest	0.52	0.96	1.87	(0.23)	3.70	8.97	11.09	6.78
Minority interest	–	–	–	–	–	–	0.07	0.17
Net earnings for the year	0.52	0.96	1.87	(0.23)	3.70	8.97	11.02	6.61
Earnings per share								
Basic	0.04	0.06	0.08	(0.01)	0.09	0.19	0.20	0.12
Fully diluted	0.04	0.06	0.09	(0.01)	0.09	0.18	0.20	0.12

*1998 and 1999 figures are reported in Canadian GAAP; all other years are in U.S. GAAP.
Source: Company files.

[3]Of Q1 2005 earnings of $0.12, approximately $0.07 was an extraordinary gain arising from an upward valuation of Opta Minerals as a result of the sale of minority interest in an initial public offering.

EXHIBIT 2   SunOpta: Balance Sheet (US$ millions)

Years*	1998	1999	2000	2001	2002	2003	2004	Q1 2005
Assets								
Current assets								
Cash and cash equivalents	0.36	1.80	0.64	10.82	9.05	21.99	8.08	10.64
Accounts receivable	2.39	4.58	8.23	8.38	18.14	26.24	38.45	41.87
Inventories	1.81	5.39	9.60	13.82	22.99	34.78	49.54	57.76
Other current assets	0.10	0.79	2.79	3.18	2.11	5.38	6.89	4.43
	4.66	12.57	21.26	36.19	52.29	88.39	102.96	114.70
Assets held for sale	–	–	–	–	–	6.01	0.21	–
Property, plant and equipment	3.66	6.76	30.24	30.53	36.68	44.76	62.41	65.52
Goodwill and intangibles	1.19	2.46	7.05	11.04	14.92	25.08	43.93	43.72
Deferred income taxes	–	–	–	–	9.89	9.02	6.83	7.31
Other assets	0.60	0.46	2.90	1.95	1.16	0.49	3.83	3.37
Total assets	10.11	22.25	61.45	79.71	114.93	173.76	220.18	234.62
Liabilities								
Current liabilities								
Bank indebtedness	–	–	2.14	1.21	3.96	–	–	6.82
Accounts payable and accrued liabilities	1.84	6.39	12.15	12.83	19.66	24.66	35.67	28.51
Customer and other deposits	–	1.02	0.79	1.39	0.42	1.78	0.43	2.03
Current portion of long-term debt	0.44	0.73	4.27	2.63	11.56	3.84	4.82	4.95
Current portion of long-term payables	0.15	0.15	0.24	1.07	3.46	0.74	1.55	0.47
	2.43	8.28	19.60	19.13	39.07	31.02	42.47	42.77
Long-term debt	0.88	1.86	15.54	14.01	25.10	21.20	31.00	29.77
Long-term payables	0.47	0.38	1.33	1.60	1.51	1.59	1.23	1.13
Future income taxes	–	0.36	0.95	1.82	–	–	–	–
	3.78	10.88	37.41	36.56	65.67	53.81	74.70	73.67
Minority interest	–	–	–	–	–	–	1.38	10.20
Shareholders' equity								
Capital stock	2.80	7.01	14.26	35.88	38.02	96.67	105.79	106.00
Contributed surplus	2.91	2.91	2.91	2.91	2.91	3.33	3.33	3.33
Retained earnings	0.54	1.50	3.37	3.14	6.84	15.81	26.82	33.43
Cumulative other comprehensive income	0.07	(0.05)	3.50	1.23	1.49	4.15	8.16	7.99
	6.33	11.37	24.04	43.15	49.26	119.95	145.48	160.95
	10.11	22.25	61.45	79.71	114.93	173.76	220.18	234.62

*1998 and 1999 figures are reported in Canadian GAAP; all other years are in U.S. GAAP.
Source: Company files.

EXHIBIT 3 SunOpta: Key Financial Figures and Ratios (US$ millions)

Years*	1998	1999	2000	2001	2002	2003	2004	Q1 2005
Average num-ber of shares outstanding	14,702,000	17,384,644	22,975,986	32,220,352	41,547,302	46,094,627	53,971,986	56,271,430
Earnings per share								
Basic	0.04	0.06	0.08	(0.01)	0.09	0.19	0.20	0.12
Fully diluted	0.04	0.06	0.09	(0.01)	0.09	0.18	0.20	0.12
Growth rates								
Sales	21.8%	114.3%	130.5%	34.9%	30.9%	64.7%	53.8%	38.0%
EPS (Fully diluted)	300.0%	56.8%	63.5%	−108.0%	N/A	100.0%	11.1%	300.0%
Price ratios								
P/E	16.81	14.72	16.44	–	35.00	51.28	35.90	10.63
Price/sales	0.63	0.47	0.50	0.76	1.08	2.14	1.27	0.83
Price/book value	1.37	1.24	1.41	1.62	2.66	3.55	2.66	1.78
Financial condition								
Net profit margin	3.7%	3.2%	2.7%	−0.3%	3.1%	4.5%	3.6%	7.7%
Long-term debt/equity ratio	0.21	0.23	0.82	0.39	0.74	0.21	0.25	0.22
Interest coverage	6.82	4.64	2.30	0.79	3.62	5.28	10.58	10.75
Book value/share	0.43	0.65	1.05	1.34	1.19	2.60	2.70	2.86
Investment returns								
Return on equity	8.2%	8.4%	7.8%	−0.5%	7.5%	7.5%	7.6%	4.1%
Return on net operating assets**	7.4%	7.7%	5.1%	2.3%	6.4%	7.2%	8.6%	1.6%

*1998 and 1999 figures are reported in Canadian GAAP; all other years are in U.S. GAAP.

**Operating earnings/net operating assets (which are total assets minus A/P and accrued liabilities, customer and other deposits, current portion of long-term payables, long-term payables and future income taxes).

Source: Company files.

EXHIBIT 4   SunOpta: Key Acquisitions Timeline[*]

	Distribution	Grains/ingredients/packaging	Opta Minerals
2005			
Jul		**Pacific Fruit Processors**– $8.9 million Fruit-based ingredients production	
Jun		**Earthwise Processors**– $4 million Organic/Specialty IP–GMO grains production **Cleugh's Frozen Foods Inc.**– $2.2 million Natural/organic fruits/vegetables production	
May			**Hillcrest Abrasive**– $550,000 Coal-based abrasive production
Apr		**Organic Ingredients Inc.**– $2.3 million Purchased remaining stake	
2004			
Sep	**Kofman-Barenholtz**– $3.2 million Canada-wide kosher frozen/groceries	**Organic Ingredients Inc.**– $2.3 million Certified organic ingredients	
May	**SnapDragon Foods**– $878,000 Canada-wide frozen/organic **Supreme Foods**– $8.3 million Eastern Canada specialty/kosher		
Apr		**General Mills Facility**– $11.7 million Oat fibre production	**Distribution A&L**– $381,000 Specialty abrasives
Mar	**Distribue-Vie**– $900,000 Eastern Canada organic fresh/produce		
2003			
Dec		**Dakota Gourmet (Sonne)**– $1.85 million Natural/organic snacks	
Nov		**SIGCO Sun Products**– $8.5 million Sunflower products	
Oct	**Pro-Organics Marketing**– $5.0 million Canada-wide certified organic produce		

EXHIBIT 4 (continued)

May		**Kettle Valley—** $2.7 million Natural/organic fruit snacks	
2002			
Dec	**Simply Organic—** $187,000 Ontario organic produce	**Opta Foods Ingredients—** $28.6 million Food ingredients/oat fibre	
Nov	**Wild West Organic—** $900,000 Western Canada organic/natural		
Oct		**Organic Kitchen—** $300,000 Organic meats (poultry/pork)	
2001			
Oct			**Virginia/Int'l Materials—** $3.0 million Abrasives supplier/garnet production
Mar		**First Light Foods—** $1.8 million Soy milk production	
2000			
Oct			**Temisca**—CDN$1.7 million Sand deposits
Sep		**Northern Food & Dairy—** CDN$11.2 million Soy milk manufacture/food ingredients	
Mar			**PECAL—** CDN$4.7 million Coated sand/foundry mixes
1999			
Aug		**Sunrich—** CDN$6.8 million Specialty grains (non-GMO, IP) and food ingredients	
1995			
Nov			**Barnes Environmental** (49%) Purchased remaining stake
Jan			**Barnes Environmental** (51%) Silica-free abrasives/minerals

*At the time of the case, the June and July 2005 acquisitions were pending but had not been announced. In addition, the General Mills Facility (April 2004) is considered by the company to be a significant facility acquisition, with its revenues counted as part of internal growth.

Source: Company files.

EXHIBIT 5   SunOpta: Seed to Table Business Model

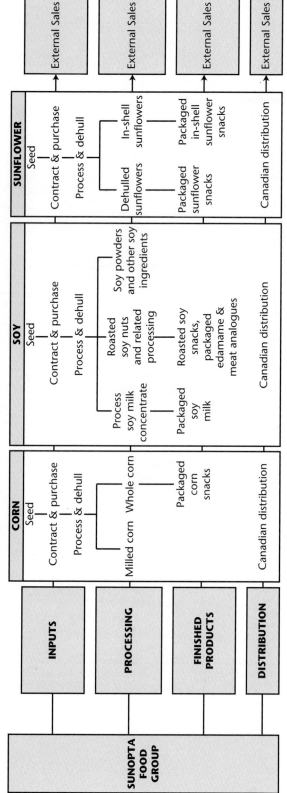

Source: Company files.

EXHIBIT 6 SunOpta: Organization Chart

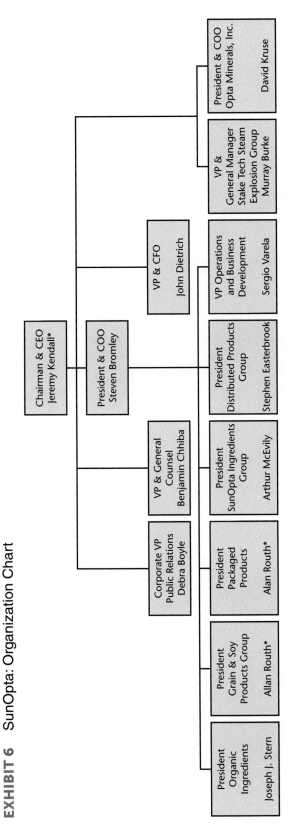

*Member, Board of Directors
Source: Company files.

EXHIBIT 7   SunOpta: Value System

SunOpta's Value System

Our values include conducting our business in a manner which demonstrates:

> Mutual respect for those with whom we work and serve;

> Compassion, honesty and support in all our interactions, while maintaining and developing a culture which builds on the passion of our people and the industry;

> Respect for the environment, where we pledge to minimize our impact and to support sustainable agricultural and environmental practices;

> Providing our customers with the highest quality of products and services, which are generally free of genetic modification and chemical treatment;

> Management of our Company with the highest ethical standards, in a transparent manner, dedicated to achieving an above average return for our shareholders; and

> Being active in the communities where we work by supporting consumer education as to the benefits of natural, organic and healthy food products.

Our value system has been adopted by our Board of Directors and is fully supported by management and employees. As our Company continues to grow, we will stand strongly behind these values, remaining focused on our mission to produce and distribute "good for you", healthy, natural, organic and specialty food products, inherently benefiting the health of our consumers and sustaining the integrity of the earth.

Source: Company files.

EXHIBIT 8 SunOpta: Stock Prices

Closing price at month end (except daily price, April/May 2005)	Stock price	
May 17, 2005	$4.38	
May 5, 2005	$4.40	
May 4, 2005	$4.59	First quarter results released
May 3, 2005	$4.52	
May 2, 2005	$4.55	
April 29, 2005	$4.61	
April 28, 2005	$4.59	
April 27, 2005	$4.71	
April 26, 2005	$4.70	
April 25, 2005	$4.62	
April 22, 2005	$4.59	
April 21, 2005	$4.67	
April 20, 2005	$5.00	
April 19, 2005	$4.96	
April 18, 2005	$4.91	
April 15, 2005	$4.97	
April 14, 2005	$5.15	
April 13, 2005	$5.15	
April 12, 2005	$5.30	Stock repurchase announced
April 11, 2005	$5.00	
Mar-05	$5.10	
Feb-05	$6.39	
Jan-05	$7.08	
Dec-04	$7.18	
Nov-04	$6.05	
Oct-04	$6.29	
Sep-04	$7.76	
Aug-04	$6.55	
Jul-04	$7.30	
Jun-04	$8.53	
May-04	$8.08	
Apr-04	$9.39	High of $11.45 on April 6, 2004
Mar-04	$9.89	
Feb-04	$10.21	
Jan-04	$9.64	
Dec-03	$9.23	
Dec-02	$3.15	
Dec-01	$2.17	
Dec-00	$1.48	
Dec-99	$0.81	
Dec-98	$0.59	

Source: Company files.

EXHIBIT 9   Selected Comparable Companies

Company	Latest 12 months	Latest 12 Months Revenue	EBITDA	EBIT	Net	Margins Gross	EBITDA	EBIT	Net	Enterprise value	Enterprise value/LTM Revenue	EBITDA	EBIT	Net	A/R days	Inv. turns	Debt/ mkt cap.
Hain Celestial	6/04	544,058	54,155	45,878	27,008	70.5%	10.0%	8.4%	5.0%	747,682	1.4	13.8	16.3	27.7	32	5.0	15.5%
United Natural Foods	7/04	1,669,952	70,144	58,484	31,986	19.8%	4.2%	3.5%	1.9%	899,702	0.5	12.8	15.4	28.1	16	7.6	5.1%
Whole Foods Market	9/04	3,864,950	341,206	229,315	137,113	34.8%	8.8%	5.9%	3.5%	2,543,178	0.7	7.5	11.1	18.5	6	18.2	6.4%
Wild Oats Markets	1/05	1,048,164	18,975	−8,942	−40,019	28.3%	1.8%	−0.9%	−3.8%	369,046	0.4	19.4	−41.3	−9.2	1	14.1	59.2%
SunOpta	12/04	306,251	22,317	15,198	11,016	19.1%	7.3%	5.0%	3.6%	411,820	1.3	18.5	27.1	37.4	31	5.9	8.0%

Enterprise value calculation

Company	Date	Common shares O/S (000)	Share price	Market value ($000)	LT debt	Minority interest	Pref	Cash	EV
Hain Celestial	6/04	37,065	$18.10	670,877	104,294	—	—	27,489	747,682
United Natural Foods	7/04	40,118	$21.67	869,357	43,978	—	—	13,633	899,702
Whole Foods Market	9/04	62,407	$41.29	2,576,785	164,770	—	—	198,377	2,543,178
Wild Oats Markets	1/05	28,489	$ 8.81	250,988	148,675	—	—	30,617	369,046
SunOpta	12/04	53,972	$ 7.18	387,519	31,003	1,378	—	8,080	411,820

Notes: Hain Celestial is a manufacturer of branded, packaged natural and organic foods. United Natural Foods is a U.S. wholesaler of natural and organic foods. Whole Foods Markets and Wild Oats Markets are large natural and organic food retailers.

Enterprise value is sometimes used as an alternative valuation method to market capitalization. It is calculated as market capitalization plus debt, minority interest and preferred shares *minus* cash and cash equivalents. It is equivalent, in some ways, to the theoretical takeover price of a company. A buyer taking over a company, for example, would take on the company's debt, but would pocket its cash.

Source: SEC 10-K Filings; stock prices from finance.yahoo.com

Guest-Tek Interactive Entertainment: International Sales

GUEST-TEK AND THE GLOBAL OPPORTUNITY

The chief executive officer (CEO) of Calgary-based Guest-Tek Interactive Entertainment Ltd. (Guest-Tek) considered whether and how his company should grow its business overseas. Ninety-seven per cent of Guest-Tek's 2003 revenue was derived from North American hotels—a market he knew would eventually become saturated. Guest-Tek had listed publicly several weeks earlier, in January 2004. Both internal and external investors now demanded results. Other geographic markets held the promise of new growth and competitors were already pursuing those opportunities. The CEO had to decide on a course of action.

COMPANY BACKGROUND

Guest-Tek was founded in Calgary, Alberta, Canada, in March 1997, and since then had established itself as a leading provider of high-speed Internet access in hotels in North America and, to a lesser extent, abroad. Guest-Tek sold its Internet solution, which was branded as GlobalSuite, to three-, four- and five-star hotels and installed access points in guest rooms, meeting rooms and common areas. Guest-Tek then maintained a post-installation network and provided technical support for GlobalSuite users through a toll-free, 24-hour telephone line. Users were typically business travellers who connected with their own laptop computers. GlobalSuite was a premium high-speed Internet access solution that was easy to use for travellers and convenient for hotel managers.

Nigel Goodwin prepared this case under the supervision of Professor Laurie Milton solely to provide material for class discussion. The authors do not intend to illustrate either effective or ineffective handling of a managerial situation. The authors may have disguised certain names and other identifying information to protect confidentiality.

Ivey

Richard Ivey School of Business
The University of Western Ontario

GlobalSuite's industry-leading 99 per cent user success rate,[1] together with Guest-Tek's comprehensive service package for both guests and hotel managers, had secured some of the world's finest hotel chains and management groups as clients (see Exhibit 1 for Guest-Tek's client list). The company had also raised sales to $17.2 million[2] for the 9 months ending December 31, 2003 (see Exhibit 2 for Guest-Tek's income statement) and successfully completed an initial public offering (IPO) of $44.6 million. Virtually all of the company's activities were run from the head office in Calgary with a staff of fewer than 150 (see Exhibit 3 for an allocation of Guest-Tek's staff by department).

THE HOSPITALITY INDUSTRY

The hospitality industry encompassed many segments, including hotels, rental properties, military housing, student housing and timeshare units, plus bars, coffee shops, restaurants, airports and train stations. Guest-Tek focused its efforts on serving hotels and, more specifically, on those in the three-, four- and five-star range. To this point in time, the company had concentrated almost exclusively on its home continent, North America (see Exhibit 4 for Guest-Tek's revenue by geographic region). The company had left the other geographic markets in Europe, Asia-Pacific and South America largely unexplored, with limited direct sales to date.

Business travellers who frequented North American three-, four- and five-star hotels had come to expect or even require Internet access. One industry survey found that as many as 87 per cent of business travellers checked e-mail or accessed the Internet from their laptops on a daily basis while on the road. There was general agreement in the industry that these travellers preferred high-speed Internet access to dial-up access for speed, convenience and cost effectiveness. Many travellers cited broadband services as an important factor in selecting accommodations. As a result, hotel managers were adopting high-speed Internet access as a way of attracting guests, competing with other properties and deriving additional revenue. This competitive edge had been particularly important for hotel managers during the recent downturn in the industry when Severe Acute Respiratory Syndrome (SARS), global security concerns and other political, social and economic events had raised anxiety about travel. Hotel managers hoped that high-speed Internet access would position them to capitalize on the expected recovery.

THE NORTH AMERICAN MARKET

With 64,500 hotels and more than 5 million hotel rooms, North America was second only to Europe on both dimensions. More importantly from Guest-Tek's perspective, though, was the fact that 40 per cent of the world's business travel was conducted in North America—more than in any other geographic region.

North America led the world in terms of both the proportion of total hotels equipped with high-speed Internet access (referred to as the penetration rate) and the frequency with which the service was used by guests (referred to as the usage rate).

---

[1]Guest-Tek measured user success as the percentage of users achieving a high-speed Internet connection when using GlobalSuite; user success rates among Guest-Tek's competitors were typically much lower, and in some cases were as low as 50 per cent.

[2]Financial figures in this case are presented in Canadian dollars, unless otherwise noted.

Both penetration and usage rates were rising sharply. Also, hotel managers increasingly viewed such access as a competitive necessity or a guest amenity and were cutting user fees or offering access for free.

High-speed Internet access-enabled properties were typically in the four- and five-star hotel categories. These hotels normally installed the service in all of their guestrooms, as well as in meeting rooms and common areas. When installation in four- and five-star hotels approached saturation (which was expected to happen within two to three years), several access providers planned to reach out to the two- and three-star categories for more growth opportunities. Fewer hotels in those categories could afford 100 per cent installation. Consequently, many opted to install services in a portion of rooms, to be used either on a trial basis or in rooms reserved for business travellers.

North America was home to 85 different hotel brands (see Exhibit 5 for more information on the North American hotel industry), as well as independent boutique hotels. Guest-Tek was a certified supplier to eight of those brands: Accor, Carlson Hospitality, Choice, Hilton, Hyatt, InterContinental Hotel Groups, Marriott and Starwood. In total, GlobalSuite had been installed with 35 different brands and 40 independent hotels. In fiscal year (FY) 2003, no single brand represented more than 11 per cent of Guest-Tek's revenue.

GLOBALSUITE SOLUTION

To answer the demand for high-speed Internet access, Guest-Tek's research and development team had developed GlobalSuite as an easy-to-use or "plug-and-play" solution. In other words, hotel guests could connect their own laptops and gain access to the Internet, corporate e-mail and other applications quickly and without changing their settings. Guests typically connected by plugging their laptops into ports or "nodes" located in the guestrooms and public areas, including conference rooms and business centres; those ports were in turn connected to a network throughout the hotel.

Wireless solutions were becoming increasingly common in the industry, allowing guests with wireless network interface cards to connect from hotspots located in lobbies, bars and other public areas and sometimes in the guestrooms themselves. Not only were wireless solutions convenient for guests, they were less demanding in terms of infrastructure and were therefore less expensive for hotels. By February 2004, 70 per cent of Guest-Tek's installations involved some degree of wireless functionality.

The wide variety of laptop configurations and network settings often made access difficult, but GlobalSuite's technology was reliable and easy to use regardless of laptop settings and technical challenges. Guests who still experienced difficulty could call the technical support desk and receive help in a variety of languages, including English, French, Spanish, Dutch, Cantonese, Mandarin, Japanese, Arabic and Hindi. GlobalSuite was also a secure solution suitable for business use. The proprietary software was regarded as best-in-class technology and was guarded closely as intellectual property.

GlobalSuite had been developed with the hotel manager in mind as a complete or "turnkey" system, requiring little knowledge or effort on the manager's part. Installation services were provided by Guest-Tek's highly skilled operations and deployment teams. Network equipment was sourced from high-quality manufacturers, including Cisco Systems, Hewlett-Packard, Dell and Paradyne Networks. Following an installation, Guest-Tek trained hotel staff to use the system, monitored and managed the system, acted as an Internet service provider (ISP) and offered free software upgrades. Guest-Tek thus offered a complete solution designed for high-quality service and peace of mind.

Additional features and benefits were designed to appeal to hotel managers who had the option to set access prices or provide the service free of charge, to track and report on usage and to customize the user interface with the hotel's own brand. Global-Suite was a best-in-class solution designed for clients who were willing to pay a premium. Depending on the size of an installation and the user fees that a hotel manager was willing to set, payback for the system could be achieved within 12 to 18 months.

BUSINESS MODEL

Once a hotel had signed a contract to purchase GlobalSuite, Guest-Tek deployed its own project managers and installation professionals to the hotel to set the system up. By managing the installation with its own people, Guest-Tek maintained control over the timelines, costs and quality. Installation work required only a few days and typically took place within four to six weeks of a contract being signed. The company could install the solution in 40 to 50 hotels per month. Installation capacity had doubled over the previous year, due to better processes and the addition of new staff.

An installation typically generated one-time revenues for Guest-Tek from the software license, installation services and networking equipment. These revenues could total between US$100 and US$350 per room, depending on the hardware involved, with a gross margin of 35 to 45 per cent. Guest-Tek also derived recurring revenues from ongoing software and hardware maintenance and from call centre support. Recurring revenues totalled between US$3 and US$4 per room, per month. A 99 per cent customer retention rate ensured the sustainability of the recurring revenue.

NORTH AMERICAN COMPETITION

Guest-Tek faced direct competition in North America from a number of other Internet solution providers. Chief among these were Wayport and STSN. These companies were running systems in approximately 600 North American hotels each as of December 2003, as compared to Guest-Tek's roughly 360 installations at that time. Other providers trailed behind (see Exhibit 6 for a breakdown of the competition in North America).

Wayport, based in Austin, Texas, provided wired access, but was also a leader in wireless solutions. Wayport had preferred vendor status with Four Seasons and was also building the Wayport brand by providing access in airports and 75 McDonald's restaurants in California. STSN, of Salt Lake City, Utah, was partially owned by Marriott and most of STSN's installations were at Marriott hotels. GoldenTree Communications, a spin-off of a Korean hardware manufacturer, was also a notable competitor in North America. With low prices and what Guest-Tek's executives believed to be a more basic solution, GoldenTree appealed to three-star hotels as well as budget-conscious four-star hotels. StayOnline, another notable North American provider, was similar to Wayport in its focus on wireless applications.

In-room entertainment companies, cable companies, ISPs, data networking companies and local telephone network operators also offered Internet access. These companies used different technology and offered a variety of benefits to various segments of the market. In-room entertainment companies, for example, provided Internet access through television sets outfitted with keyboards. This rudimentary solution did not allow users to connect with their own laptops. Some of these companies, particularly the telecommunications companies (telcos), were attempting to include hotels in their broader strategy to set up wireless public access points, known as hotspots. Hotspots could be set up at virtually any location, including coffee shops, airports, office buildings and shopping malls. Guest-Tek, as a niche solution provider, recognized that these companies were penetrating the market, but did not consider them to be direct competitors.

In the CEO's estimation, Guest-Tek was very strong compared to its competitors on key competitive elements, which included comprehensive solutions, ease of deployment, wireless capability, security, connectivity rates and end-user support. The subsequent supplier certification from various hotel brands, including Hilton, Hyatt and Marriott, gave Guest-Tek a strong competitive message. Finally, Guest-Tek was reasonably priced, relative to other premium service providers.

GUEST-TEK'S SALES AND MARKETING DEPARTMENT

Guest-Tek's revenue generation was overseen by the vice-president of sales and marketing. He held an undergraduate finance degree and an MBA in enterprise development from the University of Calgary. Known as an ambitious and energetic entrepreneur, he was keenly interested in growing Guest-Tek.

The VP of sales and marketing had a staff of 24 and was responsible for all geographic regions. Within North America, the VP had the help of a sales director; the sales director managed the sales staff directly, while the VP managed the region at a strategic level and actively participated in major deals. The VP also had the help of a consultant who provided advice on the European market. There were no sales and marketing staff allocated to the other geographic regions.

Sales were pursued through direct and indirect channels, with direct being the principal channel in North America and indirect being the principal channel in the other geographic regions. Direct sales were conducted by Guest-Tek sales representatives working at Guest-Tek's head office and travelling to visit potential customers. Indirect sales were pursued through partnerships and alliances with complementary service providers and through independent agents who sold GlobalSuite on a freelance basis.

A marketing director reported to the VP of sales and marketing and supported the sales activities by managing the Guest-Tek brand and creating demand for Global-Suite. Marketing activities included telemarketing, direct mail, communication with media and industry analysts, advertising and trade shows. The marketing director had a total staff of eight.

The VP of sales and marketing additionally oversaw a value-added solutions director. This manager was charged with finding ways to sell new products and services to existing clients. This function was seen as a way to derive additional revenue in a market that was becoming saturated. Value-added solutions were also viewed as tools for enhancing customer loyalty and ensuring recurring service and maintenance revenue for GlobalSuite installations. The value-added solutions director was assisted by two other staff members.

DIRECT SALES

The direct sales process began with Guest-Tek inside sales representatives contacting groups of hotels that shared common ownership or common management and contacting individual hotels. The inside sales representatives' objective was to generate leads for Guest-Tek's direct sales representatives. There were five inside sales representatives working under the direction of a coordinator. The direct sales representatives followed up on those leads, promoted GlobalSuite to the hotel owners and managers and attempted to close deals. Guest-Tek employed 10 direct sales representatives. All inside and direct sales representatives reported to the sales director for North America. The direct sales method was the exclusive method employed in North America, and the sales team was now extending this method to Latin America as well. All direct sales activities were managed out of Guest-Tek's head office.

Inside and direct sales representatives preferred to work with hotel ownership and management groups rather than individual hotels. Convincing one such group to purchase GlobalSuite usually resulted in sales to multiple properties. The sales representatives also targeted hotels that fell under brands such as Hilton, Hyatt and Marriott, which had granted Guest-Tek preferred vendor status and wished to see consistency across their properties. While the hotels under these brands did not necessarily have to follow advice from the brand level, preferred vendor status was a strong selling point for Guest-Tek.

Inside and direct sales employees had revenue quotas and were compensated partly through commission. All North American sales were priced and recorded in U.S. dollars but overseas sales could also be priced and recorded in local currency.

The direct sales approach had driven Guest-Tek's rapid growth despite an inherently long sales cycle. A contract required a significant capital commitment from the hotel's decision maker, who typically had to obtain approval from many layers of ownership and management. The direct sales approach allowed Guest-Tek representatives to build relationships with clients and influence them throughout the decision-making process. The full process, from generating interest to building a relationship and finally signing a contract, could take between 4 and 12 months and occasionally even longer.

INDIRECT SALES THROUGH RESELLERS

The indirect sales method most commonly involved partnerships with technology resellers who licensed GlobalSuite software as part of their own solution. In this case, Guest-Tek collected one-time revenue for the software license but took no other part in the deal and undertook no other efforts for marketing, operations or otherwise. Guest-Tek's only activity in this process was to manage the relationship with the reseller. This method had been employed in Europe, the Middle East and Africa through French technology reseller Locatel.

The relationship with Locatel had been relatively easy to manage. Initial meetings to broker the deal had been conducted at Guest-Tek's office in Calgary and at Locatel's office in Paris, France, and a Guest-Tek technical representative had later been sent to Paris to train Locatel personnel. The relationship was managed by Guest-Tek's business development team, and since Locatel installed the solution, Guest-Tek project managers and operations teams were not involved.

The reseller channel was a low-cost and low-risk method of entering new markets, particularly when Guest-Tek did not have expertise or presence in those markets. As the CEO explained, "Inbound demand mitigates risk, because a knowledgeable partner is coming to us with opportunities." However, the reseller retained a significant portion of the revenue and Guest-Tek had no control over the installation or support aspects of the solution and consequently could not control the quality, the customer experience or the user experience. Furthermore, the CEO felt that this channel was too passive.

INDIRECT SALES THROUGH AGENTS

Guest-Tek also sold GlobalSuite indirectly through agents, although this method was less common. Agents were independent technology salespeople selling the full Global-Suite solution as well as other products and solutions from other vendors. They were self-employed freelancers who took a percentage of the revenue from each sale. Agents were familiar with GlobalSuite but under no obligation to sell it over other solutions.

Guest-Tek did not drive this strategy and any sales generated this way were essentially viewed as bonus sales. The company's efforts were limited to providing the agents with information to help them sell GlobalSuite and offering the agents better commissions to encourage them to favour it. There were currently two agents operating for Guest-Tek in the Latin American region: one in Argentina and the other in Trinidad.

THE EXPANSION CHALLENGE

Guest-Tek's share offering, completed on February 6, 2004, brought the company net proceeds of $28.3 million (see Exhibit 7 for the intended allocation of the funds). These funds would allow Guest-Tek to grow by eliminating some of the financial constraints that had inhibited the company in the past. However, public status brought new shareholders and higher expectations, and the CEO knew that these people were watching Guest-Tek's market position very closely. The company's sales had grown quickly over the past two years and the CEO felt pressure to continue that pace.

One promising avenue for growth was the international market. "Guest-Tek has established a strong position with the industry in North America," the CEO stated in a recent earnings release. "We are working aggressively to repeat this success on a global scale." To that end, $3.0 million of the IPO proceeds had specifically been allocated for international sales and marketing initiatives. Guest-Tek had young, energetic and entrepreneurial leaders and employees, and there was a general feeling within the ranks that the company could "take on the world." Also, the company's executives believed that they could make up for their lack of international experience with their superior technology, turnkey solution, technical expertise, sales skills and hotel market expertise.

However, international sales could be framed as both an opportunity and a competitive requirement because the North American branches of hotel brands wanted the solutions they chose to also be available to their international branches. In other words, hotel brands wanted to deal with global players. Finally, international sales could also be considered as a risk because Guest-Tek was unfamiliar with those markets.

KEY DECISION MAKERS

As a rapidly growing company with expectations to match, Guest-Tek's business decisions were driven principally by the sales, marketing and business development personnel. The CEO would ultimately make the decision with substantial input from the VP of sales and marketing, who viewed international expansion as an excellent opportunity and the most natural avenue for growing the company.

Guest-Tek's founder, who was also the former CEO and the former executive vice-president of business development, would also have some input in the decision-making process. While no longer an executive of the company, the founder held a seat on the board of directors. He held a bachelor of commerce degree specializing in the hospitality industry. Prior to founding Guest-Tek, he had spent several years as an analyst for economic diversification and business development. The founder strongly favoured international expansion. The founder and the VP of sales and marketing had known each other for years, even before the VP of sales and marketing joined the company, and the two had held many positive conversations about international expansion.

Feasibility and practical aspects had to be considered as well as market potential; therefore, the CEO would also consider the opinions of several other executives. These executives were supportive of international expansion, but cautioned that there would be challenges. There was a general feeling that risks could be mitigated by working with partners such as Locatel and by selling to international hotel management groups, ownership groups and brands that were already customers in North America.

Guest-Tek's vice-president of operations was an industrial engineer with an MBA from the same graduating class as the VP of sales and marketing. She had joined Guest-Tek in 2000. With her dual training, she provided a balanced opinion of both operations and business. She believed that the required changes to the software would be minimal, but cautioned that hardware standards and prices would vary considerably between countries. The company would face a learning curve upon entering each new region and each new country. The VP of operations accepted these challenges and was supportive of international expansion.

The vice-president of research and development was also supportive of international expansion. With a doctorate in computer science from the University of Calgary, postdoctoral fellowships at both MIT and Stanford University and experience with several high-tech startups, he had a deep understanding of the technological ramifications facing Guest-Tek. He suggested that his department's only challenge would lie in translating GlobalSuite's user and manager interfaces into multiple languages. GlobalSuite's user interface was already available in English, French and Spanish, and additional translation would be a straightforward task. Translation of the management interface—that part of the solution used by hotel managers for pricing and billing, reporting and other administrative work—would be a much more complicated, expensive and time-consuming project.

There was also the question of multilingual service through Guest-Tek's user support hotline. Support was currently offered in the same three languages—English, French and Spanish—on a full-time basis and only partial coverage was available in other languages.

Guest-Tek's chief financial officer was also an important figure in the decision-making process and a supporter of international expansion. She was a chartered accountant with a strong business background. She was keenly aware of the expectations that Guest-Tek now faced from investors and analysts and recognized the need for revenue growth. Additional funds from the IPO had been allocated to expanding Guest-Tek's operational capacity, so growth could be achieved profitably.

GEOGRAPHIC CHOICES

The outstanding questions to those involved revolved around which markets were the most attractive, how those markets should be pursued and how the overseas business should be managed. These were difficult questions to answer because Guest-Tek had only basic information on the overseas markets and had no staff with overseas experience or expertise, aside from a recently retained consultant for the European region. The CEO preferred to gather as much information as possible before making a decision in an unfamiliar area, but in this case adequate information was not to be found internally. Without reasonable information, he was more reactive and preferred to entertain proposals from knowledgeable partners, but as explained previously, that was considered a passive strategy. The CEO had set an ambitious goal of deriving 15 to 20 per cent of new installation revenue outside North America in FY2005—a goal that might require more proactive efforts. With this in mind, the CEO considered what he did know about the opportunities before him.

EUROPEAN MARKET

Guest-Tek had historically looked beyond North America to the European market as a possible avenue for expansion. Europe featured 67,500 hotel properties and nearly 6 million hotel rooms, which were often combined with the 14,000 properties and roughly 670,000 rooms in the Middle East and Africa, and referred to as the broader Europe, Middle East and Africa (EMEA) region. However, a higher concentration of hotels and steeper demand for high-speed internet access made the United Kingdom and continental Europe the focus.

Penetration and usage rates were growing in Europe, but trailed behind North American rates and were not expected to fully catch up. In general, there was less business travel in Europe than in North America, and guests demanded less internet service. However, European hotel managers were beginning to perceive high-speed internet access as a necessary service offering, and the market was becoming more demand-driven, with strong growth expected for 2004 and beyond. European hotel managers were also more inclined to pay higher prices for better solutions. Industry sources suggested that growth in high-speed internet access in homes and offices was particularly noticeable in France and Italy. The CEO also knew that within Europe, the busiest destinations for both European and American business travellers were the United Kingdom and Germany. The proliferation of wireless technology was expected to bolster the European industry since many of Europe's hotels were historic and managers preferred less intrusive and less damaging infrastructure.

Guest-Tek's CEO resisted the temptation to discuss Europe as a single market since he perceived little homogeneity across the continent. Countries varied considerably in culture, language, business practices, the balance between business and pleasure travel, internet use and broadband penetration among the general population (see Exhibit 8 for a comparison of broadband access in OECD [Organisation for Economic Co-operation and Development] countries). Adoption of high-speed internet access in hotels also varied accordingly. Hotel communities in different countries varied in the extent to which they welcomed a solution provider from North America. Some did not mind, while others preferred to deal with local providers or at least local offices of global providers.

European countries also differed from Canada and the United States in terms of hotel structure. Firstly, the majority of European hotels were independent or affiliated with voluntary chains that demanded less in terms of conformity and standards. Guest-Tek's preferred provider approach might not be as effective in these situations.

Secondly, European hotels tended to be smaller than North American hotels, resulting in smaller sales. It was often more difficult to convince a manager of a small hotel to accept the high price of a premium high-speed internet access solution. Furthermore, the CEO believed that the European property and room totals had been inflated by small lodging establishments catering only to leisure travellers. Thus, while the totals for Europe were higher than those for North America, the CEO believed that the effective market for Guest-Tek was actually smaller in Europe.

A variety of providers were now targeting Europe, most notably European telcos, such as British Telecom and France Telecom, offering hotspots and other technologies. However, Guest-Tek perceived its most direct competition in the European market as coming from North American solution providers who viewed Europe as a natural growth area as the North American market approached saturation. As the most notable example, STSN was believed to have at least 100 European installations. Wayport was smaller than STSN in Europe but also had a presence. Several Asian niche providers were also entering Europe. One such company, interTouch, had completed 36 installations by mid-2003.

Guest-Tek had so far approached EMEA sales indirectly through a partnership with Locatel, which had a relationship with the Accor hotels and had installed Global-Suite in 33 hotels as of January 2004. As explained previously, indirect sales had been a low-cost and low-risk method of introducing GlobalSuite to the market. The CEO wondered whether the time had come to sell more proactively. Guest-Tek was not prohibited from selling directly in markets where Locatel had a presence.

LATIN AMERICAN MARKET

High-speed internet access penetration and usage rates among Latin America's 21,000 hotels and nearly 1 million hotel rooms were widely believed to trail behind North America's rates, although exact figures for Latin America were unavailable. A higher ratio of pleasure travel to business travel in Latin America resulted in lower demand for high-speed internet access among travellers. Lower penetration in Latin homes and offices also limited demand in hotels. The low demand was exacerbated by a poor communications infrastructure that raised the cost for a solution. Hotel managers charged higher users fees to fund cost recovery, and this practice further discouraged use.

In a more positive light, the CEO viewed Latin America as a relatively easier market to approach than Europe or Asia-Pacific because he believed Latin America had more internal homogeneity. However, in his experience, this internal homogeneity sometimes led Latin American clients to favour Latin American vendors.

Guest-Tek had thus far approached South America as an extension of the company's North American activities. Activity had been modest to date. Since beginning direct sales efforts to Latin America from its Calgary headquarters in June 2003, Guest-Tek had sold to at least one major hotel in Aruba, Chile, Costa Rica, Dominican Republic, Mexico, Panama and Puerto Rico. Some additional demand came from Hilton and other existing customers and from the two agents who sold Global-Suite among other solutions. Each opportunity was carefully and individually evaluated and only accepted if it presented a comfortable return on investment. In this way, Guest-Tek had mitigated its risk by reacting to inbound opportunities. In total, Guest-Tek had nearly a dozen installations in Latin America. Based on these results, the CEO considered the establishment of a regional office with a larger direct sales force.

ASIA-PACIFIC MARKET

The Asia-Pacific region, with 54,700 hotel properties and nearly 4 million hotel rooms, also caught the CEO's attention. Its usage rate actually rivalled that of North America, and both usage and penetration rates were expected to rise quickly in a revived economy. Guests were demanding high-speed internet access in spite of user fees that doubled or even tripled North American fees. Many foreign and local providers were stepping in to answer the demand.

The Asia-Pacific region, like Europe, was diverse. Cultures, languages, business communication styles and high-speed Internet access penetration and usage varied widely. Some countries or districts within the region, including Hong Kong, were approaching hotel high-speed Internet access saturation, while the market in other countries was still nascent. Countries with high residential and business broadband adoption reportedly had high hotel adoption as well, and Japanese hotel managers in particular demanded the service.

Unfortunately, Guest-Tek had little knowledge of the region and detailed assessments of the various countries were not available; in fact, the CEO ventured to say that this was the region that Guest-Tek understood least. Guest-Tek had few relationships in the area and no staff members with Asian expertise. This lack of familiarity and knowledge had clearly influenced Guest-Tek's approach to the region in the past. Guest-Tek had not proactively pursued deals and had only installed services when approached by hotels. As with opportunities in Latin America, inbound opportunities were carefully evaluated on an individual basis and only accepted on the grounds of a comfortable return on investment. Although the CEO didn't know for certain, Guest-Tek's experience in Asia-Pacific so far supported the widely held belief that it was a difficult market for foreigners to enter.

The Asian preference for a different business model was one aspect of the market that was known to Guest-Tek. In this region, solution providers were often expected to provide the solution, including software, hardware and installation services at no charge, in exchange for a share of the user fees. This model, usually referred to as "revenue share," required a great deal of capital and involved a high degree of risk for the solution provider. This model had been commonplace in North America five years earlier, but had proved to be unsustainable, and many providers following that model had filed for bankruptcy. In fact, Guest-Tek had employed that model to some degree in the company's early stages, but had abandoned it before shifting to its current model. The demand for revenue share contracts on the part of Asian hotel managers ran counter to Guest-Tek's proven strategy, and the CEO was reluctant to revisit the matter.

Most of the high-speed Internet access solutions in Asia were provided by larger telcos, including China Mobile, China Telecom, NTT Communications, Japan Telecom and Yahoo Broadband Japan, and most of the solutions were based on different technologies, including hotspots. There were only a few providers in the region that were similar to Guest-Tek in terms of their solution and business model. They were generally locally based, like Australia's interTouch, which had more than 100 installations in the region.

MANAGEMENT OF INTERNATIONAL BUSINESS

International expansion not only posed questions of how and where to sell Global-Suite, but also how to manage the business and actually install the solution. Up to that time, Guest-Tek's direct sales activities had been conducted from Guest-Tek's head office in Calgary, with personal visits by sales and account managers to the hotel properties as necessary. When a contract was signed, a project manager and an operations team were dispatched from the Calgary office to the hotel property to install the solution. Travel to overseas properties for both sales and installations could be costly due to the time and distance involved. Since, to date, international sales were relatively rare, coordination from the head office had been wise and feasible.

This situation could change, however, if Guest-Tek were to make a more concerted effort overseas. The option that immediately came to mind was to set up local offices with local presence, knowledge, connections and acceptance. Such offices, though difficult to staff, might provide a competitive advantage. An overseas office could be built with transplanted North American personnel, local personnel or some mix of the two. Present Guest-Tek employees had little overseas experience. None of the executives had worked overseas, and, beyond the one direct salesperson pursuing Latin America and the consultant providing advice on Europe, there were no employees with significant international knowledge. The CEO preferred to promote people from within the company, but knew also that international expansion would require an international experience base.

The establishment of overseas offices would also force questions about management and control. International offices could operate as closely managed extensions of the North American office under the CEO or the VP of sales and marketing, or they could be run as relatively autonomous units. The CEO wanted to replicate the Guest-Tek culture and ensure quality of operations, but with limited information about the markets, he was unsure of how well the North American management style would translate into the regions in question. He was also unsure of what level of overseas activity could effectively be managed by executives in the head office and at what point a region required or deserved its own autonomous leadership.

Of course, the option of pursuing indirect sales was still available and was somewhat attractive. Reseller and agent relationships were relatively easy to manage and would not require a buildup of staff levels. Resellers and agents would already have presence and expertise in the markets in question. However, the CEO was not certain that the more passive nature of indirect sales would fulfill his mandate for expansion.

THE CEO'S CHALLENGE

Understanding the new investors' demands for revenue growth, the CEO had to decide whether or not Guest-Tek should pursue overseas opportunities. He felt he had to decide quickly, given that the North American market would eventually become saturated and competitors were already pursuing international opportunities. Should Guest-Tek expand overseas? If so, which markets should it enter? And how should the overseas operations be managed?

EXHIBIT 1   Guest-Tek Client List, 2003

Ownership group / chain	Properties
Marriott International	132
Hyatt Corporation / Hyatt International Corporation	42
InterContinental Hotels Group	37
Hilton Hotels Corporation	34
Starwood Hotels & Resorts Worldwide	20
Accor Hotels	20
Carlson Companies	18
Best Western International	8
Ritz-Carlton Hotel Company	6
Independent, boutique and other	87
Total	404
Geographic Region	**Properties**
North America	358
International	46
Total	404
Guestrooms	80,700

Note: Figures as of November 30, 2003.

Source: Guest-Tek Prospectus, January 30, 2004.

EXHIBIT 2   Guest-Tek Income Statement, FY2001–FY2003 (in CDN$)

	Year ended March 31			Six months ended September 30	
	2003	**2002**	**2001**	**2003**	**2002**
Revenue:					
New installations	$7,294,666	$ 2,733,589	$ 1,134,780	$9,705,524	$2,615,911
Recurring revenue	1,406,428	810,783	400,917	1,333,641	591,972
	8,701,094	3,544,372	1,535,697	11,039,165	3,207,883
Expenses:					
Cost of goods and services sold	4,597,565	2,032,882	1,194,804	6,147,837	1,633,172
Selling, general and administrative	2,694,619	1,922,727	1,728,720	1,897,504	1,130,086
Research and development	551,216	556,804	456,467	273,488	270,079
Foreign currency loss	37,558	1,320	—	175,144	1,942
Interest expense (income), net	37,726	(6,468)	171,277	53,256	15,464
Write-down of property and equipment	—	—	810,544	—	—
Amortization of property and equipment	151,687	122,100	264,360	85,964	67,644
	8,070,371	4,629,365	4,626,172	8,633,193	3,118,387
Income (loss) from operations	630,723	(1,084,993)	(3,090,475)	2,405,972	89,496
Government assistance for research & development	175,709	—	—	—	54,803
Income (loss) before income taxes	806,432	(1,084,993)	(3,090,475)	2,405,972	144,299
Income taxes (recovery)	(440,000)	—	—	(185,122)	—
Net income (loss)	$1,246,432	$(1,084,993)	$(3,090,475)	$2,591,094	$ 144,299

Note: Six month figures are unaudited.

Source: Guest-Tek Prospectus, January 30, 2004.

EXHIBIT 3   Guest-Tek Staff by Department

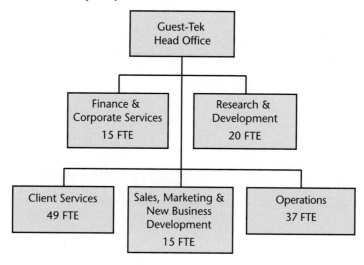

EXHIBIT 4   Guest-Tek Revenue by Geographic Region, FY2001–FY2003

	Year ended March 31			Six months ended September 30	
	2003	2002	2001	2003	2002
Canada	$1,192,855	$ 977,309	$ 907,240	$ensp781,478	$ 812,562
United States	7,203,772	2,567,063	628,457	10,021,236	2,343,616
Other	304,407	—	—	236,451	51,705
Total	$8,701,034	$3,544,372	$1,535,697	$ 11,039,165	$3,207,883

Source: Guest-Tek Prospectus, January 30, 2004.

EXHIBIT 5   North American Hotel Industry by Segment (as of November 2003)

Segment	Upper upscale	Upscale	Midscale w/ F&B	Midscale w/out F&B	Economy	Independent
Rating	5–4-star	4-star	3-star	3-star	2-star	Various
Representative brands	Four Seasons	Crown Plaza	Best Western	Amerihost	Budget Inn	Various
	Hilton	Doubletree	Four Points	Comfort Inn	Days Inn	
	Hyatt	Novotel	Holiday Inn	Country Inn	Econo Lodge	
	InterContinental	Radisson	Park Plaza	Hampton Inn	Motel 6	
	Ritz-Carlton	Residence Inn	Ramada	Signature Inn	Super 8	
Target client	Luxury / corporate	Corporate	Ec. bus. traveller	Ec. bus. traveller	Travelling sales	Various
Hotels	1,794	2,370	5,097	6,980	10,330	29,271
Rooms	658,316	380,236	643,490	628,155	810,445	1,728,300
Rooms per hotel	367	160	126	90	78	59

Notes: Figures for U.S. and Canada only. F&B refers to food and beverage service. Ec. bus. traveler refers to economy business traveller.
Source: Smith Travel Research Database, November 26, 2003. Cited in Guest-Tek Prospectus, January 30, 2004.

EXHIBIT 6 HSIA Installations in North America, by Company
(as of November/December 2003)

	Upper upscale	Upscale	Midscale w/ F&B	Midscale w/out F&B	Economy	Unclassified	Total
Wayport	296	101	78	53	12	56	596
STSN	254	277	7	28	—	24	590
Guest-Tek	100	145	21	26	9	57	358
GoldenTree	17	95	25	78	8	21	244
Stay Online	8	79	17	7	1	11	123
Broadband Hospitality	4	37	8	63	—	4	116
V-Link	78	—	—	—	—	1	79
Suite Speed	3	4	4	9	—	10	30
Indirect competitors	368	350	469	581	209	418	2,395
Total	1,128	1,088	629	845	239	602	4,531

Note: Figures for U.S. and Canada only. GoldenTree had 142 pending installations under construction. F&B refers to food and beverage service.
Source: Roger Sharma, "North American Market Analysis", Guest-Tek, December 2003.

EXHIBIT 7 Intended Allocation of Proceeds from Guest-Tek's
IPO (figures in CDN$)

Millions	Allocation
$2.0	Increasing operational capacity for deployments
3.0	Expanding international sales and marketing initiatives
5.0	Advancing new product offerings
15.0	Funding disciplined, strategic acquisitions
3.3	Supplying working capital for general corporate purposes
$28.3	Proceeds to the corporation

EXHIBIT 8   Broadband Access in OECD Countries (as of June 2003)

Country	Penetration
Korea	23.2%
Canada	13.3%
Iceland	11.2%
Denmark	11.1%
Belgium	10.3%
Netherlands	9.2%
Sweden	9.2%
Switzerland	9.1%
Japan	8.6%
United States	8.3%
Austria	7.0%
Finland	6.6%
OECD	6.1%
Norway	5.4%
Germany	4.8%
EU	4.6%
Spain	4.2%
France	4.1%
Portugal	3.7%
United Kingdom	3.6%
Italy	2.8%
Luxembourg	2.3%

Note: Penetration figures per 100 inhabitants. Only countries with at least 1.0% penetration are shown.
Source: OECD.

Palliser Furniture Ltd.: The China Question

In September 2003, Art DeFehr, president of Canada's second-largest furniture company, Palliser Furniture Ltd., of Winnipeg, Manitoba, was pondering whether to significantly expand the company's relationship with China. Ever since Palliser set up a plant in Mexico in 1998, the company had faced increasing competitive pressures from Asia, especially from China.

THE MEXICO INVESTMENT 1998

In 1998, Palliser set up a leather furniture manufacturing facility in Saltillo, Coahuila, Mexico, to serve the Midwest and southern North American market. Palliser continued to ship products from its Winnipeg plants to the northern United States and Canadian markets. The Mexican facility would expand Palliser's leather manufacturing capacity, which was also part of its strategic shift from producing wood furniture to more leather products.

In 1997, DeFehr had considered the China option. Beginning in the mid-1990s, Taiwanese furniture manufacturers started to establish plants in Mainland China, and China's household furniture exports to the U.S. market had increased quickly. However, in 1997, China was not making much leather furniture. This would have been a proactive move to respond to the emerging low-cost Asian furniture-manufacturing sector. DeFehr nonetheless chose Mexico over China for several reasons:

1. The Mexican location, which was close to the Texas border, would provide a lower distribution cost structure for Palliser. Prior to 1998, Palliser had difficulties absorbing the higher freight cost when the company shipped products from Winnipeg, Manitoba, Canada, across the U.S.-Canada border to the south.

Jing'an Tang prepared this case under the supervision of Professor Paul W. Beamish solely to provide material for class discussion. The authors do not intend to illustrate either effective or ineffective handling of a managerial situation. The authors may have disguised certain names and other identifying information to protect confidentiality.

Copyright © 2004, Ivey Management Services   Version: (A) 2009-10-08

Ivey

Richard Ivey School of Business
The University of Western Ontario

2. At the time, China's leather furniture sector was small and inexperienced. Tanneries in China were not suitable for making leather furniture and the leather had to be imported. Moreover, although there had been leather cutting and sewing workers in the garment business in China, they had little experience in producing leather furniture. In Mexico, there were more industry skills. One other major firm in the volume furniture business, Leather Trend, built products in Tijuana (a Mexican city near San Diego, California) and shipped across the continent to other cities in the United States. Other firms in Mexico were all very small businesses.

3. At that stage, the foreign investments in China were mainly joint venture operations. DeFehr wanted to own a business; he did not want a joint venture (JV) and he did not want to contract the work and noted:

> I did not feel comfortable owning something in China. I still have certain discomfort. There are millions of examples of joint ventures in China. The JV partners were pushed out after some time. In contrast, in Mexico it was easy to wholly own a business.

4. Palliser had manufactured its products mainly in Canada with only a small portion of products being assembled in the United States in 1997. As a first stage of expansion, Palliser considered Mexico an ideal choice because it was closer to the U.S. market, and it was more manageable compared with offshore sites.

Since being established, the Mexican facility had been working well, operationally. It started to ship products to the United States, especially to the southern states, in 1999. Because of reduced costs and similar quality, Palliser's Mexican-made products were well accepted.

There had been some problems, however, with the Mexico investment. Palliser had issues with the Mexican taxation practices and had disagreements with the local taxation authorities. According to Kliewer, senior vice-president in finance,

> (Their) way of interpreting the law was just so discretionary. What they allow and what they don't allow were not clear. For example, the inflation adjustment was very problematic . . . It is a bit hard to plan for that. These are things you learned as you go on.

It had taken longer than planned to recover the initial investment. For instance, Palliser did not anticipate all the shipping costs accurately. The company had not anticipated the extra tariff fees associated with cross-border shipments leaving Mexico. Moreover, there had been other costs involved in shipping products across the Mexico-U.S. border because the trucks from Mexico could not cross the border; goods had to be transferred to U.S. trucks, which resulted in extra charges. DeFehr called it a "friction cost." According to Palliser calculations, the friction costs of crossing the Canadian border were around US$1[1] for a leather sofa, but the friction costs for the same sofa built in Mexico would be US$12. (The friction costs from China would have been approximately $10.)

As another example, the order allocation process initially favoured the Canadian facility. While the Mexico plant essentially produced the same products, orders were given to the Winnipeg plants first and the balance was allocated to Mexico. As a result, the Mexico plant had to fight with headquarters for orders. Palliser acknowledged and corrected the issue, a move that had a positive impact on the Mexican overhead recovery rate.

---

[1]All currency in CDN$ unless otherwise specified.

It could also be noted that the decision to set up a facility in Mexico had relied upon the competitiveness resulting from the North American Free Trade Agreement (NAFTA). Palliser had yet to focus on how to lower the costs through changes in its Mexican supply chain. Mexico was, in a sense, trying to build its competitiveness on a more limited framework.

THE FURNITURE INDUSTRY SINCE 1998

Since the late 1990s, the world furniture industry had undergone tremendous change. The most significant trend was the rise of China. In 2002, China's total furniture output value was US$20 billion, accounting for 10 per cent of the world's total furniture output value. In the past 5 years, China's furniture exports had grown at an annual rate of over 30 per cent. Countries with heavy demand for furniture products had flocked to China to make purchases. China's export of household furniture to the United States accounted for almost 40 per cent of the market, while exports to Japan accounted for about 15 per cent of Japan's total furniture demand. IKEA, the top-selling furniture company in the world, had shifted its purchasing centre from Singapore to Mainland China.

With the prospect of cheaper labour and high-quality workers in China, American, Japanese and Italian firms had established factories in China. Natuzzi, an Italian firm that was the No. 1 furniture manufacturer in the world, built a plant in Shanghai. DeCoro, another Italian furniture company, set up a plant in Dongguan, Gongdong province. Taiwanese firms had also built more than 500 furniture plants in Mainland China. Three U.S. office furniture firms with annual production values of US$1.5 billion, US$2.7 billion and US$3 billion, respectively, had all constructed production bases in Shanghai. China's furniture capacity had increased dramatically. Guangdong province, the biggest furniture manufacturing province, produced one-third of China's total furniture production.

The rise of China had shifted the world furniture market competition structure. It had affected most furniture firms' profit margins. Natuzzi's income dropped 70 per cent, and sales dropped 10 per cent in the second quarter of 2002. Firms in the North American furniture industry felt the pressure most. The market share of all household furniture imports in the U.S. domestic market increased between 1993 and 2002, from 20.4 to 38.9 per cent, while the market share of all office furniture imports increased from 9.1 per cent to 23.8 per cent during the same period. U.S. furniture imports in 2002 grew 13 per cent to US$14.2 billion. China fuelled much of that growth, accounting for 40 per cent of total U.S. imports in 2002. That year also marked the fifth out of the last six years in which total Chinese furniture exports to the United States jumped 30 per cent or more (see Exhibits 1, 2, 3 and 4).

The contributing factors were multifold, including China's cheaper labour and comparable product quality and design. Palliser managers estimated that the labour cost in China was around US$3 day; in Mexico, about US$32; while in Canada, it was around US$90 a day. Chinese workers usually worked more than 10 hours a day, 6 days a week. There were no unions nor union pressure. The leather furniture business in China did not need to deal with any environmental problems, although there were many concerns with tannery operations. Chinese firms did not pay much income tax, nor did they bear many social costs, such as health and insurance costs for employees. The Chinese currency was pegged to the U.S. dollar and, to many people, was arguably undervalued. The combination of these factors gave China a strongly competitive position. Furniture from China could be 20 to 30 per cent cheaper than the same products that were produced in North America. Exhibit 5 provides the comparison of cost bases for some wood furniture components.

Under the weight of the competitive pressure, many U.S. firms moved manufacturing sites offshore. In July 2003, some furniture makers in America jointly protested to the American government about the severe impact the Chinese furniture manufacturers were having on the American wood bedroom furniture industry. They submitted anti-dumping applications seeking industry protection.

Total Canadian shipments of furniture and bedding hit a record $4.76 billion in 2002, capping 10 years of almost continuous growth (see Exhibit 6). According to a survey conducted by Statistics Canada, there were 630 residential furniture and bedding manufacturers in Canada in 1999—the last year for which figures were available. Canada's furniture and bedding producers could be segmented into four categories: exporters, non-exporters, bedding producers and importers. The exporters were by far the largest group. While the 19 exporters did some business in Europe, South America and the Middle East, more than 95 per cent of all Canadian furniture exported was sold to U.S. retailers.

Canadian furniture producers were employing a variety of strategies to remain competitive in an increasingly uncertain North American economy. The impact of China had not been felt as deeply in Canada as it had been in the United States. Unlike their American counterparts, many of which had moved much of their production offshore, almost every one of the top ten Canadian producers (see Exhibit 7) had recently made, or was making, a big investment in their business.

While others followed a balancing act to remain as low-cost manufacturers, some Canadian manufacturers became active importers, focusing on specialized lines not being produced domestically. Two examples illustrate this approach. Dorel Industries tried to develop a strong capability to source a wide variety of products designed by Dorel and manufactured in Asia. In 2002, the company established a new division called Dorel Asia, whose mission was to develop product suitable for North America that was built cheaply and efficiently in the Pacific Rim. A second company, Shermag Inc., launched a new import division to expand its offerings of labour-intensive, traditionally styled bedroom and dining room furniture. These goods complemented the more technology-driven, casual contemporary furniture that Shermag made in its factories in Quebec and New Brunswick.

PALLISER'S STRATEGY SINCE 1998

Cost Leadership

The Mexico investment was part of Palliser's cost leadership strategy. Palliser negotiated with its Brazilian partners to be part of its supply chain for the Mexico plant. Brazil was the No. 1 source of leather in the world. Raw leather was delivered from Brazil to Mexico, where Palliser processed the leather (cutting and sewing) for redistribution to its U.S. and Canadian locations. Although it was more expensive than that in China, processing leathers in Mexico was still much cheaper than producing in Canada.

Quick Delivery

Quick delivery was another strategy. Purchasing from China meant a minimum delivery time of six to seven weeks, which translated into high inventory cost for those importers buying Asian products. Alternatively, Palliser focused on a custom manu-facturing strategy with a delivery time of three weeks. Custom business was Palliser's premium business. The company was able to charge a slight premium for the service that could eliminate customers' inventory cost. According to DeFehr, Palliser was still making most of its money from the plants in Canada, which were strong at specialty order businesses. As the China threat developed, more and more competitors estab-lished factories offshore. However, in doing so, they became less flexible, either in time or in variety. For example, the cycle time of the specialty businesses of the Italian producers DeCoro and Natuzzi was around 90 days.

The quick delivery strategy had been working very well until September 11, 2001 (9/11). After 9/11, because the airlines cut their flights and airfares had risen, it became very expensive to ship leather from Brazil to Mexico by air. If shipping by ocean, the quick delivery advantages over China would soon disappear. Palliser was working with Brazilian suppliers, seeking solutions.

Value Enhancement

Palliser was committed to delivering annual value improvements to its customers. For instance, if the company offered some products for $500 last year, it would try to offer the equal value of products at $400 this year. Such improvements were driven by process and product redesign. The first step was to identify those products where Palliser had absolute advantages or relative advantages in the North American mar-ket. Palliser still considered the North American market to be its first priority. Palliser considered developing a product using oak in Canada. Oak had a similar price around the world. Products could be built with a rustic and low grade of oak, with rough and simple machine-driven designs. By leveraging the low-cost material and leveraging the machine-driven design, the value would be similar to that produced in China.

At the same time, Palliser tried to remain a volume producer. Using Mexico and China to do cutting and sewing, Palliser was still doing low-price business. Beyond Mexico, the company was sourcing substantial quantities of finished goods from Asian countries, such as China, Thailand and Indonesia. Another way to enhance value was to produce machine-made and capital-intensive products instead of labour-intensive furniture. The new products that Palliser was going to produce were all less labour-intensive.

EQ3, a New Marketing Initiative

In the late 1990s, Palliser started a new marketing program called EQ3. Palliser real-ized that there was an opportunity in the market place, which had been underserved. A trend in the furniture industry was that consumers were becoming more fashion con-scious, design conscious and more educated. EQ3 was a new concept that was designed to meet this market trend. It was not about one piece of furniture, but about everything in the home with fashionable designs. Palliser recruited some product managers from IKEA and designers from many regions the world over, such as Sweden, Hong Kong and Italy. Most people in the new EQ3 team were in their late 20s and early 30s.

After two years of market research. Palliser introduced in-store EQ3 galleries through its traditional retailers in the United States and Canada in October 2001, but these galleries did not work well in the traditional store channels, which did not under-stand or draw in the target customer. In late 2002, Palliser started building new chan-nels. The company set up the first two dealer-owned EQ3 stores—one in Toronto, Ontario, and the other in Grand Rapids, Michigan. These stores started offering unique storefront with the new image and the right advertising and catalogues, which customers could identify with. This distribution channel was developed outside of the traditional channel and had been very successful.

Motion Business

In the North American marketplace, the motion business was one of the fastest-growing categories. Motion products referred to furniture that could be adjusted, such as recliners. Palliser started to make motion products at the same time it started to make leather furniture. Several years ago, Palliser's sales in motion products were around $26 million dollars. In 2003, sales were expected to be nearly $100 million.

Previously, motion products were mainly considered to be products that would go in the basement, not something that could be a focal point in the living room or family room. But in recent years, with better leathers and the popularity of leather furniture in the market place, furniture companies had been able to utilize leather to make motion products more attractive, fashionable and contemporary. People were willing to put them in their living room, family room and home theatres. Leather had made motion products more fashionable. For example, the leather recliner became one of the most popular household furniture items for every American family and sofas and love seats were becoming more fashionable too.

On average, from a labour perspective, motion products required 25 to 30 per cent more labour than standard products. Motion products were more technical and required more skill to produce.

Palliser had motion product factories in Winnipeg, Manitoba; Airdrie, Alberta; and Saltillo, Mexico. The latter plant, called "Las Colinas," was set up in 2000. Each of these factories operated at the same scale, but production costs in Mexico were much cheaper. The lower labour rate in Mexico might translate into a $75 savings for a sofa $1,000 in retail value. If making the same product in Asia, the possible savings could be $120 to $130 dollars for a product with a retail value of $1,000.

Currently, Palliser realized advantages in the North American marketplace by offering good value in motion products with colour options, good service, delivery and good quality. Traditionally, even the large Asian companies, which had considerable exports to North America, had not been successful in the motion business. The lengthy lead time had been a contributing factor, but in the last year, motion products were starting to come from Asia. For instance, DeCoro now produced motion products in China. In the last international furniture show, DeCoro displayed around 10 new motion product styles.

Palliser's approach to motion products was vinyl-leather match design. DeCoro's approach was all-leather style. By producing in China, DeCoro was able to provide the same product at a lower cost than Palliser offered. For example, Palliser could offer a leather-vinyl sofa at $999 retail, while DeCoro could offer $999 for an all-leather sofa retail. Thus, for the same product, DeCoro would have approximately a $200 advantage over Palliser's retail price. In the stationary category, several years ago, Palliser was providing leather-vinyl products. As a result of competition from Asia, which was offering all-leather products at the same price point, Palliser stopped producing leather-vinyl stationary products. The same shift might be anticipated in the motion product market.

Rach, director of motion products at Palliser, pointed out that contributing factors to cheap production in Asia were not only the leather for less money, but other components were cheaper too, such as the wood for the frame, the foam and the packaging materials.

PALLISER'S ASIAN PRESENCE

Palliser had several small factories in Indonesia, did contract work in Thailand and China and had an office in Taiwan and two offices in Mainland China, (one in Shanghai and another in Guangzhou).

Taiwan

Furniture exports from Asia were driven by people from Taiwan, who developed the expertise first, starting around 20 years ago. Palliser set up an office in Taiwan in 1985. It mainly imported final furniture products to the North American market.

Taiwanese firms were the first investors to go to Mainland China. In contrast to Palliser, Taiwanese firms did not go to Indonesia because Mainland China was closer and the culture was the same, therefore they preferred to invest in Mainland China. Also, the Chinese had had a bad experience in Indonesia in the 1960s, and there had been a recent reoccurrence of this experience. Many Chinese people who were sent there to do quality work flew to Indonesia in the morning and flew back home to China at night. Some people considered Indonesia an investment place with a lot of uncertainty.

Indonesia

Palliser had several factories in Indonesia. Some were owned, some used 100 per cent contracting and others used partial contracting. Palliser provided loans to one of the plants in 1997 when the plant experienced difficulties during the Asian financial crisis. The loan ended up with Palliser's controlling interests in that factory. The other two plants were owned by Palliser. Compared with Palliser's production facilities in Canada and in Mexico, these operations were very small. The total investment amount was approximately CDN$500,000. Indonesia was more like a training ground for Palliser in Asia. Palliser sent full-time Canadian staff into those local operations.

DeFehr had worked and kept in touch with Indonesia for almost 20 years, and he felt comfortable investing there. In terms of the risk concerns in Indonesia, DeFehr provided the following logic:

> By going to Indonesia, I separate myself from the face-to-face competition with these Chinese businesses for factory space, materials and other things. As a result, I am not competing with the best capital in the business. Will Indonesia be better than China in five years? I don't know, and you don't know either. So we make the bet . . . . We try to go to places that others might consider difficult. Because we are alone, you may get a little bit of a premium by being there.

Thailand and Mainland China

Beyond Indonesia, Palliser had a lot of contract work in Thailand as well. Local plants manufactured furniture components or finished products according to the design provided by Palliser.

Currently, Palliser contracted cutting and sewing work to a Chinese factory in Haiyin, a city south of Shanghai. The factory processed leather cover for its motion products. According to Rach, director of Palliser motion products,

> Chinese workers were very good at making leathers now. One of the advantages came from their larger tannery and their experience in the garment industry, especially the leather garment industry.

These leather covers were shipped back to Winnipeg, where they were uphol-stered. Almost $1 million of monthly sales were from Asia. Cutting and sewing covers in China had enabled Palliser to make a leather sofa at 8 to 10 per cent less than that in Canada. In retail, there is around one price point ($100) difference. That was the only component that Palliser outsourced from China for motion products. For a sofa with a total cost of $625, the cutting and sewing cost was around $250. It cost approximately $30 to $33 per seat to transport a sofa from China to North America.

DeFehr had certain concerns about doing business in China. Although many for-eign firms had set up plants in China, few of them had been successful.

Finding the right partner was another concern. DeFehr felt that Chinese partners were not committed, long-term OEM suppliers. He was not comfortable building long-term relationships in China. This might be due to the fact that a level of trust had not been established yet.

DeFehr was also concerned about the product itself. If a product had a well-established brand, no one else could easily make it and sell to the market. But a sofa and chair usually were not branded products. People could easily imitate and sell them. There-fore, if the products were exclusive, either technologically or brand-wise, the partnership relationship could work. Most furniture products were not exclusive.

Realistically, Palliser could not ignore China anymore. The resources in China were phenomenal, both in labour quantity and quality. People in China were working more and more efficiently than people in North America and in other developing coun-tries. According to Tielmann, senior vice-president of marketing,

If you look at India, Indonesia and Thailand, there are real differences. The value you get from China is one of the best worldwide. Another interesting thing was the Chinese Yuan, which was tied to the U.S. dollar. It had stayed that way for a while and might be that way for a long time yet. This could avoid currency fluc-tuations, which is different from Indonesia and Thailand. Also, the exchange rate was very advantageous for export.

TOP MANAGEMENT'S ASIAN EXPERIENCE

DeFehr had been to China many times, both on political and business issues. His first visit to China was with his family in 1983 as guests of the government. He had started visit-ing Taiwan regularly on furniture business in 1985. He had regularly visited Mainland China since 1992. Most recently, he had visited Beijing, Shanghai, Shenzheng, Dong-guan, Qsingdao, Tianjin and other coastal cities. Those were cities where the Chinese furniture businesses were concentrated.

DeFehr had extensive experience with Asian culture. He had lived in Asia, but he had never lived in Mexico. His two children were born in Asia. He had lived in Bangladesh, Thailand, and he travelled to Cambodia, India and many other Asian countries. Asia, to DeFehr, was very much home. However, because both of his par-ents were from the former Soviet Union, and he had experienced dealing with commu-nist governments, he did not think he was comfortable doing business in a communist environment.

Most members of Palliser's top management had been to China. As the director of motion products, Rach visited China more frequently. He went to China at least three times a year. As China's furniture business had become stronger in recent years, the top management team had shifted much more attention to Asia.

THE DECISION

Products from China had increasingly become threats to most furniture manufacturers in North America and the pressures on Palliser had been increasingly felt. In April 2003, Palliser conducted its first layoff in the Winnipeg factory.

Palliser had production facilities in Canada, Mexico and Indonesia, and the company experimented with cutting and sewing leather in China. DeFehr had to decide whether to significantly expand Palliser's relationship with China and discern what form that relationship might follow. Should it be an investment, either wholly or partly owned? Should it be through subcontracting? To build Palliser's competitive advantages, DeFehr summarized:

> What we are considering right now is how to take advantage of our particular organizational and geographic situation to counter the advantages that the people in lower-cost environments have.

EXHIBIT 1 All Household Imports by Significant Countries in the U.S. Market (US$ millions)

	1998	1999	2000	2001	2002	CAGR
China	1,550.5	2,235.6	3,001.6	3,423.2	4,832.8	37.9%
Canada	1,301.4	1,584.7	1,837.4	1,744.2	1,739.6	16.4%
Italy	760.3	917.8	1,140.1	1,107.7	1,139.3	14.5%
Mexico	641.0	704.7	764.2	699.9	729.1	13.1%
Indonesia	323.1	407.3	450.7	445.4	492.0	16.0%
Taiwan	687.2	722.1	701.1	502.1	477.6	−7.5%
Malaysia	384.0	443.1	452.3	407.9	467.4	10.8%
Thailand	165.2	210.5	253.7	261.1	338.3	9.5%
Phillipines	214.0	241.1	269.2	223.8	217.7	8.4%
Brazil	53.4	74.8	96.9	135.2	209.5	23.6%

CAGR—Compounded Annual Growth Rate.
Source: Company files.

EXHIBIT 2 Wood Household Imports by Significant Countries in the U.S. Market (US$ millions)

	1998	1999	2000	2001	2002	CAGR
China	794.0	1,141.0	1,650.7	1,897.6	2,893.6	40.1%
Canada	947.5	1,182.9	1,368.5	1,306.7	1,267.7	17.1%
Italy	306.4	392.6	460.4	453.6	484.3	15.2%
Malaysia	340.4	396.4	399.5	364.4	414.5	11.3%
Indonesia	254.6	332.2	373.4	376.7	414.2	19.2%
Mexico	353.7	371.9	392.8	372.2	372.1	10.8%
Thailand	149.7	188.2	225.8	226.7	297.7	9.7%
Taiwan	381.7	402.7	349.4	280.5	260.2	−8.7%
Brazil	52.0	70.3	92.6	126.1	187.9	23.3%
Philippines	83.9	99.6	118.6	109.8	109.2	15.0%

Source: Company files.

EXHIBIT 3   Upholstered Household Imports by Significant Countries in the U.S. Market (US$ millions)

	1998	1999	2000	2001	2002	CAGR
Italy	363.6	412.9	559.3	529.0	528.6	14.5%
China	46.6	83.6	127.6	172.8	312.9	53.8%
Mexico	111.8	139.0	170.5	172.3	208.6	27.3%
Canada	95.8	122.8	156.2	161.5	184.3	19.7%

Source: Company files.

EXHIBIT 4   Metal and Other Household Imports by Significant Countries in the U.S. Market (US$ millions)

	1998	1999	2000	2001	2002	CAGR
China	541.3	766.7	938.7	1,033.6	1,235.5	44.0%
Canada	181.9	185.4	205.2	167.7	183.4	13.0%
Taiwan	240.9	256.7	282.4	177.2	178.0	−6.0%
Mexico	150.6	164.8	171.0	126.2	121.0	8.0%
Italy	61.3	85.4	82.0	85.9	85.0	15.0%

Source: Company files.

EXHIBIT 5   Wood Furniture Cost Comparison

	American-made[1]	Chinese-made[2]	Difference
Bed headboard	100.00	89.00	11%
Nightstand	95.00	80.22	16%
Chest	109.00	88.76	19%
Entertainment centre	211.00	159.54	24%
Armoire	474.00	330.00	30%
Rolltop desk	275.00	181.50	34%

[1]Costs are as if the product were in a U.S. warehouse, ready to ship to retailers.
[2]For the Chinese, shipping is included.
Source: Furniture/Today, May 26, 2003.

EXHIBIT 6   The Canadian Furniture Market (CDN$ millions)

	2002	2001	2000	2001–2002 change	1997–2001 change
Total industry shipments	4,760	4,307	4,106	10.5%	54.9%
Total exports	2,153	2,018	1,924	6.7%	87.9%
Export to the United States	2,036	1,911	N/A	6.5%	N/A
Total imports	1,443	1,252	1,134	15.3%	54.7%
Imports from the United States	489	509	N/A	−3.9%	N/A
Total domestic shipments	2,607	2,289	2,182	13.9%	34.2%

Source: Statistics Canada.

EXHIBIT 7   Canada's Top 25 Furniture and Bedding Producers (CDN$ millions)

Rank	Company name	Home base	2002	2001	Change
1	Dorel Inds.	Montreal, Quebec	712.9	701.7	1.6%
2	Palliser Furniture	Winnipeg, Manitoba	518.8	493.6	5.1%
3	Shermag Inc.	Sherbrooke, Quebec	188.0	163.2	15.2%
4	Canadel Furniture	Louiseville, Quebec	155.0	135.0	14.8%
5	Sealy Canada	Toronto, Ontario	139.7	121.1	15.4%
6	Simmons Canada Inc.	Mississauga, Ontario	130.9	120.1	9.0%
7	La-Z-Boy Canada Ltd.	Waterloo, Ontario	117.9	100.9	16.8%
8	Magnussen Home Furnishings	New Hamburg, Ontario	106.8	N/A	N/A
9	Gusdorf Canada	Montreal, Quebec	105.0	94.0	11.7%
10	South Shore Inds.	Sainte-Croix, Quebec	100.0	100.0	0.0%

Source: Furniture/Today, June 2, 2003.

CASE 22

Canadian Solar

In late September 2009, Dr. Shawn Qu, CEO, president, chairman and founder of Canadian Solar, was constantly on the move. His company, a NASDAQ-traded solar cell and module manufacturer, had grown at a compound annual growth rate (CAGR) of 135.7 per cent over the last 5 years, from $9.7 million in revenues in 2004 to $705 million in 2008 (see Exhibit 1 for key financials). The strong growth had been spurred by an increasing number of government incentive programs to encourage the adoption of solar photovoltaic (PV)[1] technology. For the past couple of years, solar energy was seen to be the world's fastest-growing industry. However, the credit crunch and global economic downturn, combined with changes to Spain's incentive program, had put the worldwide PV industry into oversupply for the first half of 2009. During the summer, demand changed again. Forecasts were exceeded, causing a temporary undersupply of ready-to-install solar modules. The fluctuating solar demand had caused analysts to change their financial outlook for Canadian Solar several times throughout 2009. In mid-2009, a Deutsche Bank analyst had predicted full-year sales to come in at $395 million with net losses at −$18 million, only to revise the outlook two months later to sales of $574 million and net income of $49 million.

Part of the increasing positive outlook was attributed to government incentive programs. Of particular interest to many players, including Canadian Solar, were proposed incentive programs in China and Canada. In Ontario, for example, the details of the provincial government's incentive program for green energy—the Feed-in Tariff (FIT) program—had just been released with specific requirements for domestic content. Although registered as a Canadian company, Canadian Solar had the bulk of its production operations in China; namely, seven facilities dedicated to the manufacture

Richard Ivey School of Business
The University of Western Ontario

Jordan Mitchell wrote this case under the supervision of Professor Paul W. Beamish solely to provide material for class discussion. The authors do not intend to illustrate either effective or ineffective handling of a managerial situation. The authors may have disguised certain names and other identifying information to protect confidentiality.

[1]Solar photovoltaic (PV) technology is one of the main types of solar electric power. It is the main focus of this case.

of different solar PV components. And, even though the company's "bases" were in China and Canada, 89.5 per cent of 2008 revenues came from Europe. Company management expected that to change rapidly as they were planning, or had already established, new sales offices in South Korea, Japan, China, Italy, Spain, Germany, the United States and Canada.

When looking at the relatively nascent and rapidly growing solar PV industry, replete with a mix of diverse competitors, Qu and other Canadian Solar senior managers wondered how best to compete in the increasingly "global" PV industry.

SOLAR ENERGY

Solar energy was divided into three main categories: solar electric, solar thermal and concentrating solar. Solar electric converted the sun's energy into electricity, and solar thermal used the sun for heating or cooling. Concentrating solar power mixed solar electric and solar thermal, as it used small optical mirrors to collect solar energy and convert the sunlight to heat. The heat was then applied to a liquid or gas to turn a turbine, thereby creating electricity.

The other important distinction in solar energy was between "grid-tied" and "off-grid" applications. Grid-tied applications were solar-electric systems that were connected to an electricity utility grid (in nearly all jurisdictions, electricity utility grids were heavily regulated by government bodies and were often separate from electricity providers). Grid-tied applications were either "ground mount" or "rooftop"—ground mount applications were typically in a field or desert area and were either solar PV or concentrating solar power. Grid-tied rooftop projects ranged from 1 kilowatt to 10 kilowatts (kW) on residential homes to larger projects of 10 kilowatts to 5 megawatts (MW) on commercial buildings.

Off-grid applications were defined as a system completely independent of the main electricity grid. Off-grid applications ranged from tiny solar cells in pocket calculators to solar-thermal systems for hot water tanks in residential homes. In the last few years, off-grid applications had become popular for road lights, signs and parking metres whereby a solar module was placed on top of the apparatus to provide power at night through a battery. Off-grid applications were also seen as one solution to providing power in isolated rural areas.

PHOTOVOLTAIC CELLS[2]

The main tenet of solar-electric power was the photovoltaic (PV) cell, which used the "photovoltaic effect" to generate electricity. When sunlight hit a PV cell, electrons bounced from negative to positive, thus producing electricity. In order to generate electricity, a PV cell required a semiconductor material and positive and negative poles.[3]

The most common semiconductor material for PV cells was silicon.[4] For most solar applications, the silicon was refined to 99.9999 per cent purity, which was known

---

[2]This section draws upon *SBI*, "The U.S. solar energy market in a world perspective," March 2008, pp. 2–30.

[3]Phosphorous was often used as the negative pole and boron was often used as the positive pole.

[4]Silicon was found in sand, rocks or soil as silicon oxide (SiO_2); the process for manufacturing silicon involved heating silicon oxide with a carbon material like coke or coal at high temperatures to remove the oxygen.

as 6N silicon (the number "6" referred to the number of "9s"). Companies such as Canadian Solar had commercialized products with lower grades of silicon for solar applications. For example, upgraded metallurgical-grade silicon (UMG-Si) was one such type of lower grade silicon. It was 99.999 per cent pure (or 5N for five "9s"). UMG-Si was a by-product of the aluminum smelting business and historically had been less expensive than 6N silicon.

The three types of PV cells were polycrystalline ("poly"), monocrystalline ("mono") and amorphous ("thin-film"). Poly PV cells used silicon in its refined state, whereas mono took the refinement a step further, thus creating higher efficiency (the drawback with mono PV was the higher cost of production vs. poly). The third type, thin-film, was substantially different in that it did not have crystalline silicon, but rather a painted or printed semiconductor. There were six main types of materials used in thin-film, although three had not yet been proven to be commercially viable.[5]

The basic process of constructing a crystalline PV cell began by forming cylindrical ingots from the semiconductor material. The ingots were then cut into very thin disc-shaped wafers. The wafer was etched with hydrofluoric acid and washed with water, creating a PV cell. To create a usable "solar module" (also called a "solar panel"), a series of PV cells were placed in between a sheet of glass held in by an aluminum frame and plastic backing connected to a cable plug. In most installations, a number of modules were used to make up an array. The array was then connected to an inverter (to convert the electricity from direct current [DC] to alternating current [AC]).

Solar modules were rated by their capacity in watts (W). Most solar PV modules were rated between 80W and 250W. Larger solar modules (200W+) weighed approximately 20 kilograms and were sized 1.6 metres long, 1 metre wide and 4 to 5 centimetres thick. Solar efficiency—the amount of sunlight energy converted to electricity—ranged between 12 and 18 per cent for most PV modules. However, breakthroughs were constantly being achieved—as of mid-2009, the highest PV cells had efficiency ratings slightly above 23 per cent. As a general rule of thumb, one to two per cent efficiency was deducted from the rating of the cell to determine the rating of the module (i.e., an 18 per cent efficient cell would have a 16–17 per cent efficient module).

The cost of PV cells was a constantly moving target. In securing contracts with large volumes, it was common for PV manufacturers to offer discounts of 10 to 30 per cent on the price of a module. In large-scale projects, many buyers saw PV modules more as a commodity product and were largely concerned with the price per watt. From 2007 to 2009, the selling price of a solar PV (from a PV module manufacturer to a customer) had increased slightly from $3.50 per watt to around $4, before dropping to approximately $2.50 per watt (put another way, the price for one 200W solar PV crystalline module was about $500 as of mid-2009).

A major driver behind the price of solar PV was the price of silicon. A temporary silicon shortage around mid-2008 pushed the spot price of silicon to over $500 per kilogram (up from around $25 per kilogram in 2004). However, by mid-2009, that price had fallen to around $60 per kilogram.[6] As the supply of silicon increased

---

[5]The six types of materials used in thin-film technology were: amorphous silicon (a-Si); copper indium diselenide (CIS); copper indium gallium diselenide (CIGS); cadmium telluride (CdTe); gallium arsenide (GaAs); and thin-film silicon.

[6]Edgar Gunther, "Solar polysilicon oversupply until 2013?" August 3, 2009, http://guntherportfolio. com/2009/08/solar-polysilicon-oversupply-until-2013, accessed August 18, 2009.

along with greater manufacturing efficiencies, the cost for crystalline PV modules was expected to fall below $1 per watt in two to three years.

Many industry insiders debated whether thin-film modules held more promise, given their lower cost versus poly and mono modules. As of August 2009, the price of thin-film was reported at $1.76 per watt, versus $2.50 per watt for silicon modules.[7] Despite silicon's current higher price, crystalline silicon supporters often pointed to the fact that thin-film would have trouble competing as the price of crystalline modules dropped. Additionally, poly- and monocrystalline silicon modules typically enjoyed higher efficiencies than thin-film and required less space, fewer mounting systems and less cabling for the same power output.

In addition to the cost of the module itself, the cost of installation ranged from $4 to $8 per watt. Developers of utility-scale PV projects also had to be mindful of the real estate cost and electricity transmission costs. All tallied, the cost of solar PV was between $0.15 and $0.35 per kilowatt-hour (kWh) versus non-renewable sources of energy (between $0.03 and $0.15 per kWh). As scale efficiencies grew along with technological breakthroughs, many insiders felt that the cost of solar would be competitive with non-renewable sources in a three-to-five year time horizon (this was referred to in the industry as reaching "grid parity").

THE GLOBAL SOLAR INDUSTRY

In 2008, solar PV experienced its largest increase to date by growing 5.6 gigawatts (60.8 per cent) to 14.73 gigawatts (GW) in 2008.[8] (On a global level, solar power accounted for under one per cent of all electricity generation.) Geographically, total installed capacity was split: 65 per cent in Europe, 15 per cent in Japan and 8 per cent in the United States. In 2008, the strongest market was Spain, which represented nearly half of the installations due to its aggressive Renewable Energy Feed-in Tariff (referred to as REFIT or FIT) program, which guaranteed electricity rates for certain renewable projects. Even though Spain dominated the PV market in 2008, the Spanish government had placed a 500MW cap on annual installations for the next two years, given uncontrollable growth. Thus, Spanish PV installations were expected to drop substantially in 2009. Germany was the second-largest market, capturing 26.7 per cent of worldwide installations during the year (Germany was one of the first countries in the world to introduce a FIT program). Other leading solar countries were the United States (6 per cent of worldwide installations), South Korea (5 per cent), Italy (4.9 per cent) and Japan (4 per cent).

The future of the global PV market largely hinged on government initiatives and renewable support schemes. The European Photovoltaic Industry Association (EPIA) predicted two scenarios: a moderate scenario without heavy government incentives; and a policy-driven scenario with some support initiatives present. Under the first scenario, EPIA projected that cumulative solar PV power would equate to 54.8GW in 2013 (representing a CAGR of 30 per cent). The second scenario resulted in global installed PV power being 85.8GW by 2013 (CAGR of 42.3 per cent). Exhibit 2 shows some highlights from different world markets and Exhibit 3 gives EPIA's moderate and policy-driven scenarios for the top 13 markets.

---

[7]Quote from www.solarbuzz.com, accessed August 11, 2009.

[8]By comparison, the global installed capacity of wind power grew by 29 per cent, from 93.9GW in 2007 to 121.2GW in 2008.

Germany was expected to be the top market for the next few years, given the government's continuing Renewable Energy Law (*Erneuerbare-Energien-Gesetz* or EEG). As a successor to an earlier law passed in 1991, the EEG came into effect in 2000 as part of Germany's aim to derive 12.5 per cent of the country's energy from renewable sources by 2010 (the goal was surpassed in 2007 when Germany reached 14 per cent and was modified to reach a new goal of 27 per cent renewable by 2020). In 2009, the EEG was updated: For PV solar, the feed-in rates were between €0.33 and €0.43 per kWh ($0.46 to $0.60 per kWh) depending on the size of the project. The EEG called for those rates to decrease by 8 to 10 per cent in 2010 and 9 per cent after 2011, but guaranteed the rates for a period of 20 years.[9] Despite the decreasing feed-in rates over the next few years, the EPIA believed that the rates were sufficient to encourage installations. Furthermore, PV solar was expected to remain strong as a result of high public awareness and support of renewables, the skilled PV industry and accessible financing opportunities through Kreditanstalt für Wiederaufbau (KfW).[10]

The story of Spain's boom and subsequent bust had become a hot topic in the solar industry. Through laws in 2004 and 2007, the Spanish government created an attractive Feed-in Tariff (FIT), giving up to €0.44 per kWh ($0.62 per kWh) for solar projects installed before September 2008. In spite of the original cap of 400MW, the country was flooded with demand for projects and in an 18-month period (from the passing of the 2007 law to September 2008), about 3GW of PV solar energy were installed. The heavily unanticipated installations were estimated to cost taxpayers about $26.4 billion, causing a public backlash against the government.[11] In 2008, the Spanish government placed a new cap of 500MW on installations and backed off the Feed-in Tariffs to €0.32 to €0.34 per kWh ($0.45 to $0.48 per kWh).[12] Despite the new cap, Spain was seen as a key market in the long term due to its government's high renewable target (the government wanted 20 per cent of consumed energy to come from renewables by 2020).[13]

Prior to the boom in Germany and Spain, Japan had had one of the strongest solar PV markets in the world, up until 2006, when the government stopped supplying subsidies. The majority of its PV installations were in residential applications (different from other markets where commercial applications were the norm). Recently, the government had set new targets of reaching over 50GW of installed PV power by 2030 and had implemented national and regional support mechanisms. The country's Feed-in Tariff schemes promised an initial rate of 50 yen per kWh ($0.50 per kWh) for solar installations.[14]

---

[9]"Act Revising the Legislation on Renewable Energy Sources in the Electricity Sector and Amending Related Provisions—Renewable Energy Sources Act—EEG 2009," www.erneuerbare-energien.de/inhalt/42934/3860, accessed August 18, 2009.

[10]*European Photovoltaic Industry Association (EPIA)*, "Global market outlook for photovoltaics until 2013," March 2009, p. 7.

[11]Paul Voosen, "Spain's solar market crash offers a cautionary tale about feed-in tariffs," August 18, 2009, www.nytimes.com/gwire/2009/08/18/18greenwire-spains-solar-market-crash-offers-a-cautionary-88308.html?pagewanted=2, accessed August 18, 2009.

[12]"Spain makes changes to solar tariff," September 29, 2008, www.renewableenergyworld.com/rea/news/article/2008/09/spain-makes-changes-to-solar-tariff-53698, accessed August 18, 2009.

[13]"Plan de Energías Renovables 2011–2020," http://www.plane.gob.es/plan-de-energias-renovables-2011–2020, accessed August 17, 2009.

[14]*Energy Matters*, "Japan announces solar feed in tariffs," February 25, 2009, www.energymatters.com.au/index.php?main_page=news_article&article_id=335, accessed August 17, 2009.

The U.S. market also held great promise, given President Obama's support of renewable energy and several state programs targeted at rolling out renewables. California, Arizona, New Mexico, Texas, Vermont and several other states had, or were in the process of enacting, incentives and stimulus programs. In 2010 many expected that the United States would enact a federal incentive program—one source suggested that the bill would guarantee a 10 per cent return over 20 years for renewable projects under 20MW.[15] Nearly all of the PV manufacturers had set up offices in the United States given the future potential in what many believed would become the world's largest market by the middle of the next decade.

A number of other policies and support mechanisms had also been implemented or were in the design phase in countries as far-reaching as Italy, Greece, France, Israel, South Korea, China and Canada.

In Canada, the main program was Ontario's FIT, announced in early 2009 with a start date of October 1, 2009. Ontario's FIT would replace the 2006 Standard Offer Program, which gave PV solar rates of CDN$0.42 per kWh and other renewable sources rates of CDN$0.11 per kWh.[16] In North America's first FIT program, renewables could garner between CDN$0.08 and CDN$0.802 per kWh, depending on the scale of the project. Smaller-scale solar rooftop systems for residential homes would receive the highest rates, between CDN$0.539 and CDN$0.802 per kWh. Larger-scale solar (less than 10MW) would receive CDN$0.443 per kWh. The program called for domestic content to make up 40 per cent on projects less than 10kW and 50 per cent of the project cost on projects over 10kW (after January 1, 2011, domestic requirements would rise to 60 per cent). See Exhibit 4 for more details on Ontario's FIT program.

In July 2009, the Chinese government announced major subsidies for utility-scale solar projects. The conditions of receiving the subsidies required that the project have a minimum of 300kW peak and be built in one year with longevity of 20 years. The subsidy would be 20 yuan ($4) per watt, with the overall goal of reaching 10GW of installed power by 2020.[17]

PLAYERS IN THE GLOBAL PV MARKET

Globally, there were hundreds of PV cell and module manufacturers. On the supply side of PV manufacturers, there were raw material suppliers for goods such as silicon, glass, substrates, metal and cables, as well as specialized equipment manufacturers to make solar components such as furnaces, sawing machines, printing machines and laminators. On the buyer side of PV manufacturers, there were several potential customers. Consumer electronics, automotive and industrial product companies integrated solar cells into their products for resale (examples ranged from solar cells in garden lamps through to cells used on marine buoys). For grid-tied applications, the typical customers were project developers, utility companies, solar installation companies, distributors, wholesalers, governments, construction companies and building owners.

---

[15]James Murray, "US lawmakers outline plan for feed-in tariff bill," *Business Green*, August 5, 2009, http://www.businessgreen.com/business-green/news/2247352/lawmakers-outline-plan-feed, accessed August 19, 2009.

[16]"Ontario's Standard Offer Contracts," March 22, 2006, www.energyalternatives.ca/content/SOC.htm, accessed August 18, 2009.

[17]Jim Bai and Leonora Walet, "China offers big solar subsidy, shares up," *Reuters*, July 21, 2009.

Barriers to entry were considered fairly low due to the low capital requirements and medium-low technological know-how to make a PV module. However, product warranties were one barrier that was becoming more important. For example, smaller manufacturers struggled to sell modules for use in bank-financed large-scale projects because of requirements from the banks for greater assurances that 25-year product performance warranties would be upheld. Some analysts also predicted more vertical integration both from silicon producers, specialized suppliers of PV cells and customers (such as project developers). Complementary players such as inverter manufacturers or rack suppliers were not considered to pose an immediate vertical integration threat.

The top 10 producers accounted for 55.3 per cent of PV module sales in 2008. Exhibit 5 shows the market shares of both PV module and PV cell producers. Some observers divided the market into three groups based on geography, market strength, size and quality perception. The first group competed on the basis of price and used China as a manufacturing base, the second was made up of up-start companies with a point of technological differentiation, and the third consisted of Japanese electronic firms with established brand names. The market could also be divided simply into more recent start-ups and established incumbents.

A powerful contingent of emerging PV module companies were the four companies which used China as their primary manufacturing base: Suntech, Yingli Green, Trina Solar and Canadian Solar. All were vertically integrated in that they produced ingots, wafers, cells and modules and used their access to low-cost labour for a cost advantage. Canadian Solar's management believed its company to be unique in that it combined elements of Western management and engineering with a low-cost Chinese production base.

Of the specialized start-ups, two main groups of companies existed: those producing complete PV modules and those focusing on the production of PV cells only. PV module start-ups competed more on tailored propositions, customer relationships and service, technological differences and price. For example, First Solar used cadmium telluride as a semiconductor, which allowed it to deliver a lower price per watt. SunPower competed by offering solar systems complete with inverters for easy residential and commercial installation. Both U.S. companies had the majority of their production in low-cost Asian countries, namely Malaysia and the Philippines.

Up-starts such as Germany's Q-Cells and Solar World, Taiwan's Motech and Gintech and China's JA Solar produced PV cells only and sold the cells to module producers. Q-Cells had surpassed Sharp in terms of total PV cell production in the last couple of years. The five PV cell companies competed on technology, relationships with module producers and price.

Of the incumbents, Japanese electronics multinationals such as Sharp, Kyocera and Sanyo all had long histories developing PV solar. They typically competed on the strength of their brand recognition, research and development, strong distribution and in some cases, exclusive rights with large-scale customers. Sharp had begun developing PV solar in 1959 and had dominated the world market for much of the last 50 years. While Sharp had historically sold mono- and polycrystalline PV, they had begun investing in thin-film technology in 2005. In addition to its four plants in Japan, the company produced PV solar products in the United States, the United Kingdom and Thailand. To expand production even further, Sharp was seeking joint venture partners to build solar module factories in other countries (in late 2008, the company inked a deal with Italy's Enel for a joint venture plant in Italy).

Japan's second-largest PV solar manufacturer, Kyocera, produced a range of PV products in a network of factories split between Japan, China, the Czech Republic and

Mexico. Japan's third major player, Sanyo, produced nearly all of its PV offerings in its home country. It had invested heavily in developing its own thin-film technology (called HIT for Heterojunction with Intrinsic Thin-layer), which it claimed had the highest efficiency of any solar PV cell in the world (its efficiency was 23 per cent).[18] Sanyo sold its complementary batteries with its PV solar products and had reorganized its business to satisfy its master plan of becoming a "leading provider of environment and energy-related products."[19] Sanyo's strong position in PV solar and related products was one of the key reasons for Panasonic taking a key ownership stake in Sanyo in late 2008.[20]

Other multinationals also participated in PV solar, namely Japan's Mitsubishi, Britain's BP and U.S. companies General Electric and Chevron. Mitsubishi began developing PV solar technology in the 1970s and offered complete packages including the PV module and inverter. As of 2009, Mitsubishi claimed to have one of the highest efficiencies of any poly PV cell (18.9 per cent).[21] Its production capacity was about 200MW. BP Solar also had about 30 years of history in the solar industry. With a capacity of 200MW, it produced poly and mono PV cells and modules in five plants located in Australia, Spain, the United States, India and China. However, in a recent move to focus on its core business of petroleum, its parent company, BP, had announced that it would be closing factories in Australia, Spain and the United States and shifting to a mix of its lower-cost plants and sub-contractors in China.[22] (Shell divested its solar operations in 2006 and 2007—the majority of the assets were purchased by Germany's SolarWorld.)[23]

BACKGROUND ON CANADIAN SOLAR

Canadian Solar was established by Qu in October 2001 in Markham, Ontario. In tandem, a production facility in Changshu, China, registered as CSI Solartronics was set up as a wholly owned subsidiary. Qu, a graduate of applied physics at Tsinghua University (B.Sc.) and the University of Manitoba (M.Sc.), had completed a doctoral degree in material science from the University of Toronto (Ph.D) and extensive post-doctorate work on semiconductor optical devices and solar cells. In 1996, he joined Ontario Hydro (now Ontario Power Generation) as a research scientist, where he worked on the development of a next-generation solar technology called Spheral Solar™. In 1998, he joined ATS (Automation Tooling Systems), working in several capacities, such as product engineer, director for silicon procurement, solar product strategic planning, as well as technical vice president for one of ATS's subsidiaries.

---

[18]"Sanyo develops HIT solar cells with world's highest energy conversion efficiency of 23.0%," May 21, 2009, http://us.sanyo.com/News/SANYO-Develops-HIT-Solar-Cells-with-World-s-Highest-Energy-Conversion-Efficiency-of-23-0-, accessed August 16, 2009.

[19]Sanyo Annual Report 2008, December 31, 2008, p. 9.

[20]"Panasonic and SANYO agree to capital and business alliance," http://sanyo.com/news/2008/12/19-1.html, accessed August 17, 2009.

[21]"Mitsubishi electric breaks own record with world's highest conversion efficiency rate of 18.9% for multi-crystalline silicon photovoltaic cells," February 18, 2009, www.mitsubishielectricsolar.com/news, accessed August 19, 2009.

[22]Ed Crooks, "Back to petroleum," *Financial Times*, July 7, 2009.

[23]Terry Macalister, "Big Oil lets sun set on renewables," *The Guardian*, December 11, 2007, www.guardian.co.uk/business/2007/dec/11/oil.bp, accessed August 19, 2009.

Qu left ATS to establish Canadian Solar; he commented on the opportunity he saw at the time:

> In 2001, solar was still a very small industry. A lot of my colleagues from the PhD program in applied physics were involved in fibre optics for the telecommunications industry. I believed that solar had great prospects and thought I could easily spend my career in the solar industry. Because solar was such a small part of ATS, it did not get a lot of management attention. Around 2000, I started thinking of starting my own company and worked on the business plan. At that time, the major players were small solar divisions in multinationals. My idea largely focused on areas that I felt they were not addressing: rural electrification with solar, the low-cost production of solar cells and solar modules, building integrated solar products and consumer solar products. It just so happened the first product was a consumer solar product for the automotive industry.

Canadian Solar's first contract was to manufacture and sell a solar charger to Audi-Volkswagen for use in its automobiles being manufactured in Mexico. Audi-Volkswagen required that Canadian Solar become ISO9001 and ISO16949 certified. Management saw the certification as an essential part of raising Canadian Solar's quality credibility in the early stages of the company. Canadian Solar established two additional solar module manufacturing plants in Suzhou, China, incorporated as separate companies: CSI Solar Technologies in August 2003 and CSI Solar Manufacturing in January 2005. The company purchased solar cells and silicon raw materials from a small group of companies, such as Swiss Wafers (Switzerland), Kunical (United States), Luoyang Zhong Gui (China) and LDK (China).

While continuing to supply Audi-Volkswagen (eventually receiving the accolade of class-A supplier), Canadian Solar's management saw a great opportunity to develop solar modules for electricity generation for residential and commercial applications in 2004. Qu commented:

> In early 2004, with the change of Germany's FIT program, I identified a major increase in demand for solar PV modules for buildings. Within three to four months, we were able to switch gears to large solar modules. The decision to spin-off the company from ATS in 2001 when we did was vital—had I waited until 2004, I would not have had the time to build the team and capabilities to make this switch into larger solar modules.

By the end of 2004, nearly three-quarters of Canadian Solar's sales were derived from selling standard solar modules to distributors and system integrators based in Germany, Spain and China. The company made initial contact with its customers through international trade shows. By the end of 2005, the top 5 customers accounted for 68.2 per cent of total sales. Most sales were made with non-exclusive, three-month sales contracts. It was normal that the customer paid 20 to 30 per cent of the purchase as prepayment and the remainder in advance of the shipment from China. In China, sales of solar modules were associated with development projects in conjunction with Chinese governmental organizations and the Canadian International Development Agency (CIDA); for example, in the spring of 2005, the company installed a demonstration power plant in a rural area of the province of Jiangsu.

With sales of standard solar modules accelerating, Canadian Solar turned to venture capital (VC) funding. Qu stated, "Up until 2005, we had grown without any VC involvement. We received an investment from HSBC and Jafco Ventures [a VC from Japan with $350 million under management] and then started preparing for an IPO."

In November 2006, the company listed on the NASDAQ, raising $115.5 million. The proceeds were to be used to purchase and prepay for solar cells and silicon (35 per cent); expansion into solar cell manufacturing (45 per cent); and general funding purposes (20 per cent). The initial public offering (IPO) enabled it to expand into solar cell manufacturing, resulting in the following facilities: CSI Solarchip for solar cells and modules; and CSI Advanced and CSI Luoyang for solar modules. By the end of 2007, the company had established four solar cell production lines, taking total cell capacity to 120MW.

Canadian Solar's management established a sales office of two people in Phoenix, Arizona, and a European office of three people near Frankfurt, Germany, in December 2007. All sales in Spain were done through an independent distributor. As Qu said, "We serviced these growing markets from China and Canada. The decision to open up the offices in 2007 was a logical move given that the majority of sales were coming from those markets." On the production side, the company expanded to seven factories, including a solar module manufacturing site in Changshu and an ingot and wafer manufacturing site in Luoyang. The continued expansion in China was complemented by a high-profile BIPV (Building Integrated Photovoltaic) module roof project as part of the 2008 Beijing Olympic Games. At the close of 2008, the company was recognized as one of the top 10 fastest-growing companies in China by Deloitte Asia, given its sales had more than doubled from $302.8 million in 2007 to $705 million in 2008.

In 2009, the company underwent a number of changes in its international configuration. To respond to market opportunity in South Korea, it established a two-person sales office. In Canada, it established an international development office of three people in Ottawa to focus specifically on projects in Latin America and the Middle East, given its working history with CIDA. In the United States, the company moved the Phoenix office to San Ramon, California, to be located closer to the heart of the U.S. solar movement and to take advantage of the favourable Californian incentives. It opened a warehouse at the office site to store finished solar modules. In China, it opened a PV research and development facility at its head office in Suzhou. As of the end of 2008, the company had 3,058 employees: 2,742 in manufacturing, 251 in general and administrative, 36 in research and development and 29 in sales and marketing.[24]

CANADIAN SOLAR'S MODEL

The company described itself as an "inverted flexible vertical integration business model." This meant that the company had higher capacity as it went further downstream in the manufacturing process of each component of a solar module. Graphically, this could be illustrated as:

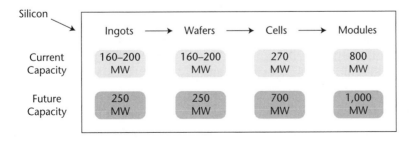

---

[24]Canadian Solar Annual Report 2008, 20-F, www.sec.gov, December 31, 2008, p. 74.

The rationale behind the "inverted vertical integration" model was to allow for flexibility in short-term demand shifts by purchasing ingots, wafers and cells from other manufacturers and to free the company from the capital investment required to have equal capacity of each component. The company believed that it would lead to a lower manufacturing cost base in the long term, as well as superior production yields, better inventory control and efficient cash management.

Canadian Solar also had been one of the first solar companies to initiate a recycling process for reclaimable silicon from discarded, broken or unused silicon wafers and ingots at two of its plants in Suzhou and Changshu. The process involved a substantial amount of labour, and analysts believed that Canadian Solar had a competitive advantage in recycling silicon. However, in the 2008 Annual Report, the company stated, "As a result of the oversupply of silicon materials that developed in the fourth quarter of 2008, we expect this aspect of our operation to be less significant in the foreseeable future."[25] The company also became a member of the Belgian organization PV CYCLE in mid-2009. PV CYCLE promoted a take-back and recycling of PV modules that had reached the end of their useful life.[26]

Products

Canadian Solar offered a portfolio of products ranging from 0.3W to 300W. It split its offerings into two main divisions: standard and specialty. The company used both its own branding and manufactured white label products for other OEMs. With a few exceptions, all products were standardized for the global market.

The company offered three types of products:

1. Standard: Standard modules were used for both ground mount and rooftop systems and were available in both mono and poly.
2. e-Modules: e-Modules were a recent product introduction which were aimed at providing a lower-cost product for smaller roof-top systems. e-Modules were lower cost because they used upgraded metallurgical-grade silicon (UMG-Si) instead of pure silicon.
3. BIPV (Building Integrated Photovoltaic): Finally, BIPV were intended to be used as a building material in a roof, skylight or façade.

Standard modules were all tested and certified by various international standards. Product performance warranties were normally 25 years, depending on the product. Prices were negotiated on the quantity ordered but were between $2 and $3 per watt. Margins ranged from 13 to 18 per cent for standard and e-Modules and were 15 to 20 per cent on BIPV products. Canadian Solar's strategy was to maintain comparable prices to its primary Chinese competitors.

Specialty products included items to be used in battery chargers, GPS tracking systems, street and traffic lights, garden lights, marine lights and other home systems. Prices varied greatly depending on the level of customization; margins were usually around 15 to 20 per cent for specialty items.

---

[25]Canadian Solar Annual Report 2008, 20-F, www.sec.gov, December 31, 2008, p. 30.

[26]"Canadian Solar becomes member of PV Cycle," July 21, 2009, http://phx.corporate-ir.net/phoenix.zhtml?c=196781&p=irol-news, accessed November 20, 2009.

Production Facilities

The company produced all of its products in its seven plants in China. The seven factories had been set up because of Chinese government incentives to establish operations in specific jurisdictions. For example, the Luoyang factory, located approximately eight hours by road from the central offices of Suzhou, was set up at the request of the government-owned silicon supplier in Luoyang.

In late 2008, Canadian Solar's then vice-president of corporate and production development, Robert Patterson, was asked if production facilities would be opened closer to areas of demand:

> Not yet. We got our hands full in terms of how fast we're growing and also our capital requirements going into our current plants. We'd probably have to stabilize our current supply stream and then we would address whether we'd want to do assembly plants in various locations. If you're based in China, you have an advantage on an assembly basis, mainly because of the labour content of a solar cell or solar module. So, it would be a future thing, not ruled out.[27]

Sales Offices

Canadian Solar had seven sales offices outside of China (domestic Chinese sales were done primarily from Suzhou and Shanghai). In mid-2009, the company opened an office in Kitchener, Ontario, and shifted its official headquarters there from Markham. The Kitchener office (eight people) was responsible for the development of Canadian sales with a focus on the Ontario market, given the recently introduced FIT program. The Ottawa office (four people) was the international sales office for projects in the Middle East and Latin America and initially also housed the company's investor relations manager. Opportunities in the Middle East and Latin America were developed through a combination of trade shows, bids on public tenders and CIDA-sponsored development projects.

The United States was primarily covered through the 10-person facility in San Ramon, California, which included business development managers and a warehouse. Additionally, there was a sales representative located in a satellite office in New York state.

The company's office in Munich, Germany, was responsible for the coordination of all sales efforts in Europe. The top five German customers accounted for just over half of the company's corporate sales. The customers were utility-scale developers and distributors of roof-top solar projects. With a total of 15 people, the office was responsible for managing the independent sales agent in Spain, as well as establishing new offices.

Canadian Solar served the Asian market through its sales forces at the principal Chinese office in Suzhou and offices in Seoul, South Korea (two people) and Tokyo, Japan (eight people). In Japan, due to the popularity of solar PV in residential applications, Canadian Solar was developing a complete systems package, which included the solar PV modules, racking systems, inverter and monitoring devices.

---

[27]Interview with Robert Patterson, VP corporate & production development, by Mark Osborne, Photovoltaics International, December 3, 2008, www.pv-tech.org/solar_leaders_video_clips/_a/canadian_solar_vp_robert_patterson_talks_umg_si_product_lines_150mw_plus

Marketing

Due to the small size of the PV industry, the company focused on building its brand through industry tradeshows and publications such as *Photon International* and *PV Technology*. In early 2009, the company had recently re-branded itself to emphasize its "Canadian" roots by changing its logo to read "Canadian Solar" instead of the previous "CSI" (standing for "Canadian Solar International"). Hanbing Zhang, the company's director of global marketing, explained:

> No one really understood what CSI meant—with Canadian Solar, we don't need to explain. As a country, Canada is well received around the world. People from all over have a connection to Canada; for example, Koreans send their kids to learn English in Canada and many Europeans have relatives in Canada. It is seen as a peaceful and environmentally aware country. By emphasizing the Canadian image, we can further differentiate from the other Chinese manufacturers.

Development Projects

In addition to its role as a producer, Canadian Solar was becoming more active in the development of both ground mount and rooftop commercial projects. Typically, Canadian Solar partnered with a solar developer, system integrator or utility to carry out the tasks involved in commercial solar development such as engineering, construction, financing, negotiation of the power purchase agreements (PPAs) and the operation of the solar project.

In its largest project to date, in 2009, Canadian Solar formed a strategic alliance with China-based Guodian Power Development to build and operate two 50MW PV power plants in China. Historically, most of Canadian Solar's development projects had been focused on providing power to rural areas in China.[28]

Financials

For the past three years, Canadian Solar posted losses. In 2008, the net loss was $9.4 million. The global economic crisis caused the company to have higher than normal interest expenses on short-term loan facilities, increases in the allowance for doubtful accounts and a major inventory write-down (caused by both a weakening in demand and the rapidly declining price of silicon).

In June 2009, Deutsche Bank analysts projected Canadian Solar's revenues to be $395 million with a loss of $18 million, and wrote:

> [Canadian Solar] is a smaller, upstream solar PV company, struggling with weak fundamentals in a highly competitive industry where capital is still a constraint for its solar PV customers amidst a credit contraction environment. Upside risks include: a rapid demand rebound, minimal average sales price declines, a weakening U.S. dollar and more favourable policy and incentive programs. Downside risks include: gauging end demand for company products amidst industry demand destruction, rapid average sales price declines/high input costs dislocating business

[28]Canadian Solar Prospectus, October 12, 2009, www.sec.gov, p. 5.

model assumptions, capital constraints hindering operational flexibility and managing currency dislocations.[29]

However, by August 2009, Deutsche Bank had raised its estimates to revenues of $574 million and net income of $49 million for 2009, stating:

> Canadian Solar posted 2Q09 results well ahead of expectations on strong shipments growth [in markets like the Czech Republic, Korea and Italy], further aided by favourable FX trends (i.e., $0.14 contribution to EPS) and prior inventory write-downs . . . we believe the company is gaining share in new markets.[30]

Deutsche Bank rated the stock a "hold" and Oppenheimer rated it an "outperform." As of September 25, 2009, Canadian Solar's stock price closed at $16.74 (the 52-week range was from $3.00 to $19.91).

CONSIDERATIONS GOING FORWARD

Some industry observers believed that the solar PV industry needed to regroup and get back to basics. Consultants from BCG wrote:

> In order to thrive in and not merely survive the harsh reality of today's market, PV suppliers need to take a critical look at their business model and operations. . . . To negotiate this far more challenging environment, PV suppliers will need to refocus their attention on the basics: relative cost position, go-to-market effectiveness and an understanding of key market segments and channels.[31]

Having been on a track of dynamic growth since inception, it was now Canadian Solar's opportunity to strategically think about any changes to its international strategy. Qu stated:

> In terms of the solar industry, the first step is to determine the market and follow the renewable policies closely. For the next two to three years, we've determined that we will be focusing on 10 countries: Canada, China, Germany, Spain, Italy, France, Czech Republic, South Korea, Japan and the United States.
>
> There is plenty of competition. First, the established players, such as Sharp and Sanyo, have powerful brands. From a technology standpoint, a company like FirstSolar clearly has a different product with their thin-film technology, and the question is, "Which technology wins?" The other U.S. competitor is SunPower, which has high efficiency and a high price premium. Out of the Chinese producers, Suntech is slightly different than others since they combine Australian engineering with Chinese production, much like we combine Canadian engineering with Chinese production. The other potential threat is the possibility that some upstream silicon makers will adapt their business models to start producing

---

[29]"Canadian Solar: Notes from the Deutsche Bank alternative energy conference," *Deutsche Bank*, June 10, 2009, p. 3.

[30]"Canadian Solar: New market penetration drives solid shipments," *Deutsche Bank*, August 6, 2009, p. 1.

[31]"Back to the Basics: How photovoltaic suppliers can win in today's solar market," *The Boston Consulting Group*, p. 1.

modules downstream. After the financial crisis, I think the industry realizes that silicon is not precious and there could be an increasing trend for silicon producers to move downstream to capture more value.

When I look back at my original business plan, we've greatly exceeded our initial revenue projections. The business has changed substantially from its initial focus—this illustrates that one of the key skills in this industry, and any start-up for that matter, is the ability to see changes in the marketplace and adapt the business accordingly.

EXHIBIT 1   Canadian Solar Financials

USD million, Years ended Dec. 31	2006	2007	2008
Net revenues	**68.2**	**302.8**	**705.0**
Cost of revenues	55.9	279.0	634.0
Gross profit	**12.3**	**23.8**	**71.0**
Operating expenses:	0.0	0.0	0.0
Selling expenses	2.9	7.5	10.6
General and administrative expenses	7.9	17.2	34.5
Research and development expenses	0.4	1.0	1.8
Total operating expenses	11.2	25.7	46.9
Income (loss) from operations	**1.1**	**–2.0**	**24.1**
Other income (expenses):			
Interest expense	–2.2	–2.4	–11.3
Interest income	0.4	0.6	3.5
Loss on change in fair value of derivatives	0.0	0.0	0.0
related to convertible notes	–8.2	0.0	0.0
Gain on foreign currency derivative assets	0.0	0.0	14.5
Debt conversion inducement expense	0.0	0.0	–10.2
Foreign exchange gain (loss)	–0.5	2.7	–20.1
Other–net	0.4	0.7	0.0
Income (loss) before income taxes	–9.0	–0.4	0.5
Income tax benefit (expense)	–0.4	0.2	–9.9
Net loss	–9.4	–0.2	–9.4
Loss per share–basic and diluted	–0.5	0.0	–0.3
Shares used in computation–basic and diluted	19.0	27.3	31.6
Total current assets		219.9	339.0
Total assets		**284.5**	**570.7**
Total current liabilities		59.2	172.7
Total liabilities		**158.2**	**238.6**
Total stockholders' equity		126.3	332.2
Total liabilities and stockholders' equity		**284.5**	**570.7**

Source: Canadian Solar Annual Report, 20-F, www.sec.gov, December 31, 2008, p. 54.

EXHIBIT 2   Highlights from World Markets

Country	Comments
Germany	Leading market for solar PV with strong financing available
	Over 40,000 people were employed in the PV sector
	The Renewable Energy Law (Erneuerbare-Energien-Gesetz or EEG) promised rates of $0.46 to $0.60 per kWh for solar PV with digression in 2010 and 2011
	The country had some of the world's largest solar parks (e.g., the 40MW Waldpolenz Solar Park)
	Over 100,000 roof-top solar PV applications had been installed
Spain	Historical strength had been on utility-scale solar parks
	The Spanish market would undergo a major decrease in 2009 and 2010 due to the government's cap of 500MW
	Potential growth beyond 2013 was still seen to be strong due to experience with renewables and long-term targets
Japan	Historical strength had been with solar PV on residential homes due to the "Residential PV System Program," which ended supplying subsidies in 2006
	In December 2008, the government was renewing its focus on solar with the aim to have solar power installed on 70 per cent of new homes. Furthermore, it wanted 14GW of installed PV power by 2020
United States	The Investment Tax Credit (ITC), state programs and the potential of a federal-level FIT were expected to boost solar PV in 2010 and beyond
	The challenge was seen to be a lack of financing
	The United States had some of the world's largest solar PV parks (e.g., Nellis Solar Power Plant, NV, 15MW)
	California was the leading state for solar roof installations due to programs such as the "Million Solar Roofs" vision and the "California Solar Initiative"
Italy	The country had a competitive FIT program and a net-metering scheme (allowing PV system owners to get credits for their produced electricity)
	Italy had no cap for PV installations
South Korea	The country's FIT program was seen as promising; however, the devaluation of the Korean currency and the placement of a cap of 500MW on the FIT in October 2008 were expected to dampen the number of installations
	Observers believed that strong political support for solar PV still existed and expected the market to grow in 2010
France	The government had a favourable FIT program for BIPV; however, the growth had been stalled by long administrative procedures to connect the systems to the grid
	France was expected to adopt a FIT program for non-BIPV applications for commercial roofs, which would be the source of its growth over the next few years
Czech Republic	The Czech government introduced a FIT program in 2008 and was one of the premiere Eastern European growth countries for solar PV
Portugal	Portugal had several large-scale PV and concentrating solar power plants but had not yet introduced a FIT program or similar incentive scheme
Greece	Greece was seen to have one of the most favourable FIT programs in Europe
	The country had a pipeline of 3.5GW of PV projects
	Bureaucracy and lengthy administrative procedures were seen to be barriers for installations in 2008
Israel	Solar-thermal (solar water heaters) were very popular, being present in 90 per cent of Israeli homes
	Israel was extensively used for research and development due to the country's high level of solar irradiance
	A FIT scheme was passed in 2008 and the market was expected to grow
India	India was expected to develop slowly but held great potential due to efforts for both on- and off-grid projects (off-grid projects were a specialty area for project developers—e.g., Shell Solar had had a division dedicated to off-grid solar PV development in India)
China	The new incentive program was expected to boost solar PV applications both for residential, commercial and utility-scale applications
Canada	Ontario's solar PV applications were expected to grow under the proposed FIT program
	The FIT program required that, for projects up to 10kW, the minimum domestic content was 40 per cent and for projects greater than 10kW, the domestic content was 50 per cent for projects with a commercial operation date prior to January 1, 2011. For projects thereafter, domestic content needed to be 60 per cent

Source: Compiled by case writer.

EXHIBIT 3   EPIA Predictions by Market

Country	Type	2006	2007	2008	2009E	2010E	2011E	2012E	2013E
Belgium	EPIA Moderate	2	18	48	100	70	80	90	100
	EPIA Policy-Driven				175	125	130	140	160
Czech Republic	EPIA Moderate	0	3	51	80	90	110	140	170
	EPIA Policy-Driven				100	160	200	220	240
France	EPIA Moderate	8	11	46	250	340	600	900	1,000
	EPIA Policy-Driven				300	500	850	1,200	1,400
Germany	EPIA Moderate	850	1,100	1,500	2,000	2,000	2,300	2,600	3,000
	EPIA Policy-Driven				2,500	2,800	3,200	3,600	4,000
Greece	EPIA Moderate	1	2	11	35	100	100	100	100
	EPIA Policy-Driven				52	200	450	700	900
Italy	EPIA Moderate	13	42	258	400	600	750	950	1,250
	EPIA Policy-Driven				500	800	1,100	1,400	1,600
Portgual	EPIA Moderate	0	14	50	40	50	100	160	230
	EPIA Policy-Driven				50	80	180	350	500
Spain	EPIA Moderate	88	560	2,511	375	500	500	550	800
	EPIA Policy-Driven				375	500	600	650	1,500
Rest of Europe	EPIA Moderate	12	17	28	120	140	200	300	450
	EPIA Policy-Driven				250	325	400	525	625
Japan	EPIA Moderate	287	210	230	400	500	700	1,000	1,100
	EPIA Policy-Driven				500	1,000	1,200	1,500	1,700
USA	EPIA Moderate	145	207	342	340	1,000	1,200	1,500	2,000
	EPIA Policy-Driven				1,200	3,000	3,400	3,900	4,500
China	EPIA Moderate	12	20	45	80	100	300	600	1,000
	EPIA Policy-Driven				100	150	600	1,200	2,000
India	EPIA Moderate	12	20	40	50	60	80	120	300
	EPIA Policy-Driven				100	200	250	300	600
South Korea	EPIA Moderate	20	43	274	100	150	220	300	400
	EPIA Policy-Driven				200	350	450	700	1,000
Rest of the world	EPIA Moderate	153	125	126	250	300	300	300	350
	EPIA Policy-Driven				400	600	800	1,000	1,600
TOTAL	**EPIA Moderate**	**1,603**	**2,392**	**5,559**	**4,620**	**6,000**	**7,540**	**9,610**	**12,250**
	EPIA Policy-Driven				**6,802**	**10,790**	**13,810**	**17,385**	**22,325**
CUMULATIVE	**EPIA Moderate**	**6,770**	**9,162**	**14,730**	**19,350**	**25,350**	**32,890**	**42,500**	**54,750**
	EPIA Policy-Driven				**21,532**	**32,322**	**46,132**	**63,517**	**85,842**

Source: European Photovoltaic Industry Association (EPIA), "Global market outlook for photovoltaics until 2013," March 2009, p. 6.

EXHIBIT 4   Ontario's Feed-in Tariff (FIT) Program

Renewable fuel	Size tranches	Contract price cent/kWh
Biomass	≤ 10MW	13.8
	> 10MW	13.0
Biogas		
On-farm	≤ 100kW	19.5
On-farm	> 100kW ≤ 250kW	18.5
Biogas	≤ 500kW	16.0
Biogas	> 500kW ≤ 10MW	14.7
Biogas	> 10MW	10.4
Waterpower	≤ 10MW	13.1
	> 10MW ≤ 50MW	12.2
Landfill gas	≤ 10MW	11.1
	> 10MW	10.3
Solar PV		
Any type	≤ 10kW	80.2
Rooftop	> 10kW ≤ 250kW	71.3
Rooftop	> 250kW ≤ 500kW	63.5
Rooftop	> 500kW	53.9
Ground mounted	≤ 10MW	44.3
Wind		
Onshore	Any size	13.5
Offshore	Any size	19.0

Domestic Content Requirements: The minimum requirements of Ontario-based content: 40% for MicroFIT (projects less than 10kW) and 50% for FIT (projects over 10kW) for projects reaching commercial operation by the end of 2010. For projects with commercial operation after January 1, 2011, domestic content increases to 60%.

	Designated activity	Qualifying percentage
1.	Silicon that has been used as input to solar photovoltaic cells manufactured in an Ontario refinery.	10%
2.	Silicon ingots and wafers, where silicon ingots have been cast in Ontario and wafers have been cut from the casting by a saw in Ontario.	12%
3.	The crystalline silicon solar photovoltaic cells, where their active photovoltaic layer(s) have been formed in Ontario.	10%
4.	Solar photovoltaic modules (i.e., panels), where the electrical connections between the solar cells have been made in Ontario, and the solar photovoltaic module materials have been encapsulated in Ontario.	13%
5.	Inverter (to convert the electricity from direct current [DC] to alternating current [AC]), where the assembly, final wiring and testing have been done in Ontario.	9%
6.	Mounting systems, where the structural components of the fixed or moving mounting systems have been entirely machined or formed or cast in Ontario. The metal for the structural components may not have been pre-machined outside Ontario other than peeling/roughing of the part for quality control purposes when it left the smelter or forge. The machining and assembly of the mounting system must entirely take place in Ontario (i.e., bending, welding, piercing and bolting).	9%
7.	Wiring and electrical hardware that is not part of other designated activities (i.e., items 1, 2, 3 and 5 of this table), sourced from an Ontario supplier.	10%
8.	All on- and off-site labour and services. For greater certainty, this designated activity shall apply in respect of all contract facilities.	27%
	Total	**100%**

Source: Ontario Power Authority, http://fit.powerauthority.on.ca, accessed October 30, 2009.

EXHIBIT 5   Market Shares and Gross Profits by PV Module Producers

2008 Rank	PV Supplier	HQ	2008 % of total MV shipments	2008 Gross profit (%)
1	Suntech	China	7.2	23.7
2	Sharp	Japan	7.2	16.0
3	First Solar	U.S.	6.9	54.4
4	Yingli Green Energy	China	4.4	21.9
5	Kyocera	Japan	4.2	25.9
6	Sunpower	U.S.	3.4	25.3
7	Trina Solar	China	3.3	19.7
8	Sanyo	Japan	2.8	15.8
9	Canadian Solar	Canada/China	2.6	10.7
10	Solar World	Germany	2.6	N/A
	Top 10 Total		**44.7**	
	Others		**55.3**	
	Total Module Shipments in GWs		**6.3**	

N/A = not available

Source: IMS Research and company files.

MARKET SHARES PV CELL PRODUCERS

2008 Rank	2007 Rank	PV Supplier	HQ	2007 % of Total MW	2008 % of Total MW	08/07 % Change	2007 % of Total $	2008 % of Total $	08/07 % Change
1	1	Q-Cells	Germany	10.9	9.4	48	14.5	12.2	43
2	4	First Solar	U.S.	5.8	8.3	144	6.2	9.0	147
3	2	Suntech	China	10.2	8.2	37	9.0	7.2	36
4	3	Sharp	Japan	9.0	8.0	51	8.0	7.3	56
5	6	Motech	Taiwan	4.9	4.8	67	4.1	4.0	70
6	5	Kyocera	Japan	5.7	4.6	37	5.0	4.0	38
7	10	JA Solar	China	3.7	4.6	108	4.6	5.8	117
8	9	Yingli Green Energy	China	4.0	4.5	93	3.3	3.8	95
9	12	Gintech Energy	Taiwan	3.1	4.4	144	2.6	3.6	141
10	8	Solar World	Germany	4.7	4.0	44	4.9	3.8	32
		Top 10 Total		**62.0**	**60.8**	**67.0**	**62.0**	**60.6**	**67.0**
		Others		**38.0**	**39.2**	**75**	**38.0**	**39.4**	**77**
		Cell & Panel PV Total		**3.57GW**	**6.0GW**	**70**	**$8.1b**	**$13.85b**	**71**

Source: "Japanese solar cell manufacturers losing market share, says IC Insights," July 22, 2009, www.pv-tech.org/news/_a/japanese_solar_cell_manufacturers_losing_market_share_says_ic_insights

Resuming Internationalization at Starbucks[1]

By 2009, Starbucks had achieved a global reach of almost 17,000 stores in 56 countries. The company had enjoyed tremendous growth over the previous two decades. Between 2007 and 2009, however, Starbucks' relentless march had been slowed by three forces: increasingly intense competition, rising coffee bean prices and a global economic recession. To remain profitable, the company started to scale back its overseas operations. In 2010, as the world gradually emerged from the economic downturn and as prospects for growth improved, Starbucks was faced with a critical strategic decision: Should the company resume its international expansion and once again intensify its commitments in overseas markets? If so, what approach should the company take? Had the pace of Starbucks' internationalization (i.e., the rate of opening new stores abroad), the rhythm of its internationalization (i.e., the regularity by which stores were opened abroad) and the geographical scope of its internationalization (i.e., the number of new countries entered) affected the company's performance in previous years?[2] What could Starbucks learn from its prior internationalization within the coffee industry to guide its future international strategy?

BACKGROUND

In 1971, the first Starbucks store was opened in Seattle to sell coffee beans and coffee-making equipment. The current chief executive officer (CEO), Howard Schultz, joined

Rob Alkema, Mario Koster and Christopher Williams wrote this case solely to provide material for class discussion. The authors do not intend to illustrate either effective or ineffective handling of a managerial situation. The authors may have disguised certain names and other identifying information to protect confidentiality.

Richard Ivey School of Business
The University of Western Ontario

---

[1]This case has been written on the basis of published sources only. Consequently, the interpretation and perspectives presented in this case are not necessarily those of Starbucks or any of its employees.

[2]Freek Vermeulen and Harry Barkema, "Pace, rhythm, and scope: Process dependence in building a profitable multinational corporation," *Strategic Management Journal*, 2002, vol. 23, pp. 637–653.

the company in 1982. After a vacation in Italy, he became enthusiastic about bringing the Italian coffee-drinking culture to the United States. He was especially excited about opportunities for selling coffee and espresso products—Italian style—but was not able to convince Starbucks' owners at the time. Schultz ended up opening his own coffee bar, Il Giornale. In 1987, Schulz bought the Starbucks store, renamed the Il Giornale stores to Starbucks and started to open new stores in the United States and Canada. In 1992, the company went public. In 1996, with the home market becoming increasingly saturated, Starbucks opened its first outlets outside North America, in the Far East. Ever since, the company had pursued a relentless international expansion. By 2009, Starbucks had grown to nearly 17,000 stores in 56 countries worldwide (see Exhibit 1). Starbucks' stock had performed well over this period (see Exhibit 2). Schultz's initial reading of the global market for coffee appeared to have been correct: Up to 2007 at least, global markets for specialty coffee continued to grow in size, particularly in high- and middle-income countries (see Exhibits 3 and 4).

THE COFFEE INDUSTRY

The energizing effect of the coffee bean was thought to have been discovered in Yemen[3] and Ethiopia[4] in the 13th century. By the 16th century, this discovery had reached other parts of the Middle East, Persia, Turkey and Northern Africa and eventually spread to Europe, Indonesia and the Americas.[5] In the 17th century, coffee houses, which were already popular in Europe, began to open in the United States.[6] At this time, coffee was sold in the form of whole beans out of a barrel, intended to be ground by the consumer at home. By the late 1990s, the coffee industry accounted for $80 billion in sales.[7] The largest markets were the European Union (35 per cent), the United States (25 per cent) and Japan (9 per cent).[8] By 2010, 501 billion cups of coffee[9] were being consumed yearly, and retail sales had grown by 6.9 per cent annually to reach $48.2 billion.[10] Worldwide consumption was expected to be 130.03 million bags (at 60 kg per bag) according to a 2010/11 forecast by Fortis Bank.[11] According to the International Coffee Organization (ICO), the historical annual growth rate of coffee consumption was approximately 2.5 per cent. This rate fell to 1 per cent in 2009/10, during the economic

---

[3]Bennett Alan Weinberg and Bonnie K. Bealer, *The world of caffeine: The science and culture of the world's most popular drug*, Routledge, New York, 2001.

[4]John K. Francis, "Coffea arabica L. RUBIACEAE," factsheet of the U.S. Department of Agriculture, Forest Service. Available at http://www.fs.fed.us/global/iitf/pdf/shrubs/Coffea%20arabica.pdf, accessed July 29, 2010.

[5]Bennett Alan Weinberg and Bonnie K. Bealer, *The world of caffeine: The science and culture of the world's most popular drug*, Routledge, New York, 2001.

[6]Food Info, "History of coffee." Available at http://www.food-info.net/uk/products/coffee/hist.htm, accessed July 29, 2010.

[7]Mark Pendergrast, *Uncommon grounds: The history of coffee and how it transformed our world*, Basic Books, New York, 1999, p. 418.

[8]"Product profile: Coffee," Third United Nations Conference on the Least Developed Countries, May 16, 2001, pp. 4–6.

[9]Mike Chronos, "Which countries consume the most coffee?" Available at http://ezinearticles.com/?Which-Countries-Consume-the-Most-Coffee?&id=3876423, accessed July 29, 2010.

[10]Packaged Facts, *Coffee and ready-to-drink coffee in the U.S.: The market and opportunities in retail and foodservice*, 6th edition, Packaged Facts, Rockville, MD, 2010.

[11]Reuters, "Fortis NL trims global coffee surplus forecast," May 24, 2010.

recession. In the 1970s, when the economy was struggling, U.S. consumption of coffee dropped from 33.4 to 26.7 gallons per capita.[12] Some commentators argued this decrease also could have been a consequence of both media reports stressing the downsides of caffeine and the high price of coffee at that time (well above $1 per pound). Exhibit 3 illustrates coffee consumption in kilograms per capita per year, and Exhibit 4 shows coffee consumption in metric tons per year.

DEMAND FOR SPECIALTY COFFEE

Since the early 1990s, the popularity of specialty coffee had been on the rise. Between 1995 and 2008, the percentage of U.S. adults drinking specialty coffee on a daily basis had risen from around 3 per cent to around 17 per cent.[13] Between 2001 and 2007, the sales of specialty coffee in the United States had risen from $8 billion to $13 billion.[14] Coffee imported by specialty roasters increased from 1 million 60-kg bags in 1985 to more than 2.7 million bags in 1999.[15] In this same period, the share of specialty coffee retail sales (compared with total coffee retail sales) in the United States grew from 5 per cent to 37 per cent.[16] From the early 2000s, coffee consumers had shown an increasing preference for premium coffee over regular coffee and had been willing to pay a higher price for premium coffee. The beans used for specialty coffee (Arabica instead of Robusta) had higher quality, were richer in flavour and contained half as much caffeine as commercially mass-produced coffee. From 1981 to 2006, the market share of specialty coffee increased from 1 per cent to 20 per cent.[17] In the United States, specialty coffee accounted for $13.65 billion in sales in 2009, approximately one-third of the $40 billion U.S. coffee industry.[18] Coffee shops often served specialty coffee and had enjoyed a fivefold increase of sales in this product line between 2000 and 2010.[19]

INCREASING COMPETITION, RISING SUPPLIER PRICES AND FAIR TRADE

As of 2006, Starbucks faced severe competition in both its home and overseas markets. Between 2000 and 2005, the number of coffee shops in the United States increased by 70 per cent, reaching a total of 21,400: approximately one shop for every 14,000

---

[12]United States Department of Agriculture, "U.S. agriculture—Linking consumers and producers." Available at http://www.usda.gov/news/pubs/fbook98/ch1a.htm, accessed July 29, 2010.

[13]AccuVal Associates, Inc., "Coffee beans: Slowly cooling supply heating up pricing." Available at http://www.accuval.net/insights/industryinsights/detail.php?ID=101, accessed July 29, 2010.

[14]Ibid.

[15]Specialty Coffee Association of America (SCAA), "1999 coffee market summary," SCAA, Long Beach, CA, November 1999, p. 2.

[16]Ibid.

[17]Ted Lingle, "The state of the specialty coffee industry," *Tea and Coffee Trade Journal*, July 2007, accessed August 8, 2008. Available at http://www.allbusiness.com/manufacturing/food-manufacturing-food-coffee-tea/4510403-1.html, accessed July 29, 2010.

[18]Dan Bolton, "Coffee industry shifts under tough economy," *Specialty Coffee Retailer*, August 2009. Avaliable at http://www.specialty-coffee.com/ME2/Audiences/dirmod.asp?sid=&nm=&type=MultiPublishing&mod=PublishingTitles&mid=8F3A7027421841978F18BE895F87F791&AudID=464620AE3F20454894C8CB7CEF72A481&tier=4&id=71C474258D2F46AEAD2BA59307E8002B, accessed July 29, 2010.

[19]Specialty Coffee Association of America, *The Mintel coffee report*, 2006.

Americans.[20] The number of independently operated coffee shops fell from 61 per cent in 1999 to 52 per cent in 2001.[21] Starbucks acknowledged that its primary competitors for coffee beverage sales were quick-service restaurants and specialty coffee shops. Starbucks had numerous competitors in all markets in which the company operated. On the one hand, Starbucks faced competition from domestic coffeehouses such as Caribou Coffee (in the eastern and mid-west United States) and Diedrich Coffee (in California and the western United States). The company also faced increasing worldwide threats from international retailers such as McDonald's. Nowhere was the severe competition more conspicuous than with McDonald's entry into the specialty coffee sector: McDonald's offered premium coffee, only cheaper. McDonald's already had 14,000 stores in the United States and, compared with Starbucks, catered to a wider range of demographic segments. It also enjoyed increased traffic from its variety of well-established breakfast options. McDonald's coffee sales increased 15 per cent in 2006. Starbucks did not initially consider McDonald's to be a competitor, believing that its own approach to marketing coffee was distinct. Many Starbucks' customers, however, were also customers of McDonald's and other fast-food chains.

In January 2008, McDonald's made an aggressive foray in the battle for high-end coffee drinkers when it announced it would install coffee bars in all 14,000 of its U.S. locations. Aggressive marketing campaigns also emphasized the large cost differential. That said, Starbucks and McDonald's *did* collaborate on the distribution of one of Starbucks' brands: McDonald's brewed Seattle's Best brand coffee, a brand owned by Starbucks.

Starbucks became concerned by these competitor moves, and Schultz was reported as having said that the company itself was to blame: Its focus had been more on expansion and not on improving customer service.[22] To get the company back on track, Starbucks said it would slow the pace of U.S. store growth and renew its focus on its store-level unit economics.[23] As a counter-manoeuvre against McDonald's, Starbucks launched a cheaper alternative to the market: Starbucks Via, an instant coffee. With the launch of this instant-brew coffee, Starbucks entered a new growth market, the $21 billion global instant coffee category.[24] Starbucks had earlier launched a drive-through service, which had been an important element of McDonald's service. As a result of these recent initiatives, Starbucks' overall market share remained resilient (see Exhibit 5).

Another threat to Starbucks was the rise in purchases of specialty coffee for use at home. During the 1990s, Starbucks foresaw this trend and stepped into the specialty coffee grocery channel. However, also stepping into this channel were the big conventional supermarket coffee producers: Procter & Gamble, Nestlé, Kraft Foods and Sara Lee. Starbucks introduced bottled frappuccino and, later, in 1996, introduced espresso drinks for the grocery channel in partnership with Pepsi-Cola. In 1997, Starbucks introduced a home espresso machine and, in 1998, signed a licensing agreement

---

[20]Dan Bolton, "Coffee industry shifts under tough economy," *Specialty Coffee Retailer*, August 2009. Available at http://www.specialty-coffee.com/ME2/Audiences/dirmod.asp?sid=&nm=&type=MultiPublishing&mod=PublishingTitles&mid=8F3A7027421841978F18BE895F87F791&AudID=464620AE3F20454894C8CB7CEF72A481&tier=4&id=71C474258D2F46AEAD2BA59307E8002B, accessed July 29, 2010.

[21]Specialty Coffee Association of America Report 1999.

[22]Isabel Goncalves, "Starbucks' Schultz back as McDonald's increases competition," *International Business Times*, January 7, 2008. Available at http://www.ibtimes.com/articles/20080107/starbucks-schultz-mcdonalds.htm, accessed July 29, 2010.

[23]Ibid.

[24]Lisa Baertlein, "Starbucks debuts Via instant coffee in U.S., Canada," *Reuters*, September 28, 2009.

with Kraft Foods to market and distribute the Starbucks' specialty coffee beans to more than 25,000 American grocers. In 2003, Starbucks acquired the Seattle Coffee Company and, with it, two brands of specialty coffee in the grocery sector. The impact on domestic sales is shown in Exhibit 6. In 2008, the total American specialty coffee grocery channel accounted for $915 million, 27.7 per cent of total grocery coffee sales. This market share grew by an annual growth rate of 12 per cent, which was high compared with the annual growth rate of 3 per cent for traditional coffees.[25]

In addition to the increased competition in the specialty coffee space, Starbucks also faced pressures from the coffee bean supply chain. The average wholesale price for coffee had increased twofold between 2001 and 2010, from US$0.41 per pound at its lowest point in September 2001 to US$1.42 per pound in June 2010 (see Exhibit 7). This price increase was the result of a constant increase in coffee consumption (see Exhibit 4) combined with a shortfall in coffee available for export. Production in the largest coffee-producing country (Brazil) dropped dramatically in 2004, following a similar dramatic drop for the second-largest coffee producer (Vietnam) in 2003. Brazil's production fell from 48.5 million bags to 28.5 million bags, and Vietnam's production fell from 14.77 million bags to 11.25 million bags.[26] The production levels of the largest coffee-producing countries historically had a huge effect on coffee prices. Back in 1975, Brazil (the largest producer at that time) had been struck by a severe frost. The world price doubled overnight and soared to eight times its pre-frost level.[27]

Starbucks also faced pressure to embrace fair trade coffee. The popularity of fair trade coffee had affected the whole coffee industry. Under a fair trade agreement, producers were guaranteed a fair price consisting of a floor price of $1.26 per pound and an additional $1.41 per pound for certified organic coffee.[28] From 2002 to 2004, the United States Agency for International Development (USAID) invested more than $57 million in coffee projects in more than 18 countries in Latin America, East Africa and Asia in an effort to create sustainable supplies of coffee.[29] In the mid-1990s, the coffee industry attracted criticism on environmental and economic grounds, which placed the supply of the Arabica bean at risk.[30] The solution to these issues lay in the use of differently cultivated coffee beans: certified organic coffee beans that were environmentally friendly, so-called shade-grown coffee. These coffee beans had been shown to have a positive influence on wildlife and bird habitat, and they offered a higher compensation to third-world coffee farmers.

[25]Dan Bolton, "Ten 2010 trends: 10. Grocery growth," *Specialty Coffee Retailer*, August 2009. Available at http://www.specialty-coffee.com/ME2/Audiences/dirmod.asp?sid=&nm=&type=MultiPublishing&mod=PublishingTitles&mid=8F3A7027421841978F18BE895F87F791&tier=4&id=0F3C8471126447439A66C0FF07866405&AudID=464620AE3F20454894C8CB7CEF72A481, accessed July 29, 2010.

[26]Ibid.

[27]John Madely, "Coffee price rise is just a hill of beans," *The Observer*, April 4, 2004. Available at http://www.guardian.co.uk/business/2004/apr/04/theobserver.observerbusiness11, accessed July 29, 2010.

[28]Global Exchange, "Frequently asked questions about fair trade coffee," 2009. Available at http://www.globalexchange.org/campaigns/fairtrade/coffee/faq.html, accessed July 29, 2010.

[29]United States Agency for International Development (USAID), "USAID supports coffee growers around the globe," USAID, Washington, September 15, 2004. Available at http://www.usaid.gov/press/factsheets/2004/fs040915.html, accessed July 29, 2010.

[30]Daniele Giovannucci, *Sustainable coffee survey of the North American specialty coffee industry*, Specialty Coffee Association of America (SCAA) and North American Commission for Environmental Cooperation, 2001, p. 7.

One problem, however, was that these differently cultivated beans often did not meet the same quality level as other beans. Starbucks hesitated in switching to different coffee beans.[31] In early 2000, Starbucks had been publicly blamed for its conventional coffee cultivation, which reportedly had involved child labour.[32] In that same year, Starbucks signed a licensing agreement to sell fair trade, organic and shade-grown coffee in the United States and Canada. This agreement was the start of a new direction in Starbucks' strategy. In 2001, Starbucks committed to purchase one million pounds of fair trade–certified coffee and donated money to support the well-being of coffee farmers. In 2002, the first corporate social responsibility program report was published, and a licensing agreement was signed to sell fair trade coffee in all Starbucks' operating countries. In 2005, Starbucks increased its fair trade coffee purchasing to 10 million pounds and thus became North America's largest buyer of fair trade coffee. Fair trade coffee sales in the United States grew by 32 per cent in 2008.[33]

STARBUCKS' GROWTH, INTERNATIONALIZATION AND PERFORMANCE

Between 1993 and 2009, Starbucks experienced substantial growth. In 2007, Starbucks had a presence in 56 countries through approximately 17,000 stores. Revenues grew from $160 million in 1993 to $10 billion in 2009. Starbucks originally started within the U.S. market and expanded abroad when it perceived the domestic market to be saturated. The first move Starbucks made outside of the United States was to expand into Canada in the early 1990s. From 1996, the company started to enter more distant countries in the Far East, such as Japan, Singapore, Philippines, Taiwan and Thailand. Over the period from 1996 to 2009, the company entered 56 countries (see Exhibit 1).

When entering a foreign market, Starbucks' strategy was to retain its core service and product offering as much as possible, while adapting to local demands in the host country, where appropriate. Examples of local adaptations included serving tea in Japan and China and omitting the siren from the logo in Muslim countries. Depending on knowledge gained about the host market and, in particular, the perceived level of risk, Starbucks adopted various modes of entry, using local partners and licensed joint ventures in certain countries and company-operated, wholly owned subsidiaries in other countries. The company often ended up buying out the local partner where joint ventures were successful and the local market had potential.

Starbucks' revenues grew, on average, 30 per cent per year between 1993 and 2009, in line with the company's growth in the number of stores (see Exhibit 8). Exhibit 9 shows the relationship between relative growth of numbers of stores and revenues. Although the company as a whole expanded, the speed of expansion diminished over the years. In the early 1990s, the growth in stores (and revenues) was approximately 70 per cent. In 1996 and 1997, the year-on-year growth increased in foreign stores, but

---

[31]Alison Stanley, "Starbucks coffee company," business case, Trustees of Dartmouth College, Tuck School of Business, Hanover, NH, 2002, p. 15.

[32]Global Exchange, "Frequently asked questions about fair trade coffee," 2009. Available at http://www.globalexchange.org/campaigns/fairtrade/coffee/faq.html, accessed July 29, 2010.

[33]K. Jesse Singerman and Tony Olson, "Sustained demand for fair trade products in economic downturn," *TransFair USA*, November 2009. Available at http://www.transfairusa.org/content/about/news/n_0910.php, accessed July 29, 2010.

declined in domestic stores. After a period of relatively high overall growth (1993 to 2002), the growth of the company slowed to approximately 20 per cent per year (from 2003 to 2008). Finally, growth of stores dropped even further in 2009 (see Exhibit 9). This decline coincided with the global recession, intensifying competition (particularly in the home market) and supply chain pressures.

Measuring performance through return on assets (ROA) gives insight into long-term profitability.[34] Exhibit 10 shows the relationship between Starbucks' ROA and its relative growth in the number of stores and countries entered between 1993 and 2009. Between 1996 and 2000, Starbucks had a period of high international growth, which was accompanied by moderate performance. During this period, the rate of growth of foreign stores consistently exceeded the rate of growth of domestic stores. ROA ranged between 7 per cent and 10 per cent. From 2003 and 2008 was a more stable period for new stores and countries entered, and this was accompanied by a higher ROA. In this phase, ROA reached 15 per cent, but the rate of growth of foreign stores fell to that of domestic stores. Between 2008 and 2009, the performance of the company dropped markedly compared with previous years: ROA fell back to approximately 7 to 8 per cent, and the number of new countries entered approached zero.

PACE OF STARBUCKS' INTERNATIONALIZATION

Pace of internationalization was measured by the relative growth in the number of foreign stores per year. Exhibit 11 shows the relationship between the pace of Starbucks' internationalization and its performance over the 17 years from 1993 to 2009, inclusive. The X-axis represents performance (ascending) and the Y-axis represents the pace of internationalization. Domestic and foreign growth rates are shown as separate lines. The downward slope indicates a negative association between pace and performance. The slopes for domestic and foreign expansion bear resemblance although the effect for foreign expansion is more pronounced than domestic expansion. The best performing years were the years characterized by a slower pace of internationalization (i.e., 2004, 2005, 2006 and 2007).

Four years (i.e., 1993, 1997, 1998 and 2001) stand out from this trend. In 1993, the pace of Starbucks' internationalization was moderate, but ROA was at its second lowest level in the 17-year period. One explanation for this low ROA could be that year's 115 per cent increase in firm assets, partly as a result of the opening of a second roasting plant. Conversely, the pace of internationalization was high in 1997 and 1998 but ROA was only moderate. In this period, Starbucks acquired Seattle Coffee Company in the United Kingdom, which included 65 stores already generating revenue. The acquisition enabled Starbucks to expand at a faster pace in the United Kingdom, without loss of performance. In 2001, Starbucks' high pace of internationalization was accompanied by an above-average ROA of 10.85 per cent. The reason for these results may lie in Starbucks' expansion strategy, announced in the previous year's annual report:

> Starbucks strategy for expanding its retail business is to increase its market share in existing markets and to open stores in new markets where the opportunity exists to become the leading specialty coffee retailer.[35]

---

[34]Michael A. Hitt et al., "International diversification: Effects on innovation and firm performance in product-diversified firms," *Academy of Management Journal*, vol. 40, no. 4, pp. 767–798.

[35]Starbucks Annual Report, 2000.

In 2001, Starbucks opened 252 additional stores in the United Kingdom. These U.K. stores accounted for approximately 75 per cent of the total expansion for that year (a total of 337 new stores were opened in 2001). In addition, Starbucks entered Thailand with the opening of 25 stores and Australia with the opening of 18 stores. These 3 countries accounted for approximately 90 per cent of Starbucks' international expansion in that year.

RHYTHM OF STARBUCKS' INTERNATIONALIZATION

Rhythm refers to the regularity by which a company such as Starbucks internationalizes. It is an indicator of the variation in international expansion over time. Exhibit 12 shows the relationship between Starbucks' rhythm of internationalization and performance in four-year blocks between 1994 and 2009. The rhythm of Starbucks' internationalization is measured through the kurtosis of the number of foreign stores over each four-year time period.[36] A higher kurtosis implies a more irregular rhythm, and a lower kurtosis implies a more regular rhythm. The first two blocks (i.e., 1994–1997 and 1998–2001) were characterized by high volatility in Starbucks' internationalization. These two blocks both represented high-growth periods for the company, particularly in terms of new countries entered (see Exhibit 11). Correspondingly, performance was lower in these periods. Performance was highest in the second two blocks (i.e., 2002–2005 and 2006–2009). The highest four-year ROA appears in the period 2002–2005. In the two periods 2002–2005 and 2006–2009, the rhythm of international expansion became much more regular and less volatile. During this phase of stable growth, almost no volatility occurred, and Starbucks was able to consolidate and improve its performance.

Exhibit 12 shows a link between a lower kurtosis and higher returns for Starbucks. Downward slopes are visible for both domestic and foreign stores: For both national and international expansion, a more regular rhythm is associated with higher ROA. The trend line for the slope of the foreign kurtosis is steeper, implying performance is potentially more sensitive to the rhythm of foreign expansion than to domestic expansion. Contrary to the overall pattern, the company's domestic expansion was extremely regular between 1994 and 1997, yet Starbucks experienced a period of relatively low ROA. However, the foreign expansion path in the same time period was much more irregular. Again, the rhythm of the foreign expansion appears to influence Starbucks' ROA to a larger extent than domestic rhythm. The foreign countries entered during this irregular period happened to be those countries where the company faced higher cultural differences for the first time: those in the Far East and the Middle East (see Exhibit 1). In the period 2006–2009, a higher performance might have been expected when compared with the period of 2002–2005 because the company had a more regular expansion;

---

[36]Formula to calculate the rhythm of the internationalization process, according to Freek Vermeulen and Harry Barkema, "Pace, rhythm, and scope: Process dependence in building a profitable multinational corporation," *Strategic Management Journal*, 2002, vol. 23, pp. 637–653. Note: n=number of observations; x_i=number of expansions in year i; s=standard deviation of the number of expansions.

$$Kurtosis = \left[\frac{n(n+1)}{(n-1)(n-2)(n-3)} \Sigma \left(\frac{x_i - \bar{x}}{s} \right)^4 \right] - \frac{3(n-1)^2}{(n-2)(n-3)}$$

however, Exhibit 12 shows the expected higher performance was not the case. This latter period coincided with the global economic recession and intensifying competition.

SCOPE OF STARBUCKS' INTERNATIONALIZATION

The geographical scope, or scope, is measured by the relative growth of the number of countries added to the company's portfolio over a given period of time. The geographical scope of Starbucks' expansion path is shown in Exhibit 13. A downward slope implies a negative association between scope and returns, which, however, was not the case: The slope is rather flat. In the first three years of the analysis (1993–1995), Starbucks was solely represented in the United States and Canada: The company had not yet internationalized into countries outside North America. Exhibit 14 shows the same analysis with these years excluded. The graph clearly shows a downward slope. Once Starbucks embraced international expansion in 1996 and thereafter, higher returns were generally gained in the years in which the scope of internationalization was low.

However, Starbucks experienced some exceptions to this general rule. In 1998, the scope of Starbucks' internationalization was high. That same year, Starbucks acquired the Seattle Coffee Company, which provided 65 stores and a presence in prime locations in the United Kingdom. This one-off acquisition enabled Starbucks to expand with a broader geographical scope and to tap into existing revenue channels in the United Kingdom. Similarly, in 2000, the trend line suggests Starbucks should have had a higher performance because it had relatively low country growth. As seen in Exhibit 11, pace was moderately high that year. Conversely, in the years 2008 and 2009, Starbucks had relatively low new country growth but performance was suppressed. Again, these results can be explained by the economic recession.

RATIONALIZATION AND THE POST-RATIONALIZATION DECISION

Starbucks' success in growing its business at home and abroad was legendary. However, the company had received criticism on a number of fronts: for growing too fast, for cannibalizing turnover in closely located stores, for decreasing product quality and company image and for driving out small, independent competitors.[37] Furthermore, after 2007, demand for Starbucks' products was badly hit by the global economic recession. All in all, these factors led the company to embark on a rationalization program between 2008 and 2010 and to close nearly 1,000 company-operated stores. According to Starbucks' 2009 annual report:

> Starbucks' actions to rationalize its global store portfolio have included the planned closure of nearly 1,000 Company-operated stores globally. At the end of fiscal 2009, nearly all of the approximately 800 US Company-operated stores, 61 stores in Australia and 41 Company-operated stores in other International markets had been closed. The remaining International store closures are expected to be completed by the end of fiscal 2010.

---

[37]"Store wars: Cappuccino kings," *BBC News*, June 9, 2004 (first transmitted February 12, 2003).

These closures resulted in approximately $580 million in cost savings, but also affected earnings by lease termination and severance costs. Approximately 70 per cent of the stores that were closed had been open for fewer than 3 years.

Now, in mid-2010, as CEO Schultz looked forward, he needed to decide again how to approach international markets. The world was gradually emerging from the economic downturn, and prospects for growth were improving. Starbucks was now faced with some critical strategic decisions: Should the company resume its international expansion and once again intensify its commitments in overseas markets? If so, what approach should the company take? Had the pace, rhythm and scope of its previous internationalization in the coffee industry affected company performance? How should Starbucks formulate and execute its international strategy going forward?

EXHIBIT 1   Starbucks' Internationalization Timeline

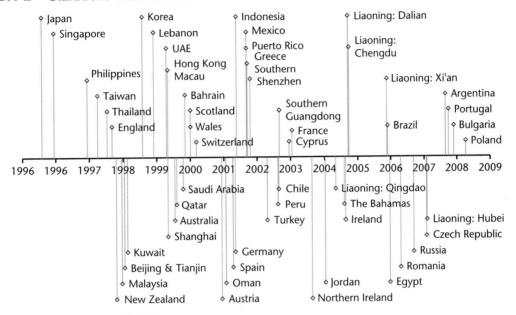

Source: Starbucks annual reports 1993–2009.

EXHIBIT 2   Starbucks' Stock versus Market Performance (Index)

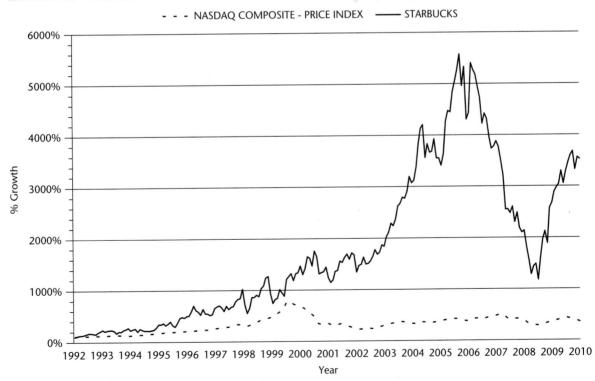

Source: Thomson Reuters Datastream (Monthly index, July, 1992 = 100%).

EXHIBIT 3   Coffee Consumption in Kilograms Per Capita by Region and Country Income

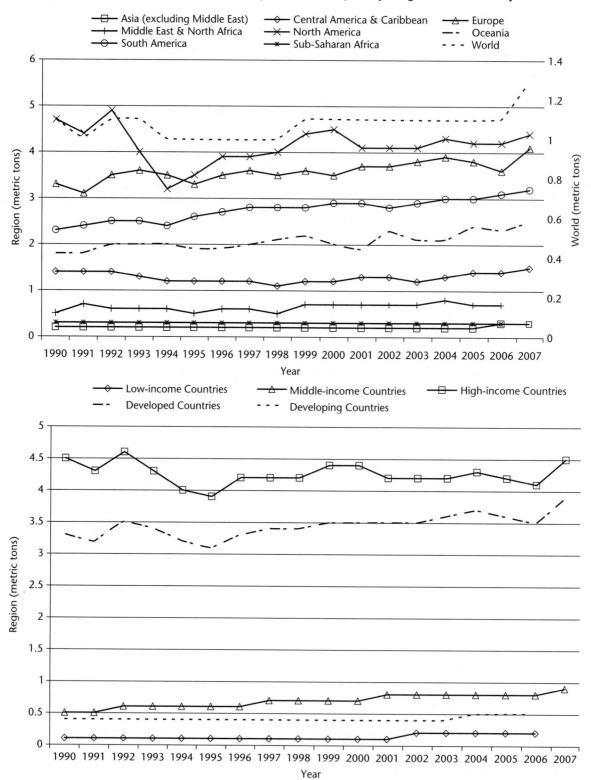

Source: International Coffee Organization (ICO), "Historical coffee statistics," ICO, London, 2008. Available at http://www.ico.org/historical. asp, accessed 29 July 2010.

EXHIBIT 4   Coffee Consumption in Metric Tons by Region and Country Income

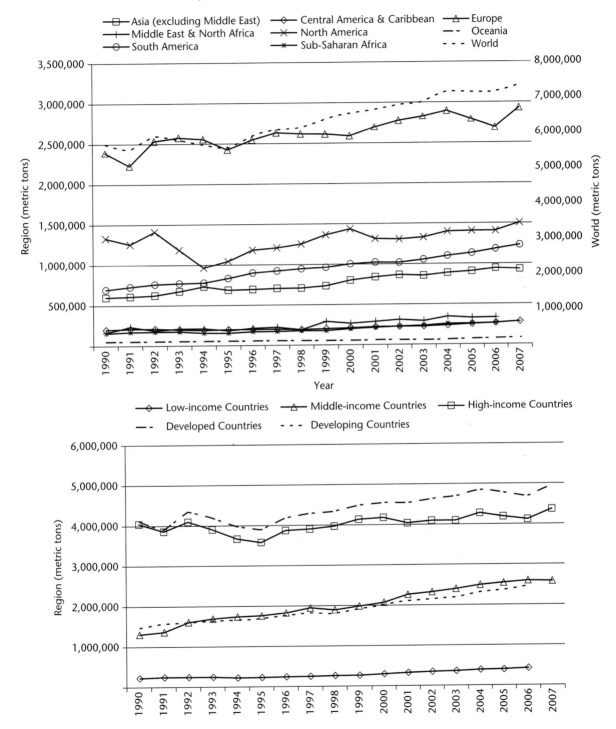

Source: International Coffee Organization (ICO), "Historical coffee statistics," ICO, London, 2008. Available at http://www.ico.org/historical. asp, accessed July 29, 2010.

EXHIBIT 5   Starbucks' Estimated Market Share (2007–2009)

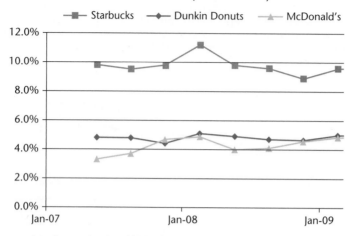

Source: Big Research, "Consumer intentions and actions (CIA) survey," May 2009. Available at http://www.bigresearch.com/news/
big052809.htm, accessed July 29, 2010.

EXHIBIT 6   Starbucks' Stores and Revenues from Grocery Channel (2002–2009)

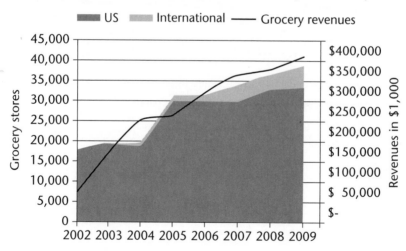

Source: Starbucks annual reports 2002–2009.

EXHIBIT 7 Composite Coffee Price (1998–2010)

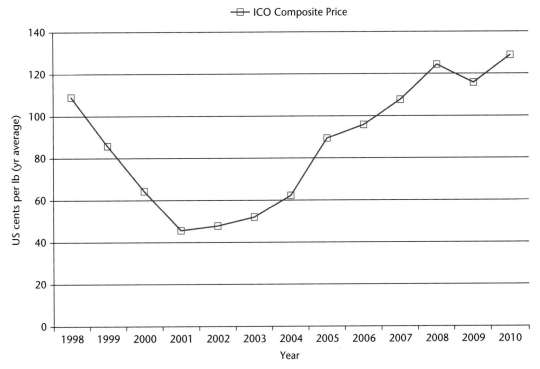

Source: International Coffee Organization (ICO), "Historical coffee statistics," ICO, London, 2008. Available at http://www.ico.org/historical. asp, accessed July 29, 2010.

EXHIBIT 8 Starbucks' Revenue Versus Absolute Store Growth

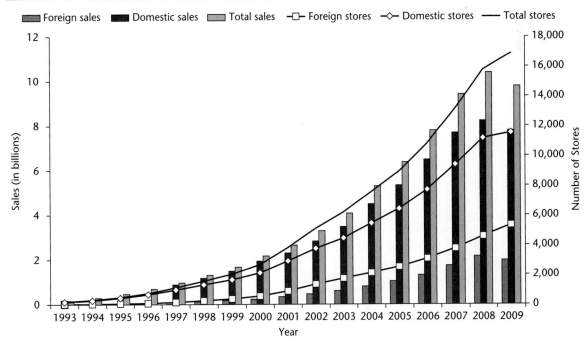

Source: Starbucks annual reports 1993–2009; and Thomson Reuters Datastream.

EXHIBIT 9 Starbucks' Revenue versus Relative Store Growth

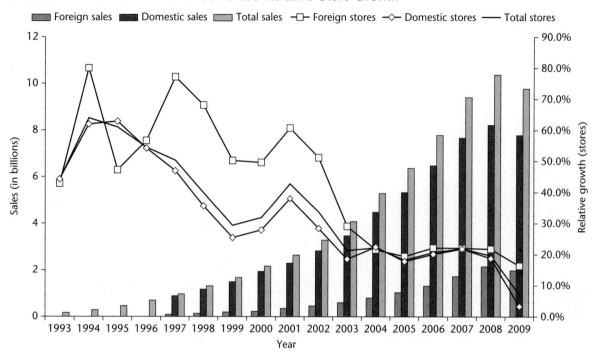

Source: Starbucks annual reports 1993–2009; and Thomson Reuters Datastream.

EXHIBIT 10 Starbucks' Performance (Return on Assets) versus Relative Growth (Stores and New Countries)

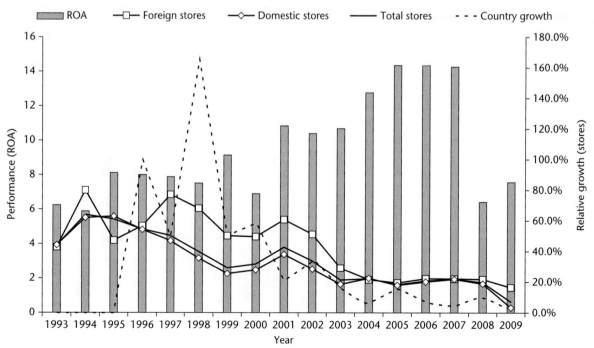

Source: Starbucks annual reports 1993–2009; and Thomson Reuters Datastream.

EXHIBIT 11 Pace of Starbucks' Internationalization

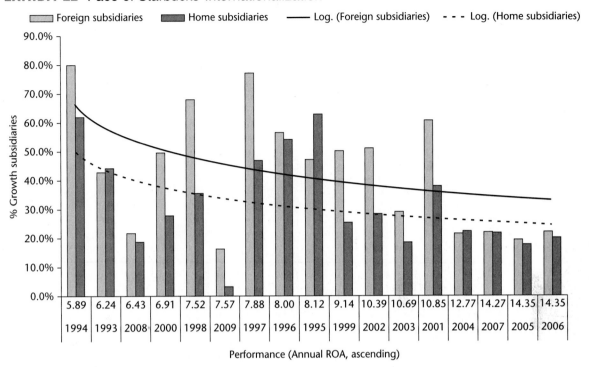

Source: Starbucks annual reports 1993–2009; and Thomson Reuters Datastream.

EXHIBIT 12 Rhythm of Starbucks' Internationalization

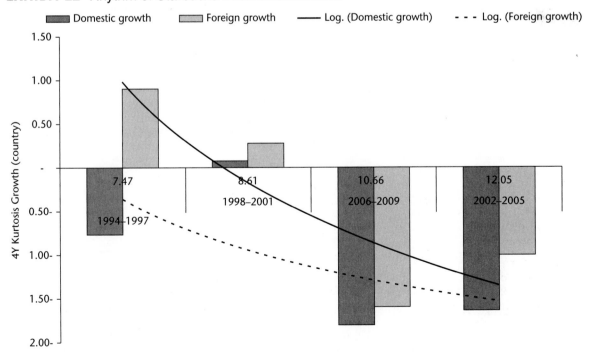

Source: Starbucks annual reports 1993–2009; and Thomson Reuters Datastream.

EXHIBIT 13 Scope of Starbucks' Internationalization (1993–2009)

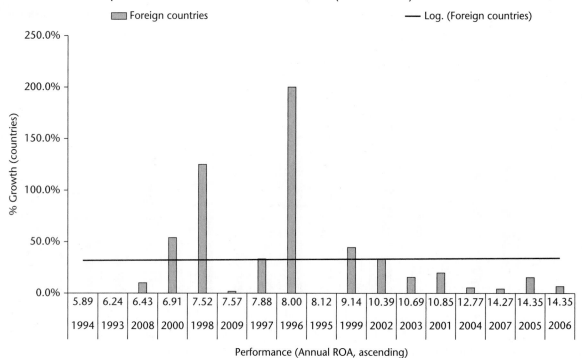

Source: Starbucks annual reports 1993–2009; and Thomson Reuters Datastream.

EXHIBIT 14 Scope of Starbucks' Internationalization (1996–2009)

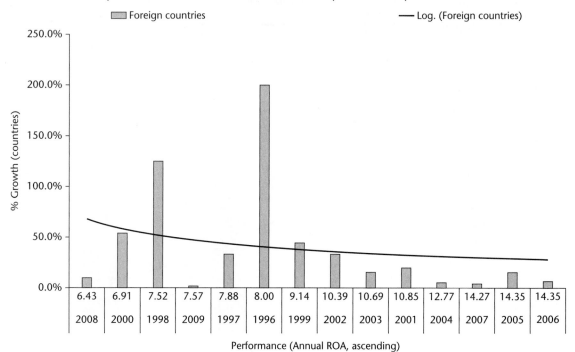

Source: Starbucks annual reports 1993–2009; and Thomson Reuters Datastream.

Chabros International Group: A World of Wood

CHABROS INTERNATIONAL GROUP

On December 30, 2009, as a result of the global economic crisis, Chabros International Group, a leading wood company headquartered in Lebanon, reported a drastic drop in lumber and veneer sales in its largest market, Dubai. Antoine Chami, Chabros' owner and president, had to decide what to do. Should he close parts of his Serbian sawmill that had cost him more than $11 million to acquire and expand 2 years ago to meet Chabros' increasing sales volume at the time? Should he try to re-boost his company's sales to use his sawmill's available capacity? If so, should Chabros try to increase its sales within the countries where it already operated, or should it expand into a new country? Would Morocco, among other countries, be the best country to expand into? Was it the right time to embark on such an expansion?

CHABROS INTERNATIONAL GROUP'S HISTORY

Chami's father and uncles founded Chabros in the 1960s. The name *Chabros* came from *Chami Brothers*. Originally, Chabros operated only in Lebanon and dealt only with veneers; that is, the different kinds of wood surface (see Exhibit 1 for a more detailed definition of wood veneer). In 1978, Chabros became wholly owned by Chami's father, and Chami took full charge after the death of his father in 1987. At that time, the political, security and economic situation in Lebanon was very unstable. The country was undergoing a civil war, so Chabros' primary goal was survival. In 1991, the civil war ended; however, the country's economic situation remained relatively unstable despite slow gradual improvement.

Bassam Farah wrote this case under the supervision of Professor Paul W. Beamish solely to provide material for class discussion. The authors do not intend to illustrate either effective or ineffective handling of a managerial situation. The authors may have disguised certain names and other identifying information to protect confidentiality.

Richard Ivey School of Business
The University of Western Ontario

After 1991, Chabros occasionally serviced Lebanese customers located in Dubai, an emirate in the United Arab Emirates (UAE). Dubai clients purchased their products from Chabros in Lebanon and shipped them to Dubai. Here, Chami and his top management team thought, "Why don't we send sales representatives from Lebanon to Dubai to market our products there?" Thus the first internationalization attempt started when Chabros sent one of its sales representatives, Nicholas Mousalli, to Dubai to study the wood market, analyze wood prices and market Chabros wood products (i.e., lumber and veneer).

The year 1998 marked the first direct exporting activities to Dubai. After making a couple of successful deals exporting wood from Chabros in Lebanon to customers in Dubai, Mousalli suggested opening a branch in Dubai. Chami implemented this suggestion immediately, opening Chabros' first branch in a 200 square metre rented warehouse. Chabros was not registered as a company in Dubai until the next year, when Chabros bought its own warehouse. In 1999, Chabros celebrated the birth of its first foreign subsidiary, the Dubai subsidiary, under the name Chabros Wood Trading (see Exhibit 2).

Chabros Dubai was a great success. Armed with this success and an ambition to make Chabros a global player in the worldwide wood industry, Chami decided to go to Saudi Arabia. However, Saudi Arabia was a huge market and, alone, Chabros did not have the required financial resources to enter such an enormous market. Chami convinced two of his Italian suppliers, who witnessed Chabros' success in Dubai, to partner with him to enter the Saudi Arabian market. In 2001, Chabros Riyadh was established. It was initially established in Riyadh, Saudi Arabia, as an international joint venture (IJV), with Chabros owning 50 per cent of its shares and each of the two Italian partners owning 25 per cent. However, given the cultural distance between European and Arab countries, the Italian partners found it difficult to adapt to the Saudi Arabian mentality and the Saudis' way of doing business. The first Italian partner sold his shares to Chabros one year after the establishment of the IJV, and the second Italian partner sold his shares to Chabros two years later. By 2004, Chabros Riyadh was a subsidiary wholly owned by Chabros Lebanon.

Prior to 2003, demand for wood (lumber and veneer) soared in the UAE, Saudi Arabia and Qatar, and Chabros experienced a great shortage in the supply of European wood. The sales generated by Chabros far exceeded the production capacity of Chabros' European supplier. To reduce this supply shortage and secure the largest quantity possible of European wood, in 2003, Chabros opened an office in Serbia, called Chabros Serbia, and financed its Serbian supplier to increase its sawmill's production capacity. Despite the financing provided, the Serbian supplier's pace of production capacity increase was very slow. As a consequence, Chami asked himself, "Why don't we acquire our Serbian supplier and quickly expand the sawmill's production capacity to meet our sales needs?" In 2007, Chabros acquired its Serbian supplier for $1.4 million, and the sawmill started operating under the name of Wood World Trading as a Chabros manufacturing subsidiary.

Given the Dubai and Riyadh internationalization successes, and despite the European wood supply shortage that the company faced, Chami and his top management team decided to go to Qatar. Qatar was attractive because it was a small, natural gas–rich country that was following the path of its neighbour, Dubai, in fast economic growth. They went to Qatar in 2004 and opened a new subsidiary, Chabros Doha.

Between 2004 and 2008, Chabros opened four new subsidiaries, albeit for different purposes. First, in 2005, Chabros opened a subsidiary in Muscat, Oman, to access new markets to sell its wood products (lumber and veneer). Then, later in that same year, it opened a subsidiary in Cairo, Egypt, to access a new market where it could sell its supply of lower-quality lumber and veneers. In 2006, it opened a second subsidiary in the UAE, in Abu Dhabi. In 2007, it opened a second subsidiary in Saudi Arabia, in Jeddah. The last two subsidiaries were opened to increase Chabros' sales volume and take advantage of lower prices associated with purchasing larger quantities. Later, Chabros benefited from production economies of scale after acquiring the Serbian sawmill.

Chami opened Chabros Cairo for a specific strategic purpose. At first, Chami, like his major competitors, bought and sold only the higher-quality veneers; that is, veneers graded "A" and "AB." However, later, by being exposed to different methods of wood production around the globe, he quickly learned that in their typical production process, sawmills produced veneers of different qualities, including "B" quality. Further, he learned that when a veneer trader bought only higher-quality veneers, for instance "A" and "AB" qualities, sawmills usually charged that trader higher prices than they would have charged a trader who bought all the different qualities of veneer that they produced. Thus, in most cases, when a trader bought only "A"- and "AB"- quality veneers, the sawmill charged that trader prices as if he/she bought all the different qualities of veneer and assigned the lower-quality veneer that was left at the sawmill, the "B"-quality veneer, a value of zero, assuming that it would not be sold. That was because it was much more difficult for a sawmill to sell its lower-quality veneers. Moreover, by being subjected to different national markets and their dissimilar product demands, Chami learned that Egypt was a market for lower-quality, rather than higher-quality wood. Thus Chami opened Chabros Cairo to market its "B"-quality veneer. This way, Chabros could buy and/or manufacture all the different qualities of wood (lumber and veneer) for the same price as the higher-quality wood alone. Then it could sell the "A"-quality wood in Dubai and the "AB"-quality wood in Saudi Arabia and Lebanon for some profit, while selling the "B"-quality wood in Egypt for approximately 100 per cent profit, when compared to trading only higher-quality wood.[1]

CHABROS INTERNATIONAL GROUP IN 2009

By 2009, Chabros had already established eight subsidiaries/offices in six countries other than Lebanon, namely Serbia, the UAE, the Kingdom of Saudi Arabia (KSA), Qatar, Oman and Egypt. While four countries hosted one subsidiary each, the UAE and Saudi Arabia hosted two each. These subsidiaries constituted Chabros International Group (for a map of the Middle East and North Africa (MENA) region and parts of Europe, including Serbia, see Exhibit 3).

When Chabros was first established, it was involved in trading only one type of wood, veneer, and just in Lebanon. However, by 2009, Chabros International Group was involved in two areas of business: production and trade. It produced several species of European lumber of different qualities and traded different qualities of diverse species of lumber and veneer among countries in many areas of the world. For example, it imported lumber and veneer from the United States, Europe, Asia, Africa and Australia, and exported them to the Middle East and North Africa (MENA) region and European countries, namely the UAE, Saudi Arabia, Qatar, Oman, Egypt, England, Germany, Denmark, Spain and Turkey.

---

[1]"B"-quality wood (lumber and veneer) was used for making lower-quality wooden doors, closets, furniture and internal decorations, etc.

Chabros International Group's Sales, Profits and Market Share

From 2005 to 2008, Chabros International Group experienced rapid growth in sales volume. In 2005, Chabros' sales were $60 million, whereas in 2008 they became $100 million, an increase of 67 per cent within only 3 years. However, 2009's sales suddenly dropped by $10 million (see Exhibit 4). This was due entirely to the drastic fall in Chabros Dubai's sales. In 2009, while Chabros' other subsidiaries experienced either relatively stable or somewhat improved sales, Chabros Dubai suffered from a 30 per cent decline in its sales. In 2008, Chabros Dubai contributed $50 million to the group's $100 million total sales, whereas in 2009 it contributed only $35 million to the group's $90 million total sales. This represented a 30 per cent drop in Chabros Dubai's sales from 2008 to 2009 and a 10 per cent aggregate increase in sales in all of Chabros' other subsidiaries.

Chabros Dubai maintained its position as Chabros International Group's leading subsidiary in terms of sales volume despite its severe sales drop in 2009. Even after the global economic crisis, Chabros Dubai ranked first in terms of sales among its Chabros counterparts, while Chabros Riyadh ranked second and Chabros Doha ranked third (see Exhibit 5).

Between 2005 and 2008, veneer sales grew 33 per cent, from $30 million to $40 million, whereas lumber sales grew 100 per cent, from $30 million to $60 million. In 2009, veneer and lumber sales dropped by $5 million each (see Exhibit 6). Thus veneer sales dropped by 14.3 per cent while lumber sales dropped by only 9 per cent. In 2009, Chabros International Group sold its veneer products at an average price of $3 per square metre and its lumber products at an average price of $1,000 per cubic metre. This translated into sales of 11,666,666 square metres of veneer and sales of 55,000 cubic metres of lumber. According to Chami, although Chabros started as a veneer company, because Chabros was considered the market leader in veneer in the MENA region, at that moment it had more potential and freedom to grow its lumber business than its veneer business.

Despite Chabros' rapid sales growth from 2005 to 2008, its percentage net profits from sales did not vary much and ranged between 6 per cent and 6.8 per cent. However, net profits suddenly dropped to 4.1 per cent in 2009 (see Exhibit 7).

According to Chami, Chabros International Group was considered the largest trader of veneer in the MENA region. It represented more than half of the supply of veneer in that region. Chabros had a lumber market share of around 20 per cent in both the UAE and Qatar and around 1 per cent in both Saudi Arabia and Egypt (see Exhibit 8).

Chabros International Group's Suppliers, Distributors, Employees and Customers

Chabros International Group bought its different kinds of veneers from suppliers (veneer manufacturers) all over the world, but mainly from suppliers in the United States, Italy, China and Ghana. In contrast, Chabros produced most of its European lumber species in its Serbia sawmill and imported its non-European lumber species from non-European countries. In terms of distribution, Chabros International Group's subsidiaries used their own trucks to distribute their products within the countries they operated in. However, Chabros Serbia used its trucks to distribute its products all over

Europe and to transport them to Chabros' Trieste wood terminal, where containers were loaded and shipped to other countries in the world. Transportation costs (i.e., truck and/or train transportation costs, plus shipping costs) of wood from Chabros Serbia to Chabros' MENA region subsidiaries ranged from $60–80 per cubic metre and made up only around 10 per cent of the total cost. Customs duties constituted 4 to 10 per cent of the total cost.

In 2009, Chabros International Group's workforce consisted of more than 500 employees. Chabros Dubai had the largest number of employees, at 180, while Chabros Abu Dhabi and Chabros Muscat had the fewest, at 10 employees each (see Exhibit 9).

Chabros International Group's customers ranged from wholesalers to building contractors to carpentries to retailers, as well as end users. However, Chabros International Group's customers differed from country to country. In the Arab Gulf, the company's customers were mainly building contractors who designed and manufactured wooden doors, closets and decorations for buildings (residential, business or governmental), towers, hotels, restaurants, etc. In Lebanon, its customers included wood wholesalers, retailers and furniture manufacturers. In Europe, its customers were mainly retailers.

Chabros International Group's Competition, Competitive Advantages/Disadvantages and Strategies

Chabros International Group competed with firms in two industries: the hardwood industry (as opposed to the softwood industry) and the veneer industry. According to Chami, hardwood was used mainly for making doors, closets, furniture and internal decorations, etc., whereas softwood was used mostly for making building components, windows, paper and external decorations. Chabros International Group faced local, regional and global competition. Locally, in the different countries where it operated, Chabros was competing with other small- and medium-sized hardwood and veneer suppliers, mainly domestic small- and medium-sized retailers and wholesalers, who usually did not import wood from abroad and who were typically servicing small- and medium-sized subcontracting companies and carpentries. Regionally, Chabros was competing with hardwood and veneer suppliers that operated only at the MENA region level; that is, companies that traded wood only in the MENA region. And globally, Chabros was competing with the largest global hardwood and veneer companies. These included American, European and Asian hardwood and veneer companies, such as General Woods and Weston in hardwood and General Woods and Fritz Kohl in veneer, which Chabros bid against for huge projects, including towers, hotels and government buildings, in Dubai, Doha and Riyadh, to name but a few locations.

Chabros International Group had several competitive advantages over its rivals. First, it provided its customers with more varied and more customized wood products than did most of its competitors. Moreover, Chabros built distinctive strategic relationships with its key suppliers.

Second, Chami had more than 25 years' experience in evaluating and choosing the best kinds of veneers to trade in. Such experience was very valuable, rare and difficult to imitate. Unlike trading in lumber, which was considered a commodity, trading in veneer required taste and expertise. Chami tried to transfer this capability to other partners and top managers at the company. Such a capability of evaluating and choosing the best veneer was important because, for veneer, the grades "A," "AB," and "B," which implied that the higher the grade the fewer the knots in the veneer, did not mean a lot. Customers bought a certain kind of veneer not because it was graded "A," "AB," or "B," but because they liked its design and pattern. So the sales of veneer were a function of the tastes of different customers in different countries. Chami had a very good understanding of the tastes of different categories of customers in many different countries. When Chami first opened in Dubai, he had much greater expertise in buying veneers than his local competitors. Even in 2009, because of this great expertise that he had acquired buying veneers over the years, he still personally inspected most of the veneers that Chabros bought.

Third, Chabros International Group was, on the one hand, a wood manufacturer and, on the other hand, a wood wholesaler. Having such a dual strategic posture gave Chabros an advantage over competitors who were solely manufacturers and competitors who were solely wholesalers. Being simultaneously a manufacturer and a wholesaler gave Chabros strategic flexibility. Being a low-cost wood manufacturer of European wood species, Chabros was able to sell the different kinds and qualities of European wood at lower prices than most of its wholesale competitors. And by being a wood wholesaler, Chabros was able to purchase the non-European wood species from the manufacturers with the lowest prices and compete with the manufacturers with the higher prices. For example, consider the situation where Chabros, as a wholesaler, had the choice to buy veneer from two different American veneer manufacturers. The first manufacturer, because of its distance from the forests, was manufacturing veneer at a cost of $1.50 per square metre and selling it at a price of $1.70 per square metre, whereas the second manufacturer, because of its proximity to the forests, was manufacturing the same veneer at a cost of $1.40 per square metre and selling it at a price of $1.50 per square metre. Chabros bought the veneer from the second manufacturer at $1.50 per square metre, a price equal to the cost that the first manufacturer was incurring to produce its veneer. In addition, Chabros received the *wood* once it paid for it, whereas the manufacturer paid for the *trees* three to four months before the veneer was available for sale. Chabros, in this case as a wholesaler, had a better competitive position than its manufacturing competitor.

Fourth, given Chabros International Group's size, the company benefited from economies of scale. To serve wider and bigger markets, Chabros bought bigger quantities and all the different qualities of wood instead of buying only smaller quantities or only higher qualities of wood (i.e., "A" and/or "AB"). This was because Chabros had higher sales and greater variety in markets that demanded more quantities and different qualities of wood (e.g., selling veneer of "A" quality to the UAE, "AB" quality to Saudi Arabia and Lebanon and "B" quality to Egypt), which ultimately lowered the cost of wood for Chabros.

Finally, according to Chami, Chabros had an advantage over its non-MENA region competitors (e.g., European, American and/or Asian competitors) in that it simultaneously understood and adapted to its Western suppliers and MENA countries' customers. This was because the majority of Chabros' employees were Lebanese and Lebanese people were known to be very adaptable due to their culture, which had emerged as a mixture of their Arabic roots and a French tinge. Lebanese people were Arabs who had been colonized for several decades by the French empire. This made them open to both Western and Arabic cultures. They gained the twin capabilities of being able to understand and adapt to the behaviours of their Western suppliers and speak the language of their MENA countries' customers, thus facilitating Chabros' business between the East and West.

While Chabros International Group had several competitive advantages, it also had some disadvantages. First, being a wood manufacturer sometimes put Chabros at a disadvantage. While being a veneer wholesaler sometimes gave Chabros an advantage over other veneer manufacturers, being a lumber manufacturer put Chabros in the reverse situation and sometimes gave it a disadvantage compared to lumber wholesalers. For example, in 2008, when the euro reached $1.55, Chabros's Russian supplier was able to sell Chabros' Dubai subsidiary the same lumber that Chabros produced at its Serbian sawmill at a lower price. This was because Chabros' Serbian sawmill's costs and prices were in euros, whereas the Russian supplier's costs and prices were in U.S. dollars. At that point, Chabros had to cut down on its production in Serbia and sell from its Russian supplier's/competitor's production.

Second, not having seriously worked on Chabros' image and brand name somehow put the company at a disadvantage. Thus, while Chabros was operating in seven MENA countries, the Chabros brand name was not very well known in the region, not to mention in its parent country, Lebanon.

To grow his company and to increase his profits, Chami followed several strategies. Due to the wood supply shortage that Chabros encountered during the early 2000s, one of the earlier strategies that he followed was acquiring his Serbian supplier, which had not been able to meet Chabros' sales demands, for $1.4 million and investing another $10 million to expand the sawmill's capacity so that it could meet Chabros' increasing sales demands.

Another strategy that Chami followed was not to sell large quantities with small margins, but rather to provide customers with a greater variety of wood products and qualities so that they could satisfy all their lumber and veneer needs with Chabros, and find the lumber and veneer they could not find elsewhere. For example, while its competitors were selling only 10 kinds of wood (lumber and veneer), Chabros was selling 40, and while its competitors were selling only 1 or 2 qualities of wood, Chabros was selling 3 or 4.

A third strategy was expanding into countries with a high demand for European lumber species. This way, he could supply these countries with lumber produced at Chabros Serbia's sawmill rather than with lumber produced by other lumber-supplying/producing companies. By following this strategy, he could sell more of his products at higher margins yet at prices lower than other rival domestic importers. Chami planned to expand into two new countries every year if possible.

A fourth and, in Chami's view, extremely important strategy that he followed was his flexible payment strategy. Chami not only did not ask his customers for any letters of credit (L/Cs), but also offered them flexible payment terms. For example, even if he agreed that a customer paid within 90 days, contrary to his non-MENA region competitors, he did not take any legal action if that customer was one or two, or even three, months late to pay. Moreover, because he did not ask for any L/Cs, customers were able to ask for different kinds of wood products, sizes and qualities without going through the hassle of applying for a new L/C or adjusting a previously existing L/C. As a consequence, customers loved to work with Chabros.

All these advantages and strategies helped Chabros International Group grow very fast; however, not for very long. . .

THE CRISIS

On December 30, 2009, Chami reviewed his company's end-of-year financial statements. Chabros Dubai's sales had dropped by 30 per cent and Dubai was Chabros International Group's largest market! To make things worse, Chami had just invested more than $11 million to buy his Serbian sawmill and multiply its capacity only 2 years earlier! In 2007 and 2008, 100 per cent of the wood produced by Chabros Serbia's sawmill was sold by Chabros' MENA subsidiaries. However, at the end of 2009 Chabros' MENA subsidiaries bought only 50 per cent of the sawmill's production. The 2008 global economic crisis created a 2009 Chabros financial crisis!

Shocked, Chami went into crisis mode. He had to find solutions, and he had to find them fast. He started asking himself, "What to do now? How to control the damage and save the company? How to overcome this financial crisis? Should we close parts of the mill and reduce its capacity to match our markets' current demand? Or should we, despite the global downturn in demand, try to re-boost sales to match our Serbian sawmill's excess capacity? If we reduce the mill's capacity, how much of that capacity should be reduced? If we decide to re-boost sales to match the mill's existing capacity, how should we do that? Is now the right time to follow such a growth strategy? If we decide to follow a growth strategy, which growth strategy should be followed? Should we follow a market penetration, product development, market development, or diversification strategy?" (See Exhibit 10 for explanations of each of these different strategies.) All these and other questions raced through Chami's head.

Chami immediately called his top management team for an urgent meeting. In the meeting, he expressed his concerns about his company's financial situation. He requested that his management team work with him on finding solutions fast. The future seemed uncertain and the team did not know what to expect. However, Chabros had good financial and human resources and had very good knowledge of its wood business.

To overcome the current situation, Chami and his team members explored different alternatives. They explored the alternative of closing parts of their Serbian sawmill (they recognized that by closing half of the sawmill, they would reduce the number of the sawmill's employees by half and thus save $400,000 per year in salaries). They looked at the alternative of trying to re-boost Chabros' sales. They examined the different strategies that they could follow if they decided to try and grow the company's sales. They thought about whether they could increase Chabros' market share in the countries where it already operated—i.e., follow a market penetration strategy—and if so, which existing markets/countries to penetrate. They contemplated the different countries that they would expand into if they decided to follow a market development or diversification strategy. They gave special attention to Morocco because they were particularly interested in it. Although they did not do a strengths, weaknesses, opportunities and threats (SWOT) analysis and did not prepare financial estimates for the other potential target countries, they did so for Morocco (see Exhibits 11, 12 and 13). They even asked themselves whether they should change their product mix—that is, focus on lumber more than on veneer, although veneer was the basis of the company, or focus on veneer more than lumber. To decide upon a course of action, they gathered information related to these alternatives (this information is available in Exhibits 14 and 15). All these alternatives had their benefits and risks. Chami and his top management team had to decide which course of action to follow, and they had to decide very quickly.

EXHIBIT 1 Glossary of Terms

Wood veneer: In woodworking, **veneer** refers to thin slices of wood, usually thinner than three millimetres (an eighth of an inch), that are typically glued onto core panels (typically, wood, particle board or medium-density fibreboard) to produce flat panels such as doors, tops and panels for cabinets, parquet floors and parts of furniture. They are also used in marquetry. Plywood consists of three or more layers of veneer, each glued with its grain at right angles to adjacent layers for strength. Veneer beading is a thin layer of decorative edging placed around objects such as jewellery boxes.

Veneer is obtained either by "peeling" the trunk of a tree or by slicing large rectangular blocks of wood known as flitches. The appearance of the grain and figure in wood comes from slicing through the growth rings of a tree and depends upon the angle at which the wood is sliced.

Lumber: Boards or planks that have been sawn (usually on all four sides) or split from large harvested logs. Though this term is often used interchangeably with "timber," "lumber" specifically refers to this wood product within the wood-products industry. Lumber appears in a wide variety of end uses, including construction, flooring, panelling and furniture.

Note: Additional information about Chabros International Group can be found on the company's website: www.chabros.com

EXHIBIT 2 Chabros Intl. Group's Subsidiary Growth by Year

	Office/Subsidiary location		Office/Subsidiary purpose
Year	Country	State/city	
1969	Lebanon	Beirut	Headquarters
1998–1999	United Arab Emirates (UAE)	Dubai	Sales subsidiary: Cut and sold mainly *higher-quality* imported wood (lumber and veneer) usually within the country but sometimes to nearby countries
2001	Kingdom of Saudi Arabia (KSA)	Riyadh	Sales subsidiary: Cut and sold mainly *higher-quality* imported wood (lumber and veneer) usually within the country but sometimes to nearby countries.
2003	Serbia	Sremska Mitrovica	Import office: Purchased wood from Europe and exported it to the Middle East and financed the Serbian sawmill from 2003–2007.
2004	Qatar	Doha	Sales subsidiary: Cut and sold mainly *higher-quality* imported wood (lumber and veneer) usually within the country but sometimes to nearby countries.
2005	Oman	Muscat	Sales subsidiary: Cut and sold mainly *higher-quality* imported wood (lumber and veneer) usually within the country but sometimes to nearby countries.
2005	Egypt	Cairo	Sales subsidiary: Cut and sold mainly *lower-quality* imported wood (lumber and veneer) usually within the country but sometimes to nearby countries.
2006	UAE	Abu Dhabi	Sales subsidiary: Cut and sold mainly *higher-quality* imported wood (lumber and veneer) usually within the country but sometimes to nearby countries.
2007	KSA	Jeddah (on the sea)	Sales subsidiary: Cut and sold mainly *higher-quality* imported wood (lumber and veneer) usually within the country but sometimes to nearby countries.
2007	Serbia	Loznica	Manufacturing subsidiary (sawmill): Bought and sawed trees, dried the wood and exported/sold the different qualities of the wood to the MENA region and Europe.

EXHIBIT 3   Map of Middle East and North Africa and Parts of Europe, Including Serbia

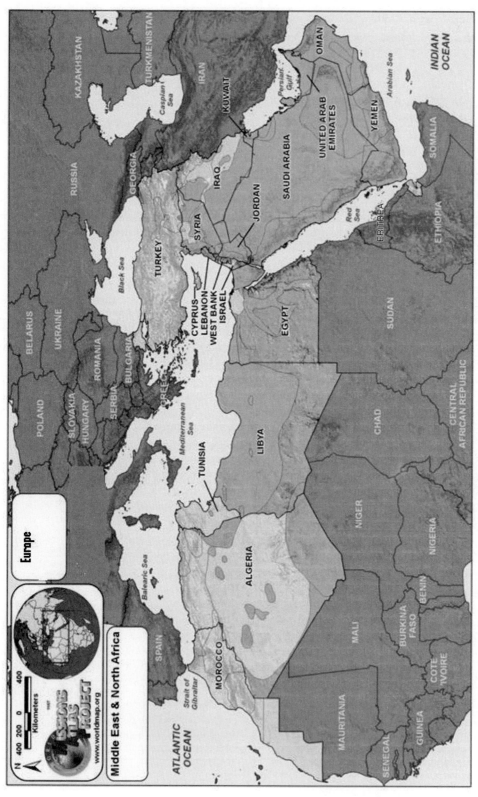

Source: WorldMap, http://worldmap.org/maps/prepared/regional/middle%20east%20and%20north%20africa/MiddleEast_NorthAfrica_jfilm.jpg

EXHIBIT 4   Chabros Intl. Group's Sales in US$ (millions)

Year	Sales
2005	$ 60
2006	$ 72
2007	$ 85
2008	$100
2009	$ 90

EXHIBIT 5   Sales Ranking of Chabros Intl. Group's Subsidiaries in 2009

Sales Rank	Subsidiary/office
1	Dubai
2	Riyadh
3	Doha
4	Beirut
5	Cairo
6	Muscat
7	Jeddah
8	Abu Dhabi

EXHIBIT 6   Chabros Intl. Group's Product Category Sales in US$ (millions)

Year	Veneer	Lumber	Total
2005	$30	$30	$ 60
2008	$40	$60	$100
2009	$35	$55	$ 90

EXHIBIT 7   Chabros Intl. Group's Net Profits from Sales (%)

2005	6.0
2006	6.5
2007	6.8
2008	6.7
2009	4.2

EXHIBIT 8   Chabros Intl. Group's Market Share by Country in 2009 (%)

Country	Market Share	
	Lumber	Veneer
UAE	20	>50
Qatar	20	>50
KSA	1	>50
Lebanon	2	>50
Oman	5	>50
Egypt	<1	10

EXHIBIT 9   Chabros Intl. Group's Employee Distribution in 2009

Chabros Subsidiary/office	Number of employees
Dubai	180
Loznica	140
Riyadh	70
Beirut	35
Jeddah	30
Doha	25
Cairo	15
Abu Dhabi	10
Muscat	10
Total number of employees	**515**

EXHIBIT 10 Different Growth Strategies Available to Chabros Intl. Group

	Products		
	Market Penetration	**Product Development**	**Existing Markets**
	(more sales and/or more subsidiaries) *Same markets (e.g., same countries), Same products (e.g., same wood products)*	(new products) *Same markets (e.g., same countries), New products (e.g., new wood products)*	
Markets	**Market Development**	**Diversification**	**New Markets**
	(new markets) *New markets (e.g., new countries), Same products (e.g., same wood products)*	(new products for new markets) *New products (e.g., new wood products), New markets (e.g., new countries)*	
	Existing Products	**New Products**	

EXHIBIT 11 Morocco's (Casablanca's) SWOT Analysis for 2010

Strengths

- Specialized know-how
- Known E.U. quality standards
- Capacity to consistently supply the market with similar-quality products
- Moroccans' positive perception of projects accomplished in Dubai

Opportunities

- No serious competent local rivals
- Big market currently served mainly by imports
- High demand for Chabros Serbia's European lumber species
- Very few sellers of veneer
- Morocco is not passing through a recession
- Morocco's currency, the dirham, is pegged to the euro, similar to Serbia's currency, the dinar, which reduced Chabros International Group's exchange rate risk

Weaknesses

- Lacking local relational networks, particularly with customers and government
- Chabros is not known in Casablanca
- Chabros does not know which Moroccan customers are creditworthy and which ones are not; the company does not use letters of credit (L/Cs)

Threats

- Supply contracts exclusively awarded to historically well-established suppliers (monopoly)
- Possible entry of new foreign competitors
- Possible changes in taxes and tariffs
- Possible tacit collusion of local competitors

EXHIBIT 12 Morocco's (Casablanca's) Financial Estimates for 2010 (US$ thousands)

Sales	$6,000
Cost of goods sold	$4,800
Gross profit margin	$1,200
Operational expenses	$ 480
Earnings before interest & taxes	$ 720

EXHIBIT 13 Morocco's Local Legal and Fiscal Characteristics in 2010

- Tariffs on lumber are 5%
- Tariffs on veneer boards that are ready to use are 35%
- Tax exemption on profit for the first 5 years, then tax of 30%
- Value added tax (VAT) on lumber is 14%
- Moroccan law guarantees re-transfer of capital, annual transfer of dividends and transfer of capital in case of termination
- Capital can be 100% foreign
- Income tax around 18%
- Sales can be made abroad

EXHIBIT 14 Market Selection: Major Economic Indicators

(1)	(2) Country	(3) Market size: Population (million)	(4) GNI per capita, Atlas method (current US$)[1]	(5) Wealth of consumers: GNI per capita, PPP (current international $)[2]	(6) Likely future growth rate: GDP per capita average annual growth rate 2000–2008 (%)
1.	Algeria	34,373	4,190	7,890	1.4
2.	Bahrain	775	25,420	33,430	*2.4
3.	Egypt	81,527	1,800	5,470	2.5
4.	Iran	71,956	**3,540	**10,850	2.7
5.	Iraq	30,711	–	–	–
6.	Jordan	5,906	3,470	5,720	2.2
7.	Kuwait	2,728	**43,930	**53,480	*1.8
8.	Lebanon	4,194	6,780	11,750	2.6
9.	Libya	6,294	12,380	16,270	*1.8
10.	Morocco	31,606	2,520	4,190	2.2
11.	Oman	2,785	**14,330	**22,170	*2.1
12.	Qatar	1,281	–	.	–
13.	Saudi Arabia	24,646	17,870	24,500	0.4
14.	Syria	20,581	2,160	4,490	1.3
15.	Tunisia	10,328	3,480	7,460	3.4
16.	United Arab Emirates	4,485	–	–	*−0.1

1. GNI per capita, Atlas method (current US$): GNI per capita (formerly GNP per capita) is the gross national income, converted to U.S. dollars using the World Bank Atlas method, divided by the mid-year population. GNI is the sum of value added by all resident producers plus any product taxes (less subsidies) not included in the valuation of output plus net receipts of primary income (compensation of employees and property income) from abroad. GNI, calculated in national currency, is usually converted to U.S. dollars at official exchange rates for comparisons across economies, although an alternative rate is used when the official exchange rate is judged to diverge by an exceptionally large margin from the rate actually applied in international transactions. To smooth fluctuations in prices and exchange rates, a special Atlas method of conversion is used by the World Bank. This applies a conversion factor that averages the exchange rate for a given year and the two preceding years, adjusted for differences in rates of inflation between the country, and through 2000, the G-5 countries (France, Germany, Japan, the United Kingdom and the United States). From 2001, these countries include the euro area, Japan, the United Kingdom and the United States. Source: World Bank national accounts data and OECD National Accounts data files.

2. GNI per capita, PPP (current international $): GNI per capita based on purchasing power parity (PPP). PPP GNI is gross national income (GNI) converted to international dollars using purchasing power parity rates. An international dollar has the same purchasing power over GNI as a U.S. dollar has in the United States. GNI is the sum of value added by all resident producers plus any product taxes (less subsidies) not included in the valuation of output plus net receipts of primary income (compensation of employees and property income) from abroad. Data are in current international dollars. Source: World Bank, International Comparison Program database.

– : Not available

*Data refer to years or periods other than those specified in the column heading, differ from the standard definition or refer to only part of a country.

**Data are for year 2007 because data for year 2008 are not available.

Source: Data in columns (3), (4), & (5) are from the World Bank's Data Catalog, http://data.worldbank.org/data-catalog. Data in column (6) are from "UNdata record view GDP per capita average annual growth rate," UNdata, http://data.un.org/Data.aspx?d=SOWC&f=inID%3a9 3%3bcrID%3a100%2c107%2c116%2c21%2c24%2c29%2c38%2c55%2c57%2c58%2c63%2c67%2c73%2c86%3btimeID%3a5&c=1,3,5, 6&s=crEngName:asc,sgvEngName:asc,timeEngName:desc&v=1. All data were collected during August 2010 for year 2008, unless otherwise stated or year was not applicable for variable.

EXHIBIT 15 Market Selection: Major Political, Legal, Commercial and Geographical Characteristics

(1) (2) Country	(3) Political system: Voice & accountability (0%–100%)[1]	(4) Legal system: Rule of law (0%–100%)[2]	(5) Commercial system: Ease of doing business (1–183)[3]	(6) Geographical distance from Lebanon (kilometres)
1. Algeria	17.8	26.8	136	3,309
2. Bahrain	24.0	69.4	20	1,672
3. Egypt	14.4	52.6	106	920
4. Iran	8.2	23.0	137	2,173
5. Iraq	12.0	1.0	153	728
6. Jordan	26.9	64.1	100	365
7. Kuwait	32.7	70.8	61	1,210
8. Lebanon	35.6	26.3	108	0
9. Libya	2.4	29.2	–	1,974
10. Morocco	27.9	51.7	128	3,991
11. Oman	16.8	74.6	65	2,398
12. Qatar	25.5	77.5	39	1,754
13. Saudi Arabia	5.3	59.8	13	1,425
14. Syria	4.8	34.4	143	306
15. Tunisia	11.5	58.9	69	2,424
16. United Arab Emirates	20.7	72.2	33	2,098

1. Voice and Accountability (VA)—Measuring perceptions of the extent to which a country's citizens are able to participate in selecting their government, as well as freedom of expression, freedom of association and a free media. The 0%–100% indicates rank of country among all countries in the world. A value of 0 corresponds to the lowest rank and 100 corresponds to the highest rank.

2. Rule of Law (RL)–Measuring perceptions of the extent to which agents have confidence in and abide by the rules of society, and in particular the quality of contract enforcement, property rights, the police and the courts, as well as the likelihood of crime and violence. The 0%–100% indicates rank of country among all countries in the world. A value of 0 corresponds to the lowest rank and 100 corresponds to the highest rank.

3. Ease of Doing Business—Economies are ranked on their ease of doing business, from 1–183, with first place being the best. A high ranking on the ease of doing business index means the regulatory environment is conducive to the operation of business. This index averages the country's percentile rankings on 10 topics, made up of a variety of indicators, giving equal weight to each topic.

– : Not available.

Source: Data in columns (3), (4), & (5) are from the World Bank's Data Catalog, http://data.worldbank.org/data-catalog. Data in column (6) are from distancefromto.net, www.distancefromto.net/country-distance-from/Lebanon. All data were collected during August 2010 for year 2008, unless otherwise stated or year was not applicable for variable.

Dell Inc. in 2009[1]

INTRODUCTION

On January 6, 2009, a senior executive at Dell Inc. (Dell) was preparing for an investor relations meeting. The company, founded by Michael S. Dell (Michael) in 1983, had originally focused on selling desktop computers. Over the next two decades, Dell grew to be the world's leading supplier of computer systems and was well regarded for its low-cost, direct model that provided it with an edge over competitors. In 2003, in recognition of Dell's increasingly broad product lineup, the company changed its name from Dell Computer Corporation to Dell Inc. To support the fast pace of growth, Dell had opened new manufacturing plants and customer service facilities in Europe, Asia and North America.

In March 2004, after more than two decades at the helm, Michael stepped down as chief executive officer (CEO) to make way for Kevin Rollins, Dell's chief operating officer. Rollins had continued Dell's focus on driving costs out of the company's supply chain and expanding into foreign markets. Starting in 2006, however, Dell had started to lose market share as competitors imitated its innovations. By the start of 2007, as a result of poor financial performance, Rollins resigned as CEO to make way for the return of Michael.

Irregularities in Dell's financial statements had prompted a restatement for the years 2003 to 2006. By mid-2007, Dell had relinquished its market share leadership to a resurgent competitor, Hewlett-Packard (HP). In an attempt to stem market share

Richard Ivey School of Business
The University of Western Ontario

[1]This case has been written on the basis of published sources only. Consequently, the interpretation and perspectives presented in this case are not necessarily those of Dell Inc. or any of its employees.

losses, Dell branched out into selling its personal computers (PCs) through retailers and emphasized the design component in its product lineup. In addition, the company was working on a $3 billion annual cost reduction plan. On September 5, Dell announced that it would sell most or all of its manufacturing facilities within 18 months.

As the senior executive reviewed the historical information on his company and its competitors, he wondered how to best to convey to skeptical investors that Dell's strategy would get the company back on track and its stock price growing again.

DELL

From an early age, Michael Dell had shown interest in entrepreneurship. At age 12, he devised a stamp auction that netted him $1,000. During his last year in high school, he made $18,000 selling papers for the now-defunct *Houston Post* and bought his first BMW.[2] In 1983, at the age of 19, as a freshman at the University of Texas at Austin, Michael founded a business selling computer dealers' excess inventory by mail. Because demand was very strong, Michael was able to fund his company's early growth internally, without having to seek venture capital. Within two years, from Michael's dormitory room, Dell Computer achieved $34 million in sales. The company focused on assembling computers for end-users who valued the ability to customize their machines. Dell by-passed intermediaries by going direct to end-users: All products were ordered by telephone, fax or via direct sales. The company grew popular with businesses, which preferred to order computers preconfigured to their specifications.

In October 1987, after the market crash, Dell completed a private placement through Goldman Sachs with the intent of growing the company. Dell raised another $30 million in 1988, earning Michael $18 million. By 1991, sales had reached $800 million. After achieving $2 billion in sales in 1992, Dell suffered its first major setback. The firm was in a liquidity crisis as it rushed to expand, and design flaws appeared in its notebook computers. Recognizing that he needed to build a senior management team, Michael recruited seasoned executives from firms such as Motorola and Apple to handle day-to-day operations.[3] In 1994, Dell ended its four-year attempt to sell computers through retailers. The same year, an informal team at Dell launched Dell.com, loading the site first with technical support information and then with price guides that enabled customers to mix, match and price components.[4]

By 1995, the company had recovered and continued to pull ahead of its competitors. Purchases by governments and large corporations, which generally ordered higher-end, preconfigured systems, pushed the average end-user's price for a Dell computer to $2,600, or 15 to 40 per cent higher than the prices of its closest competitors.[5] Dell achieved this combination of lower costs and higher margins by focusing on high-margin customers instead of initiating price wars and by relying on direct marketing rather than retail sales. Corporate customers were willing to pay more for Dell products because of quantifiable savings. A financial services customer based in Charlotte, North Carolina, described some of these savings:

[2]Rahul Jacob, "The resurrection of Michael Dell," *Fortune*, September 18, 1995, p. 117.
[3]Andrew E. Serwer, "Michael Dell turns the PC world inside out," *Fortune*, September 8, 1997, p. 76.
[4]Daniel Roth, "Dell's big new act," *Fortune*, December 6, 1999, p. 152.
[5]Rahul Jacob, "The resurrection of Michael Dell," *Fortune*, September 18, 1995, p. 117.

For us, having the right technology is do or die. We need to have 50 PCs available at any given time for delivery within 24 hours. But our resellers were never able to provide us with that. (Before we purchased Dell machines), UPS would deliver the PC, and a purchasing guy would open the box, pull out the machine, tag it, power it up, and program its electronic address. Then he would put the PC back in the box and store it in a holding station. Later, another guy would take the PC out of the box again, load in our software and stick it back in the box. Then it would go to someone's desk to be installed. If we were doing this in an office outside of Charlotte, we'd have to send a guy there for two days. Can you believe how much money we were throwing out the window? Dell could tag and address the machines and load our software in its factory. That alone saves us $500,000 a year.[6]

Dell built each desktop computer to order and carried minimal inventory in its factories, where each computer was made to order, yet the whole process from telephone call to loading onto a delivery truck took just 36 hours. Orders were instantly relayed to one of Dell's plants. Suppliers knew to deliver components within an hour after they were ordered. Components such as computer chips, boards and hard drives were kept in trucks that were backed up into delivery bays 50 feet from the beginning of the production line. After the computers were assembled, they were loaded straight onto trucks, resulting in no inventory of finished goods.[7] This attention to operational efficiency allowed Dell to achieve inventory turns of 15 times a year in 1995, compared with the 4 to 7 turns for manufacturers that sold through resellers and retailers. In an industry where component costs dropped 15 per cent or more annually, the increase in inventory turns translated into a gross margin advantage of 1.8 per cent to 3.3 per cent.[8] Dell filed process patents for the steps it had developed to build, customize and ship a computer. Whereas a standard computer assembly line involved 130 "touches," or interventions, by staff, Dell's efficiencies reduced that number to 60.[9]

By 1996, Dell.com was selling notebook computers, desktop computers and servers. The move to the Internet paid off in more than just increased revenues. It also helped the company cut costs: Its sales, general and administrative expenses were reduced from 15 per cent in 1994 to 9 per cent in 1996, with the expectation of more cost savings to come. For example, Dell created websites to show each customer the configuration of every computer bought, the price paid and a timeline of when Dell planned to introduce the next version of the computer. Dell's top 33 suppliers—from which Dell purchased 90 per cent of its goods—had a separate valuechain.dell.com website that provided data on how suppliers measured up to Dell standards, the orders they had shipped and the best way to ship.[10]

Although Dell had moved into new markets and products, its desktop and notebook computers still accounted for 83 per cent of its revenue in 1999. To complement hardware sales, Dell diversified its product lineup to include low-cost storage systems and services. In 2000, Dell made its first acquisition designed to reach its objective of being a top supplier of Internet infrastructure products. Dell was already

[6]Andy Serwer, "Michael Dell rocks," *Fortune*, May 11, 1998, p. 58.

[7]Andrew E. Serwer, "Michael Dell turns the PC world inside out," *Fortune*, September 8, 1997, p. 76.

[8]Rahul Jacob, "The resurrection of Michael Dell," *Fortune*, September 18, 1995, p. 117.

[9]Carlos Grande, "Facing up to the new computer world," *Financial Times*, February 16, 2001, FT.com, accessed October 10, 2008.

[10]Daniel Roth, "Dell's big new act," *Fortune*, December 6, 1999, p. 152.

the second-largest major supplier of servers in the world, with its PowerEdge servers accounting for 40 per cent of industry growth in the product category.

At the end of 2000, Dell was the number one firm in U.S. PCs, worldwide PCs for large and medium businesses and worldwide workstation shipments. Dell had grown at least twice the industry rate in every product category, customer segment and regional market it competed in. It had the best performing stock in the Standard & Poor's index of the 500 largest U.S. corporations in the 1990s. Dell's products won more than 300 awards for dependability and quality. In its annual report, Dell attributed these achievements to its direct business model, its focus on execution and its understanding of customer needs.

Dell's anti-hierarchical, cost-focused corporate culture was evident to customers who visited its head office. Dell's white office buildings were plain and sterile. Inside, workspace was divided into rows of cubicles, except for four offices, which were shared interchangeably by two vice-chairs, a director and Michael. The hallways were mostly devoid of art. A senior vice-president previously with Motorola recalled finding the "411" feature for directory assistance blocked because it was too expensive. She described her health insurance card as:

> barely cardboard. There's no such thing as a free lunch. The first week, I asked my assistant to lunch. I didn't realize it was going on my personal credit card. I mean, just about everything goes on my personal credit card.

Dell's hiring practices were designed to weed out anyone who would slow the company down. Newcomers were told they had to be comfortable with a high level of ambiguity. Long-time executives were hard-pressed to draw an organization chart: To make the company more nimble, departments were divided up when they became too big.[11]

Despite poor economic conditions following the end of the Internet bubble, Dell continued its growth in 2001, becoming the number one firm in global market share for the first time in its history. The company was growing beyond its reliance on desktop computers: Sales of server and storage systems, workstations, notebook computers, services and peripheral products represented more than half of Dell's revenues and two-thirds of its profit. Dell targeted market segments where profit margins were high and product standards had stabilized. According to Mort Topfer, a vice-chair formerly with Dell:

> We know what we are and what we're not. We're a really superb product integrator. We're a tremendously good sales-and-logistics company. We're not the developer of innovative technology.

A Dell mantra was that today's technology was tomorrow's commodity. Dell waited until the cost of that technology fell low enough for it to be put into computers at state-of-the-art factories and then sold direct at a cheap price, which allowed the company to gain market share.[12]

Dell continued to have the industry's lowest cost structure. Because systems were built only after they were ordered, inventory was kept to a minimum, allowing Dell to pass on to its customers any reductions in component costs. In 2001, Dell held an average five days of inventory, a record low for the firm. Customers continued to rank Dell number one in service and customer satisfaction in leading industry surveys. Interactions between Dell salespeople and their customers seemed to focus on data, not on

---

[11]Betsy Morris et al., "Can Michael Dell escape the box?" *Fortune*, October 16, 2000, p. 92.

[12]Betsy Morris et al., "Can Michael Dell escape the box?" *Fortune*, October 16, 2000, p. 92.

relationship building. As a result, not all customers at Dell were treated equally. Dell's data enabled it to know how profitable each customer was. More profitable customers received better treatment, such as special pricing or enhanced customer service. Dell even used sales and service data to identify unprofitable customer accounts to be dropped in the future.

In 2002, industry demand for computer systems and services declined due to worldwide economic weakness. Dell's revenues fell from $31.9 billion in 2001 to $31.2 billion in 2002. Yet Dell held on to its number one market share position globally. Contributing to this hold on the top spot was Dell's standing as the leading server supplier in the United States with a 27 per cent gain in customer demand; it sold twice as much storage capacity in 2002 than in 2001; and it further reduced its days of inventory to four days. Dell Direct Store stand-alone kiosks, staffed by Dell employees, began appearing in U.S. shopping malls. In April 2002, in the midst of a slumping market, Dell set an internal goal to double sales to $60 billion by 2007.

Dell continued to set records in 2003 as shipments, revenue and earnings per share increased at double-digit rates. To ensure that it continued to deliver strong results, Dell invested in leadership training programs. Dell's growth and expansion in newer markets resulted in 35 per cent of Dell's worldwide team being new to the company in the past two years. Dell emphasized its success was based on a commitment to "customers, colleagues, direct relationships, global citizenship and winning with integrity."[13]

In 2003, acknowledging its expansion into other hardware products, Dell dropped the word "computer" from its company name. Kevin Rollins, president and chief operating officer, stated that Dell aimed for 30 to 40 per cent of the global market for all the products it made. The company sought out the biggest "profit pools," picked those with close "adjacencies" to those markets Dell already served to reduce the risk of wandering into unknown territory and applied its core competencies to enter the market. According to Rollins, "Our goal is to shrink the profit pool and take the biggest slice. Our gross margins are in the 18 to 19 per cent range: We don't need 40 per cent."[14]

Dell brought its operating philosophy to its service business as well, which generated $4 billion in 2002. Michael stated:

> The fact is that you can put some mystical notion on lots of these services, but if you look at them in detail, look at what's really going on, you'll find that many of the things that [services people] are doing are highly repeatable. We are in effect commoditizing services. There is no reason why this can't occur.[15]

In 2004, Dell was the world's leading supplier of computer systems for the second consecutive year. In the U.S. market, it had been the leading supplier for the past five years. Its business was profitable in every geographic market, customer segment and product category. Its product shipments grew 26 per cent, 3 times the average of other companies. Dell coined the term "the Dell Effect" to explain the increase in customer value as a result of Dell entering a new product category: A drop in price and an increase in value. Dell identified four strategic initiatives that would help the company continue to grow: driving global growth, attaining product leadership, continuously improving the customer experience and enhancing Dell's winning culture. Product leadership was defined as "bringing to market exactly what customers want, when

---

[13]Dell 2003 Annual Report, p. 6.

[14]Richard Waters, "Dell aims to stretch its way of business," *Financial Times*, November 12, 2003, FT. com, accessed October 10, 2008.

[15]Fiona Harvey, "Michael Dell of Dell Computer," *Financial Times*, August 4, 2003, FT.com, accessed October 10, 2008.

they want it, for the best value in the industry."[16] Dell extended its product line-up to include inkjet printers, digital music players, LCD television and computer monitors, handheld computers and digital projectors.

In 2005, Dell was well ahead of its plan to reach $60 billion in sales by the end of 2007. Thus, a new goal—reaching $80 billion in sales by 2009—was set. The company seemed to be expanding beyond PCs as evidenced by the non-PC products, such as servers, storage systems, services and printers, which accounted for more than half of its revenue and an even greater portion of its operating income.

In 2006, manufacturing plants and customer service facilities were opened in Germany, Scotland, Ireland, India, El Salvador, Canada, Japan, China, the Philippines and the United States. Dell continued to attribute its success to its direct model: direct customer relationships, information over inventory, world-class manufacturing, superior customer information and execution excellence. In 2006, Dell stopped selling digital music players.

Dell Underperforms

Starting in 2006, Dell began losing share in the U.S. consumer segment to HP, Apple and other vendors. Analysts attributed Dell's share losses to a number of factors, including Dell's own internal issues (e.g., exiting the low-end of the market), growth of units sold through retail and competitive pressure from HP and Apple. Another viewpoint suggested that improving technology and decreasing cost reduced the need for customization. Many components that cost extra in the past now came as standard-issue items in retail PCs. Prices for PCs had dropped by half since the late 1990s. Dell was also losing market share as competitors imitated its supply chain innovations and lowered their prices.[17]

Michael Dell Returns as CEO

On January 31, 2007, after months of poor financial performance and negative news coverage, Kevin Rollins resigned as CEO, making way for Michael Dell to return to his former role as CEO. In addition to sluggish sales and profit, Dell was under investigation by the Securities and Exchange Commission for accounting irregularities that related to the timing and recognition of income and expenses. An investigation that had begun in August 2006 identified evidence that certain adjustments, typically at the close of the quarter, appeared to have been motivated by financial targets. The investigation also found that, in some cases, business unit personnel had not provided complete information to corporate headquarters and, in other instances, purposefully incorrect or incomplete information about these activities had been provided to internal or external auditors. To correct the irregularities, Dell restated its financial statements from 2003 to 2006. The change to net revenue for each annual period led to a reduction of less than one per cent of the previously reported revenue for the period. The cumulative change to net income from 2003 to 2006 was a reduction of between $50 million and $150 million (compared with previously reported net income of more than $12 billion for the restatement period). The adjustments did not have a material effect on the current balance sheet and did not have a material effect on cash flows.[18]

---

[16]Dell 2004 Annual Report, p. 3.

[17]Chris Nuttall and Richard Waters, "Rollins' rate sealed by falling margins," *Financial Times*, February 2, 2007, p. 24.

[18]"Dell independent investigation completed; will restate financials," http://www.dell.com/content/topics/global.aspx/corp/pressoffice/en/2007/2007_08_16_rr_000?c=us&l=en&s=corp, accessed September 1, 2008.

In 2007, Dell lost its lead as the world's top personal computer maker to Hewlett-Packard. After the first quarter of 2007, Dell's global market share of PC shipments had dropped to 15.2 per cent from 18.2 per cent a year earlier. During the same period, Hewlett-Packard's PC shipments had risen from 16.5 per cent to 19.1 per cent. The consumer market, it seemed, had changed significantly in the past three years, and Dell was trying to catch up.

Dell Adds Retail as a New Channel and Expands Its Service Offering

In June 2007, Dell began selling two models of its low-end Dimension personal computers in 3,500 Wal-Mart stores in the United States, Canada and Puerto Rico. Michael announced the new retail strategy to employees by noting that "the direct model has been a revolution, but is not a religion."[19] Speaking to a reporter, Bob Pearson, a spokesperson for Dell, added that the Wal-Mart relationship was not a pilot program. Rather, it was the "first step in our global retail strategy rollout. Stay tuned. There will definitely be more, and it will be global."[20] Dell had experimented with retail before. In the early 1990s, it had sold computers through a number of mass merchandisers, such as Best Buy, Costco and Sam's Club, but it had ended that practice in 1994, citing low profit margins.[21]

On the day of Dell's announcement, its shares closed down 1.4 per cent to US$25.89 per share. Dell's share price had never recovered since its fall from an all-time high of US$139.88 per share reached in February 1998 (see Exhibit 1 for Dell's historical share prices). Dell no longer offered detailed financial guidance—Michael called the earnings promises a trap that "caused us to, every turn of the crank, think a little bit more short-term until ultimately we sort of drove ourselves off the cliff."[22] An analyst estimated that, in 2007, Dell's consumer business was operating at breakeven, whereas profit margins at competitors' consumer segments were 5.0 per cent for HP, 3.2 per cent for Lenovo and 2.1 per cent for Acer.[23]

Observers' comments included the following:

- "We've been telling Dell for years that they need to explore a retail strategy," said an analyst from Forrester Research. "They need to learn about how retail exposes your product to a variety of customers."[24]
- "It smacks of a little desperation," said Tim Ghriskey, chief investment officer for Solaris Asset Management, a tech industry investor.[25]

By December 2007, Dell had announced that its PCs would be carried in further 6,500 locations, following partnerships with Staples, Best Buy, Gome, Carrefour,

---

[19]Erica Ogg, "What Wal-Mart means to Dell," CNET News.com, May 24, 2007.

[20]Patrick Seitz, "Hmm, hell can freeze over," *Investor's Business Daily*, May 25, 2007, p. A04.

[21]Matt Richtel, "Coming soon to Wal-Mart: 2 low-end PCs from Dell," *The New York Times*, May 25, 2007, p. 4.

[22]Jon Fortt, "Dell bleeds from its own price cuts," http://bigtech.blogs.fortune.cnn.com/2008/08/28/dell-bleeds-from-its-own-price-cuts/, accessed September 1, 2008.

[23]Chris Whitmore and Joakim Mahlberg, "Enterprise edge #140," *Deutsche Bank*, June 2, 2008, p. 5.

[24]Peter Svensson, "Dell opts to sell its PCs at Wal-Mart," *The Seattle Times*, May 25, 2007, p. D1.

[25]Loren Steffy, "Wal-Mart isn't the answer to Dell's myriad problems," *Houston Chronicle*, May 30, 2007, p. 1.

Bic Camera and Carphone Warehouse. The intention was to develop, in each of the 20 countries in which it competed, one to two retail partnerships. In addition to its retail strategy, Dell started to sell through "re-sellers," outside companies that designed and installed computer systems for small businesses and corporate clients.[26]

Dell stepped up its acquisitions of complementary firms (see Exhibit 2).

Changes to Manufacturing

In conjunction with its new focus on expanding beyond direct sales, Dell started to modify its manufacturing model to support the retail effort. Michael recruited Michael Cannon, the chief executive of Solectron, a leading contract manufacturer, to revamp Dell's supply chain.[27] Dell shifted its focus to make high-volume products, sacrificing configurability and time-to-market.

Dell was targeting $3 billion in annual cost savings by 2011 through two cost-saving initiatives: "Reduce COGS" (cost of goods sold); and "Decrease Opex" (operating expenses). Seeking a reduction in COGS, Dell would optimize its global manufacturing network, redesign its supply chain, cut development time, design for customer requirements and reduce complexity. To decrease operating expenses, Dell would reduce compensation and benefit costs, decrease headcount, improve productivity and tighten discretionary spend.

Of the $3 billion, 25 per cent, or $750 million would come from personnel reductions and the rest would come from a combination of improved product design, development and manufacturing.

Full system manufacturing would be outsourced to partners located in low-cost countries such as China (see Exhibit 3 for Dell's 2007 manufacturing footprint). These partners would build computers to retailers' forecasts, directly shipping full systems to the retailer (see Exhibit 4 for an analyst's estimation of the cost savings).

On September 5, 2008, the *Wall Street Journal* reported that Dell had approached two contract manufacturers to take over its plants. The report suggested that the discussions were at an early stage but that the move could help Dell cut costs.[28]

By the end of fiscal 2008, Dell PCs were being sold in more than 12,000 retail outlets; however, the Dell Direct Store kiosks in the United States were closed. The company also introduced a redesigned PC named "XPS One." It was "perhaps the most beautiful Dell ever, (reflecting) a sea of change in design we're bringing to customers," said Michael. "This all-in-one premium consumer electronics system offers the best in style, entertainment, design and features."[29] See Exhibits 5 and 6 for Dell's financial statements.

During the company's fiscal 2008 review, Michael stated that Dell's strategy would be to focus both on becoming more competitive by reducing costs and on growing the company in the consumer, enterprise and emerging markets. To ensure that the

---

[26]Kevin Allison, "Dell's long view irks investors," *Financial Times*, August 31, 2008, FT.com, accessed October 10, 2008.

[27]Kevin Allison, "Dell considers plan to outsource production and sell its factories," *Financial Times*, September 6, 2008, p. 19.

[28]Kevin Allison, "Dell considers plan to outsource production and sell its factories," *Financial Times*, September 6, 2008, p. 19.

[29]"A focus on growth priorities," *Fiscal 2008 in Review*, http://www.dell.com/content/topics/global.aspx/about_dell/investors/financials/index?~ ck=ln&c=us&l=en&lnki=0&s=corp, accessed August 30, 2008.

focus on products that appealed to consumers was not lost, Dell separated its product design department into consumer and commercial teams.

COMPETITION

In the second quarter of 2008, HP was the top global PC vendor with an 18.9 per cent share of units. Dell had 16.4 per cent of the market, and key competitors Acer Inc., Apple, Inc. and Lenovo had 9.5 per cent, 3.5 per cent and 7.9 per cent respectively.[30]

Acer Inc.

Acer Inc. (Acer), previously named Multitech, was founded in 1976 by seven Taiwanese entrepreneurs, who launched the company as a distributor of electronic parts and a consultant in the use of microprocessor technologies. Acer grew in size when it purchased Texas Instruments' notebook division in 1997. Acer outsourced its PC production to contract manufacturers; however, in 1999, it spun off its manufacturing arm, Wistron Corp., both to focus on Acer-brand PCs and to avoid conflicts of interest with its contract manufacturing services.[31]

Acer strengthened its U.S. presence by purchasing Gateway Inc. in 2007 and Packard Bell in 2008. In 2008, Acer was a Taiwanese multinational electronics manufacturer and the third-largest computer manufacturer in the world after Hewlett-Packard and Dell. Its product lineup included desktop and notebook PCs, personal digital assistants (PDAs), servers and storage, peripherals and e-business services for business, government, education and home users.[32]

Acer, which sold its products mainly through retail channels, had three branded offerings. Its Acer brand competed on price, typically offering its products at less than US$1,200.[33] The company achieved these lower prices by focusing on cost management both in its manufacturing operations and in the Linux operating system it chose to install on notebooks. Acer's Gateway, Packard Bell and eMachine brands were positioned in the medium- to high-end range. According to Acer, the decision to choose Linux's operating system over Microsoft's reduced costs, decreased computer boot-up to 15 seconds and extended battery life from 5 to 7 hours.[34]

Apple, Inc.

Founded in 1976, Apple Inc. (Apple) designed, manufactured and marketed desktop and notebook computers, portable digital music players, mobile phones, software, services, peripherals and networking solutions. Apple targeted the premium consumer (75 per cent of sales), the education sector (10 to 15 per cent of sales) and creative professional market (10 to 15 per cent of sales) with its lineup of stylish

---

[30]Chris Whitmore and Joakim Mahlberg, "Enterprise edge #140," *Deutsche Bank*, August 4, 2008, p. 3.

[31]Bear, Stearns Analyst Report on, "Acer Inc.," October 9, 2006, p. 15.

[32]Wikipedia, entry for "Acer Inc.," http://en.wikipedia.org/wiki/Acer_Inc., accessed September 9, 2008.

[33]SinoPac Securities Analyst Report on, "Acer," May 22, 2008, p. 5.

[34]Iain Thomson, "Acer bets big on Linux," http://www.vnunet.com/vnunet/news/2218172/acer-pushes-linux-hard, accessed October 6, 2008.

desktop and notebook computers.[35] For example, in the consumer desktop market, Apple's lineup did not offer a low-cost model, despite the 83 per cent of total consumer market units being accounted for in the sub-$1,000 segment. Similarly, in the consumer notebook market, Apple was largely absent from the sub-$1,200 segments of the market, which excluded it from 70 per cent of the total market.[36] After experimenting with failed consumer products, such as digital cameras, portable CD audio players, speakers, video consoles and TV appliances, Apple launched the iMac in 1998, returning the company to profitability for the first time since 1993. In May 2001, Apple opened the first Apple retail stores in Virginia and California. The same year, it introduced the iPod portable digital audio player, of which 100 million units were sold by 2008.

Apple's PC lineup included the iMac and the MacBook Air, a popular, ultra-thin notebook introduced in January 2008. Apple products were available at mass merchandisers, specialty stores and through the company's 200-store network of Apple retail stores. Apple was known in the industry for its aesthetic design and distinctive advertising campaigns.[37] On the strength of its design, Apple achieved, from its lineup of computers, gross margins in the 30 per cent range, exceeding the PC industry average by more than 1,000 basis points.[38]

Apple generated half its revenue directly through its retail stores, direct sales force and online stores. The balance of sales was generated from third-party wholesalers and resellers. The company operated 208 retail locations and planned to increase the number of locations to 242 by the end of fiscal 2008. Apple's computers were sold at a total of approximately 10,000 retail locations worldwide.[39] Apple's key differentiator was its ability to design and market a total product. It was the only company in the computer industry to design its own operating system, hardware, applications and related services. The result was often a product that was better integrated, easier to use and more aesthetically consistent than its competitors'. Since the launch of its distinctly designed iMac computers in 1998, Apple had tried to regain its footing in the PC industry by working with developers, investing in branding campaigns and offering Windows users in-depth Mac training.[40]

These efforts seemed to have little impact until, in 2005, Apple announced its intent to switch to the Intel platform from the IBM PowerPC architecture. By embracing the industry standard, Apple attracted a wider array of PC-centric software developers. Second, Apple launched Boot Camp in 2006, a software utility that allowed Mac users to run the Windows operating system on Mac hardware. Third, it enabled support for Windows through third-party virtualization software. These three efforts reduced the perceived switching costs for Windows users.[41] Apple's products were mainly produced by Taiwanese contract manufacturers, such as Hon Hai Precision Industries, Quanta and Pegatron.[42]

---

[35]Yair Reiner and Michael Suh, "Apple Inc.," *Oppenheimer*, May 21, 2008, p. 9.

[36]Bill Shope et al., "Apple Inc.," *Credit Suisse*, August 7, 2008, p. 20.

[37]Anne Fisher, "America's most admired companies," *Fortune*, March 17, 2008, pp. 65–67.

[38]Bill Shope et al., "Apple Inc.," *Credit Suisse*, August 7, 2008, p. 19.

[39]Yair Reiner and Michael Suh, "Apple Inc.," *Oppenheimer*, May 21, 2008, pp. 12–13.

[40]Yair Reiner and Michael Suh, "Apple Inc.," *Oppenheimer*, May 21, 2008, p. 9.

[41]Bill Shope et al., "Apple Inc.," *Credit Suisse*, August 7, 2008, p. 25.

[42]Yair Reiner and Michael Suh, "Apple Inc.," *Oppenheimer*, May 21, 2008, p. 22.

Hewlett-Packard

Hewlett-Packard (HP) grew from its roots as an engineering and medical company to an information technology corporation. In 1999, HP spun off its engineering and medical businesses as Agilent. In 2002, HP merged with Compaq Computers, becoming a major player in desktops, notebooks and servers.

Mark Hurd, HP's current CEO, refocused the company away from building and marketing the PC as a commodity item. Besides making PCs more attractive to consumers, HP included user-friendly features, such as the ability to check e-mail and appointments without having to wait for the machine to boot up. HP's marketing team pitched their PCs as a personal reflection of consumers' desires and needs. Using the tagline "The computer is personal again," HP developed advertisements featuring entertainers such as Shawn "Jay-Z" Carter.[43] HP's Personal Systems Group (PSG) included sales of PCs, handheld devices, digital entertainment systems, calculators and related accessories, software and services. Desktops and notebooks represented more than 90 per cent of PSG's revenue and gross profit.[44] In 2007, PSG represented approximately 35 per cent of HP's revenues and 18.3 per cent of operating profits.

HP branded its PCs based on the customer segment served. The company's HP Compaq products were sold into the commercial market, while its HP Pavilion and Compaq Presario products targeted consumers. In the consumer segment, the HP Pavilion line was the high-end brand, positioned above the Compaq Presario products. Analysts expected HP's PSG group to maintain operating margins of between 5.1 and 5.4 per cent from 2008 to 2010. HP's PCs were sold through a retail network of approximately 80,000 stores. In PCs, HP's large presence in the consumer retail market for notebooks positioned the company to take advantage of industry growth in the shift to mobility. In addition, the majority of HP's PC growth in recent years was a result of sales through its indirect distribution channel—70,000 third-party resellers who sold HP services as part of their solutions.[45,46]

HP outsourced most of its manufacturing to contract manufacturers, including Flextronics, Celestica, Solectron, Sanmina and Jabil Curcuit for desktop PCs and servers, and Taiwan-based original design manufacturers (ODMs) Quanta, Inventec, Wistron and Compal for notebook PCs. HP utilized Intel and AMD processors for the company's desktop and notebook product lines.[47] Hard disk drives were supplied by Seagate and Western Digital. HP relied on Intel, AMD, Canon and Hitachi for much of its research and development (R&D). Given that the company outsourced the bulk of its manufacturing and R&D, HP could manage costs and avoid significant margin decreases in a slowing demand environment.[48] See Exhibit 7 for an overview of HP's supply chain.

From 2004 to 2006, PSG's margin improved by 300 basis points, a result of increased leverage with Intel as HP started to use AMD processors (150 basis points);

[43]"BusinessWeek's top global brands–HP stages a turnaround," *The Digital Mindset Blog*, http://www.communities.hp.com/online/blogs/kintz/archive/2007/07/30/HPPost4045.aspx, accessed September 1, 2008.

[44]Jesse Tortora, "Hewlett-Packard Co.," Prudential Equity Group, LLC., October 19, 2006, p. 17.

[45]Bill Shope et al., "Hewlett-Packard," *Credit Suisse*, August 7, 2008, p. 5.

[46]"HP services partners," http://h20219.www2.hp.com/services/cache/78952-0-0-225-121.html, accessed September 22, 2008.

[47]Jesse Tortora, "Hewlett-Packard Co.," Prudential Equity Group, LLC., October 19, 2006, p. 17.

[48]Jesse Tortora, "Hewlett-Packard Co.," Prudential Equity Group, LLC., October 19, 2006, p. 26.

supply chain improvements and leveraging of purchasing across divisions to secure lower pricing on components such as hard disk drives, panels and memory (100 basis points) and a broader selection of notebooks (50 basis points).[49] To enhance its service business, HP announced in May 2008 that it was purchasing EDS for $13.9 billion. On one hand, EDS enhanced HP's offerings in IT and applications outsourcing. There was also the potential for significant cost synergies, or shifting general and administrative costs offshore. In addition, synergies would come from improvements in supply chain, real estate and process improvement. On the other hand, analysts believed that turning EDS around would be a distraction to HP.[50]

Lenovo Group Limited

Lenovo Group Limited (Lenovo) was the largest PC manufacturer in China and the fourth-largest PC manufacturer worldwide after HP, Dell and Acer. Formerly named Legend Group Ltd. and New Technology Developer Incorporated, the company was restructured and separated into two entities. One of the entities, Lenovo, became a PC manufacturer. In 2005, Lenovo purchased IBM's PC Division for $1.27 billion and, post-transaction, IBM held an 18.9 per cent share in Lenovo. For 18 months after the transaction, Lenovo had the right to use the IBM brand name, and it owned the "Think" brand. Following the transaction, Lenovo hired six key executives from Dell with supply chain expertise. One of the Dell executives, William Amelio, became Lenovo's new president and chief executive officer.

A key change for Lenovo, after the IBM PC Division purchase, was that notebook computer sales became the company's largest contributor, accounting for about half of revenues in 2006, a striking contrast from late 2004, when Lenovo did not sell notebooks. More than 50 per cent of Lenovo's revenues were generated from the Asia Pacific market, where PC sales growth was twice the global average.[51] Lenovo sold computers to large businesses and to consumers via both online sales and distribution to retailers. Lenovo's global advertising operations were centralized in Bangalore, India, to leverage the low-cost skilled labour base in the region.[52] Logistics, sales and warranty services were brought in house.[53] To maintain the quality and look of its ThinkPad computers, Lenovo's in-house manufacturing was supported by a Japan-based research and development centre.[54]

Three-quarters of Lenovo's manufacturing took place at its 10 plants around the world. Lenovo had primary PC manufacturing plants in China, the United States, Mexico, Brazil, Scotland, Hungary, India, Malaysia, Japan and Australia. If deemed necessary, Lenovo would contract manufacturers on a temporary basis until the production could be transferred to a Lenovo plant. Analysts expected that cost savings from procurement and reductions in sales, general and administrative expenses would boost operating margins from 1.1 per cent in 2006 to 3.4 per cent in 2011.[55]

---

[49]Jesse Tortora, "Hewlett-Packard Co.," Prudential Equity Group, LLC., October 19, 2006, p. 30.

[50]Bill Shope et al., "Hewlett-Packard," *Credit Suisse*, August 7, 2008, p, 15.

[51]Manish Nigam and Venugopal Garre, "Lenovo Group," *Credit Suisse*, July 31, 2006, p. 6.

[52]David Hannon, "Lenovo does global supply chain right," http://www.purchasing.com/article/CA6489110.html, accessed September 22, 2008.

[53]Leon Chik, "Lenovo Group," *HSBC*, February 1, 2007, p. 4.

[54]Leon Chik, "Lenovo Group," *HSBC*, February 1, 2007, p. 12.

[55]Leon Chik, "Lenovo Group," *HSBC*, September 13, 2006, p. 22.

PREPARING FOR THE INVESTORS' MEETING

Like Steve Jobs' return to Apple Inc., Michael Dell's return to Dell had sparked significant changes to its business with the objective of improving its stock price. However, a year-and-a-half later, the market had not responded favourably to Michael's return. During Dell's fiscal 2008 review, Michael acknowledged that, despite the growth in revenue in the past 10 years, Dell had lost its way:

> It is fair to say that as we got to the end of that 10-year period, our strategy wasn't working as well as it had previously. Moreover, as we evolved, we lost focus and allowed our cost structure to become non-competitive.[56]

Michael seemed to be optimistic, however, that the turnaround effort was making progress:

> Since our inception, Dell has the availability of technology for millions of businesses and enabled millions of people to get online for the first time. Now, more than ever, we are advancing this mission through new ways of listening to and reaching customers, and by expanding and customizing our product and service portfolios. Dell is evolving at one of the most exciting points in our industry's history. Our team has a clear focus on what we must do to increase our growth and competitiveness. We are committed to sustaining and building on the gains we made in fiscal 2008.[57]

To prepare for the investors' meeting, the senior executive started to assemble detailed speaking notes that described Dell's competitive advantage, the evolution of its business model and its prospects for the future.

---

[56]http://www.dell.com/content/topics/global.aspx/about_dell/investors/financials/index?c=us&l=en&s=corp, accessed October 10, 2008.

[57]"A clear focus and inspiration," *Fiscal 2008 in Review*, http://www.dell.com/content/topics/global.aspx/about_dell/investors/financials/index?c=us&l=en&s=corp, accessed September 20, 2008.

EXHIBIT 1   Dell Inc.'s Historical Share Prices

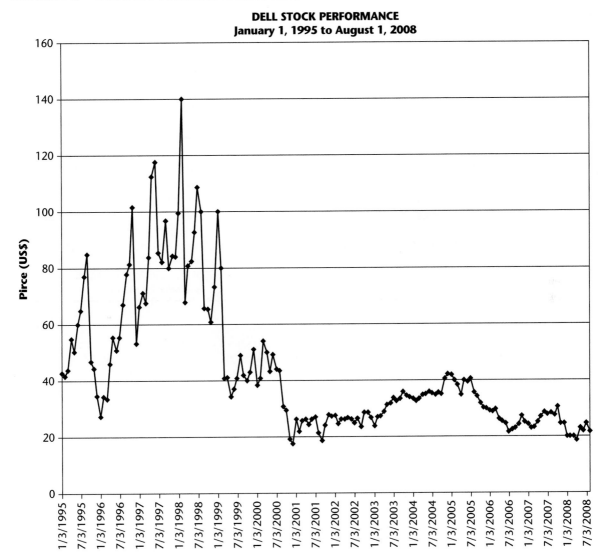

DELL STOCK PERFORMANCE
January 1, 1995 to August 1, 2008

Source: ca.finance.yahoo.com, accessed August 15, 2008.

EXHIBIT 2   Acquisitions of Complementary Firms

To expand its menu of services, Dell stepped up its acquisitions of complementary firms:

Date	Company	Product or service
May 2006	Alienware	High-end computers targeted at the gaming market
November 2006	ACS	IT services provider focusing on Microsoft, VMware and RSA Security
June 2007	Silverback Technologies	Remote management services sold through resellers
August 2007	Zing	Wi-Fi music players
August 2007	ASAP	IT infrastructure management services
November 2007	Everdream	Remote management services sold through resellers
November 2007	EqualLogic	Storage area network management services
February 2008	MessageOne	E-mail continuity, compliance, archiving and disaster recovery

EXHIBIT 3   Dell Inc.'s Manufacturing, Distribution and Design Facilities

Americas properties

Description	Principal locations	Owned (square feet)	Leased (square feet)
Headquarters	Round Rock, Texas	2.1 million	
Business Centres	• Canada–Edmonton and Ottawa • El Salvador–San Salvador • Oklahoma–Oklahoma City • Panama–Panama City • Tennessee–Nashville • Texas–Austin and Round Rock	1.1 million	1.9 million
Manufacturing and distribution	Brazil–Hortolândia • Florida–Miami (Alienware) • North Carolina–Winston-Salem • Ohio–West Chester • Tennessee–Lebanon and Nashville • Texas–Austin	2.9 million	700,000
Design Centres	Texas–Austin and Round Rock	700,000	100,000

Europe, Middle East and Africa properties

Description	Principal locations	Owned (square feet)	Leased (square feet)
Headquarters	Bracknell, England	100,000	100,000
Business Centres	• Germany–Halle • France–Montpellier • Ireland–Dublin and Limerick • Morocco–Casablanca • Slovakia–Bratislava	400,000	1.5 million
Manufacturing and distribution	• Limerick and Athlone (Alienware) • Poland - Lodz	1.0 million	

Asia Pacific and Japan properties

Description	Principal locations	Owned (square feet)	Leased (square feet)
Headquarters	Singapore		50,000
Business Centres	• China–Dalian and Xiamen • India–Bangalore, Gurgaon, Hyderabad and Mohali • Japan–Kawasaki • Malaysia–Penang and Kuala Lumpur • Philippines–Metro Manila	300,000	3.2 million
Manufacturing and distribution	• China–Xiamen • Malaysia–Penang • India–Chennai	1.1 million	150,000
Design Centres	• China–Shanghai • India–Bangalore • Singapore • Taiwan–Taipei		500,000

Source: Dell 2008 10-K filings.

EXHIBIT 4   Cost Savings from Manufacturing in China

	Typical cost structure for PC manufacturers	Savings from manufacturing in China	Total cost savings
Materials	75%	15%	11.3%
Labour (direct/indirect)	12%	75%	9.0%
Overhead/equipment	7%	25%	1.8%
Other	6%	15%	0.9%
Total	**100%**		22.9%

Source: Deutsche Bank estimates and company reports.

EXHIBIT 5 Dell Inc.'s Balance Sheets, 1996 to 2008

	2008	2007	2006	2005	2004	2003	2002	2001	2000	1999	1998	1997	1996
Assets													
Total current assets	19,880,000	19,939,000	17,706,000	16,897,000	10,633,000	8,924,000	7,877,000	9,491,000	7,681,000	6,339,000	3,912,000	2,747,000	1,957,000
Total long-term assets	7,681,000	5,696,000	5,403,000	6,318,000	8,678,000	6,546,000	5,658,000	3,944,000	3,790,000	538,000	356,000	246,000	191,000
Total assets	27,561,000	25,635,000	23,109,000	23,215,000	19,311,000	15,470,000	13,535,000	13,435,000	11,471,000	6,877,000	4,268,000	2,993,000	2,148,000
Liabilities													
Total current liabilities	18,526,000	17,791,000	15,927,000	14,136,000	10,896,000	8,933,000	7,519,000	6,543,000	5,192,000	3,695,000	2,697,000	1,658,000	939,000
Total long-term liabilities	5,206,000	3,405,000	3,053,000	2,594,000	2,135,000	1,664,000	1,322,000	1,270,000	971,000	861,000	278,000	250,000	236,000
Total liabilities	23,732,000	21,196,000	18,980,000	16,730,000	13,031,000	10,597,000	8,841,000	7,813,000	6,163,000	4,556,000	2,975,000	1,908,000	1,175,000
Shareholders' equity													
Total equity	3,829,000	4,439,000	4,129,000	6,485,000	6,280,000	4,873,000	4,694,000	5,622,000	5,308,000	2,321,000	1,293,000	1,085,000	973,000
Total liabilities & equity	27,561,000	25,635,000	23,109,000	23,215,000	19,311,000	15,470,000	13,535,000	13,435,000	11,471,000	6,877,000	4,268,000	2,993,000	2,148,000

Source: Mergentonline, SEC filings.

EXHIBIT 6 Dell Inc.'s Income Statements, 1996 to 2008

	2008	2007	2006	2005	2004	2003	2002	2001	2000	1999	1998	1997	1996
Revenue	61,133,000	57,420,000	55,908,000	49,205,000	41,444,000	35,404,000	31,168,000	31,888,000	25,265,000	18,243,000	12,327,000	7,759,000	5,296,000
Cost of goods sold	49,462,000	47,904,000	45,958,000	40,190,000	33,892,000	29,055,000	25,661,000	25,445,000	20,047,000	14,137,000	9,605,000	6,093,000	4,229,000
Gross profit	11,671,000	9,516,000	9,950,000	9,015,000	7,552,000	6,349,000	5,507,000	6,443,000	5,218,000	4,106,000	2,722,000	1,666,000	1,067,000
Selling, general & administrative	7,538,000	5,948,000	5,140,000	4,298,000	3,544,000	3,050,000	2,784,000	3,193,000	2,387,000	1,788,000	1,202,000	826,000	595,000
Other operating expenses	86,000	27,000	70,000	129,000	201,000	244,000	695,000	347,000	412,000	169,000	137,000	79,000	57,000
Depreciation & amortization	607,000	471,000	393,000	334,000	263,000	211,000	239,000	240,000	156,000	103,000	67,000	47,000	38,000
Operating income	3,440,000	3,070,000	4,347,000	4,254,000	3,544,000	2,844,000	1,789,000	2,663,000	2,263,000	2,046,000	1,316,000	714,000	377,000
Net income	2,947,000	2,583,000	3,572,000	3,043,000	2,645,000	2,122,000	1,246,000	2,177,000	1,666,000	1,460,000	944,000	518,000	272,000

Source: Mergentonline, SEC filings.

EXHIBIT 7   Hewlett-Packard Supply Chain Overview

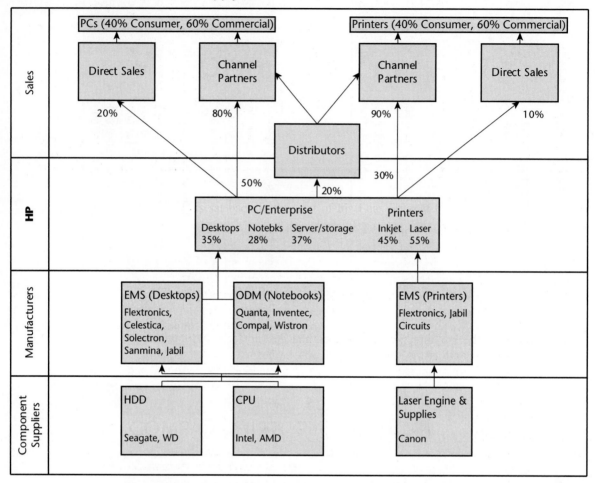

Source: Jesse Tortora, "Hewlett-Packard Co.," Prudential Equity Group, LLC, October 19, 2006, p. 25.

Coral Divers Resort (Revised)

Jonathon Greywell locked the door on the equipment shed and began walking back along the boat dock to his office. He was thinking about the matters that had weighed heavily on his mind during the last few months. Over the years, Greywell had established a solid reputation for the Coral Divers Resort as a safe and knowledgeable scuba diving resort that offered not only diving, but also a beachfront location. Because Coral Divers Resort was a small, but well-regarded, all-around dive resort in the Bahamas, many divers had come to prefer Greywell's resort to the other crowded tourist resorts in the Caribbean.

However, over the last three years, revenues had declined; for 2008, bookings were flat for the first half of the year. Greywell felt he needed to do something to increase business before the situation worsened. He wondered whether he should add some specialized features to the resort to help distinguish it from the competition. One approach would be to focus on family outings.

Rascals in Paradise (Rascals), a travel company that specialized in family diving vacations, had offered to help him convert his resort to specialize in family diving vacations. Rascals had shown him the industry demographics indicating that families were a growing market segment (see Exhibit 1) and suggested the changes that would need to be made at the resort. Rascals had even offered to create children's menus and to show the cook how to prepare the meals.

Another potential strategy for the Coral Divers Resort was to focus on adventure diving. Other resort operators in the Bahamas were offering adventure-oriented deep-depth dives, shark dives and night dives. The basic ingredients for adventure diving (i.e., reef sharks in the waters near New Providence and famous deep-water coral walls) were already in place. However, either of these strategies, creating a family vacation resort or an adventure diving resort, would require changes and additions to the

Professors Paul W. Beamish and Kent E. Neupert prepared this case with assistance from Andreas Schotter solely to provide material for class discussion. The authors do not intend to illustrate either effective or ineffective handling of a managerial situation. The authors may have disguised certain names and other identifying information to protect confidentiality.

IVEY

Richard Ivey School of Business
The University of Western Ontario

current operations. Greywell was not sure whether any of the changes was worth the time and investment or whether he should instead try to improve on what he was already doing.

A final option, and one that he had only recently considered, was to leave New Providence and relocate elsewhere. At issue here was how much he might be able to recover if he sold Coral Divers Resort and whether better opportunities existed elsewhere in the Bahamas or around the Caribbean.

SCUBA DIVING INDUSTRY OVERVIEW

Skin diving was an underwater activity of ancient origin in which a diver swam freely, unencumbered by lines or air hoses. Modern skin divers used three pieces of basic equipment: a face mask for vision, webbed rubber fins for propulsion and a snorkel tube for breathing just below the water's surface. The snorkel was a J-shaped plastic tube fitted with a mouthpiece. When the opening of the snorkel was above water, a diver was able to breathe. When diving to greater depths, divers needed to hold their breath; otherwise, water entered the mouth through the snorkel.

Scuba diving provided divers with the gift of time to relax and explore the underwater world without surfacing for their next breath. Scuba was an acronym for self-contained underwater breathing apparatus. Although attempts to perfect this type of apparatus dated from the early 20th century, it was not until 1943 that the most famous scuba, or Aqualung, was invented by the Frenchmen Jacques-Yves Cousteau and Emil Gagnan. The Aqualung made recreational diving possible for millions of non-professional divers. Although some specially trained commercial scuba divers descended below 100 metres (328 feet) for various kinds of work, recreational divers never descended below a depth of 40 metres (130 feet) because of increased risk of nitrogen narcosis, an oxygen toxicity that causes blackouts and convulsions.

The scuba diver wore a tank that carried a supply of pressurized breathing gas, either air or a mixture of oxygen and other gases. The heart of the breathing apparatus was the breathing regulator and the pressure-reducing mechanisms that delivered gas to the diver on each inhalation. In the common scuba used in recreational diving, the breathing medium was air. As the diver inhaled, a slight negative pressure occurred in the mouthpiece, prompting the opening of the valve that delivers the air. When the diver stopped inhaling, the valve closed, and a one-way valve allowed the exhaled breath to escape as bubbles into the water. By using a tank and regulator, a diver could make longer and deeper dives and still breathe comfortably.

Along with scuba gear and its tanks of compressed breathing gases, the scuba diver's essential equipment included a soft rubber mask with a large faceplate; long, flexible swimming flippers for the feet; a buoyancy compensator device (known as a BC or BCD); a weight belt; a waterproof watch; a wrist compass; and a diver's knife. For protection from colder water, neoprene-coated foam rubber wet suits were typically worn.

Certification Organizations[1]

Several international and domestic organizations trained and certified scuba divers. The most well-known organizations were PADI (Professional Association of Diving

---

[1]Information on the certifying agencies has been drawn from materials published by the various organizations.

Instructors), NAUI (National Association of Underwater Instructors), SSI (Scuba Schools International) and NASDS (National Association of Scuba Diving Schools). Of these, PADI was the largest certifying organization.

Professional Association of Diving Instructors The Professional Association of Diving Instructors (PADI), founded in 1967, was the largest recreational scuba diver training organization in the world. PADI divers comprised 70 per cent of all divers. The diving certificate issued by PADI through its instructors was acknowledged worldwide, thus enabling PADI-certified divers wide access to diving expeditions, tank filling and diving equipment rental and purchase. Worldwide, PADI had certified more than 16.5 million recreational divers. In 2007, PADI International issued nearly 1 million new certifications.

In addition to PADI's main headquarters in Santa Ana, California, PADI operated regional offices in Australia, Canada, Switzerland, Japan, Sweden, the United Kingdom and the United States. PADI offices served more than 130,000 individual professional members and more than 5,300 dive centres and resorts in more than 180 countries and territories. Translations of PADI materials were available in more than 26 languages. PADI comprised four groups: PADI Retail Association, PADI International Resort Association, professional members and PADI Alumni Association. The three association groups emphasized the "three E's" of recreational diving: education, equipment and experience. By supporting each facet, PADI provided holistic leadership to advance recreational scuba diving and snorkel swimming to equal status with other major leisure activities, while maintaining and improving the organization's excellent safety record. PADI courses ranged from entry levels (such as scuba diver and open water diver certifications) to master scuba diver certification and a range of instructor certificates. Via its affiliate, Diving Science and Technology (DSAT), PADI also offered various technical diver courses, including decompression diving, Trimix diving and gas blending for deep sea diving. In 1995, PADI founded Project AWARE to help conserve underwater environments. Project AWARE information was integrated into most courses, and divers were offered the opportunity to exchange their standard certificate for an AWARE certificate by making a donation to the program when applying for a new certificate.

National Association of Underwater Instructors The National Association of Underwater Instructors (NAUI) first began operation in 1960. The organization was formed by a nationally recognized group of instructors known as the National Diving Patrol. Since its beginning, NAUI had been active worldwide, certifying sport divers in various levels of proficiency from basic skin diver to instructor. NAUI regularly conducted specialty courses for cave diving, ice diving, wreck diving, underwater navigation and search and recovery.

Industry Demographics[2]

Scuba diving had grown steadily in popularity over the last 20 years. From 1989 until 2001, certifications had increased an average of 10 per cent each year; and increases had continued to be steady, despite more difficulties surrounding air travel because of the events of September 11, 2001, and the bleaching impact of climate change on

---

[2]This section draws from results of surveys conducted by scuba diving organizations and publications for the years 1991 to 2007.

coral reefs. In 2007, the total number of certified divers worldwide was estimated to be more than 22 million. The National Sporting Goods Association, which conducted an annual sports participation survey, projected the number of active divers in the United States at 2.1 million, and market share data from resort destinations showed 1.5 million active travelling U.S.-based scuba divers, not including resort divers.

Approximately 65 per cent of the certified scuba divers were male, 35 per cent were female and about half of all scuba divers were married. Approximately 70 per cent of scuba divers were between the ages of 18 and 34, and approximately 25 per cent were between the ages of 35 and 49 (see Exhibit 2). Scuba divers were generally well educated: 80 per cent had a college education. Overwhelmingly, scuba divers were employed in professional, managerial and technical occupations and earned an average annual household income of $75,000, well above the national average. Forty-five per cent of divers travelled most often with their families, and 40 per cent travelled most often with friends or informal groups.

People were attracted to scuba diving for various reasons; seeking adventure and being with nature were the two most often cited reasons (identified by more than 75 per cent of divers). Socializing, stress relief and travel also were common motivations. Two-thirds of all divers travelled overseas on diving trips once every three years, whereas 60 per cent travelled domestically on dive trips each year. On average, divers spent $2,816 on dive trips annually, with an average equipment investment of $2,300. Aside from upgrades and replacements, the equipment purchase could be considered a one-time cost. Warm-water diving locations were generally chosen two-to-one over cold-water diving sites. Outside of the continental United States, the top three diving destinations were Cozumel in Mexico, the Cayman Islands and the Bahamas.

According to a consumer survey, the strongest feelings that divers associated with their scuba diving experiences were excitement and peacefulness. In a recent survey, these two themes drew an equal number of responses; however, the two responses had very distinct differences. The experience of excitement suggested a need for stimulation, whereas experience of peacefulness suggested relaxation and escape. Visual gratification (beauty) was another strong motivation for divers, as were the feelings of freedom, weightlessness and flying.

Under PADI regulations, divers needed to be at least 10 years old to be eligible for certification by the majority of scuba training agencies. At age 10, a child could earn a junior diver certification. Divers with this certification had to meet the same standards as an open water diver but generally had to be accompanied on dives by a parent or another certified adult. At age 15, the junior diver certification could be upgraded to open water status, which required a skills review and evaluation. Youth divers required pre-dive waivers and release forms signed by a parent or guardian until they reached age 18. Recently, PADI added a so-called bubble-maker program, which allowed children as young as age 8 to start scuba diving at a maximum depth of 2 metres (6 feet). The program was conducted by PADI instructors in sessions that typically lasted one hour, and no pre-training was required. However, few dive centres had adopted the program because of the additional investment in special child-sized equipment and the low student-to-instructor ratio, which made the program uneconomical. On the other hand, children's programs increased the family friendliness of scuba diving.

In general, most dive centres maintained a cautious approach to young divers, based on the concept of readiness to dive. An individual's readiness to dive was determined by physical, mental and emotional maturity. Physical readiness was the easiest factor to assess: Was the child large enough and strong enough to handle scuba equipment? A regular air tank and weight belt can weigh more than 40 lbs. (18 kgs).

Mental readiness referred to whether the child had the academic background and conceptual development to understand diving physics and perform the arithmetic required for certification. The arithmetic understanding was needed to determine a diver's allowable bottom time, which required factoring in depth, number of dives and length of dives. Emotional readiness was the greatest concern. Would the junior diver accept the responsibility of being a dive buddy? Divers never dived alone, and dive buddies needed to look out for and rely on each other. Did young divers comprehend the safety rules of diving and willingly follow them? Most dive centres therefore accepted students from age 10, but the final determination of readiness to dive rested with the scuba instructor. Instructors were trained to evaluate the readiness of all students before completion of the course work and would only award a certification to those who earned it, regardless of age.

DIVING IN THE BAHAMAS[3]

New Providence Island, the Bahamas

New Providence Island was best known for its major population centre, Nassau, a community whose early development was based on its superb natural harbour. As the capital of the Bahamas, it was the seat of government and home to 400 banks, elegant homes, ancient forts and a wide variety of duty-free shopping. Nassau had the island's most developed tourist infrastructure, exemplified by its elegant resort hotels, casinos, cabaret shows and cruise ship docks. More than two-thirds of the population of the Bahamas lived on the island of New Providence, and most of these 180,000 people lived in or near Nassau, on the northeast corner of the island.

Because thousands of vacationers took resort-based diving courses (introductory scuba courses taught in resort pools), Nassau had become known as a destination for both an exploratory first dive and more advanced diving. As a result, many professional dive operations were located in the in the Nassau area (see Exhibit 3). Although all dive operations offered resort courses, many also offered a full menu of dive activities designed for more advanced divers. Within a 30-minute boat ride of most operations were shipwrecks, beautiful shallow reefs and huge schools of fish.

In contrast to the bustle of Nassau, the south side of New Providence Island was quieter and more laid back. Large tracts of pine trees and rolling hills dominated the central regions, while miles of white sand beach surrounded the island. At the west end of the island was Lyford Cay, an exclusive residential area. Nearby, the Coral Harbour area offered easy access to the sea. Although golf and tennis were available, the primary attractions were the good scuba diving and the top-quality dive operators.

The southwest side of the island had been frequently used as an underwater film set. The "Bond wrecks" were popular diving destinations for divers and operators. The Vulcan Bomber used in the James Bond film *Thunderball* had aged into a framework draped with colorful gorgonians and sponges. The freighter, Tears of Allah, where James Bond eluded the tiger shark in *Never Say Never Again,* remained a popular dive attraction in just 40 feet of water. The photogenic appeal of this wreck had improved with age as marine life increasingly congregated on this artificial reef.

---

[3]The content in this section is based on information drawn from *The islands of the Bahamas dive guide*, published by the Bahamas Ministry of Tourism, Commonwealth of the Bahamas, in conjunction with the Bahamas Diving Association, retrieved from http://www.bahamasdiving.com/6729/with_flash/html/index-5.html, accessed on April 10, 2008.

Natural underwater attractions, such as Shark Wall and Shark Buoy, were popular dive spots. Drop-off dives, such as Tunnel Wall, featured a network of crevices and tunnels beginning in 30 feet of water and exiting along the vertical wall at 70 or 80 feet. Southwest Reef offered magnificent coral heads in only 15 to 30 feet of water, with schooling grunts, squirrelfish and barracuda. A favourite of the shallow reef areas was Goulding Cay, where Elkhorn coral reached nearly to the surface.

TYPES OF DIVING

A wide array of diving activities was available in the Bahamas, including shark dives, wreck dives, wall dives, reef dives, drift dives and night dives. Some illustrative examples follow.

Shark Diving

The top three operators of shark dives in the Caribbean were located in the Bahamas. Although shark diving trips varied depending on the dive operators, one common factor was shared by all shark dives in the Bahamas: the Caribbean reef shark (Carcharhinus perezi). When the dive boat reached the shark site, the sound of the motor acted as a dinner bell. Even before the divers entered the water, sharks gathered for their handouts.

Long Island in the Bahamas was the first area to promote shark feed dives on a regular basis. This method began 20 years ago and had remained relatively unchanged. The feed was conducted as a feeding frenzy. Sharks circled as divers entered the water. After the divers positioned themselves with their backs to a coral wall, the feeder entered the water with a bucket of fish, which was placed in the sand in front of the divers, and the action developed quickly. At Walker's Cay, in Abaco, the method was similar except for the number and variety of sharks in the feed. Although Caribbean reef sharks made up the majority of sharks seen, lemon sharks, bull sharks, hammerhead sharks and other species also appeared.

The shark feed off Freeport, Grand Bahama, was an organized event in which the sharks were fed either by hand or off the point of a polespear. The divers were arranged in a semi-circle with safety divers guarding the viewers and the feeder positioned at the middle of the group. If the sharks became unruly, the food was withheld until they calmed down. The sharks then went into a regular routine of circling, taking their place in line and advancing to receive the food. Although the sharks often came within touching distance, most divers resisted the temptation to reach out.

Shark Wall, on the southwest side of New Providence, was a pristine drop-off decorated with masses of colourful sponges along the deep-water abyss known as the Tongue of the Ocean. Divers positioned themselves along sand patches among the coral heads in about 50 feet of water as Caribbean reef sharks and an occasional bull shark or lemon shark cruised mid-water in anticipation of a free handout. During the feeding period, the bait was controlled and fed from a polespear by an experienced feeder. Usually 6 to 12 sharks were present, ranging from 4 to 8 feet in length. Some operators made two dives to this site, allowing divers to cruise the wall with the sharks in a more natural way before the feeding dive.

The Shark Buoy, also on the southwest side of New Providence, was tethered in 6,000 feet of water. Its floating surface mass attracted a wide variety of ocean marine life, such as dolphin fish, jacks, rainbow runners and silky sharks. The silky sharks were typically small, three to five feet long, but swarmed in schools of 6 to 20, with the sharks swimming up to the divemaster's hands to grab the bait.

From the operator's standpoint, the only special equipment needed for shark dives were a chain mail diving suit for the feeder's protection, feeding apparatus and intestinal fortitude. The thrill of diving among sharks was the main attraction for the divers. For the most part, the dives were safe; only the feeder took an occasional nip from an excited shark.

Recently, shark feeding had come under attack from environmentalists for causing a change in the feeding behaviour of sharks, which had led to the loss of their natural fear of humans. In addition, some rare but fatal accidents had been prominently exposed through TV news channels and newspapers. For example, in 2001, Krishna Thompson, a 34-year-old New York banker, lost a leg, and very nearly his life, when he was attacked just off the beach at Lucaya Golf and Beach Resort in Freeport, Grand Bahama. Thompson successfully sued the resort for failing to warn guests that local dive operators sold shark-feeding tours at sites located less than a mile from the hotel beach. In April 2002, TV shark show daredevil Erich Ritter went into severe shock and nearly lost his left leg after he was bitten by a bull shark that he had attracted to shallow water with fish bait.

In spite of opposition from a small but well-funded group of U.S. dive industry insiders including PADI, DEMA, *Scuba Diving* magazine and *Skin Diver* magazine, the Florida Fish and Wildlife Conservation Commission banned shark feeding in 2001. However, shark feeding remained legal in the Caribbean, and, despite its dangers, was on the rise. Divers participating in shark dives were required to sign waivers before the actual dive. As noted by the fine print in most life insurance and travel insurance policies, claims for scuba-related accidents were excluded.

Wreck Diving

Wreck diving was divided into three levels: non-penetration, limited penetration and full penetration. Full penetration and deep wreck diving should be attempted only by divers who have completed rigorous training and have extensive diving experience. Non-penetration wreck diving referred to recreational diving on wrecks without entering an overhead environment that prevented direct access to the surface. Divers with open water certification were qualified for this type of diving without any further training, provided they were comfortable with the diving conditions and the wreck's depth. Limited penetration wreck diving was defined as staying within ambient light and always in sight of an exit. Full penetration wreck diving involved an overhead environment away from ambient light and beyond sight of an exit. Safely and extensively exploring the insides of a wreck involved formal training and mental strength. On this type of dive, a diver's first mistake could be a diver's last.

Wall Diving

In a few regions of the world, island chains, formed by volcanoes and coral, have been altered by movements of the earth's crustal plates. Extending approximately due east-west across the central Caribbean Sea was the boundary between the North American and Caribbean crustal plates. The shifting of these plates had created some of the most spectacular diving environments in the world, characterized by enormous cliffs, 2,000 to 6,000 feet high. At the cliffs, known as walls, divers could experience, more than in any other underwater environment, the overwhelming scale and dynamic forces that shape the ocean. On the walls, divers were most likely to experience the feeling of free motion, or flying, in boundless space. Many of the dives in the Bahamas were wall dives.

Reef Diving

Reefs generally were made up of three areas: a reef flat, a lagoon or bay and a reef crest. The depth in the reef flat averaged only a few feet with an occasional deeper channel. The underwater life on a shallow reef flat could vary greatly in abundance and diversity within a short distance. The reef flat was generally a protected area, not exposed to strong winds or waves, making it ideal for novice or family snorkelers. The main feature distinguishing bay and lagoon environments from a reef flat was depth. Caribbean lagoons and bays could reach depths of 60 feet but many provided teeming underwater ecosystems in as little as 15 to 20 feet, making this area excellent for underwater photography and ideal for families because it was a no decompression stop diving site.[4] The reef's crest was the outer boundary that sheltered the bay and the flats from the full force of the ocean's waves. Since the surging and pounding of the waves was too strong for all but the most advanced divers, most diving took place in the protected bay waters.

FAMILY DIVING RESORTS

The current average age of new divers was 36. As the median age of new divers increased, families became a rapidly growing segment of the vacation travel industry. Many parents were busy and did not spend as much time with their children as they would have preferred. Thus, many parents who dived would have liked to have a vacation that would combine diving and spending time with their children. In response to increasing numbers of parents travelling with children, resort operators had added amenities ranging from babysitting services and kids' camps to dedicated family resorts with special facilities and rates. The resort options available had greatly expanded in recent years. At all-inclusive, self-contained resorts, one price included everything: meals, accommodations, daytime and evening activities and water sports. Many of these facilities offered special activities and facilities for children. Diving was sometimes included or available nearby.

For many divers, the important part of the trip was the quality of the diving, not the quality of the accommodations, but for divers with families, the equation changed. Children, especially younger children, could have a difficult time without a comfortable bed, a television and a DVD player, no matter how good the diving promised to be. Some resorts that were not dedicated to family vacations made accommodations for divers with children. Condos and villas were an economical and convenient vacation option. The additional space of this type of accommodation allowed parents to bring along a babysitter, and the convenience of a kitchen made the task of feeding children simple and economical. Most diving destinations in the Bahamas, the Caribbean and the Pacific offered condo, villa and hotel-type accommodations. Some hotels organized entertaining and educational activities for children while parents engaged in their own activities.

---

[4]A decompression stop is a safety requirement for dives below 30 feet. It lasts typically between 1 to 5 minutes at 3 to 6 metres (10 to 20 ft). During the stop, "micro-bubbles" in the bloodstream that are present after every dive leave the diver's body safely through the lungs. If they are not given enough time to leave safely, it can cause the symptoms and injuries known as decompression sickness.

Because the number of families vacationing together had increased, some resorts and dive operators started special promotions and programs. On Bonaire, an island in the Netherlands Antilles, August had been designated family month. During this month, the island was devoted to families, with a special welcome kit for children and island-wide activities, including eco-walks at a flamingo reserve, snorkeling lessons and evening entertainment for all ages. In conjunction, individual resorts and restaurants offered family packages and discounts. Similarly, in Honduras, which had very good diving, a resort started a children's dolphin camp during summer months. While diving family members were out exploring the reefs, children aged 8 to 14 spent their days learning about and interacting with a resident dolphin population. The program included classroom and in-water time, horseback riding and paddle boating.

Rascals in Paradise

One travel company, Rascals in Paradise (Rascals), specialized in family travel packages. The founders, Theresa Detchemendy and Deborah Baratta, were divers, mothers and travel agents who had developed innovative packages for diving families. According to Detchemendy, "The biggest concern for parents is their children's safety, and then what the kids will do while they're diving or enjoying an evening on the town." The Rascals staff worked with a number of family-run resorts all over the world to provide daily activities, responsible local nannies and child-safe facilities with safe balconies, playgrounds and children's pools.

Rascals also organized family weeks at popular dive destinations in Belize, Mexico and the Cayman Islands. Family week packages accounted for more than 50 per cent of Rascals' bookings each year. On these scheduled trips, groups of three to six families shared a teacher/escort, who tailored a fun program for children and served as an activities director for the group. Rascals' special family week packages were priced based on a family of four (two adults and two children, aged two to eleven) and included a teacher/escort, one babysitter for each family, children's activities, meals, airport transfers, taxes, services and cancellation insurance (see Exhibit 4) but not airfare. For example, in 2007, a seven-night family vacation at Hotel Club Akumal, on the Yucatan coast, cost US$2,080 to US$3,100 per family. Rascals also packaged independent family trips to 57 different condos, villas, resorts and hotels, which offered scuba diving. An independent family trip would not include a teacher/escort and babysitter (see Exhibit 5) and a seven-night family trip to Hotel Club Akumal would cost between US$624 and US$1,779, depending on the season and the type of room. Here also, the airfare was not included.

Rascals personally selected the resorts with which the company worked. "We try to work with small properties so our groups are pampered and looked after," said Detchemendy. "The owners are often parents and their kids are sometimes on the property. They understand the characteristics of kids." Typically, Detchemendy and Baratta visited each destination, often working with the government tourist board to identify potential properties. If the physical structure were already in place, adding the resort to the Rascals booking list was easy. If modifications were needed, then Detchemendy and Baratta met with the property's management to outline the facilities needed to include the resort in the Rascals program.

Rascals evaluated resorts according to several factors:

• Is the property friendly toward children and does it want children on the property?
• How does the property rate in terms of safety?

- What facilities does the property have? Is a separate room available that could be used as a Rascals room?
- Does the property provide babysitting and child care by individuals who are screened and locally known?

A successful example of this approach was Hotel Club Akumal, in Akumal, Mexico. Detchemendy and Baratta helped the resort expand its market reach by building a family-oriented resort that became part of the Rascals program. Baratta explained:

> In that case, we were looking for a place close to home, with a multi-level range of accommodations, that offered something other than a beach, that was family-friendly and not in Cancun. We found Hotel Club Akumal, but they didn't have many elements in place, so we had to work with them. We established a meal plan, an all-inclusive product and designated activities for kids. We went into the kitchen and created a children's menu and we asked them to install a little kids' playground that's shaded.

The resort became one of Rascals' most popular family destinations.

Rascals offered two types of services to resort operators interested in creating family vacations. One was a consulting service. For a modest daily fee plus expenses, Baratta or Detchemendy, or both, would conduct an on-site assessment of the resort, which usually took one or two days. They would then provide a written report to the resort regarding needed additions or modifications to the resort to make it safe and attractive for family vacations. Physical changes might include the addition of a Rascals room and child-safe play equipment and modifications to existing buildings and structures, such as rooms, railings and docks, to prevent child injuries. Rascals always tried to use existing equipment or equipment available nearby. Other non-structural changes could include the addition of educational sessions, play times and other structured times for entertaining children while their parents were diving. The report also included an implementation proposal. Then, after implementation, the resort could decide whether or not to list with Rascals for bookings.

Under the second option, Rascals provided the consulting service at no charge to the resort; however, any requests for family bookings were referred to Rascals. Rascals would then list and actively promote the resort through its brochures and referrals. For resorts using the Rascals booking option, Rascals provided premiums, such as hats and T-shirts, in addition to the escorted activities. This attention to the family differentiated a Rascals resort from other resorts. Generally, companies that promoted packages received net rates from the resorts, which were 20 to 50 per cent lower than the rack rates. Rascals, in turn, promoted these special packages to the travel industry in general and paid a portion of its earnings out in commissions to other travel agencies.

Rascals tried to work with its resorts to provide packaged and prepaid vacations, an approach that created a win-win situation for the resort managers and the vacationer. Packaged vacations, also known as all-inclusive vacations, followed a cruise ship approach that allowed the inclusion of many activities in the package. For example, such a package might include seven nights' lodging, all meals, babysitting, children's activities and scuba diving. This approach allowed the vacationer to know, upfront, what to expect. Moreover, the cost would be included in one set price, so that the family would not have to pay for each activity as it came along. The idea was to remove the surprises and make the stay enjoyable. The resort operator could bundle the activities together, providing more options than might otherwise be offered. As a result, the package approach was becoming popular with both resort owners and vacationers.

In its bookings, Rascals required prepayment of trips, which resulted in higher revenues for the resort since all activities were paid for in advance. Ordinarily, resorts that operated independently might require only a two- or three-night room deposit. The family would then pay for the balance of the room charge on leaving, after paying for other activities or services they used. Although vacationers might think they had a less expensive trip this way, in fact, pre-paid activities were generally cheaper than a la carte activities. Moreover, purchasing individual activities potentially yielded lower revenues for the resort. Rascals promoted prepaid vacations as a win-win, low-stress approach to travel. Rascals had been very successful with the resorts it listed. Fifty per cent of its bookings were repeat business, and many inquiries were based on word-of-mouth referrals. All in all, Rascals provided a link to the family vacation market segment that the resort might not otherwise have access to. It was common for Rascals-listed resorts to average annual bookings of 90 per cent.

CORAL DIVERS RESORT

Coral Divers Resort (Coral Divers) had been in operation for 10 years. Annual revenues had reached as high as $554,000. Profits generally had been in the two per cent range, but for the past two years, the business had experienced losses. The expected turnaround in profits in 2007 had never materialized (see Exhibit 6). Although the resort was not making them rich, the business had provided an adequate income for Greywell and his wife, Margaret, and their two children, Allen, age 7, and Winifred, age 5. However, revenues had continued to decline. From talking with other operators, Greywell understood that resorts with strong identities and reputations for quality service were doing well. Greywell thought that the Coral Divers Resort had not distinguished itself in any particular aspect of diving or as a resort.

The Coral Divers Resort property was located on a deep-water channel on the southwest coast of the island of New Providence in the Bahamas. The three-acre property had beach access and featured six cottages, each with its own kitchenette, a full bath, a bedroom with two full-sized beds and a living room with two sleeper sofas. Four of the units had been upgraded with new paint, tile floors, a microwave, a colour TV and a DVD player. The two other units ranged from "adequate" to "comfortable." Greywell tried to use the renovated units primarily for families and couples and housed groups of single divers in the other units (see Exhibit 7). Also on the property was a six-unit attached motel-type structure. Each of these units had two full-sized beds, a pull-out sofa, sink, a refrigerator, a microwave and a television. The resort had the space and facilities for a kitchen and dining room, but neither a kitchen nor a dining room was in use. A small family-run restaurant and bar was available within walking distance.

Greywell had three boats that could each carry from 8 to 20 passengers. Two were 40-foot fibreglass V-hull boats powered by a single diesel inboard with a cruising speed of 18 knots and a protective cabin with dry storage space. The third was a 35-foot covered platform boat. Greywell also had facilities for air dispensing, equipment repair, rental and sale and tank storage.

Coral Divers Resort, which was affiliated with PADI and NAUI, had a staff of 11, including 2 boat captains, 2 mates, a housekeeper, a groundskeeper, a person who minded the office and the store and 4 scuba diving instructors. Greywell, who worked full-time at the resort, was a diving instructor certified by both PADI and NAUI. The three other diving instructors had various backgrounds: One was a former U.S. Navy SEAL working for Coral Divers as a way to gain resort experience, another was a local

Bahamian whom Greywell had known for many years and the third was a Canadian who had come to the Bahamas on a winter holiday and had never left. Given the size of the operation, the staff was scheduled to provide overall coverage, with all of the staff rarely working at the same time. Greywell's wife, Margaret, worked at the business on a part-time basis, taking care of administrative activities, such as accounting and payroll. The rest of her time was spent looking after their two children and their home.

A typical diving day at Coral Divers began around 7:30 a.m. Greywell would open the office and review the activities list for the day. If any divers needed to be picked up at the resorts in Nassau or elsewhere on the island, the van driver would need to leave by 7:30 a.m. to be back at the resort for the 9 a.m. departure. Most resort guests began to gather around the office and dock about 8:30 a.m. By 8:45 a.m., the day's captain and mate began loading the diving gear for the passengers.

The boat left at 9 a.m. for the morning dives that were usually "two tank dives;" that is, two dives utilizing one tank of air each. The trip to the first dive site took 20 to 30 minutes. Once there, the captain would explain the dive, the special attractions of the dive and tell everyone when they were expected back on board. Most dives lasted 30 to 45 minutes, depending on the depth. The deeper the dive, the faster the air consumption. On the trip down, divers were always accompanied by a divemaster, who supervised the dive. The divemaster was responsible for the safety and conduct of the divers while underwater.

After the divers were back on board, the boat would move to the next site. Greywell tried to plan two dives that had sites near each other. For example, the first dive might be a wall dive in 60 feet of water, and the second might be a nearby wreck 40 feet down. The second dive would also last approximately 40 minutes. If the dives went well, the boat would be back at the resort by noon, which allowed time for lunch and sufficient surface time for divers who might be interested in an afternoon dive. Two morning dives were part of the resort package. Whether the boat went out in the afternoon depended on the number of non-resort guest divers contracted for afternoon dives. If enough paying divers were signed up, Greywell was happy to let resort guests ride and dive free of charge. If there were not enough paying divers, no afternoon dive trips were scheduled, and the guests were on their own to swim at the beach, sightsee or just relax. When space was available, non-divers (either snorkelers or bubble-watchers) could join the boat trip for a fee of $15 to $25.

Greywell's Options

Greywell's bookings ran 90 per cent of capacity during the high season (December through May) and 50 per cent of capacity during the low season (June through November). Ideally, he wanted to increase the number of bookings for the resort and dive businesses during both seasons. Adding additional diving attractions could increase both resort and dive revenues. Focusing on family vacations could increase revenues because families would probably increase the number of paying guests per room. Break-even costs were calculated based on two adults sharing a room. Children provided an additional revenue source since the cost of the room had been covered by the adults, and children under 10 incurred no diving-related costs. However, either strategy, adding adventure diving to his current general offerings or adjusting the focus of the resort to encourage family diving vacations, would require some changes and cost money. The question was whether the changes would increase revenue enough to justify the costs and effort involved.

Emphasizing family diving vacations would probably require some changes to the physical property of the resort. Four of the cottages had already been renovated.

The other two also would need to be upgraded, which would cost $15,000 to $25,000 each, depending on the amenities added. The Bahamas had duties of up to 35 per cent, which caused renovation costs involving imported goods to be expensive. The attached motel-type units also would need to be refurbished at some point. The resort had the space and facilities for a kitchen and dining area, but Greywell had not done anything about opening these facilities.

The Rascals in Paradise people had offered to help set up a children's menu. He could hire a chef, prepare the meals himself or offer the concession to either the nearby restaurant or someone else. He would also need to build a children's play structure. An open area with shade trees between the office and the cottages would be ideal for a play area. Rascals would provide the teacher/escort for the family vacation groups, and it would be fairly easy to find babysitters for the children as needed. The people who lived on this part of the island were very family-oriented and would welcome the opportunity for additional income. From asking around, Greywell determined that between $5 and $10 per hour was the going rate for a sitter. Toys and other play items could be added gradually. The Rascals people had said that, once the program was in place, Greywell could expect bookings to run 90 per cent capacity annually from new and return bookings. Although the package prices were competitive, the attraction was in group bookings and the prospect of a returning client base.

Adding adventure diving would be a relatively easy thing to do. Shark Wall and Shark Buoy were less than an hour away by boat. Both of these sites featured sharks that were already accustomed to being fed. The cost of shark food would be $10 per dive. None of Greywell's current staff was particularly excited about the prospect of adding shark feeding to their job description. But these staff could be relatively easily replaced. Greywell could probably find an experienced divemaster who would be willing to lead the shark dives. He would also have to purchase a special chain mail suit for the feeder at a cost of about $15,000. Although few accidents occurred during shark feeds, Greywell would rather be safe than sorry. His current boats, especially the 40-footers, would be adequate for transporting divers to the sites. The other shark dive operators might not be happy about having him at the sites, but they could do little about it. Shark divers were charged a premium fee. For example, a shark dive would cost $115 for a two-tank dive, compared with $65 for a normal two-tank dive. He figured that he could add shark dives to the schedule on Wednesdays and Saturdays without taking away from regular business. Although he needed a minimum of 4 divers on a trip at regular rates to cover the cost of taking out the boat, 10 or 12 divers would be ideal. Greywell could usually count on at least eight divers for a normal dive, but he did not know how much additional new and return business he could expect from shark diving.

A third option was for Greywell to try to improve his current operations and not add any new diving attractions, which would require him to be much more cost efficient in his operations. For example, he would have to strictly adhere to the policy of requiring a minimum number of divers per boat, and staff reductions might improve the bottom line by 5 to 10 per cent. He would need to be very attentive to materials ordering, fuel costs and worker productivity in order to realize any gains with this approach. However, he was concerned that by continuing as he had, Coral Divers Resort would not be distinguished as unique from other resorts in the Bahamas. He did not know the long-term implications of this approach.

As Greywell reached the office, he turned to watch the sun sink into the ocean. Although it was a view he had come to love, a lingering thought was that perhaps it was time to relocate to a less crowded location.

EXHIBIT 1   U.S. Population Demographics 1980, 1990 and 2000

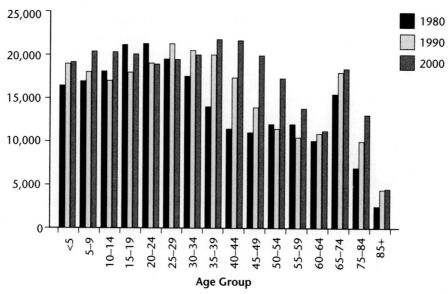

Note: Numbers are in the thousands.

Source: U.S. Bureau of the Census, 2000. Retrieved from http://factfinder.census.gov/servlet/QTTable?_bm=y&-geo_id=01000US&-qr_name=DEC_2000_SF1_U_DP1&-ds_name=DEC_2000_SF1_U, accessed on April 10, 2008

EXHIBIT 2   U.S. Diver Demographics: Age of Divers

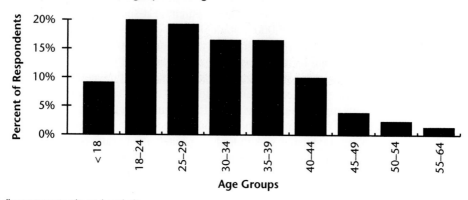

Source: PADI diver survey results and analysis.

EXHIBIT 3 Names and Location of Diving Operators in the Bahamas

Abaco
Above and Below Abaco
Brendal's Dive Center International
Dive Abaco
Dive Guana
Froggies Out Island Adventures, Ltd.
Treasure Divers

Andros
Coral Caverns Dive Resort
Kamalame Cay Resort
Seascape Inn
Small Hope Bay Lodge
Tiamo Resort

Bimini
Bill & Nowdla Keefe's Bimini Undersea
Scuba Bimini

Cat Island
Hawk's Nest Resort & Marina

Eleuthera/Habour Island
Cape Eleuthera Divers
Ocean Fox Divers
Valentine's Dive Center

Exuma
Exuma Scuba Adventures

Live-Aboard Dive Boats
Aqua Cat Cruises
Blackbeard's Cruises
Cat Ppalu Cruises
Explorer Ventures
Juliet Sailing and Diving
Nekton Diving Cruises
Sea Dragon
The Dream Team, Inc.

Long Island
Cape Santa Maria Beach Resort
Reel Divers at Grotto Bay
Stella Maris Resort Club

New Providence Island/Nassau
Bahama Divers Ltd.
Coral Divers Resort
Land Shark Divers
Stuart Cove's Dive South Ocean

San Salvador
Riding Rock Resort

Source: The Bahamas Diving Association membership.

EXHIBIT 4   Rascals in Paradise Pricing Guide, Rascals Special Family Weeks

Destination	Price	Notes
Bahamas		
South Ocean Beach	$3,120 to 3,970	Lunch not included.
Small Hope Bay	$3,504	Scuba diving included. Local host only.
Mexico		
Hotel Buena Vista	$2,150 to 2,470	
Hotel Club Akumal	$2,080 to 3,100	Lunch and airport transfer not included.

Note: Prices are based on a family of four with two adults and two children aged two and eleven. Rates are per week (seven nights) and include (except as noted): accommodations, Rascals escort, meals, babysitter, children's activities, airport transfers, taxes and services and a $2,500 cancellation insurance per family booking. Airfares not included.

EXHIBIT 5   Rascals in Paradise Pricing Guide, Independent Family Trips

Destination	Price	Notes
Bahamas		
South Ocean Beach	$1,355 to 1,771	
Small Hope Bay	$2,860 to 3,560	All meals, bar service, babysitter and diving included.
Hope Town Harbour Lodge	$962 to 1,121	
Treasure Cay	$875 to 1,750	
Stella Maris, Long Island	$1,547 to 2,597	
Mexico		
Hotel Buena Vista	$1,232 to 1,548	All meals included.
Hotel Club Akumal	$624 to 1,779	
Hotel Presidente	$1,120 to 1,656	
La Concha	$655 to 963	
Plaza Las Glorias	$632 to 1,017	

Note: Prices are based on a family of four with two adults and two children aged two and eleven. Rates are per week (seven nights) and include accommodations and applicable taxes. These rates are to be used as a guide only. Each booking is quoted separately and the amount charged depends on season, type of accommodation, ages and number of children, meal and activity inclusions. All prices are subject to change. Some variations apply. Airfares not included.

EXHIBIT 6   Comparative Balance Sheets as at June 30 (US$)

	2007	2006	2005
Assets			
Current assets			
Cash	5,362	8,943	15,592
Accounts receivable	2,160	8,660	2,026
Inventories	5,519	6,861	9,013
Prepaid expenses	9,065	8,723	8,195
Total current assets	22,106	33,187	34,826
Fixed assets			
Land	300,000	300,000	300,000
Building	200,000	200,000	200,000
Less: accumulated depreciation	(70,000)	(60,000)	(50,000)
Boats	225,000	225,000	225,000
Less: accumulated depreciation	(157,500)	(135,000)	(112,500)
Vehicles	54,000	54,000	54,000
Less: accumulated depreciation	(32,400)	(21,600)	(10,800)
Diving equipment	150,000	150,000	150,000
Less: accumulated depreciation	(90,000)	(60,000)	(30,000)
Total fixed assets	579,100	652,400	725,700
Total assets	**601,206**	**685,587**	**760,526**
Liabilities			
Current liabilities			
Accounts payable	1,689	4,724	1,504
Bank loan	20,000	–	2,263
Mortgage payable, current portion	25,892	25,892	25,892
Note payable, current portion	40,895	40,895	40,895
Total current liabilities	**88,476**	**71,511**	**70,554**
Long-term liabilities			
Mortgage payable, due in 1996	391,710	417,602	443,494
Note payable, 5-year	81,315	122,210	163,105
Total Long-term liabilities	473,025	539,812	606,599
Total liabilities	**561,501**	**611,323**	**677,153**
Shareholders' equity			
Jonathan Greywell, capital	44,879	44,879	44,879
Retained earnings	(5,174)	29,385	38,494
Total shareholders' equity	39,705	74,264	83,373
Total liabilities and shareholders' equity	**601,206**	**685,587**	**760,526**

EXHIBIT 6   (Continued)

	2007	2006	2005
Revenue			
Diving and lodging packages	482,160	507,670	529,820
Day diving	11,680	12,360	14,980
Certifications	5,165	5,740	7,120
Lodging	2,380	1,600	1,200
Miscellaneous	1,523	1,645	1,237
Total revenues	**502,908**	**529,015**	**554,357**
Expenses			
Advertising and promotion	15,708	15,240	13,648
Bank charges	1,326	1,015	975
Boat maintenance and fuel	29,565	31,024	29,234
Cost of goods sold	762	823	619
Depreciation	73,300	73,300	73,300
Dues and fees	3,746	4,024	3,849
Duties and taxes	11,405	18,352	17,231
Insurance	36,260	34,890	32,780
Interest, mortgage, note and loan	40,544	40,797	41,174
Management salary	31,600	31,600	31,600
Office supplies	12,275	12,753	11,981
Professional fees	11,427	10,894	10,423
Repairs and maintenance, building	15,876	12,379	9,487
Salaries, wages and benefits	196,386	194,458	191,624
Telephone and fax	9,926	9,846	7,689
Trade shows	14,523	14,679	14,230
Utilities	20,085	19,986	17,970
Vehicles, maintenance and fuel	12,753	12,064	11,567
Total expenses	**537,467**	**538,124**	**519,381**
Net income	**(34,559)**	**(9,109)**	**(34,976)**
Retained earnings, beginning	**29,385**	**38,494**	**3,518**
Retained earnings, ending	**(5,174)**	**29,385**	**38,494**

Note: Bahama$1=US$1

EXHIBIT 7   Coral Divers Resort Pricing Guide, Family Dive Vacations

Destination	Duration	Price	Notes
Bahamas			
Coral Divers Resort		$1,355 to 1,455	Standard accommodations, continental breakfast and daily two-tank dive included.
Coral Divers Resort		$1,800 to 1,950	Deluxe accommodations, continental breakfast and daily two-tank dive included.

Note: Prices are based on a family of four with two adults and two children ages two and eleven. Rates are per week (seven nights) and include accommodations and applicable taxes. Rates will be dependent on season, type of accommodation, ages and number of children. All prices are subject to change. Airfares not included. Prices dropped to $600 to $700 per week for the standard package and $800 to $900 for deluxe accommodation if diving was excluded.

Tavazo Co.

In June 2010, Naser Tavazo, one of the three owner/manager brothers of both Tavazo Iran Co. and Tavazo Canada Co., was considering the company's future expansion opportunities, including further international market entry. Candidate cities of interest were Los Angeles, Dubai and other cities with large Iranian diasporas. Another question included where to focus on the value chain. Should the family business use its limited resources to expand its retailer business into more international markets, or to expand its current retailer/wholesale activities within Canada and Iran?

BACKGROUND

Tavazo was a family business operated by three brothers: Naser, Khosro and Parviz. The business was originally started by their grandfather. He had started his career as a gardener in Eastern Azerbaijan province in Iran in 1929 when he was 18 years old. Later, he moved to Tabriz, the capital city of the province, and dried his gardens' fruits using sunlight. From his small processing site, he distributed to small retail stores. Difficulties dealing with distributors led him to rent a store and sell dried fruits from his and neighbouring gardens directly to customers. The store started with fruits such as apples, peaches and apricots. Then, to the store's product list, he added seeds, which he roasted in a big pan at the store.

As the store's business grew, he added nuts such as pistachios and cashews, which were not the products of Azerbaijan. Pistachios thrived in areas with cool winters and long, hot summers. They were drought-resistant and very tolerant of high summer temperatures, but could not tolerate excessive dampness and high humidity. Central provinces in Iran, such as Kerman and Yazd, were the main sources of Iranian pistachio

Majid Eghbali-Zarch wrote this case under the supervision of Professor Paul W. Beamish solely to provide material for class discussion. The authors do not intend to illustrate either effective or ineffective handling of a managerial situation. The authors may have disguised certain names and other identifying information to protect confidentiality.

Richard Ivey School of Business
The University of Western Ontario

production. He purchased raw pistachios from the central provinces and displayed and sold them in the store after roasting them.

Their grandfather was 23 years old when he married. Later, his three sons joined him to grow the business. Meanwhile, the manufacturing site was equipped with drying machinery which burnt sulphur to dry the fruits, as well as roasting machinery for nuts and seeds.

In 1962, the grandfather passed away and his elder son, together with his teenage sons Naser, Khosro and Parviz, moved to Tehran, the capital of Iran. He bought a store in a prestigious location in Tehran, as well as a warehouse and manufacturing site in Karaj, a city 50 kilometres from Tehran, and started the same business his father had years ago. After Iran's 1979 revolution, the two younger sons came back from Italy, where they had completed their higher education. The unstable institutional environment and unfavourable job market in Iran led them to decide to continue their father's business, despite the fact it was unrelated to their education.

THE CURRENT SITUATION

By 2010, the family business was vertically integrated as grower, manufacturer, retailer and exporter. The current mark-up figures, as well as the sales contribution of each section in the value chain, are illustrated in Exhibit 1.

Historically, nuts and dried fruit had been considered commodities in Iran. The three partner brothers felt an advantage in continuing their ancestors' way of differentiating the Tavazo products and tried to provide nuts and dried fruits as a branded product as opposed to a commodity product. The store had loyal customers who came to Vali-E-Asr Street just to buy nuts from Tavazo.

In mid-March, before Nowrouz,[1] the first day of the New Year in the Iranian calendar, the nuts and dried fruits market in Iran would experience a seasonal surge in demand, in addition to the steady demand throughout the year. Iranians had been celebrating Nowrouz for more than 2,500 years. Families had the tradition of getting together, visiting senior family members and exchanging gifts. Guests were served mostly nuts, cookies and fruit during the Nowrouz parties. Yalda night, the longest night of the year, was the other occasion that created a seasonal demand for Tavazo. The night was celebrated by going to the house of the eldest person in the family, eating nuts and reading Hafiz[2] poems.

Growing

The company grew only a small portion of what it sold, and this mainly focused on fruits. Most supplies were purchased from gardeners and farmers across Iran. The relatively strong financial resources of the business, as well as its insistence on high-quality products, had made the company's network of suppliers a valuable asset. The company purchased the farmers' products months in advance of the harvest season. This was considered an advantage against rivals who could not do so for financial

---

[1]Nowrouz is the Persian word for the new Iranian year and means "the new day."

[2]Hafiz was a prominent Iranian poet who lived from 1320 to 1389 AD. His poems are intriguing and complex. In addition to reading the poems, some Iranians open his poem book and use the random poem that comes up for fortune-telling purposes. Although the majority of Iranians do not believe in the ability of poems to predict the future, they still do it for fun.

reasons. Also, Tavazo knew that high-quality products were not abundantly available. Farms or gardens with high-quality nuts and fruits were limited. Therefore, the company did its best to develop a long-term relationship with its suppliers so that they would see little advantage in switching to Tavazo's rivals.

As part of a heart-healthy diet, many people ate tree nuts with some regularity, either as a snack, as part of a recipe or as some kind of treat. Unlike many vegetable plants, nut trees grew for a long time before their first harvest. A walnut tree, for instance, performed best after 30 years and a pistachio tree took approximately 7 to 10 years to reach significant production. Year-to-year production levels were not consistent, even after a tree had reached its prime. Many nut trees that produced a large crop one year would have a smaller yield the following year in order to build up internal nutrients.

Iran's diverse climate and agricultural lands made it a source of high-quality agricultural products, which shaped a significant pillar of the Tavazo business in Iran and, later, in international markets. Iran was the largest producer of pistachios in the world followed by the United States, Turkey, Syria and China (see Exhibit 2). Pistachios were a major contributor to Tavazo's sales, accounting for about 20 per cent of total sales. Other nuts and fruits for which Iran had a substantive worldwide market share were berries, apricots, dates, cherries, apples, figs, almonds and walnuts. Exhibit 3 illustrates Iran's worldwide rank in the production of select fruits and nuts.

Manufacturing/Processing

Dried fruits and nuts, the two main categories of Tavazo products, had different manufacturing processes.

For nuts, time was of the essence once they were picked. They needed to be hulled promptly for proper dehydration. If the outer shell was left on too long, the quality of the nut (and, in turn, the price it could command) would decline. The next stage was sorting the nuts and categorizing by size. Then, if some nuts, such as pistachios, were supposed to be roasted, they would go through the salting and roasting stage and eventually be ready for delivery to retail stores.

Tavazo conducted all manufacturing operations in house. Advanced drying and roasting machines were acquired to keep the quality of the products to a high standard.

The manufacturing process for dried fruits was different to some extent. After the fruit was picked from the tree, collected and transported to the manufacturing site, it was washed, sorted, had its stones removed and was chopped or sliced. Then it was spread in pots and placed on shelves in an area which was smoked by burning sulphur and other drying materials.

Tavazo Retail Store

Retailing was the main focus of Tavazo Co. in Iran. The Tavazo brothers believed that presenting and selling nuts and dried fruits was a special skill that only retailers specializing in nuts and dried fruits held. Therefore, they devoted a significant effort to presentation, in-store packaging and sales at the retail store. Customers could browse the store, choose a product, fill special Tavazo bags with the desired amount and have the bags sealed with a packaging machine available in the store. Also, they could choose among the gift packaging boxes or baskets offered in the Tavazo store. Exhibit 4 illustrates decorative handicraft pots and some gift boxes and baskets specifically designed for presenting Tavazo products at its store in Toronto. Gift boxes/baskets carried a modest additional cost for customers.

Tavazo Brand and the Case of Imitators

The store was known to offer slightly premium-priced products. However, customers who had quality as their first priority would choose Tavazo for their purchases, both year-round and for special occasions. By 2010, the brand was more of a retail brand and did not have as much strength in the upstream of the value chain. However, Naser Tavazo believed that the company's relationship with growers and its tendency towards careful and high-quality manufacturing had a significant impact on its success in retailing. Focusing on customer satisfaction and excellent product quality made the Tavazo brand well known among nuts retailers in Tehran, a city which had about 10 million of the 70 million people in Iran.

Trained in a traditional business environment, the Tavazo brothers were not originally aware of the importance of brand management. While the performance of the Tavazo nuts store was strengthening the brand, imitators started to pop up all around Tehran, using Tavazo as the name of their stores. After a short time, there were 28 such stores in Tehran and other cities in Iran. This caused the family to register the brand and take imitators to court. Naser Tavazo remembered a quote by one fake Tavazo store owner in court:

> Well, I thought every store that sold nuts should be named Tavazo!

The fake stores were banned from using the Tavazo name as a result. However, afterwards each used a prefix or suffix to Tavazo both to keep the name and to obey the lawful order of the court.[3] Further follow-ups required more legal expenditure, which was recognized as uneconomic at the time.[4]

Iran's Economy

After Iran's revolution in 1979, the economic, as well as business, environment in Iran became volatile. Many large companies were nationalized and the economy moved toward more government intervention. Later, the Iranian government tried to change its policy towards more privatization and encouragement of foreign firms investing in Iran, a policy that met with little success.

Iran's economy had been performing relatively strongly in recent years, supported by high oil prices and expansionary fiscal and monetary policies.[5] Notwithstanding this, many believed the growth was not proportionate to the country's resources and potential. Iran's economy was marked by reliance on the oil sector, which provided the majority of its revenue. After oil, which constituted 80 per cent of the country's revenue, chemical and petrochemical products, fruits and nuts and carpets held the next rankings in the country's sources of revenue. As of 2009, the country's major export partners were China (16.6 per cent), Japan (11.9 per cent), India (10.5 per cent), South Korea (7.5 per cent) and Turkey (4.4 per cent), and the major import partners were the United Arab Emirates (15.1 per cent), China (13.5 per cent), Germany (9.7 per cent), South Korea (7.2 per cent), Italy (5.3 per cent), Russia (4.8 per cent) and India (4.1 per cent).

The country had been using a managed floating exchange rate regime since unifying multiple exchange rates in March 2002. The rial, the local currency, had been

---

[3]Examples of the new names were Tavazo-North and Tavazo-Bazaar.

[4]$200,000 to $300,000 was the estimated legal cost for the follow-up at that time.

[5]International Monetary Fund's Country Report No. 10/74, www.imf.org, accessed September 23, 2010.

pegged to the U.S. dollar ever since. This policy made the exchange rate unrealistically low and caused imports to seem more profitable and attractive than local production and exports.[6]

ENTERING CANADA

In the 1990s, Tavazo Co. was steadily moving forward and, although it had started exporting nuts, especially pistachios, to some countries like the United States, it had not planned any significant growth. In 1988, after their father passed away, the three brothers decided to leave Iran in search of a more stable and developed environment in which to live, and to further their children's education. They began to consider whether they could expand their business into a foreign market. Among the countries on their list were the United States and Canada, the two major destinations for the Iranian diaspora. Due to a lower government tariff on nuts and dried fruits, they chose Canada. The U.S. government had encouraged aggressive growth in domestic U.S. pistachio production during the past three decades, the result of which was a tariff of around 400 to 500 per cent on imported pistachios. Coupled with the increased global demand, pistachio production had jumped from 1,179 tons of production in 1978 to around 175,000 tons in 2009.[7] The Tavazo partners believed that by entering Canada, they would have access to its southern neighbour too.

A friend helped the family to go to Canada and believed that the overall living conditions, as well as the business, environment fitted their situation well. As a result, the three owner/manager partners of Tavazo Co., together with their families, immigrated to Canada in 1995 under the business immigration program. After their initial settlement and adjustment to life in Toronto, the brothers contemplated starting a similar business in Canada.

Since they did not have an already developed market in Canada, and since the majority of their products were to be imported from Iran in bulk, they had to consider a warehouse to store the imported products to be sold over time. To be exported, nuts and dried fruits were to be packed, kept in industrial fridges and transported by ships equipped with fridges.[8] The destination warehouse had to have refrigerators too. The brothers bought a warehouse facility in Richmond Hill (a suburb of Toronto) and equipped it with the necessary requirements.

For some products, the manufacturing process was split between Iran and Canada. A major example was roasted pistachios. In order for the product to be of the highest quality, the roasting process was to be done as close to the point of sale as possible. Therefore, pistachios were refrigerated and transported from Iran to Canada, and the roasting process was done in the company's facility in Richmond Hill. An additional advantage was that raw nuts could be kept in the refrigerated warehouses for up to two years without changing taste or colour. Later, they could be roasted based on the demand from the market.

The brothers started by wholesaling the imported products and distributing them to retail stores. Although the majority of the target retail stores at that stage were those with ethnic products, mainly Iranian and Afghan stores in Toronto, the Tavazo brothers

---

[6]The inflation rate was 13.6 per cent as of 2009 and 25.6 per cent as of 2008. The local currency would depreciate against the U.S. dollar each year by approximately these figures, whereas the controlled exchange rate policy would not let it happen in reality.

[7]http://faostat.fao.org

[8]The products were exported to Canada through a trading company based in Iran.

did their best to familiarize others with their high-quality Iranian nuts and dried fruits as well. In 2010, on average, 70 per cent of the Tavazo retail store customers were Iranians and 30 per cent were other nationalities. Naser Tavazo was surprised at the growth of the number of Chinese customers, who constituted around half of non-Iranian customers.

> We had participated in trade fairs in Canada and the United States during our stay in Canada. When we presented samples of Iranian high-quality pistachios and dried fruits, some said they had not seen such large pistachios before and they doubted if they were really pistachios.

Notwithstanding this, the Iranian diaspora in Toronto was a proper starting point. The majority of Iranians abroad knew the brand and the quality positioning that the company had. They understood that the premium-priced high quality of Tavazo products compared very well to the extant Iranian and American pistachios and nuts available on the market. Naser Tavazo noted:

> When we were in Iran, we had export orders from Canada that were very price sensitive. They requested very low-priced pistachios regardless of the size and quality. When we offered higher-quality pistachios, they were wondering if the market would pay for the higher price. It took time and effort since we entered Canada to establish a market receptive to higher-quality and premium-priced products.

Meanwhile, the Tavazo brothers had to consider the management of the Iranian side of the business. On one hand, Tehran's retail store was still active and manufacturing facilities in Karaj needed supervision and control. With the expansion of the business, someone needed to be physically present in Iran to facilitate the day-to-day issues that could come up. Good relations with suppliers were historically a valuable asset for the company, but needed close supervision and maintenance. Another need for a physical presence of a decision maker was plausible change in regulations (e.g., customs tariffs, or other restrictions) in Iran. On the other hand, the brothers had all moved to Canada with their families. They decided to solve the need for managing Iran's facilities in a rotating way. Each of the three brothers would spend four months of the year in Iran and the rest in Canada. The respective brother's family had the choice of staying in Canada, or having a trip to Iran to reconnect with family and friends.

Dealing with retailers had its own challenges and difficulties. Many retailers were grocery stores with a variety of products and were not as specialized in the presentation and sales to customers of nuts and dried fruits. Retailers' poor sales performance, together with their financial weakness, resulted in an increase in the number of non-sufficient funds (NSF) cheques received by Tavazo. Many of the products were returned as a result. A more important factor for Tavazo that made its relations with retailers weaker was the harm to the Tavazo brand. Weak presentation and shelving of Tavazo products in stores made the brand decline, which was not in accordance with what Tavazo had strived for over the years.

The difficulties of dealing with retailers led the brothers to think of having their own retail store, as they had in Iran. They knew that they should have the store somewhere on Yonge Street, near where the majority of Iranians were residing and where the Iranian Plaza was located. A Thornhill store (near Richmond Hill) was chosen after an attractive offer was received. The store was decorated like the company's retail store in Iran and products were presented similarly. The company stopped distributing to the stores that were harming the brand through poor sales performance and presentation. Later, in 2010, the company's second retail store in Canada was inaugurated in Richmond Hill.

Exhibits 5 and 6 illustrate the statement of earnings and the balance sheet of the company in 2009.

Products

Nuts, dried fruits and vegetables, spices, cookies and other Iranian ethnic food products, such as saffron and caviar, were the main products of Tavazo in Iran and Canada. Exhibit 7 includes some rough estimates of the sales contribution of each category. Among the products, pistachios were the largest contributor in the sales figures.

COMPETITORS

Retailing accounted for the majority of the Tavazo business. No significant Iranian competitor existed. Of course, the remaining Tavazo imitators in Iran sometimes attracted uninformed new customers by claiming that they were the original Tavazo. In Canada, the closest retailer to Tavazo in terms of product presentation was Bulk Barn. The market and product positioning of the companies, however, was quite different. For example, in October 2010, the average retail price for natural, salted, unbranded pistachios was $26 per kilogram at Bulk Barn, while Tavazo sold its pistachios for $20-$30 per kilogram, depending on size.

In wholesale, there were a few companies in Canada which could be considered Tavazo's competitors.[9] Naser Tavazo, however, believed that the limited strength of the company in the wholesale area had made it more cooperative than competitive. In fact, North American Co. and Tavazo sometimes sold Iranian and American nuts and pistachios to each other.

THE FUTURE OF TAVAZO

After a successful entry into Canada, the Tavazo family business was contemplating further growth. The challenge was to determine the direction of future business expansion. One option was to exploit current geographic markets, expanding more inside Iran and Canada and focusing more on the upstream of its value chain as a wholesaler. Alternatively, the business could pursue more geographic diversification and entry into other international markets with or without Iranian diasporas.

Iranian Diasporas

For Tavazo, Iranian diasporas could be a solid starting point at the time of entry to a new geographic market. The Tavazo brand recognition among Iranians was an asset that differentiated the company from its export and retail competitors. Iran had a vast diaspora abroad. Some had gone abroad in search of higher education and quality of life. Others had done so for political reasons. The United States hosted over a million Iranians, whose socioeconomic characteristics were reported to be significantly above average.[10] The United Arab Emirates, due to its proximity to Iran and its being

---

[9]North America Co., Genesis Co. and John Vince Co. were some examples.

[10]The percentage of Iranians over 25 years old who had obtained a bachelor's degree or higher, for example, was 57.2 per cent in comparison to 24.4 per cent for the rest of the U.S. population. Percentage-wise, Iranian-Americans held five times the number of doctorates than the national average. Also, the per capita average income for Iranian-Americans was 50 per cent higher than that of the nation (Source: Iranian Studies Group at the Massachusetts Institute of Technology).

a convenient hub for Iranian businessmen and tourists, hosted some 400,000 Iranians. Canada was third with some 120,000 Iranians, followed by Qatar and Germany, with numbers fast approaching 100,000 each. Other countries with large concentrations included Sweden, with approximately 54,000 Iranians; the United Kingdom, home to some 43,000 Iranians; and Israel, home to some 48,000 Persian Jews.

Candidate Cities

By 2010, the three brothers had had frequent discussions about how to expand their business. Whenever they discussed more geographic expansion (see Exhibit 8 for the top pistachio importer nations in the world), cities such as Vancouver, Los Angeles and Dubai were mentioned. Business expansion in the current geographic markets of Tehran and Toronto often had its proponents in the family discussions as well. While the brothers were aware of the match between the company's capabilities and the opportunities for further geographic diversification, they were often concerned with the financial and managerial resources required for diversification. They had the experience of entering Canada and were therefore aware that each market entry entailed initial set-up and market penetration costs.

Recently, on a trip to visit some family and friends in Los Angeles, the city with the largest population of Iranians in the United States, Parviz Tavazo had collected some data on start-up costs for a new store and discussed these with his brothers when he came back to Toronto. The monthly rental cost for a store in a decent neighbourhood and the required warehouse space cost were $2,500 and $1,500, respectively. He had estimated some $20,000 for store renovation and decoration and around $30,000 as the required financials for store and warehouse inventory. Furthermore, for store management, one of the family members would have to move and live in the new location. The other major restriction for Tavazo in the U.S. market was the challenge of importing Iranian products (especially pistachios) into the United States.

Having the second-highest population of overseas Iranians, Dubai was the other alternative on the table. Apart from the Iranian diaspora there, many Iranians travelled to Dubai for business, vacations and shopping. The number of Iranians travelling to Dubai was 970,000 in 2009. The generally rich Arab population of Dubai could contribute to the potential target market as well. The costs and challenges of starting and running a business in Dubai were, to a great extent, similar to those in Tehran.

A major disadvantage of Dubai for the Tavazo family was its rather similar living environment to Tehran. Although the city was famous in the Middle East for its modern infrastructure, attractive entertainment and fancy shopping malls, the higher education system was no stronger than in Iran, if not weaker. No members of the Tavazo family seemed interested in moving to Dubai on a permanent basis.

Family Business Limitation

As in every family business, the number of family members was considered to be a limited resource. The three partner brothers had four children between them, who were mostly university or college students. Only one of them had a business-related education. The three others were studying law and engineering. Further expansion of the business would probably require the family partners to bring in a non-family member partner or manager. The traditional family ambiance in the business would require a radical change and adjustment to accommodate a non-family member.

The Tavazo brothers had to decide whether to enter new geographic markets or to focus on the current markets and expand within them as retailers. They could also vertically integrate and expand by focusing more on the wholesale side. As a family, they had to contemplate their limitations and strengths in order to exploit opportunities and respond to threats to the business that they had inherited from their grandfather.

EXHIBIT 1   Tavazo Co. Value Chain Price Mark-ups and Current Business Focus

	Farms & Gardens	Manufacturing	Wholesale & Exports	Retail Stores
Mark-up (in %)	10	10	15	20
% of current business	2	6	12	80

EXHIBIT 2   Top Pistachio Producer Nations in the World

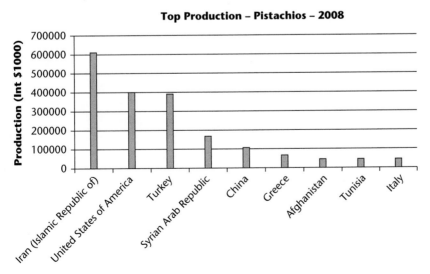

Top Production – Pistachios – 2008

Source: http://faostat.fao.org/site/339/default.aspx, accessed October 6, 2010.

EXHIBIT 3   Iran's Rank in Global Production of Nuts and Fruits

Global production rank (Value-based)	Commodity	Global production rank (Value-based)	Commodity
1	Pistachios	7	Pumpkins, squash and gourds
1	Berries	7	Sour cherries
2	Watermelons	7	Onions, dry
2	Apricots	7	Grapes
2	Cucumbers and gherkins	8	Tangerines, mandarins
2	Dates	8	Kiwi fruit
3	Cherries	8	Oranges
3	Apples	8	Lemons and limes
3	Figs	8	Lentils
4	Almonds, with shell	8	Spices
4	Walnuts, with shell	10	Potatoes
4	Indigenous sheep meat	10	Persimmons
6	Peas, dry	10	Tea
6	Hazelnuts, with shell	10	Natural honey
6	Chick peas	12	Plums and sloes
7	Peaches and nectarines	13	Melon seed
7	Tomatoes	13	Eggplants (aubergines)

Source: http://faostat.fao.org

EXHIBIT 4   Tavazo Company's Store Appearance and Gift Baskets

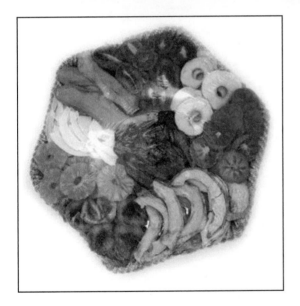

EXHIBIT 5   Tavazo Canada Co. Statement of Earnings (2009) (in $000s)

Sales	$495
Cost of sales	$250
Gross margin	$245
Expenses	
Administrative and selling expenses	$ 70
Interest and bank charges	$ 5
Depreciation	$ 2
Total expenses	$ 77
Net profit (loss) before income taxes	$168

Note: Financial figures are estimates.

EXHIBIT 6   Tavazo Canada Co. Balance Sheet (2009) (in $000s)

Current assets	
Cash	$ 80
Accounts receivable	$ 10
Inventory	$ 60
Property, plant and equipment	$600
Subtotal	**$750**
Current liabilities	
Bank indebtedness	$400
Accounts payable and accrued liabilities	$ 45
Subtotal	**$445**
Retained earnings	**$305**

Note: Financial figures are estimates.

EXHIBIT 7   Tavazo Canada Co. Product Sales Contribution

Product	Sales contribution (%)
Pistachios	20
Almonds	10
Walnuts	15
Seeds	10
Hazelnuts	5
Cashews	5
Dried fruits, vegetable, spices, etc.	35

Source: Company estimates.

EXHIBIT 8 Top Pistachio Importing Nations (2007)

Rank	Area	Quantity (tons)
1	China, Hong Kong	55,031
2	Germany	41,373
3	China	29,915
4	Russian Federation	20,749
5	Netherlands	16,729
6	United Kingdom	15,040
7	Spain	13,101
8	Italy	11,533
9	France	11,073
10	Luxembourg	10,612
11	Belgium	9,235
12	India	7,777
13	Saudi Arabia	5,426
14	Mexico	4,879
15	Lebanon	4,613
16	Japan	3,742
17	Israel	3,478
18	Pakistan	3,359
19	Canada	3,241
20	Lithuania	3,180

Source: http://faostat.fao.org/site/342/default.aspx

CASE 28

Victoria Heavy Equipment Limited

Brian Walters sat back in the seat of his Lear jet as it broke through the clouds en route from Squamish, a small town near Vancouver, British Columbia, to Sacramento, California. As chairman of the board, majority shareholder and chief executive officer, the 51-year-old Walters had run Victoria Heavy Equipment Limited as a closely held company for years. During this time, it had become the second-largest producer of mobile cranes in the world, with 2007 sales of $150 million and exports to more than 30 countries. But in early 2008, the problem of succession was in his thoughts. His son and daughter were not ready to run the organization, and he personally wanted to devote more time to other interests. He wondered about the kind of person he should hire to become president. There was also a nagging thought that there might be other problems with Victoria that would have to be worked out before he eased out of his present role.

COMPANY HISTORY

Victoria Heavy Equipment Limited (Victoria) was established in 1917 in Victoria, British Columbia, to produce horse-drawn log skidders for the forest industry. The young firm showed a flair for product innovation, pioneering the development of motorized skidders and later, after diversifying into the crane business, producing the country's first commercially successful hydraulic crane controls. In spite of these innovations, the company was experiencing severe financial difficulties in 1970 when it was purchased by Brian Walters Sr., the father of the current chairman. By installing tight financial controls and paying close attention to productivity, Walters was able to turn the company around, and in 1977, he decided that Victoria would focus exclusively on cranes and go after the international market.

Richard Ivey School of Business
The University of Western Ontario

Paul W. Beamish and Thomas A. Poynter wrote this case solely to provide material for class discussion. The authors do not intend to illustrate either effective or ineffective handling of a managerial situation. The authors may have disguised certain names and other identifying information to protect confidentiality.

At the time of Brian Walters Sr.'s retirement in 1990, it was clear that the decision to concentrate on the crane business had been a good one. The company's sales and profits were growing, and Victoria cranes were beginning to do well in export markets. Walters Sr. was succeeded as president by his brother James, who began to exercise very close personal control over the company's operations. However, as Victoria continued to grow in size and complexity, the load on James became so great that his health began to fail. The solution was to appoint an assistant general manager, John Rivers, through whom tight supervision could be maintained while James Walters' workload was eased. This move was to no avail, however. James Walters suffered a heart attack in 1992, and Rivers became general manager. At the same time, the young Brian Walters, the current chairman and chief executive officer, became head of the U.S. operation.

When Brian Walters took responsibility for Victoria's U.S. business, the firm's American distributor was selling 30 to 40 cranes per year. Walters thought the company should be selling at least 150. Even worse, the orders that the American firm did get tended to come in large quantities, as many as 50 cranes in a single order. This played havoc with Victoria's production scheduling. Walters commented, "We would rather have 10 orders of 10 cranes each than a single order for 100." In 1997, when the U.S. distributor's agreement expired, he offered the company a five-year renewal if it would guarantee sales of 150 units per year. When the firm refused, Walters bought it, and in the first month fired 13 of the 15 employees and cancelled most existing dealerships. He then set to work to rebuild, only accepting orders for 10 cranes or less. His hope was to gain a foothold and a solid reputation in the U.S. market before the big U.S. firms noticed him.

This strategy quickly showed results, and in 1998, Walters came back to Canada. As Rivers was still general manager, there was not enough to occupy him fully, and he began travelling three or four months a year. While he was still very much a part of the company, it was not a full-time involvement.

VICTORIA IN THE EARLY 2000S

Victoria entered the early 2000s with sales of approximately $75 million and by 2007, partly as a result of opening the new plant in California, had succeeded in doubling this figure. Profits reached their highest level ever in 2005, but declined somewhat over the next two years as costs rose and the rate of sales growth slowed. Financial statements are presented in Exhibits 1 and 2. The following sections describe the company and its environment in the early 2000s.

Product Line

The bulk of Victoria's crane sales in the late 1990s and early 2000s came from a single product line, the LTM 1000, which was produced both in its Squamish facility (the firm had moved from Victoria to Squamish in the early 1920s) and its smaller plant in California, built in 2001. The LTM 1000 line consisted of mobile cranes of five basic sizes, averaging $750,000 in price. Numerous options were available for these cranes, which could provide uncompromised on-site performance, precision lifting capabilities, fast highway travel and effortless city driving. Because of the numerous choices available, Victoria preferred not to build them to stock. The company guaranteed 60-day delivery and "tailor-made" cranes to customer specifications. This required a large inventory of both parts and raw material.

Walters had used a great deal of ingenuity to keep Victoria in a competitive position. For example, in 2004, he learned that a company trying to move unusually long and heavy logs from a new tract of redwood trees in British Columbia was having serious problems with its existing cranes. A crane with a larger than average height and lifting capacity was required. Up to this point, for technical reasons, it had not been possible to produce a crane with the required specifications. However, Walters vowed that Victoria would develop such a crane, and six months later, it had succeeded.

Although the LTM 1000 series provided almost all of Victoria's crane sales, a new crane had been introduced in 2006 after considerable expenditure on design, development and manufacture. The $975,000 A-100 had a 70-ton capacity and could lift loads to heights of 61 metres, a combination previously unheard of in the industry. Through the use of smooth hydraulics, even the heaviest loads could be picked up without jolts. In spite of these features, and an optional ram-operated tilt-back cab designed to alleviate the stiff necks which operators commonly developed from watching high loads, sales of the A-100 were disappointing. As a result, several of the six machines built were leased to customers at unattractive rates. The A-100 had, however, proven to be a very effective crowd attraction device at equipment shows.

Markets

There were two important segments in the crane market—custom-built cranes and standard cranes—and although the world mobile crane market was judged to be $945 million in 2007, no estimates were available as to the size of each segment. Victoria competed primarily in the custom segment, in the medium- and heavy-capacity end of the market. In the medium-capacity custom crane class, Victoria's prices were approximately 75 per cent of those of its two main competitors. The gap closed as the cranes became heavier, with Victoria holding a 15 per cent advantage over Washington Cranes in the heavy custom crane business. In heavy standard cranes, Victoria did not have a price advantage.

Victoria's two most important markets were Canada and the United States. The U.S. market was approximately $360 million in 2007, and Victoria's share was about 15 per cent. Victoria's Sacramento plant, serving both the U.S. market and export sales involving U.S. aid and financing, produced 60 to 70 cranes per year. The Canadian market was much smaller, about $66 million in 2007, but Victoria was the dominant firm in the country, with a 60 per cent share. The Squamish plant, producing 130 to 150 cranes per year, supplied both the Canadian market and all export sales not covered by the U.S. plant. There had been very little real growth in the world market since 2002.

The primary consumers in the mobile crane industry were contractors. Because the amount of equipment downtime could make the difference between showing a profit or loss on a contract, contractors were very sensitive to machine dependability, as well as parts and service availability. Price was important, but it was not everything. Independent surveys suggested that Washington Crane, Victoria's most significant competitor, offered somewhat superior service and reliability, and if Victoria attempted to sell similar equipment at prices comparable to Washington's, it would fail. As a result, Victoria tried to reduce its costs through extensive backward integration, manufacturing 85 per cent of its crane components in-house, the highest percentage in the industry. This drive to reduce costs was somewhat offset, however, by the fact that much of the equipment in the Squamish plant was very old. In recent years, some of the slower and less versatile machinery had been replaced, but by 2007, only 15 per cent of the machinery in the plant was new, efficient, numerically controlled equipment.

Victoria divided the world into eight marketing regions. The firm carried out little conventional advertising, but did participate frequently at equipment trade shows. One of the company's most effective selling tools was its ability to fly in prospective customers from all over the world in Walters' executive jet. Victoria believed that the combination of its integrated plant, worker loyalty and the single-product concentration evident in their Canadian plant produced a convinced customer. There were over 14 such visits to the British Columbia plant in 2007, including delegations from China, Korea, France and Turkey.

Competition

As the world's second-largest producer of cranes, Victoria faced competition from five major firms, all of whom were much larger and more diversified. The industry leader was the Washington Crane Company, with 2007 sales of $600 million and a world market share of 50 per cent. Washington had become a name synonymous around the world with heavy-duty equipment and had been able to maintain a sales growth-rate of over 15 per cent per annum for the past 5 years. It manufactured in the United States, Mexico and Australia. Key to its operations were 100 strong dealers worldwide with over 200 outlets. Washington had almost 30 per cent of Canada's crane market.

Next in size after Victoria was Texas Star, another large manufacturer whose cranes were generally smaller than Victoria's and sold through the company's extensive worldwide equipment dealerships. The next two largest competitors were both very large U.S. multinational producers whose crane lines formed a small part of their overall business. With the exception of Washington, industry observers suggested that crane sales for these latter firms had been stable (at best) for quite some time. The exception was the Japanese crane producer Toshio, which had been aggressively pursuing sales worldwide and had entered the North American market recently. Sato, another Japanese firm, had started in the North American market as well. Walters commented:

> My father laid the groundwork for the success that this company has enjoyed, but it is clear that we have some major challenges ahead of us. Washington is four times our size and I know that we are at the top of their hit list. Our Japanese competitors are also going to be tough. The key to our success is to remain flexible—we must not develop the same kind of organization as the big U.S. firms.

Organization

In 2001, a number of accumulating problems had ended Brian Walters' semi-retirement and brought him back into the firm full time. Although sales were growing, Walters saw that work was piling up and things were not getting done. He believed that new cranes needed to be developed, and he wanted a profit-sharing plan put in place. One of his most serious concerns was the development of middle managers, given a perceived lack of depth. The root cause of these problems, Walters believed, was that the firm was overly centralized. Most of the functional managers reported to Rivers, and Rivers made most of the decisions. Walters concluded that action was necessary: "If we want to grow further, we have to change."

Between 2001 and 2004, Walters reorganized the firm by setting up separate operating companies and a corporate staff group. In several cases, senior operating executives were placed in staff/advisory positions, while in others, executives held positions in both operating and staff groups. Exhibit 3 illustrates Victoria's organizational chart as of 2005.

By early 2006, Walters was beginning to wonder "if I had made a very bad decision." The staff groups weren't working. Rivers had been unable to accept the redistribution of power and had resigned. There was "civil war in the company." Politics and factional disputes were the rule rather than the exception. Line managers were upset by the intervention of the staff VPs of employee relations, manufacturing and marketing. Staff personnel, on the other hand, were upset by "poor" line decisions.

As a result, the marketing and manufacturing staff functions were eradicated with the late-2007 organizational restructuring illustrated in Exhibit 4. The services previously supplied by the staff groups were duplicated to varying extent inside each division.

In place of most of the staff groups, an executive committee was established in 2006. Membership included the president and head of all staff groups and presidents (general managers) of the four divisions. Meeting monthly, the executive committee was intended to evaluate the performance of the firm's profit and cost problems, handle mutual problems, such as transfer prices, and allocate capital expenditures among the four operating divisions. Subcommittees handled subjects such as research and development (R&D) and new products.

The new organization contained seven major centres for performance measurement purposes. The cost centres were:

1. Engineering; R&D (reporting to Victco Ltd.)
2. International Marketing (Victoria Marketing Ltd.)
3. Corporate staff.

The major profit centres were:

4. CraneCorp. Inc. (U.S. production and sales)
5. Victco Ltd. (supplying Victoria with components)
6. Craneco (Canadian production and marketing)
7. Victoria-owned Canadian sales outlets (reporting to Victoria Marketing Ltd.)

The major profit centres had considerable autonomy in their day-to-day operations and were motivated to behave as if their division was a separate, independent firm.

By mid-2007, Brian Walters had moved out of his position as president, and Michael Carter, a long-time employee close to retirement, was asked to take the position of president until a new one could be found.

Walters saw his role changing.

> If I was anything, I was a bit of an entrepreneur. My job was to supply that thrust, but to let people develop on their own accord. I was not concerned about things not working, but I was concerned when nothing was being done about it.

In the new organization, Walters did not sit on the executive committee. However, as chairman of the board and chief executive officer, the committee's recommendations came to him and ". . . they constantly tried me on." His intention was to monitor the firm's major activities rather than to set them. He did have to sit on the product development subcommittee, however, when "things were not working . . . there was conflict . . . the engineering group (engineering, R&D) had designed a whole new crane and nobody, including me, knew about it." Mr. McCarthy, the VP of engineering and R&D, called only five to six committee meetings. The crane his group developed was not to Walters' liking. (There had been a high turnover rate in this group, with four VPs leaving since 2005.) Recognizing these problems, Walters brought in consultants to tackle the problems of the management information system and the definition of staff/line responsibilities.

In spite of these moves, dissatisfaction still existed within the company in 2008. The new organization had resulted in considerable dissension. Some conflict centred on the establishment of appropriately challenging budgets for each operating firm, and even more conflict had erupted over transfer pricing and allocation of capital budgets. In 2007–08, even though requested budgets were cut equally, lack of central control over spending resulted in over expenditures by several of the profit and cost centres.

The views of staff and the operating companies' presidents varied considerably when they discussed Victoria's organizational evolution and the operation of the present structure. Diane Walters, the president of Victoria International Marketing, liked the autonomous system because it helped to identify the true performance of sections of the company: "We had separate little buckets and could easily identify results." Furthermore, she felt that there was no loss of efficiency (due to the duplication of certain staff functions within the divisions) since there was little duplication of systems between groups, and each group acted as a check and balance on the other groups so that "manufacturing won't make what marketing won't sell." Comments from other executives were as follows:

> The divisionalized system allowed me to get closer to my staff because we were a separate group.

> We ended up with sales and marketing expertise that was much better than if we had stayed under manufacturing.

> If you (run the firm) with a manufacturing-oriented organization, you could forget what people want.

> In a divisionalized system, there was bound to be conflict between divisions, but that was not necessarily unhealthy.

Some executives saw the decentralized, semi-autonomous operating company structure as a means of giving each person the opportunity to grow and develop without the hindrance of other functional executives. Most, if not all, of the operating company presidents and staff VPs were aware that decentralization brought benefits, especially in terms of the autonomy it gave them to modify existing practices. One senior executive even saw the present structure as an indicator of their basic competitive stance: "Either we centralize the structure and retract, or we stay as we are and fight with the big guys." With minimal direction from Brian Walters, presidents were able to build up their staff, establish priorities and programs and essentially, were only held responsible for the bottom line.

Other executives believed that Victoria's structure was inappropriate. As one put it, "The semi-independence of the operating companies and the lack of a real leader for the firm has resulted in poor co-ordination of problem solving and difficulty in allocating responsibility." As an example, he noted how engineering's response to manufacturing was often slow and poorly communicated. Even worse, the executive noted, was how the priorities of different units were not synchronized. "When you manufacture just one product line, all your activities are inter-related. So when one group puts new products first on a priority list, while another is still working out bugs in the existing product, conflict and inefficiencies have to develop."

The opposing group argued that the present organization was more appropriate to a larger, faster-growing and more complex company. As one senior executive put it,

"We're too small to be as decentralized as we are now. All of this was done to accommodate the Walters' kids anyway, and it's now going to detract from profitability and growth." Another executive stated that, rather than being a president of an operating company, he would prefer to be a general manager at the head of a functional group, reporting to a group head. "If we had the right Victoria Heavy Equipment president," he said, "we wouldn't need all these divisional presidents." Another continued,

> Right now, the players (divisional presidents and staff VPs) run the company. Brian Walters gives us a shot of adrenaline four or six times a year, but doesn't provide any active leadership. When Brian leaves, things stop. Instead, Brian now wants to monitor the game plan rather than set it up for others to run. As we still only have an interim president (Carter); it is the marketplace that leads us, not any strategic plan or goal.

THE NEW PRESIDENT

Individual views about the appropriate characteristics of a new president were determined by what each executive thought was wrong with Victoria. Everyone realized that the new president would have to accommodate Brian Walters' presence and role in the firm and the existence of his two children in the organization. They all generally saw Brian as wanting to supply ideas and major strategies, but little else.

All but one of Victoria's executives agreed that the new president should not get involved in day-to-day activities or in major decision making. Instead, he should "arbitrate" among the line general managers (subsidiary presidents) and staff VPs and become more of a "bureaucrat-cum-diplomat" than an aggressive leader. As another put it, "The company will drive itself; only once in a while he'll steer a little."

THE 2008 SITUATION

Due to the proliferation of subprime mortgages in the U.S. and the subsequent decline in real estate and construction, industry analysts predicted a decline of 10 per cent in world crane sales, which totalled 1,200 units in 2007, and as much as a 30 per cent decrease in the North American market in 2008. Victoria's sales and production levels were down. Seventy-five shop floor employees had been laid off at Squamish, bringing total employment there to 850, and similar cuts were expected in Sacramento. Worker morale was suffering as a result, and the profit-sharing plan, which had been introduced in early 2007 at Walters' initiative, was not helping matters. In spite of the optimism conveyed to workers when the plan was initiated, management had announced in October that no bonus would be paid for the year. Aggravating the problem was the workforce's observation that while certain groups met their budget, others did not, and hence all were penalized. This problem arose because each bonus was based on overall, as well as divisional, profits.

Many of the shop-floor workers and the supervisory staff were also disgruntled with the additions to the central and divisional staff groups, which had continued even while the workforce was being reduced. They felt that the paperwork these staff functions created was time-consuming and of little benefit. They noted, for example, that there were four or five times as many people in production control in 2008 as there were in 2002 for the same volume of production. In addition, they pointed out that, despite all sorts of efforts on the part of a computer-assisted production control group, inventory levels were still too high.

Brian Walters commented on the 2008 situation and his view of the company's future:

What we are seeing in 2008 is a temporary decline in the market. This does not pose a serious problem for us and certainly does not impact on my longer term goals for this company, which are to achieve a 25 per cent share of the world market by 2012 and reach sales of $375 million by 2021. We can reach these goals as long as we don't turn into one of these bureaucratic, grey-suited companies that are so common in North America. There are three keys for success in this business—a quality product, professional people and the motivation for Victoria to be the standard of excellence in our business. This means that almost everything depends on the competence and motivation of our people. We will grow by being more entrepreneurial, more dedicated and more flexible than our competitors. With our single product line, we are also more focused than our competitors. They manage only by the numbers—there is no room in those companies for an emotional plea, they won't look at sustaining losses to get into a new area, they'll turn the key on a loser . . . we look at the longer term picture.

"The hazard for Victoria," Walters said as he looked out of his window toward the Sacramento airstrip, "is that we could develop the same kind of bureaucratic, quantitatively oriented, grey-suited managers that slow down the large U.S. competitors." "But that," he said, turning to his audience, "is something I'm going to watch like a hawk. We need the right people."

EXHIBIT 1   Victoria Balance Sheet for the Years 2003–2007 ($000s)

	2003	2004	2005	2006	2007
Assets					
Current assets					
Accounts receivable	12,492	11,940	14,664	15,768	16,426
Allowance for doubtful accounts	(439)	(465)	(423)	(445)	(474)
Inventories	31,729	36,637	37,047	38,439	40,567
Prepaid expenses	178	156	234	159	193
Total current assets	43,960	48,268	51,522	53,921	56,712
Advances to shareholders	1,950	1,950	1,950	1,950	1,950
Fixed assets: Property plant and equipment	10,260	10,470	10,312	11,029	11,083
Total assets	$56,170	$60,688	$63,784	$66,900	$69,745
Liabilities and shareholders' equity					
Current liabilities					
Notes payable to bank	$11,599	$12,328	$13,887	$15,241	$16,998
Accounts payable	14,568	17,029	15,814	15,697	16,479
Accrued expenses	1,611	1,678	2,613	2,251	1,732
Deferred income tax	628	600	594	612	517
Income tax payable	817	1,038	918	780	774
Current portion of long-term debt	1,368	1,336	1,300	1,332	1,354
Total current liabilities	$30,591	$34,009	$35,126	$35,913	$37,854
Long-term debt	9,426	9,165	9,030	9,007	9,171
Total liabilities	40,017	43,174	44,156	44,920	47,025
Shareholders' equity					
Common shares	300	435	442	585	652
Retained earnings	15,853	17,079	19,186	21,395	22,068
Total shareholders' equity	16,153	17,514	19,628	21,980	22,720
Total liabilities and shareholders' equity	56,170	60,688	63,784	66,900	69,745

EXHIBIT 2   Victoria Income Statement for the Years 2003–2007 ($000s)

	2003	2004	2005	2006	2007
Revenue					
Net sales	95,079	116,566	129,519	142,329	151,414
Costs and expenses					
Cost of sales	73,857	89,755	95,994	107,727	113,712
Selling expense	11,205	13,851	16,402	17,155	19,656
Administrative expense	4,026	5,800	8,235	8,692	10,557
Engineering expense	2,013	2,533	2,748	2,923	3,163
Gross income	3,978	4,627	6,140	5,832	4,326
Income taxes	1,621	1,921	2,445	2,257	1,881
Net income	2,357	2,706	3,695	3,575	2,445

EXHIBIT 3   Victoria Organizational Structure, 2001–2005

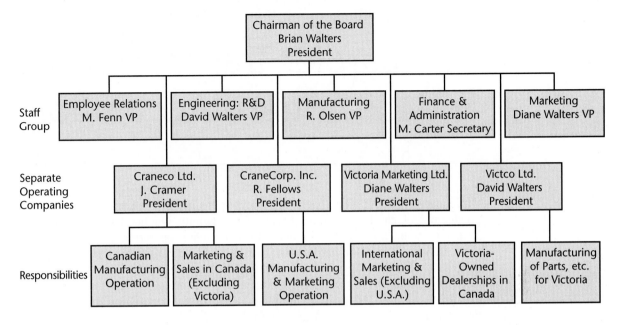

EXHIBIT 4   Victoria Organizational Structure, Late 2007

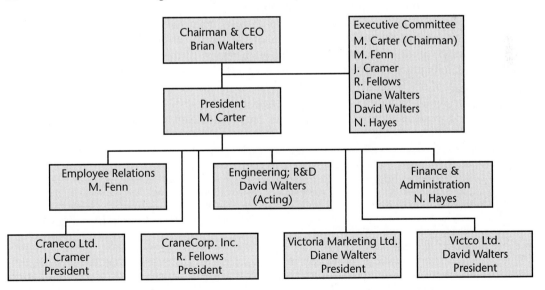

Bombardier Transportation and the Adtranz Acquisition

On January 10, 2001, it had been only one month since Pierre Lortie was appointed president and chief operating officer of St. Bruno, Quebec-based Bombardier Transportation (BT).[1] BT was one of three major operating groups of Montreal, Canada-based Bombardier Inc. (BBD) and, with 2000 revenues amounting to CDN$3.45 billion, it was one of the world's largest manufacturers of passenger rail cars. In an effort to expand BT's presence in the global rail equipment industry, executives at BBD had recently completed a successful negotiation for the acquisition of Adtranz from DaimlerChrysler for US$725 million. At approximately twice the size of BT, Adtranz (headquartered in Berlin, Germany) would not only expand BT's revenues and geographic scope but would significantly increase its competencies in propulsion systems and train controls and would complete its product portfolio. However, before the deal could close, BT required, among others, the regulatory approval of the European Commission (EC). Lortie was well aware that the EC process could be long and protracted.

Although Lortie had not been directly involved in the acquisition decision or negotiations, he was a supporter of the merger efforts. As he assumed his new responsibilities, Lortie began a thorough review of the work accomplished and the planning efforts undertaken to ensure an efficient integration of the two entities. As part of this process, he undertook a series of one-to-one meetings with members of his senior management team. The meetings were designed to measure the strengths and weaknesses of his key managers, but also to discuss the strategic and operational priorities.

David Barrett prepared this case under the supervision of Professor Allen Morrison solely to provide material for class discussion. The authors do not intend to illustrate either effective or ineffective handling of a managerial situation. The authors may have disguised certain names and other identifying information to protect confidentiality.

---

[1]St. Bruno was located on the south shore of the St. Lawrence River, in the suburbs of Montreal.

BT was structured into five geographically based operating units—North America, Atlantic Europe, Continental Europe, Mexico and China—and one market/functional unit, Total Transit Systems, which focused on turnkey projects. In contrast, Adtranz was organized around product segments (i.e., high-speed trains, cars, subway trams) and functions (i.e., bogies, drives, car bodies) making its structure and allocation of responsibilities quite foreign to Bombardier. Although each business complemented the other nicely and constituted a good strategic fit, the organizational structures were incompatible. Even though BT's management team in Europe had not been involved in the discussions and reviews with Adtranz that had preceded and immediately followed the deal, they were keenly aware of the organizational issues and eager to establish their position as soon as the nod could be given to proceed with the takeover.

On January 10, 2001, Lortie had just finished his first in-depth meeting with Rick Dobbelaere, vice-president of operations of Bombardier Transportation, Atlantic Europe. Dobbelaere had come prepared with questions about how BT and the senior management team would set priorities during the interim period while awaiting EC approval. He presented these to Lortie in question form:

> Do we sit and await approval from the EC before taking steps towards the potential integration of Adtranz? Should we focus our planning on ways to improve the product quality and reliability of Adtranz equipment with existing customers? Should we start to institute personnel changes within BT in anticipation of the merger, and if so, at what pace? Do we focus on top-line revenue growth or start to immediately focus on bottom-line cost cutting?

Dobbelaere was highly respected, not only within the Atlantic Europe division but throughout Bombardier, and Lortie was aware that his concerns and questions were shared by others, particularly in Continental Europe.[2] But Lortie realized that he faced additional issues, including concerns over BT's ongoing operating performance. As Bombardier expected EC approval of the acquisition within a matter of weeks, Lortie and his team had little time to waste.

BOMBARDIER COMPANY HISTORY

The Early Years

In 1921, at the age of 19, Joseph-Armand Bombardier opened a garage in Valcourt, Quebec, where he earned his living as a mechanic. Early in his life, he looked for a solution to the problem of travelling the snow-covered roads near his village, which kept many people isolated during the long winter months. Over a 10-year period, Bombardier used his garage to develop multiple prototypes of a vehicle that would make winter travel easier. In 1936, he submitted his B7 prototype, the precursor to today's snowmobile, for patent approval. This seven-seat passenger model sported a revolutionary rear-wheel drive and suspension system, both major innovations at that time.

After receiving an initial 20 orders, Bombardier assembled a work crew of friends and family to manufacture the B7s. Customers included country doctors, veterinarians, telephone companies and foresters. By 1940, Bombardier had built a modern

---

[2]BT Continental Europe was based in Berlin and included six manufacturing facilities in Germany and one each in Austria and the Czech Republic.

factory in his village that had an annual capacity of 200 units. In 1942, Bombardier incorporated his business as L'Auto-Neige Bombardier Limitee (ANB). Shortly thereafter the company began to receive orders from the Canadian government for specialized all-track vehicles for use by the armed forces efforts during the Second World War. Between 1942 and 1946, ANB produced over 1,900 tracked vehicles for the Canadian armed forces. Although not a profitable venture, the war-time manufacturing experience allowed Bombardier to refine his manufacturing process and develop competence in government relations.

The 1950s saw technological advances in lighter engines, improved tracking and high-performance synthetic rubber. In 1959, Bombardier achieved his lifelong dream when ANB introduced a one-passenger snowmobile. At an original price of CDN$900, the Ski-Doo sported 5-foot wooden skis, a coil spring suspension system and could travel at speeds of up to 25 miles per hour (mph). Sales increased from 225 units in 1959 to 2,500 units in 1962 and 8,000 units in 1964. Joseph-Armand Bombardier died in 1964, leaving a CDN$10 million company to his son, Germain.

In 1966, Germain Bombardier passed on the presidency to his 27-year-old brother-in-law, Laurent Beaudoin, and in 1967, the company name was changed to Bombardier Limited. In 1969, the company went public with the intention of utilizing the funds to vertically integrate and increase its manufacturing capability. BBD grew as the market for snowmobiles rapidly expanded in the late 1960s and early 1970s. The North American snowmobile market grew from 60,000 units to 495,000 units in the period between 1966 and 1972, and BBD captured one-third of this market. Between 1966 and 1972, BBD's sales soared from CDN$20 million to CDN$180 million, while profits rose from CDN$2 million to CDN$12 million. Under Beaudoin's leadership, the company pushed into the lucrative U.S. market, unveiled new products and utilized aggressive marketing initiatives to drive the business. In 1970, the company completed the acquisition of Austrian-based Lohnerwerke GmbH. Lohnerwerke's subsidiary, Rotax, was a key supplier of engines for Bombardier Ski-Doo snowmobiles and also a tramway manufacturer. This provided BBD with its first entry, albeit involuntarily, into the rail business. The energy crisis of the mid-1970s put the brakes on the snowmobile industry, and when the dust settled, the largest of the six remaining manufacturers was BBD.

Bombardier Begins To Diversify

Laurent Beaudoin, the chief executive of Bombardier, realized that in order to reduce cyclical risks and ensure its long-term survival, the company needed to diversify into other products beyond snowmobiles. To bolster sagging snowmobile sales, Beaudoin began to seek out opportunities for BBD within a more broadly defined transportation industry. In the late 1960s and early 1970s, BBD made several strategic acquisitions.

Transportation In 1974, snowmobiles represented 90 per cent of BBD revenues. By securing a CDN$118 million contract (US$99.14 million) with the city of Montreal to supply the local transit authority with 423 subway cars, BBD had made its first major move to diversify its revenues away from its predominant snowmobile business. Using rubber-wheeled cars licensed from the supplier to the Paris subway system, BBD's work won positive reviews from Montreal commuters. Further contracts followed, including supplying 36 self-propelled commuter rail cars to Chicago in 1977, 21 locomotives and 50 rail cars to Via Rail Canada in 1978, 117 commuter cars to New Jersey Transit Corporation in 1980, 180 subway cars to Mexico City in 1982 and 825 subway cars to the City of New York, also in 1982.

The mid-1980s was a turbulent time in the rail transportation industry, and BT looked to capitalize on industry uncertainty by purchasing companies at low prices and growing its market share through these acquisitions. Pullman Technology was acquired in 1987, Transit America in 1988 and controlling interests in rail equipment companies in France and Belgium in 1988. In the early 1990s, BT also acquired Concarril (Mexico's top rail manufacturer), as well as UTDC in Canada. These acquisitions and investments established BT as one of the leading supplier of rail cars and cemented its international reputation.

Aerospace In 1973, BBD commenced diversification into the aerospace business with the acquisition of a controlling interest in Heroux Limited of Longueuil, Quebec. Heroux designed, manufactured and repaired aeronautical and industrial components at its two Canadian plants. In 1986, following an international bidding contest, BBD acquired struggling Canadair from the Canadian government at a total cash and share price of CDN$293 million. By applying aggressive marketing tactics, cost-cutting measures and tight controls, BBD was quickly able to turn operations around. Subsequent acquisitions of Short Brother PLC (an aircraft producer in Northern Ireland) in 1990, Learjet Corporation in 1990 and a controlling stake in de Havilland in 1992 and the remaining interest in 1997 firmly entrenched BBD in the civil aircraft industry. During the 1990s, BBD introduced a series of new planes, including the Lear 60, the Challenger 600-3A, the Challenger 604 and the Lear 45. BBD delivered its first Canadair Regional Jet in 1992 and its first Global Express business jet in 1999, the CRJ 700 (75-seat jet) in 2001.

Corporate Balance By the early 1990s, BBD had diversified to the point where snowmobile sales represented less than 15 per cent of the company's revenues. BBD still controlled 50 per cent of the Canadian market and 25 per cent of the U.S. market for snowmobiles, but BBD had clearly established itself as a diversified company. By 1992, sales had increased to US$3.43 billion and profits to US$104 million. While, in many cases, the companies acquired by Bombardier were in poor shape, observers noted that the majority of Beaudoin's deals and acquisitions had been turned around and were making money.

Different operating groups at BBD took centre stage at different times during the 1990s (see Exhibit 1). In 1994, the recreational products group seemed to surge forward, fuelled by increased snowmobile sales and sales of Sea-Doo watercraft, first introduced in 1968. Profits from this group represented 37 per cent of the company's profits and made the recreational products group central to the company's success. The mid-1990s saw a boom in the aerospace group as both regional and business jet sales took off with the expanding economy. Many observers credited Bombardier with creating an entirely new commuter jet segment as the result of product innovation. Aerospace group sales grew from 1996 levels of US$3.16 billion to 2000 levels of US$7.79 billion. In 2000, the aerospace group represented 66 per cent of the company's revenues and 85 per cent of its profits.

BT continued to grow during this period as well. BT was awarded a prestigious contract to produce specialized rail cars for the huge Eurotunnel engineering project. In early 1995, Waggonfabrik Talbot KG of Germany was acquired for $130 million cash. In late 1997, BT acquired DWA Deutsche Waggonbau GmbH of Berlin for CDN$518 million (approximately US$359.52 million) and thus doubled its train and subway car manufacturing capacity in Europe. In December of that year, BT secured a US$1.18 billion contract with Virgin Rail Group of Great Britain to supply 78 diesel/electric multiple units and rail cars. In November 1999, the company entered into a joint venture to construct a manufacturing facility in China and to subsequently build 300 inter-city mass transit railcars for the Chinese Ministry of Railways (see Exhibit 2).

Bombardier Growth Philosophy

BBD sought acquisition opportunities that allowed it to add value to the business through the application of its existing competencies. Acquisitions were typically not viewed solely as financial plays, but as a way for BBD to complement or strengthen its existing businesses. BBD prided itself on thoroughly evaluating target companies so that pay-back was not reliant on the divestiture of some aspect of the acquired business. In negotiations, BBD had also shown that it was not afraid to walk away from a deal if it meant overpaying for a business. But once a deal was completed, BBD had a reputation for being patient in the integration of the acquired company.

In addition to a strong track record of integrating acquisitions, BBD had strengths in product costing and tendering. It also had extensive experience in product assembly. Whether aircraft, recreational products or rail cars, most products made by BBD were assembled, as opposed to manufactured. Utilizing external suppliers and adopting just-in-time delivery methods resulted in substantially reduced inventory levels, throughput time and assets. BBD sought ways to control product technology and design, assembly and distribution while outsourcing other non-core functions.

When taking over a business, BBD tried to eliminate waste and turn around underperforming assets by applying tried and tested management approaches over time as opposed to rushing to replace existing methods. This approach to acquisitions had garnered strong employee support over the years as workers realized that BBD would invest in new products and thus protect jobs. When BBD entered the aerospace industry through acquisitions, it did not replace existing staff. Instead, it used personnel from BT to teach successful approaches and manufacturing methods developed elsewhere in the organization. Transfers were not all one way; aerospace also shared its best practices in engineering management. With a commitment to excellence in assembly, inventory and management control, the aerospace group and BT were both able to make significant gains in productivity and product quality.

Despite the similarities in operating strategy, BBD's businesses differed in important ways. Bombardier's rail business was counter-cyclical versus other businesses in the company. An event such as an energy crisis would affect the rail industry differently than recreation or aerospace. Also, technology and product development were somewhat different across the businesses. In recreational and aerospace products, a Ski-Doo or business jet was developed for the market in general, while in rail, each customer had unique requirements and demanded tailor-made products. Generic rail cars simply did not exist. Customer demand varied according to a wide range of factors, including car size, weight, number of doors, propulsion system and so on. Other variables included the materials being used (steel versus aluminum), the type of car being produced (tramway, subway, inter-city or high-speed rail) and the infrastructure interface (track width).

BT was well regarded for its competencies in assembling rail cars, but it had no in-house expertise in propulsion systems, locomotives and switching and communications gear. Mark Cooper, vice-president of supply management of the inter-city trains for Adtranz, commented on Bombardier's reputation:

> Overall, Bombardier had a good level of credibility in the market place, despite being the smallest of the four rail manufacturers and rail service providers. It was seen to be one of the most effective in terms of its ability to deliver contracts and to manage and govern itself.

THE GLOBAL RAIL TRANSPORTATION INDUSTRY

In 2001, the railway transportation industry could be divided into six distinct segments: services, propulsion and controls, total transit systems, rail control solutions, rolling stock and fixed installations. Bombardier was absent from the last segment, which it considered as non-strategic and quite distinct in nature from the others.

1. Services included the planning and implementation of high-quality production and maintenance programs for both new and existing systems. Services also included the development of long-term process improvements to both systems operation and rolling stock maintenance.
2. Propulsion and Controls provided the diesel and electric motors, traction drives and control systems for trains.
3. Total Transit Systems provided a process through which manufacturers developed and supplied complete transportation systems and services. Working in partnership with local civil contractors and suppliers, manufacturers designed, integrated, installed and delivered a broad range of technologies—from large-scale urban transit systems to airport people-movers.
4. Rail Control Solutions were required to operate safe and efficient railways. Customers needed effective and "fail-safe" rail control and signalling equipment and systems.
5. Rolling Stock included subway cars, locomotives, inter-city/regional trains, high-speed trains, tram cars and light rail.
6. Fixed Installations referred to the building of rail infrastructure.

Public Policy and the Role of Governments in Regulating the Industry

The role of transportation and, with it, the attitudes and values of the public and government differed considerably from country to country and from continent to continent. Differences in public policy affected travel behaviours in a major way. While the cost of raw fuel amongst developed nations varied only marginally, fuel taxation levels differed by up to 800 per cent. As a result, public policy decisions affected not only the demand for fuel, but also the demand for public transportation as an alternative to the automobile. Because of lower gasoline taxes and the promotion of automobile travel in the United States, public transport ridership was three to nine times lower there than in European countries.

Most industry analysts believed that European policies promoting reductions in congestion, pollution abatement, urban development, traffic safety and energy conservation would continue and that support for public transportation systems would continue for the foreseeable future. The question was whether the United States would embrace European norms as congestion increased in that country. The combination of greater geographic distances, car-friendly culture, efficient and large air travel systems and aversion to government subsidies convinced many that U.S. rail policy would take a great many years to significantly change in a direction that supported an increase in rail transportation usage and investment.

Government regulations significantly affected industry structure in one other important way. Because U.S. passenger trains frequently shared tracks with freight trains, the government mandated that U.S. passenger rail cars be reinforced and strengthened in order to sustain collisions without collapsing with the ensuing high casualties that would result. As a result, U.S. trains were substantially heavier than European trains and were uncompetitive and poorly adapted to markets outside North America. European Union standards were widely embraced by governments and customers throughout the world, particularly in emerging economies such as China and India.

Infrastructure Model

A common perception in both Europe and the United States was that the rail industry, as a whole, was best designed to operate as a monopoly. High sunk costs, low marginal costs and demands for managerial coordination perpetuated this opinion. However, the emerging approach in the European Union (EU) was to separate the high-speed train industry and subject its component parts to competition. Although the potential technical, economic and social gains associated with this approach were perceived as exceptional, the process was often complicated by different national visions of how the industry should be divided between public and private ownership. Most countries opted to retain state ownership of infrastructure with the creation of a state agency to manage it. However, rolling stock companies were slowly becoming privatized. In 1998, the United Kingdom became the first country in the EU to totally privatize its rail system, including both infrastructure and rolling stock (see Exhibit 3).

The U.K. model of privately owned infrastructure and rolling stock had its troubles. The government was forced to operate the infrastructure element of the system when Railtrack, the private company it selected to manage the vast U.K. rail infrastructure (nearly 23,000 miles of track and 2,500 stations), went bankrupt in October 2001. Also, some in the United Kingdom worried about safety risks associated with spreading accountability across multiple for-profit companies. Conversely, the French model of public-owned train operator had been a tremendous success. As one industry observer remarked,

> France was operating state-of-the-art 300 km/h trains on a new network of rail lines dedicated to fast passenger service, and making money doing it. Britain was operating 1960s technology, 200 km/h trains on the nation's undependable and failing 19th century freight/passenger network, and losing money.[3]

Despite the success of the publicly operated French system, the EU was not designed to promote monopolistic, country-centred railroad companies. As a result, the U.K. model of privatized rolling stock and state-operated infrastructure more closely fit the cultural and social paradigm emerging in the EU and was thus being adopted cautiously and to differing degrees throughout the EU. During the latter half of the 1990s, public sector funding gradually shifted from supporting nationally subsidized rail systems to include more significant involvement from local municipal governments and the private sector. The belief was that by shifting to private ownership of rolling stock, the railway industry would eventually emulate the automobile or air transport models. Airlines worked with governments to secure terminals and immediate air space and runways, while operating and maintaining their own or leased airplanes. In effect, the airlines rented the infrastructure. Many believed that rail companies should operate in a similar fashion.

---

[3]Andersen, Svein and Eliassen, Kjell (2001), *Making policy in Europe*, London, Sage, p. 72.

High-speed Trains

By the early 2000s, the European Commission continued to rank the development of a Europe-wide high-speed train infrastructure as its highest investment priority in transportation infrastructure. The Community of European Railways (COER), a continent-wide association of railway companies, asserted that high-speed rail services were especially appropriate for the 200-kilometre to 300-kilometre distances between heavily populated urban centres. Most of Europe fit this profile with mobility increasing as the prospects of a single European market progressed. But for Europe to fully benefit from the one market model, decisions in infrastructure policy required a European, and not a nationalistic, approach. However, many predicted that the tendency for governments to protect national producers would be detrimental to the continent-wide objectives for many years to come.

Customers

The privatization of many national railways had changed the financing arrangements and customer base within the European rail car industry. In the past, manufacturers like BT sold directly to government-operated railroads. However, with the privatization of rolling stock operations increasing in Europe, leasing arrangements were now available to operators. In the United Kingdom, equipment manufacturers sold to one of three large rail equipment leasing companies (ROSCO) owned by one of three large British banks (Bank of Scotland, HSBC or Abbey National Bank), which then leased the new rolling stock to the train operators. This lease-versus-purchase option reduced up-front costs for rolling stock operators and significantly decreased their overall capital requirements. It also put a premium on standardized trains—necessary to protect residual values. This, in turn, significantly reduced the incentives to purchase rolling stock from within a rail operator's home country.

In countries with private rail operators, revenues were generated through ticket sales and government subsidies, while expenses were incurred through infrastructure franchise fees, day-to-day train maintenance, fuel and labour costs and leasing expenses. Since leasing costs on old, existing stock were much cheaper than on new equipment, operators preferred to delay purchases for as long as possible. When equipment was ordered, rail operators would sometimes seek additional delays by complaining that delivered equipment suffered from low reliability, which prevented it from meeting defined service standards the operators had committed to achieve in order to gain the concession from the government to operate the train service. This, in turn, caused manufacturers to incur late delivery charges and inventory costs as rail cars piled up in shipping yards awaiting minor repairs or adjustments. Many observers believed that these dysfunctional practices would be repeated in other European nations as they evolved to private operating models.

DAIMLERCHRYSLER AND ADTRANZ HISTORY

Although the roots of Chrysler go back to 1920 in the United States, the history of Daimler-Benz dates to the 1880s in Germany, and to the efforts of two inventive engineers—Gottlieb Daimler and Carl Benz. After a series of initiatives, Daimler-Benz was officially incorporated in 1926 and began producing cars under the Mercedes-Benz brand.

By the 1980s, competition in the global automobile market had increased dramatically, and Daimler-Benz was looking to diversify its business. Between February 1985 and February 1986, the company acquired three conglomerates[4] for a combined US$1.11 billion. The cash expenditures of these 1985/86 acquisitions put a strain on its balance sheet, and by mid-1993, Daimler-Benz reported its first loss since the Second World War. In 1994, operations recovered somewhat, with the company showing US$750 million in profits. But in 1995, the company's fortunes sagged again as it reported a loss of US$4 billion—the largest in German industrial history.

In 1995, Daimler-Benz's chief executive officer (CEO), Edvard Reuter, was forced to resign and was replaced by the aerospace division head, Jurgen Schrempp. One of Schrempp's first moves as CEO was the acquisition of 50 per cent of the rail division of Swedish-Swiss ABB Asea Brown Boveri Ltd., in exchange for US$900 million cash from Daimler-Benz. This joint venture formed the new ABB Daimler-Benz Transportation (Adtranz). Adtranz would become the largest rail service provider in the world, with annual sales of US$4.5 billion.

By the mid-1990s, Robert Eaton had assumed the position of CEO at Chrysler at a time when the economic conditions in the automobile industry included an excess manufacturing capacity and an Asian economic crisis. Industry analysts were projecting an annualized global overcapacity of 18.2 million vehicles by the early 2000s. It came as no surprise that both Eaton and Schrempp were seeking partners due to the inevitable consolidation within the industry.

DaimlerChrysler AG was formed in November of 1998 when Daimler-Benz and Chrysler merged in a US$37 billion deal. In 1998, the newly formed company had revenues of US$130 billion, factories in 34 countries and sales of 4.4 million vehicles, making it the fifth-largest automobile manufacturer in the world. In 1999, DaimlerChrysler acquired the remaining 50 per cent of Adtranz from ABB for US$472 million.

ADTRANZ

Although the name Adtranz dated back only as far as 1995, the multiple production facilities that comprised the company dated back to the 19th century. By the time of the DaimlerChrysler merger, the rail business in Europe had narrowed to four primary players: Alstom (France), Siemens (Germany), Adtranz and Bombardier. Unlike Altsom and Siemens, which had strong single country affiliations, Adtranz facilities and staff were a collection of multiple companies in multiple countries across the continent. Many of these companies also had a history of unstable ownership. For example, since 1989, the Adtranz facility in Derby, England, had experienced the following ownership changes: 100 per cent British Rail Engineering, then 40 per cent ABB, 40 per cent Trafalgar Rail and 20 per cent employee ownership, then 100 per cent ABB, then 50 per cent DaimlerChrysler and 50 per cent ABB and finally 100 per cent DaimlerChrysler. Each new ownership group brought its own philosophies to

[4]Daimler owned 50 per cent of Motoren-und Turbinen-Union (a manufacturer of aircraft engines and diesel motors for tanks and ships) and bought the remaining 50 per cent for $160 million. Daimler purchased 65.6 per cent of Dornier (a privately held manufacturer of spacecraft systems, commuter planes and medical equipment) for $130 million. Daimler additionally purchased control of AEG (a high-technology manufacturer of electronic equipment, such as turbines, robotics, data processing and household products) for $820 million.

manufacturing, sales, contract tendering, personnel, etc. Mark Cooper commented on the cultural challenges in Adtranz:

> I don't think that Adtranz has had enough time to fully develop its own culture. Every two years there seems to have been a change of ownership, a change in structure, a change in values and a change in processes. So under those circumstances, you don't get a good sense of who you are.

In the late 1990s, Adtranz represented less than three per cent of DaimlerChrysler's revenues. Revenues of US$3.3 billion were recorded at Adtranz in 1999, and in 2000, after years of continual losses, Adtranz reported its first year of break-even results. Although Adtranz revenues were up over 15 per cent in 2000, the annual revenue growth over the previous 4 years averaged only 4.5 per cent. Given the complexity of the business and its peripheral role in DaimlerChrysler's overall strategy, many observers believed DaimlerChrysler would eventually divest its rail business.

Production Challenges

Although DaimlerChrysler's assembly process and knock-down capabilities had been introduced, Adtranz's reputation for producing high-quality products was poor. In particular, Adtranz was having quality, reliability and certification problems with its core Electrostar and Turbostar model trains designed for the U.K. market (see Exhibit 4). In 2000, the Electrostar model had only eight trains in service as customers were refusing to accept this train. Reliability was achieved under the terms of the contract.[5] The Turbostar had 279 trains in service, but only 86.5 per cent were available for operation. Reliability was also not achieved under the terms of the contract. Deciphering the causes of these reliability problems was a challenge for BT managers. Neil Harvey, director of public affairs at BT, provided one common interpretation:

> In terms of the reputation of Adtranz's products and its overall reputation as a company, many believed there was a certain amount of mismanagement. In particular, some felt that too many contracts were being bought, and there was often very poor follow-through on products, production and subsequent support.

In addition, Adtranz's customer support function and its initial contract bidding processes were viewed by some as inadequate. Many at BBD believed that Bombardier's structured governance system, manufacturing controls and proven bidding systems would be excellent complements to Adtranz.

A STRATEGIC ACQUISITION FOR BOMBARDIER

Despite awareness that certain management practices needed adjustment, BBD viewed the acquisition of Adtranz as a smart strategic move for several reasons. Europe was the nexus of technological advances in the industry. Asia and South America primarily utilized European engineering concepts and had a history of failing to develop new technologies on their own. North American trains were too heavy and, hence, more expensive and costly to operate compared to the refinements in other world markets

---

[5]Reliability is measured as the total distance travelled by the rail car between breakdowns. The total performance of all rail cars is then averaged together to get the mean reliability number as a factor of distance travelled by each train model. This is then measured in subsequent periods to evaluate performance and reliability levels going forward.

and therefore not competitive. Also, the green movement and strong government support signalled long-term growth in the demand for rail transportation in Europe.

Not only did BBD find the European rail market attractive, but it was increasingly interested in balancing the revenue streams produced by its various groups. Strengthening the company's rail business was viewed as an important move to counter-balance Bombardier's growing, but cyclical, aerospace group. Dr. Yvan Allaire, executive vice-president at BBD, explained this strategic perspective: "Bombardier's value for shareholders is as a premium diversified company, not as an aerospace company."

Although margins were often lower in rail, (in 2000, margins for the aerospace group were 11 per cent—more than twice that of the transportation group) the industry benefited from the traditional business practice of advance and progress payments from customers. These payments translated to a low level of net utilized assets and very positive cash flow, contingent on a growing backlog of orders. These cash flows provided BBD with capital that was utilized throughout the company. Allaire explained this possibility:

> Transportation is a huge cash generator. While the margins are low, cash is large in this business. In fact, we have traditionally financed a large part of the investment in the aerospace sector from cash coming from transportation. A lot of people don't understand this.

Although low-margin businesses traditionally had profit levels driven by cost control, in the rail transportation industry, variability and project management performance were additional key drivers. For example, penalty charges for late delivery of each car generally amounted to 10 per cent of the value of it. In comparison, period costs in sales, general and administration (SG&A) accounted for six per cent of expenses. Preliminary investigation by BT managers indicated that repair and late delivery charges amounted to nearly 20 per cent of Adtranz's expenses. By applying BT's production and cost control systems, it was thought that acquiring Adtranz would provide substantial upside potential to raise profits.

Finally, BT had a strong reputation for its expertise in subway, trams and light rail cars. Adtranz had expertise in propulsion systems, high-speed and inter-city cars and signalling systems. While the acquisition would clearly strengthen Bombardier's global reach, it would also bring needed technology and product expertise to the electrical locomotive, high-speed train, propulsion and train control/communications. Closing this gap was becoming an imperative in Europe. For instance, in 2000, Bombardier was precluded to bid on the largest order ever awarded in the United Kingdom because Siemens, Alstom and Adtranz had refused to sell the propulsion system to them. In addition, Adtranz—at over twice the size of BT—would add $2.7 billion in backlog to maintenance and services, while providing more service facilities for customers in the European marketplace.

THE ACQUISITION

Financial analysts had anticipated that DaimlerChrysler would seek a sales price of 25 to 30 per cent of 1999 revenues of US$3.3 billion. However, ongoing problems in DaimlerChrysler's automobile business may have hastened their unloading of the non-core asset. Although Alstom and Siemens were BBD's main competitors in the rail industry, neither competed to acquire Adtranz, in part because of the beliefs that the European Commission would probably not approve of the merger due to their current strong positions in several market segments.

On August 4, 2000, BBD announced its intention to buy Adtranz for US$715 million. In its negotiations with DaimlerChrysler, BBD agreed to pay the purchase price in two installments of cash—one at closing and one six months later. Under the deal, Bombardier also agreed to the assumption of certain debt. For the deal to proceed, regulatory approval was notably required in both the EU and the United States. Given the complimentary operations of both companies in the United States (mechanical versus propulsion), U.S. approval was never a significant issue. However, matters were different in Europe, where it was initially estimated that the approval process would take between four and six months.

In negotiating the deal, DaimlerChrysler insisted on a limited due diligence process. In response, it was determined that any disagreement between the asset valuation done by BBD and the value given by DaimlerChrysler would lead to adjustments in a manner agreed upon; however, if adjustments exceeded a given amount, BBD could claim that there had been a material adverse change. This disagreement would then be submitted to an independent arbitrator for adjustment. Allaire commented on the limited due diligence process:

> It was certainly the first time that Bombardier agreed to go into an acquisition without first doing full due diligence. DaimlerChrysler basically said, "Look, have your people do an initial review and don't worry about the rest—we'll give you an equity guarantee. Adjustments will have to be made to the price if the provisions already taken in our books are not sufficient.

DaimlerChrysler had good reasons for wanting to limit the due diligence process. A new management team had just been put in place and was supposedly making progress streamlining Adtranz's operations. It was a natural concern that the management team would be seriously demoralized if Bombardier was invited in, only to later walk away from the transaction. And, secondly, Adtranz had serious worries about opening their books to a direct competitor. For Bombardier to come in and examine their pricing, cost structure, contracts and so on would have been off-limits under EU competition rules governing mergers and acquisitions.

NEGOTIATIONS WITH THE EUROPEAN COMMISSION

With the negotiations complete, BBD then applied to the EC for regulatory approval. Since 1990, the system for monitoring merger transactions in Europe had been governed by the Merger Regulation Committee of the European Commission. The Merger Regulation Committee eliminated the need for companies to seek approval for certain large-scale mergers in all European countries separately and ensured that all such merger requests received equal treatment. The control of mergers and acquisitions was one of the pillars of the EU's competition policy. When companies combined through a merger, acquisition or creation of a joint venture, this generally had a positive impact on markets: Firms became more efficient, competition intensified and the final consumer benefited from higher quality goods at lower prices. However, mergers that created or strengthened a dominant market position were prohibited in order to prevent abuses. A firm was in a dominant position when it was able to act on the market without having to account for the reactions of its competitors, suppliers or customers. A firm in a dominant position could, for example, increase its prices above those of its competitors without fearing any significant loss of sales.

In order to merge competing companies in Europe, the approval of the EC's merger task force was required. A review was comprised of two phases. Phase 1 involved a preliminary review, although full approval could be granted at this stage. Should

Phase 1 identify potential competitive issues or conflicts associated with the proposed merger, a deeper investigation proceeded to Phase 2. This second phase could take months or years to complete as the depth and breadth of the investigation increased.

While many mergers were ultimately approved by the EC merger task force, this was in no way guaranteed. During the prior year, Alcan's proposed purchase of Pechiney was turned down by the task force. And GE's proposed acquisition of Honeywell was facing growing opposition. With this track record, some feared that the EC might have a bias against North American companies buying European businesses.

BBD utilized a negotiation strategy that it hoped would prove successful in gaining regulatory approval. It identified potentially contentious issues in advance and developed tactics to minimize disagreement. In order to comply with the likely EC demands, BBD volunteered to divest non-strategic transportation assets in Germany and to extend, for several years, a series of supply contracts with smaller companies based in Austria and Germany. BBD was the main customer for these small suppliers and, with the acquisition of Adtranz, technologies previously purchased from these companies could now be manufactured within the newly assembled Bombardier/Adtranz. The few years of continued sales to BBD allowed these small companies to transition into new industries or to find new customers.

On a separate matter, BBD realized that the market share of the combined companies might be an issue for certain product segments in certain countries and so tried to shape the focus of the merger task force to the European market in total and not to any specific country. Primary geographical areas of concern were Germany, Austria and the United Kingdom. The German market was a key area with annual sales over US$1.8 billion; in Germany, Bombardier/Adtranz would have had a 50 per cent share. Concessions were made to ensure that a third competitor (Stadler) was allowed to strengthen its position in the German regional train market. Allaire, who led the negotiating team at the EC, commented on the efforts to win regulatory approval:

> You always have to make concessions—that's part of the deal over there. You don't get through the EC review process without some concessions, unless you are buying something totally unrelated. But if there is any relatedness, the acquiring party must come up with concessions that will make the transaction acceptable.

For BBD, the preliminary result of the negotiation was not a Phase 1 approval, but a shortened Phase 2 process because issues were identified in Phase 1 and solutions were already designed. BBD believed, in March 2001, that Phase 2 would conclude within a month or so of further negotiations. While BBD was pleased with the results of its efforts to this point, the company had no firm guarantees that the transaction would be approved, or if approved, under what final conditions and timelines.

PIERRE LORTIE

A graduate of Université Laval (Canada) and Université de Louvain (Belgium), Pierre Lortie was both an engineer and an economist by training. He also received an MBA with honours from the University of Chicago. Prior to taking over BT, Lortie had been president and chief operating officer of Bombardier Capital (2000–2001). He had also been president and chief operating officer of Bombardier International (1998–2000), president of Bombardier Aerospace, Regional Aircraft (1993–1998) and president of Bombardier Capital Group (1990–1993). Before joining Bombardier in 1990, Lortie had been chairman, chief executive officer and president of Provigo Inc.—a major, Quebec-based retailer (1985–1989)—and president and chief executive officer of the Montreal Stock Exchange (1981–1985).

Over the years, Lortie had developed a reputation within BBD as a turnaround expert. His movements throughout BBD corresponded with the transformation of under-performing businesses into market leaders within a few years of his taking the helm. His philosophy included a combination of approaches: strong and decisive leadership, hands-on management, good relationships with existing personnel and the development of pride within those on the team. He also believed in the importance of rapidly achieving small, visible wins in order to build the support necessary to make subsequent larger changes. Lortie summarized his approach:

> You have to figure out the business model and focus everything on the key factors. You also have to work with the people . . . making sure they are focusing on what has to be done . . . helping them, coaching them and removing roadblocks. You should never forget that people like successes and being on the winning team.

Lortie recognized that his style and methods of change management were in some ways different than approaches taken by others in turnaround situations. Although aware of the need to streamline costs, he did not follow the traditional approach of implementing massive, short-term, cost-cutting tactics as an initial step in the turnaround plan. Instead, he focused first on creating a healthy operating environment through the implementation of reporting and governance systems aimed at monitoring key metrics and assessing current and potential success. His main objective was to ensure a balance between cost reduction or restructuring initiatives and revenue growth. He strongly held the view that balance was necessary because halting growth would hurt the market performance of a company far more than would a failure to rapidly reduce costs.

In promoting change, he not only engaged and empowered people at all levels, he also sought to create the trust and credibility necessary for a leader to implement further, more difficult changes that may be required based on assessment of the metrics. Lortie commented on the rationale behind his move to BT:

> My job at Bombardier has been to turn around operations that were not doing well. This is what I did at Bombardier Capital and Regional Aircraft. When Bob Brown (CEO of BBD) asked me to take over the job at transportation, he was concerned that there were difficulties in the current transportation group and high expectations involving the Adtranz merger. He felt that the magnitude of the task of stitching together the two organizations and rapidly delivering acceptable performance required someone who had a track record. There was some concern that I had not been at Bombardier Capital long enough to complete the restructuring process I had set in motion. But Adtranz was going to be Bombardier's biggest acquisition ever and getting it right seemed to be more important than keeping me at Capital.

Determining a Course of Action

While Lortie was a veteran of Bombardier and had participated in the strategic plan and budget reviews of the group over the years, he admitted knowing relatively little about Bombardier Transportation operations, per se. But he was convinced that the process for building and operating trains was not dissimilar to commercial aircraft. Many of the key success factors were thought to be the same. Beyond this core belief, Lortie faced an overwhelming number of decisions. He summarized the long list:

> What was the best way for us to leverage the potentially increased size of Bombardier Transportation? Should we take a top-line approach to results or a bottom-line approach? How can we tailor the integration to balance revenue and cost initiatives? How do we reconcile the fundamentally incompatible organizational structures,

particularly in Europe? How do we go about designing the "best" organizational structure under the circumstances? How should we proceed to approve new bids (those arising in the first few weeks and longer term) and ensure they are profit-making propositions? How should we develop and instill a project management culture in an organization that has no such tradition (or lost it)? How do we get management focused on the operations, on "getting it right," avoid finger pointing at former Adtranz management, create a climate conducive to teamwork while conducting a thorough due diligence of all Adtranz contracts and operations? How and when should Bombardier integrate its manufacturing philosophies into the existing Adtranz operations? What should Bombardier do to minimize tensions and maximize teamwork with personnel changes imminently on the horizon? How should those personnel changes be made? Who, in the management ranks of Adtranz and BT, should I keep and who should I replace, and how should I go about the process of making these decisions? Should the headquarters of the merged companies be located in St. Bruno, Quebec, Berlin or a more neutral city like Brussels, Paris or London? And finally, what kind of style should I use in leading the organization forward? How directive should I be versus participative in making decisions?

The Richard Ivey School of Business gratefully acknowledges the generous support of The J. Armand Bombardier Foundation in the development of these learning materials.

EXHIBIT 1   Bombardier Revenue and Profit History, 1992 to 2001 (CDN$ millions)

Fiscal year*	Overall	Transportation	Aerospace	Recreational products	Capital	Other
2001e	16,101	3,043	10,562	1,687	1,033	(224)
2000	13,619	3,446	8,126	1,473	739	(165)
1999	11,500	2,966	6,444	1,628	571	(109)
1998	8,509	1,679	4,621	1,633	245	332
1997	7,976	1,597	4,011	1,866	162	341
1996	7,123	1,575	3,309	1,641	140	459
1995	5,943	1,310	2,981	1,111	112	430
1994	4,769	1,312	2,243	791	97	323
1993	4,448	1,238	2,228	556	58	367
1992	3,059	726	1,519	391	56	366

Profits Before Taxes—Segmented by Division

Fiscal year*	Overall	Transportation	Aerospace	Recreational products	Capital	Other
2001e	1,428	121	1,237	86	(15)	—
2000	1,124	174	904	18	28	—
1999	827	148	682	(46)	43	—
1998	627	85	462	1	64	16
1997	606	63	270	212	47	14
1996	461	100	150	174	42	(6)
1995	346	66	141	117	22	(1)
1994	207	(24)	137	76	14	4
1993	151	(73)	181	29	7	7
1992	121	4	137	(9)	(12)	2

EXHIBIT 1   (Continued) Revenue—Segmented by Region

Fiscal year*	Overall	Canada	Europe	United States	Asia	Other
2001e	16,101	1,241	4,757	8,592	471	1,040
2000	13,619	1,013	4,362	7,139	327	779
1999	11,500	900	4,049	5,497	259	796
1998	8,509	962	2,260	3,964	760	563
1997	7,976	949	2,342	3,712	605	367
1996	7,123	4,504	1,779	841	—	—
1995	5,943	3,619	1,536	789	—	—
1994	4,769	2,696	1,431	642	—	—
1993	4,448	2,335	1,675	438	—	—
1992	3,059	1,331	1,373	355	—	—

e–estimate

*fiscal year ends January 31. As a result, 2001 data essentially covers results from 2000.

Source: Company files.

EXHIBIT 2   Overview of Bombardier Businesses in 2000

Businesses	Leadership Position
Recreational Products Group Snowmobiles (Ski-Doo) Personal watercraft (Sea-Doo) Small engines (Rotax) All-Terrain vehicles Neighbourhood electric vehicles (NEV) Sport boats	No. 2 globally No. 1 globally No. 1 in ultra-light aircraft engines Launching No. 1 globally
Transportation Group Mass transit and systems	No. 1 in North America No. 4 in Europe
Aerospace Group Business jets (Challenger, Global Express, Learjet 31A, 45, 60) Commercial aircraft (Canadair Regional Jet, Dash 8) Amphibious Aircraft (CL415)	No. 2 globally No. 1 in 29–50 seat globally No. 1 globally
Capital Group Dealer inventory financing Commercial industrial financing Railcar leases Manufactured housing mortages Targeted consumer financing	Strong positions in niche markets

Bombardier Inc.

Source: Adapted from McKinsey Quarterly, 1997, Volume 2.

EXHIBIT 3   Growing Privatization of the European Union Rail Industry

Partial Deregulation:
Germany
Sweden
Denmark
Netherlands
Switzerland
Italy

Nationalized:
undergoing process of change

Privatization:
United Kingdom

Commercialization:
France
Spain
Portugal
Belgium
Norway
Finland
Austria
Ireland
Turkey

Source: Company files.

EXHIBIT 4 Bombardier's Electrostar

Intercity Transport

Electrostar* Electric Multiple Unit, Class 375/377
United Kingdom

Bombardier Transportation is responsible for supplying 182 Class 375/377 Electrostar* trains to the UK Govia owned rail operator, South Central Ltd. These state of the art, air-conditioned electric trains are either three or four cars in length. Each vehicle has two wide sliding powered doors per side capable of handling the passenger densities and flows required by busy urban and sub-urban services.

The trains operate at speeds up to 160 km/h on suburban services south of London. 15 of the 4-car trainsets are dual voltage capable of both 25 kV AC 50 Hz overhead and 750 V DC third rail operation. The remaining 167 electric trainsets in 3 and 4-car formations are single DC voltage only.

Particular attention has been paid to the provision of a high degree of reliability, safety and maintainability whilst ensuring low whole life costs.

The Class 375/377 Electrostar trains have a high level of passenger comfort with a very quiet interior environment and are fully compliant with the requirements of the Disability Discrimination Act. A modern passenger information system linked to the Global Positioning System relays messages in both visual and audible form. Each car will be fitted with a closed-circuit television surveillance system for enhanced internal security, allowing the driver to view car interiors whilst the train is stationary.

BOMBARDIER *TRANSPORTATION*

Source: Company files.

CASE 30

Challenges of Growth at Protegra

Wadood Ibrahim was looking through the window of Protegra's business building, focusing on a duck pond that employees made last summer for hosting a family of jolly birds that somehow landed on the company premises. The CEO of this growing consulting firm had many reasons for satisfaction. In 2008, Protegra celebrated its 10th birthday with good financial results (see Exhibit 1), added prestigious awards to its already rich collection (see Exhibit 2), maintained employees that came happily to work, attracted new talent, expanded the project portfolio, acquired a small software development company and advanced its national and international recognition. Protegra employees embraced two strategic thrusts that made the Protegra way: a unique organizational culture of a flat, professional organization and the combining of two areas of consulting—business performance and software development.

A seasoned business leader and entrepreneur, Ibrahim knew that strengths and opportunities were usually countered by challenges. He knew that the steady increase in the company's size and international expansion of operations could challenge the Protegra way. The question ringing in Ibrahim's mind was how could Protegra keep growing while maintaining the culture of a small organization and the overall unique organizational design?

BACKGROUND

Protegra was established in 1998 in Winnipeg, Manitoba, when three friends decided to deploy their rich experience from the information technology (IT) industry to build a dream company. Ibrahim explained:

> We wanted to create a place where we actually wanted to work, where all the organization members could be what they wanted to be. The other motivator was

to create quality software, while delivering on schedule and budget. We stated these intentions in the very name of the company, which joined the words "professional" and "integrity." "Protegra" stands for "professionals with integrity."

After immigrating to Canada and obtaining his computer science degree and an M.Sc. in industrial engineering, Ibrahim worked as an IT professional in several organizations before turning entrepreneur.

Protegra started out, with the three founding members and a few employees, by developing software for the gaming and financial industries. Until 2004, the strategic direction was toward developing software products for sale. Then, after some heated discussion, a majority in the company decided against that course. The new course was toward developing custom software to be offered along with business performance consulting. The later competence emerged opportunistically out of the company's effort to engineer its own processes according to a lean methodology. After implementing lean operations, one client asked if Protegra could customize internal processes in the client's organization. Protegra took on the challenge and provided a process-improvement solution, accompanied with custom-built software and training. The client was satisfied. Protegra realized from this experience that there existed a market for offering both business performance and information systems consulting.

In the mid-2000s, Protegra was one of the fastest-growing small companies in Canada, expanding its client base into the United States, Europe and Japan. Its clients were both for-profit and non-profit organizations. In 2008, the company had 67 employees and generated about $7.8 million in revenue. Protegra had achieved a number of awards, including the Best Small and Medium Employer in Canada in 2009 and Manitoba's awards for the project of the year and for best business practices in 2006.

PROTEGRA'S STRUCTURE

Protegra was a flat organization. There was just one level of management, represented in the operations team that oversaw projects, financial results and anything else requiring immediate attention, and the client relationship management team that oversaw sales and marketing. Ibrahim, the only remaining founding member of the company, served on both teams. While working in a collaborative, peer-based fashion that defied titles, the team members used some traditional titles in communication with external parties (e.g., manager and director). The intention was to avoid confusing the clients and partners with their unorthodox organizing and management philosophy.

Darlene Smith, director of human resources, explained that the term "management" had a different meaning in the company. "We don't actually have people who manage people. Nobody really reports to the one who happens to have that title of manager. Our management is about managing the responsibilities in a particular area—not people."

Protegra had no external stakeholders, as it was entirely employee-owned. Even the two retired founding members had to sell back their shares before leaving. Shares were offered to all the employees, and half of them had chosen to buy. A share of profits had been regularly distributed to the shareholders after the annual employee bonus had been covered. The remaining profits were reinvested in the company for future growth.

Protegra's flat organizational structure was supported by intensive horizontal communication. Ibrahim explained, "We don't hide information. We all share both the good news and the bad news. Assuming that employees are unable to handle bad news is condescending. The only information that we don't share is private and personal information."

Every Protegra employee could freely talk to anyone else, ask questions, make proposals and initiate communication via different channels for the sake of professional development and other shared goals. Dan Perron, practice leader for business performance consulting, explained how horizontal communication had been deployed in tracking organizational performance: "The operations team has a very rigorous planning process. We use our balanced scorecard to track our performance, and every month we report on it. Every employee can see the reports anytime. As well, everybody can provide feedback."

This flat organization was also flexible since Protegra did not have many rules and regulations. "A lot of organizations react to a few 'bad apples' that can land in any organization, and in defence they create all sorts of procedures and policies," commented Ibrahim. "However, I think we should make the organization work for the majority, and then the 'bad apples' will be squeezed out anyway."

Even though it offered consulting services in two areas—information systems and organizational performance—and had clients in several industries, Protegra was not differentiated in a functional sense. Rather, the basis of its organization was the project team. Usually engaging between two and five members, a project team was assembled of professionals with competencies fitting the project needs. Competencies were the skills falling into three categories: technical, critical thinking and interpersonal. Combinations of competencies provided the basis for roles a team member could fill, such as application developer (programmer), technical architect, application architect, business analyst, consultant and project manager.

Although these different roles existed, collaboration rather than hierarchy reigned in the team context. For example, an application architect, who took care of the overall design of application software and the coordination of work, usually had as much say in project decisions as a project manager. A technical architect, who was closest to developers and could do some coding, also participated in making important decisions within a project team. Terry Bunio, internally known as delivery lead and externally as delivery manager, remarked, "Project managers and architects are on equal footing at Protegra. This is different from the industry practice that puts a project manager above everyone else on the team. A project manager should be a supporting role, not a directing role. The direction should come from your team."

Sean Bueckert experienced this democratic, shared leadership in many projects he worked on in different roles: "When some big technical decision came up, we would summon people together and start discussing what our options were, what was good, what bad. . . . And then we made a decision as a team."

In project-driven organizations, project staffing had usually been a challenging task, particularly when different projects had to compete for the same resources. At Protegra, there was a resourcing process that took advantage of the shared leadership practice. This process specified objectives to be rated in deciding on team member assignment. The employee-related objectives included the employee's career goals, expertise and wishes. Other criteria were the growth of Protegra's sales and portfolio and the value the company was able to deliver to the customer. Members of the operations team and leaders of affected projects individually rated a professional to be assigned, and then they discussed the ratings.

Differences in ratings were always reconciled, noted Bunio, since Protegra professionals shared an understanding of priorities. For example, a more demanding project that involved the solving of a business problem usually had a competent professional on board even though this person could be already engaged in some simpler work in another project. Once an assignment was decided, the professional was asked to join a team. But the assignee could refuse the assignment. However, nobody had ever used this right. Bunio explained: "I'd have a good discussion with them, and if the assignment was not great, I'd let them know that this fact was noted and that it would be taken into consideration the next time we make assignments."

PROTEGRA'S CULTURE

Protegra had a strong organizational culture that influenced many other aspects of the organization. This culture was in many respects unique, and it had been a major attraction point for a number of job applicants, as well as a key to retaining and engaging existing employees. Protegra's culture had three focal points: employee, client and professionalism.

The employee focus was expressed in the saying "People come first," which Ibrahim and other Protegrans had readily cited on many occasions. Built into the foundations of the company since its inception, the employee focus was equally shared by new organization members. Jennifer Glen, who filled a new role of employee relationship facilitator, explained what part of the Protegra culture attracted her: "I was looking for a place where I could submit my ideas and feel like they were being heard, where I could work autonomously and feel that the company was about more than earning a profit." She pointed out that Protegra's culture was not bound to limitations of traditional organizations in which managers assumed that people's abilities were much more limited than they really were.

The focus on employees surfaced in several values. One was *Respect for Others*. Bueckert commented, "And even if you enjoy the work in a company, the people might ruin it. But they can also make it better. So I think the people have to be friendly, respectful, good to get along with and provide a comfortable, respectful, enjoyable work environment. And we have that here at Protegra."

Protegra had a formal process of complaining for the employees who felt offended by the language or acts of others. A team of peers with a changing membership considered the complaint and ensured that the case was brought to a resolution in compliance with Protegra's culture.

While many organizations could be touted for nurturing respectful employees, at Protegra this value dove-tailed with a less usual one—*Avoid Bad Politics*. Protegrans believed that talking about others behind their backs, manoeuvring to promote one's agenda, blocking others and similar acts belonged to bad politics that had no place in their company. Director of human resources Smith admitted that, right at her start at Protegra, she took this aversion to bad politics with caution: "I quickly realized that there was indeed no backstabbing at this place. I wasn't getting employees coming into my office to talk about a conflict they were having with other employees." She explained that bad politics was blocked by several characteristics that made Protegra a different place. One was a lack of hierarchy that otherwise could facilitate building personal empires around a rank. Other blockers of bad politics were peer-based decision-making, collaboration and teamwork. Since people were moving from one team to another, an employee would ultimately get to know everyone else. This dynamic facilitated self-control and self-awareness of one's reputation on the part of every Protegra employee.

Protegrans believed that "the world is your oyster." The professional world was there for everyone to discover, open and explore. This was yet another aspect of employee focus, which could be translated into a value of *Empowerment and Self-Actualization.* Ryan Caligiuri, who, right after graduation, became communications coordinator at Protegra, noted that taking on leadership responsibilities was an important expectation that Ibrahim and the company set before him. "They looked to me for guidance on the things I was hired for. If I didn't know something, I had to get myself educated. This has really made my job fun, opened it up and empowered me as a person because I've been in charge of my career. The world really is my oyster!"

Uwe Schmitz, technical architect, provided more illustrations of the value of *Empowerment and Self-Actualization:*

> I think that everyone at Protegra has the freedom to exercise as much creativity, to take as much ownership and to guide different parts of the organization as they wish. We can bite off as much as we wish. I don't ask anyone for permission. I just do it, and then I shop it around with my colleagues. Honestly, I don't think I'm working, I'm having fun.

Another pillar of Protegra's culture was the focus on the client. In their consulting engagements, Protegrans were expected to do their best in order to deliver the best value for their clients. This implied creating quality software and business solutions that were based on advanced knowledge and technologies and that made a beneficial difference on the client's side. Protegrans believed that the foci on the client and on the employee were complementary. This was formulated through the value of *Three Wins.* If employees enjoyed their project work, they won. If employees won, the client won too, because they had gotten the best value from such project work. The third win resulted from these two and applied to Protegra as a whole. A happy client acted as the best advertisement and usually came back for more.

Schmitz interpreted the effect of the Three Wins equation on software development: "If our developers can solve a programming problem in three lines of code rather than 30, that's in everybody's best interest because every line of code costs money to create and to maintain."

Protegra had discovered that a repeat customer was most likely to accept this entire equation. The repeat customer was able to understand that Protegra also needed to win by making a profit, or the company would not be around when its service was needed again.

The atmosphere of a professional organization was the third pillar of Protegra's culture. Its foundations were in project-based teamwork. Perron learned teamwork flying on the C-130 Hercules, a 14,400 horsepower military transport aircraft. Through his military experience, Perron developed an unshakeable enthusiasm toward teamwork:

> It was amazing what a small team could accomplish while handling the gigantic aircraft in all kinds of situations, including missions to perilous combat zones. We aviators shared principles of self-discipline, leadership, team problem solving and team-based performance evaluation. These principles equally apply to consulting work at Protegra.

While being the foundation of the organizational structure, the project team was supported by a set of values favouring peer-based relationships over hierarchy. One such value was *Open Communication.* Perron explained how it worked for him: "I'd come and have a conversation with anybody, and ask them what they think. And people would give me their opinions, as everybody here was free to say what they think, and there was no fear of failure."

Like the crew of a Hercules aircraft, Protegra nurtured *Shared Leadership,* which materialized in the peer-based decision-making in project teams, as well as in the operational team. Leadership was also shared in the entire organization among professionals initiating some action that others responded to. Glen provided several examples of shared leadership practices:

> Anyone can become an internal or external thought leader in some area. The internal thought leader is considered the go-to-person for a particular methodology or technology. That person might give our internal Lunch-and-Learns, do coaching and mentoring on that particular area or maintain our internal wiki on that subject. The external thought leader may give presentations at conferences on behalf of Protegra, create an external blog or write a white paper.

Trust was another salient value in this professional culture. It stemmed from *Shared Leadership* and *Open Communication,* as well as from the people focus. Trustfulness pre-empted the space for individual competition and bad politics.

Part of this professional culture was the management of material resources. For example, a programmer could have an office because the work involved extensive confidential communication with a client. However, the project manager on the same project could be seated in an open cubicle. Protegrans maintained that this allocation of offices should not be a matter of entitlement but rather result from common sense and real needs.

Continuous Improvement was another aspect of Protegra's professional culture. "That's where we really get a lot of joy here, as people keep thinking of how to make things better," remarked Bunio. Perron explained that *Continuous Improvement* was practiced both at the strategic and operational levels. The former began with the strategic planning process that involved all the employees in a process ending with an annual launch conference. Starting from broad targets for the year, everybody was to reflect on the previous year, and to share what was learned and how to build on that knowledge in the next year.

Continuous Improvement pertained to the individual level as well. A good professional was deemed one who continually improved personal knowledge. Protegrans regularly used organized knowledge-sharing events. They also learned on their own at home or in the office when there was no immediate project work to be done. Since the learning time was not billable and Protegra lived on billable hours, knowledge acquisition required a delicate balancing with the consulting work.

The professional culture at Protegra was rounded up by a set of beliefs and practices characterizing the company's way of working. These were based on the assumption that a *lean approach* was the desirable way of operating for both Protegra and its clients.

LEAN APPROACH TO CONSULTING

In its consulting practices, Protegra used a lean methodology. Perron recalled that this methodology had developed early in Protegra's life by combining concepts from Toyota's lean manufacturing approach, some methods described in the consulting literature and the professional experience and ideas of Protegrans of the time. Essentially, Protegra's lean methodology tended to streamline the job on the consultant side, as well as provide streamlined solutions to the client. Put another way, both the purpose of the consulting process and the result of consulting were to maximize efficiency.

The consulting process aimed at identifying a gap between goals and reality. This gap constituted the problem to solve. Analysis then turned to discovering a root cause to the problem. "Usually, information exchange, information translation, information retrieval and data structure were root causes of problems, which then call for looking for IT solutions," noted Perron. Still, Protegra consultants would not come to an engagement with the intention of merely selling yet another piece of software. The information part of the solution first had to be conceived of in terms of the lean principles of value for the end-client and waste elimination. An example was the practice of re-entering the same data, which reduced the efficiency of the pertinent work task or process. The software solution had to eliminate the redundant data entry as the root cause.

The lean methodology involved examining various aspects of the client organization, including governance, reward mechanisms, remunerations and incentives. It also engaged the client in problem solving. Perron pointed out that organizations were often unaware of the problem-solving capabilities of their own staff. Why were employees not identifying problems or solving problems? Not because they could not do it, but because they were not asked to do so.

A showcase of the lean methodology was the project for Loewen Windows, a large manufacturer of wooden windows and doors for the luxury market, located in Steinbach, Manitoba. The goal of the project was to enhance lean manufacturing by improving the efficiency of key organizational processes and quality assurance. In accord with the lean principle of high-bandwidth communication and collaboration with the client, Protegra's consultants worked with many employees at Loewen to document and define the client's measures of success and the value delivered to customers. Consultants also collaborated with a client's multi-occupational team to identify root causes to problems and to solve them.

In the Loewen project, the consultants also addressed the governance of the organization, following the principle that root causes could be in that area. Loewen's information systems were thoroughly examined as well. The solutions rested on engaging the resources of the organization to train and empower employees, re-engineering processes and innovating information systems. Loewen was satisfied with innovations that fit its strategy. It particularly praised Protegra's expertise and partnership-creating capability.

Part of the lean methodology was the process for developing and maintaining software—Protegra's Lean Software Life Cycle. Schmitz explained the principles behind this cycle. One was iterative development that created system functions and user interface through iterations, while using the client's continuous feedback to improve the computer code. The client would get to see and evaluate code early and often, thus helping developers avoid delivering something that was not desirable, which would be considered waste from the lean perspective. The client had the opportunity to test the prototype and figure out if something needed to be changed.

The Lean Software Life Cycle welcomed changes of system requirements. While this principle would usually complicate the developer's job, it was used to increase the quality of software and its value for the client. Another principle was to defer commitment to technical details until the last responsible moment in order to provide the user with flexibility. For example, instead of predefining certain parameters and thus forcing always the same way of running software, design allowed for configurable settings that the user could enter while the software was running. Deferring the decision to the last responsible moment also applied to the selection of technologies to be built into an information system.

The development process included meetings devoted to reflecting on accomplishments and deciding on necessary adjustments. This principle stemmed from the cultural value of continuous improvement. Lastly, the software package had to be optimized as a whole, which included answering questions: How should software be updated? How should the data be fed into the information system? How should the solution be adapted to the changing business requirements? The software was thoroughly tested before the final release. Schmitz stressed that the quality test went beyond determining if the software performed the required work for the client. Complying with functional requirements was rather assumed, and the real measure of quality was the reliability, performance and other non-functional requirements of software.

The overarching value of waste elimination or efficiency maximization drove continuously the system development work. For example, the Lean Software Life Cycle prescribed a number of project documents, but only some were considered critical and thus mandatory, while others were left to the discretion of project teams.

INFORMATION SYSTEMS AT PROTEGRA

Protegra was a paperless company. One could search in vain for paper folders in the offices and cubicles of the company's building. The employees would get their pay stubs e-mailed to them. Even family photos were usually maintained on small digital displays rather than in paper photo frames. Developed in house, all information systems were customized to internal needs. Microsoft technology was the main development platform, while Java and other platforms were used when it was appropriate.

Reporting Systems

Protegra's information systems enabled its unique organization design. The flat organization and the cultural focus on people had strong support in reporting systems that were accessible to all employees. There was a whole range of dashboards that one could view via the company's intranet. These covered finances, client relationships, offerings (see Exhibit 3), sales, project delivery, human resources, building management and so on. For example, the dashboard for client relationship management showed the forecast for sales and weekly reports on accomplishments. The human resources dashboard provided, among other information, an updated picture of the assignment of employees to projects. Every employee was authorized to access these dashboards at any time.

Every dashboard showed goals based on the internal balanced scorecard methodology and the actual achievement. For example, the users could monitor the project delivery dashboard to understand where a particular project was in terms of planned/ accomplished billable hours and budget. Colours were used to indicate how plans related to reality: Red meant a gap between the realization and a goal, while green indicated a goal achievement.

With the exception of the parts based on face-to-face communication, the sales process was entirely electronic. The sales management system was based on a particular sales methodology, and it supported the entire sales process. Its start point was a set of steps creating an "opportunity pipeline." The system user filled online templates for sales opportunities in order to identify a buyer prospect. Meetings, decisions and other subsequent steps were tracked in succession, and a resulting sales plan was posted. This system contained all potential opportunities and provided current information on the sales forecast, win/loss ratio, closing cycle and other details.

Particular data were entered in the sales system by those responsible for performing particular steps in the sales process. This principle applied to other systems as well, thus supporting the Protegra culture, in which process drivers were trusted and empowered to handle the data they created. From the perspective of information system use, this principle meant that many systems in the company were used in the self-service manner. Another example of self-service systems was the entering of billable hours directly by members of project teams. This was done through a project management system. Data from the system fed into the project delivery dashboard, which was also used on the basis of self-service. The human resource director used the information on billable hours too, and created utilization reports showing every employee in the company along with the billable per centage of their transpired work hours.

Both the process and the system for employee evaluation rested on self-service. Every team member evaluated the work of other teammates and of himself or herself. The evaluation form was online and it asked about a qualitative evaluation of performance and of possible areas of improvement. This information was later used for various purposes, including the calculation of bonuses at the end of the fiscal year. The culture of trust ensured the validity of the employee evaluation information.

Project Management Systems

Every project, internal and external alike, had a SharePoint site for storing and sharing the project documentation, such as announcements, diagrams, change requests, status reports, financial aspects, milestones and completed work. Configuration management was also supported. Microsoft Team Foundations Server was used for work item tracking, source code repository, build management/continuous integration and bugs tracking.

Part of the project management system was also the test servers and websites that supported high-bandwidth communication with clients in the course of a project. Thus the client could get online access via a virtual private network (VPN) to certain project documentation and preliminary deliverables. In the Loewen project, the client could remotely access the drawings, communications and other relevant project documents. The client reciprocated by providing Protegra's consultants with online access to floor maps, databases, scheduling and any other information the consultants requested.

Bueckert noted that keeping the communication with clients this way was important, particularly when developing enterprise-level software. This software demanded that an extensive system infrastructure was built first, which then allowed developing functionality that made sense to the end user. Letting clients see, by themselves, the progress of the work on the system infrastructure did help to maintain trust on the client side.

Knowledge Work Systems

Dedicated information systems expanded the scope of practices in the area of knowledge acquisition and sharing. One such tool was called "Idea Funnel." The front end was an online form that any employee could use to submit some innovation-relevant idea. A two-member team with a changing membership would receive the proposal and perform a triage by assigning the proposal to some employee that the proposal could concern. The recipient of the proposed idea would then decide on taking ownership over the idea and on implementing it. The following downstream steps were the defining of a solution, collecting the feedback to it and the final go/no go decision. All these steps were recorded in the Idea Funnel. The ideas submitted ranged from work process improvement to augmenting the space for socializing.

A content mapping application was available for facilitating learning from past projects. The user could run a search based on keywords and identify projects that

accrued with the relevant experience. For example, if one wanted to learn about challenges related to partner engagement, the search would result in finding the relevant lessons learned in the previous projects. Every employee could access this application via the company's intranet.

Protegrans used blogging for sharing knowledge. This was also deemed a good way of getting the thoughts of those colleagues who were either uncomfortable with public speech or who might not be able to be heard out in the open. In addition, blogging was considered a good way of developing written communication skills. Finally, wikis were used in order to convey and document knowledge in a more systematic way.

Communication Systems

E-mail was the major communication channel, second only to face-to-face communication. It provided an electronic trail to the project work, meetings, decisions, company events and the like. E-mail was the system of choice during a multi-year project for a client in Luxembourg in Europe. It helped coping with the time difference and establishing a good rapport with the client, in spite of the inherent limitations of e-mail technology. The use of e-mail was enhanced by applying a desktop search engine for searching through e-mail messages, attachments and files in various formats that were stored on the hard drive.

Protegrans also used an instant messaging (IM) system based on Microsoft Communicator software. Being fully integrated with a calendar application, the IM system had awareness capability. This meant that the availability status of every person logged into the intranet locally or via a VPN connection was shown by an indicator. Thus it was clear if a person was available for contact or if perhaps he/she was at a meeting, in which case the meeting's location and timing were also tacked.

An electronic bulletin board based on the SharePoint platform was also available for teamwork and company-wide discussions. The telephone technology of choice was voice over IP (VoIP). It allowed employees to deploy soft phones on their laptops and to phone from any place where the Internet connection was available.

Other electronic tools at Protegra included several locators, mapping spatially the people and professional development books that were in circulation. The intranet also supplied complete coverage of meetings and presentations and social information (events, announcements, birthdays, anniversaries, etc.).

CHALLENGES AHEAD

In 2007, Protegra doubled in size. One of the challenges engendered by the rapid growth was the preservation of the company's culture. New employees were joining and Protegra professionals were increasingly dispersed in the global space. Protegra's key challenge became how to keep growing while ensuring the preservation of the organizational culture that made Protegra a special place and successful enterprise. In 2008–2009, Protegra directly addressed this challenge through a strategy called "enduring culture." Expected behaviours that reinforced cultural values were collaboratively defined in all areas of the company. A course for teaching the Protegra way was created. Key aspects of the culture were graphically depicted in an animated presentation called "Perpetual Culture Machine," which provided an easy method for new employees to begin learning the company's culture (see Exhibit 4).

Organizational communication helped the enduring culture strategy by conveying the culture via new methods. These included the creation of cultural stories that conveyed the main cultural values. Stories were published as cartoons in a new publication entitled "Planet Protegra." For example, one story talked about how two software developers teamed up on their own initiative and worked over a weekend in order to respond to a client's request. Another method was publishing the "Fact of the Week," a brief narrative that promptly conveyed some cultural value. One such narrative explained why some Protegrans had offices while others did not.

While the enduring culture initiatives helped new employees adopt the Protegra way, the culture was likely to keep being challenged by the expected increase in the spatial dispersion of operations. Ibrahim and his teammates were aware that it might be increasingly difficult to maintain the company's culture if the personal contact among Protegrans was diminished. The key cultural values of open communication, trust and shared leadership had been practised just in the face-to-face setting. The lean methodology of system development also favoured collaboration through direct interaction as the way of working that allowed for the quickest communication.

The tension between culture and growth created a number of questions awaiting prompt answers. How could the values of the professional and people-focused organization be preserved when professionals were not located in the same space? Were some modifications of the culture needed? Did Protegrans need to go through some training for working in the distributed team mode? And crucially important for this technology company, how was Protegra supposed to leverage its systems for communication, knowledge work and project management in order to preserve its culture while growing? Would Protegrans need to explore new information technologies and systems in the process of transforming into a larger high-touch and high-tech organization?

EXHIBIT 1   Protegra's Financial Results

	2008	2007	2006
Revenue	$7,827,425	$6,912,308	$5,643,079
Expenses	$7,228,430	$6,052,981	$5,384,776
Profit*	7.65%	12.43%	4.58%

*Profit before taxes, excluding tax credits for research and development. All figures are in Canadian dollars.

EXHIBIT 2   Awards

Protegra was recognized as one of 2009's top 75 **Best Workplaces in Canada.**

In 2009, Protegra was selected as the **#1 Best Small and Medium Employer in Canada** by the Globe and Mail and Queen's School of Business.

In 2008, Protegra was **one of Manitoba's 50 Fastest Growing Companies** for the third consecutive year, as ranked by Manitoba Business Magazine.

Protegra was recognized as **one of Canada's fastest growing companies,** as selected by Profit Magazine in 2004, 2005 and 2006.

Protegra was awarded the **Project of the Year (2006)** by the Project Management Institute, Manitoba chapter, for the company's online Parks Reservation System, developed in collaboration with Manitoba Conservation.

Protegra was a finalist for the **"Outstanding Medium Business Award"** from the Manitoba Chamber of Commerce for the past four years (2004, 2005, 2006 and 2007).

Protegra received a 2006 **"Best in Business Practices Award"** from Manitoba Business Magazine, in recognition of its outstanding business management and industry success.

Source: www.protegra.com/News/AwardsAndDistinctions.aspx

EXHIBIT 3   Protegra's Offerings in Business Performance Consulting

Business Innovation Workshop for Executives and Senior Managers	Performance Consulting
Strategic Planning, including Balanced Scorecard	Organizational Design
Process Improvement, including Analysis and Modelling	Change Management
Business and Data Architecture, and Unified Business Modelling	Value Stream Analysis
Business Analysis	Survey Design, Development and Analysis
Workshop Design and Facilitation	Training Design, Development and Delivery
Infrastructure Design, including Business Continuity Planning and Disaster Recovery	Database Reviews and Operational Data Store Design
Gap and/or Fit Analysis	Decision Making and Problem Solving

Source: Protegra, 2007.

EXHIBIT 4   Perpetual Culture Machine

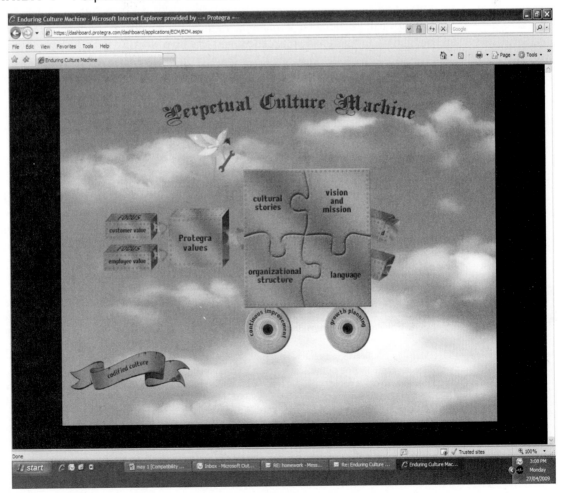

Source: Company files.

CCL Industries Inc.: Building and Maintaining an Effective Board

"I have to work harder to ensure stakeholders don't think of CCL as a 'controlled' company. As CEO, *I* am accountable for the outcome of our decisions, not the board."

Donald Lang reflected on the relationship between himself, president and chief executive officer (CEO) of CCL Industries Inc. (CCL), and the CCL board of directors. CCL had recently undertaken a major change in strategy when the planned and publicly announced sale of one of CCL's major divisions was abruptly cancelled.

"We had specific conditions and they ultimately were not met, so I decided to cancel the deal. I then had to explain the rationale to the board." Fortunately for Lang, he and the CCL board had an excellent and effective working relationship. It was not always this way. In the past, the CCL board was much less involved and less effective. Through hard work, the CEO/board team was on pace to meet its goal of being the world's premier packager of consumer products by 2005. In order to ensure this goal was attained, Lang and the board felt that there were issues that needed to be addressed to further the improvements they had made over the years.

CCL INDUSTRIES INC.

CCL was founded in 1951 by Stuart Lang Sr., his brother and Stuart's two sons, Gordon and Jim.[1] It was Gordon, however, who built CCL into the preeminent aerosol, custom manufacturing, rigid packaging and labelling business in North America. Fifty years after its founding, sales topped $1.6 billion (see Exhibit 1) and CCL employed 7,500 people around the world.

Richard Ivey School of Business
The University of Western Ontario

Trevor Hunter prepared this case under the supervision of Professor Larry Tapp solely to provide material for class discussion. The authors do not intend to illustrate either effective or ineffective handling of a managerial situation. The authors may have disguised certain names and other identifying information to protect confidentiality.

[1] For a comprehensive history of CCL Industries, see D.B. Davies, *Magic in the mist: The exciting and improbable saga of CCL Industries 1951–2001*, CCL Industries Inc., 2001.

CCL was originally named Connecticut Chemicals Limited and originated as a joint venture with an American company. Under the leadership of Gordon Lang, Conn-Chem (as it was more widely known in the early days) eventually outgrew its American parent and repatriated the balance of the equity it didn't own.

Through a number of acquisitions, the lines of business expanded beyond aerosols. To reflect this change of direction, the company's name was further shortened to CCL Industries Inc. in 1980.

Essentially an outsourcer to major packaged goods and consumer products firms, CCL produced some of the best-known name brands in the world, yet was largely unknown to the general public. The company produced its various products in close association with its customers and was divided into four divisions:[2]

1. CCL Custom Manufacturing—was the largest contract manufacturer of outsourced consumer products in North America and the United Kingdom. Products included some of the best-known brand names in the world for personal care, household, over-the-counter (OTC) pharmaceutical, oral care and specialty food products.

2. CCL Container—provided packaging solutions to the major global consumer products manufacturers from locations in North and Central America. Products included aluminium aerosol containers, tubes and jars.

3. CCL Plastic Packaging—from operations in the United States, this division produced plastic tubes, tamper-evident closures, dispensing closures, lined closures and jars.

4. CCL Label—was the largest North American printer of identification and information labels (paper and film pressure sensitive) with plants located in the United States, Canada, Europe, Mexico and Puerto Rico.

CCL first went public in 1972. Its shares consistently performed well on the Toronto Stock Exchange (TSE) until the 1976 "ozone scare." Reports issued by the Environmental Protection Agency (EPA) and the Food and Drug Administration (FDA) had suggested that chloro-fluorocarbons (CFCs), the propellant in aerosol cans, lead to depletion of the earth's ozone layer. These reports seriously injured the global aerosol market. By this time, CCL had both diversified its product line (sufficiently that a decrease in aerosol sales did not cripple the firm) and converted away from use of CFCs (which were ultimately banned in the United States in 1978 and in Canada in 1979). Nevertheless, the "ozone scare" significantly depressed CCL's share price.

Sensing an opportunity, management repurchased all outstanding shares and took CCL private. The firm went public again in 1980 and has remained public since then.

Donald Lang

Although he was the son of the man who built CCL, Donald Lang was not automatically given the job of president and CEO.

After graduating from the HBA program at the Richard Ivey School of Business (formerly Western Business School), Lang worked at Nabisco Canada for two years. He knew that he wanted to eventually work at CCL, but felt it was important to gain some management experience in a larger, more formalized organization prior to joining CCL Industries.

---

[2]This information was taken from the CCL website, www.cclind.com

He entered the business in a plant operations role in 1982. By 1993, he had been appointed president of CCL Custom Manufacturing and later, president and chief operating officer (COO) of CCL. Finally, he became CEO in 1999. Although by 2002 he had held the top management position in CCL for only three years, he had been involved with the corporation's governance as a member of the board of directors since 1991.

During his time as a board member, Lang had been considered a catalyst for change. He had often not agreed with the processes or extent of involvement of the CCL board. He had been only a minority voice, however, and was unable to effect change. When Lang wrote a letter that suggested he might resign from the board should not be forthcoming, the board responded by agreeing to some initial modifications.

The CCL Board

From its incorporation, CCL had only three board chairs. The first was Gordon Lang. In discussion with the board, a succession plan was developed whereby he would step down from his position, but would be recognized for his contributions with the new title founder chairman. The chairman title and corresponding responsibilities were appointed to the then-current president and CEO, a longtime senior CCL manager. In 1999, the first independent board chair, Jon Grant, was appointed (see Exhibit 2).

In the heydays of CCL's rapid growth in the 1960s and 1980s, the board could arguably have been characterized as a rubber stamp to management. The senior management of CCL was composed of longtime employees who had been hired by Gordon Lang and had worked their way up the ladder through hard work. There was no doubt that they were exceedingly hard-working and competent, but decisions were made with the expectation that once made, they would have to be approved by the board.

A quote from Edward W. Dobson, former executive vice-president and chief administrative officer and one of the builders of CCL, illustrates this point well: "We didn't have time for regular meetings, memos, reports or a rigid management structure. We just talked about it, made a decision and did it."[3]

Donald Lang recalls:

After we went public we were trying to make the bridge to a public structure but we still clung to our past. We brought in outside directors, but we were still only providing a rubber stamp. The firm's managers were not being held accountable for their actions. Then we had U.S. directors who were getting frustrated with the situation and pushed for a change. I was in a better position as COO and together we were able to make the necessary changes.

It was Donald Lang who ultimately instigated a formal evolution of the board, including a change in the nominating and governance committee chairman, the hiring of a search company for new directors and a succession plan for his father to retire as chairman with the long-term plan of separating the chairman and CEO roles.

Lang commented, "Unfortunately business performance has to get pretty bad before the board is compelled to take any action against a CEO. When I was appointed CEO, I wanted to make sure the CEO was held accountable to the board." The

[3]Quoted in D.B. Davies, *Magic in the mist: The exciting and improbable saga of CCL Industries 1951–2001*, CCL Industries Inc., 2001, p. 49.

separation of the CEO and chairman roles was advocated by Lang, even though he was the incoming CEO.

The focus on accountability went beyond management however. In 1994, the board itself decided to bring in a consultant to assist in a board self-evaluation. The purpose of the evaluation was to improve the process and contribution the board made to the operations of CCL, to ensure it was acting as more than a rubber stamp. Three annual evaluations followed until 1997, when they were stopped. Lang suggested that the evaluations were both not welcomed by the board members and had received negative feedback:

> During that time (i.e., the period between 1994 and 1997), the company's strategy lacked focus. There was a need for the board to work better together and to be more aligned. They were not interested in being evaluated when there were other issues that were considered a higher priority.

Lang was convinced that self-evaluation was critical to the success of the board as an effective group. "The intention (of the evaluations) was good, but the execution was wrong. We needed to find a better way to make them a priority and make them work," said Lang. A new evaluation process was introduced in 2000 that received more positive feedback. The addition of new directors, with differing opinions than those on the board from 1994 to 1997, helped improve the reception and effectiveness of the evaluations.

In order to give structure to CCL's governance policies, a document titled "Statement of Governance Policies of the Board of Directors of CCL Industries Inc." was prepared in 1994. This document was updated regularly and was given to every current and new director. Its purpose was to:

> Set forth the mandates and principles adopted by the board of directors of CCL Industries Inc. for the good stewardship of the company. It is intended as guidance for the board, for each director and for the committees of the board in the exercise of their respective responsibilities in the governance of the company.

The document contained policies on the following:

- The mandate of the board as a whole;
- The mandates of the audit, human resources, nominating and governance and environment and occupational health and safety committees;
- The composition of the board
  - Related and unrelated directors
  - The role of the chair
  - The composition of committees;
- The role of a director
  - Access to management and independent counsel;
- New directors
  - Criteria for new director selection
  - Orientation and training for new directors;
- Duties of the president and CEO;
- Performance assessment procedure for the president and CEO; and
- Proceedings and meetings
  - Meeting procedures
  - Information.

The following is a list of some of the specific activities undertaken by the board that Lang felt significantly improved the performance of the board after his appointment as CEO in 1999:

1. The appointment of a non-executive board chair. Aside from the skills and experience Board Chair Jon Grant brought to the position, the fact that there was independence at the top allowed for constructive challenging of the CEO and other senior executives that pushed for performance, clarity and accountability.

2. Grant, like Lang, was interested in bringing in more unrelated directors to further enhance the independence of the board. Members were selected strategically. The contribution and skill set each potential member could bring and how each prospect could help improve CCL's performance were heavily considered.

3. On average, Lang expected that directors should spend one day's worth of preparation briefing themselves on the materials the corporation sent them one week in advance of meetings for each four-hour board meeting, aside from their additional roles on the various committees.

4. Board committees were chaired by outside directors with functional executives acting as secretaries. There was thus more direct contact between board members and other senior executives. Senior executives were also required to make presentations to the board on topics of business plans. This gave the board more freedom to critique their strategies directly and assess the ability of the senior executives the CEO had hired and promoted.

5. A two-day board member retreat entirely devoted to strategic planning was instituted. Day one involved presentations from the divisional presidents that included an exchange of ideas and opinions. Day two was reserved for the board and the CEO only. The CEO was challenged and pushed, while at the same time the experience and skills of the board members were leveraged.

6. One board meeting per year would be held at one of the manufacturing sites as an opportunity to better understand the business details.

7. One half-hour was set aside at every meeting for the board to meet without the CEO present. This time allowed for frank discussion on such issues as CEO performance, compensation, evaluation or any other sensitive topic.

8. It was usual for the board members to meet for dinner informally the night preceding the CCL board meeting with, and sometimes without, management, which offered another opportunity for directors to converse and build a stronger relationship.

9. The splitting of the CEO and chair positions was a shift from the way the roles had been conceived and institutionalized at CCL in the past. There was frequent contact between Lang and Grant, and a good working relationship was fostered. Lang was accountable to Grant, but while Lang often consulted Grant, decisions were made by Lang. As a non-executive chair, Grant was an "outsider." Although the two worked together closely, Lang ran the business.

10. Board agendas were very detailed and included:
    - Scheduled time for outside directors discussions
    - General background information
    - Consent agenda items;
      – Items that could be approved with one motion, past board minutes, for example
    - Committee reports
    - Operations update

All pertinent information was included in advance briefing books, including a summary of the resolutions to be proposed.

11. The amount and type of documentation directors received was revamped. Agendas were set one month before the meeting and materials were delivered to directors no less than one week before the meeting. If an item missed the agenda, it had to be held for the next meeting (emergencies excepted). Thus, senior executives that wanted something on the board agenda had to be sure that their timing was on schedule. Meetings were scheduled on a two-year rotating basis to ensure full attendance. There was a conscious attempt to strike a balance between providing too much detail (thus overwhelming the directors) and too little information.

These and other measures had led many of the directors to feel that the CCL board was one of the most effective on which they had served.

MOVING FORWARD

Although the CCL board and Lang had made an effective team and understood and fulfilled their roles with accountability, there were still issues that needed improvement. The latest board evaluation had resulted in some concerns that needed to be addressed.[4]

Three main areas in which the board could be strengthened emerged from the evaluation: the strategic planning process, succession planning and board composition.

Strategic Planning

While the directors noted that this process had improved over the years and that the value of the two-day retreat was clear, they felt that more of their time should be spent on reviewing strategic opportunities and risks and the plans for execution, rather than management reports. There was concern over a lack of clarity and direction on the part of the board. While unanimity was not the goal, greater consensus was desired. Concerns as to how to reach a consensus in a timely and effective manner were raised. The directors felt that, in order to effectively aid in the strategic planning process, they needed to be involved in the process on a more regular basis. The content, amount and timing of the information they received regarding strategic planning needed to be reviewed. Did they need more information? Should they meet more often? Who should be at the meetings? What sort of information should they receive? These questions needed to be addressed.

Succession Planning

Nearly all the directors felt that more time needed to be spent on the issue of succession planning. Many felt that this issue was often considered secondary, which is why it had not been given its due attention. An annual discussion regarding potential successor candidates for all senior positions was suggested. The discussion would centre on their readiness, development plans, retention risk and compensation.

Another issue of key personnel involved a lack of clarity of the role of the board's HR committee and the degree of support the committee received. The HR committee

---

[4]This information is drawn from a report prepared by Patrick O'Callaghan & Associates for CCL Industries Inc.

saw part of its role as challenging the CEO on whether the senior executives were not only experts in their area, but also strategic thinkers and could take work off the desk of the CEO. This followed the philosophy of CCL founder Gordon Lang, who said, "I hired good people and then got out of their way. I had no time to constantly look over people's shoulders or question their every decision."[5] Perhaps the content of the annual reviews needed to be changed. Perhaps the HR committee needed a broader scope for potential candidates.

A further important issue that needed attention was the development of an emergency plan in case of an accident involving the CEO or other senior executives.

Board Composition

Although the majority of board members was composed of "outside and non-related" directors, there was a concern regarding the skills and experience that were needed at the board level to assist with strategic planning in the coming years. Criteria for future directors included:

- U.S. or international background (with a concern regarding the logistics problem for international directors)
- Experience in corporate finance and mergers and acquisitions
- Information technology experience
- A current CEO of a significant-sized public corporation operating internationally
- Human resources experience

Although the board was always looking for the best candidate, there was a clear recognition of the lack of women and visible minorities at the board level. While not looking to fulfill a quota, there was a desire to break away from the "white male" stereotype characteristics of many boards.

THE CURRENT SITUATION

After the change in strategy, Lang recognized the need and potential for greater board involvement in the strategic activities of CCL. As this sort of activity could be the norm in the future, the need for flexible, nimble strategic planning, along with informed governance, would only increase in the face of competition and global uncertainty.

In 2002, CCL operated in nine countries around the world. There was a global economic slowdown and decreased consumer confidence. The effects of the terrorists' attacks on September 11, had further exacerbated the poor economic conditions. Acquisitions and divestitures, keys to CCL's growth strategy, would be difficult in the coming years, particularly in new markets around the world.

The challenge was to develop and execute strategy and appropriately develop and leverage the skills and experience of the board. Clearly, the board was working well now; however, there were issues regarding strategic planning, succession planning and composition that needed to be addressed if it was going to fulfill its role as steward in the future business environment facing CCL. Making changes to the board as an anticipatory change tended to be difficult, especially when the change affected something

---

[5]Quote taken from in D.B. Davies, *Magic in the mist: The exciting and improbable saga of CCL Industries 1951–2001*, CCL Industries Inc., 2001, Prologue.

that was working well. What needed to be done to increase the involvement of the board? How could the board's concerns be handled? Was it time to update or overhaul CCL's governance policies? There was a fine line between governing and running the firm, and neither Lang nor Grant wanted to cross that line.

The Richard Ivey School of Business gratefully acknowledges the generous support of CCL Industries Inc. in the development of these learning materials.

EXHIBIT 1 Selected Financial Data from the CCL 2001 Annual Report for Years Ending 2000 and 2001 (in thousands of dollars, except for per-share data)

	2001	2000
Sales	1,600,497	1,589,087
EBITDA	159,879	183,295
Depreciation, amortization of other assets	73,439	75,351
Interest	32,415	36,560
Income from operations before unusual items, income tax and goodwill amortization	54,025	71,384
Unusual items (net)	7,684	18,776
Earnings before income taxes and goodwill amortization	46,341	52,608
Income taxes	7,993	13,156
Earnings before goodwill amortization	38,348	39,452
Goodwill amortization, net of tax	13,457	12,798
Net earnings	24,891	26,654
Per class B share		
Earnings before goodwill amortization	1.08	1.04
Earnings before unusual items	0.83	1.10
Net earnings	0.70	0.70
Cash flow before unusual items	3.39	3.47
At year end		
Total assets	1,454,991	1,392,820
Net debt	435,755	486,139
Shareholders' equity	563,704	558,201
Net debt to equity ratio	0.77	0.87
Return on average equity	4.4%	4.7%
Net debt to total capitalization	43.6%	46.5%
Book value per share	16.52	15.22

EXHIBIT 2　Profile of CCL Industries Inc. Board of Directors

Jon Grant—Chairman of the Board of CCL Industries Inc.

Chairman of the board of the Laurentian Bank of Canada and former Chairman of Canada Lands Company Limited and a director of CCL since 1994. Former chairman and CEO of the Quaker Oats Company of Canada Limited, former chairman of Scott Paper Limited and former chairman of the board of governors of Trent University. Mr. Grant is also a director of AXA Pacific Insurance Company. He is currently chairman of the Ontario Board of the Nature Conservancy of Canada.

Donald G. Lang—President and CEO, CCL Industries Inc.

CEO of CCL Industries since June 1999, in addition to his previous role as president. Mr. Lang was appointed president and chief operating officer of CCL in April 1998. Prior to his appointment as COO, he was president of the company's largest division, CCL Custom Manufacturing. Mr. Lang has served on CCL's Board of Directors since 1991. Additionally, he is a member of the Advisory Committee at the Richard Ivey School of Business. Mr. Lang holds an Honours Bachelor of Arts degree from the Richard Ivey School of Business, University of Western Ontario.

Stuart W. Lang—President of CCL Label International

Mr. Lang has held progressively senior positions throughout the Custom and Label Manufacturing divisions in Canada, Mexico and Europe since joining the company in 1982 and has served as a director of CCL Industries since 1991. Mr. Lang has a BSc. in Chemical Engineering from Queen's University. Prior to this, he played for the CFL's Edmonton Eskimos for eight years.

Paul J. Block

Chairman and CEO of Proteus Capital Associates. Previously, Mr. Block was chairman and president of Revlon International. Mr. Block is a board member of the China Retail Fund and the Shanghai-Syracuse University International School of Business. He is also a member of the Advisory Board of the Syracuse University School of Management. Mr. Block has served as a director of CCL since 1997.

Dermot G. Coughlan

Former chairman and chief executive officer of Derlan Industries Limited. A director of CCL Industries Inc. since 1991, Mr. Coughlan is also a director of Mackenzie Financial Corporation and chairman of a number of North American and international manufacturing companies.

Stephan J. Friedman

Senior partner with the international law firm of Debevoise & Plimpton. Mr. Friedman was previously executive vice-president and general counsel of the Equitable Companies Inc. He served as Commissioner of the Securities and Exchange Commission and as deputy assistant secretary of the Treasury for Capital Markets Policy. Mr. Friedman also serves on the boards of the American Ballet Theatre, the Practising Law Institute and the United Way of New York City.

Albert Gnat

Partner at Lang Michener, a Toronto law firm. A director of CCL since 1973, Mr. Gnat also serves on the boards of CamVec Corporation, GEAC Computer Corporation Limited, Leitch Technology Corporation, IKEA Limited, MDC Corporation, Rogers Communication and Vitran Corporation.

Jean-René Halde

President and chief executive officer of Irwin Toys and was president and CEO of Livgroup Investments, which succeeded Livingston Group where he was president and CEO from 1995–2000. Prior to this, he served as president and CEO to Culinar Inc. Mr. Halde's other directorships include the boards of Bracknell Corporation and the Institute of Corporate Directors.

Lawrence G. Tapp

Dean of the Richard Ivey School of Business since 1995. He also served as Executive-in-Residence and Adjunct Professor, Faculty of Business, University of Toronto from 1993–1995; vice-chairman, president and CEO of Lawson Mardon Group Ltd. (a packaging conglomerate) from 1985–1992. He has served as a director of CCL since 1994.

Source: CCL Industries Inc. website, http://www.cclind.com/corp_profile_directors_bio.html

Currie Road Construction Limited (A)

In December 2008, Martin Cook, president of Currie Road Construction Limited, a British Columbia-based road construction and maintenance firm, was contemplating U.S. market entry. Having investigated the opportunity to establish an operation in Houston, Texas, Cook now needed to make his decision.

THE B.C. ROAD CONSTRUCTION AND MAINTENANCE INDUSTRY

The construction and maintenance of Canada's highways and roads fell under the jurisdiction of the provincial and municipal governments. In B.C., for example, the primary government funding agency responsible for the construction and maintenance of the major transportation structures (i.e., highways, roads, bridges) was the Ministry of Transportation and Infrastructure (MTI). As well, each municipal government (e.g., City of Victoria) was also responsible for constructing and maintaining certain roadways in its respective jurisdiction.

With the 2010 Winter Olympic Games slated to be held in the Vancouver area, the B.C. Road Builders and Heavy Construction Association, which represented approximately 100 road construction and maintenance companies in B.C., acknowledged that the transportation and infrastructure projects associated with the Games had been a boon to the Association's members. However, the onset of an economic recession was now casting a shadow of uncertainty over the continuing prosperity of the industry in B.C. More specifically, with the forecasted downturn in government revenues, it was unclear whether the MTI would be in a position to continue funding major improvements to B.C.'s road infrastructure. A competing perspective suggested that the Canadian federal and provincial governments would follow the example of their American

Professor Paul Beamish prepared this case solely to provide material for class discussion. The author does not intend to illustrate either effective or ineffective handling of a managerial situation. The author may have disguised certain names and other identifying information to protect confidentiality.

Richard Ivey School of Business
The University of Western Ontario

neighbours and accelerate infrastructure spending in an effort to stimulate economic recovery.

Competition in the road construction industry was fierce. Exhibit 1 presents market share data and the contract value for a majority of the road construction work awarded by MTI in 2008. This was only for new construction work awarded by the MTI and excluded work tendered by the municipal governments. The industry was fragmented among many competitors.

A tendering process was used by both the MTI and municipal governments to award work to contractors. A tender document was broken down into specific stages where a cost was assigned for each stage (i.e., stage one—survey stake out; stage two—shrubbery removal; stage three—direct excavation). A unit cost was attached to each stage so that if a cost overrun occurred that was beyond the control of the contractor, then MTI would pay the contractor for the overrun. A contract was awarded on a lowest cost basis among those contractors who prepared a tender for a specific job. There was no limitation on the number of jobs a contractor could bid for as long as the company was qualified (i.e., total dollar value of work the company could do per year) and the qualification associated with each tender call (i.e., assets of company) was satisfied. As a result, often as many as ten companies bid on one job at a time in B.C., thus making it extremely difficult to gain market share.

In order to stay profitable, construction companies had a number of options. The first was to invest in costly capital equipment. This was critical in this labour-intensive industry because equipment breakdowns were a major reason for cost overruns on a job. A second option was to integrate vertically backwards into the commercial end of the industry. This involved owning an asphalt production plant and/or a sand and gravel operation. Large amounts of money were required, as well as a strategic decision to compete in a related industry. The third option was to compete in markets other than B.C. (i.e., the U.S., Ontario, Alberta). With this option, the firm risked an incomplete understanding of the market, the competitors and the customer (i.e., government agencies responsible for road construction/maintenance have varying specifications and methods of doing business in each province or state). The final option was to diversify into an unrelated industry (e.g., concrete, housing or transportation). This option also involved a great deal of risk because of market unfamiliarity and the large amounts of capital required.

Background Information on Cook

Cook graduated from the University of Manitoba with a Bachelor of Science degree in 1984 and immediately accepted a job as an asphalt engineer with Shell Canada Limited (SCL). It was in the asphalt division that Cook established a working relationship with David Thomas that would have a significant effect on both their future careers within SCL. By the early 1990s, Cook was elevated to the position of asphalt sales manager for Western Canada. Not totally satisfied with the constraints of a large corporation, he turned down two excellent promotional opportunities within SCL.

In 1994, Cook and Thomas discussed the possibility of entering into business together in the asphalt-related products market. The business would supply road asphalt and other oil-based by-products to the consumer. On January 1, 1995, Cook and Thomas left SCL and formed a company called Costal Asphalt Limited (Costal). They each contributed their personal savings of $30,000 into this company. As Cook said, "When we left Shell we did not know where we were going. We had to first find a place to set up our plant and then find the necessary financing. However, we knew we had a good idea."

Development of Costal Limited

Cook and Thomas approached the B.C. Ministry of Small Business, Technology and Economic Development and the Federal Business Development Bank for financial support for Costal. They were turned down because their proposal was determined to be infeasible. The banks also would not provide any financing because Cook and Thomas had no personal assets for use as collateral. However, they were able to get financial support from Mark Currie and Evan Clarry, owners of Currie Road Construction Limited. The deal was structured so that Currie Road Construction owned 51 per cent of Costal and Cook and Thomas, 49 per cent. After payment of a $200,000 loan to Currie and Clarry, the equity position would become 50 per cent Currie, 25 per cent Cook and 25 per cent Thomas. It took one and a half years to repay the original $200,000 loan.

In 1997, Costal entered into a joint venture with an investor (Jake Garner) to purchase a profitable road construction company, A.A. McLeod Construction Limited (McLeod), in the Queen Charlotte area in British Columbia. Garner was responsible for the day-to-day operations and management of the firm.

From 1997 to 2000, Cook and Thomas concentrated primarily on expanding Costal operations by opening up terminals in Calgary and Edmonton. McLeod continued to be profitable under Garner's direction. Costal's success to this point was attributed mainly to the dedication of Cook and Thomas. It was not unusual for either partner to work seven days a week, fifteen hours a day. During this period, Cook's responsibilities included answering the phone, pouring 425°F asphaltic product into 25 kilogram containers in the shop and taking care of financial matters, as well as "pounding the pavement to drum up business." This hard work paid off for Cook and Thomas—Costal was profitable from its inception. Over this period, their management skills and business know-how increased enormously.

In 2000, Cook and Thomas wanted to further vertically integrate forward. They attempted to purchase a profitable road construction company in Victoria (similar in size to McLeod), but the deal fell through. At the same time, Currie Road Construction was offered for sale. Currie and Clarry had received a serious offer from a British-based company to purchase Currie; however, they desired to sell it to Canadian investors if they could be found. Cook and Thomas saw this as an excellent opportunity to become fully integrated in the road construction industry in B.C. Because Currie was a major customer for Costal product, a change of ownership could jeopardize this account. Also, the purchase of Currie by another firm could have a negative effect on Costal's operations since Currie owned 50 per cent of Costal. Up to this time, Currie and Clarry were silent partners in Costal; they never interfered with the management of Costal and McLeod and the valuable long-term assets on Currie's balance sheet.

Currie Road Construction Limited

Currie Road Construction was one of the oldest and largest road maintenance and construction companies based in B.C. Its history dated back to 1933, when Eugene Boyle built the foundations upon which Currie would grow and prosper for the next 75 years. During that time, Currie participated in building such large projects as the Trans-Canada Highway and the Alaskan Highway. The company enjoyed enormous success in the '60s and '70s when governments were spending huge amounts of money to build Canada's transportation infrastructure. However, during the late 1970s and early 1980s, Canada's infrastructure was nearing completion and the industry was shifting away from new construction of road systems to reconstruction and maintenance of the existing road networks.

Cook and Thomas decided that with the purchase of Currie Road Construction, Cook would leave Costal and become president of Currie. There was too much at stake to allow someone else to run the company for them; this was a major acquisition that could cause the collapse of everything they had achieved to date if not managed properly.

On November 15, 2000, Cook took over total control of Currie's operations. During the negotiations to purchase Currie for $21.2 million, Currie had indicated that he expected Currie to make a profit of $1 million for the fiscal year (ending March 31) of 2001. However, much to Cook's surprise, Currie experienced a net operating loss of $1.3 million instead.

Despite the poor performance in 2000, Cook believed that Currie was still a good deal. The company owned valuable pieces of real estate (e.g., two golf courses) whose potential value was enormous. As well, Currie owned and operated asphalt production plants in key strategic locations in the province, and owned valuable land north of Vancouver that contained large amounts of aggregate used in the construction process and in the asphalt production plants. Having an asphalt supply was extremely important in the road construction business.

Cook identified some critical problems with Currie's operations initially. A glaring problem was that they were still competing heavily in the highway road construction segment of the market, yet they were losing money. Currie had failed to recognize that the market was undergoing a change from new highway construction to reconstruction and road maintenance. Road construction placed much greater emphasis on earthmoving (excavating, drilling, blasting) than road maintenance, where the emphasis was more on grinding and recycling. In addition, Currie's equipment was old and tended to break down. This led to cost overruns and reduced profit margins on all jobs.

Another problem was that Currie was an old company which had old ways of doing business. The majority of the senior level management had been with the company for over 30 years; in fact, a lot of them had started out as equipment operators and worked their way up into management. Currie lacked fresh "blood" in the organization; the environment was changing dramatically; and management was not able to realize this or keep up with it.

The employees of Currie were very dedicated and loyal to the company. A great majority were immigrants who had worked for Currie for many years. However, Cook noticed that some of the older employees had become comfortable and complacent with their positions, and hence their motivation had dropped. As Cook stated, "We had a lot of old employees who were getting late in their years and did not have too much drive. It was imperative that we get their productivity to increase dramatically."

For the next three years, Cook concentrated on restructuring the organization in terms of personnel and operations. The key was to identify those people in management who were able to make the quantum leap from the "old school" to the "new school." Those who were not able to adapt had to retire. Also, Currie had to re-orient itself in the market by making the transition from the heavy construction end of the business to the road maintenance end where the profit margins were higher.

By 2004, Cook felt that he had moulded Currie into a more aggressive and stronger competitor in the road construction market. He had removed all the older management that could not adapt to Currie's new environment and, as a result, the senior management staff was much leaner and more aggressive. Secondly, Cook hired two key people to the management staff: One brought valuable experience to the commercial side of the business and the other to the equipment operations area. Finally, Cook had rationalized the operations in some areas and expanded efforts in other areas.

Cook identified six key strategic decisions that were made:

1. Entered into a joint venture operation with a successful and experienced sand and gravel company to develop Currie's 500 acres of gravel deposits north of Vancouver.

2. Made a commitment to become the leader in the pavement maintenance market in B.C. This required investing in specialized technologies required to engage in activities such as recycling, road surface scarifying and pavement profiling. Recycling was a process whereby the existing pavement surface was removed (i.e., by grinding machines or by using backhoes to completely tear it up) and used along with virgin aggregate to form a new recycled mix of asphalt. The new mix was then re-laid on the roadway using the usual procedures. This process required additional equipment installed in the asphalt production plant. Pavement profiling was a process whereby a machine (i.e., a grinder) with a large rotating drum containing carbide teeth planed the surface of the road to various depths. The material removed from the road could be used in a recycled asphaltic mixture or it could be used as subgrade material in another project. This process was used to remove surface distress appearing in the pavement. As well, it corrected the pavement profile to allow for proper drainage and to correct curb heights. Road surface scarifying was a process in which a machine heated up the pavement and removed the surface distress. The removed material was treated with an emulsion to rejuvenate its properties and then re-laid.

3. Increased Currie's presence in the road calcium segment of the market. Calcium was sprayed on dirt roads to control the amount of dust.

4. Obtained operating authority to transport petroleum products (for Currie and commercially) in Alberta and several surrounding northern U.S. states.

5. Rationalized Currie's operations in Burnaby, moving away from road construction and concentrating on supplying materials (i.e., asphalt and aggregate) and carrying out winter operations (i.e., snow removal and sanding).

6. Purchased a road surfacing company in Alberta. This made Currie one of the dominant firms in this market.

These changes had a positive effect on Currie's income statement. Exhibit 2 presents a financial summary of Currie's performance from 2001 to 2008. Since 2003, Currie had been a profitable company.

A major burden upon Currie's profitability was the interest owing on the $20.0 million loan. The original plan was to repay the bank the entire debt by 2006. However, owing to the economic deceleration associated with the stock market slowdown between 2000 and 2002, Currie was not able to make any interest payments until 2007. Cook was able to get the bank to agree to capitalize the interest payments over that time.

In 2004, Currie was able to sell some property in order to pay off some of the outstanding debt. As well, the company seemed to be going in the right direction, and as Cook stated, "We were able to see faintly the light at the end of the tunnel."

The Proposed Houston Division

In the summer of 2007, Cook had business dealings with Brad Carlyle. Carlyle worked for a pipeline construction company in the Calgary area. Prior to this job, he worked in Houston, supervising the expansion of a rapid transit system. In December 2007, Carlyle arranged to have lunch with Cook. Over lunch, Carlyle told Cook about the opportunities that he saw in the Houston market. Carlyle knew that Currie was looking to expand its operations and he felt that the Houston market was one area that Currie should seriously consider. Currie Road Construction had previously only worked in the U.S. as a subcontractor on several road rehabilitation projects.

Carlyle indicated to Cook that he wanted to return to Houston. He believed that he was capable of developing a successful division in this market for Currie. Carlyle had made some valuable contacts within both the government and the construction industry that would be very beneficial. As well, he knew the market and the way it functioned. Cook was impressed with Carlyle's enthusiasm and his belief in the Houston market. Although Carlyle did not have a civil engineering background and was not totally comfortable with road construction techniques, Cook had full confidence in his ability to "learn on the job." Cook indicated that he would get back to Carlyle very soon.

As a result of this meeting, Cook and Thomas decided that it would be worthwhile to spend a few days in the Houston market in order to get a better feeling for its potential. None of Currie's senior management people had experience in this market. In mid-January 2008, Cook, Thomas and Carlyle spent three days in Houston meeting with Texas Department of Transportation (TxDOT) officials and touring the area. During this brief stay, a large amount of positive information was gathered about the prospects of entering this market. The TxDOT officials were excited about Currie entering the market because a recent combines investigation found that a large number of the old, established road construction firms were guilty of price fixing and collusion. As a result, they were barred from bidding work for one to two years.

Texas was also undergoing growth, and government officials realized that improvements to the infrastructure were required to ensure this growth. As a result, the government had made it a priority to upgrade the highways, bridges and roadways throughout the state. Cook and Thomas were astonished at the amount of money budgeted to infrastructure upgrading. It was approximately US$1,400 million a year, roughly 4.5 times more than the amount allocated by the MTI in B.C.

Even more enticing about this market was the fewer number of competitors compared with the competition in B.C. The average number of contractors bidding per job was approximately four.

Further discussion regarding the Houston market took place between Cook, Thomas and Carlyle. More visits to Houston followed.

The main reason to enter this market, according to Cook, was because "It offered an opportunity to get better utilization out of our specialized machinery. Instead of having our grinding machines and scarifiers sit idle during the winter months, we could find work for them in Houston. Additionally, there were only five firms identified by the Asphalt Recycling & Reclaiming Association as being headquartered in the state of Texas."

Cook's orientation for the Houston market was to concentrate primarily on the road maintenance activities of pavement grinding and scarifying operations where Currie was strongest. It was thought that by going in small, Currie could get a better understanding of the market, make some key contacts in government and develop a good reputation within the industry by doing quality work. Because the road maintenance techniques which Currie possessed were more advanced than those in use in Texas, the company realized it would take a little time to demonstrate their merits to the key government contacts. Currie planned to eventually reproduce its B.C. operations in Texas, where there were no companies totally vertically integrated. Once Currie was established in Texas, it would be able to compete in the nearby surrounding states: Florida, Georgia, North and South Carolina, Tennessee, Alabama and Louisiana.

The proposed organizational chart for the Houston operations is presented in Exhibit 3. Carlyle would report directly to Cook on all matters concerning operations. If the entry took place, Cook planned to spend time overseeing the move to Houston. However, after operations were running, Cook did not plan on spending much time in Houston because Currie did not have much slack in the management ranks. The existing people were all so extended that U.S. entry would have to be delayed if Brad Carlyle, or someone like him from outside existing management, was not available.

Subsequent Thinking

Early in the fall of 2008, it appeared that the prospect of expanding into the Texas market might be derailed by the collapse of global credit and equity markets, as well as the rapid onset of an economic recession. However, the dramatic downturn in the U.S. economy prompted federal lawmakers to consider implementing unprecedented stimulus spending in order to revive the economy and to avoid an impending depression. By February 2009, the U.S. Congress was anticipated to sign into force the American Recovery and Reinvestment Act, which would inject more than $100 billion into infrastructure spending. Approximately $27 billion of this infrastructure spending was earmarked for highway and bridge construction. More than $4.5 billion of this was slated for projects approved by the TxDOT. The TxDOT's commissioners were anxious to quickly identify "shovel-ready" projects and scheduled nearly $2.75 billion worth of project bid dates to occur between April and December 2009 (see Exhibit 4 for the monthly gross value of projects subsequently scheduled for tender throughout 2009). Exhibit 5 lists a sample of the types of projects that were being subsequently scheduled for tender in April 2009. With the broad slowdown in the economy, competition for these lucrative projects was expected to be fierce.

At the same time, Canadian lawmakers were beginning to consider similar stimulus spending. Cook informally learned that the B.C. government was considering more than $880 million in infrastructure spending, although the timelines for implementation were not as aggressive as they were in Texas, and it was unclear how much would be directed to the MTI for road construction and maintenance projects.

Although Currie's primary strength was in road maintenance, the decision was made to get involved in the road construction end of the business if Currie entered the Texas market. There were two reasons for this strategy. The first was to generate some cash flow in order to cover the operating expenses until the grinding and scarifying operations picked up. Secondly, according to information provided by Carlyle, the market appeared to be made of gold; it offered easy access to abnormal profits.

Although little public data was available, the competition in this market was primarily family-owned companies. These firms were cash rich and were not accustomed to much competition. As Cook described them, "They are a bunch of old-time southern contractors who are financially very strong and wealthy, primarily from the price fixing that had occurred." One additional key player in the market was ARRON, a subsidiary of Petro Oil, one of the largest corporations in the United States.

If they proceeded, Cook and Carlyle decided that Currie would buy new equipment since abnormal profits seemed to be present. While Currie would normally lease and/or rent equipment for new operations initially in order to minimize investment in a new market, this would reduce profit margins slightly. It was felt that Currie could be competitive and easily make even more than four per cent net profit on revenue with new equipment.

Carlyle felt there would be no problem locating supervisors and equipment operators given the rising rate of unemployment. Due to the large population growth occurring in the southern states and the minor influence of labour unions, Carlyle felt he would be able to hire blue-collar employees at about half the wage rate that Currie was paying its employees in B.C. Carlyle would be responsible for hiring all the blue-collar employees; however, he would require Cook's approval in hiring supervisors.

If Currie decided to enter this market, the Houston subsidiary would utilize Currie's existing centralized control systems. In 2006, Currie had paid $30,000, and invested a further $140,000, for a fully integrated job costing/receivable/ledger cost reporting and accounting system, which was one of the most comprehensive of any firm in the industry. For each of the 200 active accounts that Currie was working on, it received a monthly cost analysis (see Exhibit 6, for example). This allowed the company to see costs broken down by subcategory on each job for the current month, to date, to complete and forecasted final—all versus the original plan. For *any* given job, it might be several years before all of the relevant costs had been accounted for and the accounts closed off.

In light of the rapid developments associated with the anticipated economic stimulus spending in both B.C. and Texas, Cook realized that if he were to enter the U.S. market at all, he would have to decide soon.

EXHIBIT 1 2008 Market Share Ranking (MTI)*

	Total contracts: 682	Total value: $697,354,600		Total tons: 4,455,751
Rank	Contractor	Contracts	$ Value	Market %
1	ARC Holdings Ltd.	46	130,963,194	18.78
2	TCN Construction	14	66,876,306	9.59
3	Arvac Construction	14	41,353,128	5.93
4	Jean Ltd.	7	35,286,143	5.06
5	Pey Ltd.	7	24,756,088	3.55
6	Atlas Construction Ltd.	4	22,873,231	3.28
7	RAC Paving	25	22,524,554	3.23
8	Dunn Construction	28	20,711,432	2.97
9	Alden Ltd.	18	19,177,252	2.75
10	Currie Road Construction	14	18,828,574	2.70
11	Gant Paving Ltd.	4	17,852,278	2.56
12	Lyee Construction Ltd.	11	17,364,130	2.49
13	Rant Construction Ltd.	28	16,945,717	2.43
14	Rome Construction Ltd.	11	16,039,156	2.30
15	Ram Brothers Construction	4	14,435,240	2.07

*Figures may be disguised
Source: Company files.

EXHIBIT 2 Currie Road Construction Limited Financial Summary (Yearly) ($000s)

Year	Current assets	Current liabil.	Long-term debt	L.T.D. interest	Revenue	Net income	F.A. purch.
March 2001*	10,962	9,074	17,948	—	13,798	−2,740	1,146
March 2002	12,012	11,292	19,450	1,802	44,760	4,248	0
March 2003	12,058	8,646	23,836	2,780	42,318	306	2,674
March 2004	10,228	7,940	21,002	3,262	46,866	7,438	2,272
March 2005	10,126	5,728	20,560	3,908	46,534	2,050	3,990
March 2006	20,956	14,102	22,056	4,190	59,568	4,338	4,164
Feb. 2007	18,578	7,176	25,910	4,210	69,404	2,288	3,390
Feb. 2008	25,966	16,290	13,654	3,326	81,842	1,480	4,618

*2001 values are for an eight-month period
Source: Company files.

EXHIBIT 3   Proposed Organization Chart: Houston, 2009

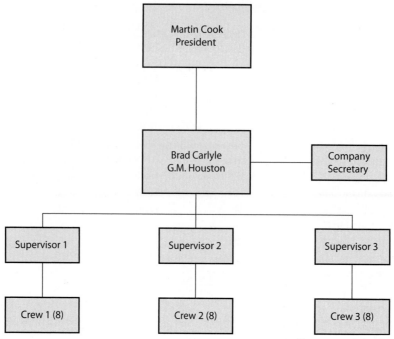

Source: Company files.

EXHIBIT 4   Gross Estimated Value of Transportation Infrastructure Scheduled for Bidding in Texas During 2009

Month scheduled for bidding	Estimated gross value of projects
April	$ 397,026,973
May	$ 151,320,643
June	$1,256,350,277
July	$ 258,887,573
August	$ 260,255,403
September	$ 118,414,267
October	$ 52,717,115
November	$ 198,285,487
December	$ 57,499,031
Total:	$2,750,756,768

Source: Company files.

EXHIBIT 5 Sample of Transportation Infrastructure Projects Scheduled for Bidding in Texas During April 2009

District	County	Highway	Project ID	Estimated value	Project description
Tyler	Anderson	US 84	12301034	$ 6,491,332	WIDEN ROADWAY
Odessa	Andrews	SH 115	54801036	$ 5,604,394	REPAIR ROADWAY
Wichita Falls	Archer	SH 25	13705028	$ 3,763,273	WIDEN ROADWAY
Amarillo	Armstrong	US 287	4203038	$13,712,239	REPAIR ROADWAY
Corpus Christi	Bee	US 181	10007045	$ 3,999,719	RESURFACE ROADWAY
Waco	Bell	SH 317	1505043	$ 1,671,882	RESURFACE ROADWAY
Waco	Bell	SH 201	353402002	$ 1,840,469	INTERSECTION
Austin	Blanco	US 281	25301047	$ 1,261,109	RESURFACE ROADWAY
Houston	Brazoria	SH 35	17803138	$ 5,258,533	RESURFACE ROADWAY
Houston	Brazoria	FM 524	100402014	$ 2,402,836	RESURFACE ROADWAY
Bryan	Brazos	SH 21	11604096	$ 1,414,670	RESURFACE ROADWAY
Bryan	Brazos	FM 60	50601093	$ 1,554,118	RESURFACE ROADWAY
Bryan	Brazos	FM 1179	131601053	$ 461,440	RESURFACE ROADWAY
Brownwood	Brown	US 67	5406090	$ 2,251,374	RESURFACE ROADWAY
Bryan	Burleson	FM 60	64803046	$13,606,472	WIDEN ROADWAY
Atlanta	Cass	SH 77	27703024	$ 3,320,478	WIDEN ROADWAY
Atlanta	Cass	SH 43	56901048	$ 1,409,474	WIDEN ROADWAY
Lubbock	Castro	FM 1055	129101012	$10,533,348	REPAIR ROADWAY
Beaumont	Chambers	SH 61	24203068	$ 1,631,534	RESURFACE ROADWAY
Beaumont	Chambers	IH 10	50803090	$ 1,241,392	RESURFACE ROADWAY
Childress	Childress	CR	92508017	$ 2,157,148	REPLACE BRIDGE
San Antonio	Comal	FM 306	310601012	$ 8,532,728	REBUILD ROADWAY
Wichita Falls	Cooke	IH 35	19402088	$ 3,580,759	RESURFACE ROADWAY
Waco	Coryell	US 84	5503023	$14,282,449	CONSTRUCT LANES
Dallas	Dallas	FM 1382	104702044	$ 2,246,574	TRAFFIC SIGNAL
San Angelo	Edwards	SH 55	23502043	$ 3,306,441	CONSTRUCT BRIDGE
Houston	Fort Bend	US 90A	2706055	$ 1,740,866	RESURFACE ROADWAY
Houston	Fort Bend	FM 521	11103054	$ 1,178,514	RESURFACE ROADWAY
Houston	Fort Bend	SH 36	18801036	$ 1,901,213	REPAIR ROADWAY
Houston	Fort Bend	FM 1093	125802031	$ 1,453,262	RESURFACE ROADWAY
Houston	Fort Bend	FM 3155	322301009	$ 294,857	RESURFACE ROADWAY
Bryan	Freestone	FM 80	45603015	$ 6,239,325	REPAIR ROADWAY
San Antonio	Frio	FM 140	74804036	$ 1,258,462	CURB & GUTTERS

Source: Company files.

EXHIBIT 6   Currie Road Construction Ltd. Cost Analysis for Period Ended _____

	Cost for Month		Cost to Date		Cost to Complete		Forecasted Final		Planned*		Variance
	Unit	Cost	Unit	Cost	Unit	Cost	Unit	Cost	Unit	Cost	
100—Contract Costs											
110—Construction Costs											
198—Cost of Operations											
200—Traffic Control											
Quantity											
Man Hours											
Labour											
Man Hours											
Supervisor											
Permanent Materials											
Other Construction Costs											
Equipment											
TOTALS											
210—Erosion Control											
Quantity											
Man Hours											
Labour											
Permanent Material											
Other Construction Costs											
Equipment											
TOTALS											
220—Lump Sum Construction											
Quantity											
Man Hours											
Labour											
Permanent Material											
Other Construction Costs											
Equipment											
Hired Equipment and Operator											
Hired Equipped/Operated											
Minority Business Enterprises											
TOTALS											

*Equals original bid cost
Source: Company files.

Online Piracy: Jaywalking or Theft?

In September 2009, Brian Lee purchased a computer game developed by a major company and, like some other customers, was experiencing difficulty running it. The source of the problems was a highly restrictive system of digital rights management (DRM),[1] which, while more or less universally disliked, was causing serious technical problems for a minority of users. Lee began to share his experience on the company's message board and was soon engaging in a debate about online piracy with a company representative. He was curious about piracy in the file-sharing age and wondered why it would be wrong to download a pirated version of the game with the DRM circumvented.

THE DIALOGUE

Brian: I have been a loyal supporter of your company for over a decade, but that is going to change. I pre-ordered your newest game and since it arrived a week ago, I have tried repeatedly to run it, but my DVD-ROM drive will not recognize the disc. Updating drivers at the request of technical support did not fix the problem. In fact, technical support insinuated that I must be using a pirated version, which is outrageous. Many people on this message board are experiencing problems running the game and yet, for the most part, our computers are perfectly capable according to the box's specifications. It seems that many of the difficulties customers are experiencing result from the new system of DRM employed by the game. When it was announced months ago that the

IVEY

Richard Ivey School of Business
The University of Western Ontario

[1]DRM is a broad term for methods of controlling access to digital material. Examples of DRM include FairPlay for iTunes, which prevented songs purchased from the iTunes Store from playing on competitors' digital music players; region codes on DVDs; installation limits and online activation requirements in computer games; and copying and printing restrictions in e-books.

game would use this form of DRM, some were skeptical, particularly because it entailed an installation limit of five times. Yet we all expected to play the game through at least once! The retailer from which I purchased the game will not issue a refund or allow an exchange for a different game. It did permit me to swap for another copy of the same game in case the first copy was defective, but I did so and my problems remained. Also, when I tried to sell the game, I discovered that the used computer games market is now virtually non-existent due to DRM. Thus, I am out $60 and hours of time and I will never give business to your company again.

Customer Support: Dear Brian, we regret that you are experiencing this problem. It has come to our attention that a minority of users (approximately two per cent) are having trouble running the game because of DRM conflicts. We encourage you to stay in touch with technical support until a solution is reached. We are aware of the unpopularity of what seems like a draconian anti-piracy system and can assure you that our decision to use it was not taken lightly. We deemed it necessary after our games were pirated 50,000 times in 2008. That equates to 50,000 stolen games—50,000 lost sales! We deeply regret the problems our customers face due to DRM, but we believe their frustration is better directed at the pirates who have forced us to take these measures.

Brian: Technical support has stopped replying to my e-mails. Nonetheless, I would like to respond to one of your points; namely, where you claim you lost 50,000 sales in 2008 after your games were "stolen" 50,000 times. It is incorrect to equate an illegal game download with a game stolen off a store shelf, because in the latter instance each game stolen represents a physical, and likely irretrievable, loss for the company, whereas software piracy entails illegal duplication. While piracy certainly cuts into your company's profits, you cannot assume that each user of a pirated software program would have purchased the retail version if a pirated version was unavailable.

Customer Support: I acknowledge that an illegally downloaded piece of media does not equate perfectly with a lost sale. However, I will in turn point out a misconception that many piracy advocates believe—that if they are morally obligated to pay for content, it should merely be the materials cost (e.g., a couple dollars for a DVD, booklet and case). But this neglects to factor in all the labour involved in the creation of the content, and it suggests that intellectual property itself is worthless. How is a record company supposed to pay salaries if it receives money for the raw materials cost of CDs but not also for the creativity on the CDs? As Mark Helprin writes in *Digital Barbarism*, "The advocates of 'music sharing' think that, because the Beatles, half of whom are dead, have hundreds of millions, or perhaps even billions, of dollars, and the people who would filch a song or two may have to buy their salad one tomato at a time and use milk crates as chairs, these expropriations are somehow mathematically justified. They aren't, and not merely because their cumulative effect has destroyed the music industry. . . . It doesn't matter if you steal a lot or a little, or if you get away with it, or not: theft is ugly."[2] I regret your problems, but I stand firm in my belief that piracy is always wrong.

Brian: I do believe intellectual property is of monetary value, and indeed, I have never used pirated content. However, this is the first time I have been unable to run purchased content. While I have been waiting (hopefully not in vain) for a patch to fix the game, I have researched online piracy and have learned some surprising facts. Your assertion that "piracy is always wrong" is probably off the mark. In *Free Culture*,

---

[2]Mark Helprin, *Digital barbarism*, HarperCollins, New York, 2009.

Lawrence Lessig defines four different types of file sharers: a) those who "use sharing networks as substitutes for purchasing content"; b) those who "use sharing networks to sample music before purchasing it"; c) those who "use sharing networks to get access to copyrighted material that is no longer sold or that they would not have purchased because the transaction costs off the Net are too high"; and d) those who "use sharing networks to get access to content that is not copyrighted or that the copyright owner wants to give away."[3] Of course, type A is unambiguously wrong, and type D is perfectly acceptable. The grey area falls within types B and C. Some think it not unreasonable that users illegally download and "sample" a program or album before buying it and, admittedly, doing so quickly eliminates many weak, overpriced products from consideration. Also, some who sample products will then buy them, and a few of these converted pirates would never have known about these products had they been unavailable in pirated form. As for acquiring content no longer manufactured or commercially available but still copyrighted, I see no harm in this. Waiting for content with a "dead copyright" to enter the public domain is increasingly unrealistic considering the average copyright term in the United States has ballooned from 32 years in 1973 to 95 years in 2003.[4] In addition, it can be next to impossible to locate copyright holders of dormant works.

By the way, are there any updates on the patch?

Customer Support: We are actively working on a patch, although if we are unsuccessful, we might arrange for a refund or a coupon for our products.

As for type B file sharing, I find this sense of entitlement preposterous, and I doubt there is conclusive evidence that pirates often purchase works they have illegally sampled. Type C file sharing also involves a sense of entitlement. Indeed, pirates are abetted by a sense of entitlement that coincides with the new potential for massive accumulation of content and information. This sense of entitlement, Mark Helprin believes, stems from a faulty belief in endless, ubiquitous wealth; the relative youth of the anti-copyright movement and its adherents; the view that intellectual property is not property; and the expectation of paying for media not with cash, but through subjection to nonstop commercials, banners and other advertising intrusions.[5] It is plain to see that there is a slippery slope in both types B and C. Conscientiously sampling content with a genuine willingness to buy good content turns into carelessly "sampling" everything and buying nothing. Rigorously searching the web and store bargain bins for an old underground album before downloading a pirated version as a last resort quickly degenerates into conducting a 30-second web search, conveniently concluding the album is commercially unavailable and downloading an illegal copy. Besides, there are legal means for acquiring rare content, such as eBay. The point is that types B and C quickly become type A. Ultimately, we can fret about the details, but it is fair to conclude that piracy is utterly harmful not only to content creators, but also to users. Increased piracy drives up prices and necessitates measures that occasionally cause problems for paying customers such as yourself. Nobody likes intrusive DRM, but the fact remains that a mere four per cent of video games entering production will earn a profit.[6] Worldwide, more than a third of all software used in 2007 was pirated, causing lost revenues to the

---

[3]Lawrence Lessig, *Free culture*, Penguin Books, United States, 2005.

[4]Ibid.

[5]Mark Helprin, *Digital barbarism*, HarperCollins, New York, 2009.

[6]Koroush Ghazi, "PC game piracy examined," June 2009, www.tweakguides.com/Piracy_1.html

software industry of approximately $48 billion,[7] and DRM is a logical response to this reality. Critics of DRM hold that because DRM is sometimes circumvented, it should cease to exist. By this logic, because locks on houses are often broken, we should not bother to lock our houses.[8] The point of DRM is deterrence, and it performs this function more or less admirably.

Brian: But at what cost? DRM can undoubtedly be expensive and tricky to maintain for companies, and the drawbacks for consumers are even worse. Much of the DRM used in games, for example, is so intrusive that it remains on a user's computer after a game is uninstalled. If it retains the potential to collect information about a user's computer after the user has removed the program, is it much better than malware?[9] Installation limits are also troubling. Users are constantly formatting their hard drives or uninstalling programs to free up space, and a limit of three or five installations is unfair. Of course, I am posting here simply because of the impasse DRM has brought me to, and I sense that in time we will look back on most of these anti-piracy measures with disbelief. Remember DRM audio CDs? They suffered a quick demise after it was discovered that Sony BMG was including rootkits on their DRM CDs, causing potential security vulnerabilities for customers' computers.[10] More recently, Steve Jobs, the driving force behind Apple, has identified the folly of DRM in iTunes and has succeeded in relaying his opinion to the big four record companies, who control the distribution of 70 per cent of the world's music,[11] so that the iTunes Store is now DRM-free. Fairplay, iTunes's DRM, used to mean that only iPods could play tracks purchased from iTunes, that tracks purchased from iTunes would not play on competing music players, and that there were other limitations, such as only being able to access purchased tracks on a maximum of five computers. Unsurprisingly, many other digital music players and online music stores employed their own systems of DRM. Yet the vast majority of worldwide music sales were still in the form of CDs and thus were DRM-free, so it was silly and overly complex for music distributed online, which comprised a small portion of music sales, to be saddled with these different forms of DRM. Even Bill Gates himself criticized DRM, saying it has "huge problems."[12]

Customer Support: DRM is not perfect, and the anti-piracy measures of the future will undoubtedly look different from those used now. But no good comes of piracy and necessary steps need to be taken to prevent it.

Brian: Is it entirely true that no good comes of piracy? While I recognize the harm caused by piracy, it has brought certain inadvertent benefits. Jeff Raikes, when he was president of the Microsoft Business Division, stated, "Our number one goal is that we want people to use our product. If they're going to pirate somebody, we want it to be us rather than somebody else . . . . What you hope to do is over time you hope to convert

---

[7]Note that pirated software does not include pirated music or movies. *Business Software Alliance*, "Online software scams: A threat to your security," October 2008, www.bsa.org/files/Internet_Piracy_Report.pdf

[8]Koroush Ghazi, "PC game piracy examined," June 2009, www.tweakguides.com/Piracy_1.html

[9]Malware, also known as malicious software, is software made to break into or disrupt a user's computer without the user's permission. The term encompasses viruses, trojan horses, spyware, rootkits, etc.

[10]Robert McMillan, "Settlement ends Sony rootkit case," *PC World*, May 23, 2006, www.pcworld.com/article/125838/settlement_ends_sony_rootkit_case.html

[11]Steve Jobs, "Thoughts on music," February 6, 2007, www.apple.com/hotnews/thoughtsonmusic

[12]Cyrus Farivar, "CE-Oh no he didn't! . . ." *Engadget*, December 14, 2006, www.engadget.com/2006/12/14/ce-oh-no-he-didnt-part-xxi-gates-tells-consumers-to-ditch-dr

them to licensing the software, legally licensing it."[13] Regarding the competition in China between Microsoft Windows and Linux, a free open-source operating system, Bill Gates said, "It's easier for our software to compete with Linux when there's piracy than when there's not."[14] And generally speaking, have not many of the technological and cultural milestones in the West been inextricably linked to piracy? Consider Hollywood, born of pirates evading the patent laws of Thomas Edison, the inventor of filmmaking.[15] What about the United States, which neglected to recognize foreign copyrights for the first hundred years of its existence?[16] How about extensive "borrowing" and refining by Disney?[17] It was Rupert Murdoch who said that without Napster, there was no Internet, and we can see that high-speed Internet boomed due to Napster.[18] In Canada, Bell had 51,000 high-speed Internet customers when Napster launched in June 1999. By 2002, this number had jumped to 1.1 million.[19] Consider the iPod now. Hank Berry, former Napster CEO, said, "Without Napster, there is no iPod, period . . . . Remember that the iPod launched two years before the iTunes store was around, so you have a two-year period where essentially the only source of music for people's iPods was people doing their own ripping from their own CD collection and getting things from Napster or some other service."[20] I could go on—Youtube, cable television, radio, VCRs, CD burners, tape recorders; all these technologies owe a debt to piracy, and many could not have thrived without it.

Customer Support: I cannot say I share your utopian vision of piracy. I will grant that much of the technology we use today is or was associated with piracy, but whether we should be proud of this is another question. You seem to champion piracy and imply that theft is a key driver of innovation. Indeed, there are many likeminded individuals on the web and you would find a better reception for your views at the Pirate Bay, the famous torrent[21] indexing site. In case you were unaware, BitTorrent has taken the baton of file sharing from the older generation of peer-to-peer (P2P) programs like Napster, and while there are plenty of sites from which to download torrents, none is as famous as the Pirate Bay, which is the centre of an anti-copyright, counter-culture movement touting "freedom of information" to justify facilitating massive piracy. But if you ask me, the four men who own the Pirate Bay are just masquerading as revolutionaries, and their grievances about the supposed greed of corporate America lose credibility when you consider that the site racks up millions of dollars a year in ad revenues, not to mention donations. They do not simply promote and facilitate piracy, they get rich off of it. And as a result, they have been sentenced to serve a year in jail and pay millions of dollars in fines. As a matter of fact, following their sentencing,

---

[13]*Computer Business Review,* "Microsoft admits piracy benefits," March 16, 2007, www.cbronline.com/news/microsoft_admits_piracy_benefits

[14]David Kirkpatrick, "How Microsoft conquered China," *CNN Money*, July 17, 2007, http://money.cnn.com/magazines/fortune/fortune_archive/2007/07/23/100134488

[15]Lawrence Lessig, *Free culture*, Penguin Books, United States, 2005.

[16]Ibid.

[17]Ibid.

[18]*The Globe and Mail,* "Download decade," 2009, www.theglobeandmail.com/news/technology/download-decade

[19]Ibid.

[20]Ibid.

[21]A torrent is a small file that contains the metadata needed to download a larger file (e.g., a game or movie) from a network of users. BitTorrent is the protocol through which torrents function, and some sources estimate that BitTorrent traffic accounts for half of all the traffic on the Internet.

the "business" has been sold to a gaming company for nearly $8 million. The company, Global Gaming Factory X, promises that the Pirate Bay will introduce legitimate business models with which to pay content owners, but the owners of the Pirate Bay seem to tell a different story, suggesting the sale will not affect the site.[22] Only time will tell. Suffice it to say, I find it repugnant to see my company's work available on the Pirate Bay for free under the pretence of "freedom of information." The fact that the Pirate Bay has many loyal fans hardly legitimizes it—is it surprising that people flock to its banner after using it to steal thousands of dollars of free content? You even have a Norwegian socialist party launching filesharer.org, a website where users are supposed to post their mugshots to demonstrate they are "criminals" like the owners of the Pirate Bay. I doubt the pro-piracy movements, political or otherwise, offer coherent, realistic plans for intellectual property rights. What they do offer is a tired communitarian philosophy, or worse—anarchy.

Brian: Geez, why are we talking about anarchy? I'm still trying to get my computer game working.

Customer Support: Fair enough. But my little rant is due to the fact that if my company cannot generate revenues, people like me lose their job.

Brian: Nobody wants you to lose your job. But can we get back to my problem? On Google, I searched for the name of the game plus the word "torrent" and was astounded at the depth of matches. The torrent sites offer a version of the game that is complete, yet cracked, so that the DRM is removed.[23] This means that following a few hours' download time, I could install a pirated copy of your game and it would probably play successfully (since there is no potential for a DRM incompatibility), not to mention present fewer hassles than the retail version. I am somewhat confounded that BitTorrent is resilient to the legal problems that defeated Napster, but I would wager that BitTorrent survives because the standard BitTorrent client does not feature a built-in search engine for torrents (these must be downloaded from a site like the Pirate Bay) and because torrents only contain metadata and not "real data."

Companies do not seem to be giving enough thought to the future of the relationship between the Internet and intellectual property. In my view, this is where our focus should lie, so I have compiled a list of technological and other ways that content could be protected from piracy. In fact, I have created a new message board thread because this is such an important topic (see Exhibit 1).

At this juncture, I must say that it has been weeks since I first notified technical support of my problems and that the assistance I have received has been disappointing, if not unethical. When I first explained my problem, tech support provided me with a customer complaint number and asked a question about my computer hardware, then received a response, sent another question, received another response and stopped replying. When I e-mailed to ask why they stopped responding, they gave me a new customer complaint number, started asking the same questions as before and again stopped replying. They have issued four customer complaint numbers now and I suspect they keep placing me at the top of the queue so that I give up trying. They have never apologized or indicated a serious effort to fix my problem, and especially disconcerting is their suggestion that I am using a pirated version and that this must be the source of my difficulties (ironically, a pirated version would probably play fine).

---

[22]*CBC News*, "Pirate Bay site sold to Swedish gaming company," June 30, 2009, www.cbc.ca/arts/music/story/2009/06/30/pirate-bay-sold-gaming-company.html

[23]To crack software is to modify it in order to remove protection such as the requirement of CD checks or serial numbers.

As a former part-time business student, I detect a weakness in your service recovery. In fact, in my view, it is so bad that it is bordering on immoral. I found an old ethics textbook which says that the minimal moral obligation of a business organization toward customers is "Accurately labeled, safe goods and services of good value. Adequate customer information. Respect promises on delivery and performance."[24]

Customer Support: I take issue with your claim that the company has conducted itself unethically in response to your problem. We care deeply about customers' concerns, though, unfortunately, technical support is overstretched and cannot always provide immediate assistance. I can assure you we are operating in accordance with ethical standards. But remember, if users object to the glitches, installation limits and other hassles brought on by DRM in games, they should not forget that the pirates are the offending party, not us.

Brian: Whatever you say! Did you read the new thread about ways to cut down on online piracy?

Customer Support: Yes, I read it over and it's interesting stuff. At this time, I regret to inform you that, due to cash flow issues, we cannot issue a refund. Furthermore, we have been unsuccessful in developing a patch. Thank you for your understanding.

---

[24]Frederick Bird and Jeffrey Gandz, *Good management: Business ethics in action*, Prentice-Hall Canada Inc., Scarborough, Ontario, 1991, p. 111.

EXHIBIT 1   A Few Ways to Reduce Piracy

The first way to reduce piracy is to launch an attack against file-sharing technologies such as BitTorrent. The idea of stifling technology in order to protect copyrights is not unprecedented in recent decades. Jack Valenti, when he was president of the Motion Picture Association of America, was virulently opposed to VCRs, calling them "tapeworms": "When there are 20, 30, 40 million of these VCRs in the land, we will be invaded by millions of 'tapeworms,' eating away at the very heart and essence of the most precious asset the copyright owner has, his copyright."[1] Quashing file-sharing technologies would be an overreaction, causing technological regression, and is impractical. Much more realistic is the prospect of Internet service providers (ISPs) blocking access to file-sharing sites like the Pirate Bay and, as I understand, that site is blocked in Denmark. One problem with this measure is that torrent indexing sites are almost ubiquitous; another is that some ISPs are reluctant to offer restrictive access to the Internet because it undermines the free, limitless nature of the technology. France just narrowly rejected legislation to enact a three-strikes policy, whereby users who illegally download copyrighted content would be warned twice before their Internet was cut off. A common means by which ISPs reduce traffic is "throttling," where download speeds of BitTorrent users are mitigated, and this is inadvertently an anti-piracy measure. Finally, it is evident that monitoring piracy on the Internet and then pursuing the culprits is incredibly unpopular—witness the notorious efforts of the Recording Industry Association of America to sue casual P2P users for hundreds of thousands of dollars.

There is, of course, the DRM question. DRM has arguably proven unsuccessful with digital music but is still a factor in PC games, e-books (e.g., to control copying and printing), Blu-rays and DVDs (e.g., region codes), operating systems and even ring tones. The very fact of my writing this post speaks to one of DRM's shortcomings—inconveniencing legitimate customers, whether through bogging down the experience or stopping it altogether. An alternative to the sort of DRM that irritates computer gamers is selling games through Steam, an online distribution system (somewhat like an iTunes for games) that requires users to log in and, for some games, be connected to the Internet. This could be considered "DRM-lite." Most games sold on Steam do not use a separate system of DRM; hence, most do not have installation limits or disc checks (since Steam games are all downloaded), and do not leave remnants of DRM on the computer after removal.

Bundling software with new computers is an effective method of combating software piracy. Another good method is cloud computing, in which software functionality lies on a vendor's server instead of on a local PC.[2] Another possibility is software asset management, which helps users keep track of software licenses. The potential rise of streaming media services offering a vast archive of high-quality media could mitigate the appeal of downloading media illegally (and perhaps with lower quality) through BitTorrent. Last.fm is an innovative Internet radio site that streams free music with ads and offers a premium service for a small subscription fee. Spotify streams free ad-supported music to computer users and is experimenting with a subscription model for mobile phone users. These business models accept that the current generation, rightly or wrongly, feels entitled to music for free or for dirt cheap.

Moving on, there are ways to protect content that are rooted more in ideology than technology. Does overpriced content significantly increase piracy rates? Certainly some users engage in piracy out of a belief that big business does not need or deserve their money. However, the correlation between price and piracy rates is difficult to gauge for general Western populations. On the other hand, many users in the developing world are simply too poor to pay for content, whether it costs $2 or $20, and, unsurprisingly, the highest software piracy rates in the world are in Georgia (95 per cent), Bangladesh (92 per cent), Armenia (92 per cent) and Zimbabwe (92 per cent), while the lowest piracy rates are in North America (21 per cent) and Western Europe (33 per cent).[3] Finally, globalization means that emerging markets will increasingly value legitimate software and will be more active in cracking down on intellectual property violations. This seems to be playing out in China right now.

It is plausible that some tweaking of copyright laws is in order. For example, Canada has not updated its copyright law since 1997, two years before the release of Napster.[4] As well, some argue that people need to change their perceptions about piracy—should it remain illegal to download "abandonware," that is, software no longer sold or supported and for which no one is actively asserting copyright ownership? The following system could be implemented for users who want to draw from, or publishers who want to make available, orphan works: "In the

---

[1]Lawrence Lessig, *Free culture*, Penguin Books, United States, 2005.

[2]Sixth Annual BSA-IDC Global Software Piracy Study, May 2009, http://global.bsa.org/globalpiracy2008/index.html

[3]Ibid.

[4]*The Globe and Mail*, "Download decade," 2009, www.theglobeandmail.com/news/technology/download-decade

EXHIBIT 1   (Continued)

absence of a claimant, a notice could be posted on a universal copyright Internet notice board. After a reasonable time and no response, a potential user or publisher could be granted permission to use or publish, with royalties held in escrow for yet another period, until they were claimed. And if they were not claimed, they could be directed to a fund of some sort, or revert to the payer. These simple steps would make orphan works available and protect the copyright holders at the same time."[5] Are copyright terms in general too long? In the United States, the only software that has entered the public domain due to copyright expiration is software published before 1964 that was not renewed in its copyright during its 28th year following publication; for unpublished software, the copyright lasts 70 years plus the life of the author, regardless of when it was written.[6] Hopefully Creative Commons[7] will grow in popularity so that content creators can conveniently permit their work to be available to others with minimal restrictions if they so desire. New possibilities for abandonware and orphan works, as well as the availability of a more flexible copyright, could reduce the scope of what is considered piracy and copyright infringement.

More sample or trial versions[8] of software, music and movies could reduce piracy rates to a small degree. Evolving attitudes, perhaps influenced through educational initiatives, could present purchasing content as classy and pirating as reprehensible. The public should be informed that pirated content frequently comes with malware and that unpaid taxes on pirated content can hurt communities.

To end, I would like to share a scheme proposed by Harvard law professor William Fisher to solve the problem of online piracy: "Under his plan, all content capable of digital transmission would (1) be marked with a digital watermark . . . . Once the content is marked, then entrepreneurs would develop (2) systems to monitor how many items of each content were distributed. On the basis of those numbers, then (3) artists would be compensated. The compensation would be paid for by (4) an appropriate tax."[9] Thus, users would simply download what they wanted and taxes would compensate content creators according to how much their work was downloaded. Lawrence Lessig has proposed a slight modification to this scheme.

---

[5]Mark Helprin, *Digital barbarism*, HarperCollins, New York, 2009.

[6]Stephen Fishman, *The Public domain: How to find and use copyright free writings, music, art & more*, NOLO, 2008.

[7]Creative Commons is a non-profit organization devoted to providing a "some rights reserved" alternative to the traditional "all rights reserved" copyright.

[8]Trial versions generally offer limited features and/or expire after a specified term.

[9]Lawrence Lessig, *Free culture*, Penguin Books, United States, 2005.

CASE 34

Barrick Gold Corporation-Tanzania[1]

By March 2009, Canadian mining company Barrick Gold Corporation (Barrick) had only been operating in the Lake Victoria Zone in Tanzania for a decade. In the same year, Barrick had adopted a new name for its business in Tanzania, African Barrick Gold PLC (ABG), which was also listed on the London Stock Exchange. The company was widely considered to be one of the more "responsive" global corporations in the mining industry.[2] Its extensive mining activities in the region employed thousands of local people, and Barrick was engaged in social development projects in various Tanzanian communities.[3] By October 2010, the company operated four main gold mining sites in the country.[4]

Despite Barrick's efforts to support social development initiatives in the Lake Victoria Zone over the past decade, discontent and resistance at one of its mining sites in North Mara still remained. This area posed challenges. A key question was why the tension and violence had not stopped in certain mining sites in the North Mara mining area, and whether there was much more Barrick could reasonably be expected to do to resolve the problem.

BACKGROUND ON TANZANIA

Tanzania was a developing country located in East Africa, with a total land size of 945,087 square kilometres. It had one of the highest levels of unemployment and

Professors Aloysius Newenham-Kahindi and Paul W. Beamish wrote this case solely to provide material for class discussion. The authors do not intend to illustrate either effective or ineffective handling of a managerial situation. The authors may have disguised certain names and other identifying information to protect confidentiality.

---

[1]This case has been written on the basis of published sources only. Consequently, the interpretation and perspectives presented in this case are not necessarily those of Barrick Gold Corporation or any of its employees.

[2]www.barrick.com/CorporateResponsibility/BeyondBorders/default.aspx, accessed March 24, 2009.

[3]www.barrick.com/News/PressReleases/PressReleaseDetails/2010/Barrick-Named-to-Dow-Jones-Sustainability-World-Index-for-Third-Consecutive-Year/default.aspx, accessed September 27, 2010.

[4]www.tanzaniagold.com/barrick.html, accessed October 1, 2010.

poverty in sub-Saharan Africa. Its economy was heavily dependent on agriculture, which accounted for half of the gross domestic product (GDP), provided 85 per cent of the country's exports and employed 90 per cent of the workforce. Topography and climatic conditions, however, limited cultivated crops to only four per cent of the land area. Industry was mainly limited to processing agricultural products and light consumer goods.

Like most developing nations, Tanzania had a very weak national institutional and legal system. It also had a very high rate of corruption.[5] The country needed support from foreign direct investment (FDI) and transnational corporations (TNCs) in order to promote businesses, employment and other opportunities for its citizens. Tanzania wanted its institutions to be more transparent and accountable, and to regulate the activities of FDI and TNCs in addressing the country's social and ecological issues. Both local and international not-for-profit organizations (NFOs), however, had continued to create a significant impact with respect to promoting responsive behaviour in corporate governance practices, positively influencing all involved stakeholders and other social actors to address social issues.

Following independence in 1961, Tanzania opted for a socialist command economic and institutional system, with socialist policies (*Ujamaa* in Swahili) being implemented in 1967. The emphasis of these policies was to promote cooperative institutions and collective villages with the aim of building an egalitarian society, eliminating ethnic and gender barriers and creating a common language of Swahili for all. Within the practice of Ujamaa, the country had managed to unite its ethnic groups under a common language, with the result that the central government had created strong post-colonial nationalistic ideologies, unity, ethnic harmony and peace among its people. Compared to many post-colonial sub-Saharan African countries that went through civil and ethnic strife and conflicts after independence in the 1960s and 1970s, Tanzania under Ujamaa appeared to be a successful model.

Towards the end of the 1980s, however, Tanzania began to experience significant economic stagnation and social problems. To combat these issues, in the early 1990s, the government sought to privatize its economy and reform its institutions in order to attract foreign investment. The introduction of the famous post-Ujamaa Investment Act of 1997 was intended to encourage free market and trade liberalization in the country. Investment in various private sectors such as mining, tourism, fishing, banking and agriculture under foreign-owned TNCs served to bolster the country's reforms by creating employment opportunities for the local economy.

As the country continued to privatize and reform its national institutional and legal systems, many foreign companies sought to invest in its economy. The Tanzania Investment Centre (TIC) was created in the early 2000s as a tool for identifying possible investment opportunities and aiding potential investors in navigating any procedural barriers that might exist during the process of investment in the country.[6] The liberalization of the banking industry in 2002, for example, saw the former Ujamaa Cooperative and Rural Development Bank replaced by the Commercial Rural Development Bank (CRDB) and the National Microfinance Bank (NMB), which promoted community investments across the country. In February 2009, the Tanzania Private Sector Foundation (TPSF) was created with the aim of strengthening the entrepreneurial culture among its citizens, by providing communities and individuals across the country with entrepreneurial business ideas and grants. In June 2009, the government

[5]See data on Tanzania at www.transparency.org
[6]www.tic.co.tz, accessed April 1, 2009.

started an ambitious national resolution under the so-called "Kilimo Kwanza" policies (meaning "Agriculture First" in Swahili) to boost the standard of living among
the *eighty per cent* of citizens who relied on agriculture for their livelihood.[7] It was
based on Green Revolution principles aimed at boosting Tanzania's agriculture into
the modern and commercial sector, and mobilizing for-profit organizations (FPOs),
such as local private businesses and foreign-owned TNCs, in the country to increase
their investment engagement with the agriculture sector, both at the macro and micro
levels (i.e., along with local communities).

In order to ensure that there was sufficient security and peace for private and
foreign-owned investors (i.e., TNCs), in 2005, the government introduced a new entity
called "Tanzania Security Industry Association." The association was based on local,
professional private security firms and groups whose main tasks were to safeguard
business firms' activities rather than letting the firms rely on local police forces. The
largest and best-known local security firm was Moku Security Services Limited, based
in Dar Es Salaam, which had over 13,000 employees across the country. Other security
groups with over 400 employees were Ultimate Security Company, Dragon Security,
Tele-security Company Limited, and Group Four Security Company. Private security
employees were mainly retired army and police officers; young people who had lost
their previous jobs following the collapse of the Ujamaa policies that provided "jobs
for everyone and for life;" and individuals who sought better remuneration in the security sector than in the government public sector. However, due to increased demand
for better security across businesses, many foreign-owned TNCs sought the services
of security firms from abroad, mainly from South Africa's professional security firms,
such as the South African Intruder Detection Service Association (SAIDS). Some security personnel had combat experience, which helped them handle sophisticated forms
of crime and intrusion.

The Tanzanian economy continued to grow and create job opportunities, training
and innovative development prospects for its people. Earlier, the country had introduced new mining legislation, such as the Mining Act of 1998 and the Mining Regulation Act of 1999, in order to harmonize investment relations between FDI and local
interests. However, in April 2010, the government passed another new mining Act, following consultations with civil society groups such as the Foundation for Civil Society
Tanzania (FCST), companies and other stakeholders. The legislation of a new mining
Act imposed a new form of royalties that required all TNCs and local companies to be
listed in the country and gave the state a stake in future projects.[8]

The country possessed vast amounts of natural resources like gold, diamond, copper, platinum, natural gas and zinc deposits that remained underdeveloped. It was one
of the more peaceful countries in sub-Saharan Africa. In order to attract and protect
the interests of FDI and TNCs and, of course, its own people, Tanzania had attempted
to harmonize its investment practices and labour legislation. In order to create responsible institutional policies, in February 2010, the National Assembly of Tanzania
enlisted a group of local environmental and toxicity experts to investigate environmental and toxic effects on the people and livestock in the North Mara gold mine in Tarime
District, Mara Region, by the Tigithe River.[9]

---

[7]www.actanzania.org/index.php?option=com_content&task=view&id=121&Itemid=39, accessed
February 12, 2010.

[8]www.mining-journal.com/finance/new-tanzanian-mining-act, accessed September 27, 2010.

[9]www.dailynews.co.tz, accessed February 10, 2010.

For a number of reasons, Tanzania was a willing host nation for FDI. The country needed the input of TNCs in order to create employment and prosperity. In return, Tanzania could provide TNCs with low-cost labour and a readily available labour force. Low labour costs were an opportunity to support a host nation's development policy in attracting FDI and ultimately in creating a knowledge-based society in the midst of the globalization challenges that were faced by so many developing countries. Furthermore, Tanzania continued to create a local business environment in conjunction with various TNCs' global business interests in order to generate sustainable development policies and practices. It also engaged in market development initiatives that represented innovative learning opportunities and entrepreneurship ventures for its citizens.

LAKE VICTORIA BACKGROUND

Tanzania's Lake Victoria was surrounded by the three East African countries of Kenya, Tanzania and Uganda. The lake itself was named after the former queen of England, Queen Victoria, and stood as the world's largest tropical lake and the second-largest freshwater lake after Lake Superior in North America. Covering a total of 69,000 square kilometres, the lake was as large as the Republic of Ireland and lay in the Rift Valley of East Africa, a 3,500-mile system of deep cracks in the earth's crust, running from the Red Sea south to Mozambique. Lake Victoria was the source of the Nile River, which passed through the Sudan and Egypt and finally reached the Mediterranean Sea.

Lake Victoria Zone in Tanzania

The Lake Victoria Zone consisted of the three regions of Mwanza, Mara (formerly called Musoma) and Kagera (formerly called Bukoba), and was one of the most densely populated regions in Africa. Population growth around Lake Victoria was significantly higher than in the rest of sub-Saharan Africa. During the last five decades, population growth within a 100-kilometre buffer zone around the lake had outpaced the continental average, which had led to growing dependency and pressure on the lake's resources.

Prior to the mining extraction boom in the early 1990s and following the collapse of Ujamaa, most people living in this region were mainly engaged in rudimentary forms of fishing, agricultural farming and keeping cattle, as well as other forms of cooperative activities that had been engineered by the country's former Ujamaa policies. Irrigation was limited to a small scale and often used rudimentary technologies to support both individual and cooperative farming activities. Noted for its temperate climate, the area had a mean temperature of between 26 and 30 degrees Celsius in the hot season and 15 and 18 degrees Celsius in the cooler months. The area was rich with tropical vegetation and fruits such as bananas, mangoes, corn, pineapple and many others. The lake was essential to more than 15 million people, providing potable water, hydroelectric power and inland water transport, as well as support for tourism and wildlife.

The area remained one of the most fertile for farming activities and continued to attract immigrants from other regions of the country, as well as from Tanzania's neighbours in the war-torn populations of Burundi, Rwanda and the Democratic Republic of Congo. The presence of hundreds of TNCs engaged in various activities in the area was the main "draw" for these immigrants, who came seeking employment and new sources of livelihood.

The resulting population increase in the Lake Victoria Zone created several problems with respect to the lake and the environment. According to a report by World Watch Institute in Washington, D.C., the once clear, life-abounding lake had become murky, smelly and choked with algae. It had been reported that:

> The ecological health of Lake Victoria has been affected profoundly as a result of a rapidly growing population, clearance of natural vegetation along the shores, a booming fish-export industry, the disappearance of several fish species native to the lake, prolific growth of algae, and dumping of untreated effluent by several industries. Much of the damage is vast and irreversible. Traditional lifestyles of lakeshore communities have been disrupted and are crumbling.[10]

As a result of the overuse of natural resources in the area, the traditional lifestyles of the lakeshore communities were significantly disrupted, a situation that prompted both social and ecological concerns for the area and its residents.

The fishing industry was badly affected in the region following the introduction of Nile perch (Lates Niloticus) and Nile tilapia (Oreochromis Niloticus) into the lake. For example, in the 1980s, a survey of the lake revealed an abrupt and unexpected increase in numbers among the Nile perch, constituting 80 per cent of all fish in the lake. In spite of working harder, local fishermen caught fewer fish since the populations of smaller fish, which traditionally had been the fishermen's primary source of livelihood, became decimated. In addition, the big, oily Nile perch, generally referred to as "Mbuta," swam too far out in the open waters for the little local fishing boats and was too big to be caught in the locals' unsophisticated nets.

In response to an increased international demand for the Nile perch, commercial fishing fleets owned by foreign firms displaced local fishermen and many women in lakeside communities who worked as fish processors. The processing of fish, traditionally performed by women, was gradually taken over by large filleting plants. The women resorted to processing fish waste, commonly referred to as *mgongo-wazi,* or "bare-back" in Swahili. The waste, comprised of fish heads, backbones and tails, was sun-dried and then deep-fried and sold to local people, who were drawn to its low price and nutritional value. Many fishermen were forced to look for alternative sources of livelihood, mainly seeking employment in extractive mining corporations and other industries as manual labourers.

The water hyacinth posed another threat to the health of Lake Victoria. With the deceptive appearance of a lush, green carpet, the hyacinth was in fact a merciless, free-floating weed, reproducing rapidly and covering any uncovered territory. First noticed in 1989, the weed spread rapidly and covered areas in all three surrounding countries. It formed a dense mat, blocking the sunlight from reaching the organisms below, depleting the already-low concentrations of oxygen and trapping fishing boats and nets of all sizes. The hyacinth was also an ideal habitat for poisonous snakes and disease-carrying snails that caused bilharzias. The government, in partnership with other international agencies, had tried desperately to control the weed. Its most promising approach involved harvesting the hyacinth and using it either for compost or for biogas production.

The health implications associated with the declining state of the lake were extensive. Dumping untreated sewage in the lake and nearby rivers exposed people to water-borne diseases, such as typhoid, cholera and diarrhea, and chronic forms of malaria. The Lake Victoria Zone was known to have the most dangerous types of malaria in the

---

[10]www.cichlid-forum.com/articles/lake_victoria_sick.php, accessed April 1, 2009.

world. As fish prices soared, protein malnutrition became a significant threat for communities living in the zone. Lack of regular income also meant that many people in the area could not afford to be treated for waterborne typhoid, yellow fever and various forms of tropical worms, such as tapeworms and hookworms.

Mining in Tanzania

Gold mining activities around the Lake Victoria Zone in Tanzania started during the German colonial period in 1894, when Tanzania was called Tanganyika. The First and Second World Wars accelerated the demand for gold production in the region and, following the introduction of Ujamaa in 1967, mining became a state-directed activity. By nationalizing the industry, the government hoped to capture more benefits from mining through the creation of local employment, direct spending on social services for mining communities and higher budget revenues from having a direct stake in the business. However, despite these high hopes, the mining sector failed to stimulate the industrialization of the country's economy. During Ujamaa, the production of gold declined significantly due to limited government funding and limited technological know-how within the industry. Mining activities that were performed illegally by small-scale operators contributed to several environmental and social problems.[11]

The collapse of Ujamaa in 1990s, however, resulted in new opportunities for the country to attract mining companies from Canada, the United Kingdom, Australia and South Africa, all of whom were interested in gold exploration and development activities. Following successful exploration mining activities that began in 1995, Barrick invested in Tanzania in 1999 at the Lake Victoria Zone. It acquired gold reserves in the Bulyanhulu mine, located in northwest Tanzania, East Africa, approximately 55 kilometres south of Lake Victoria and approximately 150 kilometres from the city of Mwanza; Buzwagi near Kahama District; Tulawaka in Biharamulo, Kagera Region; and later at the North Mara gold mine in the northwestern part of Tanzania in Tarime District of Mara Region, approximately 100 kilometres east of Lake Victoria and 20 kilometres south of the Kenyan border.

According to the Tanzanian Mineral Authority and Tanzania Chamber of Minerals and Energy (TCME), since 2000, production of gold had been growing, making the Lake Victoria Zone one of the most attractive areas for employment opportunities, as well as for business opportunities in other industries. Tanzania was Africa's third-largest producer of gold, after Ghana and South Africa.[12] Tanzania was also richly endowed with other minerals, including cobalt, copper, nickel, platinum group metals and silver, as well as diamonds and a variety of gemstones. The energy sector was dominated by natural gas. Commercial quantities of oil had yet to be discovered. In 2008, TCME reported that a total of US$2 billion in the past decade had been injected into the Tanzanian economy by mining TNCs, and, in total, mining TNCs had paid the government over US$255 million in taxes within the same period.[13]

In 2002, Tanzania joined the African Union's development blueprint, an endeavour that was governed by the New Economic Partnership for African Development (NEPAD), to oversee an African Mining Partnership (AMP) with global mining corporations. The goal of this partnership was to promote sustainable development and

---

[11]www.douglaslakeminerals.com/mining.html, accessed February 26, 2009.

[12]www.mineweb.co.za/mineweb/view/mineweb/en/page67?oid=39782&sn=Detail, accessed May 1, 2009.

[13]Ibid.

best-practice guidelines for African governments as a way to ensure that their mining laws protected ecological and community welfare, while maximizing remittances from the mining TNCs to the government budgets in a transparent and accountable way.

The country did, however, develop competitive tax packages and incentives to attract TNCs to invest in high-risk and complex exploration areas such as the Lake Victoria Zone. The government did not devise a practical and engaging strategy to utilize mining resources and revenues paid by TNCs to support the local communities that were situated around mining sites and who had lost their livelihood, homes, health, natural resources and recreation with little or no compensation.[14] Also, the government did not come up with a concrete strategy to deal with the chronic sewage and environmental issues in the area.

Like any TNC engaged in extractive mining activities in a developing country, such as Tanzania, with so many social problems and legal and institutional weaknesses, Barrick had faced conflicting pressures with regard to the way it engaged in locally based community social partnership (see Exhibit 1). Such partnerships were meant to address the social problems of unemployment, poverty, diseases and environmental concerns in a sustainable way. Barrick strictly followed Western legal and property approvals to legitimize its mining activities in the country. It also continued to face challenges with respect to its efforts to strike a balance between its global strategies and those of the local subsidiary operations in Tanzania. Mineral wealth continued to fuel and prolong violent behaviour by local communities mainly in North Mara, thus failing to diversify economic growth and contribute to the development of communities in the Lake Victoria Zone. Corruption and weak institutional capabilities to enact or enforce the democratic, transparent and agreed-upon rules and laws that governed the operation and taxation of mining activities were a source of ongoing problems.[15] Also, some local communities did not see the potential benefits of large corporations in their communities.

BARRICK GOLD CORP. IN TANZANIA

As a gold producer on the world stage, Barrick used advanced exploration technological systems for its mining development projects.[16] The company owned one of the world's largest gold mineral reserves and a large land position across its subsidiary mining extraction activities. These were located across the five continents of North America, South America, Africa, Australia and Asia. As one of the largest Canadian mining companies, Barrick shares were traded on the Toronto and New York Stock Exchanges and on other major global stock index centres in London, as well as on the Swiss Stock Exchanges and the Euronext-Paris. It was a shareholder-driven firm. Barrick invested in Tanzania in 1999, following the completion of exploration activities that had started in 1995. The company's initial mining activities were limited to Bulyanhulu in Kahama Dictrict until 2004, when it expanded to other areas surrounding the Lake Victoria Zone.

Socialization was part of the corporate culture used to manage human resources (HRM)[17] in Tanzania. Each mining site had a training department. Barrick recruited

---

[14]"The challenge of mineral wealth in Tanzania: Using resource endowments to foster sustainable development," International Council on Mining & Metals, 2006.

[15]www.revenuewatch.org/our-work/countries/tanzania.php, accessed May 1, 2009.

[16]www.tanzaniagold.com/barrick.html, accessed, May 1, 2009.

[17]www.barrick.com/CorporateResponsibility/Employees/AttractingRetaining/default.aspx, accessed April 24, 2009.

university graduates who worked on administrative activities in corporate offices, and assigned manual labourers to mining sites to work along with expatriates and locals who had experience in mining activities. Also, the company was involved in developing the so-called Integrated Mining Technical Training (IMTT) program, a joint project with the Tanzania Chamber of Minerals and Energy and the Tanzanian government. The goal was to offer locals the skills they needed to participate in the country's burgeoning mining sector and to reduce the industry's reliance on foreign-trained expatriates.[18] Barrick used its Global Succession Planning Program (GSPP) that provided expatriates with a chance to increase their knowledge and expertise by transferring them into assignments at other Barrick sites in Tanzania and sites in other countries where the company operated.[19] The major role of GSPP was to instill the corporate culture through the training of employees regarding various mining technology skills, and to run the company's daily practices in accordance with the corporate business interests of the company.

Mission, Vision and Values

Given the questionable reputation of some global mining corporations with respect to sustainable development projects in developing societies, Barrick's core vision and values were to continue finding, acquiring, developing and producing quality reserves in a safe, profitable and socially responsible manner. Barrick claimed to promote long-term benefits to the communities in which it operated and to foster a culture of excellence and collaboration with its employees, governments and local stakeholders.

The company followed global corporate social responsibility standards as part of its larger global business strategies, using the vocabularies of business ethics, human rights and development. Among these strategies, the company placed significant emphasis on its social relationships with local communities and the right to operate in their land.[20]

Building Social Development Initiatives

Barrick was committed to making a positive difference in the communities where it operated. The company focused on responsible behaviour as its duty, as well as creating opportunities to generate greater value for its shareholders, while at the same time fostering sustainable development in the communities and countries where it operated. As a global TNC, Barrick strove to earn the trust of its employees, of the communities where its subsidiary operations were based, of the host nations' governments and of any other persons or parties with whom the company was engaged in the sustainable development of mineral resources.[21]

In 2008, the corporation established a locally based mining institution in Moshi, Kilimanjaro Region. The aim of the institute was to provide training skills and

---

[18]www.barrick.com/Theme/Barrick/files/docs_csr/BeyondBorder2008July.pdf#page=4, accessed September 27, 2010.

[19]www.barrick.com/CorporateResponsibility/Employees/AttractingRetaining/default.aspx, accessed September 27, 2010.

[20]www.barrick.com/CorporateResponsibility/OurCommitment/default.aspx, accessed September 27, 2010.

[21]www.barrick.com/CorporateResponsibility/default.aspx, accessed March 25, 2009.

opportunities for Barrick's mining sites and other mining TNCs in the country.[22] Local individuals involved in the training program included fresh university graduates in engineering and geology and dedicated individuals from local communities where Barrick operated. Such an initiative supported Barrick's sense of corporate responsibility towards these two groups of people by providing tangible benefits to their communities in the form of employment opportunities and cooperative relationships.

Yet among community leaders and NFOs, there was clear discontent regarding the various foreign companies:

"The government has not addressed the role of foreign companies in our communities. Some communities have been compensated by the government to clear land for the mining company, but some did not receive any money. Most communities would tell you what was given to them by the government, which is very little. They cannot build a house and send children to school and so on. They feel their livelihood is gone forever."

"The mining corporation does not compensate people nor does it explain why it is operating in our communities. Of course, these companies have official binding contracts and the right to operate in our communities from the government. Local communities are in despair … the government is nowhere to be seen! The people are angry with the government and the mining company."

"People are not happy with the government. They are aware of the extent of corruption among the government officials in the region and districts, but they cannot confront the government the way they are now confronting the mining company. They think that the company might be more sympathetic to them than the government would be with respect to offering them jobs and other opportunities."

"The company has initiated several development projects in our communities [North Mara] in education, health and infrastructure. But we do not have jobs to access these better equipped services (education and health) nor essential means to support us to build community enterprises where we could apply our local skills in many activities. Though the company is doing very good projects here, we are still unhappy with the company. Our problems are long-term; they need serious engagement with us."

"The company discharges water to the land, which is causing lots of environmental problems on our farms such as land erosion and polluting of the rivers. We have more mosquitoes, snakes and snails at the moment than any time in our lives because of stagnant water caused by the company's water discharge. The exploration and explosive activities conducted at night on mining sites have caused shockwaves, panic and sleepless nights among neighborhood villages, making big cracks on community farms and land."

Two community leaders (representing local stakeholders' interests) commented:

"The other night we were all suddenly shaken by the mining blast tremor. Initially, we thought it was the so-called earthquake ("Tetemeko la Ardhi" in Swahili). What is on all the people's minds here in Bulyanhulu is, 'When will all this end?'"

[22]www.ippmedia.com/ipp/guardian/2008/04/11/112164.html, accessed February 13, 2009.

"We need a mutual partnership with foreign companies investing in our communities. There are so many potential benefits we can get from the company with respect to jobs and skill development; also, the company can learn a lot from us when it comes to negotiation strategies with our communities. If the company responds positively to our concerns, we will strive to protect its business interests here and it will operate in harmony in our communities. But the government needs to sit with local communities and tell them why the government has allowed the company to come to practice mining in their land and tell us what potential benefit it will bring in our communities. For the time being, the company is left to itself to address these issues with the local communities."

Amid this climate of discontent among the native Tanzanians, Barrick's mining operations were subject to some hostilities from local stakeholders. In response, the company put into place several CSR initiatives that were aimed at developing sustainable benefits within the communities and around its business operations in the core mining sites of Tulawaka, Bulyanhulu and Buzigwa. Two NFO officials in Mwanza cut to the nature of the problem:

"The company initially attempted to collaborate with local communities and the local government to address the social and ecological issues during its initial stage of entry into the country. But it was not easy to find serious stakeholders right away. Because of the nature of the local institutions, it was also not easy to have things done quickly due to the degree of bureaucracy and the culture of corruption."

"The recent protests in North Mara from local communities can be resolved only if the government, company and other social awareness groups sit together to address this situation. Shooting protestors, closing the mining site and sending employees home without pay won't solve the problem in the long run. And the company's legal insistence of its right to operate in the communities isn't enough to convince these angry communities."

"The company is not wrong at all … it has followed all legal procedures and has the right to be here [in the Lake Victoria Zone], but for local communities, legal papers are NOTHING. The company finds people very unpredictable. The answer is so simple: it is all about deep understanding, integration, and building a trusting relationship."

"Mining companies are granted too many tax contracts and subsidies in order to create jobs. During this process, it is very possible for companies to avoid paying taxes that would actually benefit poor countries. There are often 'secret contracts' with corrupt government officials. The lack of institutional capacity is also a major problem; the people have not been made to see how these companies can benefit our poor societies. That's why there is still so much poverty, and that's why communities around the mining sites are angry and desperate."

Several local communities felt they were isolated when it came to the social issues that concerned them, e.g., land issues, compensation, employment, and how the presence of the company in their communities would benefit them generally. According to community leaders, few projects were initiated by the company within the various neighbourhood communities, and the ones that were enacted showed a lack of any significant sense of local ownership and influence; they did not possess the diverse forms of institutional infrastructure that fostered accountability values in communities and in the management of the company itself. As a consequence, local communities lost interest in pursuing most of the developmental projects that Barrick had initiated.

Following community tensions with Barrick between 2007 and 2009, a different strategy was developed. Implementing a locally based interaction model that promoted mutual partnership with communities seemed like the best strategic legitimacy approach. In early 2009, Barrick encountered discontent from the local communities, as well as from the local media, activists groups and lobby groups, who felt that the company had not done enough to promote sustainable and inclusive development in the communities where it operated. Barrick's new mining site at North Mara was featured several times in the media.[23] Two local NFOs commented on the dispute:

> "The government needs to educate its people as to what benefits TNCs would bring to its citizens; the mining company is extracting our natural resources, causing environmental degradation and pollution, and displacing people, all with a lack of accountability, and is not doing enough for the host communities to create prosperity, jobs, local innovation and entrepreneurship initiatives."

> "The source of discontent is from local communities and small-scale miners who feel neglected by the government. We strongly feel that their livelihoods have been destroyed with little or no compensation. They also feel that the government and local authorities have been giving foreign investors much attention at the expense of local people. Corruption and lack of accountability on the government side is the source of all these problems. The company is caught in the middle!"

Creating a Corporate Responsive Agenda

Barrick developed a responsive initiative to deal with the company's challenges in its international business activities abroad, including Tanzania. It established a community department in all four mining areas to oversee development initiatives. It also adopted standardized global CSR strategies as part of its larger international and localization business strategies, stating that "as a global corporation, we endorse the definition of Corporate Social Responsibility as proposed by the World Bank—Corporate Social Responsibility is the commitment of business to contribute to sustainable economic development—working with employees, their families, the local community and society at large to improve the quality of life, in ways that are both good for business and good for development."[24]

1. Education in partnership with local communities Through its newly established community department, Barrick had made a concerted attempt to identify self-employment opportunities to the communities around the Bulyanhulu gold mine. In

---

[23]Several protests by local communities against Barrick's mining activities in Tanzania had been reported. See www.protestbarrick.net/article.php?list=4type&type=12, accessed February 17, 2009.

[24]www.barrick.com/CorporateResponsibility/Ethics/PoliciesStandards/default.aspx, accessed February 17, 2009.

partnership with local governments, NFOs and communities, the company had used educated locals to promote a broad array of social entrepreneurship skills in a variety of areas such as finance, accounting and marketing (see Exhibit 2).

The communities surrounding the mine needed a great deal of support in terms of education in order to be able to exploit the area's potential. By 2008, Barrick had committed to working closely with eight villages, before expanding to another eight villages along the Bulyanhulu-Kahama road in Bulyanhulu. Seven of the eight villages were in the Bugarama ward and one was in the Mwingilo ward, but all were located in the Bulyanhulu mining area.

2. Community-based entrepreneurship In collaboration with local community authorities, Barrick went on to assist several community groups that already possessed local skills and entrepreneurship initiatives and which had local resources to generate business activities. Other community development projects had also been started and were engineered under the same procedure of governance.

3. Health Barrick committed itself to upgrading the Sungusungu Health Centre into what became called the Nyamongo Hospital in the Bulyanhulu area under the so-called phase I. Organized by the Evangelical Lutheran Church in the area, several NFOs had entered into an agreement with the local district office and the village councils to provide health care that was affordable to the many local residents to treat diseases such as malaria, waterborne diseases, typhoid, yellow fever and other epidemiology problems. The community trust committed $30,000 towards beds and fittings and for a general upgrade to the hospital. Barrick's overall objective was to make health services available to many disadvantaged communities, and to attempt to curb the number of deaths that occurred among pregnant women when they travelled from the poor communities to the district hospital.

4. Environment The Lake Victoria Zone was one of the most densely populated areas in sub-Saharan Africa, but it was also one of the most polluted and environmentally affected places in the world. Barrick, in cooperation with local government authorities, had been working to provide opportunities to the residents of the mining areas to orient themselves with mining operations. The company was creating environmental awareness in order to create local "ambassadors," who could then go out and speak positively about the mining sites to other communities. Adequately addressing the issues of water toxins on rivers and the lake and land degradation had been the major challenge for Barrick.

Protests from so-called "secondary" stakeholders that included local communities, artisanal miners, peasant farmers and their families and local not-for-profit organizations (NFOs) had occurred to address specific social, environmental and land heritage and resettlement issues. All these stakeholders had widely varying claims, interests and rights. In addition, subgroups and individuals with multiple and changing roles and interests existed. They included manual mining workers who felt they had been unfairly dismissed from their jobs with little or no compensation, and felt unjustly treated by either Barrick or the Tanzanian labour court system. Local communities also had expressed anger at the level of noise caused by heavy machines during mining explorations at night and the extent of the company's impact on land in their neighbourhoods. There were also individuals, mainly unemployed youths, who were engaged in intrusion, vandalism and theft at the mining sites.

Barrick had relied on the Tanzanian anti-riot police force, known as "Field Force Unit" (FFU), to quell large-scale mob criminal behaviour and demonstrations at the mining sites. Also, Barrick had relied on the Tanzanian legal system and government to protect its business activities in the region. However, the behaviour of the FFU, the weak government institutional system and the loyalty of administrative workers to Barrick had increased anger, frustration and resentment among communities, small-scale artisanal miners and NFOs. The FFU had been regarded by local communities as brutal and uncompromising during confrontations. Responses by the FFU had even led to death,[25] long-term imprisonment of community campaigners' leaders, intimidation and harassment.[26] The government had been viewed as lacking vision and leadership to reap the benefits of the mining activities in the region and had been criticized for failing to protect the interests of its citizens.

CONCLUSION

By 2010, a variety of corporate social responsibility (CSR) initiatives were established based on ABG's commitment to building a sustainable relationship with local communities. The overall aim was to ensure that the company would build mutual respect, active partnerships and a long-term commitment with its secondary stakeholders, who tended to have disparate goals, demands and opinions. Mutual respect, it was argued, was important if such relationships were to be lasting, beneficial and dynamic. In addition, the company had used its social development department in each of the mining sites to develop practical guidelines in order to facilitate the implementation of its organizational values and mission, including building long-term relationships of mutual benefit between the operations and their host communities, and to avoid costly disputes and hostilities with local stakeholders.[27] Although significant progress and successful collaborations had evolved across local communities at its mining sites, African Barrick Gold still faced serious, unique problems and increased pressure to manage conflicts and reconcile stakeholders' demands in places such as North Mara.

---

[25]A recent incident at a Barrick mining site in the Mara region had led the Tanzanian FFU to kill an intruder. See www.protestbarrick.net/article.php?list=type&type=12, accessed April 17, 2009.

[26]For the behaviour of Tanzania's FFU in quelling demonstrations, see www.protestbarrick.net/article.php?id=369, accessed April 17, 2009.

[27]Further CSR programs are available at www.barrick.com/CorporateResponsibility/default.aspx, accessed February 24, 2009.

EXHIBIT 1   Three Types of Engagement Behaviours

Dimension	Transactional	Transitional	Transformational
Corporate Stance	"Giving Back" Community Investment	"Building Bridges" Community Involvement	"Changing Society" Community Integration
Communication	One-Way	Two-Way	Two-Way
# of Community Partners	Many	Many	Few
Nature of Trust	Limited	Evolutionary	Relational
Frequency of Interaction	Occasional	Repeated	Frequent
Learning	Transferred from Firm	Transferred to Firm	Jointly Generated
Control over Process	Firm	Firm	Shared
Benefit & Outcomes	Distinct	Distinct	Joint

Source: F. Bowen, A. Newenham-Kahindi and H. Irene, "Engaging the community: A synthesis of academic and practitioner knowledge on best practices in community engagement," Canadian Research Network for Business Sustainability, Knowledge Project Series, Ivey School of Business, 1:1, 2008, pp. 1–34.

EXHIBIT 2   Barrick Spending on Corporate Social Responsibility in Tanzania

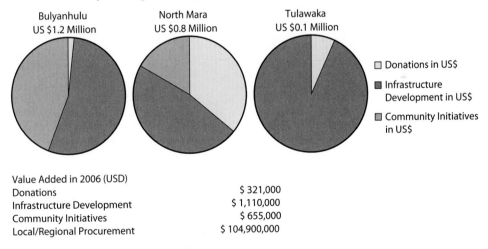

Value Added in 2006 (USD)	
Donations	$ 321,000
Infrastructure Development	$ 1,110,000
Community Initiatives	$ 655,000
Local/Regional Procurement	$ 104,900,000

2006 Environmental, Health & Safety Performance

Note: Total amount of money in U.S. dollars spent on health & safety training and emergency response training in 2006

Source: www.barrick.com/Theme/Barrick/files/docs_ehss/2007%20Africa%20Regional%20Rpt.pdf, accessed April 30, 2009.

EXHIBIT 3   Total Amount of Money Spent on Community Development
Projects, 2006

COMMUNITY	2006	2005	2004	2003
Donations in US$				
Bulyanhulu	20,193	14,000	410,000	485,000
North Mara	294,220	50,0000	0	0
Tulawaka	6,778	7,662	5,894	N/A
Infrastructure development in US$				
Bulyanhulu	631,222	3,570,000	4,374,000	572,000
North Mara	389,384	360,000	350,000	100,000
Tulawaka	89,020	43,697	6,250	N/A
Community initiatives in US$				
Bulyanhulu	519,793	609,000	0	0
North Mara	135,015	0	Not measured	
Tulawaka	304	0	0	N/A
Regional purchases of goods & services in US$				
Bulyanhulu	65,600,000		Not measured	
North Mara	37,700,000		Not measured	
Tulawaka	1,600,000		Not measured	

Source: www.barrick.com/Theme/Barrick/files/docs_ehss/2007%20Africa%20Regional%20Rpt.pdf,
accessed April 30, 2009.

FIJI Water and Corporate Social Responsibility—Green Makeover or "Greenwashing"?[1]

"Bottled water is a disaster, for several reasons. First there's the issue of the sustainability of underground aquifers, from where much of the bottled water is drawn. And then there's the carbon footprint. Water is heavy, and transporting it around the world uses a lot of energy."

Jeff Angel, Total Environment Centre, Sydney, Australia[2]

"We survived before we had water in bottles. It is unnecessary. When you see water imported from Fiji in plastic bottles, you know it's bad for the environment all round."

Lee Rhiannon, Australia's Greens MP[3]

"I think the world is slowly going insane. No thanks but I prefer water in bottles, that way you know it's clean and you know, healthy. Not a sacrifice people should make when plastic bags are still rampant. Those Greens are extremists and I don't see this 'tap water alternative' ever being viable."

Anthony L., N.S.W.[4]

"Consumers who choose FIJI Water will actually be helping the environment by taking carbon out of the atmosphere with every purchase."

Thomas Mooney, senior vice-president, sustainable growth, FIJI Water, Los Angeles, California[5]

Richard Ivey School of Business
The University of Western Ontario

[1]This case has been written on the basis of published sources only. Consequently, the interpretation and perspectives presented in this case are not necessarily those of FIJI Water LLC. or any of its employees.
[2]"Disaster in a bottle," *Sydney Morning Herald,* April 24, 2007.
[3]Kelly Fedor, "Greens call for ban on bottled water," *Livenews.com,* March 22, 2008.
[4]A reader's comment posted on Livenews.com on March 22, 2008.
[5]"FIJI Water becomes first bottled water company to release carbon footprint of its products," Press Release from FIJI Water, April 9, 2008, www.bevnet.com

2008 was a trying year for FIJI Water LLC., a U.S.-based company that marketed its famous brand in more than a dozen countries out of its bottling plant located in the Fiji Islands. The company was facing some complex challenges to achieve its goal of a carbon negative outcome at its production plant and in the transportation of its products, and to convince its consumers and other stakeholders that it was leading the industry in carbon footprint disclosure and offset. The environmental protest against bottled water in general, and FIJI brand in particular, in the United States, the United Kingdom and other developed countries was gathering steam as the message on the carbon impact of bottled water was more and more widely publicized to consumers. FIJI Water was singled out as a primary example of "water insanity" due to the fact that the product was shipped from a remote island in the South Pacific to its main markets thousands of miles away. In response to this protest, the company launched a new promotion campaign under a slogan, "every drop is green," only to be immediately accused by environmentalist groups of engaging in greenwashing activities. The claim was also challenged by government watchdogs in some countries where FIJI Water was sold.

At the same time, the company's relationships with the Fiji government were at the lowest point. The government accused FIJI Water of transfer price manipulations and seized hundreds of containers carrying FIJI brand water. After assessing the company's contribution to the Fiji economy, the government tried to impose a hefty tax on exported water, and the company took the drastic action of laying off its employees in Fiji to pressure the government to repeal the initial 20-cents-a-litre tax that would have greatly reduced FIJI Water's profitability by increasing its tax bill by about FJ\$50 million per year. The company intensified its PR activities, focusing on its contributions to the local communities, to show how good a corporate citizen it was in Fiji.

THE PRODUCT CONCEPT AND COMPANY BACKGROUND

The product concept was developed in the early nineties by David Gilmour, the Canadian-born owner and founder of Fiji's renowned Wakaya Island Resort. Simply put, the concept was to bottle Fiji natural artesian water and market it both locally and internationally as a unique and exotic product. An important aspect of the product concept was to bottle the water straight from the source—the source being an old artesian aquifer containing tropical rainwater, filtered for 450 years through layers of volcanic rock. The aquifer was found in the Yaqara Range of the Nakauvadra Mountains. Being separated by 1,500 kilometres of ocean, far away from major polluting sources, and being formed before any industrial activity could contaminate it, the water could only be of the purest quality and of distinct taste. Moreover, this silica-rich water was attributed anti-aging and immunity-boosting properties. The product was expected to appeal to health-conscious and image-oriented consumers.[6]

To extract and bottle Fiji's artesian water, in 1993 Gilmour founded a company under the name Nature's Best. In 1995, the company's name was changed to Natural Waters of Viti Ltd. The first bottling plant was built in 1996 at the cost of FJ\$48 million

---

[6]James McMaster and Jan Nowak, "Natural Waters of Viti Limited—Pioneering a new industry in the Fiji Islands," *Journal of the Australian and New Zealand Academy of Management*, 9:2, 2003 (Special Edition on Management Cases).

at Yaqara in Ra, on land sub-leased from the Yaqara Pastoral Company. The plant was built where the source of artesian water had been found.[7] The site was in a remote and underdeveloped rural area of the island of Viti Levu that was poorly served with public infrastructure. The unpolluted, pristine location of the water source and factory guaranteed that the artesian water was of the highest purity. However, the site's remoteness from the capital city of Suva, where Fiji's main port is located, entailed higher road transport costs compared to other alternative mineral water sources. In 1996, FIJI Water LLC. corporate headquarters was established in Basalt, Colorado, to handle the product distribution in the United States, which was intended to be the main market for FIJI Water.

The production process began with the extraction of the water from a bore-hole. The water was then channelled through a pipe into the factory, treated and bottled in 4 bottle sizes: 0.33, 0.5, 1.0 and 1.5 litres. Using imported bottle caps, PET resin and labels, the bottles were manufactured by the company on its premises and were filled with water during the same production cycle. Bottles were packed into cartons for shipment to domestic and international markets. The cartons were made in Fiji by Golden Manufacturers.[8]

Rising demand for FIJI Water led to the construction of a new 110,000-square-foot, state-of-the-art bottling plant, completed in 2000. Demand continued to build in the 2000s, leading to the airlifting of a new bottling line in 2004 to help increase capacity to more than 50 million cases a year. The design and construction of the factory was regarded as among the best in the world, with high-quality and high-speed production capability.

In 2004, the company was sold by its main shareholder, David Gilmour, to Roll International Corporation for an undisclosed price. Roll International was controlled by one of Hollywood's richest couples, Stewart and Lynda Resnik.[9] Following this acquisition, FIJI Water's corporate headquarters was moved to Los Angeles. While the Fiji Islands-based operation focused on mineral water extraction, bottling and transportation within Fiji, the corporate headquarters handled marketing and logistics functions worldwide. The new owner expanded the Fiji plant's production capacity by adding a new (third) bottling line in 2006. In 2007, the state-of-the-art factory could churn out more than a million bottles of FIJI Water a day.[10]

As of 2008, FIJI Water marketed its bottled mineral water in about a dozen countries in North America (including Mexico and the Caribbean), Asia-Pacific, Europe and the Middle East. It was marketed as FIJI Natural Mineral Water in Europe and as FIJI Natural Spring Water in Australia. The two main markets for the product were the United States and Australia.

In the latter part of 2008, the bottling plant at Yaqara had about 400 employees. Of the total number of employees, only about 10 per cent were employed with the administration, finance and management sections; the rest were factory-floor workers.

---

[7]Reserve Bank of Fiji, "Natural Waters of Viti Limited," Briefing Paper, August 2001, p.1; and Ed Dinger, "Fiji Water LLC.," International Directory of Company Histories, 74, 2003.

[8]Ibid.

[9]Roll International also owned such companies as POM Wonderful, which produced and marketed juices and fresh pomegranates; Telesfora, the largest online flower shop in the world; Paramount Farms, the largest grower and producer of pistachios and almonds in the world; and Paramount Citrus, a leader in the California orange and lemon markets (www.roll.com).

[10]Charles Fishman, "Message in a bottle," Fast Company, 117, July/August 2007, p. 110.

The company employed only a handful of expatriates and placed an emphasis on the hiring, training and advancement of the inhabitants of nearby villages, most of whom had little or no employment opportunities prior to Natural Waters of Viti Ltd. locating its factory at Yaqara. The company claimed to be one of the highest-paying employers in Fiji.[11]

THE GLOBAL MARKET FOR BOTTLED WATER— CONSUMPTION TRENDS

Sales of FIJI Water in the domestic market were relatively very small. More than 90 per cent of all production was exported. Therefore, for FIJI Water, global trends in bottled water consumption and demand were of paramount importance.

Since the beginning of the last decade, the beverage product category had been shaken by rapidly changing consumer preferences that had led to a radical shift away from traditional beverages and toward "New Age" products, like bottled water. In fact, bottled water had been the fastest growing segment of the entire beverage business. As Exhibit 1 shows, between 2002 and 2007, the world's bottled water consumption was increasing by 7.6 per cent annually and by 2007 reached close to 50 billion gallons (approximately 185 billion litres). As a result, by 2007, bottled water had become the second-largest beverage category, after soft drinks.

As Exhibit 1 also indicates, the United States was the world's leading consumer of bottled water in 2007. Americans drank 8.8 billion gallons of bottled water, as compared to 5.8 billion consumed by Mexicans and 4.8 billion consumed by Chinese. Altogether, the top 10 consuming nations accounted for 73 per cent of the world's bottled water consumption in 2007. However, it should be pointed out that China's consumption grew the fastest among the top three consumers in the world between 2002 and 2007, at the compound annual rate of 17.5 per cent, which was twice the world's average. Therefore, China was expected to become the largest consumer of bottled water in the world in the next decade. Another emerging big consumer of bottled water was India. Although not among the leading bottled water consuming nations in 2007, India had experienced one of the fastest growth rates in the world during the period shown in Exhibit 1, even faster than China.[12]

When per capita consumption was taken into account, the nations' ranking looked different (see Exhibit 2). In 2007, the United Arab Emirates, Mexico and Italy showed the highest consumption per person in the world, and the United States was ranked ninth, with only a slightly higher consumption per capita than Hungary and Switzerland. It is noteworthy that Australia and the United Kingdom, two markets of interest to FIJI Water, were not among the biggest consumers of bottled water in the world, neither in terms of total consumption nor per capita.

In 2007, Europe and North America were the biggest regional markets for bottled water, accounting for 30.9 and 30.7 per cent of the world's sales volume, respectively. Asia accounted for 24.3 per cent and the rest of the world accounted for 14.1 per cent.[13]

---

[11]Company website: www.fijiwater.com

[12]"The global bottled water market. Report 2007," Beverage Marketing Corporation, January 2008.

[13]Ibid.

FIJI WATER'S INTERNATIONAL MARKET EXPANSION

While responding to those world market trends, FIJI Water had made its strategy revolve around capturing international market opportunities and strongly positioning the brand in large and growing markets for bottled water, but markets that were not overly price competitive, as FIJI Water, right from the beginning, was designed to be a premium brand. The first, and critical, international market to conquer was the United States.

Conquering the U.S. Market

To begin its international market expansion, FIJI Water was first launched in California in 1997, using Los Angeles and Palm Beach as a beachhead for a subsequent and gradual roll-out of the product across the United States. In 1998, the company entered the sophisticated New York market, firmly positioning itself on the East Coast. At the same time, FIJI Water was also introduced to the Canadian market, starting with the country's West Coast. The North American market provided the company with tremendous growth opportunities. The U.S. market in particular was so embracing that after about five years of the product's presence there, FIJI Water had achieved the second selling position in the U.S. market among imported still water brands, and in 2008, it had climbed to the number one position among imported bottled waters in the United States.[14] Such a strong market position had been achieved in the market where competition was fierce and which was characterized by industry consolidation and the increasing dominance of major soft drink companies in bottled water marketing, such as Coca Cola and PepsiCo, which had entered the market with their own proprietary brands, Dasani and Aquafina, respectively. At the same time, FIJI Water had benefited from the overall beverage market trend that had shown a major shift in beverage consumption preferences in the United States.

As Exhibit 3 shows, the per capita consumption of bottled water in the United States increased from 13.5 gallons in 1997, when the FIJI Water brand was introduced to the U.S. market, to 29.3 gallons in 2007, thus more than doubling. This was part of the exponential growth trend in bottled water consumption over a longer period, although growth clearly accelerated after 1990.[15]

The above shifts in the consumption of beverages could be linked to changing lifestyles and growing concerns of the effects of sweetened carbonated drinks on people's health. The baby boom generation, which constituted about a third of the total population in North America, had become obsessively health-conscious and fitness-oriented. Bottled water had become popular among the younger generation as well. Over the last decade, bottled water had gained a reputation of not only being healthy, but also a fashionable, elegant and "trendy" drink.

In 2007, total U.S. bottled water sales surpassed 8.8 billion gallons, a 6.9 per cent advance over 2006's volume level. That translated into more than 29 gallons per person, which meant U.S. residents drank more bottled water annually than any other beverage,

---

[14]"FIJI Water becomes first bottled water company to release carbon footprint of its products," Press Release from FIJI Water, April 9, 2008, www.bevnet.com

[15]"The global bottled water market. Report 2007," Beverage Marketing Corporation, January 2008.

other than carbonated soft drinks (CSDs). While CSDs still had volume and average intake levels more than twice as high as those of bottled water, the soft drink market had been struggling because of competition from bottled water. Per capita consumption of bottled water had been growing by at least one gallon annually, thereby more than doubling between 1997 and 2007. In 2007, U.S. consumers spent $15 billion on bottled water, more than on iPods or movie tickets.[16]

As Exhibit 4 shows, sales of non-sparkling bottled water by far exceeded sales of its sparkling counterpart. Also, between 2000 and 2007, non-sparkling water's sales grew faster than those of sparkling water. At the same time, it is noteworthy that imported bottled water constituted only a little more than two per cent of the total sales of this product category, and imports tended to fluctuate widely from one year to another. The biggest sellers in the U.S. market were local brands, such as Arrowhead, Poland Spring, Zephyrhills, Ozarka, Deer Park and Ice Mountain. The market was dominated by four large companies: Nestlé, Coca Cola, PepsiCo and Danone. Nestlé had the largest market share of all—in 2007, the company's brands of bottled water accounted for 26 per cent of total sales of the product category.[17]

During the product's introduction into the U.S. market, FIJI Water LLC. was responsible for the marketing and logistics of FIJI brand. The company had two senior VPs, in charge of the East Coast and the West Coast, respectively, reporting to the company's CEO, Mr. Doug Carlson.[18]

The successful launch of FIJI Water in the United States was attributed to a skilful marketing strategy and the high quality of the people who drove the initial marketing campaign.[19] FIJI Water LLC.'s marketing personnel were able to differentiate the FIJI brand in a crowded market where about 400 brands of bottled water competed with each other. This was mainly achieved through unique product positioning, innovative packaging, premium-product pricing, effective distribution and image-creating publicity. The latter had elevated this otherwise mundane commodity to celebrity status.

Due to its light mineralization, FIJI Water was characterized by a smooth taste and no aftertaste. The light mineralization also gave the water a clean, pure taste. Many U.S. consumers instantly liked the taste of the water and, having tried it, repurchased the product in preference to the more mineralized waters. FIJI Water had been top-rated in taste tests sponsored by such influential magazines and guides as Chicago Magazine, Cook's Illustrated Buying Guides and Men's Health. Taste therefore was one of FIJI Water's main advantages over other bottled water brands. The company continued to educate the consumer about the difference between purified, spring and artesian bottled water.[20] In addition to superb taste, the water had a high level of silica, the ingredient that was believed to promote rejuvenation and anti-aging. Another distinct aspect of the product was its purity, stemming from the fact that the source of the water was a virgin, unpolluted ecosystem, located 1,500 kilometres away from any metropolitan and industrial area, and the fact that the water was 450 years old, thus formed before industrial pollution could affect its purity. All this added to the mystique that the product seemed to be surrounded by in the minds of consumers. Due

[16]Fishman, "Message in a bottle," July/August 2007, p. 110.
[17]Ibid., p. 115.
[18]McMaster and Nowak, "Natural Waters of Viti Limited—Pioneering a new industry in the Fiji Islands," 2003, p. 42.
[19]Paul Yavala, "Fiji Water travels," *The Fiji Times*, November 2000, p. 4.
[20]www.fijiwater.com

to FIJI Water's superb taste, purity and mystique, a premium-product positioning had been followed right from the beginning.

Although of paramount importance, the product content was only part of the successful marketing equation. Another important element was packaging. For many years, all bottles containing natural water were the same—round, with paper labels. Packaging, one of the most fundamental ways to differentiate a product, was not used as such a tool in bottled water markets. Over the last decade, both companies and consumers had discovered the power of packaging in bottled water brand positioning and imagery. FIJI Water had utilized the power of packaging to its benefit. Natural Waters of Viti Ltd. was the first company in the industry to use a square bottle and this had become the product's signature trait. Furthermore, since FIJI was the only brand that came from a tropical paradise—not a cold, mountainous region—the packaging reflected that in an artful and compelling way: Consumers could see that immediately when they looked at the unique square bottle bearing bright, three-dimensional graphics.[21]

FIJI Water's packaging was initially designed by a New York-based advertising agency and had been refined several times since its original design. When the brand was introduced to the U.S. market, its square-shaped bottle was unique and had great appeal to consumers. The gold border on the label gave an image of quality. The blue cap was colour-coordinated with the blue waterfall and the blue-green colours in the see-through labels. Consumers had reported favourably on the attractive label with the Pacific image and see-through waterfall. Later on, the company had redesigned the labelling and added new features to the bottle's front and back labels. The front label, in addition to the brand name, featured a pink hibiscus flower, a national flower of the Fiji Islands. In a new version of the bottle design, the inside of the back label, instead of a waterfall, displayed a large palm frond, which was amplified when the bottle was filled with water, and the outside of that label explained the water's distinct characteristics, such as its remote and pristine source and its unique mineral composition. In fact, in 2008, FIJI Water had four different outside back labels, each of which illustrated a unique image and communicated a different part of the FIJI Water story; they included "bottled in Fiji," "what ecosystem is your water from," "what is artesian water" and "untouched by man."

Similarly to packaging, a premium-price policy reinforced the product's high-quality image. Anyway, high freight costs between Fiji and the United States would have made a low- or even medium-price policy impossible. FIJI Water's price was higher than that of most brands offered to U.S. consumers. For example, in the Californian market, FIJI Water was positioned slightly below Perrier, but above Evian.

Another important factor that had contributed to FIJI Water's success in the U.S. market was its distribution. Having good distributors was important, in that it enabled the brand to be well-placed in, and readily available to, the market. While in Fiji the company used exclusively Coca Cola Amatil to distribute its product, in the U.S. market, the product was sold by numerous distributors, including wholesalers, retail chains and individual retailers. In addition to stores, the product was sold on the premises of many high-end restaurants and hotels. The product was also available online in the continental United States. To support the brand's continued growth, FIJI Water LLC. had expanded distribution beyond exclusive retailers to include mass merchandisers, convenience stores, drug stores and even gas stations.[22] This intensification of

---

[21]Nancy Christy, "Age of enlightenment," *Beverage Aisle*, August 2001.

[22]Heather Landi, "Paradise in a bottle," *Beverage World*, November 2007, p. 24.

distribution might sound like a contradiction of the product's exclusive positioning, but the company representatives claimed that it was all part of "the affordable luxury" strategy.

Destined for the U.S. market, FIJI Water was shipped from the ports of Suva or Lautoka on Viti Levu to three major distribution centres in the United States—Los Angeles, New Jersey and Miami. It was then distributed throughout most of the United States. Initially, the physical distribution to and within the United States was contracted out to specialized logistics firms, which delivered the product to a variety of distributors, who then carried it through their distribution channels. Occasionally, these logistics firms delivered the product directly to consumers. In 2000, FIJI Water entered into an exclusive distributorship agreement with Cadbury Schweppes. This partnership was crucial to FIJI Water's aggressive expansion and success in the U.S. market, where the FIJI brand was available at tens of thousands of outlets. Canadian shipments were sent to Vancouver, the only location where the product was initially available. In 1999, FIJI Water appointed Brio Industries Inc. as Canada-wide Master Distributor of the FIJI brand.[23] In 2008, the U.S.-market distributorship agreement with Cadbury Schweppes was extended to cover Canada also. Since February of that year, FIJI Water had been exclusively distributed by Cadbury across Canada among grocery, convenience, drug and most other retail stores.[24]

Building an image of the high quality, uniqueness and class of the product was another aspect of this successful marketing campaign. At the beginning, FIJI Water did very little "formal" or paid advertising, which included only some printed advertisements placed in in-flight magazines, such as those of Air Pacific. The brand achieved an explosive growth early on, mostly through word-of-mouth advertising, free product placement and targeted sampling. According to Thomas Mooney, senior vice-president of sustainable growth, the company continued its focus on introducing new customers to the brand and converting them to "brand evangelists." While doing so, FIJI Water targeted locations and venues that resonated with the brand's premium image. Said Mooney, "It's different to get a bottle of water after walking off the subway than it is to get a bottle at an after-party following the Oscars."[25] In fact, the product had received a lot of publicity through movies, as Hollywood celebrities, such as Tom Cruise, Pierce Brosnan, Whoopi Goldberg and Vin Diesel, and popular singers, such as Michael Bolton, Tina Turner and Jessica Simpson, had eagerly endorsed the product. FIJI Water had also become a favourite at the dining tables of some of New York's better restaurants and hotels, including Jean Georges, Four Seasons Restaurant, Pierre Hotel, Trump International Hotels & Towers and the Carlyle and the Paramount. And there were celebrity chefs using FIJI Water as a cooking ingredient in their kitchens, such as *Sam the Cooking Guy*, an Emmy-Award winning TV show.

In 2007, the company launched a new marketing campaign, aiming at communicating the core benefits of FIJI Water. Revolving around the theme "untouched," the campaign followed an integrated marketing communication approach, combining advertising, PR, direct marketing, product placements and event marketing. The advertising part of the campaign used a striking blue-colour creative copy that brought

---

[23]"Brio Industries Inc. appointed Canada-wide Master Distributor of Fiji Water," *Business Wire*, Vancouver, British Columbia, April 15, 1999, http://findarticles.com/p/articles/mi_m0EIN/is_1999_April_15/ai_54381790

[24]"Canadians have a taste for FIJI Water," FIJI Water Press Release, Toronto, Ontario, March 10, 2008, www.nkpr.net/pressreleases/FW_Cadbury_Schweppes_Release.pdf

[25]Heather Landi, "Paradise in a bottle," *Beverage World*, November 2007, p. 24.

out the pristine nature, magical allure and mystery that the Fiji Islands embodied. The advertising campaign was developed by FIJI Water's in-house creative agency and used both out-of-home (OOH) and print media.[26]

In sum, the secret of FIJI Water's success in the United States seemed to lie in its marketers' ability to elevate the world's simplest drink to celebrity status. FIJI Water was much more than just pure, good-tasting liquid. It was a promise of good health, refinement, status and exclusivity. It evoked images of unspoiled natural beauty and purity. It was a tropical paradise captured in a bottle!

Expanding into the Australian Market

With the tremendous success achieved by FIJI Water in the United States, the firm entered the Australian market in 2003 from a position of strength. As shown earlier, Australia was not among the leading bottled water consuming countries. However, the country's relatively large market and, more importantly, its proximity to Fiji made it an attractive market to enter. Moreover, before the product was launched in Australia, many Australians visiting Fiji had a chance to develop a taste for FIJI Water. It was common to see Australian vacationers returning from Fiji carrying cartons of FIJI Water with them back home. This created awareness of, and even pent-up demand for, the product before it was officially launched.

The product was initially introduced to select hotels and restaurants, before becoming available in gourmet, deli and independent convenience stores. In 2005, FIJI Water gained national distribution in more than 400 Coles supermarkets, and in 2007, FIJI Water's Australian subsidiary signed a national distribution agreement with Cadbury Schweppes Australia.[27] At that time, Cadbury Schweppes had a national market share of about eight per cent, with its Cool Ridge, Spring Valley Twist and FIJI Water brands.

The Australian bottled water market had sustained a high growth rate in the past decade and was predicted to continue to grow strongly in the next one. FIJI Water was emerging as a major brand in the premium market segment and was facing stiff competition. The Australian bottled water market was very competitive, and it was also less consolidated than the U.S. market. In Australia, about one thousand brands of bottled water competed for market share. Coca-Cola Amatil's Mount Franklin was Australia's leading water brand and was sourced from select Australian springs.

According to the Australasian Bottled Water Institute (ABWI) website, consumer research suggested that although bottled water was consumed in Australia by people of varying age groups and occupations, a large majority of them tended to be young singles and couples, in particular females, aged between 14 and 35 years. In terms of psychographics, bottled water consumers could be described as being more health-conscious, progressive and socially aware.[28]

Another Fiji company, whose brand name was Island Chill, with a very similar bottle design to FIJI Water, successfully entered the Australian market a few years after FIJI Water's launch there. Island Chill also contained silica and had been well-received in the Melbourne market. Although Melbourne was initially Island Chill's primary sales focus area, the brand was expanding to other Australian cities. The noticeable similarities in bottle shape and label design between the FIJI Water and

---

[26]FIJI Water Press Releases, www.fijiwater.com, accessed July 23, 2008.

[27]"National packaging covenant," FIJI Water (Australia) Pty Ltd., Annual Report, July 2006–June 2007, South Yara, Victoria, Australia.

[28]www.bottledwater.org.au

Island Chill brands had led to a trademark dispute between the two companies in both Australia and the United States. According to the Island Chill website's press centre, in February of 2007, the Federal Court of Australia ruled in favour of Island Chill, dismissing FIJI Water's complaint against Island Chill.[29] In the United States, the dispute was settled outside of court in June of 2008, when Island Chill agreed to remove the hibiscus flower from its bottle's label.[30]

Experiencing a Backlash in the U.K. Market

One year after FIJI Water entered the Australian market, it made an attempt to crack the U.K. market. The company launched FIJI brand through the supermarket chains Waitrose and Selfridge's, department stores Harvey Nichols and Harrods, and a number of specialty stores carrying whole-food products.

Soon after the brand had arrived in Britain, FIJI Water gained the reputation as the best-travelled bottled water in the country.[31] The fact that the product had to travel 10,000 miles to reach the British consumer could not escape the attention of environmentalist and conservation groups, in a country where quality of tap water was among the highest in the world. In a newspaper article published in 2004, an official from the Food Commission was reported to have said that "it was ludicrous to bring water from the other side of the world when essentially the same product was available out of the tap."[32] At the same time, it was noted that the most popular French bottled water brands—Evian and Vittel—travelled "only" between 400 and 460 miles to reach Britain. As a result of this backlash, FIJI Water had so far been largely unsuccessful in penetrating the U.K. market. Moreover, FIJI Water's appearance in the United Kingdom had fuelled the debate around the environmental impact of bottled water.

In 2008, British environmentalists and conservationists took up the war against bottled water. They were joined by some political leaders and government officials as well. For example, the mayor of London and the CEO of Thames Water Authority launched a campaign called "London on Tap" to encourage consumers to order tap water in restaurants.[33] Their message to consumers was that using less bottled water would help tackle climate change by cutting carbon emissions with its production, storage, transport and disposal. Campaign partners included London Remade, the Crafts Council and WaterAid and the supporters included Friends of the Earth and London Sustainability Exchange.

On January 18, 2008, the BBC broadcast a TV special that featured FIJI Water in a Panorama documentary called "Bottled Water—Who Needs It?" It gave a critical analysis of the negative impact the success of the U.K. bottled water industry was having on the environment.[34] It pointed out that, "In the UK last year we spent nearly £2 billion buying bottled water, yet a billion people around the world don't have access to safe drinking water" and that "Sales of bottled water have boomed in recent decades, growing 200-fold from the 1970s. But a litre of one of the UK's most popular French mineral waters generates up to 600 times more CO2 equivalent than a litre of Thames

---

[29]www.islandchill.com/press.html

[30]"Island Chill and Fiji Water end trademark dispute," *Foodbev.com*, June 24, 2008.

[31]"Bottle of water that has travelled the world," *The Daily Telegraph*, November 3, 2004.

[32]Ibid., p. 3.

[33]Hannah Marriott, "Bottled water under fire: How industry responded," *PRWeek (UK)*, February 21, 2008.

[34]The documentary can be accessed from http://news.bbc.co.uk/2/hi/programmes/panorama/7247130.stm

tap water."[35] The programme travelled to Fiji, where they visited the FIJI Water bottling plant, Fijian villages and hospitals, noting that one in three Fijians did not have access to safe tap water. The documentary was wrapped up with the following statement: "Indeed Fiji Water would make the case that if you really care about the plight of Fijians, you should buy Fiji water as it provides jobs and income for the islands. But tell people here on the street that we buy bottled water from Fiji and most will still roll their eyes and ask: Why?"[36] The 2008 BBC Panorama story focusing on FIJI Water had 3.5 million viewers!

Growing concerns about bottled water's harmful effects on the environment might have caused a reversal of a growing trend in bottled water consumption in the United Kingdom. For the first time in years, a nine per cent drop of retail sales of bottled water was reported in the first quarter of 2008.[37] This was largely attributed to an Evening Standard campaign to get Londoners to turn to tap water instead of buying expensive and environmentally harmful bottled water. A fifth of diners in London restaurants were reported to opt for tap water. The government's Food Standards Agency banned bottled water from its offices. This move was followed by a growing number of Whitehall departments doing the same, including Downing Street. Food and health lobby group "Sustain" launched a campaign for government departments and official bodies to turn to tap water. The campaign's director, Richard Watts, believed it had worked. He said, "This looks to be the first ever recorded fall in bottled water sales. It is a significant development. The message about bottled water being unnecessary, expensive and damaging to the environment is finally getting through."[38]

WORLDWIDE CONTROVERSIES OVER BOTTLED WATER'S IMPACT ON THE ENVIRONMENT

In the last 10 years, the high sustained global growth rate of bottled water sales of about eight per cent per annum had been a triumph of modern marketing and a dynamic, profitable segment of the beverage market for the growing number of producers. FIJI Water had been very successful in gaining market share in this rapidly growing industry. Advertising campaigns had promoted bottled water as a healthy alternative to high-calorie CSDs and purer alternative to tap water. The advertisements focused on its pristine pureness, safeness and better taste compared to tap water. However, conservationists pointed out that the price of bottled water was about 500 to 1,000 times higher than that of tap water. Since the launch of FIJI Water in the United Kingdom, the bottled water industry had been under attack in the media and FIJI brand had been singled out for criticism by environmental groups and by a BBC documentary that had been widely broadcast.

The Swiss-based conservation group World Wide Fund for Nature had published a research study it funded, which found that bottled water was often no healthier or safer to drink than tap water and it had used the findings to argue strongly that bottled water was not only environmentally unfriendly, but also a waste of money.[39]

---

[35]Ibid.

[36]Ibid.

[37]Lucy Hanbury, "Bottled water sales dry up as London turns to tap," *Evening Standard*, April 14, 2008.

[38]Ibid.

[39]Catherine Ferrier, "Bottled water: Understanding a social phenomenon," Discussion paper commissioned by WWF, April 2001.

Another watchdog, Corporate Accountability International, had mounted a campaign called "Think Outside the Bottle."[40] The group advocated ending state contracts with bottled water suppliers, promoting water systems and improving the quality of water infrastructure.

According to Janet Larsen's article "Bottled Water Boycotts," in 2007 city governments, high-class restaurants, schools and religious groups from San Francisco to New York to Paris were ditching bottled water in favour of tap water.[41] The U.S. Conference of Mayors, which represented some 1,100 American cities, discussed at its June 2007 meeting the mayors' role in promoting the consumption of municipal tap water, and many city councils were banning the purchase of bottled water for their employees. In the same year, New York City launched a campaign to persuade people to cut back on bottled water and return to tap water. San Francisco's mayor banned city employees from using public money to buy imported water, while Chicago's mayor imposed a five-cents-a-bottle tax on plastic bottles to compensate for the financial burden bottled water caused for municipal waste disposal systems.[42] It was somewhat ironic that in the United States, more than a quarter of bottled water was just purified tap water, including Pepsi's top-selling Aquafina and Coca-Cola's Dasani.

FIJI WATER'S "CARBON NEGATIVE" CAMPAIGN

In response to the environmentalists' criticism, in 2008, FIJI Water LLC. launched a "carbon negative" PR campaign, claiming that it was the first bottled water company to release carbon footprint of its products.[43] It had also joined the Carbon Disclosure Project Supply Chain Leadership Collaboration and had started working with the Carbon Disclosure Project (CDP), the world's largest investor coalition on climate change, to disclose its own, and its suppliers', carbon emissions. As measurement is the first step to managing and reducing carbon emissions, FIJI Water Company estimated its total annual carbon footprint at 85,396 metric tons of CO2eq. This was for the base year ending June 30, 2007.[44]

While measuring its carbon footprint, FIJI Water calculated its carbon emissions across every stage in the product lifecycle: starting from producing raw materials for packaging, through transporting raw materials and equipment to the plant, manufacturing and filling bottles, shipping the product from Fiji to markets worldwide, distributing the product, refrigerating the product in stores, restaurants and other outlets, to disposing/recycling the packaging waste. It estimated that about 75 per cent of its carbon emissions resulted from the operations of supply chain partners. The company also looked at carbon emissions from its administrative and marketing activities. At the same time, the company launched a product-specific emissions disclosure via a website (www.fijigreen.com). The website provided consumers with access to product lifecycle emissions data and analysis for each of the company's products. The company's senior VP for sustainable growth, Mooney, argued that "the only way

---

[40]"Corporate Accountability International: Challenging abuse, protecting people," www.stopcorporate-abuse.org

[41]Janet Larsen, "Bottled water boycotts," Earth Policy Institute, 2007.

[42]Lucy Siegle, "It's just water, right? Wrong. Bottled water is set to be the latest battleground in the eco war," *The Observer*, February 10, 2008, p. 30.

[43]"FIJI Water becomes first bottled water company to release carbon footprint of its products," April 9, 2008, www.bevnet.com

[44]Ibid.

consumers can turn their good environmental intentions into good decisions is to give them the information they need regarding the emissions associated with the products they buy."[45]

As part of its "carbon negative" campaign, FIJI Water was planning to offset its total carbon footprint by 120 per cent, by removing from the earth's atmosphere not only all the emissions its activities produced, but also an additional 20 per cent. In that sense, the company's impact on carbon emissions would be negative. To achieve this goal, FIJI Water had undertaken a number of steps towards sustainable growth. These steps included:

- reducing packaging by 20 per cent
- supplying at least 50 per cent of the energy used at its bottling plant with renewable energy
- optimizing logistics and using more carbon-efficient transportation modes
- restoring degraded grasslands in the Yaqara Valley by planting native tree species
- supporting recycling programs for plastic PET bottles

According to a company press conference held in April 2008, FIJI Water had already implemented several measures to reduce its carbon emissions. By optimizing its logistics, the company had reduced trucking miles by 26 per cent on average. FIJI Water's 1.5-litre bottle had been redesigned to reduce the packaging by 7 per cent. The company had also managed to reduce motor fuel consumption in Fiji by 50 per cent by using more fuel-efficient trucks in transporting its products from the plant to ports.[46]

All in all, the above sustainable growth commitment provided FIJI Water with an opportunity to use that commitment as a PR pitch: The sale of every bottle of FIJI Water would result in a net reduction of carbon in the atmosphere! In other words—"every drop is green," as the company's website emphasized.

CONSERVATIONISTS' ATTACKS ON FIJI WATER'S GREEN MAKE-OVER

Conservation groups had not been impressed by FIJI Water's claim that it was going carbon negative. It was perceived as pure greenwashing at its best. The 10th edition of the Concise Oxford English Dictionary recognizes the word "greenwash," defining it as "Disinformation disseminated by an organisation so as to present an environmentally responsible public image." Greenwashing was defined in law in Australia by the Competition and Consumer Commission that ensured compliance with the Commonwealth Trade Practices Act 1974. The Act contains a general prohibition on "conduct that is misleading or deceptive or is likely to mislead or deceive." Section 53 of the Act prohibits a corporation from representing that "goods or services have sponsorship, approval, performance characteristics, accessories, uses or benefits they do not have."

Conservation groups argued that the new website launched by FIJI Water in 2008 to sell its carbon negative message failed to provide a detailed description of the actual calculation of its carbon footprint and its reduction by the measures that were promised to be implemented in the future. At the same time, the groups pointed to the basic

[45]Ibid.

[46]"FIJI Water becomes first bottled water company to release carbon footprint of its products," FIJI Water Press Release, Los Angeles, April 9, 2008, www.bevnet.com

carbon footprint advantages of consuming local tap water. They argued that the new slogan "every drop is green" was straightforward greenwashing pushed to its limits.

The Food and Water Watch website posted a blog, entitled "Greenwashed: Fiji Water Bottles the Myth of Sustainability," about FIJI Water's carbon negative claim that summarized the response of the environmental watchdogs.[47] The website stated: "Corporate attempts to label their products as 'green' for the sake of turning a fast buck are nothing new. Corporations exist, after all, in order to make money, and capitalizing on whatever is capturing the public's collective imagination is often the best way of doing so. But *Fiji* Artisanal *Water*'s entree into the green movement strikes us as particularly suspect. The company has recently launched *fiji*green.com, a website outlining the ways in which their *water* is 'good for the environment.' If you're anything like us, you are probably wondering how this claim could be true. It can't."[48]

The Greenwash Brigade (part of the Public Insight Network), a U.S. organization of environmental professionals that are dedicated to exposing "greenwash" as they examine eco-friendly claims by companies, was quick to respond to FIJI Water's claim that it was going carbon negative. In an article by Heidi Siegelbaum on June 6, 2008, titled "Fiji Water by the Numbers," she summarized FIJI Water's environmental impact by the following numbers:

- 5,500 miles per trip from Fiji to Los Angeles;
- 46 million gallons of fossil fuel;
- 1.3 billion gallons of water;
- 216,000,000 pounds of greenhouse gases.[49]

And she commented, "Fiji is using staggering amounts of energy, water, and fossil fuels to take a naturally occurring product (which is not regulated like drinking water here in the US), put it in an inherently problematic container and then have that forever-container tossed into landfills or incinerators all over America (and Asia, where we have a healthy export market for plastics)."[50]

Tony Azios summarized the reaction in the United States to the response of bottled water companies to the environmental protests, as follows: "Even as bottled water companies continue to see increased sales, the recent raft of negative media coverage and activist campaigns against the industry has caused a product once seen as fundamentally green and healthy to lose some of its luster. Now, brand-name bottlers are scrambling to reposition their products by upping their green credentials to fend off further consumer backlash fermenting in churches, college campuses, and city halls across the country."[51]

Rob Knox, in his article titled "Green or Greenwashing? Fiji Water," was also not convinced that "every drop is green."[52] His evaluation of the green makeover was that it was greenwashing. Knox reported, "[. . .] In March they took out a massive booth at the Natural Products Expo, part of a larger 'hey we're green now' campaign by the company. The booth featured a gigantic banner proclaiming 'every drop is green'."

[47]www.foodandwaterwatch.org/blog/archive/2008/05/02 greenwashed-fiji-water-bottles-the-myth-of-sustainability
[48]Ibid.
[49]Heidi Siegelbaum, "Fiji Water by the numbers," June 6, 2008.
[50]Ibid.
[51]Ibid.
[52]Robert Knox, "Green or greenwashing? Fiji Water," www.greenopia.com/USA/news/15063/7-16-2008/Green-or-Greenwashing?-Fiji-Water

He continued: "Allow me free reign to mock Fiji for a moment. Let's discuss what every drop of Fiji water is—and here's a hint, it's not green. Every drop of Fiji water is imported from Fiji. That's right, the Fiji that is an island in the middle of the Pacific Ocean, thousands of miles from the mainland United States. This company takes water, which can be found in rather large quantities in the US, all the way from Fiji to your neighborhood. Every drop of Fiji water represents thousands of miles in completely unnecessary transportation and hundreds of gallons of fuel, all so you can drink expensive water from a pretty bottle."[53]

In 2007, Pablo Päster, an engineer and MBA, claimed to have undertaken a thorough and exhaustive study of the cost of bringing a litre of FIJI Water to America that was reported about on the Treehugger website in an article by Lloyd Alter, entitled "Pablo Calculates the True Cost of Bottled Water." His study found that, "In summary, the manufacture and transport of that one kilogram bottle of Fiji water consumed 26.88 kilograms of water (7.1 gallons), .849 kilograms of fossil fuel (one litre or .26 gallons) and emitted 562 grams of Greenhouse Gases (1.2 pounds)."[54]

RELATIONS WITH THE FIJI GOVERNMENT

Natural Waters, the Fiji Islands-based production subsidiary of FIJI Water LLC., played an important role in the Fiji economy, particularly as a source of export earnings. While in 1998, FIJI Water brand exports ranked 14th among product categories exported from Fiji,[55] its position among exports had climbed to number 2 in 2007, bringing FJ$105 million in export earnings.[56] Only sugar, whose exports in 2007 stood at FJ$185 million, brought more export revenues than bottled water, which was virtually all accounted for by FIJI Water. Since export revenues from sugar had been on the decline since 2000, there was a possibility that bottled water would soon become the number one export earner for Fiji, provided the Fiji government did not do any harm to the rapidly growing bottled water industry. The stand-off between Fiji's bottled water companies and the government over the 20-cents-per-litre export duty and excise in 2008 might put a brake on this industry's growth and erode a substantial part of Fiji's export earnings. In 2007, bottled water accounted for almost 10 per cent of Fiji's total export revenues.[57]

Taxation Issues

Over the last decade, the Fiji government had observed the rapid growth of a new export industry led by FIJI Water.[58] When Natural Waters of Viti Ltd. was established, it applied to the government for financial incentives under the Tax Free Factory Scheme and was granted a thirteen-year tax holiday from the government. Also, it was granted approval to import the plant and equipment for its factory free of import duty.[59]

---

[53]Ibid.

[54]www.treehugger.com/files/2007/02/pablo_calculate.php

[55]McMaster and Nowak, "Natural Waters of Viti Limited—Pioneering a new industry in the Fiji Islands," 2003.

[56]Fiji Islands Bureau of Statistics, "Key statistics: Overseas merchandise trade," March 2008, p. 71.

[57]Ibid.

[58]According to *Fiji Times* (August 12, 2008, p. 2), FIJI Water accounts for 98 per cent of bottled water exports from Fiji.

[59]McMaster and Nowak, "Natural Waters of Viti Limited—Pioneering a new industry in the Fiji Islands," 2003.

The success of FIJI Water was very evident to all citizens of Fiji as they observed the large number of trucks transporting containers of bottled water to the ports of Lautoka and Suva using the Queen's Highway. FIJI Water received positive media reports and was a sponsor of the Fiji Exporter of the Year Awards. A film was made about the company's past growth and plans for the future, and was broadcast several times on the local TV station Fiji One.

It was not until 2008 that the government started to review the potential tax contribution that could be levied on the bottled water industry. FIJI Water appeared to provide little direct benefit to government revenue because of the tax-free status granted by earlier governments. One could argue that the damage caused to the national roads and bridges by the huge number of heavily laden trucks carrying FIJI Water might have exceeded the road and fuel tax, and that the citizens of Fiji were subsidizing FIJI Water. The bottling plant of FIJI Water was fully automated with state-of-the-art equipment and featured a highly capital-intensive production process employing a relatively small workforce, given the volume of exports.

On July 4, 2008, without any prior consultation with the industry, the Fiji government imposed a 20-cents-per-litre export duty on all mineral water exports and the same level of excise duty on mineral water sold for domestic consumption.[60] This new tax was put into effect by amending the Customs Tariff Act (Amendment) (No. 3) Promulgation 2008 And Excise Act (Amendment) (No. 1) Promulgation 2008.[61]

The local media reported that the interim finance minister, Mahendra Chaudhry, said, "The main purpose of this new duty was to stimulate conservation of our scarce natural resources."[62]

These new taxes came into effect on July 1, 2008. In a press statement released on July 20 by Fiji Islands Revenue and Customs Authority chief executive officer, Jitoko Tikolevu, it was announced that "Should there be a change in the rates in the future as decided by government, the Authority will refund any excess revenue collected from these taxes."[63]

Based on FIJI Water's export levels, the new export tax would result in the company paying many millions to the government coffers. In 2006, FIJI Water exported 119,000,000 litres of bottled water to the United States. Applying a tax of 20-cents-per-litre to this level of export to the United States would result in a tax bill of FJ$24 million to FIJI Water just for its exports to one market. It was likely that FJIJ Water could end up paying as much as FJ$50 million for the new tax.[64]

FIJI Water and the nine other companies immediately mounted a campaign against the new tax. They first threatened to cease production and to lay workers off. They issued press releases that argued the new tax would destroy the whole industry and greatly undermine foreign investor confidence, which was already at a low level. The 10 bottled water companies formed an industry association and appointed a spokesperson to lead the media campaign. They argued that this sudden decision by the Cabinet was made without thorough analysis of the economic costs and benefits. They stated that the government did not have detailed information on company costs and profitability, and that the firms could not absorb the ill-conceived new tax that would have a major negative impact on the whole economy. It would be the death

---

[60]"Cabinet approves Tariff, Excise Act," *Fiji Times*, July 4, 2008.

[61]Ibid.

[62]Ibid.

[63]"Duty on bottled water remains," *Fiji Times*, July 20, 2008.

[64]FIRCA Press Release, July 21, 2008, www.frca.org.fj/docs/firca/press_releases/Press Release 21.07.pdf

knell of this new export industry and would greatly reduce export earnings and foreign exchange earnings, and lead to job losses and slower economic growth. They pointed out that it would undermine the government's economic development strategy, which was based on increasing the level of investment and export-oriented growth.

The new industry association comprising 10 firms—Warwick Pleass, FIJI Water, VTY, Mr Pure, Island Chill, Aqua Pacific, Diamond Aqua, Tappoos Beverage, Fresh Spring Limited and Minerals Water of Fiji—lobbied the members of the Military Council and the media and gained strong support of the local newspapers. The main local newspaper, the Fiji Times, published an editorial in July 2008 calling for the sacking of the interim minister of finance, who was seen as the architect of this new tax. The bottled water industry was required to make its submissions to the Finance Ministry on the new tax.

A critical issue was the likely impact of this new tax on both foreign and local investment. It was seen as moving the goal posts after the start of the game. Foreign investor confidence was already at a very low level because of the military takeover of the democratically elected government in December 2006. Investors are not attracted to a country where the taxation environment can alter dramatically overnight without consultation.

On July 23, 2008, Natural Waters of Viti Ltd. laid off about 400 workers and shut down operations, along with five other major exporting companies. The following day, the Fiji Times, the leading local newspaper, published an editorial comment on the so-called "Water Debacle."[65] The editorial stated that "the closure of Fiji Water's operations yesterday shows what happens when governments take draconian measures to impose unrealistic taxes on large corporate entities. This major contributor to the national economy has closed its doors, sent staff home and deprived the nation of $3 million in export revenue per week." The editorial continued, stressing the importance of FIJI Water operations for the livelihood of workers and their families, for tax revenues, as well as for retail revenues in the nearby towns of Rakiraki and Tavua. It also pointed out the impact of the plant closure on dockworkers and drivers.[66]

Also the following day, a spokesperson for the bottlers, Jay Dayal, said they had decided to take legal action, as their patience had been exhausted. The bottlers had filed for a judicial review over the government decision to impose the 20-cents-per-litre tax.[67] On the same day, FIJI Water released a statement saying that the lawsuit was caused by the lack of movement by the interim government on the imposition of tax by Fiji Islands Revenue and Customs Authority (FIRCA), pending a final decision by the interim Cabinet. "Unfortunately, FIJI Water must take this action because we have now reached a critical juncture where we can no longer effectively operate our business," the statement said. "We have neither sold nor exported any product since July 1, forcing us to cancel multiple port calls from various shipping lines. As long as the crisis continues, the nation of Fiji will continue to lose approximately FJ$3 million in export revenue each week (more than FJ$150 million annually)."[68]

Behind the scenes, the bottlers were very active in seeking the support of the media and key decision makers, trade unions, village leaders and local chiefs as well

[65]"Water Debacle," *Fiji Times*, July 24, 2008.

[66]Ibid.

[67]"Fiji water bottlers file suit against government, Association says 20-cent tax will kill industry," Radio New Zealand International, www.rnzi.com

[68]"Fiji Water shuts down operations," *Fiji Daily Post*, July 24, 2008.

as lobbying interim ministers and members of the Military Council. One of the bottlers described the tax-induced crisis as "like a war had broken out or a bomb had exploded." There were tens of millions of dollars at stake that could be collected from the bottlers.

On July 25, 2008, the Fiji government made an announcement that it had decided to drop the new tax. This decision by interim Prime Minister Commodore Voreqe Bainimarama was praised by the proprietors of water bottling companies.[69] Immediately after the announcement of the repeal of the tax, the major bottled water-exporting companies resumed production and re-employed the hundreds of workers who had been laid off.[70]

FIJI Water had, for a number of years, been a sponsor of the Fiji Exporter of the Year Awards, an annual event to celebrate successful exporters. On August 3, 2008, FIJI Water's local CEO, David Roth, announced the company's decision to withdraw its sponsorship of the Awards because of the lack of support of FTIB during the taxation dispute.[71] David Roth said, "Fiji Islands Trade and Investment Bureau (FTIB) did not provide any support or assistance towards the bottled water industry during this struggle, and in fact FTIB's chairman publicly supported the imposition of the unreasonable and draconian excise and export duties, in spite of many of us trying to explain to him that his assumptions about our businesses were simply incorrect." Roth added that the company's decision to withdraw had nothing to do with its attitude toward others in government.[72]

In November 2008, the Fiji government re-introduced the disputed water tax as part of the 2009 budget in a different form. It was called "water resource tax" and was progressive depending on the amount of water extracted. For extractions up to 4,999,999 litres, it was set at 0.11 cents per litre; for extractions between 5,000,000 and 9,999,999 litres, it was 0.22 cents per litre; and an extraction volume of 10,000,000 litres or more would attract a tax of 0.33 cents per litre.[73] The tax was to be imposed only on extracted (artesian) water; companies engaged in the bottling of rainwater or purified tap water would be exempt from the tax. The tax was supposed to be collected from January 2009. It was expected that the Fiji government would collect FJ$1.5 million through the water extraction tax.[74]

Transfer Pricing

In January 2008, the government became concerned that FIJI Water was engaging in transfer price manipulations, selling the water shipments produced in Fiji at a very low price to the company headquarters in Los Angeles. It was feared that very little of the wealth generated by the company was coming into Fiji as foreign reserves from export earnings, which Fiji badly needed to fund its imports. Seemingly, FIJI Water was funnelling most of its cash to the United States.

As a result of these concerns, FIRCA decided to take action against FIJI Water and it halted exports in January 2008 at the ports by putting 200 containers loaded with FIJI

---

[69]Margaret Wise, "Sigh of relief as State drops tax," *Fiji Times*, July 25, 2008.

[70]"Bottled water back in action," Fiji Live website, July 24, 2008.

[71]"Fiji bottlers reconsider boycott decision," Fiji Live website, August 3, 2008.

[72]Ibid.

[73]PriceWaterhouseCoopers, 2009 Fiji Islands Budget Summary, November 21, 2008.

[74]"$1.5 million expected from water tax," Fiji Live website, November 21, 2008.

water bottles under armed guard, and issued a statement accusing FIJI Water of transfer price manipulations. FIRCA's chief executive, Jitoko Tikolevu, said, "The wholly US-owned Fijian subsidiary sold its water exclusively to its US parent at the declared rate, in Fiji, of US$4 (NZ$5) a carton. In the US, though, the same company then sold it for up to US$50 a carton."[75]

Natural Waters of Viti Ltd. immediately filed a lawsuit against FIRCA with the High Court of Fiji. The High Court issued an interim order, allowing the company to resume shipment of the embargoed containers upon payment of an FJ$5 million bond to the Court.[76]

The U.S. ambassador to Fiji, Larry Dinger, issued a barely veiled threat to Fiji. "The example [the authority] and the interim government set regarding fair and impartial treatment in this case will surely have a major impact on global perceptions of Fiji's investment climate. American companies have to receive fair and impartial treatment around the world. That applies in Fiji, too. 'Rule of law' and a 'level playing field' are critically important factors when there are commercial disputes, and those elements have a major impact in decisions by foreign investors, including American investors, on where they will direct their funds," he stated.[77]

A press release by FIRCA, issued in January 2008, noted that FIJI Water had received advice from international law firm Baker & McKenzie, which conducted an economic study on transfer pricing and declared what the company was doing in Fiji was fair. FIRCA rejected the claim by stating that "FIRCA will not passively accept the verdict of Baker & McKenzie without itself having access to the information on which same is based, and to the instructions on which same is based, and without the opportunity to conduct its own transfer pricing study based on such matters and upon the profitability of Natural Waters of Viti Limited."[78]

The FIJI Water dispute with the government over transfer pricing attracted the attention of the University of the South Pacific economist Sukhdev Shah, who published an article on "The True Cost of Water" in the Fiji Times on January 24, 2008, to give the general public a lecture on the complexities of transfer pricing. He stated that "Multinational companies as represented by FIJI Water are capable of spreading their risks across countries where they do business. They do this by shifting most of their profits and asset holdings to their affiliates in low-tax countries that are also considered safe. Given a choice between US and Fiji, FIJI Water would definitely take a bet on US - partly for the reason of lower tax obligation but mostly because it can be a safe-haven."[79]

RELATIONS WITH THE LOCAL COMMUNITY

The company had recognized the importance of establishing and maintaining good relations with the five neighbouring Fijian villages that were the traditional landowners of the Yaqara basin, where the bottling plant was located. These villages were Drauniivi, Togovere, Naseyani, Nananu and Rabulu. FIJI Water's bottling plant drew most of its workforce from these villages. It employed a young workforce and most of

---

[75]Michael Field, "Fiji-US row brews over water exports," *The Dominion Post*, January 21, 2008.

[76]"High Court set to rule in Fiji Water case," *Fiji Times*, February 8, 2008.

[77]Field, "Fiji-US row brews over water exports," January 21, 2008.

[78]"Press Release," Fiji Islands Revenue & Customs Authority, January 11, 2008, p. 3.

[79]Sukhdev Shah, "The true cost of water," *Fiji Times*, January, 24, 2008.

the workers had not previously had a wage job, but had been engaged in subsistence farming and fishing activities. The company provided its staff with on-the-job training in operating the sophisticated production line. In return, its workers showed a lot of enthusiasm, loyalty and pride in working for the company. Through strong leadership, FIJI Water had established an excellent work environment with good interpersonal relationships among the workforce. The company supported children's education. To assist the children in getting an early start, it had constructed a kindergarten classroom in each village to provide early childhood education. The company had also provided the preschools with equipment, educational material, teacher training and other support.

In March 2002, the company voluntarily established an independently administrated community development trust fund and allocated FJ$275,000 to it. The trust fund was established after a series of negotiations with the members of the community. It was designed to support village projects to improve the hygiene and sanitation of the community. Through this fund, the company intended to finance projects to supply potable water to the villages and reticulate it to the households. It also aimed at supporting projects to reduce pollution and improve hygiene. Through improving the quality of hygiene and sanitation, it was hoped to improve the health of the villagers and of the workforce of the company.[80]

As a result of the above-described trust fund, Draunivi and Togovere were first provided with clean, safe drinking water. The water supply project was then extended in 2008 to cover three other villages in the vicinity of the bottling plant—Naseyani, Nananu and Rabulu.[81] Moreover, in the same year, FIJI Water teamed with the Rotary Club in Suva to fund the Pacific Water for Life Trust. The Trust provided funds for developing the infrastructure, expertise and skills needed to supply clean, safe and sustainable water to more than 100 communities, schools, health centres and nursing stations throughout Fiji.[82]

Natural Waters of Viti Ltd. was a strong believer in contracting out. It had contracted out services to a local company that employed tens of people in the following functions: transport of workers to and from work; security office to guard the factory; the preparation of food for workers in the canteen; ground maintenance; and laundry.

In recognition of FIJI Water's involvement in local community development in Fiji, in 2004, the U.S. State Department honoured the company with the Award for Corporate Excellence for Outstanding Corporate Citizenship, Innovation and Exemplary International Business Practice. The award was presented to FIJI Water founder David Gilmour by Secretary of State Colin Powell in October 2004, who remarked, "Fijians take special pride in their island's tranquil beauty and Fiji Water has matched their passion with action . . . More than a good corporate citizen, Fiji Water is a good neighbour to all the people of Fiji."[83] Ironically, two months later, FIJI Water was sold by Gilmour to Roll International.

---

[80]McMaster and Nowak, "Natural Waters of Viti Limited—Pioneering a new industry in the Fiji Islands," 2003.

[81]www.fijiwater.com

[82]Ibid.

[83]"Here's to you: Fiji Water," *Beverage World*, March 8, 2007.

WHAT NEXT?

In 2009 and beyond, FIJI Water will continue facing complex CRS challenges. It will have to live up to its promise of becoming a carbon negative company. Any attempt to engage in greenwashing will be quickly identified and protested by environmental groups. Keeping true to its slogan "every drop is green" will require substantial new investment in a renewable energy plant and equipment and in tree-planting offset activities.

FIJI Water's tax-free concession granted by the Fiji government for 13 years in 1995 came to an end in October 2008, and the company will be required to pay corporate tax in Fiji. The new water resource tax, although much lower than the draconian 20-cents-a-litre excise, is nevertheless likely to erode the company's profitability by adding about FJ$1 million to its costs every year. This is expected to coincide with a slow-down of growth or even stagnation of FIJI Water sales in its main markets due to the global recession.

Maintaining good relations with the Fiji government will be vital. A series of ads sponsored by FIJI Water, placed in the popular daily Fiji Times in late 2008 and early 2009, was focused on letting the public (and the government!) know how good a corporate citizen the company is. The ads highlighted FIJI Water's contribution to creating new jobs, improving education and raising standards of living in Fiji. In January 2009, FIJI Water donated US$0.5 million to Fiji's National Disaster, Relief and Rehabilitation Fund, which was created by the Prime Minister's Office in the aftermath of devastating floods.[84] Clearly, FIJI Water was making efforts to live up to its good corporate citizenship claim. But is it enough to dispel government officials' and ordinary citizens' doubts about FIJI Water's positive contribution to the local economy and community?

Designing and implementing a sustainable growth strategy and a socially and environmentally responsible marketing plan will require dealing effectively with the promise to go carbon negative, as well as meeting the demanding needs of customers, clients and other stakeholders. Will FIJI Water be able to successfully navigate through these rough waters of corporate social responsibility? What should it do to breathe new life into this otherwise clever marketing strategy?

James McMaster is a professor at the Graduate School of Business, The University of the South Pacific, and Jan Nowak is a professor at the Central European University Business School.

---

[84]"Fiji Water donates to PM's Relief Fund," Press Release, Fiji Government On-line, January 27, 2009.

EXHIBIT 1   Global Bottled Water Market Leading Countries' Consumption and Compound Annual Growth Rates, 2002–2007

Rank, 2007	Countries	Consumption in millions of gallons		CAGR* 2002/07
		2002	2007	
1	United States	5,795.6	8,823.0	8.8%
2	Mexico	3,898.6	5,885.2	8.6%
3	China	2,138.4	4,787.8	17.5%
4	Brazil	2,541.8	3,621.1	7.3%
5	Italy	2,558.2	3,100.9	3.9%
6	Germany	2,291.5	2,743.2	3.7%
7	Indonesia	1,622.5	2,400.6	8.2%
8	France	2,225.6	2,283.2	0.5%
9	Thailand	1,277.0	1,533.1	3.7%
10	Spain	1,191.4	1,284.0	1.5%
	Top 10 subtotal	**25,540.7**	**36,462.2**	**7.4%**
	All others	9,054.2	13,407.3	8.2%
	WORLD TOTAL	**34,594.9**	**49,869.6**	**7.6%**

*Compound annual growth rate

Source: "The global bottled water market. Report 2007," Beverage Marketing Corporation, January 2008.

EXHIBIT 2 Global Bottled Water Market per Capita Consumption by Leading Countries, 2002–2007

Rank, 2007	Countries	Consumption in Gallons per Capita	
		2002	2007
1	United Arab Emirates	35.2	68.6
2	Mexico	37.7	54.1
3	Italy	44.2	53.3
4	Belgium-Luxembourg	32.7	39.5
5	France	37.1	35.8
6	Germany	27.8	33.3
7	Spain	29.7	31.7
8	Lebanon	24.9	29.3
9	United States	20.1	29.3
10	Hungary	13.5	28.5
11	Switzerland	24.2	28.2
12	Slovenia	18.8	25.2
13	Austria	20.9	25.0
14	Czech Republic	21.1	24.6
15	Croatia	14.9	24.3
16	Saudi Arabia	23.8	24.1
17	Cyprus	21.4	24.0
18	Thailand	20.1	23.6
19	Israel	12.4	23.2
20	Portugal	19.9	22.4
	GLOBAL AVERAGE	**5.6**	**7.6**

Source: "The global bottled water market. Report 2007," Beverage Marketing Corporation, January 2008.

EXHIBIT 3   U.S. Bottled Water Market per Capita Consumption, 1997–2007

Year	Gallons per Capita	Annual % change
1997	13.5	–
1998	14.7	8.3%
1999	16.2	10.2%
2000	16.7	3.5%
2001	18.2	8.6%
2002	20.1	10.6%
2003	21.6	7.2%
2004	23.2	7.5%
2005	25.4	9.7%
2006	27.6	8.4%
2007	29.3	6.4%

Source: "The global bottled water market. Report 2007," Beverage Marketing Corporation, January 2008.

EXHIBIT 4   U.S. Bottled Water Market Volume and Growth by Segment, 2000–2007

Year	Non-sparkling		Domestic sparkling		Imports		Total	
	Volume*	Change	Volume*	Change	Volume*	Change	Volume*	Change
2000	4,443.0	—	144.2	—	137.9	—	4,725.1	—
2001	4,917.3	10.7%	144.0	−0.1%	123.9	−10.1%	5,185.3	9.7%
2002	5,487.5	11.6%	149.5	3.8%	158.7	28.0%	5,795.7	11.8%
2003	5,923.9	8.0%	152.6	2.1%	193.3	21.8%	6,269.8	8.2%
2004	6,411.3	8.2%	166.8	9.3%	228.6	18.2%	6,806.7	8.6%
2005	7,171.4	11.9%	185.0	10.9%	182.5	−20.2%	7,538.9	10.8%
2006	7,899.9	10.2%	189.3	2.3%	164.3	−10.0%	8,253.5	9.5%
2007	8,435.7	6.8%	201.2	6.3%	186.0	13.2%	8,823.0	6.9%

*Millions of gallons.

Source: "The global bottled water market. Report 2007," Beverage Marketing Corporation, January 2008.

Strategic Leadership at Coca-Cola: The Real Thing[1]

In recent years, The Coca-Cola Company (Coca-Cola) has seen a much lower rise in its stock price compared with the exceptional 5,800 per cent rise during the 16-year tenure of its well-known chief executive officer (CEO) Robert Goizueta. After Goizueta's untimely death from cancer in October 1997, the company witnessed some tumultuous times, and Goizueta's three immediate successors have not lasted for even half as long as his total tenure (see Exhibit 1). Coca-Cola's CEO succession process was widely regarded as being ad hoc, and each succession story had its own peculiarities and intrigues. The leadership styles of CEOs at Coca-Cola differed and were often a source of interest in the media and the investment community, where many speculated on the type of leadership that was needed at the helm.

In general, leadership styles can be described as managerial, visionary or strategic.[2] In this categorization, *managerial leaders* are considered those who are risk averse, reactive and for whom goals are based on the past and on necessities, as opposed to goals arising from desires and dreams. Such leaders relate to people according to their roles in the decision-making process, see themselves as conservators and regulators of the existing order and involve themselves in situations and contexts characteristic of day-to-day activities. They are concerned with, and are more comfortable in, functional areas of responsibility, ensuring compliance to standard operating procedures. These leaders exhibit linear thinking and are deterministic, i.e., they believe their choices are determined by their internal and external environments.

Version: (A) 2008-10-16

Richard Ivey School of Business
The University of Western Ontario

---

[1] This case has been written on the basis of published sources only. Consequently, the interpretation and perspectives presented in this case are not necessarily those of The Coca-Cola Company or any of its employees.

[2] W. Glenn Rowe, "Creating wealth in organizations: The role of strategic leadership," *Academy of Management Executive*, February 2001, pp. 81–94.

In contrast, *visionary leaders* are proactive; they shape ideas and they change the way people think about what is desirable, possible and necessary. They are given to risk taking. They bring fresh approaches to long-standing problems, concern themselves with ideas and relate to people in intuitive and empathetic ways. They feel separate from their environment, working in, but not belonging to, their organizations. Such leaders are concerned with ensuring the future of the organization, especially through development and management of people. They engage in multifunctional and integrative tasks, they know less than their functional area experts, utilize non-linear thinking and believe in strategic choice, i.e., their choices make a difference to their organizations and, through their organizations, to their environment.

Strategic leaders are a synergistic combination of managerial and visionary leadership. They oversee both operating (day-to-day) and strategic (long-term) responsibilities, apply both linear and non-linear thinking and emphasize ethical behaviour and value-based decisions. Strategic leadership is defined as the ability to influence those with whom you work to voluntarily make decisions on a day-to-day basis that enhance both the long-term viability of the organization and the organization's short-term financial stability.[3]

GOIZUETA IS IT![4]

Background

Robert Goizueta was born in Havana, Cuba, in 1931, a scion of a major sugar industry family in Cuba. Goizueta's maternal grandfather immigrated to Cuba from Spain, and, despite a lack of education beyond high school, was able to save enough money to buy a sugar refining business and some real estate during the Cuban depression. His grandfather's focus on the importance of cash made an early impression on Goizueta. After attending a Jesuit school in Cuba, Goizueta moved to a private academy in Connecticut for a year to improve his English. His outstanding performance and connections at the academy helped him gain admission to Yale University, where he majored in chemical engineering with an eye to a possible future in the family business.

When he returned to Cuba, he chose not to join the family business. Instead he answered a blind advertisement in a newspaper that led to a job as an entry-level chemist at The Coca-Cola Company in Havana. "It was going to be a temporary thing for me, $500 a month—my friends thought I was absolutely crazy," he recalled. However, he soon rose to become chief technical director of five Cuban bottling plants. Then, in 1959, Fidel Castro came to power and Coca-Cola's Cuban operations came under a strong threat of takeover.

The family escaped to Miami, where Goizueta, his wife, three children and a nursemaid shared a motel room for a month. Fortunately, Goizueta landed a job with Coca-Cola in a new Miami office. His only possessions of value were 100 shares of Coca-Cola stock in a New York bank and US$40. He later recalled the importance of that experience:

> You cannot explain that experience to any person. That was ten times more important than anything else in my life. It was a shocker. All of a sudden you don't

---

[3]Ibid.

[4]Slogans used in titles retrieved from The Coca-Cola Company website, Heritage section, http://www.thecoca-colacompany.com/heritage/ourheritage.html, accessed on March 22, 2008.

own anything, except the stock. One hundred shares! That's the only thing I had. It brings a sense of humility. It builds a feeling of not much regard for material things.[5]

After working in the Miami office, he worked as a chemist in the Bahamas for Coca-Cola's Caribbean region and later moved back to headquarters in Atlanta, Georgia. At age 35, he was promoted to vice-president, Technical Research and Development, the youngest person to hold this position. He was then promoted to head the Legal and External Affairs department in 1975 and became vice-chairman in 1979.

Goizueta as CEO of Coca-Cola

Robert Woodruff, widely regarded as Coke's main power broker because he revitalized the company after taking over as CEO in 1923 and served in that position for decades, befriended Goizueta. Aided by a close relationship with Robert Woodruff, Goizueta moved up through the technical operations and became president in 1980, after J. Lucian Smith's resignation. When the chairman, J. Paul Austin, retired in 1981, Goizueta became chairman and CEO. At the time, the transition was seen as messy, because Woodruff (despite being retired), used his position as the company's 90-year-old patriarch to overrule Austin's choice for successor, Donald R. Keough. Woodruff's pick, the chemical engineer from Cuba, was regarded as the darkest horse in the succession process. However, Woodruff and others on the board saw Goizueta as the person needed to introduce change and improve performance.

Goizueta generously asked Keough to be his chief operating officer (COO) and president, sending the broader message that

> The day of the one-man band is gone. It would be a crime for me to try to lead the bottlers the way Don Keough can. I would look like a phony. . . . My job is to pick the people, then give them the responsibility and authority to get the job done.

Goizueta created a two-page, double-spaced document, "The Job of the Chief Executive Officer," which delineated what he could and couldn't delegate.[6] For 12 years, Goizueta and Keough complemented each other. Goizueta was known as the business philosopher, whereas Keough did more of the footwork—travelling to bottlers, meeting customers and ensuring overall operations were in shape.[7]

Goizueta stated that he had viewed Coca-Cola as having become "too conservative" and revealed his desire for major changes: "It took us a little bit longer to change than it should have. The world was changing, and we were not changing with the world." At a retreat for company executives, he unveiled a "Strategy for the '80s" and emphasized that "We're going to take risks."[8]

When Goizueta took over, the company was in multiple businesses: soft drinks, wine, coffee, tea, plastics, shrimp farming, orange groves, steam generators, industrial boilers, desalting plants and industrial water treatment. Goizueta subjected each business to a standard financial formula: Is our return on capital greater than our cost

[5]Betsy Morris, "Roberto Goizueta and Jack Welch: The wealth builders," *Fortune*, December 11, 1995, pp. 80–94.

[6]Betsy Morris, "Roberto Goizueta and Jack Welch: The wealth builders," *Fortune*, December 11, 1995, pp. 80–94.

[7]Betsy Morris, "The real story," *Fortune*, May 31, 2004, pp. 84–98.

[8]"Coke CEO Roberto C. Goizueta dies at 65," *CNN Interactive News*, October 18, 1997, http://www.cnn.com/US/9710/18/goizueta.obit.9am, retrieved April 18, 2008.

of capital? He then divested non-core businesses that did not measure up until the only business left by the late 1980s was the selling of bottled carbonated soft drinks (CSDs)—predominantly Coca-Cola and minor quantities of Sprite and Tab (a diet soft drink)—and one non-CSD beverage (i.e., Minute Maid). He stated his rule of investment: "You borrow money at a certain rate and invest it at a higher rate and pocket the difference. It's simple." He was a pioneer in promoting the idea of economic profit (i.e., after-tax operating profits in excess of capital costs) and wrote to Wall Street analysts personally about it. Today, the concept has gained ground as economic value added (EVA), a well-regarded tool for increasing shareholder wealth.

Goizueta's style was less hands-on and more intellectual. Despite the fact that Coca-Cola earned up to 80 per cent of its profits abroad, Goizueta visited only about a half-dozen countries a year and remained most comfortable defining "the character of the company" from his office at Coca-Cola's headquarters. Goizueta used rewards based on economic profit targets to motivate his management team to perform.[9] A contemporary CEO characterized Goizueta's style in the following manner: "A lot of executives can intellectualize the process, but [Goizueta] can follow through."[10]

Although Coca-Cola had never borrowed money, under Goizueta, it borrowed billions and bought out independent bottlers around the world to upgrade its own distribution systems. With Douglas Ivester as chief financial officer (CFO), the "49 per cent solution" was devised. This involved Coca-Cola buying out U.S. bottlers that were not doing well and combining them with its own bottling network. The new creation was called Coca-Cola Enterprises (CCE) and was spun off to the public, with Coca-Cola retaining a strategic 49 per cent of the stock. This arrangement helped Coca-Cola reduce its debt and divest itself of a low-return, capital-intensive business.[11]

Looking back at that time, Goizueta later commented during an interview:

> We really lost focus on who our customer was. We felt our customer was the bottler as opposed to McDonald's and Wal-Mart. So consequently, we were being either cheerleaders or critics of our bottlers. But hands off; we didn't have anything to do with it—that was their job. I think the worst thing we ever had to do was to establish a sense of direction . . . so that they know where they're going. Then you can let them have a lot of freedom.[12]

During this same interview, Goizueta emphasized the need for leaders to establish a sense of direction, so people both knew where they are going and had a lot of freedom to get there. He added that if people did not know where they were going, you do not want them to get there too fast. Finally, he encouraged people to create what can be, as opposed to what is.

Goizueta emphasized the importance of relationships. He enticed the Cisneroses (Pepsi's most venerable bottlers in Venezuela) away from Pepsi and signed the deal in the presence of three generations of the Cisneroses at Coca-Cola headquarters. "It was a very family-like gathering, to symbolize that this was to be a long-term relationship," Gustavo Cisneros recalled. "This is a people-relations business," Goizueta later said.[13]

---

[9]Patricia Sellers, "Where Coke goes from here," *Fortune*, October 13, 1997, pp. 88–91.

[10]Betsy Morris, "Roberto Goizueta and Jack Welch: The wealth builders," *Fortune*, December 11, 1995, pp. 80–94.

[11]Patricia Sellers, "How Coke is kicking Pepsi's can," *Fortune*, October 28, 1996, pp. 70–84.

[12]Betsy Morris, "Roberto Goizueta and Jack Welch: The wealth builders," *Fortune*, December 11, 1995, pp. 80–94.

[13]Patricia Sellers, "How Coke is kicking Pepsi's can," *Fortune*, October 28, 1996, pp. 70–84.

These moves were also in line with Goizueta's overall approach of developing senior managers' intimate strategic knowledge of, and engagement in, the core business. Whereas CCE and other bottlers carried out the operational details on the ground, Goizueta focused his own role and that of other senior managers on brand building, making deals and selling concentrate. Coca-Cola did not rotate its successful managers through jobs rapidly, in contrast to its main rival Pepsi. "If you do that, you can never see how good the people really are," Goizueta explained.

Goizueta encouraged calculated risk-taking, epitomized by his decision to put the Coca-Cola trademark on a new product, Diet Coke, in 1982, which turned into the most successful product launch of the 1980s. Traditionally, the company had never put the Coca-Cola trademark on other products. Goizueta invested outside the core business only on one occasion, to buy Columbia Pictures in 1982, after it went bust. He later sold it to Sony in 1989 for a large profit. He stated that this investment was not to hedge his bets, but to pile up earnings until he could sort out issues with the soft drinks business.

The new moves included launching New Coke. Based on a sweeter formula, it was a departure from the traditional Coke formula and was developed to counter Pepsi, which was doing better on taste tests. In Goizueta's words, the launch of New Coke was "the boldest single marketing move in the history of the consumer goods business." However, when New Coke bombed in 1985 and loyal customers demanded a return of the old formula, the old Coke was re-launched as "Classic Coke," and over time "New Coke" was allowed to die out. Coca-Cola learned a valuable lesson: Its brand and marketing, not the taste of the sugar water, was its asset, and Coca-Cola marketing was consequently overhauled. "I realized what I should have before," he recalled. "That this was a most unique company with a most unique product. We have a product that people have an unusual attachment to. I had never felt so bullish about it."[14]

Goizueta encouraged speedier decision-making and kept encouraging risk-taking. At a worldwide gathering of Coca-Cola's quality assurance staff, in response to a concern about all the changes taking place, Goizueta said:

> Don't wrap the flag of Coca-Cola around you to prevent change from taking place. It is extremely important that you show some insensitivity to your past in order to show the proper respect for the future.[15]

During Goizueta's reign, the company expanded both domestically and internationally, backed by the new slogan "Coke Is It!" Goizueta turned Coca-Cola around financially, organizationally and culturally, making it America's most admired company, against all expectations. Coca-Cola's stock price increased 5,829 per cent during Goizueta's tenure (see Exhibits 1 and 2). Its market value grew 34 times, from $4.3 billion to $147 billion during Goizueta's 16-year tenure. In addition, in a *Fortune* story on Goizueta in October 1997 describing "The Goizueta Effect," it was reported that revenues had increased from $4.8 billion to $18.5 billion, net income from $0.5 billion to $3.5 billion and return on equity from 20 to 60 per cent from 1981 to 1996 (see Exhibit 3).[16]

When asked what he looked for in a future successor, Goizueta agreed with his fellow interviewee, Jack Welch, General Electric's CEO, that his successor needed

---

[14]Ibid.

[15]Ibid.

[16]Patricia Sellers, "Where Coke goes from here," *Fortune*, October 13, 1997, pp. 88–91.

incredible energy, the ability to excite others, a defined vision, the capacity to find change fun and the facility to be as comfortable in New Delhi as in Denver. Goizueta added that while energy is the number one quality, two other qualities were also important—integrity and the intellectual courage to take a risk, a leap of faith, whether the leap was big or small.

Roberto Goizueta died of cancer at the age of 65 in October 1997. The 100 shares he had when he arrived in Miami were worth more than $3 million. He was a billionaire by 1997, and his belief in Coca-Cola was evidenced by the fact that, in 1995, more than 99 per cent of his personal wealth was tied up in Coca-Cola stock.[17] He was replaced by heir apparent Douglas Ivester. Some said that Goizueta's strategic planning showed in his leaving behind a solid management team. Herbert Allen, a director at Coca-Cola since 1982, stated, "Roberto has filled in behind him so well. He established at least four people who can run the company . . . and behind them are ten more people who could fill their jobs."

ALWAYS DOUGLAS IVESTER

Background

In a few ways, Ivester was comparable to Goizueta. He had his own rags-to-riches story and was regarded as a dark horse who came from corporate backwaters. Ivester was the only child of conservative Southern Baptist factory workers, raised with discipline and rigidity in the Georgia mill village of New Holland, 60 miles north of Atlanta. He described his parents as "strong savers, [with] very strong religious values," partly due to their being children of the Depression. They had very high expectations of him. When he got an A in school, his father would remark, "They give A-pluses, don't they?" As a child, Ivester worked after school doing odd jobs. He hardly had time for any extra-curricular activities or team sports.

"One thing I learned in Gainesville was to never let my memories be greater than my dreams," Ivester recalled. He graduated from the University of Georgia with an accounting major and worked as an accountant at Ernst & Whinney. Ivester headed the audit team for Coca-Cola and was recruited by Coca-Cola as assistant controller in 1979. Six years later, CEO Goizueta, impressed with Ivester's solutions to complex financial problems that helped maximize returns on investment, made him CFO.[18]

As CFO, Ivester was the brains behind getting Coca-Cola's low-return bottling operations and its debt off the company's books. Under Goizueta's leadership, Ivester helped create a separate bottling company, Coca-Cola Enterprises (CCE), and spun it off to shareholders, while keeping 49 per cent equity for Coca-Cola to control the business. Goizueta groomed Ivester and provided opportunities for varied experiences in marketing and international operations. Ivester's first operations job was as president of Coca-Cola's European operations in mid-1989. When the Berlin Wall came down later that year, Ivester cut deals with bottling plants across Eastern Europe, and his opportunism saw Coca-Cola seizing control of the region that had long been dominated by Pepsi.

As president of Coca-Cola in 1990, Ivester visited overseas markets and sent out a new message. Instead of setting goals in the traditional style, he asked executives to

---

[17]Patricia Sellers, "Where Coke goes from here," *Fortune*, October 13, 1997, pp. 88–91; Betsy Morris, "Roberto Goizueta and Jack Welch: The wealth builders," *Fortune*, December 11, 1995, pp. 80–94.

[18]Patricia Sellers, "Where Coke goes from here," *Fortune*, October 13, 1997, pp. 88–91.

think about what kind of growth would be possible in a market, and to figure out how to knock down the barriers to attain that growth. He also stated that, like Goizueta, he would remain focused on one business—non-alcoholic beverages. During his time as president of Coca-Cola USA, he spent every Saturday morning for a year learning marketing from Sergio Zyman, who went on to become Coca-Cola's global marketing boss. He added the position of chief learning officer and encouraged its first incumbent, Judith A. Rosenblum, to turn the company into "a learning organization." His goal was to capture all of the growth in Coca-Cola's markets.

Upon Goizueta's unexpected death due to cancer in 1997, Doug Ivester was the heir apparent and became CEO. However, it was rumoured that his appointment was not supported by Don Keough.[19]

Douglas Ivester as CEO of Coca-Cola

As CEO, Ivester made some important changes in positions. His competitor for the CEO position, E. Neville Isdell, was moved to head a bottler in Britain. Carl Ware, a senior vice-president, was demoted. Don Keough, who, after his retirement, had continued attending Coca-Cola board meetings as Goizueta's consultant, lost his consulting contract and his place at the boardroom table.

Ivester's personality, like Goizueta's, was seen as reserved on the surface. Yet, despite wide recognition for being brilliant, Ivester seemed to lack some of Goizueta's characteristics. Ivester was known for an obsession with a rational and orderly way of operating. He was considered arrogant and insecure, blind to his own weaknesses and not forthcoming in soliciting advice. He placed less emphasis on Goizueta's tradition of having almost daily chats with directors. During his reign, Coca-Cola alienated European regulators and several executives at major customers, such as Disney and Wal-Mart. Some major bottlers, including Coca-Cola Enterprises, were also alienated. In time, he became more and more obsessed with controlling the most minor details of every operation. To make matters worse, the Asian currency crisis occurred during his reign and affected Coca-Cola's business. The U.S. dollar, which had remained weak for a long time and had contributed to Coca-Cola's earnings, strengthened during Ivester's tenure.[20]

As CEO, continuing on in his earlier approach, Douglas Ivester was known for working seven days a week and nearly all the time. On visiting Shanghai as CEO, he was known to have walked out on the streets while the "World of Coca-Cola" travelling multi-media exhibit was going on. Ivester walked into little stores and asked why Coke was not prominently displayed on shelves and noted where fountain machines were turned off. He was known to have done similar walks as president of Coca-Cola USA, going from store to store and even identifying the hairdressing salons and laundromats where Coke couldn't be found. On one Saturday morning, he drove from Atlanta to Rome, Georgia, with a video crew to identify missed opportunities along the way.[21] He encouraged people to avoid doing things sequentially and pushed for "viral growth." As an example, he suggested if you opened offices in China, not to open them one at a time, but to have each new office assist in opening several more.[22]

---

[19]Betsy Morris, "The real story," *Fortune*, May 31, 2004, pp. 84–98.

[20]Ibid.

[21]Betsy Morris, "Doug is it," *Fortune*, May 25, 1998, pp. 71–84.

[22]Ibid.

Ivester was known to be a CEO who communicated with people at all levels and ignored hierarchy. He wanted employees to think of themselves as knowledge workers, to think of their office as the information they carried with them, supported by technology that would allow them to work anywhere. With Ivester, business planning was not done annually, but became an ongoing discussion involving top executives. Ivester focused on getting lots of information, aided by technology, which he believed was necessary for real-time decision-making. Although past CEOs had focused on letting executives find their own solutions, Ivester involved himself in finding solutions for them. Ivester explained his involvement by stating that in such a fast and complicated world, a CEO could not run a business by sitting in an office. To many, this approach sounded like micromanaging.[23]

Jack Stahl, senior vice-president and president of Coca-Cola's North America group, reported that he often got six or seven notes a day from Ivester. And Ivester expected prompt replies to all his communications, including his voice mails. Ivester went without a number two person for about a year, working instead with a flat structure that had 14 senior vice-presidents, including 6 operating heads, reporting to him directly. Ivester took less naturally to the ceremonial nature of his job, remarking to the mayor of Shanghai, "Nice place you have here" on visiting the mayor's opulent meeting room. While he delivered a message to all officials about helping China, he was known to enjoy his time most with his troops in the trenches.[24]

Ivester's thirst for information was rarely satiated and he continued delving into every little detail of the company's worldwide operations. When an executive from Coca-Cola's biggest Mexican bottler talked about tens of thousands of mom-and-pop stores, Ivester jumped in and asked, "So which are they—moms or pops?" The bottler's COO could only muster a weak response: "I think it's more moms than pops, Doug, but I'm not sure."[25]

The downturn in overseas markets, where Coca-Cola derived about three-quarters of its profits, was met head-on as an opportunity to buy bottlers, distribution and rival brands at bargain prices. Ivester was betting that the investments would help fuel growth in the future. Whereas Goizueta had handled international operations from a distance, Ivester worked 14-hour days and stayed in contact with executives worldwide through e-mail, voice mail and pagers even as the business grew in size and complexity around the world.

Under Ivester, the era of exclusive contracts in the soft drink industry became very aggressive. Coca-Cola and Pepsi pursued such contracts not only in restaurant chains, but in other locations, such as schools and convenience stores. A marketing consultant for Cadbury Schweppes remarked, "Coke is the No. 1 icon in the world; it has to be a good corporate citizen. They are not in a situation where they can create shareholder value by being a bully."

Whereas Goizueta had focused on stockholders, Ivester spent his energies on customers: "If you focus on the customer, the business will prosper, and if the business prospers, the stock will eventually be priced right."[26] However, when dozens of Belgian school children fell sick after drinking Coca-Cola products, Ivester maintained

---

[23]Ibid.

[24]Ibid.

[25]"Man on the spot," *Business Week*, May 3, 1999, pp. 142–151.

[26]Ibid.

silence for a week before going to Belgium to apologize. Coca-Cola ultimately recalled 65 million cans due to this incident. When he failed to promote Carl Ware, senior vice-president for African operations and Coca-Cola's top African-American executive, the doors opened for four past and current employees to sue Coca-Cola for racial discrimination.

Ivester took much of the credit for improvements in the bottler system, including the creation of CCE and technological improvements across the company. Some of these claims served to isolate Don Keough, Goizueta's erstwhile president and COO, who was also connected to two powerful Coca-Cola board members, Herbert Allen and Warren Buffet. Keough became the person all constituents, including customers, bottlers and employees, gradually started complaining to.[27]

Commenting on his earlier successes under Goizueta, Ivester had stated, "I look at the business like a chessboard. You always need to be seeing three, four, five moves ahead. Otherwise, your first move can prove fatal." His methodical approach extended to all areas: "I learned that marketing is not a black box," he stated, "marketing can be even more logical than finance. If you ask enough questions and listen closely, you find that people are very logical."[28] He was also reported to have once said, "I know how all the levers work, and I could generate so much cash I could make everybody's head spin." However, after Ivester's more than two years as CEO, Coca-Cola's market value remained stuck at $148 billion, compared with the $147 billion market value when Goizueta had left the helm.[29]

In early December 1999, Ivester flew to Chicago for a regular meeting with McDonald's executives and, during the same trip, also had a private meeting with Coca-Cola's two most powerful directors, Warren Buffet and Herbert Allen. The two directors informed Ivester that they had lost faith in his leadership, and it was time for a change. Don Keough, who had been Goizueta's number two person for 12 years as COO and president was said to have played a role in this meeting. Upon retirement in 1993, Keough had remained involved in Coca-Cola as a consultant and later rejoined as a director when Coca-Cola abolished its 74-year age limit for board membership. Keough was chairman at Allen & Co., Herbert Allen's small investment firm housed in Coca-Cola's building in New York.

At only age 52 and after just more than 2 years as the chairman and CEO, Ivester was pushed to retire from the position. On returning from the meeting in Chicago, Ivester publicly announced his departure from Coca-Cola: "After extensive reflection and thought, I have concluded that it is time for me to move on to the next stage of my life and, therefore, to put into place an orderly transition for this great company."[30] In reaction to the news, Coca-Cola's share price, which had already lagged the American stock market by 30 per cent over the previous 2 years, fell 12 per cent in 2 days. This drop was quite a contrast for investors who had seen the stock price rise over 5,800 per cent during Goizueta's 16-year tenure.[31] During Ivester's tenure, the stock price had dropped 12.3 per cent (see Exhibits 1 and 2).

---

[27]Betsy Morris, "The real story," *Fortune*, May 31, 2004, pp. 84–98.

[28]Patricia Sellers, "How Coke is kicking Pepsi's can," *Fortune*, October 28, 1996, pp. 70–84.

[29]Betsy Morris and Patricia Sellers, "What really happened at Coke–Doug Ivester was a demon for information," *Fortune*, January 10, 2000, pp. 114–116.

[30]"Coke CEO stepping down after difficult tenure," *CBC News*, December 6, 1999, http://www.cbc.ca/money/story/1999/12/06/coke991206.html, retrieved April 19, 2008.

[31]"New Doug, old tricks," *The Economist*, December 11, 1999, p. 55.

DOUGLAS DAFT. ENJOY.

Background

The next CEO of Coca-Cola, Douglas Daft, was born in 1943, in Cessnock, New South Wales, Australia. He received a bachelor of arts degree with a major in mathematics from the University of New England in Armidale, New South Wales. He later received a post-graduate degree in administration from the University of New South Wales.

Daft was a first-generation college student, being the first in his family to attend university. He later recalled that the opportunity had led him to develop a passion for lifelong learning about the world and different cultures. In an interview, he mentioned his profound respect for the differences and similarities of people and his experiences of cultural and intellectual diversity across Singapore, Tokyo and Beijing, which shaped him for leadership roles at Coca-Cola, one of the most international companies in the world.[32]

Daft started at Coca-Cola as a planning officer in the Sydney (Australia) office in 1969. He progressed through the company, holding positions of increasing responsibility, and became vice-president of Coca-Cola Far East Ltd. in 1982. Daft was named president of the North Pacific Division and president of Coca-Cola (Japan) Co., Ltd. in 1988. In 1991, he moved to Coca-Cola's Atlanta headquarters as president of the Pacific Group, with responsibilities including the Africa Group, the Middle and Far East Group and the Schweppes Beverage Division. He was elected president and COO in December 1999.

Douglas Daft as CEO of Coca-Cola

Daft was preparing for retirement in Australia when he was brought in to replace Ivester. It was said that Daft neither aspired to, nor was groomed for, the CEO job and was "an accidental CEO."[33] Daft had spent most of his 30 years with the company in Asia, and had succeeded as president of Coca-Cola in Japan, one of the company's most difficult and largest markets outside the United States.

Daft's personality was described as low-key, unassuming, media-shy and not communication friendly. He was known for a consensus-driven style and for avoiding conflict. He began by making changes that were seen as culturally new, such as removing flags that had traditionally flown at Atlanta headquarters: the American flag, the Georgia flag, the Coca-Cola flag and a flag to honour the visitor of the day, generally a bottler or customer. He called upon a feng shui consultant to make interior decoration changes and to rearrange telephones so that the cords would not coil in the wrong direction. Life-sized ceramic roosters were installed in the offices of Daft and two senior executives.[34]

In his first few weeks, Daft started the process of cutting 5,200 jobs to reduce costs. However, these cuts were not seen as steering the company in a clear strategic direction. Whereas Ivester's mantra had been "Think global—act local," Daft's vision leaned more toward "Think local—act local." This mindset reflected his experience

---

[32]Interview with Doug Daft, Institute of International Education. IIENetwork.org, http://iienetwork.org/?p=29253, accessed on June 21, 2008.

[33]Patricia Sellers, "Who's in charge here?" *Fortune*, December 24, 2001, pp. 76–80, 83, 86.

[34]Betsy Morris, "The real story," *Fortune*, May 31, 2004, pp. 84–98.

away from headquarters, where he had developed the idea that bureaucracy at head-quarters was a problem. Daft challenged Coca-Cola's matrix system, which, created and nurtured by Goizueta, had ensured that the finance, marketing, technical, law and quality control departments at headquarters networked with and controlled the corresponding departments in other countries. Daft's approach was to get rid of corporate bureaucracy and give more decision-making power to the field managers.

Under Daft's tenure, Don Keough's advice and attendance at board meetings was again welcomed. Under Daft's leadership and Keough's approval, several key executives who had served under Ivester were ousted. Turnover among senior managers during Daft's tenure was severe. In just more than four years, Coca-Cola had two new marketing heads, two new European operations heads and new management in the company's human resources departments and in the North America, Asia and Latin America divisions.[35]

Daft also built the company's forays into the fast-growing area of non-carbonated drinks, including bottled water and juices,[36] exemplified by Daft's attempts to buy Quaker Oats, maker of Gatorade, in 2000. Although Quaker Oats broke off talks with Pepsi and Danone, in the end the Coca-Cola board did not pass the deal. Reportedly, directors Warren Buffet and Peter Ueberroth objected, seeing the exchange of Coca-Cola's 10 per cent stock for Quaker Oats as too risky. A joint venture with Procter & Gamble Co. (P&G) was created to develop synergies between Coca-Cola's Minute Maid juices and distribution prowess with P&G's potato chip and juice brands. Ideas included developing a half-size can of P&G's Pringle's potato chips for distribution through Coca-Cola's machines and other channels. A similar deal with Nestlé was crafted to develop tea and coffee drinks using Nestlé's research and development labs. Historically, Coca-Cola had not succeeded in using its distribution and marketing to develop a presence in the high-margin premium beverage market dominated by Snapple, AriZona, SoBe and Gatorade.

These changes epitomized Daft's approach as a passionate, idea-a-minute manager, building upon intuitions from his Asia-Pacific experience. His approach contrasted sharply with Ivester's numbers-based accountant's approach to decision making. At a retreat in San Francisco, Daft asked for new ideas from 2 dozen Coca-Cola executives and, on the spot, funded 4 of the ideas with $250,000 each. Under Daft's tenure, scientists and marketers united to build new products ranging from calcium-fortified waters to vitamin-enriched drinks bearing Disney characters' names.

Coca-Cola's advertising was also overhauled, because the "Always" campaign had "lost people, lost humanity and become clinical," according to Coca-Cola's marketing director, Stephen C. Jones. In a new move, Coca-Cola began to allow bottlers to customize promotions to local events. Although Ivester had opposed tie-ins with movies, Daft made a deal with Warner Bros. Entertainment Inc. to co-market movies, such as the *Harry Potter* series, around the world.[37]

Daft announced another major step in his restructuring when he let go president and COO, Jack L. Stahl. Steve Heyer, formerly president and COO at Turner Broadcasting, was brought in as the new president. Subsequently, Daft used this time to be out in the field to improve relations with bottlers. However, Daft remained known for making quick decisions and sometimes being unsure about them later. Coca-Cola's bottlers in Colombia had faced violence, and Daft announced at an awards dinner in

[35]Ibid.

[36]"Repairing the Coke machine," *Business Week*, March 19, 2001, p. 86.

[37]Ibid.

Washington that he would have general counsel Deval Patrick investigate. However, the decision was abruptly reversed four months later, and an announcement about Patrick's resignation leaked out. At an annual meeting, stockholders were distributed leaflets by demonstrators who shouted, "Coca-Cola, killer Cola, toxic Cola, racist Cola." None of the directors faced the crowd, and Daft, seemingly losing control, unwittingly urged a child questioner to "Drink Coke, Sam," later amending the line by saying, "That is, if your parents let you."[38]

At the same meeting, Keough commented on Coca-Cola's succession plan, saying that the company would find the best candidate for the job. A very public search was launched, which included talks with Jim Kilts, CEO of Gillette, and Jack Welch, the retired CEO of GE. During Daft's tenure as CEO, Coke's stock price increased 9.15 per cent (see Exhibits 1 and 2).

THE ISDELL SIDE OF LIFE

Background

Coca-Cola's next CEO, Edward Neville Isdell, was born in Downpatrick, Northern Ireland, in 1943. He moved to Zambia in childhood and later completed a bachelor's degree in social science at the University of Capetown, South Africa. In 1966, Isdell joined Coca-Cola through the local bottling company in Zambia. Moving up on the bottling side of operations, in 1972 he became general manager of the Johannesburg bottler, the largest Coca-Cola bottler in Africa. In 1980, he became the regional manager for Australia, and the following year became the president of the bottling joint venture between Coca-Cola and San Miguel Corporation in the Philippines. Isdell was subsequently credited with turning around and renewing the entire Coca-Cola business in the Philippines.

Isdell's international career continued with a stint in Germany, starting in 1985 as president of the company's Central European division. He moved up the ranks of the company in 1989, when he was elected senior vice-president and concurrently became president of the Northeast Europe/Africa Group (later to become the Northeast Europe/Middle East group in 1992). During this phase, Isdell oversaw the company's expansion into new markets, such as India, Middle East, Eastern Europe and the Soviet Union. He became president of the Greater Europe Group in 1995.

Isdell subsequently moved to Great Britain in 1998 as CEO of Coca-Cola Beverages PLC in Great Britain. Under his watch, that company merged with Hellenic Bottling and resulted in the largest Coca-Cola bottler of that time, Coca-Cola Hellenic Bottling Company (HBC). He left Coca-Cola in 2001 to form his own investment company in Barbados.[39]

Isdell as CEO of Coca-Cola

Doug Daft's retirement announcement in February 2004 was followed by two months of speculation regarding his successor. Some wondered whether an outsider such as Gillette's president and CEO, James M. Kilts, might be the likely candidate. Instead, E. Neville Isdell was named the new chairman and CEO. Interestingly, Isdell had been

[38]Betsy Morris, "The real story," *Fortune*, May 31, 2004, pp. 84–98.
[39]The Coca-Cola Company website, http://www.thecoca-colacompany.com/ourcompany/board.html, accessed February 15, 2008.

passed over for the top job in 1997 (in favour of Douglas Ivester), despite having been Keough's preference at the time.

On accepting the position, Isdell said:

> I am both proud and humbled to be given the opportunity to help write the next chapter in this illustrious company's history. I appreciate the importance of this position and the trust placed in me by the board of directors. We are all grateful to Doug Daft for his enormous contributions and look forward to building upon the tremendous foundation he and his team have built. I am excited to get started and help shape our future.[40]

During Isdell's CEO tenure, Coca-Cola's profits rose steadily, in particular from international operations. Right at the start, Isdell had laid out his plans, based on his belief in significant future growth for the Coca-Cola brand. Some growth was expected to come from new markets, such as China and India, while further growth was still possible in the United States and Europe. Keough let his confidence in Isdell be known, mentioning that it was the first time in 119 years that the company would have a CEO who had worked on both sides of the system, referring to Isdell's experience of being involved both as a bottler and concentrate person and his experience on working 5 continents.[41] Under Isdell's leadership, Coke's stock price increased 12.9 percent. Overall, the 3 CEOs who had served after Goizueta's untimely death in 1997 had increased Coke's stock price 11.6 per cent.

EPILOGUE

In December 2007, Isdell announced that he would step down from the CEO position in July 2008 to be replaced by Muhtar Kent, the company's COO. However, Isdell would remain chairman of the board until the company's annual meeting in 2009, splitting the position of CEO and chairman at Coca-Cola for the first time. To questions on why Isdell chose this time to announce his departure, he said, "Because it's the right time. I've been working on succession since Day 1". Although a national search had been launched when Doug Daft left, there would be no doubt as to who the next CEO would be this time.

Commenting on the news, John Sicher, a beverage industry expert, remarked, "Kent understands the company and the system literally as well as anybody in the world and better than most." Deutsche Bank analyst Marc Greenberg said, "Kent has played a formative role in shaping the current course—'steady as she goes' is likely the mantra." In the position of COO, Kent saw major strategic initiatives undertaken, such as the $4.1 billion acquisition of Glacéau in 2007, strengthening Coca-Cola's position with new brands, such as vitamin water.

At the time of this announcement, Kent mentioned that he had no immediate plans to change any leadership roles but that some scope was available for fine-tuning management. He pointed out that he knew he faced challenges: "We have confidence the United States has growth left in it," he said. Regarding the bottling issues, he added, "We were at each other's throats with our bottlers a year ago—we are aligned now." [42]

---

[40]The Coca-Cola Co. 8-K report filed with SEC on 5/5/04. http://www.secinfo.com/dkrf.12f.d.htm, accessed on June 21, 2008.

[41]Betsy Morris, "The real story," *Fortune*, May 31, 2004, pp. 84–98.

[42]"Coca-Cola's CEO Isdell to step down," Associated Press, MSNBC, December 6, 2007; http://www.msnbc.msn.com/id/22127700/, accessed June 22, 2008.

As the plane headed towards Atlanta and Coca-Cola's corporate headquarters, Kent looked out at the Atlantic Ocean and thought about the company's previous illustrious leaders, their times and strategies, and wondered how he would take charge and lead the company into the future.

EXHIBIT 1   CEO Succession Timeline and Stock Price Performance at Coca-Cola

CEO	Period of Tenure	Adjusted Monthly Closing Stock Price at Beginning Month of Tenure*	Adjusted Monthly Closing Stock Price at Ending Month of Tenure*
Robert Goizueta	March 1981 to October 1997	$ 0.78	$46.23
Douglas Ivester	October 1997 to February 2000	$46.23	$40.54
Douglas Daft	February 2000 to February 2004	$40.54	$44.25
E. Neville Isdell	May 2004 to June 2008	$45.71	$51.61**
Muhtar Kent	July 2008 to present		

*Closing price adjusted for dividends and stock splits
**As of June 30, 2008

EXHIBIT 2   Coca-Cola (KO) Stock Market Performance Compared to the Dow Jones (DJI) and Standard & Poor's (GSPC) Indices

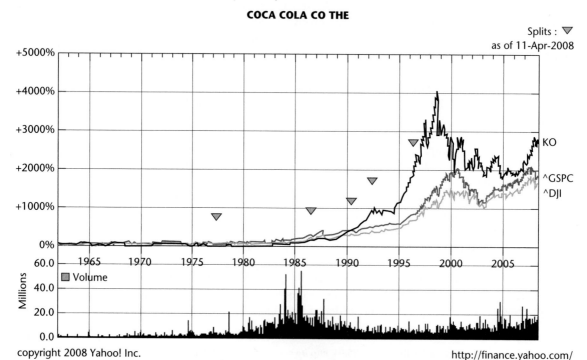

Source: Yahoo Finance website, accessed April 11, 2008. Reproduced with permission of Yahoo! Inc. YAHOO! and the YAHOO! logo are trademarks of Yahoo! Inc. ©2007 by Yahoo! Inc.

EXHIBIT 3 Graphical Comparison of Net Profit / Sales and Net Profit / Equity During the Goizueta and Ivester Time Frame

Net Profit / Sales (%)

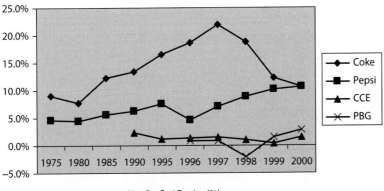

Net Profit / Equity (%)

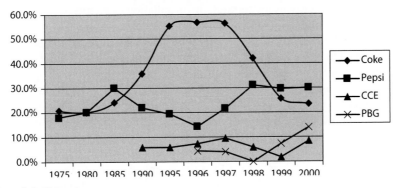

CCE: Coca-Cola Enterprise

PBG: Pepsi Bottling Group

Source: David B. Yoffie, "Cola wars continue: Coke and Pepsi in the twenty-first century," July 30, 2002, Harvard Business School, Exhibit 4, p. 19.

CASE 37

The GE Energy Management Initiative (A)

Raj Bhatt, business development manager for GE Canada[1] had recently met with executives from GE Supply, a U.S.-based distribution arm of GE Industrial, to discuss new business opportunities in Energy Efficiency. The Energy Efficiency industry focused on the reduction of energy usage through the installation of energy-efficient technologies. Bhatt had recently gained pre-qualification for GE Canada to bid on a $1 billion program to install energy-efficient technologies in all federal government buildings. He was confident that GE's expertise in lighting, motors, appliances and financing was sufficient to win at least some of the contracts. Furthermore, he saw the program as a stepping stone to building a GE business to service the Energy Efficiency needs of a range of clients.

The GE Supply executives informed Bhatt that they had already established a position in the U.S. Energy Efficiency industry, through a joint venture with a new Energy Service Company (ESCo), and had retained the services of a full-time consultant to develop the business. An ESCo, or Energy Service Company, developed, installed and financed projects designed to improve the energy efficiency and maintenance costs for facilities over a long time period, typically 7 to 10 years. ESCos generally acted as project developers for a wide range of tasks and assumed the technical and performance risks associated with the project.

The GE Supply executives were interested in the federal buildings program that Bhatt had been working on, but felt that it would be more efficiently run as a division of GE Supply, rather than as a locally managed Canadian venture. The meeting posed a dilemma for Bhatt. He was encouraged by the level of interest that already existed for Energy Efficiency within GE, but at the same time held certain misgivings about

Ken Mark revised this case (originally prepared by Joseph N. Fry and Julian Birkinshaw) solely to provide material for class discussion. The authors do not intend to illustrate either effective or ineffective handling of a managerial situation. The authors may have disguised certain names and other identifying information to protect confidentiality.

Richard Ivey School of Business
The University of Western Ontario

[1]The authors have disguised certain names, industry data and other identifying information.

folding the federal buildings program into GE Supply's nascent business. Specifically, he was concerned that a lot of interesting Energy Efficiency opportunities existed in Canada, which a U.S.-focused business would not be in a position to exploit. Bhatt left the meeting uncertain how to proceed.

GENERAL ELECTRIC (GE)

GE was one of the most respected firms in the world. From the early days of Thomas Edison, it had grown to be a diversified 54-business corporation. When Jack Welch became chief executive officer (CEO) in the early eighties, he made a series of sweeping changes. The corporate planning department was abolished, some layers of management were eliminated, and the concepts of empowerment and customer focus became the new drivers behind GE's activities. In the course of a series of divestments, acquisitions and amalgamations, GE's major criterion for holding on to a business was that it was number one or number two worldwide in its chosen industry.

Welch retired in 2001, and GE's new CEO, Jeffrey Immelt, in an effort to continue GE's tradition of innovation, implemented his own changes. Immelt made significant changes to the portfolio, divesting slow-growth businesses like insurance, and, through acquisition, he has created new businesses for GE including wind power, water and process technologies, security and life sciences. In addition, he reorganized GE into six core businesses (GE Commercial Finance, GE Consumer Finance, GE Healthcare, GE Industrial, GE Infrastructure and NBC Universal), each of which contained several units. These units were further subdivided into a number of divisions. GE Lighting was a unit of GE Industrial business, and GE Supply was a corporate business that reported directly into GE headquarters. Immelt put more emphasis on technological innovation and marketing, as two key drivers of success.

As a *Fortune* article put it, "What might look like a repudiation of Welch's legacy, though, is Welch's legacy. It was Welch who picked Jeff Immelt. And it was Welch who allegedly gave him the same instructions that his own predecessor, Reginald Jones, had given him 20 years earlier: Blow it up."[2]

Each business worked from a U.S. head office and was charged with global responsibility for its operations. This structure, which by-passed the traditional country organizations, was intended to give priority to the global demands of the businesses, rather than to national interests. International operations were structured under a vice-chairman, international, but the reality under a so-called direct-connect model was that the operating authority in each country was held by the relevant global business unit. Typically, this meant that general management roles in country operations were eliminated and that business leaders or functional managers of specific businesses reported to their headquarters in the United States, rather than through their country organization. For example, the marketing manager of GE Lighting's Canadian operations reported directly to the vice-president of marketing at GE Lighting group headquarters.

GE Canada

The shift to global management had a major impact on GE's Canadian business. Historically, GE Canada operated as a "miniature replica" of its parent company; most

---

[2]Jerry Useem, "Another boss another revolution," *Fortune*, April 4, 2004.

businesses and all functions were represented in Canada, and typically, the manufacturing plants made a full line of products primarily for the Canadian market but with some exporting possibilities. The Canadian CEO was fully responsible for the profitability of the Canadian operating divisions. This changed dramatically under the direct-connect structure implemented in the late 1980s.

With the globalization of GE businesses, the CEO of GE Canada had a vastly different role as all operations reported straight to their U.S. divisional bosses, each of whom had profit and loss responsibility. The CEO of GE Canada was directly responsible only for the activities of a very small number of employees, such as vice-presidents in finance, environmental affairs, legal, human resources and government affairs. These managers were responsible for all the uniquely Canadian issues that cropped up, such as new legislation, tax accounting, government grants and so on. In addition, there was a small business development group, consisting of three managers. Traditionally, this group had been involved in feasibility studies and new market development for the business units in Canada. Following the shift to a "direct-connect" structure, the role had become primarily one of looking for opportunities to leverage the strengths of Canadian activities on a global basis. They were also concerned with identifying new business opportunities in Canada. Bhatt, one of the business development managers, explained:

> Canada is a relatively small marketplace. Consequently, most U.S.-based business leaders have a limited awareness of the opportunities here because they have either a U.S. or a global focus. The role of business development is to attempt to identify investment or market opportunities here that they might find valuable.

There was some discussion among business development managers over the extent to which they should actively "sell" business opportunities to the GE businesses. Some felt that a proactive strategy of promoting Canadian opportunities was appropriate; others preferred to investigate only those cases where business development's involvement had been solicited. The recent decision to promote the vice-president of business development, but not replace him, added further to the uncertainty over the group's role.

Raj Bhatt

Bhatt was only 29. He had worked at GE for just one year, following a successful period at Northern Telecom and an MBA at the Richard Ivey School of Business. Bhatt stated:

> Business development is quite a challenging experience. There are lots of good opportunities in Canada, but it is sometimes difficult to achieve the level of interest and buy-in necessary to attract the appropriate attention. The Oakville lighting plant, a global manufacturing mandate, received a planned $144 million investment and is certainly our biggest success so far, but there have been a lot of ideas that failed to materialize.

The business development manager typically held that post for only two years, after which he or she was expected to take a line position in one of the businesses. Bhatt had been given a number of attractive options, but had turned them down because he was afraid that his involvement was critical to a number of projects. Specifically, he was concerned that the Energy Efficiency business opportunity he had championed up to now would die because no one else had the knowledge of, or the enthusiasm for, that particular opportunity.

ENERGY EFFICIENCY

Energy Efficiency covered the multitude of ways that energy usage could be optimized, including conservation, use of efficient equipment and off-peak usage. Energy Efficiency was originally conceived in the early 1970s as a response to rising oil prices. It recently saw a resurgence due to the environmental movement and the increasing need for cost competitiveness in the late eighties. Although strongly motivated by public opinion and government pressure, Energy Efficiency initiatives were usually sponsored by the energy supply utilities. They recognized that they could more effectively keep their investment down by reducing demand than by building expensive new power stations. There were also obvious benefits to consumers (in reduced costs) and to the environment.

The growth in utility-sponsored programs for Energy Efficiency was responsible for the formation of many Energy Service Companies (ESCos). Typically, ESCos offered the following services: [3]

- develop, design and finance energy efficiency projects;
- install and maintain the energy efficient equipment involved;
- measure, monitor and verify the project's energy savings; and
- assume the risk that the project will save the amount of energy guaranteed.

These services were bundled into the project's cost and were repaid through the dollar savings generated. ESCo projects were comprehensive, which meant that the ESCo employed a wide array of cost-effective measures to achieve energy savings. These measures often included the following: high efficiency lighting, high efficiency heating and air conditioning, efficient motors and variable speed drives and centralized energy management systems. What set ESCos apart from other firms that offered energy efficiency, such as consulting firms and equipment contractors, was the concept of performance-based contracting.

For ESCos, the first step in securing business was to respond to a request for proposal from a potential customer. ESCos were typically selected, or short-listed, and invited to bid on projects depending on their track record or reputation. The next step was to conduct a preliminary audit to estimate the investments and savings that could be generated from an energy efficiency project, a task which required significant expertise on the part of the ESCo. Then, detailed engineering helped confirm savings estimates. When an ESCo undertook a project, the company's compensation, and often the project's financing, were directly linked to the amount of energy that was actually saved. Thus, throughout the life of the project, energy savings were closely monitored.

Typically, the comprehensive energy efficiency retrofits inherent in ESCo projects required a large initial capital investment and offered a relatively long payback period. The customer's debt payments were tied to the energy savings offered under the project, so that the customer paid for the capital improvement with the money that came out of the difference between pre-installation and post-installation energy use and other costs. For this reason, ESCos led the effort to verify, rather than estimate energy savings. Most performance-based energy efficiency projects included the maintenance of all or some portion of the new high-efficiency equipment over the life of the contract, with the cost of this ongoing maintenance folded into the overall cost of the project.

Another critical component of every Energy Efficiency project was the education of customers about their own energy use patterns in order to develop an "energy

---

[3] http://www.naesco.org/about/esco.htm, accessed February 24, 2006.

efficiency partnership" between the ESCo and the customer. A primary purpose of this partnership was to help the customer understand how its energy use was related to the business that they conducted. Included in the ancillary services provided in a typical performance-based Energy Efficiency contract were the removal and disposal of hazardous materials from the customer's facility. When, for example, ballasts that contained PCBs and fluorescent light tubes that contained traces of mercury were replaced, the old equipment had to be disposed of as hazardous waste. Upgrades to heating, air conditioning and ventilation systems could involve the removal of asbestos and would also be properly disposed of by the ESCo.

The ESCo Industry in Canada

The Canadian ESCo industry was among the most advanced in the world. Both federal and provincial governments had active energy-management programs to promote "green" initiatives, and had targeted Energy Efficiency as a critical industry. Ontario Hydro and Quebec Hydro had budgets for Energy Efficiency of $800 million and $300 million respectively, in comparison to the CDN$1.5 billion budget for all U.S. utilities combined.

As a result of the utilities' involvement, the Canadian ESCo industry was growing very rapidly and one estimate put the total market potential in the billions of dollars.

Three major segments could be identified, each accounting for approximately one-third of the total volume. They were commercial, which consisted primarily of office buildings, hospitals and other public buildings; industrial, which consisted of factories and production plants; and residential, which consisted of single-family dwellings. So far, the commercial sector had been the most rewarding to ESCos, largely due to the similarities between (for example) one hospital and another. Industrial also had potential, but required knowledge of the specific process technology used in each case.

Over the past decade, the ESCo industry in Canada had experienced mixed fortunes, as companies struggled to understand the dynamics of the market. Lack of technical and risk management experience, flawed contracts, lack of financial strength and energy price collapses had all led to very low levels of profitability among major players. The recent upsurge of interest in Energy Efficiency, however, had pushed the industry onto a more steady footing. Furthermore, a shake-out had occurred, leaving only a handful of serious competitors in Canada.

ESCo Strategies

ESCos saw themselves as undertaking three useful functions with commercial and industrial customers. First, they could undertake energy audits of client sites and advise what forms of energy management were most appropriate. Second, they could engineer and provide access to a wide range of energy-efficient technologies that would normally be hard to get hold of. Third, they could install new energy-efficient equipment, under a performance contract or similar. In the Canadian industry, there were several hundred consulting engineers that participated in energy audits, but only seven "full-service" ESCos that undertook all three functions.

Performance contracting offered great potential return to ESCos, but also a high degree of risk. Following an installation, it took between 5 and 10 years before the financial benefits were realized. ESCos were paid at the time of installation by their financing partners, who recovered their costs over the lifetime of the project, but in the event that the project was badly estimated, the shortfall in revenue would have to be made up by the ESCo. Access to capital at a reasonable cost was thus critical. Some ESCos had parent companies with deep pockets. The audit and supply functions, while less lucrative, were important elements of the ESCo's business because they established legitimacy in the eyes of the customer. Many commercial clients were extremely skeptical of the estimated energy savings provided by ESCos, but if they agreed to an energy audit, there was a greater likelihood they could be sold on the merits of an installation. The credibility of the guarantee provided by the ESCo was thus of great importance.

THE GE ENERGY MANAGEMENT INITIATIVE

The Initial Opportunity

As GE business development manager, Raj Bhatt received a communication from the federal government inviting ESCos to seek to be prequalified for the implementation of performance contracts in 50,000 federal buildings in Canada. The program had a potential total value of $1 billion, which was to be split into a number of smaller contracts. Bhatt was struck by the potential fit between GE's areas of expertise and the requirements of the program. First, GE's reputation gave it a significant competitive advantage over lesser-known firms. Second, within the GE organization lay most of the components required for the energy efficiency project. ESCos had to be able to provide energy-efficient lighting, motors and controls and provide financing for the project; GE was a leading supplier of many of the required products and had a large financing division. Thus, unlike rival firms that would have to form consortia between electrical and financing companies, GE had much of the needed expertise in house. However, Bhatt also realized that all GE divisions—such as Lighting and Finance—served external as well as internal customers. It was very likely that GE divisions would be approaching, or be approached by, other ESCos seeking to start up business relationships.

What GE could not do in house, it could subcontract. For example, the engineering expertise required to estimate detailed energy savings for an entire building, over a long period of time, did not exist in house, as of yet. To manage outside contractors and, indeed, the entire energy savings project, strong project management expertise was required.

Bhatt submitted a proposal for the federal buildings program and, along with a number of other consortia, achieved "prequalification", meaning the right to bid on subsequent contracts that fell under the federal buildings umbrella. This success underlined the magnitude of the opportunity that GE was facing in the ESCo industry. Rather than limiting GE's involvement to the one-off federal buildings program, Bhatt thought there was potential for an ongoing GE business to meet the expected surge in demand for energy management services. He began to think through the best way of proceeding.

The GE Canada Executive Meeting

Bhatt's first move was to meet with the GE Canada executive group and get their reaction to his idea for an Energy Management Business. Attending were Matthew Meyer, chairman and CEO; Mike Kozinsky, vice-president of finance; and Scott Larwood, vice-president of government relations. Larwood had already been heavily involved in the federal buildings program and was in favour of Bhatt's proposal.

Bhatt:	GE Canada is very well-positioned to start an Energy Management business. We have a broader range of relevant products and services than any other ESCo, and the Ontario and Quebec Hydro programs are among the most advanced in the world.
Kozinsky (Finance)	But this is a systems business. We have never been very good at systems implementation.
Bhatt:	I realize that we may have to find partners. We are working with a small ESCo on the federal buildings project which will do all the installation work. We can identify suitable future partners as things progress.
Kozinsky:	But what is our experience in being a prime contractor? This seems to be very different from any business we have been involved with before.
Larwood: (Government Relations)	That's not quite true. The Apparatus Technical Service (ATS) business in GE Power Systems manages service contracts, and there is a lot of project experience in the States.
Meyer: (CEO)	But there seems to be a considerable risk here. What happens if we pull down a load of asbestos when we're changing a lighting system? GE is an obvious target for legal action.
Kozinsky:	And you stated earlier that there is some downside financial risk if the performance contract does not yield the expected savings.
Bhatt:	True, but the estimates are conservative. The overall financial projections are very promising, and involve very little upfront cost. Apart from the salaries of three or four employees, most costs are on a contract-by-contract basis.
Meyer:	Have you given any thought as to how this business would fit into the GE structure?
Bhatt:	One of the strengths of GE Canada is that it already taps into all the different businesses. I would like to see the Energy Management business based in Canada, and drawing from the other GE businesses as required.

Bhatt received a lot of questioning and cautioning on various aspects of the proposal, but there was consensus at the end that the project was worth pursuing. Meyer recommended that Bhatt investigate the level of interest in the U.S. businesses and at the corporate level before any formal proposal was put together.

The GE Supply Opportunity

In discussion with U.S. colleagues, Bhatt discovered that three U.S. divisions were attempting to establish their own ESCo-like initiatives. Two of them were at about the same stage of development as Bhatt. The third, GE Supply, was more advanced. They had been working with an ESCo for a number of months and had retained a well-connected consultant to advise them. Up to now, the ESCo had assumed all the risk, with GE providing its name, its products and some servicing expertise, but the division was planning to create a joint venture with the ESCo in the near future.

On hearing about the GE Supply initiative, Bhatt went to Connecticut to visit the GE Supply executives to discuss their respective plans. Present at the meeting were Bhatt, Doug Taylor, CEO of GE Supply, and Fred Allen, manager of the Energy Management business.

Taylor:
(CEO)
Last week we signed a formal alliance agreement with Wetherwell Inc. to run for 18 months. We are now actively looking for contracts.

Allen:
But the U.S. market requires some education. How is the market in Canada?

Bhatt:
There is a very promising opportunity that we are working on right now. Basically, the federal government is looking for bidders on a $1 billion program, and we have already gained prequalification.

Allen:
That beats anything we've got down here. I think there could be some real opportunities for us to work together. We have gained quite a lot of experience over the past 12 months, and combined with your market, we could have a winning combination.

Bhatt:
I am certainly interested in exploring opportunities. How do you see a Canadian Energy Management business fitting with your business?

Taylor:
We could manage the Canadian business out of our office here.

Bhatt:
That causes me some concern. The business relies on close coordination with utilities and government bodies, and a strong local presence would definitely be necessary. I must admit, we considered that management of at least part of the business should be in Canada. The opportunities in Canada are unmatched.

Taylor:
Well, there is some strength to your argument, but I don't see why this business should not fit the normal model.

Bhatt left the meeting feeling that there was a lot of work left to do in order to convince the GE Supply executives that a strong Canadian presence was needed. The opportunity that the federal buildings initiative provided could be the first in a series of lucrative contracts for GE Canada. On the flight home, he analyzed the situation and considered his next steps.

IMAX: Larger Than Life[1]

FLASHBACK 2004

In Daytona, Florida, John watched a racecar going at more than 100 miles per hour crash into a concrete barrier. John ducked to escape the debris that appeared to be flying straight at him. A few moments later, John was virtually within a racecar, next to the driver, zooming at more than 120 miles per hour around the racetrack. For the next half an hour, John experienced, in three dimensions and on a larger-than-life scale, crashing cars, dizzying turns, efficient pit crews, shining metal, burning rubber, swirling gas fumes and screaming fans. Finally, as the overhead lights at the theatre gradually lit up, the audience sitting around John started applauding. John had just witnessed a screening of the IMAX movie *NASCAR*.

NASCAR set a box-office record as an original IMAX 3D film with the highest grossing opening weekend and the highest per-screen average. At $21,579, *NASCAR's* per-screen average was higher than that of the weekend's top 10 films.[2] Reports of *NASCAR's* box-office success would have surely pleased Richard Gelfond and Bradley Wechsler, the co-CEOs of IMAX Corporation.

INTRODUCTION

Gelfond and Wechsler had bought IMAX, along with Wasserstein Perella Partners, from the original owners in 1994 for $80 million. They took it public the same year to raise capital to fund IMAX's growth. For investors in IMAX, the years since then had

Richard Ivey School of Business
The University of Western Ontario

---

[1]This case has been written on the basis of published sources only. Consequently, the interpretation and perspectives presented in this case are not necessarily those of IMAX or any of its employees.

[2]IMAX press release, March 14, 2004.

been like a ride on a rollercoaster in the IMAX film *Thrill Ride:* exciting peaks when movies achieved commercial and critical acclaim, and scary drops when analysts questioned whether a niche player such as IMAX would be able to achieve consistent growth or even survive.

NASCAR's success at the box office was evidence that the co-CEOs' efforts to reach a new audience—distinct from those typically attracted to IMAX's educational documentaries—might work. Another movie that was indicative of IMAX's emerging strategy was *The Polar Express*. *The Polar Express* was the first time a Hollywood movie would be released simultaneously in commercial multiplexes and IMAX theatres. *NASCAR* and *The Polar Express* were symbolic of the direction in which Gelfond and Wechsler had pushed the company to achieve faster growth and higher margins. The two-pronged strategy involved expanding the reach of IMAX by (a) going beyond its cloistered museum environments into multiplexes and (b) presenting Hollywood films in IMAX format.

Despite the success of *NASCAR* and *The Polar Express,* IMAX faced several questions about its future:

- Could IMAX thrive as a niche player that made large format films and systems?
- Would increasing the number of Hollywood movies released in IMAX format save the firm or dilute the IMAX brand?
- Should Hollywood movies be released simultaneously in regular and large format?

THE BACKGROUND SCORE

Since the first moving images flickered in a dark theatre, movies have captivated audiences around the world. About the time that people were getting familiar with programming their VCRs and learning to enjoy movies on the small television screen, a small group of people was developing a technology to project movies on giant screens. The idea for IMAX originated in 1967, when the success of a multi-screen theatre system at the Montreal Expo led filmmakers Graeme Ferguson, Robert Kerr and Roman Kroitor to create a large format movie system. IMAX was founded as the only company in the world that was involved in all aspects of large format films. The first IMAX film premiered in 1970 at the Fuji Pavilion in Osaka, Japan.

IMAX was listed on the NASDAQ exchange in 1994 and achieved a market capitalization of $196 million in the first year itself.[3] As of December 12, 2008, market capitalization was down to $125 million. There were about 295 theatres showing IMAX movies in 40 countries, with almost 60 per cent of the theatres in North America.[4] Almost 50 per cent of the theatres were located in museums, aquariums, zoos and other institutions, and about the same percentage had the IMAX 3D technology. The IMAX movie library at the end of 2007 stood at 226 films, some produced by IMAX, many others produced by independent filmmakers or studios such as Time Warner. In 2007/2008, some of the well-known films to be released in IMAX included *Harry Potter and the Order of the Phoenix, Shine a Light*—a film about the Rolling Stones by the famous film director Martin Scorcese—and *The Spiderwick Chronicles.*

---

[3]S. N. Chakravarty, "A really big show," *Institutional Investor*, 35:10, October 2002, p. 20.

[4]Hoover's, www.Hoovers.com

THE IMAX STORY

Scope of IMAX

The company's main sources of revenues were long-term theatre system lease and maintenance agreements, film production and distribution and theatre operations. Given its scope of operations, IMAX could be considered a part of three different industries: Photographic Equipment and Supplies (SIC code 3861), Motion Picture and Video Tape Production (SIC code 7812) and Motion Picture and Video Distribution (SIC code 7822). IMAX was a relatively small firm compared to a rival studio such as Disney/Pixar or a theatre chain such as Regal Entertainment.

In 2007, it generated $59.12 million (51.04 per cent of total revenue) from IMAX systems sales, $36.57 million (31.57 per cent of total revenue) from films and $16.58 million (14.31 per cent of total revenue) from theatre operations.[5] Order trends suggested that newer agreements were for 3D systems. The theatre leases were generally for 10 to 20 years and renewable by the customer. As part of the lease, IMAX advised customers on theatre design, supervised the installation of the system, trained theatre staff and maintained the system.[6]

Inside IMAX

Hardware: The Film Technology IMAX films were printed on films that were 10 times larger than the 35 mm films that were used in traditional multiplexes and were projected on screens that were (on average) 8 stories high (approximately 88 feet) and 120-feet-wide, or in domes that were 81 feet in diameter. Please see Exhibit 1 for a comparison of 35 mm and IMAX film sizes.

IMAX theatres were designed so that projected images stretched up to the peripheral vision of the viewer; thus the viewer was completely immersed in the scene. Each frame of an IMAX film had 15 sprocket holes to guide it through projectors (compared to 4 in each frame of a 35 mm film). The films were projected to screens by IMAX-designed projectors that had special features—a higher shutter speed, rolling loop motion and vacuum to hold the film to the lens.[7] IMAX projectors used 15,000-watt bulbs, whereas the regular 35 mm projectors used bulbs between 3,000–4,000 watts. The projectors were cooled by circulating more than 50,000 cubic feet of air and 9 gallons of distilled water per minute. These features of the IMAX projection system produced images on-screen that were brighter and sharper than those found in conventional movie theatres.

IMAX had developed the skills, knowledge and capabilities to design and assemble the critical elements involved in its projector and camera systems, though most of the components were purchased from vendors with whom it maintained long-term relationships. Strict quality control of components and end products had ensured an average service time of 99.9 per cent for its equipments installed in theatres. Company personnel visited each theatre for servicing the systems; the projection systems were serviced every three months and the audio systems were serviced once a year.

In 2007, IMAX spent almost five per cent of its sales revenue on research and development, and 50 of its 318 employees were involved in it. The company had spent

---

[5]Annual Report, 2007.

[6]Annual Reports.

[7]*Computer-Aided Engineering*, 15:8, 1996, pp. 8–9.

about $12.6 million in R&D in the past 3 years.[8] It had also received grants from Ontario Technology Fund for its R&D, and held 46 patents and had 7 patents pending in the United States.[9] IMAX had successfully developed 3D cameras and projection systems to produce realistic 3D images. The audience used polarized or electronic glasses that split the images for the left and right eye by using liquid crystal shutter lenses that were controlled by an infrared signal and opened and shut 48 times per second in coordination with the projector to create a 3D effect. Another example of the firm's technological capabilities was a lightweight 3D camera that it had developed to shoot a movie about the International Space Station in space. IMAX worked with MSM Design, a small firm owned by Marty and Barbara Mueller, and developed a camera that weighed only 90 pounds, compared to the traditional IMAX 3D cameras that weighed 228 pounds.[10] IMAX 3D projectors were also capable of projecting 2D images. The visuals were supported by six-channel digital audio that typically produced 12,000 watts of realistic, distortion-free sound. The sound systems were developed by Sonics Associates Inc., a subsidiary in which IMAX had 51 per cent ownership. The company had even developed a 3D directional sound technology that offered location and depth to the audio. A testament to IMAX's technological prowess was the 1997 Oscar Award it received for Scientific and Technical Achievement.[11]

Because of its larger size, printing and distributing IMAX films was costlier than 35 mm films. IMAX had developed digital cameras and projectors that it planned to install in theatres starting in 2008, so that it could produce and distribute its movies in digital format. While the conversion to digital format required substantial upfront investment, it was expected that this shift would allow IMAX to lower its operational costs (of film production and distribution) significantly.

Software: IMAX Films The motion picture industry produced several types of movies: horror, adventure, comedy, romantic comedy, family, drama and documentaries. Of these, the documentary segment was considered so significant that the Motion Picture Association of America (MPAA), in its annual Oscar Award ceremony, gave out separate awards for these films. While the large format film itself was a unique feature of IMAX, it had also differentiated itself by its library of films and locations. IMAX films were often educational and entertaining, and involved documentaries of natural and scientific wonders such as the Grand Canyon, space stations, etc. An IMAX film, *Fires of Kuwait*, was nominated for an Academy Award in 1993.

By locating itself in prestigious venues, such as the Smithsonian Institution in Washington, Liberty Science Center in New Jersey, the Museum of Science and Industry in Chicago and Port Vell in Barcelona, Spain, the firm had created a unique brand image. In an interview with CNN, co-CEO Gelfond noted IMAX's advantage: "IMAX is also a brand, so we don't have to pay the same kind of talent that Hollywood has to pay, which is really a huge percentage of the costs. Once you take those costs down and you look at just making the film with the world around you as the talent, you get into much more manageable budget ranges. A typical two-dimensional film at IMAX

---

[8]Annual Report, 2007.

[9]Annual Report, 2007.

[10]"Cam programming helps design 3d IMAX movie camera for NASA," *Computer Aided Engineering*, 19:3, March 2000, p. 10.

[11]W. C. Symonds, "Now showing in IMAX: Money!; The giant-screen technology will even bag an Oscar," *Business Week*, 3520, March 31, 1997, p. 80.

is about $5 million; a typical 3D film at IMAX is about $10 million."[12] Hollywood studios would have to pay a major star (such as Tom Cruise or Eddie Murphy) more than $10 million for a movie. While top movie stars were celebrities and drew huge compensation, many others involved in the production, distribution and marketing of a film were neither well known nor highly paid. In 2007, according to the Bureau of Labor Statistics (BLS), the median salary for an actor in the motion picture and video industry was about $17 per hour.[13] Some of these talents had formed unions, such as the Screen Artists Guild, to negotiate higher wages for their labour. The disruption of TV programming in spring 2008 caused by the brief Writers Guild strike was suggestive of the power such groups had on studios.

Besides stars, the other major cost of movie-making was the marketing. It was estimated that a studio spent almost 30 to 50 per cent of the total cost of production and distribution of a movie in its marketing. According to the Motion Picture Association of America (MPAA), the average cost of making and marketing a movie rose to more than $106 million in 2007, with marketing budgets averaging $36 million.[14] The marketing of the movie was done through several channels such as TV, the press, theatres, websites and promotions with retailers. Please see Exhibit 2 for average spending in each media. For example, most kids' movies released by studios, such as Disney and SKG Dreamworks, were promoted through tie-ups with restaurants such as McDonald's and Burger King, and also toy manufacturers and other retailers. The Hollywood business model used the awareness created by the presence of stars and substantial marketing budgets to draw large audiences into theatres on the opening weekend itself.[15] To achieve high ticket sales on opening weekends, large numbers of prints of the movie were distributed. In contrast, traditionally, IMAX had not marketed its films aggressively. The company did have a sales force and marketing staff at its offices in Canada, the United States, Europe, Japan and China to market its theatre systems. The movies were sold to theatres separately; as such, there was no national marketing or advertising.[16] Unlike Hollywood movies that had short lifespans in the theatre circuit and were then withdrawn for release on DVD and pay-per-view format, IMAX films were often shown in theatres for years after their release. In recent years, IMAX films had received some marketing support. For example, for IMAX movie *Everest,* producer Greg MacGillivray spent $2 million in marketing and reportedly saw a 20 to 45 per cent increase in box-office revenues at each theatre. Moreover, IMAX's alliances were helping in cross-promoting its movies. For example, for its *T-Rex: Back to the Cretaceous* 3D movie, it had a month-long promo on Showtime that was also shown in Imaginarium stores in malls across the United States.[17] The increasing number of Hollywood movies that were released in IMAX format allowed IMAX to ride on the coat-tails of marketing campaigns launched by the studios.

---

[12]D. Michael, "Bigger is better: IMAX knocking competition down to size," *CNN*, November 6, 1998, www.cnn.com/SHOWBIZ/Movies/9811/06/imax/index.html?iref=newssearch, accessed March 23, 2008.

[13]www.bls.gov/oes/current/naics4_711500.htm, accessed December 23, 2008.

[14]M. Marr, "Now playing: Expensive movies; Average cost of a film tops $100 million for first time; Valenti set to leave MPAA," *The Wall Street Journal*, March 24, 2004, p. B. 4, www.mpaa.org/researchStatistics.asp, accessed December 23, 2008.

[15]Adam Leipzig, " How to sell a movie (or fail) in four hours," *The New York Times*, November 13, 2005.

[16]D. Oestricher, "IMAX hopes for big run with Matrix," *The Wall Street Journal*, June 18, 2003, p. b5c.

[17]T. L. Stanley, "IMAX lands Showtime, GTE for 1st X-Promo," *Brandweek*, July 13, 1998, 39:28, p. 5.

IMAX films were often produced by the firm or partially or fully financed by other parties. The firm hired the talent for the film on a project-by-project basis. Most of the post-production work was performed at David Keighley Production, a wholly-owned subsidiary of IMAX. IMAX (and any investors or sponsors) shared the ownership rights for a film, while usually IMAX controlled the distribution rights. As a result, IMAX had the distribution rights to the largest number of large format films. The distributor received a percentage of the theatre box office revenues. IMAX films often remained in distribution for four or five years. (Please see Exhibit 3 for box office revenues for IMAX films.)

Generating Growth

IMAX used a two-pronged strategy to maintain its growth. First, it had sought to expand beyond its institutional environment by opening IMAX theatres within multiplexes or converting existing multiplexes' screens to IMAX format. Second, it had launched Hollywood films in IMAX format.

An IMAX Near You While early IMAX theatres were mostly located in institutional settings such as museums and aquariums, to reach a wider audience IMAX had engaged in alliances with commercial movie theatre owners.[18] It grew rapidly during the late 1990s as theatre owners such as AMC, Cinemark and Regal went on a building spree and bought IMAX systems to install in their multiplexes. According to Wechsler, this strategy backfired when IMAX could not escape the crisis that hit the theatre industry in the late 1990s because of the overbuilding during that decade. As many theatre owners filed for bankruptcy, IMAX had to engage in belt-tightening of its own because of its receivable problems. Moody's downgraded IMAX's debt of $200 million senior notes from Ba2 to B2 and a $100 million note from B1 to Caa1 because of the risk of default by customers. In response, IMAX cut $14 million in overhead, laid off 200 employees and bought back $90 million of its debt.[19] Debt remained a critical problem for IMAX (please see Exhibits 4, 5 and 6 for IMAX financials).

In recent years, IMAX entered into partnerships with AMC and Regal Cinemas to screen IMAX films in multiplexes using its MPX technology. MPX technology allowed IMAX and theatre owners to convert traditional theaters to IMAX format.[20] It was estimated that it now cost only $175,000 to retrofit a multiplex and another $500,000 to install the IMAX system.[21] Regal Cinemas had built IMAX theatres in several markets and waited to see how they performed before adding more.[22] In March 2008, it signed another agreement with IMAX for 38 more theatres, bringing the total number of Regal IMAX theatres to 52 by 2010. Regal theatres would charge $2.50 to $5.00 more than their regular feature admission for IMAX films.[23] In December 2007,

---

[18]L. Gubernick, "Hollywood Journal: Hollywood think bigger —your favorites, only taller: Can re-released movies breathe life into IMAX?" *The Wall Street Journal*, February 15, 2002, p. W. 5.

[19]Z. Olijnyk, "One giant leap," *Canadian Business,* 75:17, September 16, 2002, pp. 46–48.

[20]D. Oestricher, "IMAX hopes for big run with Matrix," *The Wall Street Journal*, June 18, 2003, p. b5c.

[21]Katy Marquardt, "Imax parlays a huge screen and 3-D tech into an experience you can't duplicate at home. Coming soon to a multiplex near you," *US News and World Report*, Feb. 6, 2008, www.usnews.com/articles/business/2008/02/06/imax-parlays-3-d-tech-into-an-experience-you-cant-duplicate-at-home.html, accessed December 23, 2008.

[22]*The Wall Street Journal*, 2000.

[23]B. Pulley, "The really big screen," *Forbes*, 172:13, December 22, 2003, p. 222; *The Wall Street Journal*, 2003.

IMAX signed a deal with AMC to install 100 IMAX digital theatres systems in 33 markets, thereby substantially increasing its presence in the U.S. market. IMAX had identified 655 multiplexes without an IMAX nearby.[24] However, IMAX co-CEO Wechsler had stated that he did not expect IMAX theatres to be ubiquitous but exclusive, like flying first-class; while co-CEO Gelfond had suggested that the IMAX experience would be so unique that it could not be replicated at home. Consistent with this vision, the theatre agreement that it recently signed gave AMC territorial exclusivity.[25] Unlike past agreements where theatres chains bought the system from IMAX, the newer agreements required the partner theatre chain to make the investment for retrofitting the theatre, while IMAX paid for the system installation in return for revenue-sharing on future ticket sales. Analysts expected that such agreements (and digital conversion) would lower IMAX's capital requirements and help it pay off its debt.[26]

Go West IMAX!

Another strategic move by IMAX to ensure its growth was the conversion of Hollywood movies into IMAX format. IMAX had developed a patented digital re-mastering (DMR) technology that allowed it to convert traditional 35 mm films such as *Harry Potter, Spiderman, Antz* and *The Simpsons* into the large-screen format and even develop 3D versions of such movies. The development of this technology was critical because merely projecting a 35 mm film on the large IMAX screen would have produced a grainy picture. According to co-CEO Gelfond, the firm invested millions of dollars to sharpen the resolution of the converted pictures and it took more than five years to develop the technology.[27] The re-mastering of *Apollo 13* took 16 weeks, while *The Matrix Revolutions* was re-mastered as it was being produced, allowing for near-simultaneous theatre and IMAX releases. As IMAX had worked out the teething problems with this technology, the costs of conversion had come down. For each print, it now cost $22,500 to convert a standard two-dimensional film and $45,000 to convert a 3D film. It was expected that moving to a digital format would further lower the conversion costs. If the conversion succeeded at the box office, more studios might be willing to spend the extra money to convert their standard 35 mm films to IMAX format.[28] This would also attract theatre chains to open new IMAX screens. Though IMAX made only 7 per cent of the box office revenue from reformatted films by other studios, compared to the nearly 30 per cent that it made on its own movies,[29] the conversion of Hollywood movies might allow IMAX to survive, according to co-CEO Gelfond.[30] An announcement to launch the *Harry Potter* movie on IMAX resulted in an almost 11 per cent surge in its stock price that day. Gelfond noted that IMAX could continue making educational films that could be screened in theatres during daytime

---

[24]D. Oestricher, "IMAX hopes for big run with Matrix," *The Wall Street Journal*, June 18, 2003, p. b5c.

[25]Katy Marquardt, "Imax parlays a huge screen and 3-D tech into an experience you can't duplicate at home. Coming soon to a multiplex near you," *US News and World Report*, February 6, 2008,www.usnews.com/articles/business/2008/02/06/imax-parlays-3-d-tech-into-an-experience-you-cant-duplicate-at-home.html, accessed December 23, 2008.

[26]Ibid.

[27]S. N. Chakravarty, "A really big show ," *Institutional Investor*, 35:10, October 2002, p. 20.

[28]*The Wall Street Journal,* 2000; *Institutional Investor*, 2002.

[29]D. Lieberman, "IMAX supersizes its plans for future flicks," *USA Today*, December 16, 2002, www.usatoday.com/tech/news/techinnovations/2002-12-16-IMAX_x.htm, accessed December 23, 2008.

[30]Z. Olijnyk, "One giant leap," *Canadian Business*, 75:17, September 16, 2002, pp. 46–48.

for families, students and tourists, while its reformatted Hollywood movies could be screened in the evening. In an interview with Amusement Business, co-CEO Wechsler noted that the IMAX strategy of moving into the commercial movie business would hopefully expand the core audience.[31] "Our research tells us that a lot of people will pay that extra $3 to $5," Gelfond said in an interview with USA Today.[32]

The first full-length Hollywood movie released on IMAX was *Fantasia 2000* in January 2000.[33] The classic *Beauty and the Beast,* which had a 20-week show on 67 IMAX screens in 2002, generated $32 million in revenue.[34] The first live-action commercial movie to be launched in IMAX format was *Apollo 13,* which generated an additional $2 million in revenue. Later, *Star Wars* was released on IMAX, followed by *The Matrix Reloaded,* which generated $11.7 million.[35] These movies were released in IMAX after their theatrical release.[36]

As more Hollywood movies were converted to IMAX format, the studios had to decide whether these should be released simultaneously in theatres and IMAX format. Could the expansion into IMAX theatres cannibalize the traditional theatrical revenues? It was found that almost 90 per cent of *The Matrix Reloaded* IMAX viewers had seen the movie in theatres earlier. *The Polar Express,* which was released simultaneously in IMAX and traditional theaters during the 2004 Christmas season, was a big hit with $45 million in revenues in the IMAX format.[37] On December 12, 2008, the movie *The Day the Earth Stood Still* was released simultaneously on IMAX and multiplex screens. At $31 million, the movie had the highest box office gross over a weekend. More than $3.8 million (about 12 per cent) of the total revenue came from IMAX theatres. Notably, the average revenue per IMAX theatre was $30,800, compared to the national average theatre revenues of $8,100.[38] Such track records should give more studios the confidence to release their movies simultaneously in commercial and IMAX theatres.

INDUSTRY DYNAMICS

Motion picture production and distribution was part of the service sector of the economy and included firms such as Disney/Pixar, MGM, Regal Entertainment, Lions Gate and Carmike. Many of the production and distribution companies were now part

---

[31]N. Emmons, "IMAX may turn toward mainstream," *Amusement Business,* 112:49, December 4, 2000, p. 1, pp. 20–21.

[32]D. Lieberman, "IMAX supersizes its plans for future flicks," *USA Today,* December 16, 2002, www.usatoday.com/tech/news/techinnovations/2002-12-16-IMAX_x.htm, accessed December 23, 2008.

[33]R. Ricklefs, "IMAX hopes to take cast screen into mainstream—a new 'Fantasia' tests film strategy of Canadian firm," *The Wall Street Journal,* December 10, 1999, p. 1.

[34]D. Oestricher, "IMAX hopes for big run with Matrix," *The Wall Street Journal,* June 18, 2003, p. b5c.

[35]T. Lowry, "Now playing at IMAX: Hit movies" *Business Week,* 3807, November 11, 2002, p. 46.; N. Sperling, "IMAX executives hoping Warner's 'The Matrix' is 'the one'," *Amusement Business,* 115:46, 2003, pp. 24–25.

[36]T. King, "Hollywood Journal: When a 'sure thing' isn't—Even the $20 million stars can't guarantee a hit; trying to ignore 'Pluto'," *The Wall Street Journal,* October 11, 2002, p. W.11.

[37]W. D. Crotty, "IMAX's screen gets bigger," *The Motley Fool,* September 15, 2005, www.fool.com/investing/general/2005/09/15/imaxs-screen-gets-bigger.aspx?terms=Imax+screen+gets+bigger&vstest=search_042607_linkdefault, accessed December 23, 2008.

[38]"IMAX rises as consumers embrace large screens," *Associated Press,* December 16, 2008,http://biz.yahoo.com/ap/081216/imax_mover.html?.v=1, accessed December 23, 2008.

of other, larger, diversified firms. For example, Columbia Pictures was now part of Sony, Warner Brothers was a subsidiary of Time Warner, Paramount Studios was part of Viacom and Pixar and Miramax were part of Disney. Over the years, media firms had sought to vertically integrate their operations by owning not only the production facilities but also distribution networks.

Film production remained a risky business. Only one in ten films ever recovered its investment from domestic theatre release; and only six out of ten movies ever recouped the original investment. Competition among movies within the same genre was so high that studios scheduled releases carefully to avoid direct competition. Thus, release dates were announced several years in advance and production was designed around preferred holiday release dates such as Thanksgiving, July 4th, Memorial Day weekends or the first weekend of May.

IMAX films faced competition from other films produced by studios such as Pixar/ Disney that were targeted for families or children. Within the large format film segment, Iwerks was the only rival to IMAX.[39] Iwerks was founded in 1986 and continued to be involved in all aspects of large format films and simulation rides. It produced films in the 15/70 and 8/70 formats; however, the focus of the firm was more on ride simulation packages located in theme parks, zoos, museums and other destinations. Iwerks had received two Academy Awards for Scientific and Technical Achievement. In 2002, Iwerks merged with SimEx (a firm founded in 1991), which was involved in ride simulation and animation production. Another firm, Megasystems, which was involved in the development of large format projection systems, production and consulting in marketing, operations and technical services, had discontinued its projection system production and was renamed Pollavision. Pollavision was now only involved in consulting (and maintenance) services for large format film theatres.[40]

Technology Trends

Potential IMAX viewers could consume many alternative sources of entertainment such as live plays, sport events, TV programs, the Internet, etc. Please see Exhibits 7 and 8 for admissions, prices and time spent on alternative entertainment sources. Viewers might choose to watch a movie on DVD, pay-per-view or video-on-demand rather than at the theatre. The development of high-definition DVD recording, big-screen TVs and cheaper home theatre projection and sound systems posed an even bigger threat to box office ticket sales. Please see Exhibit 9 for DVD sales trends in the United States. According to one estimate, almost 85 per cent of a film's revenue now came from home viewing through various channels such as DVD/VHS, cable and TV.[41] Yet, it had been found that the success of secondary sources such as DVD sales and rentals was a function of the movie's box office success.[42] According to Jack Valenti, former president of MPAA, 50 per cent of DVD viewers and almost 38 per cent of VCR movie-users were frequent moviegoers. He said, "People who love movies are eager to watch them again in different environments."[43]

---

[39]C. Booth, "IMAX gets bigger (by getting smaller)," *Time*, June 29, 1998, 151:25, pp. 48–49.

[40]www.pollavision.com, accessed December 23, 2008.

[41]E. J. Epstein, "Hollywood's death spiral," *Slate*, July 25, 2005.

[42]Bruce Orwall, "A dud at theaters will be a dud DVD," *The Wall Street Journal*, November 26, 2005, p. A2.

[43]J. Valenti, MPAA Press Release, 2002.

The development of new technologies, such as cheaper high-definition camcorders, as well as the proliferation of new distribution channels such as cable, satellite and the Internet, had also created opportunities for new independent firms to enter the industry. One such firm that leveraged its knowledge of computer technology to develop blockbuster animated films was Pixar. New firms might enter one or more parts of the film industry value chain—talent management, production, post-production, distribution, etc. Specialists in post-production processes had emerged who were responsible for editing, special effects, media transfers, subtitling, etc. However, entry into all aspects of the value chain simultaneously had been rare. A recent example of such an entry was SKG Dreamworks, a studio that was started by film industry veterans Spielberg, Katzenberg and Geffen.

Such technological changes had also increased the potential for piracy. According to the Motion Picture Association of America, the U.S. film industry lost more than $3 billion annually because of piracy. Section 8, Article 1 of the U.S. Constitution offers Congress the power to offer copyright protection. The Copyright Act of 1976 that was amended in 1982 offers strong penalties for copyright violations. (Please see www.copyright.gov/title17 for recent development in copyright law.) Violations were considered felonies and were subject to federal criminal charges and civil lawsuits. The Motion Picture Association was working closely with the U.S. Congress to enforce sentencing guidelines and improve copyright protection as newer technologies emerged and posed fresher challenges. According to Karen Randall of Vivendi, whose production *The Hulk* was released on the Internet by pirates before its theatrical release, the FBI was very cooperative and aggressive in pursuing the case.[44]

Other Trends

IMAX had to cease screening its movie *Volcanoes of the Deep Sea* in some parts of the United States, as certain religious groups were offended by its position on, and depiction of, evolution.[45] Concerns about violence and sex in movies had generated considerable efforts to organize and lobby political action to regulate the industry. For example, Tipper Gore and Lynn Cheney (spouses of former vice-presidents Al Gore and Dick Cheney, respectively) had worked hard to curtail the levels of violence, sex and vulgar language found in popular media.[46]

Another trend that might help firms such as IMAX was the increased consumption of educational entertainment. Ever since Sesame Street succeeded in educating and entertaining kids simultaneously, the "edutainment" market had grown as parents increasingly sought out play activities for their children that were educational. This trend had been attributed to increasing belief among parents that in a knowledge economy, their kids' success might depend on education. The widespread popularity among parents of the concept of the "Mozart effect"—a finding that babies that listened to Mozart recordings in the womb or at early stages after birth had richer cognitive development—was seen as evidence of their desire to produce smart kids.[47] Other trends

---

[44]S. McBride and B. Orwall, "Movie industry steps up drive against pirates," *The Wall Street Journal*, January 27, 2004, p. B1.

[45]Cornelia Dean, "A new test for IMAX: The Bible vs. the volcano," March. 19, 2005.

[46]Richard Goldstein, "Scary move: When both parties team up to target Hollywood, be afraid. Be very afraid!" *Village Voice*, October 3, 2000, p.20.

[47]Jeffrey Kluger and Alice Park, "The quest for a superkid," *Time*, April 22, 2001, www.time.com/time/nation/article/0,8599,107265-1,00.html, accessed December 23, 2008.

that were driving this growth could include higher education levels of parents and over-scheduled kids and parents.[48] As a result, zoos, museums, software, TV shows and toys were all redesigning their products to entertain and educate.

According to IMAX, more than 20 per cent of IMAX audiences were school groups. About 70 per cent of IMAX viewers were between 19 and 65 years of age, and the majority were college- or university-educated, with an average household income of more than $70,000, and with 33 per cent earning more than $100,000.[49] MPAA offered a more fine-grained analysis of demographic data on movie attendance. It reported that 12–24 year olds (38 per cent of admissions) had the largest attendance for feature films in theatres in 2007, followed by the 25- to 39-year-olds group (29 per cent of admissions).[50] The 12–24-year-olds were also frequent moviegoers (at least 1 movie per month), representing 41 per cent of frequent moviegoers. IMAX needed to figure out a way to attract this demographic.

U.S. and Global Market

In 2007, 603 movies were released in the United States and collected revenues of $9.6 billion.[51] According to the MPAA, there were 1.4 billion movie theatre attendances in the United States in 2007.[52] Jack Valenti, former president of the MPAA, noted that Americans had the highest per capita movie attendance in the world at 5.3 films a year. By excluding those who did not see at least 1 movie a year, the per capita attendance rose to 8.6 films per year.[53] Exhibit 10 displays theatre revenues, average U.S. ticket prices, attendance annual growth rate, consumer price index (CPI) and growth of the U.S. economy. Theatre owners realized that ticket prices could not go up forever, as this might drive away more viewers, so they tried to generate revenue by screening more commercials before showing the feature film. According to some experts, release of big-budget franchise movies or sequels of popular movies attenuated the adverse impact of the economy on theatre attendance.

Movies were now increasingly becoming a global industry. More than 5,000 films were released worldwide in 2007, with 7 billion attendances and annual global box office revenues estimated at $26.7 billion.[54] The Asia-Pacific region had the largest share of the global market. While Hollywood movies had always enjoyed an international audience, with globalization and the increased movement of people across national borders, movies from other regions, such as Hong Kong and India, were also finding an international audience. For Hollywood movies, a significant part of the revenues now came from outside the United States. Please see Exhibit 11 on domestic and foreign sources for the top 10 films in 2007.

---

[48]R. White, "That's edutainment," White Hutchinson Leisure & Learning Group, 2003.

[49]www.IMAX.com

[50]J. Valenti, MPAA Press Release, 2002.

[51]US Entertainment Industry: 2007 MPAA statistics. See also M. Marr, "Now playing: Expensive movies; Average cost of a film tops $100 million for first time; Valenti set to leave MPAA," *The Wall Street Journal*, March 24, 2004, p. B. 4.

[52]James Jaeger, "The movie industry," www.mecfilms.com/moviepubs/memos/moviein.htm, accessed December 23, 2008.

[53]2007 movie attendance study, MPAA.

[54]2007 international theatrical snapshot, MPAA; www.mpaa.org/International%20Theatrical%20Snapshot.pdf, accessed March 4, 2009.

THE LARGER ISSUES

At this point in its evolution, IMAX faced two critical questions. Would IMAX lose its differentiation if it exhibited too many Hollywood movies? Greg MacGillvray, who had made several films in the IMAX format, including the highly successful *Everest,* argued that IMAX ran the risk of losing its brand identity as it moved into non-educational entertainment films. He said, "There's also been a slight brand erosion given that these films have not been really educational experiences, but more entertainment experiences." According to MacGillvray, IMAX's own research showed that the brand's trustworthiness was rooted in the fact that IMAX grew up in institutional settings.[55]

Another question that the present co-CEOs had faced for several years was: Should IMAX be sold to a larger studio such as Sony, Disney or Time Warner? That is, was it too small to survive on its own? Some analysts had speculated that IMAX was ripe for acquisition. Co-CEO Gelfond had once stated, "Someday it will make sense for IMAX to be part of a studio."[56]

The author would like to thank Professors Barbara Bartkus, Alan Eisner, Jim Key, participants at a case writing workshop organized by the Society for Case Research and students at Old Dominion University for comments on earlier versions of the case. Thanks also to Lee-Hsien Pan for his research assistance.

---

[55]P. Waal, "Call in the barbarians," *Canadian Business*, 73:17, September 18, 2000, pp. 85–87.

[56]P. Waal, "The plot quickens," *Canadian Business*, 71:11, June 26–July 10, 1998, pp. 51–57.

EXHIBIT 1   IMAX Film Size

Film Frames Actual Size

© 1994 Smithsonian Institution/Lockheed Martin Corporation

15/70mm

Standard 70mm

Standard 35mm

Source: IMAX, with permission.

EXHIBIT 2 Average Marketing Spending on Various Media, 2007

Newspapers	12.9%
Network TV	16.1%
Spot TV	13.7%
Internet	5.3%
Trailers	4.9%
Other media (cable TV, radio, magazines, billboards)	24.5%
Other non-media (production/creative services, exhibitor services, promotion & publicity, market research)	22.6%

Source: www.mpaa.com

EXHIBIT 3 Box Office Revenues for IMAX Movies (in millions of $)

Rank	Title	Studio	Gross-to-date	Year
1	Everest	MFF	$87.18	1998
2	Space Station 3D	IMAX	$77.10	2002
3	T-Rex: Back to the Cretaceous	IMAX	$53.14	1998
4	Fantasia 2000	BV	$52.26	2000
5	Mysteries of Egypt	IMAX	$40.59	1998
6	Deep Sea 3D	WB	$37.09	2006
7	Magnificent Desolation	IMAX	$26.67	2005
8	Beauty and the Beast	BV	$25.49	2002
9	NASCAR 3D: The IMAX Experience	WB	$21.58	2004
10	Sea Monsters: A Prehistoric Adventure	NGC	$20.05	2007

Source: www.boxofficemojo.com. IMAX box office receipts have only recently started being tracked.

EXHIBIT 4   IMAX Corporation Annual Balance Sheet (in thousands of dollars)

Period Ending	31-Dec-07	31-Dec-06	31-Dec-05	31-Dec-04
Assets				
Current assets				
Cash and cash equivalents	16,901	25,123	24,324	28,964
Short-term investments	–	2,115	8,171	–
Net receivables	25,505	26,017	89,171	19,899
Inventory	22,050	26,913	28,294	29,001
Other current assets	2,187	3,432	3,825	2,279
Total current assets	**66,643**	**83,600**	**153,785**	**80,143**
Long-term investments	59,092	65,878	–	59,492
Property, plant and equipment	23,708	24,639	26,780	28,712
Goodwill	39,027	39,027	39,027	39,027
Intangible assets	4,419	3,782	6,030	3,931
Accumulated amortization	–	–	–	–
Other assets	10,928	6,646	9,756	7,532
Deferred long-term asset charges	4,165	3,719	10,806	12,016
Total assets	**207,982**	**227,291**	**246,184**	**230,853**
Liabilities				
Current liabilities				
Accounts payable	74,267	69,720	62,057	62,724
Short/current long-term debt	–	–	–	–
Other current liabilities	–	–	–	–
Total current liabilities	**74,267**	**69,720**	**62,057**	**62,724**
Long-term debt	160,000	160,000	160,000	160,000
Other liabilities	–	–	–	–
Deferred long-term liability charges	59,085	55,803	44,397	50,505
Minority interest	–	–	–	–
Negative goodwill	–	–	–	–
Total liabilities	**293,352**	**285,523**	**266,454**	**273,229**
Stockholders' equity				
Common stock	122,455	122,024	121,674	116,281
Retained earnings	(213,407)	(184,375)	(144,347)	(160,945)
Other stockholder equity	5,582	4,119	2,403	2,288
Total stockholder equity	**(85,370)**	**(58,232)**	**(20,270)**	**(42,376)**

Source: Annual reports.

EXHIBIT 5 IMAX Corporation Annual Income Statement (in thousands of dollars)

Period Ending	31-Dec-07	31-Dec-06	31-Dec-05	31-Dec-04
Total revenue	115,832	129,452	144,930	135,980
Cost of revenue	74,673	76,902	73,005	70,062
Gross profit	41,159	52,550	71,925	65,918
Operating expenses				
Research & development	5,789	3,615	3,264	3,995
Selling, general and administrative	44,705	42,527	39,503	36,066
Non-recurring	562	1,073	−859	−639
Others	547	1,668	911	719
Total operating expenses	51,603	48,883	42,819	40,141
Operating income or loss	(10,444)	3,667	29,106	25,777
Income from continuing operations				
Total other income/expenses net	(933)	1,036	1,004	265
Earnings before interest and taxes	(11,377)	4,703	30,110	26,042
Interest expense	17,093	16,759	16,773	16,853
Income before taxes	(28,470)	(12,056)	13,337	9,189
Income tax expense	472	6,218	934	(255)
Minority interest	0	0	0	0
Net income from continuing ops.	(28,942)	(18,274)	12,403	9,444
Non-recurring events				
Discontinued operations	2,002	1,425	1,979	800
Extraordinary items	0	0	0	0
Effect of accounting changes	0	0	0	0
Other items	0	0	0	0
Net income	(26,940)	(16,849)	14,382	10,244

Source: Annual reports.

EXHIBIT 6   IMAX Corporation Cash Flow Statement (in thousands of dollars)

Period Ending	31-Dec-07	31-Dec-06	31-Dec-05	31-Dec-04
Net income	(26,940)	(16,849)	14,382	10,244
Cash flows provided by or used in				
Operating activities				
Depreciation	17,738	16,872	15,867	14,947
Adjustments to net income	(3,520)	10,349	(8,678)	(4,577)
Changes in accounts receivables	675	(11,106)	(8,324)	(6,673)
Changes in liabilities	4,781	4,399	(11,749)	(6,830)
Changes in inventories	(1,603)	57	(383)	(283)
Changes in other operating activities	2,648	(9,659)	(1,545)	4,583
Total cash flow from operating activities	(6,221)	(5,937)	1,786	11,411
Cash flows provided by or used in				
Investing activities				
Capital expenditures	(2,150)	(1,985)	(1,597)	(320)
Investments	2,115	6,396	(7,818)	393
Other cash flows from investing activities	(702)	2,105	(1,301)	(1,435)
Total cash flows from investing activities	(737)	6,516	(10,716)	(1,362)
Cash flows provided by or used in				
Financing activities				
Dividends paid	–	–	–	–
Sale purchase of stock	420	286	3,633	558
Net borrowings	(1,714)	–	–	(29,769)
Other cash flows from financing activities	–	–	786	800
Total cash flows from financing activities	(1,294)	286	4,419	(28,411)
Effect of exchange rate changes	30	(66)	(129)	44
Change in cash and cash equivalents	($8,222)	$799	($4,640)	($18,318)

Source: Annual reports.

EXHIBIT 7   Substitute Activities to Movies in 2007

	Activity	Attendance (in millions)	Average ticket price (in $)
1	Movies	1,400	6.88
2	Theme Parks	341	35.30
3	Ice Hockey/NHL	21	44.60
4	Basketball/NBA	22	46.75
5	Football/NFL	17	65.25
6	Baseball/MLB	77	23.50

Source: MPAA, www.mpaa.com

EXHIBIT 8 Media Consumption Based on Hours per Person per Year

Filmed Entertainment	2003	2004	2005	2006	2007
Cable & satellite TV	886	909	980	997	1,010
Broadcast TV	729	711	679	676	676
Consumer Internet	153	164	169	177	181
Home video (DVD & VHS)	60	67	63	62	64
Box office	13	13	12	12	13
In-flight entertainment & mobile content	5	8	10	13	18
Subtotal	1,846	1,872	1,913	1,937	1,962
Other Entertainment					
Broadcast & satellite radio	831	821	805	778	769
Recorded music	187	196	195	186	171
Newspapers	195	192	188	178	172
Consumer magazines	122	125	124	121	119
Consumer books	108	108	107	108	108
Video games	76	78	73	76	82
Subtotal	1,522	1,520	1,492	1,447	1,421

Source: MPAA, www.mpaa.com

EXHIBIT 9 DVD Consumption in the United States (in millions of units)

	Rental DVDs	Sell-through DVDs	Total DVDs	Avg. price of DVD
2007	171.2	1,084.6	1,255.8	22.11
2006	180.2	1,129.0	1,309.2	22.29
2005	179.0	1,114.5	1,293.6	21.20
2004	149.3	1,063.3	1,212.6	20.32
2003	105.4	768.3	873.6	20.15

Source: MPAA, www.mpaa.com

EXHIBIT 10 Theatre Box Office Revenues, Average U.S. Attendance, Price and Economy

Year	Revenue (in billions $)	Ticket price (in $)	Attendance (in billions)	GDP Growth (in %)	CPI Inflation (in %)
1990	5.02	4.22	1.19	1.9	5.4
1991	4.80	4.21	1.14	-0.2	4.2
1992	4.56	4.15	1.10	3.3	3.0
1993	4.89	4.14	1.18	2.7	3.0
1994	5.18	4.08	1.24	4.0	2.6
1995	5.27	4.35	1.21	2.5	2.8
1996	5.81	4.42	1.32	3.7	3.0
1997	6.21	4.59	1.35	4.5	2.3
1998	6.76	4.69	1.44	4.2	1.6
1999	7.31	5.06	1.44	4.5	2.2
2000	7.46	5.39	1.38	3.7	3.4
2001	8.12	5.65	1.44	0.8	2.8
2002	9.27	5.80	1.60	1.6	1.6
2003	9.16	6.03	1.52	2.5	2.3
2004	9.21	6.21	1.48	3.6	2.7
2005	8.83	6.41	1.38	2.9	3.4
2006	9.14	6.55	1.39	2.8	3.2
2007	9.63	6.88	1.40	2.0	2.8

Source: National Association of Theater Owners (NATO), www.natoonline.org; Bureau of Economic Analysis, www.bea.gov; and Bureau of Labor Statistics, www.bls.gov

EXHIBIT 11 Domestic and Overseas Revenues for 2007 (in millions of dollars)

Rank	Title	Domestic	Overseas	World
1	Pirates of the Caribbean: At World's End	309.4	649.0	958.4
2	Harry Potter and the Order of the Phoenix	292.0	645.0	937.0
3	Spider-Man 3	336.5	548.9	885.4
4	Shrek the Third	321.0	470.4	791.4
5	Transformers	319.1	382.0	701.1
6	Ratatouille	206.4	409.5	615.9
7	I Am Legend	256.4	327.6	584.0
8	Simpsons Movie, The	183.1	342.4	525.5
9	300	210.6	246.0	456.6
10	National Treasure: Book of Secrets	220.0	234.0	454.0

Source: www.worldwideboxoffice.com